IN SEARCH OF ARAB UNITY

by the same author

The Emergence of the Palestinian Arab National Movement   Vol. I   1918–1929

The Palestinian Arab National Movement: From Riots to Rebellion   Vol. II   1929–1939

IN SEARCH OF
ARAB UNITY
1930 – 1945

YEHOSHUA PORATH

FRANK CASS

First published 1986 in Great Britain by
FRANK CASS AND COMPANY LIMITED
Gainsborough House, 11 Gainsborough Road,
London, E11 1RS, England

and in the United States of America by
FRANK CASS AND COMPANY LIMITED
c/o Biblio Distribution Centre
81 Adams Drive, P.O. Box 327, Totowa, N.J. 07511

Copyright © 1986 Y. Porath

British Library Cataloguing in Publication Data

Porath, Yehoshua
   In search of Arab unity 1930–1945.
   1. Arab countries—Politics and government
   I. Title
   320.917'4927   JQ1850.A3

ISBN 0-7146-3264-3 (Case)
ISBN 0-7146-4051-4 (Paper)

All rights reserved. No part of this publication may be reproduced, stored in a retrieval system, or transmitted in any form, or by any means, electronic, mechanical, photocopying, recording, or otherwise, without the prior permission of Frank Cass and Company Limited.

Typeset by Williams Graphics, Abergele, North Wales
Printed and bound in Great Britain by
A. Wheaton & Co. Ltd., Exeter

CONTENTS

	Foreword	vii
1	**Hashemite Attempts at Fertile Crescent Unity**	1
	Faysal's Syrian initiatives	4
	'Abdallah's Greater Syria project	22
	Nuri al-Sa'id's initiative	39
2	**The Ever-Present Panacea – Arab Federation as a Solution to the Palestine Question**	58
	Jewish proposals	58
	Arab initiatives	69
	Unofficial British démarches	72
	The Philby Scheme, or the proposed Saudi-led federation	80
	Official British thinking	106
3	**The Rise of Political Pan-Arabism**	149
	Pan-Arabism in Egypt	149
	Pan-Arabism in the Fertile Crescent	159
	The effect of the Palestine Arab Rebellion	162
	The growth of cultural co-operation	175
	Improvement of inter-Arab relations	179
	The effects of the early years of the Second World War	185
4	**British Policy Regarding Pan-Arabism**	197
	British reaction to Faysal's initiative	197
	Britain and 'Abdallah's Greater Syria project	203
	British reaction to Nuri al-Sa'id's initiative	216
	British attitude to Pan-Arabism	223
5	**The Formation of the Arab League**	257
	The impact of Eden's February 1943 statement: the inter-Arab consultations	257
	From the consultations to the Preparatory Committee	267
	The formation of the Arab League	284
	British attitude: the final stage	290
	British policy in the Middle East: image versus reality; London versus 'the men on the spot'	303
	Conclusions	312
	Notes	320
	Bibliography	361
	Index	366

IN MEMORY OF
YOSSEF LUNTZ,
A GREAT MAN

FOREWORD

The aim of this book is to analyse the interaction among three factors: Arab attempts, whether dynastical, political or ideological-cultural, to promote their unity; various endeavours to find a solution to the Palestine problem within a framework of Arab unity; and British policy regarding the two factors. The analysis covers the Arab countries of Asia, Palestine and Egypt, where the political and ideological developments analysed in the book took place. It is by no means a comprehensive political or ideological history of those countries; on the contrary, it assumes a certain amount of knowledge of them.

The description and analysis begin in about 1930 since in that year Iraq got its formal independence. Thus its ruler could pursue, much more vigorously than in the past, his policy of Arab unity. For many Arab nationalists Iraq had by then become the potential engine of pan-Arabism, a possible Piedmont of Arab Unity. The formation of the Arab League in 1945 was the culmination of all those factors under discussion.

British and Jewish archival source-material is the main fountainhead of information. I am well aware of the great disadvantage caused by my inability to consult Arab source-material. I tried my best to minimise the damage by drawing heavily upon memoirs of Arab statesmen and the press. I hope that one day this discrepancy will be made good. Until then my conclusions cannot be regarded as final even by myself.

During the preparation of this book I got financial support for the collection of the source-material from the Davis Institute, the Truman Institute and the Research Fund of the Faculty of Humanities, all at the Hebrew University, Jerusalem. I gladly acknowledge my deep gratitude to them all.

The Hebrew University, Jerusalem　　　　　　　　　　YEHOSHUA PORATH

1

Hashemite Attempts at Fertile Crescent Unity

From its inception in 1930 the new Iraqi state was in an ambivalent position: on the one hand, it was apprehensive of most of its neighbours, and on the other, it was bound to the Arab World and the Mediterranean through Syria. Persia, since the establishment at the end of the fifteenth century of the strong Safawi-Shi'ite dynasty had been a persistent enemy of the Ottoman Empire, which had annexed Iraq from the Safawis in 1534. Since then the boundary between these two empires along the Shatt al-'Arab river had been a permanent bone of contention. Usually when the Ottomans were engaged in a war on their western or northern frontiers the Persians would use the opportunity to encroach upon Ottoman dominions in Iraq, until they were strong enough to regain control of what the Persians grabbed. The fact that the Shi'a Holy Places of Najaf, Karbala and al-Kazimayn were located in Iraq under Ottoman-Sunni rule formed a steady source of friction.

This basic situation did not change essentially with the dissolution of the Ottoman Empire at the end of the First World War. From a Persian point of view nothing was altered as far as the boundary and the Holy Places were concerned, with the substitution of the Ottoman Sunni rule by an Arab-Hashemite Iraqi rule which was Sunni too.[1] From an Iraqi angle if there was a change it was for the worse. Persian pilgrims continued to visit their Holy Places, but now the new Iraqi ruler was much weaker than the Ottoman Sultan. The new Iraqi monarch was afraid lest the more rigorous Pahlevi ruler should exploit the existence of the Holy Places and the rights of the pilgrims to press various political demands upon Iraq. Iraq continued to claim the validity of the provision of the old Ottoman-Persian treaty which had conferred upon the former full rights of sovereignty over both banks of the Shatt al-'Arab river and brought the matter before the League of Nations.[2]

Iraqi Shi'ites looked towards Persia (Iran since 1935) for guidance, inspiration and protection. Some of the co-religionists of Persia, including schoolteachers, regarded themselves as Persians. At times they expressed loyalty to Persia or propagated the desirability of Persia taking over the Iraqi mandate from Britain. Such manifestations of attachment to Persia only increased the suspicions of Iraqi authorities towards the Persian connection of its Shi'ite population, some of whom were Persian nationals or of Persian descent.³

The Shi'ah was not the only Iranian factor threatening Iraq. The new Pahlevi Shah, after consolidating his position as head of state, adopted a more rigorous kind of nationalism and revived dreams of resurrecting the old Sassanian Empire. Iranian schoolchildren were taught to regard Ctesiphon in Iraq as the rightful capital of the Persian King of Kings. All these aggravated Iraq's apprehensions and misgivings towards its eastern neighbour.⁴

The British were aware of this situation and had no qualms about using it to their advantage in their dealings with the Iraqi authorities, reminding the Iraqis of the dangers which were confronting them over their eastern frontier and their need for a secure British support.⁵ It should be added that even after a treaty had been signed in 1937 between Iran and Iraq the latter's fears did not dissipate.

Similar fears governed Iraq's attitude towards another of its neighbours – Turkey. This power had up to 1926 endeavoured to secure the oil-rich northern district of Iraq for itself. It did not hesitate to encourage by clandestine means the Turkish population of that district to demand its annexation to Turkey.⁶ Only a very strong British position and Britain's paramount influence in the League of Nations persuaded Turkey to give up its claim to the District of Mosul and to accept the present boundary as final. However, the 1926 settlement of the District of Mosul question did not altogether alleviate Iraq's apprehensions. Iraq's political elite had grown up during the Ottoman period and could not forget that Iraq had only recently been governed from Istanbul. Some of them could not believe that the Turks had given up for good any desire to regain the lost Ottoman territories in Iraq, especially Mosul, as it contained many non-Arab (Kurds, Turkomans and Turks) inhabitants whose kith and kin lived beyond the Turkish border. According to the official Turkish nationalist ideology the Kurds were but 'mountainous Turks' to say nothing about ethnic Turks and Turkish-speaking Turkomans.⁷

Even later on, years after the question of the District of Mosual had been settled in Iraq's favour, the Kurdish concentration in that district continued to worry the Iraqis. Their governing circles were not confident enough that they could forestall a Kurdish demand for autonomy or even independence, the more so since such demands might be supported and even encouraged by the Soviet Union. Iraq felt that it needed the support of the Arabs in order to prevent such an eventuality from taking place.⁸

Less strongly felt but still important was Iraq's uneasiness about its relations with its southern neighbour, the Saudi monarchy, which succeeded in 1926 in expelling the Hashemite dynasty from Hijaz and uniting it with Najd into the Saudi Arabian kingdom. Hashemite fugitives at the Faysal's court in Baghdad were a permanent reminder of his father's ignominious fate. To this may be added various occasions of border tension arising from the complicated question of tribal wandering across the Iraq-Saudi border.[9]

All these factors drove Iraq to look for a wider framework in which it might feel more secure. This framework was to be the Fertile Crescent and specifically Syria. Together with the Arabs of Syria the Kurdish threat might look less menacing. One has also to remember that the Arab-Sunnite élite which ruled Iraq did not exceed about twenty five per cent of the population. It was only with the Sunnite Kurds that they constituted a match, at least numerically, for the Shi'ites who numbered more than fifty per cent. Therefore it may be rather reasonable to assume that Iraq's search for Sunni-Arab partners also stemmed from this consideration.

The Iraqis felt also that Syria was the land which connected them with the wider Arab world and through which passed the line of communication with the Mediterranean.[10] The development of the oil industry and the completion in the mid-thirties of the oil pipe-line to the Mediterranean through Syria made this last factor extremely important in Iraq's eyes. Such a connection with the Mediterranean was not a purely economic matter, although Iraq not infrequently stressed its desire to construct a railway to the Mediterranean coast to facilitate its commerce and other economic interests.[11] One Iraqi statesman regarded it as an alternative to the Persian Gulf, and hence it entailed a foothold in Beirut or Haifa.[12] It seems that Iraq was looking for a secure alternative to the Persian Gulf because of its weak position there. Its access to the Gulf was confined to the Shatt al-'Arab river which could not be trusted should a war break out with Iran. In such an eventuality Iran's advantageous position as a riparian along hundreds of miles of the Gulf coast would render Iraq's outlet to the high seas very precarious.

One should not forget that Syria's capital, Damascus, was the place in which Faysal had reigned after the First World War and it was there that he was crowned as an independent Arab sovereign (in his own and his followers' eyes, at least). Therefore, even disregarding any tangible interests, Damascus and Syria stood very close to Faysal's heart. What was happening in the other parts of the Fertile Crescent – Syria, Trans-Jordan and Palestine – awoke interest and a feeling of solidarity in both Iraq and its ruler. Furthermore, Faysal was convinced as early as 1933 that the French had reached an understanding with the Turks to transfer Alexandretta, Aleppo and Antioch to Turkish rule as soon as a favourable opportunity occurred. Such a loss would be a serious blow to Arab hopes and, moreover, a first step in a Turkish plan to regain Mosul. Therefore Iraq could not remain indifferent to developments in, and pertaining to, Syria.[13]

Faysal's Syrian initiatives

It is rather difficult, if not almost impossible, to know for sure when Iraq's king was motivated in his démarches towards Syria by his personal dynastic motives and sentiments and when by Iraq's state interests. However, at the very early stages of Faysal's endeavour to have a Hashemite prince installed as the ruler of Syria it seems certain that the motivation was dynastic. In April 1921, when Faysal's prospects of becoming the future King of Iraq were not yet fully certain, his envoy, General Haddad, tried to convince M. Berthelot, the French Foreign Minister, that in order to smooth the relations between the French and the Arabs within and without Syria an Arab ruler should be installed over the whole of Syria. This ruler had to be either Faysal's brother 'Abdallah or another Hashemite.[14] Thus, 'Abdallah, who had expected to become King of Iraq and in 1919 was proclaimed as such by the Iraqi–Arab nationalists working in Faysal's Syria, would have his aspirations satisfied, and the Hashemite dynasty would become the paramount force in the Arab world by gaining control over the Hijaz and most of the Fertile Crescent.

Already in that early stage of French rule in Syria such an idea did not fall on totally deaf ears, although memories of the recent conflict with Faysal's Hashemite monarchy in Syria were too vivid in the French Government's mind to rule out any substantial move towards their former enemies. Still, the French knew only too well that Faysal had not been an uncompromising enemy to their presence in Syria and that in late 1919 he had reached an agreement with their Prime Minister Georges Clemenceau which as a result of the intransigence of his nationalist followers (along with the fall of Clemenceau's government) was a little later to come to nought.[15]

And, indeed, several years later, in February 1924, the French High Commissioner for Syria and Lebanon, General Weygand, hinted in a talk with Nuri al-Sa'id that the French 'had under consideration the question whether Amir Ali, son of Hussein, could not be installed in much the same position as Faisal in Iraq in Syria'. It seems that the French were impressed by the rather smooth and tranquil situation that the British succeeded in bringing about in Iraq compared with the incessant agitation against their rule which was the order of the day in Syria.[16]

We do not know what precisely Weygand had in mind when he made this hint.[17] It looks as though the French were trying to ascertain Faysal's and Britain's possible reactions without committing themselves too much. If in 1924 the French had felt themselves to be in a disadvantageous position compared with the one held by Britain in Iraq, certainly at the end of 1925 there was much more ground for such feelings, as the Syrian revolt against their rule had reached its peak. The French were then trying to bring the revolt to an end by means of a double-edged weapon: on the one hand, they were employing harsh military measures to crush the revolt, while on the other, they were trying to gain the support of the more moderate sections of the public by expressing their readiness to negotiate, to hold elections to a representative council and to hasten the introduction of a constitution. As part of the latter task they resumed, so it seems, their contacts with Faysal. At an interview with M. Berthelot in November 1925, King Faysal was asked for his advice on solving the Syrian question. The King advocated a constitution similar to that instituted in Iraq, thus implying a Hashemite restoration.[18]

The French did not react to such a far-reaching proposition and we doubt that any intervention in the Syrian turmoil in 1925 on behalf of King Faysal could have contributed to the endeavour of finding a peaceful solution. Some of the Hashemites' staunchest supporters (the Druzes, Dr 'Abd al-Rahman Shahbandar, Nasib al-Bakri) were at the helm of the Revolt and it is doubtful that Faysal would have tried to influence them in the direction of a more moderate position, thus jeopardising their esteem for him. This same reason may also have been a source of French hesitation to carry on with their démarche. If Faysal's supporters in Syria were implicated in the Revolt it could – in the French view – damage Faysal's reliability.

But the downfall of the Hashemite monarchy in the Hijaz made the question of 'Ali, the last King of Hijaz, more imminent. In February 1926 Nuri al-Sa'id, then the Iraqi Minister for Foreign Affairs, proposed to General Weygand 'Ali's candidature for the Syrian throne. Consequently, 'Ali himself came to Beirut and had talks with the French HC on the same subject.[19] This visit, along with the publication in the summer of 1926 of an article in Le Matin by a French writer about the possibility of setting up a monarchy in Syria, gave rise to widespread interest in the topic among Syrian public opinion and the press. Thereafter, such a possibility and the imminent return of Faysal to Syria were frequently mentioned by the press in the Middle East.[20]

The next occasion for raising the possibility of installing a Hashemite prince on the throne of Syria came in 1928. In February of that year, the French High Commissioner announced the imminence of elections for a Constituent Assembly with an 'Agreement' with France to follow. This body, if it had properly functioned, could have shaped Syria's constitutional structure for many years to come. Faysal well understood this eventuality and he acted quickly. He sent emissaries to Syria to enquire of the French High Commissioner in Beirut whether or not a Hashemite prince would be regarded with favour by the French as a candidate for the throne of Syria. The High Commissioner did not consider himself authorised to commit his government on such a matter with such international implications and referred it to Paris. Through the good services of the British the views of the French Government, which were not favourable, became known to Faysal.[21]

Faysal and his followers did not confine their endeavours only to the diplomatic sphere. In 1928 they organised a monarchist party in Syria and through their mouthpiece, the Damascene newspaper *al-Mirsad*, advocated the idea that a monarchy was the only regime consistent with the country's traditions, its people's hopes and the requirement of stable government.[22] Petitions were submitted to the Constituent Assembly denouncing the article in the draft Constitution that provided for a republican regime. The members were called upon to replace it with a monarchy, mainly for two reasons: (*a*) a republican regime did not accord with the country's mentality and (*b*) according to Islamic practice, a ruler could not be a hired agent for a fixed period; Islam, therefore, did not recognise any regime but a monarchical one and since the overwhelming majority of the population was Muslim any regime but a monarchy was ruled out. Telegrams repeating these claims were cabled to the French Foreign Ministry and the press. The religious significance of this question was stressed when the monarchists asked the Muslim *'ulama'* (doctors of law) of Syria to express their authoritative reply (*fatwa*) to the following question: 'Your Eminences well know that the principles of government in Islam require a consultative (*Shura*) government relying on a King who will introduce unity and implement the laws. Therefore, is it lawful to substitute for this form of government, which has up to today unanimously been agreed upon, a republican civil form which reverts to frequent changes? Please, let us know your authoritative response'. And indeed the monarchists succeeded in obtaining a *fatwa* in support of this attitude. Also, Shaykh Taj al-Din al-Hasani, the foremost moderate leader and the then Prime Minister of Syria endorsed this view.[23]

As in the previous case, Faysal's attempts were not successful. Although two special emissaries (Tahsin Qadri and Rustum Haydar, the latter of Lebanese-Shi'ite origin) were sent by Faysal to convince the Assembly Members of his views, the majority, along with the public at large, supported a separate republican regime.[24] In the long run, this obstacle proved to be much more injurious to Hashemite designs over Syria than the French attitude. Faysal, no doubt, was aware of Syrian opposition to his proposals which were interpreted as an attempt at annexation of Syria by Iraq. It may well have been in order to alleviate such fears that he did not propose a comprehensive unification of both countries under one Parliament. What Faysal had in mind was that if he were King of both countries he would reside for half of the year in each and appoint a Regent during his absence.[25]

This cool reaction to Faysal's initiative did not deter him from attempting it again and again. On the contrary, it is very clear that the endeavour to get for himself or one of his family possession of the Syrian throne and thus be able to bring that country very close to his own had become the prime motive in Faysal's policy since the end of 1929. In September of that year, it had become apparent that Britain, since the Labour Party's rise to power, was ready to bring the mandatory regime in Iraq to an end, to replace it with a new kind of treaty relation between the two countries and to support Iraq's candidature for admission to the League of Nations.[26] Iraq realised that independence had fallen within reach. During the negotiations over the proposed treaty Faysal rejected the British demand to make the treaty of indefinite duration. He was afraid that such a precedent would be repeated by the French in Syria and thus the division between Syria permanently bound to France and Iraq permanently bound to Britain would be perpetuated.[27] Sir Francis Humphrys, the British High Commissioner for Iraq, well understood Iraq's position that the establishment of an independent Iraq state was 'the first step towards the distant goal of Arab unity'.[28] Furthermore, Iraq was the first to gain independence among the Arab countries which had hitherto been placed under foreign tutelage. Being first, Iraq felt under a special obligation to promote the independence of other Arab countries and to ensure their unity. As Taha al-Hashimi, a veteran Arab nationalist and a former Iraqi Chief-of-Staff turned statesman, put it in his *Diaries*: 'Independent Iraq was the factor that could fruitfully work for the independence of the other Arab countries and for the safeguard of [Arab] unity'.[29]

Another factor drove Faysal almost at the same time to advocate a union of the Fertile Crescent countries. This was the flare-up of the Arab-Jewish conflict in Palestine, which culminated in August 1929 in the Wailing Wall riots.[30] Faysal based his *locus standi* in the affairs of a foreign country under the mandatory rule of Britain on 'the racial and religious traditions and relations which bind me with the Arabs of Palestine'. Faysal well understood how difficult the Palestine question was for Britain, torn between two conflicting parties both of whom were armed with strong moral arguments and possessing political leverage. Therefore he suggested a scheme to solve the problem, which on the one hand would be part of a comprehensive Arab unity and on the other would relieve Britain of that burden. He hoped that the possibility of such relief might impel Britain to support his plan. Faysal's basic assumption was the possibility of reconciling the aspirations of both Arabs and Jews if the Balfour Declaration were interpreted in a less far-reaching way and Arab unity advanced by the unification of either Syria, Iraq and Palestine or of Trans-Jordan and Palestine only. Faysal was ready to admit the right of persecuted Jews to find refuge in his unified Arab state because he believed it was the prospect of becoming a subject minority within the limits of Palestine that was the threat which exasperated the Arabs. If Palestine were united with Syria and Iraq, that threat would be removed and Faysal saw no difficulty in arranging for a satisfactory development of a Jewish national home in Palestine which would be redefined in a much stricter way than previously.[31]

Faysal's propositions fell on deaf ears in London. In those days Britain did not contemplate any renunciation of its position in Palestine. In fact, it was the other way round; the early 1930s were the period when Palestine became very important in the eyes of Britain's strategists as a maritime base for its Mediterranean fleet, a fuelling post for aircraft en route to the Far East, a terminal for an Iraq oil pipeline and as a possible alternative location for the Egyptian garrison should the 1929 draft treaty with Egypt be ratified. Although the British were to some extent impressed by Faysal's moderate tone they politely rejected his suggestions.[32]

The British position that the Palestine question should be dealt with on its own merits did not discourage Faysal from pursuing his proposal, since Palestine was for him a means by which he could achieve his unity scheme, possibly serving as bait for the British. When, about a year later, he repeated his proposal in a conversation with the British President in 'Amman, he dropped Palestine from his proposed Federation of Arab States, agreeing that owing to the existence of Palestine's Holy Places this country should remain under British rule. The omission of Palestine from his proposed Federation was not permanent. In November 1932 his scheme again included Palestine and it seems that thenceforward this country became a permanent component in his and his successors' political thinking.[33]

Already in 1930 he had added the Arabian kingdom of Ibn Saud and the Yemen to the Fertile Crescent states of Iraq, Syria and Trans-Jordan. As for the former, Faysal was convinced that Ibn Saud's kingdom would go to pieces on the death of its present monarch,[34] implying that Britain, the principal foreign friend of Ibn Saud, should best preempt such a possibility by supporting Faysal's proposed federation.[35]

Soon afterwards Faysal began to substantiate his concepts by attempting to strengthen Iraq's relations with its Arab neighbours and establishing an 'Arab Alliance'. At the end of 1930 negotiations were begun between Iraq and Trans-Jordan aiming at a treaty of friendship and co-operation, which culminated in March 1931 with the signing of the treaty of friendship. The treaty was regarded a 'practical example of the good understanding which should exist between Arab Kings and Governments',[36] thus implying that other Arab countries should follow suit. More practical agreements over border relations and extradition were concluded with Egypt and the Saudi kingdom of Najd and Hijaz. Iraq also tried to persuade the Yemen to join the Alliance and Nuri al-Sa'id and Taha al-Hakimi were sent to San'a to discuss the matter with Imam Yahya.[37] A place was left open for Syria declaring that 'there is nothing to prevent her from joining this Alliance when a national government is set up in it such as will realise the aspirations of the Syrian people to liberty and independence'.[38]

However, developments in Syria were not proceeding in that direction. Since the formation of a Constituent Assembly in June 1928 the French authorities had been engaged in a political struggle with the nationalist circles over the drafting of the Syrian Constitution and the possibility of substituting for the mandatory regime a treaty relationship between France and the Levant States which would be modelled on the Iraqi precedent. This struggle reached its height in the winter of 1930 with strikes, demonstrations and the inevitable repressive counter-measures. On 14 May 1930 the High Commissioner dissolved the Constituent Assembly and promulgated by decree a constitution for Syria after deleting the controversial clauses which impinged upon the status of the mandatory regime.[39] The fact that during and after this crisis some French officials resorted to dropping hints about their readiness to see a Hashemite prince installed as a King of Syria can be interpreted either as an indicator that they had been impressed by the relative success of the British in Iraq or as an artifice which hinted to the Syrian nationalists that they might be circumvented unless they came to their senses. And, indeed, Sir Francis Humphrys, after having talked to M. Paul Lépissier, the French *chargé d'affaires* in Baghdad and a former secretary of the French High Commissioner for Syria, wrote of the latter: 'He tells me that he is convinced that the only satisfactory solution of the Syrian problem is for the French Government to follow our example in Iraq, but he laments to me in private that the Quai d'Orsay is generally overruled by the military party in Paris'.[40]

A year later an authoritative spokesman of French policy in Syria expressed similar views. When Sir Francis Humphrys visited Syria and talked with Henri Ponsot (the French High Commissioner) he was told that British policy in Iraq was right in principle, that the 1930 treaty 'while it carefully safeguarded British interests, represented a generous and a statesmanlike endeavour to meet the legitimate aspirations of the Iraqis towards independence' and that a similar policy should be pursued in Syria. As for the form of the regime he did not believe 'that any French Government would raise objections to the creation of a monarchy, if the Syrians expressed their preference for this form of government. In that case the Syrians would, he hoped, be left free to choose their own King, whether from the Hashimite family, or from the sons of Ibn Saud, or from elsewhere, he could not say'.[41] Lépissier repeated his view, but this time in public. In an interview to a Syrian newspaper he declared that 'France did not object to the assumption of the Syrian throne by ex-King Ali [Faysal's elder brother] if the Syrians wished this'.[42]

Now the French démarches were part of a general policy change. First of all in June 1931 they informed the Permanent Mandates Commission of the League of Nations of their 'intention of concluding in the near future treaties with the Governments of Syria and the Lebanon, taking into account the evolution which has taken place and the progress which has been achieved'.[43] Secondly, the French attempted to overrule Faysal's objection to the Iraqi oil pipeline to the Mediterranean passing through a French-controlled area, on the grounds that if the pipe were laid through Syria, the French would never evacuate that country. Therefore, so it seems, they tried to impress Faysal with the argument that by opposing French interests in the oil question he might endanger the prospects of his dynasty in Syria.[44]

A direct approach to Faysal had become necessary. In January 1931 M. Paul Lépissier sounded both King Faysal and Sir Francis Humphrys on the kind of condition which any prospective candidate for the throne of Syria would be likely to impose before he agreed to become king. Faysal took this seriously, consulting the British High Commissioner on the subject and resuming his activity in Syria (see later on, on p. 11). Several months later, in September of that year, Faysal visited Paris and had a talk with M. Berthelot. According to Faysal's account of the talk, Berthelot repeated that the French Government were considering the terms of a treaty which they hoped to negotiate with Syria next winter, after elections had been held and a Syrian Government had been formed. He added that although the constitution provided for a Republic, it was probable that the Syrians would prefer to have a king rather than a president. This question and the actual choice of a king were matters which the French Government would be prepared to leave entirely to the discretion of the Syrian people. Most importantly, he expressed the view that his government now realised that they had made a mistake when they expelled King Faysal from Damascus in 1920, and they would welcome the return of Faysal as King of Syria if this was the expressed verdict of the people.[45] In a public reception M. Paul Reynaud, the French Minister for the Colonies, toasted Faysal as the 'King of the Arabs' and gave him the impression that he was shortly to be invited by the French Government to accept the throne of Syria. The French Ministry of Foreign Affairs – which regarded Reynaud's words as mistaken and unfortunate, and saw to it that he did not repeat the mistake when he visited Baghdad in November – took the position that nothing in the reception exceeded customary, though cordial, treatment. Nevertheless Faysal was deeply impressed and reacted accordingly.[46]

Already in June 1931 Faysal had sent Yasin al-Hashimi, one of the more radical Iraqi statesmen, to Syria in order to win over Faris al-Khuri, the most influential Syrian nationalist leader of the Christian faith. The envoy made considerable progress in this matter[47] and Faris al-Khuri afterwards maintained pro-Iraqi leanings for many years. Faysal himself, following the talks with the French officials and what looked to him more than the required cordial reception, intensified the propaganda campaign in Syria and the Lebanon. On the same night in which the reception took place Faysal called upon Faris al-Khuri who had also come to Paris. Both agreed that the latter would immediately return to Syria to convince the leaders of the national bloc to agree to Faysal's being entrusted with the throne of Syria, which then seemed to him to be almost a settled question.[48] When Faysal returned to Baghdad he sent Rustum Haydar, one of his closest and most loyal associates who had just been appointed as Minister of Finance, to Syria and the Lebanon to carry on the pro-Faysal campaign there. His being of Lebanese origin was likely to be an advantage to him in his task. In addition to these people of public standing, Faysal also sent agents to propagandise his candidature to the throne.[49]

Faysal's Syrian supporters made use of the decisions of the Syrian Congress which had been convened in July 1919 and had resolved to demand a constitutional monarchy for a united Syria, comprising Lebanon, Trans-Jordan and Palestine. The monarchists claimed that the 1919 Congress resolutions were especially valid since its delegates had come from all parts of the 'Syrian territories' and had expressed their views in a greater atmosphere of freedom. In addition to the constitutional matter, this party had published a 48-article programme which stressed the unity of the 'Syrian Territories' and the illegality of any surrender of any part of them, and demanded, *inter alia*, the conclusion of a treaty based on national sovereignty, the formation of a patriotic (*watani*) army, the cancellation of the laws and regulations which had been enacted since the evacuation of the Turks, and the expulsion of all foreign officials except specialists who were indispensable.[50]

Internal developments also required the intensification of Faysal's propaganda campaign in Syria. In mid-November 1931 the French mandatory authorities decided to put the suspended Constitution into force and to hold elections to a Parliament. The elections were held during the next month, but the Extraordinary Session of the elected Chamber, whose purpose was to elect their officers (President, Vice-Presidents and Secretaries), took place in Damascus only on 7 June 1932. This was a long period of active political struggle between the Nationalists and more moderate factions, in an attempt at influencing the voters before the elections, and after they had been held, over the control of the Chamber. The Nationalists strongly attacked the French authorities with regard to the propriety of the elections and to their declared returns, claiming that the authorities had illegally tampered with the ballot boxes.

During these months of fierce struggle various newspapers in both Syria and Iraq constantly published articles in support of the Hashemite claim to the Syrian throne.[52] Yasin al-Hashimi again went to Syria and Lebanon to propagate the idea of unity under the Hashemites and upon his return the organ of his more nationalist party published an editorial which stressed Iraq's duties towards the not yet independent Arab countries.[53] Faysal's supporters distributed petitions in Damascus, which thousands of people signed 'in favour of entrusting to King Faisal the mission of protecting the rights of the country'. In June 1933 Faysal stayed at 'Amman en route to Europe.[54] The organisers of the petition sent a delegation which included two MPs, Jamil Mardam and Muzhir Raslan, to meet Faysal and ask him to work in international circles for the independence of Syria, Lebanon and Palestine. Now that Iraq, first among the Arab countries, had already been admitted to the League of Nations, great hopes were raised in the Arab world regarding the support and services that Iraq could and should render to 'its oppressed brethren'. This delegation claimed that the majority of the population in the Levant supported Faysal's becoming King of their countries.[55]

Faysal's direct appeal to national opinion in Syria did not bear the expected fruit. Most of the monarchist candidates failed in the elections,[56] and Faysal tried to outmanoeuvre the Nationalists by appealing to other quarters. Later, in November 1932, Faysal met various Druze leaders from Syria and enquired whether or not his candidature to the Syrian throne was acceptable to them. He promised them that he would not interfere with the affairs of their religion nor with their 'feudal' privileges. The earlier support for Faysal by the two Druze leaders from Lebanon, the brothers Shakib and 'Adil Arslan was used by Faysal to his benefit during these contacts.[57]

Although Faysal asked the British for advice regarding his policy, the British representatives avoided giving him a clear-cut clue as to their plans, since they did not want to expose their negative attitude to his ideas (see ch. 4, pp. 198–203). Ignorant of the real British attitude, Faysal was encouraged by the victory of the parties of the Left in the 1932 French elections and sent Ihsan al-Jabiri, one of the Syrian Pan-Arabists, to arrange his visit to Paris during his forthcoming visit to Europe scheduled for the following year. But the Assyrian trouble of June–July 1933 and Faysal's premature death in September of that year put an end to this démarche.[58]

In 1932 Faysal had felt a sense of urgency about the future of his plan for a confederation of Arab States under the Hashemites. He was confident that the precedent of Iraq's becoming independent of the mandatory regime would within three years be repeated in territories under the French mandate. Therefore once again one of his closest associates, this time Nuri al-Sa'id, repeated before the British the details of his proposal in order to win them over. The novelty this time was Faysal's (or Nuri al-Sa'id's) realisation that the formation of the confederation should be gradually accomplished. Once Syria had become independent and joined the proposed Union, Trans-Jordan should be released from the mandate and absorbed into Iraq. The Hijaz would in any case fall under the Hashemites upon the death of Ibn Saud, 'whose influence was now definitely on the wane'. After Trans-Jordan Faysal's next step would be an attempt at obtaining a direct settlement with the Jews as a preliminary to negotiating with His Majesty's Government for the emancipation of Palestine. This he hoped to achieve through a treaty similar to the Anglo-Iraqi Treaty of 1930 and the inclusion of that country in the proposed federation.[59]

When Faysal came to London in June 1933 for political talks Nuri al-Sa'id, his Foreign Minister at that stage, told British Foreign Office officials that he had been instructed to deliver a message that the present time would be an extremely favourable opportunity for a meeting between Dr Chaim Weizmann and King Faysal, who thought that he might be able to smooth over some of the present difficulties between Arabs and Jews in Palestine. Upon further enquiry Faysal denied that he had made such a suggestion although he would be happy to meet Dr Weizmann. Sir Francis Humphrys was convinced that the suggestion had originally been put forward by Nuri al-Sa'id, in order to manoeuvre the British Government into taking the initiative or to ensure that Dr Weizmann would be the first to approach the King. King Faysal would then agree to meet Dr Weizmann as a special favour to the British Government and subsequently would probably make undesirable capital out of his position. Since this was the British interpretation of Nuri al-Sa'id's proposition the British made no haste to react and nothing happened up to 20 July when Faysal left London. His premature death two months later prevented any continuation of this initiative, which may have originally emanated from Nuri Pasha or from the King.[60]

Whatever the importance that Faysal may have attributed to the Palestine question, it was not the only nor even the main subject that occupied Faysal's attention during his official talks in London through his last visit there in June–July 1933. In his meeting with Sir John Simon and Sir Francis Humphrys he stressed Iraq's need for a line of communication to the Mediterranean either through Syria or through Palestine, preferring the latter so long as the French remained the masters of Syria and were capable of using this proposed communication line to spread their influence into Iraq. Faysal left his interlocutors in no doubt that since the Syrians were Arabs 'it was only natural that the Arabs of Iraq should take the greatest interest in their destiny' and now that Iraq had become a full member of the League of Nations, the Iraqi Government would challenge French policy in Syria at the next meeting of the Assembly of that body. The British were not moved although they were no doubt impressed by Faysal's sincerity in expressing his desire to continue working through close co-operation with them.⁶¹

At this juncture, a group of ardent Arab nationalists were endeavouring to promote of the idea of Arab unity by its transformation into a concrete political programme and the formation of a political organisation aimed at its implementation. For them Faysal's Iraq could serve as a suitable springboard for their enterprise or even as a possible Piedmont; whereas for Faysal these Pan-Arabists were a possible source of support. Therefore, Faysal's and the pan-Arabists' courses of action necessarily crossed each other but again to no avail. Internal conflicts of interest and external pressure combined together to thwart this joint initiative.

It seems that sometime in the spring of 1931 various Pan-Arab leaders, members of the Syrian National Bloc, supporters of the Arab-Islamic trend in Egypt, radical anti-British politicians in Iraq, etc. were approached by Shakib Arslam, the Lebanese Druze of strong pan-Arab and pan-Islamic views, in order to form a radical organisation which would act for the liberation of the Arab countries, especially Syria and Palestine, from foreign rule.⁶² This far-reaching scheme did not materialise but the conviction that something had to be done did not disappear and it was quite soon revived. During the meetings of the Islamic Congress, which convened in Jerusalem in December 1931,⁶³ about 50 individuals — former members of *al-Fatah*, active supporters of Faysal's regime in Damascus in 1918–20 and resolute nationalist leaders of the day (mostly Palestinians and Syrians) — met together in the house of 'Awni 'Abd al-Hadi. They decided to lay down a Pan-Arab National Covenant as the foundation for an endeavour to convene a General Arab Congress. The Covenant had three articles:

1 That Arab countries are an indivisible unity and [that] the Arab Nation does not recognise nor agrees to any kind of division.
2 The endeavours in each Arab country should be directed towards the sole aim of total independence, safeguarding their unity and resisting any idea of being content with action for local and regional (*iqlimiyyah*) policies.
3 That imperialism in any shape or form is totally contrary to the honour and the greatest aspiration of the Arab Nation and that, in consequence, the Arab Nation should reject imperialism and resist it with all its might.

The participants also elected a Preparatory Committee to lay the groundwork for such a congress, which was composed of As'ad Daghir (Maronite Lebanese, living in Egypt), Khayr al-Din al-Zirikli (Syrian, also living in Egypt), 'Ajaj Nuwayhid (Palestinian of Lebenese Druze stock) and Subhi al-Khadra', 'Izzat Darwaza and 'Awni 'Abd al-Hadi (the last three were all Palestinians). This committee, later named the Executive

Committee of the General Arab Congress, called upon sundry Arab personalities in Syria, Iraq and Egypt, to take part in the proposed congress.

The Covenant roused interest and support in various Arab countries. In Egypt the support came mainly from the traditional supporters of Arabism, such as the newspaper *Kawkab al-Sharq* and the politicians Hamid al-Basil, and 'Abd al-Rahman 'Azzam,[64] who in early 1932 were still members of the influential *Wafd* party. And indeed, in May this party sent a letter to the organisers of the congress in which they declared their readiness for a joint action based on the three principles of the Covenant.[65] But owing to a split in the *Wafd* party, as a result of which the pan-Arabists found themselves outside the party, the possibility of its participation became unlikely. Since they did not attend any meeting of the Preparatory Committee and no other Wafdist representative had been nominated, one of the organisers complained to Mustafa al-Nahhas Pasha, leader of the *Wafd*, of this lukewarmness on the part of Egypt and urged him to ensure that the *Wafd* would be represented at the congress.[66]

The Preparatory Committee was not known of course by this failure. More Syrian, Lebanese-Muslim and Iraqi personalities (such as Shukri al-Quwatli, the brothers Nabih and 'Adil al-'Azmah, Yasin al-Hashimi and Riyad al-Sulh) joined the organisers, the preliminary discussions were carried on and the Preparatory Committee was legally registered as an association.[67] Their greatest hope was Iraq and their eyes turned towards its ruling circles more than anywhere else. The Preparatory Committee made up their minds to convene the congress at Baghdad and obtained the consent of Nuri al-Sa'id, the Iraqi Prime Minister, who in June 1932 visited Lebanon.[68] Three months later when King Faysal visited 'Amman the organisers of the congress went there to discuss with him the congress programme, its date and place, and secured his blessing on the congress being held in his capital, Baghdad.[69] Top Iraqi statesmen – Yasin al-Hashimi, Nuri al-Sa'id, Jamil al-Midfa'i, 'Ali Jwadat, Sa'id Thabit and Mawlud Mukhlis – formed an Iraqi Preparatory Committee to encourage local religious and political personalities who had been approved by King Faysal to take part in the preliminary discussion. Yasin al-Hashimi was the central figure in this committee and he went several times to Egypt to try to get more support for the congress.[70]

It was not, however, at Egypt that the Iraqi supporters of the congress were aiming but at Syria. At his meeting in 'Amman in September 1932 with the organisers of the congress, King Faysal sought their support for the proposed confederation of Iraq and Syria under his crown provided that Syria would become independent on the same lines as Iraq and they would make this plan of unity one of the principal items on the congress agenda. Shakib Arslan, 'Awni 'Abd al-Hadi, Riyad al-Sulh and the Syro-Palestinian Congress publicly supported this idea. Faysal stressed his view that the congress would bring about unity among the Arabs by substituting the pursuit of a clearly defined common aim, such as his, for the present chaos of conflicting views which divided even the active nationalists.[71] This attitude was fully shared by the Iraqi Preparatory Committee. In their published announcement they made it clear that they had 'formed a committee among us which would work in the name of Iraq for the rescue of Syria and for the implementation of the Arabs' aspirations in their various countries'. The Syrians were especially exhorted to keep up their steadfastness and unity and to rely in particular upon Iraq, and the Arab peoples in general, in the course of their struggle.[72]

The original decision of the Preparatory Committee, taken in a meeting attended by Yasin al-Hashimi, was to hold the General Arab Congress in Baghdad in the autumn of 1932. But soon afterwards it was realised that such an early date had become impossible. In the summer of 1932 some of the tribes of northern Hijaz, under the leadership of Ibn Rifadah, had revolted against the Saudi authorities. Since the latter were sure that Amir 'Abdallah of Trans-Jordan had supported the rebels, the Saudis became very suspicious towards the Hashemites and their intentions in general.

Consequently the pan-Arabists split between pro-Saudi and pro-Hashemite factions and quarrelled over the eventual place of the congress, the former advocating Mecca as a proper place while the latter stuck to Baghdad. The pro-Saudis raised an interesting argument against the suitability of Baghdad: the strong British influence there as opposed to Mecca which was free from any foreign presence and possible interference.[73] King Ibn Saud himself made public his conditions for giving his support to holding the congress: 'that the decisions were to be free from taint of personal and material interests and were directed solely towards "the advantage of the Arabs"'.[74] This view was rightly interpreted as a qualified support accorded on condition that the congress was not made the means of forwarding any personal-dynastic interest or of affecting the union of Syria and Iraq. In order to solve this impasse, Yasin al-Hashimi put forward the suggestion that the congress would advocate the union of Palestine and Trans-Jordan, and when these were united, they would be placed under the Government of Iraq. The question of Syria would be dealt with later.[75]

When this proposal was accepted and the controversy was settled, April 1933 was fixed as a possible date for holding the congress in Baghdad.[76] But now the organisers were confronted with a higher obstacle, the British negative attitude (see, for details, pp. 201–3). Faced with British pressure, Faysal tried to convince them that the congress would discuss

Arab problems in a calm and a statesmanlike manner, and would seek by constructive proposals to facilitate the solution of the difficulties which confronted Great Britain and France in their relations with the Arabs.[77] But since the British were not convinced, Faysal had to drop the idea of holding the congress at any rate till the autumn, and Yasin al-Hashimi resigned from the Iraqi Preparatory Committee.[78] In September 1933 Faysal died and the political situation in Baghdad drastically changed. The pan-Arabists continued for some time to consider the holding of the congress in an alternative place or to establish a unified all-Arab party, but such a scheme did not materialise and holding a congress without the strong backing of an independent state was regarded as purely ceremonial.[79] The failure was complete.

Faysal's policy with regard to Syria met with difficulties made not only by foreign factors, such as the British, the French or the majority of Syrian Nationalists, but also from within his own family. We have already noticed that during and upon the constitutional crisis in Syria of the winter of 1930 the French were dropping hints that they were looking for a king for Syria (see pp. 10–11 of this chapter). M. Lépissier, the French *chargé d'affaires* in Baghdad, told Faysal that the French Government had three candidates in mind, and that one of them was ex-king 'Ali, the last Hashemite King of Hijaz and Faysal's eldest brother. Lépissier added that the French Government really wished to discuss with Faysal the possible offer to 'Ali of the throne of Syria.[80]

At the same time, two French officials (M. Maurepas and Captain Terrier) even enquired of 'Ali what were his views with regard to Syria's constitutional question and told him that the French Government had come to the conclusion that the time had arrived for them to conclude a treaty with united Syria (excluding the Lebanon) on the lines of the Anglo-Iraqi Treaty of 1922. Jealous of his brother Faysal, 'Ali was moved by this French step.[81] He asked Lépissier to see to it that he would be invited for a visit to Syria and the Lebanon in order to see for himself in which directions French policy and Syrian Nationalists' aspirations were turning and to convince them to support his candidature for the throne of Syria. M. Lépissier, who was very anxious to succeed in getting Iraq's consent to the passage of the Iraqi oil pipeline through Syria, got the agreement of the French High Commissioner for Syria to invite 'Ali for a visit. And indeed, in January 1931 while 'Ali was visiting 'Amman he got this invitation and unhesitatingly accepted.

Sir Francis Humphrys suspected that M. Lépissier had been led by his own personal convictions to anticipate the adoption of a policy which the French Government had in fact no intention of pursuing.[82] The British were in a much better position to know what French policy really was and to evaluate it properly; it was even more important that not only 'Ali but also his brother and another prominent Iraqi politician accepted

Lépissier's démarches and enquiries at face value.[83] Faysal was not happy over this French step and his brother's positive response, and did not hide his reservations from the British. Syrian politicians were also aware of 'Ali's moves and of the duplicity of the French manoeuvre. None of them supported 'Ali's candidacy and Faysal admitted that 'Ali was not working on his (Faysal's) behalf.[84] Therefore, one can conclude with reasonable certainty that 'Ali's endeavour did not strengthen the Hashemite bid for the Syrian throne.

Another, and more serious, obstacle to Faysal's attempts was his brother 'Abdallah's own ambitions. For his part 'Abdallah let it be known that he opposed the candidature of either Faysal or 'Ali to the Syrian throne. The British authorities realised that 'Abdallah's opposition was connected with the latter's personal ambitions towards this position and they had to assure 'Abdallah that they had not promised Faysal to support his bid.[85] 'Abdallah was very jealous of his younger brother who had become a king while he, 'Abdallah, had to content himself with the lesser title and position of Amir, and the British Ambassador to Iraq was in 1933 of the opinion that 'Abdallah's intrigues were likely to interfere very considerably with the smooth working of Faysal's plans.[86] 'Abdallah's jealousy of his brother reached such magnitude that he resented the tokens of condolence that the Arabs of Palestine expressed in September 1933 when the body of his deceased brother reached Haifa *en route* to its last resting-place in Baghdad. More astonishing is that even a year later when the first anniversary of Faysal's death was commemorated with deep sorrow by the Arabs of Palestine 'Abdallah could not help expressing his strong feelings of censure.[87]

'Abdallah's negative attitude was not expressed only in emotional terms. He went further and tried to convince the British how dangerous Faysal was to them. He told Sir Arthur Wauchope, the High Commissioner for Palestine and Trans-Jordan that King Faysal had been and still was a sympathiser of the Arab *Istiqlal* (Independence) Party and still provided them with some of their funds. 'Abdallah stressed the extreme character of this party, implying that Faysal was committing a dangerous mistake in his support for them.[88]

Faysal for his part did not keep to himself his disappointment over his brother's attitude and he expressed this with 'unusual vehemence'. Faysal strongly resented the deal which 'Abdallah was in 1932 negotiating with the Jewish Agency according to which 'Abdallah would lease a large tract of his lands in Ghawr al-Kabd in Trans-Jordan. Faysal claimed that 'Abdallah 'had brought disgrace and humiliation on his family and all but ruin on himself'. Another source of friction between the two royal brothers was the question of their attitude to Ibn Saud. While 'Abdallah had never acquiesced in the former's occupation of the Hijaz, the Hashemite ancestral land, and nourished the hope of regaining it, Faysal had practically resigned himself to it, and in 1930 recognised the Saudi rule of his native country. Regarding this question 'Abdallah was furious with his brother and wrote him a very strong letter 'reproving him for his treachery to the Hashimite family'.[89]

This sort of mutual distrust was not kept secret and various stories were published in the newspapers of the Arab countries, particularly in Palestine and Syria. Both brothers denied them, but it looked, to put it mildly, rather strange that 'Abdallah's declaration, after having disavowed the existence of any controversy between the two brothers and having disapproved of 'securing personal benefit by the way of trading with the interests of a whole nation [the Syrian]', went further to deny recent press reports 'regarding attempts on the part of the Royal Court of Baghdad for intervention with certain quarters in connection with Syrian affairs'. It stressed that 'the Royal Diwan at Baghdad had never contemplated any interference with affairs of Syria'. As far as his aspirations and possible interference were concerned, 'Abdallah's declaration was mute. This inter-Hashemite conflict of interest led the rival claimants for the Syrian throne to concede 'the ability and competence of the Syrians to appreciate the interests of their country' and their having no need of (foreign) intervention in the affairs of Syria.[90] Thus, they weakened the argument of historical legitimacy in the Hashemite bid for the Syrian throne and strengthened the right of the Syrian people to decide their own kind of régime regardless of the 1919–20 precedent.

These inter-Hashemite conflicts, Britain's strong reservations and French duplicity were not the only obstacles in Faysal's path to the Syrian throne. The Saudi King had never ceased to worry over Faysal's designs regarding Syria and even the Hijaz, although — as we have noticed — the latter publicly recognised Saudi rule there. Therefore, Ibn Saud exerted pressure on the French not to conclude a deal with Faysal and also gave money to Syrian politicians, such as Jamil Mardam and Kamil al-Qassab (the latter being a lifelong Saudi agent), to encourage their activities against Faysal's plan.[91] The pro-Saudi politicians in Syria launched a propaganda campaign against the Hashemites and among those Syrians who preferred a monarchy to a republic, there were some who supported the candidature of Faysal, the son of 'Abd al-Aziz Al Sa'ud, and not of Faysal the First, the Hashemite King of Iraq, or another Hashemite prince.[92] Sharif Arslan the Pan-Arab activist tried to change Ibn Saud's negative attitude towards the Hashemites. He argued to him that the candidature of King Faysal was preferable to that of any possible Egyptian candidate (see below) and to a republican regime in Syria. He claimed that the French preference was for a republic, implying that it was detrimental to the Arabs and that the idea of a republican regime might one day cross the Arabian desert and reach Ibn Saud's kingdom itself.⁹³ Faysal himself had come to terms with Ibn Saud and reached friendly relations with Saudi Arabia,⁹⁴ but 'Abdallah's negative attitude towards the Saudis and his involvement in the 1932 anti-Saudi revolt of the tribes of Hijaz⁹⁵ damaged Saudi–Hashemite relations for many years to come. It seems that Faysal's dissociation from 'Abdallah, and his readiness to use his good offices to improve the relations between Ibn Saud and 'Abdallah, failed to bring about a rapprochement between the two.⁹⁶

The Hashemite bid for the Syrian throne ran into trouble with some of the other Middle Eastern countries as well. The Turkish Government expressed their uneasiness at the probability that Faysal's installation in Damascus would be nothing but a facade behind which French troops would remain in Syria. While they claimed that they did not oppose in principle a possible unity between Syria and Iraq,⁹⁷ their support of another candidate to the Syrian throne indicated the opposite (see below).

Egypt also expressed its dislike of a possible choice of any member of the Hashemite dynasty as a King of Syria. But this country was then much more disturbed by the candidature of the former Khedive 'Abbas Hilmi who in the early 1930s promoted his own candidature for the Syrian throne while engaged in diverse political activities all over the Middle East, including an attempt to bring about a solution to the Palestine question. Both the Egyptian King and his government strongly opposed 'Abbas Hilmi's candidature since they were afraid if 'Abbas Hilmi obtained the throne of Syria, he would use it to return to Egypt, where he had been deposed in 1914 and subsequently denied the right to be involved in any political activity. But the possibility of a scion of the dynasty of Muhammad 'Ali being installed on the Syrian throne pleased them and a few years later they offered the candidature of the Prince 'Abd al-Mun'im, the son of 'Abbas Hilmi.

Unlike the Egyptians the Turkish Government in 1931–33 supported this candidature⁹⁸ of 'Abbas Hilmi as he was a man who had long-established connections with Turkey and felt at home with Turkish culture.⁹⁹ But the overriding reason, so it seems, was that 'Abbas Hilmi's becoming King of Syria would ensure the separation between Syria and Hashemite Iraq. Contrary to what they once told the British Ambassador later on, the Turks admitted that they disliked the possibility of a union between these two countries and the emergence of a powerful Arab state on their southern border. They also hoped that with a good friend of Turkey sitting on the Syrian throne, they would be able to reach an agreement with regard to a ratification of the Turco-Syrian border to their advantage.¹⁰⁰ Upon the death of Faysal, however, the Turkish support for the candidature of 'Abbas Hilmi waned, as there was no longer need to block the candidature of Faysal.¹⁰¹

The sudden death of Faysal drastically changed the situation as far as the Hashemite bid for the Syrian throne was concerned. It is true that not everybody thought that such a change had taken place, but they were later proved wrong. On the fortieth day after Faysal's death, a memorial gathering took place in Baghdad, in which delegates from several Arab countries participated. The Iraqi speakers did not refer to the question of Arab unity, but the Muslim speakers from Syria and Lebanon 'urged the people of Iraq to work for unity of Iraq and Syria under a Hashemite King, swearing allegiance to King Ghazi as successor of King Faysal of Syria' and renewing the pledge made to King Faysal when he was proclaimed King of Syria in Damascus in 1919.[102]

'Ali, who survived his younger brother for two years, immediately upon his brother's death renewed his endeavours to be installed on the Syrian throne. He got in touch with French officials to discover whether now there was any prospect of his being invited to accept the throne of Syria.[103] The most influential pro-Hashemite newspaper in Syria, *Alif Ba'*, published an article in support of 'Ali's coming to the Syrian throne.[104] The French, however, were not moved. On the contrary, they resorted to their own stratagem of hinting that they were considering the possibility of substituting a monarchy for the republican regime in Syria, this time having in mind the candidacy of 'Abd al-Majid or of his father 'Ali Haydar of the rival branch of the Hashemite family (Dhaw Zayd), who had up to 1909 preceded Husayn Ibn 'Ali, the father of 'Ali and Faysal, as the Amir and Sharif of Mecca.[104a]

The French were thus simultaneously threatening the two other protagonists for power over Syria: the Syrian National Bloc and Hashemite Iraq. The Syrian Nationalists rejected the version of the treaty which the new French High Commissioner had just presented to them and relations between the French and the Nationalists were again deadlocked, and tension was increased by demonstrations, arrests and the like. The Iraqi Government had adopted a stiff position through the negotiations with the French mandatory authorities in Syria over the conclusion of a commercial agreement between Syria and Iraq. It seems rather clear that at this juncture (the end of 1933) the French wanted to pressurise both these two factors into more pliant positions. When Lord Tyrrell, British Ambassador in Paris, called on the Comte de Saint Quentin, Director of Arabian and Levant Affairs at the French Foreign Ministry, and directly asked him whether the rumours of French support for the candidature of 'Abd al-Majid Ibn Sharif 'Ali Haydar were founded or not, he did not receive a fully convincing reply. The British Ambassador got the impression that his French interlocutor was hesitant in his answer, and he was not convinced that the French Government 'were altogether a stranger to any idea that 'Abd al-Majid might one day become the candidate of their choice'.[105] It seems that such an impression exactly suited the French aims.

It should be added that such hint-dropping, whenever the French were faced with troubles either with Hashemite Iraq or with the Syrian Nationalists, continued unabated. In June 1935 Lépissier alluded to the candidacy of one of Ibn Saud's sons to the Syrian throne and in 1939 'Abd al-Majid told his brother that French '"Military authorities" assured him of their support in his candidature for the throne of Syria'.[106]

To the forces working against 'Ali one should add the Iraqi Government and King Ghazi as well. Immediately after his father's death, the latter made it clear that he would not welcome 'Ali's candidacy and both the Prime Minister (Rashid 'Ali al-Kaylani) and the Minister of the Interior (Hikmat Sulayman) assured the British Ambassador 'that the present Government did not propose to support the policy of union with Syria which was so dear to the heart of the late King Feisal'.[107]

'Abdallah's Greater Syria project

The death of King Faysal and the abstention of King Ghazi and the Iraqi Government from pursuing the unity policy of the late King left the stage vacant for the other son of Husayn Ibn 'Ali, the Amir 'Abdallah of Trans-Jordan. 'Abdallah's direct involvement in Syria goes back to the autumn of 1920. Upon the expulsion of his brother Faysal from Damascus, he organised a military force of bedouins from the 'Utaybah tribe of the Hijaz and marched with them to the north in order to liberate Syria from the French occupiers. Thus he arrived at Ma'an in the southern part of Trans-Jordan, nominally under British rule. At Ma'an he proclaimed himself to the Viceroy of Syria and called upon the members of the Syrian Congress, the bedouin shaykhs and the commanders and soldiers of the Syrian Arab forces to come to Ma'an and to re-establish the Syrian Government. In his manifesto to the Syrian people published in Ma'an, 'Abdallah stressed that the Umayyad capital Damascus would not become a French colony and that the Syrians' oath of allegiance to King Faysal I was being renewed through himself.[108]

This development posed an acute problem for the British, who refused to see a Hashemite prince using a British-controlled territory for an attack on the French. The way out of this imbroglio was secured in four talks between the British and 'Abdallah held in late March 1921 in Jerusalem. The essence of the agreement was the formation of the Emirate of Trans-Jordan with 'Abdallah as its head under the British mandate for Palestine. In return for this British support, 'Abdallah guaranteed that there would be no anti-French and anti-Zionist agitation from his Emirate and that he would not allow any other groups to make trouble. This commitment was secured from 'Abdallah after the British negotiators (T. E. Lawrence and the Colonial Secretary Winston Churchill) had promised him something rather important in respect of Syria.[109]

British official records of the March 1921 Cairo Conference and the subsequent negotiations with 'Abdallah held in Jerusalem tell us as follows:

> It was pointed out to him (Abdullah) that if he succeeded in checking anti-French action for six months he would not only convince the French Government that so far from being actively hostile to them the Sharifian family was prepared loyally to co-operate with His Majesty's Government in protecting them from external aggression, and would thus reduce their opposition to his brother's candidature for Mesopotamia, but he would also greatly improve his own chances of a personal reconciliation with the French *which might even lead to his being instated by them as Amir of Syria in Damascus* [my italics]. It was made perfectly clear to him that while they would do everything they could to assist towards the attainment of this object, His Majesty's Government could not in any way guarantee that it would be achieved.[110]

'Abdallah had a rather different version of this British pledge published in his memoirs. 'I must remain here in Trans-Jordan on the basis of an understanding with them [The British Government] and lead my people so that they will refrain from challenging the French. If this objective is achieved, France, it is hoped, will reconsider the matter, and subsequently, he [Mr Churchill] believes, there will be a possibility that after six months he will congratulate us on the return of Syria to our hands'.[111] We cannot know for sure whether 'Abdallah believed in his version or not. What is important is that about twenty years later he acted as though a far-reaching pledge in respect of Syria had been given to him by Mr Churchill.

Another point is clearer and perhaps more important. Although 'Abdallah had given the British guarantees that he would refrain from pursuing an anti-French policy from his Emirate he did not give up the vision of founding a united Syria with himself as its king. In his memoirs, articles, declarations and letters he developed a rather coherent ideology of Arabism in which Greater Syria under Hashemite rule becomes the crux of the matter.[112] He regarded the Arab Revolt of the First World War as both an Islamic and Arab act which was the foundation stone of the modern Arab revival. By means of that revolt and its bloodshed the Arabs rescued Islam from the tyrannical and infidel Young Turks, returned to the stage of history and achieved the political rights of Najd, Yemen, Iraq, Trans-Jordan and Syria.[113] As the standard-bearers of the revolt, the House of Hashim became the redeemers of the Arab nation, an indivisible unit, and its legitimate leaders. The Hashemites were descendants of the Prophet Muhammad and by leading the revolt they had acted like Muhammad himself.

This religious-political right of leadership was accepted and confirmed by the Arab National Movement and by the members of the 1919–20 Syrian Congress. Greater Syria is the historical and territorial centre of the Arab nation and Damascus its capital. Greater Syria within its natural boundaries, which is the modern version of the traditional concept of *Bilad al-Sham*, was the main territorial target of the Arab revolt.[114] Therefore the establishment of such a state would be both the culmination of the Arab revolt and the restoration of a historical-geographical unit which had been illegitimately divided into four countries: Syria, Lebanon, Palestine and Trans-Jordan.

There was also a personal factor which drove 'Abdallah towards Syria. In March 1920 when the Syrian Congress proclaimed Faysal as King of (Greater) Syria, the Iraqi activists in Damascus acted simultaneously and proclaimed 'Abdallah as King of Iraq. Although he ostensibly conceded this right to Faysal when the British arranged for Faysal to be elected King of Iraq, 'Abdallah continued to claim that by doing so the British had deprived him of his right,[115] and that therefore he was entitled to compensation in the form of the kingdom of Greater Syria.

'Abdallah's concept of Syrian unity was not contradictory to what was prevalent in those days among Arab nationalists. George Antonius, the well-known propagator of Arab nationalism, admitted in April 1936, in private it is true, that there was no connection between Iraq and Syria, that the Iraqis constituted a people on their own, that a wide desert separated Iraq and Syria, that King Faysal had erred in pursuing the unity of these two countries and that there was a strong Iraqi national feeling. Therefore, it was thought that it was only the unity of Syria, from the Taurus Mountains to the Sinai Desert, which mattered.[116]

Upon Faysal's death 'Abdallah thought that he was going to become the standard bearer of the Hashemite claim to the Syrian throne and the leader of the Arab movement for unity. His immediate reaction to the news of King Faysal's death was to indicate his intention of taking his dead brother's place as the acknowledged leader of the Arab nationalists of Iraq, Syria, Trans-Jordan and Palestine. His first step in that direction was a reconciliation with the members of the *al-Istiqlal* party, with whom Faysal had close relations but with whom 'Abdallah had been in open quarrel. Following this reconciliation 'Adil al-'Azmah (a Syrian exile living in Trans-Jordan) and 'Awni 'Abd al-Hadi and 'Izzat Darwaza (Istiqlalist leaders from Palestine) travelled to Iraq to Faysal's funeral service as members of 'Abdallah's suite. Towards King Ghazi, Faysal's young successor, 'Abdallah adopted a paternalistic attitude. During their first meeting 'Abdallah behaved as a mentor entrusted with the education of a young pupil. He also handed to him a memorandum in which he had set out the principles by which he advised Ghazi to be guided in directing the policy and administration of Iraq, covering such questions as the Euphrates tribes, the Assyrians, the Shi'ah and foreign policy. He did not fail to emphasise the need to turn to the British Ambassador for advice on important matters.[117] 'Abdallah also wanted to make public his supposedly newly acquired position as leader of the pan-Arab tendency. He prepared a proclamation, calling upon the Arabs to unite and re-establish their past glory. He gave the draft to several prominent people and asked for their remarks. The Istiqlalists promised to prepare a draft of their own, but under pressure from the Acting British Resident 'Abdallah had to shelve the text.[118]

Here we have discerned the big difference between Faysal and 'Abdallah and the latter's big handicap: while Faysal, although bound to Britain by a treaty and under the strong influence of Sir Francis Humphrys, the British Ambassador in Baghdad, was an independent Head of State, 'Abdallah was only semi-autonomous, almost totally dependent upon British guidance and subsidies. His ability to pursue an independent policy was minimal and he could not, publicly at least, act contrary to British advice and policy. The cool reaction that 'Abdallah got from King Ghazi over his patronising attitude and the negative attitude of the British sufficed to calm him down and it was only after a few years that 'Abdallah renewed his efforts to be crowned as King of Greater Syria.

After a General Strike, demonstrations and clashes in Syria lasting for two months in the winter of 1936, the French Government agreed to negotiate a treaty with the representatives of the National Bloc as their *interlocuteurs valables* and not the moderate Syrian Government. An agreement in principle was reached on 1 March, the details being left to be negotiated with a Syrian Nationalist Delegation in Paris. The period of about half a year up to September 1936 during which the negotiations were taking place was crucial for the future of Syria.[119] 'Abdallah realised that these negotiations would dictate the form of the regime as well. If the National Bloc, most of whose leaders were republican, succeeded in achieving independence and became the undisputed ruling force, 'Abdallah's chances would drastically diminish.

Therefore in April 1936 he sent messengers to the leaders of the National Bloc to put to them that Trans-Jordan and Syria should be united with himself as King, and the delegation which was to leave for Paris should first visit him in 'Amman. 'Abdallah realised that the French would strongly oppose his plan because they would view its implementation as an aggrandisement of the British sphere of influence at the expense of their own. Therefore he sent another messenger, this time to the Comte de Martel, the French High Commissioner proposing that Syria and Trans-Jordan united under 'Abdallah be divided into two spheres of influence: one British and one French. Both the High Commissioner and the Syrian nationalist leaders replied in discouraging terms; the French were interested in safeguarding their influence as much as possible, whereas the Nationalists wanted to get the greatest amount of independence and to preserve it in their own hands. They were more ready to co-operate with 'Abdallah if they were assured that his proposals had been approved by the British Government and that they could rely on British support in their forthcoming negotiations with the French.[120] Since this condition could not be met, the Syrian Nationalists persisted in their negative attitude towards 'Abdallah's démarches.

For 'Abdallah it was only the beginning. He resumed his attempts in 1937 when it began to emerge that the French were in no hurry to ratify the treaties with Syria and the Lebanon which had been concluded in September 1936 subject to ratification by the French Assemblée Nationale. First of all, he tried to arrange a meeting with King Ghazi somewhere outside Iraq, away from the influence of the Iraqi Government headed by Hikmat Sulayman, who had held a cool and reserved position as far as the Islamite pan-Arab programmes were concerned, and of the British diplomatic representatives, who strongly resented these efforts. 'Abdallah, so it seems, tried to exert pressure on Ghazi not to initiate any more of his own as far as inter-Arab relations were concerned and to let 'Abdallah have the sole initiative on behalf of the Hashemites, being, at least in his own eyes, the head of the Hashemite family since the death of his brother 'Ali.[121] His activities were intensified in 1938–9 when it became crystal-clear that the French were not going to ratify the treaties with the Levant countries. The reaction of the Syrians to the French default was very grave. They felt deceived and humiliated and some of the National Bloc leaders had second thoughts about the negative attitude they had shown in the past towards the Hashemites.[122]

In June 1938 'Abdallah tried to enhance his position on another front. In those days the Woodhead Commission was examining the practicability of the Partition Plan which had been recommended as a solution to the Palestine problem by the 1937 Palestine Commission.[123] He prepared a memorandum to be presented to the commission. And although the High Commissioner prevented its presentation, claiming that it went beyond the commission's terms of reference, it is worth considering its content, since its conveyed 'Abdallah's approach. For him the solution to the Palestine problem would be reached by the union of Palestine with Trans-Jordan under an Arab sovereign. This United Arab State would grant the Jews self-government in the Jewish areas which would be defined by a committee composed of British, Arabs and Jews. Jewish immigration 'in reasonable proportion' and land purchases would continue in the Jewish areas only. The Jews would be represented in the Parliament in proportion to their numbers. After a transitional period of 10 years a final solution would be decided and the mandate superseded by a treaty with Great Britain.[124] A success in Palestine was for 'Abdallah a possible beginning of a longer march, and an enhancement of his standing both in the eyes of the Arabs and of the British.

Simultaneously with his initiative on his main fronts — Syria and Palestine — 'Abdallah instigated an anti-Saudi propaganda campaign. Apparently some of his followers printed leaflets in the name of the 'Party of the Free Hijazis' and sent it from Baludan in Syria to prominent persons at Jedda, Mecca and Madinah, calling upon them to exert themselves and expel their Saudi rulers, who had expelled their country's rightful (i.e. Hashemite) rulers and were busily engaged in sucking the country dry and oppressing it in many ways.[125] It may have been that those who instigated the distribution of these leaflets were mainly interested in ousting the Saudis from Hijaz. But, there is another possibility that it was intended to keep 'Abd al-'Aziz Al Sa'ud's attention directed towards the internal affairs of his kingdom and to reduce his absolute opposition to 'Abdallah's moves in Syria[126] or, at least, to distract his attention from them. The Saudi King took the matter very seriously. He emphasised his fear lest the addition of Syria to the Hashemite domains should facilitate Hashemite designs against Hijaz or even Najd.[127] The leaflets of the 'Party of the Free Hijazis' could only strengthen such fears and increase Saudi opposition to a Hashemite being installed on the Syrian throne.[128] It seems that this Saudi opposition became stronger owing to the fact that the name of Amir Faysal, son of 'Abd al-'Aziz Al Sa'ud, was mentioned from time to time as a possible candidate to the Syrian throne.

As in the past, it was the French who mentioned this possibility and they did it in such a way as to be in a position to disclaim any responsibility. In April 1939 the French High Commissioner for Syria asked Ibn Saud a 'personal' question: whether or not he would agree to the appointment of one of his sons as a King of Syria on the basis of independence and protection of minorities. Ibn Saud replied in the affirmative, provided Syria were not less free than Iraq was then.[129] The content of this question became known to the public and it served the French well. It was at the peak of their quarrel with the Syrian Nationalists and this was a way of bypassing them. They saw to it that their hints and queries were made as non-committal and as vague as possible so that they could always disclaim responsibility. Only upon repeated British approaches did the French admit that a monarchy might eventually be established in Syria.[130] The 'rumours' were usually more specific and far-reaching.

Into these troubled waters, Amir 'Abdallah in 1939 again launched his boat. To some extent his chances looked promising. In 1937 the leaders of the 1925 anti-French revolt returned to Syria after being pardoned by the mandatory authorities. They included Dr 'Abd al-Rahman Shahbandar and Sultan al-Atrash. The former established the party in opposition to the ruling National Bloc which was pro-Hashemite in its policy; and the latter, a veteran of the pro-Hashemite forces in Syria, regained his very influential position inside his Druze community. Dr Shakbandar gained the support of the Bakri brothers (Fawzi and Nasib) who, during the 1916–18 Hashemite-led Arab revolt, had been the connecting link between the Arab nationalists of Syria and the Hashemites and had, up to 1938, held top political and administrative posts in the Syrian Nationalist-controlled government.

In other respects, too, 'Abdallah could rest more assured. In the past the Turks had expressed their objection to the Hashemite schemes concerning Syria. Now 'Abdallah had some ground to hope for a more positive Turkish attitude. His son Na'if had recently been appointed an aide-de-camp of the Turkish President Ismat Inönü and had let his father know that his accession to the Syrian throne was supported by the Turkish President. In order to consolidate this possible support 'Abdallah was ready to concede to the Turks another portion of northern Syria in addition to the Alexandretta region ceded to them by the French.[131] In public 'Abdallah based his claim to the throne of Syria on the need to ensure the unity of northern and southern Syria (i.e. Trans-Jordan and Palestine) and emphasised that the experience of the past few years had proved that all forms of government had failed, that only a monarchy was a solution and that the Syrians themselves desired it. This referred, no doubt, to the Syrian failure to secure the ratification of their treaty with France. But, as in the past, the Hashemite bid for Syria was not one and united. As 'Abdallah had in the early 1930s opposed his brother Faysal's initiative, so he had now to contend with opposition from Nuri al-Sa'id, who had become the standard-bearer of the Iraqi–Hashemite claim, to the detriment of 'Abdallah's own initiative.[132]

When in 1939 'Abdallah began to translate his idea into a concrete political campaign he mainly consolidated relations with the groups of his supporters in Syria and endeavoured to mobilise the support of various outside parties who might influence the course of events inside Syria.

At the end of 1938 (whether after having been encouraged to do so by 'Abdallah or not we do not know) an important Druze leader, 'Abd al-Ghaffar Pasha al-Atrash, approached Gilbert Mackereth, the British Consul in Damascus, with the request on behalf of the Druze leaders that the British should arrange the secession of Jabal al-Duruz from Syria and its annexation to Trans-Jordan. On their part, the Druze would declare their independence from Syria and their loyalty to Amir 'Abdallah. The British Consul noted that he had reason to believe that 'on occasions Amir Abdallah has shown pleasure at Druse's suggestion or implication of leaving Franco-Syrian allegiance to accept the Amir's rule'.[133] The French did not become aware of this Druze démarche. But they did detect activities by Trans-Jordanian agents in various villages in Jabal al-Duruz aimed at strengthening the connection with Trans-Jordan and the allegiance to Amir 'Abdallah. Following their complaints the British authorities made enquiries and reached the conclusion that these were very much exaggerated. The British representatives in Trans-Jordan were convinced that nothing of the sort had happened. What had really taken place was an attempt by Trans-Jordanian officials to collect taxes from Druzes in respect of orchards owned and cultivated by them on the Trans-Jordanian side of the border (finally demarcated in 1934) and which now reached fruition for the first time.[134]

It appears that British denials were sincere and made in good faith, and they certainly conveyed the official British position. But we doubt whether these British officials knew what 'Abdallah's officials and agents were secretly advocating among the Druze. The French were by no means convinced that 'Abdallah's agents were not engaged in pro-Hashemite propaganda among the Druze. Therefore they went so far as to ask the Saudis to use their good offices with the British to convince the latter 'to prevail on the Emir Abdullah to desist'.[135] It was natural that the French should be rather suspicious. When in the summer of 1941 they were engaged in re-establishing their authority in Syria (see pp. 32–3), they heard from Druze leaders in Suwayda that they had no time for Frenchmen and that they wished to join Trans-Jordan.[136]

At the same time relations with Shahbandar's followers and his party were strengthened. A delegation led by 'Abd al-Rahman Shahbandar and Fawzi al-Bakni visited 'Amman in June 1939 and discussed their common aims of ousting the National Bloc from power and putting 'Abdallah on the Syrian throne. Both sides were ready, as 'Abdallah had made clear in the past, to see United Syria divided into British and French regions of influence. Before leaving 'Amman Shahbandar declared that pan-Arabism was in danger and that Amir 'Abdallah was the only sovereign capable of realising Arab unity. He added that 'the artificial frontiers created by the various imperialist powers should be abolished. We did not come to say "The King [King Ghazi of Iraq] is dead" but rather "Long live the living King of Syria and Transjordan"'.[137] Shahbandar himself after the outbreak of the Second World War explained to the British that his opponents in Syria and Palestine (the Nationalist leaders of Istiqlal origin, Shakib Arslan, the National Bloc leaders etc.) were jeopardising the Allies' war effort and that the ground was fertile for the establishment with British backing of an Arab Confederation under 'Abdallah.[138] And in turn 'Abdallah told various Syrian politicians that the unity of Greater Syria had the backing of Great Britain.[139]

Another veteran supporter of 'Abdallah was then engaged in an attempt to recruit as many supporters as possible for 'Abdallah's cause. A delegation of the Palestinian National Defence Party led by Fakhri al-Nashashibi left for Syria and Lebanon in connection with this initiative.[140] Indeed, Palestine was an integral part of the Greater Syria scheme and the Nashashibis' Party had years ago been won over to 'Abdallah's case. But in Palestine another factor was to be found — the Jews.

With them too 'Abdallah had entertained rather cordial relations and tried to carry them along in support of his policies. Here as well his attempts were intensified in the crucial period beginning with 1939. After exchanging polite but non-committal letters,[141] 'Abdallah's supporters and messengers contacted the heads of the Jewish Agency and entered into semi-official talks. Nasib al-Bakri, the Syrian supporter of 'Abdallah, explained to Dr Bernard Joseph of the Jewish Agency in a conversation held in Jerusalem on 30 March 1940, that the formation of a Federation of Syria, Trans-Jordan and Palestine would secure the Arabs from Jewish domination and thus moderate the local (i.e. Palestinian) Arabs and make them ready to make concessions — an idea current among circles and statesmen (see chapter 2). As a first step 'Abdallah suggested to the High Commissioner that Palestine and Trans-Jordan should be united under one Arab government, safeguarding the Jewish interests by such an arrangement as would secure their immigration and land purchases.[142] Moshe Shertok, head of the Political Department of the Jewish Agency, responded that it was then premature to discuss this problem, but added 'that if the Jews discussed this proposal, it would be done from the angles of immigration, settlement and free life in the country'.[143] It must be added that the Jewish Agency tried to direct 'Abdallah's attention away from Palestine to Syria and were ready to support him as far as his bid for Syria was concerned, but it is rather clear that even in exchange for 'Abdallah's support of free Jewish immigration to Palestine and land purchase there, Shertok and even more so his more extreme colleagues in the Jewish Agency Executive (like M. Ussishkin) were reluctant to accept 'Abdallah's rule over what they regarded as their country.[142]

'Abdallah was not happy with the non-committal responses that he got from both the High Commissioner for Palestine and Trans-Jordan and from the Jewish Agency. To the British he emphasised that his programme was not necessarily anti-French since it allowed for a treaty with France as far as Syria was concerned (and a treaty with Britain for the rest, i.e., Trans-Jordan and Palestine). From the Jewish Agency he required identification with, and support of, his basic idea of uniting Syria, Palestine and Trans-Jordan under his kingship and promised in exchange settlement facilities for the Jews in Trans-Jordan and Syria as well. But the Jewish side refused to commit themselves, although Shertok expressed interest in the project and the settlement facilities in Trans-Jordan (but not in Syria) and agreed to ascertain in London and Paris the positions of the British and French Governments.[145]

In summer 1941 when the Allies occupied Vichy-governed Syria, 'Abdallah intensified his efforts aimed at winning over the Jews and again sent his messenger to the Jewish Agency. The messenger explained how beneficial for the Jewish National Home would be an agreement with 'Abdallah, but the same evasive Jewish attitude prevailed.[146] On a later occasion 'Abdallah made it clear to Shertok that Damascus was his target and that he intended to establish his capital there and not in Jerusalem. He also repeated his readiness to reach an agreement in respect of Jewish immigration to the whole area of united Syria and asked for financial support and a Jewish-launched propaganda campaign in favour of his project in Britain and in ... Syria. But the Jews had no illusions over 'Abdallah's ability to deliver the goods. They knew about his almost total dependence on the British and his weak position in Syria. The very fact that he asked the Jewish Agency to carry on a propaganda campaign in his favour in Syria, of all places, completely exposed this weakness. Therefore the Jewish Agency decided as in the past to maintain contact with 'Abdallah but not to negotiate on the problem of immigration, which was completely in the hands of the British authorities, or of Jewish support of, and propaganda for, 'Abdallah, which they were not in a position to undertake.[147]

Whatever importance 'Abdallah may have attributed to possible Jewish support, he attributed to the British a much higher degree of importance; and, indeed, his attempt to get such support was the main characteristic of his policy after the late 1930s. It is apparent that he realised how small was the support for his plan in Syria itself. On the French he could not count, whereas the British could be regarded as possible backers. He never forgot what he regarded as the 'Churchill promise' given in March 1921 (see pp. 22–3) and was sure that if any Hashemite had a chance of getting British backing it was he alone.[148]

With the outbreak of the Second World War the situation looked more promising to 'Abdallah. Certainly he remembered the days of the First World War when the whole political structure of the Middle East had changed. New Arab countries had emerged at its end and the Hashemites had become the ruling dynasty of Trans-Jordan and Iraq. Another point did not pass unnoticed by 'Abdallah: Winston Churchill, who had made the 'promise' and who had been out in the cold during the whole of the 1930s, on the outbreak of the war was invited to join the government, and appointed to the very important position of First Lord of the Admiralty and member of the War Cabinet. 'Abdallah's reaction was swift: he wrote to the British Government praising Churchill and his appointment, and asking that Churchill be told that 'I am still waiting the outcome of his promises'.[149] The British were evasive in their replies and tried to shake off 'Abdallah.[150]

Despite this discouraging response, 'Abdallah did not give up. On the contrary, upon the fall of France in June 1940 he tried again, even more earnestly. He was convinced that the French mandate had ended with the ignoble French surrender and that the Levant States had become *res nullius*. He stated his intention of (a) issuing a public statement that Trans-Jordan and Syria would thenceforth be one country under Great Britain, and of (b) preparing forces with which to occupy any part of Syria which the French might evacuate or from which they could be ejected. When 'Abdallah realised that the British were not seeking another front in the Middle East in addition to the Italian one in Libya he requested the British Resident that the 'Churchill promise would be borne in mind when the British policy to be followed in Syria was decided upon. He expressed his fear that this opportunity would be missed. Appeals from his traditional supporters in Syria – bedouin sheikhs and Druze leaders from Al-Atrash family – to include their regions in his Emirate could only pour salt on his wounds'.[151]

When the British and the Free French forces invaded Syria in June 1941, 'Abdallah was deeply disturbed. He immediately expressed his sorrow that the Trans-Jordanian Arab Legion was not taking part in the occupation of Syria.[152] Thereupon, officials of his cabinet organised a demonstration in 'Amman in support of the liberation of Syria, demanding unity with Trans-Jordan under 'Abdallah's sovereignty. A delegation of 'Amman merchants presented the same demand to the British Resident, and telegrams to the same effect were cabled by the Bedouin Sheikhs, 'prominent intellectuals' and merchants to Sir Miles Lampson, the British Ambassador in Cairo.[153] 'Abdallah's next move was to induce his Council of Ministers to present a long resolution, expressing support of the Allies' cause, calling for the unity of the 'Syrian Countries' and asking him to allow his Council of Ministers to approach the Allied Governments and 'to co-operate with them in a common endeavour to achieve the aforementioned aims'.[154] As an alternative and less far-reaching plan he put before the British the suggestion that he should be installed on the throne of Palestine and get British financial support for his propaganda campaign in Syria. He saw to it that some prominent leaders of the Palestinian National Defence Party (the Nashashibi organisation) would back his claim to Palestine by writing to him an appeal to this effect.[155]

Similar means were used in Syria. 'Abdallah had submitted to the British authorities a long petition bearing the signatures of 844 Syrians calling for the unity of Trans-Jordan and Syria and the accession of the Amir to the Syrian throne and referring to the pledges given by Britain to 'Abdallah and to his late father King Husayn of Mecca. This petition is typical of the amount of support that 'Abdallah could mobilise in Syria: most of the signatures came from the Hawran area of bedouin tribes and the Druze, and they did not include the signature of any political leader of any importance.[156] However great 'Abdallah's enthusiasm was, the British were reluctant to do anything that could be regarded as an encouragement to him and therefore they exerted pressure on 'Abdallah to desist from any public move. Even Tawfiq Abu al-Huda, his Prime Minister, realised how premature and even stupid 'Abdallah's manoeuvres were. Therefore, he let the British know that even inside his court support for 'Abdallah's policy was not unanimous.

A little later the chances of 'Abdallah looked a bit better. The Free French authorities in Syria soon made it clear that they were interpreting their declaration of independence given by General Catroux on the eve of the invasion of Syria in a very restrictive way. At most they were ready to concede independence as defined in an unratified 1936 treaty. They refused to treat the National Bloc as the main representative of the Syrian people and appointed a Syrian Government under the presidency of the moderate leader, Sheikh Taj al-Din al-Hasani, who was anathema to the Nationalists.[157] Thereupon, Faris al-Khuri, a prominent leader of the National Bloc, a President of the Syrian Council of Representatives, which had been suspended in 1939, and one of the few among them who had in the past been rather friendly to the Hashemites, wrote to 'Abdallah about the situation in Syria and dangled the crown of Syria before him. He said that once independence had been achieved the constitution could be amended so as to substitute a monarchy for the present republican form of government and then the services of 'Abdallah to the Arab cause would not be overlooked. Faris al-Khuri emphasised that he was speaking for his associates as well as on his own behalf.[158]

In our opinion the National Bloc was not really converted to 'Abdallah's cause. It seems reasonable to assume that at that time the Syrian leaders, like almost everyone else in the Middle East including the French, believed that 'Abdallah's project had the backing of the British, if it had not originated with them. Therefore, they tried to get the British to support their national claims against the French, having been disappointed by the British retreat under the Free French pressure and their agreement to install a French administration in mainly British-occupied Syria. But before long they were to learn from the British civil and military representatives in Damascus and Beirut that Britain was not supporting 'Abdallah's bid for Syria and that they could more or less count on British support for their cause against the French even without any bait.[159] Therefore this favourable attitude by Faris al-Khuri remained an isolated episode. Another point which emerges from this episode is that had Britain pursued a pro-'Abdallah policy in Syria, his support among the Syrian Nationalist politicians might possibly have increased.

Thus, till the formation of the Arab League, the end of the Second World War and the emergence in 1946 of the Levant States and Trans-Jordan as independent and separate political entities 'Abdallah had not missed any suitable political event to press his claim. A proper moment to resume his initiative came only in November 1942. Earlier, between the spring and autumn of that year Britain's position in the Middle East had been at its lowest ebb. German troops were inside Egypt after having driven out the British Forces from Libya. Then even 'Abdallah, Britain's loyallest Arab client in the Middle East, lost confidence in Britain and, believing that it was going to lose the war, thought it would be useful to 'reinsure' in the Axis Powers. At such a time 'Abdallah did not press any claim on the British, who might be very soon the losers without any goods to deliver.[160]

By late October everything looked different, as far as the course of the war in the Middle East and the British position there were concerned. On 23 October the British Eighth Army under General Sir (as he was then) Bernard L. Montgomery began the third and decisive offensive, smashed the German line at Al-'Alamein and drove the German troops under Rommel back to Libya. Two weeks later, on 8 November, an Anglo-American force commanded by General Dwight D. Eisenhower made a successful landing in Vichy-controlled North Africa.

'Abdallah immediately realised that Britain had once again become the arbiter of political fortunes in the Middle East. He presented his claims to Richard Casey, the British Minister of State Resident in the Middle East, and sent a personal letter to Churchill. His plan was now more comprehensive. In addition to his traditional demand for 'complete union' of the four components of Greater Syria he asked for a cultural union between Greater Syria and Iraq, the solution of the Palestine problem within the union in such a way that Great Britain could keep the promises to the Jews without subjecting the Arabs to the Jews, and, most interestingly, 'The creation of a system which would guarantee the contentment of the Muslim world in regard to its Holy Land [i.e. Hijaz]'. The raising of the final point indicates how much self-confidence 'Abdallah had suddenly gained and how high his aspirations now reached.[161] 'Abdallah, although discouraged by the usual cool British response, gave some publicity to his renewed bid. In a press interview he pointed to the need to promote the Arab Alliance (*Al-Hilf al-'Arabi*). He did not go into the full details of his programme and left the precise composition of the Alliance for the future, but emphasised that it should be based on an equality between the Syrian Bloc, partitioned at Versailles, and Iraq.[162] 'Abdallah was prudent enough not to mention in public the question of *Hijaz*.

This campaign was intensified a couple of months later as a reaction to Anthony Eden's reply in Parliament on 14 February 1943, to a question about the British position on the movement for Arab unity. Eden used the same phrase as he had used in his 29 May 1941 Mansion House speech and did not intend anything beyond it (see later on, pp. 255–6), but for

'Abdallah it was an ominous sign that Britain was defining its policy and aims in the Middle East and that therefore the time had come for a tougher line. Not content with another appeal to Britain through diplomatic channels, this time he approached Arab public opinion. He called upon the Arabs, in reaction to Eden's words, to initiate their own plan of union and suggested, as a first step, that a popular Congress of representatives from Syria, Trans-Jordan and Palestine should be convened to decide 'the proper form of government in *Bilad al-Sham* (the historic name of Greater Syria)'. He promised that the union would guarantee to the minorities their life and rights.[163]

Eden's words brought other reactions in the Middle East, foremost among them the invitation by Mustafa Nahhas, the Egyptian Prime Minister (see pp. 258–60), to the Arab countries to send representatives to a conference to discuss the question of unity. Tawfiq Abu al-Huda reacted in such a way as to make clear that the urgent question was to bring about the union of the Syrian Bloc and that Trans-Jordan expected that the independent Arab kingdoms would use all means at their disposal to support this aim. Having gained its unity and independence, the Syrian Bloc 'would participate in whatever the Arabs would agree upon as far as their union is concerned'.[164]

'Abdallah wanted to give as much publicity to his call as possible. Therefore he tried to arrange a broadcast by the (British) Near East Broadcasting Station at Jaffa of a declaration to the 'people of Syria, town-dwellers and nomads from the Gulf of Aqaba to the Mediterranean Sea and to the upper parts of the Euphrates' to work for unity and to organise a special Syrian conference to be held in 'Amman as the foundation stone of this unity. In addition, 'Abdallah asked the British to demand from the Egyptian and Syrian authorities that they should modify their attitude towards his attempts to rally the people of Syria to the cause of unity according to his concepts.[165]

Mustafa Nahhas' initiative and the talks he organised in autumn of 1943 annoyed 'Abdallah. He regarded it as a usurpation by Egypt (which he did not consider to be an Arab country at all) of his own right and an attempt to increase Egypt's own prestige. His claims were now voiced publicly and officially in the Amir's speeches and by his Council of Ministers. He realised that he was missing his chances and that a decision had to be taken immediately not waiting until after the end of the war when Syria might emerge as an independent state.[166] 'Abdallah was so persistent with the British since both he and the British authorities knew that he was loyal and helpful to the British and therefore had established a claim on British gratitude.[167] He felt that his long and faithful association with the British for a quarter of a century coupled with the fact that he was the senior member of the House of Hashim entitled him to expect the British to publish an emphatic statement in support of the

Amir's claim to assume the leadership of the Arab movement towards unity as defined by him.[168]

Since 'Abdallah well understood that the inter-Arab Conference of autumn 1944 (see pp. 267–83) would shape inter-Arab relations for many years to come he took the last-minute step of circulating a lengthy memorandum to the supposed participants (excepting the Saudi Arabian representatives) of the conference in which he strongly emphasised the part played by the House of Hashim in the Arab awakening and therefore his right to leadership.[169] And at the last available minute on 26 February 1945, on the eve of the constituent conference of the Arab League (see p. 288), 'Abdallah once more appealed to his 'personal friend' Winston Churchill and warned him of the dangers that Britain would face in the post-war Arab countries if it based its relations with the Arabs on unstable republican regimes and on politicians who were prone to passing and to extreme ideological influences.[170] A novel argument he used in 1944 was linked with the United States' newly established position in the Middle East and the discernible British discomfort with it. He tried to play it up and to explain to the British that against the encroaching Americans only he could be relied upon by Britain. But all these efforts and arguments did not prevail and except for general, meaningless words he could not get solid support or even a promise of support from the British Government.[171]

A permanent element of 'Abdallah's demand from the British to support his Greater Syria plan was his demand that Trans-Jordan be granted independence. When the British and Free French forces invaded Syria, they declared on 8 June 1941 the independence of Syria and the Lebanon. On the same date 'Abdallah reacted in a letter in which he expressed his joy over this grant of independence, but rather bitterly complained that while Syria and the Lebanon were being granted independence nothing was said about Trans-Jordan which had behaved towards the British so admirably. 'Abdallah more than hinted that if his country and himself were left in an inferior position compared with that of the Levant States his chances to carry them along with his plan would be severely affected.[172] And, indeed, these twin arguments – the analogy of Iraq, Syria and Lebanon and the impossibility of attaining Arab unity in the form of Greater Syria so long as Trans-Jordan remained inferior in status – were used by 'Abdallah whenever, during the Second World War, he demanded independence.[173]

However, during these decisive years of 1943–45 'Abdallah's initiative stumbled upon obstacles wherever he turned. First of all there were the Iraqis. Even before Nuri al-Sa'id launched his initiative in January 1943 to bring about an Arab unity of the Fertile Crescent (see p. 51), the leading politicians of Iraq had not accepted 'Abdallah's plan.[174] After the onset of Nuri's initiative the relations between the two became tense. 'Abdallah did not miss an opportunity to disparage Nuri in the eyes of the Iraqi Regent (see later, p. 57). But beyond the personal relations, the public in Iraq was not moved by 'Abdallah's plan[175] and Nuri publicly announced that the formation of Greater Syria was a matter completely dependent on the wishes of the population of these countries. They were entitled to decide either to form this unity or to stand each country on its own and to join the general Arab union as independent units.[176]

In Syria itself 'Abdallah never stopped advocating his cause, by establishing contacts with disgruntled politicians, distribution of leaflets etc., but his success was very meagre.[177] There was apparently one exception. In July 1942 when 'Abdallah stopped pressing his claim and the British position in the Middle East looked very bad indeed, the (underground) anti-French Syrian Nationalist Party[178] (better known as *Parti Populaire Syrien*, which is an erroneous translation of the Arabic name *al-Hizb al-Qawmi al-Suri*) approached 'Abdallah and offered to unite their efforts for Syrian unity. This party which believed in personal dictatorship as a proper form of government expressed its readiness to regard 'Abdallah's kingship of a Greater Syria as compatible with their own concept of government. In return the party asked for permission to disseminate its propaganda freely and an 'association with certain Ministries', such as Interior, Propaganda, Education and Social Affairs 'so as to let the teaching of the Party reach the people through channels of an official nature'. It is rather difficult to understand what prompted this extreme secularist, anti-religious and anti-Arabist Party to appeal to 'Abdallah, the standard-bearer of traditional Islamic Arabism. They may have thought that in the summer of 1942 even 'Abdallah could be separated from the British and make such a drastic *volte-face* in exchange for a promise of support of his plan. Anyway 'Abdallah refused to consider this proposal, informed the British authorities[179] about it and nothing of this sort happened again.

Much more important was the attitude of the Syrian National Bloc. After the settlement in November 1943 of the crisis between the Lebanese Government and the French authorities in favour of the former and after having consolidated their hold on the reins of power in Syria,[180] the Syrian Nationalists felt much more self-confident, their possible need for 'Abdallah as an ally against the French disappeared and they could rest assured of a friendly British attitude at least as far as the British representatives in the Levant were concerned. Therefore when they now had an opportunity to express their reaction to 'Abdallah's project they did it in the clearest possible voice. In September 1944 when the new Trans-Jordanian Consul at Damascus paid his first official visit to the Syrian Prime Minister Sa'dallah al-Jabiri he was told that the Syrian Government favoured the formation of Greater Syria but without alteration of the present republican regime. Trans-Jordan was part of Syria and should be reunited with republican Syria. The wishes of the inhabitants of both territories in regard to the regimes could be tested by a plebiscite. As regards Lebanon the Syrian Government desired complete reunion or, if this was not possible, reduction of Lebanon to its original (i.e. pre-1914) boundaries.[181] This statement also belittled the role of the Hashemites in the First-World War Arab Revolt and thus their claim to leadership. It was a total defiance of 'Abdallah's concepts and pretensions and it fully exposed his total failure to win over Syria to his cause. It is true that in those months when the French despaired of securing a treaty with the Syrians which would safeguard their position and interests they once more approached the Amir and asked him whether or not he would be ready to be King of Greater Syria while having treaty relations at one and the same time with Great Britain in respect of Trans-Jordan and with France in respect of Syria proper. But it came too late and the British did not like it.[182]

Even among his Druze supporters 'Abdallah was losing ground. The leading Atrash family reached the conclusion that the cause of Druze autonomy within Syria, to say nothing of secession and eventual union with Trans-Jordan, was lost. In September 1944 they therefore decided to approach the Syrian National Bloc Government and proposed full incorporation into the Syrian state, which was carried out quite smoothly.[183] Also in Palestine his Nashashibi followers were not solidly united behind his effort. If at his request some of the (Nashashibi) National Defence Party notables wrote to 'Abdallah in June 1941 in support of his project, Raghib al-Nashashibi, their leader, declined a few months later to do the same and told the British that he preferred the continuation of British rule in whatever form, including the transformation of Palestine into a Crown Colony, to its incorporation into Greater Syria under 'Abdallah's sovereignty.[184]

Outside the Fertile Crescent, the Egyptian attitude towards 'Abdallah's project was reserved,[185] although it was not expressed too frequently since Egypt was deeply immersed in its own problems. But the other important Arab country outside the Fertile Crescent, Saudi Arabia, was very hostile to any scheme of Arab unity under the Hashemites and even more under 'Abdallah. And the representatives of that country never failed to let the British know how strongly the Saudis felt about it. When in autumn 1941 a meeting between 'Abdallah and 'Abd al-Illah, the Iraqi Regent, became known, Amir Faysal, son of 'Abd al-'Aziz Al Sa'ud, made it clear to the British representative 'how detrimental it would be to his [Ibn Saud's] interest if a third neighbouring country [meaning Syria] were placed under Hashemite rule'.[186] Regarding the form of regime suitable for Syria the Saudi monarch had become a sworn republican: 'The best thing for that country [Syria] is to remain a republic. Where there is no suitable man, why put in a puppet? A King without kingly attitudes is worse than useless'.[187] When 'Abdallah began in the winter of 1943 to publicise his claim to the Syrian throne, Ibn Saud brought pressure to bear on the British to dissociate themselves from 'Abdallah. When he realised that this exactly was the British position he expressed his confidence that the British would 'be watchful over his interests'.[188] In itself the Saudi position might not look terribly important. Saudi Arabia was not a mighty power and its financial resources in the early 1940s were very meagre. However, the importance of its position originates from the fact that it was taken very seriously by the British and strongly influenced their decision-making (see chapter 4).

Nuri al-Sa'id's initiative

Another actor who tried to carry the banner of Arab unity after the death of King Faysal I was the prominent Iraqi statesman Nuri al-Sa'id. He took his first step in that direction at the end of 1935 when the internal situation of Iraq calmed down at the end of the rebellion of the Euphrates tribes. Nuri Pasha al-Sa'id then found an appropriate opportunity to sound the British Ambassador in Baghdad on the idea of forming a federation between Iraq and Trans-Jordan. Unlike the past, he added, Amir 'Abdallah was now supporting the idea. British Foreign Office officials had no doubt that Nuri was then thinking that 'the pan-Arab mantle of King Feisal has fallen on his shoulders' and that by making this suggestion Nuri was reviving Faysal's old scheme of Arab confederation which should include Syria once this country had been emancipated.[189] It was not long before officials were proved one hundred per cent right. And, as in the past with Faysal, the intractable problem of Palestine was the background against which Nuri Pasha made his proposition.

During the 1936 General Strike and the first stage of the Arab rebellion in Palestine Nuri tried to mediate between the Jews and the Arabs, and between the Arabs and the British Government. In the spring of 1936 Nuri served as Foreign Minister in the Cabinet headed by Yasin al-Hashimi and in June he came to London for talks with the British Government. On his initiative[190] on 5 June 1936, he met Dr Chaim Weizmann and made the following suggestion to him: Jewish immigration to Palestine would be suspended during the period of the Royal (Peel) Commission's enquiry;[191] the Jews should make it clear that they were prepared to accept the position of being a minority in Arab country; and the formation of the Arab Federation of States within which Nuri was prepared to offer considerable concessions to the Jews in Palestine. Apparently Dr Weizmann agreed as a gesture to stop immigration for a year. William Ormsby-Gore, the Colonial Secretary, was asked by Arthur Wauchope, the High Commissioner for Palestine, to corroborate this statement. This brought a vehement denial from Weizmann[192] and thus Nuri had to look for another outlet for his scheme. Two months later Nuri came to Jerusalem and offered his good offices as a mediator between the Palestine Government and the Higher Arab Committee (HAC). He drew up a memorandum to serve as a basis for a settlement. The memorandum stressed the 'racial ties' which bound Iraq and the Arabs of Palestine[193] and the whole episode was hailed in Palestine as a 'confirmation of Arab unity and a cord binding Palestine with this unity, so that Palestine will become an integral part of it'.[194] But the British Government rejected Wauchope's recommendation to accept Nuri al-Sa'id's mediation[195] and Nuri had to approach them directly, clarifying his real intentions.

Before approaching the British Government Nuri tried once more to enlist the Jewish Agency's support for his proposal. Rightly or wrongly, he had understood from his talk with Dr Weizmann, and from the latter's initial agreement to his ideas and later denial, that real authority among the Jews lay in the heads of the Jewish Agency Executive in Jerusalem. Therefore he approached Moshe Shertok, head of the Jewish Agency's Political Department, and repeated his basic ideas. Shertok's reply in regard to Jewish agreement to a stoppage (temporarily, at least) of immigration was emphatically negative since it would be regarded as a capitulation to the campaign of terror carried on by the Palestine Arabs. Concerning the Arab Federation idea Shertok remained non-committal.[196] Nuri therefore had to bring his proposal to the British Government without having first succeeded in bridging the gap between the Arabs and the Jews of Palestine or in achieving the latter's agreement to his proposition.

In October 1936 when the General Strike of the Palestine Arabs ended and a lull was reached in their rebellion, Nuri made his views known in full to the British Government through their Ambassador in Baghdad. The essential thing to do was to remove for all time from the hearts of the Palestine Arabs the fear of Jewish predominance. At present there were about 700,000 Arabs, as against 400,000 Jews, in Palestine and the former were afraid lest in a few years the pressure of the Jews should overcome them. Therefore the Palestine Arabs had to be shown that behind them there were 5,000,000 brother Arabs to protect them against the danger of Jewish domination. This could be done by the formation of some kind of Arab confederation. Nuri had in mind a loose union of states, a commonwealth such as the [then] British Empire in which each state would be as autonomous as any dominion. They might have a single sovereign, a *Zollverein* and a Privy Council to deal with questions of common interest. The formation of this confederation would not mean Arab acquiescence in the unrestricted flow of Jewish immigration to Palestine. It had to be restricted to maintain the present balance of population of Palestine – seven Arabs to four Jews – and future Jewish settlement on land confined to a triangle of about a million acres (about 44 million dunams) south of Haifa. It is clear that Nuri had lost hope of getting Jewish support for his scheme, since the only thing that could have ensured such support was Arab agreement to unrestricted Jewish immigration to Palestine.

In his dealings with the British Nuri thought then that the confederation should be formed of Palestine, Trans-Jordan and Iraq. As for Syria he explained that the proposed confederation would maintain the closest and friendliest relationship as long as it was allied to France and France was on its present terms with Great Britain. Similarly, the confederation would be equally willing to keep in the closest and friendliest touch with Saudi Arabia when Ibn Saud gave up his flirtation with the Italians and came into the British system of alliances like Egypt and Iraq.[197]

At the end of October 1936 a coup d'état took place in Baghdad, the main victim of which was Nuri al-Sa'id. General Bakr Sidqi became chief of staff and the real master of the country and his main civilian accomplice, Hikmat Sulayman, was appointed Prime Minister, while Nuri al-Sa'id fled from Iraq to Cairo. In his exile Nuri continued his activities, but now with much less inhibition. He established contacts with Syrian politicians and was ready to advance much further in his endeavour to gain their support and that of Ibn Saud for his plan and, possibly, for his return to power in his country. He made it plain that he wanted both countries to be included in the confederation and he was ready to have Ibn Saud as the Sovereign of this confederation, while Shukri al-Quwatli, the most prominent pro-Saudi Syrian leader, would be appointed Viceroy.[198] This *volte-face* by Nuri al-Sa'id as far as the Saudi dynasty was concerned can be explained against the background of Bakr Sidqi's coup d'état. It seems that Nuri had been convinced, and the circumstances surrounding the coup encouraged this belief[199] that King Ghazi was implicated in the coup, or at least had advance knowledge of it. Nuri therefore regarded him as responsible for his misfortune and for more than a year Nuri's pan-Arab campaign assumed an attitude of unmitigated hostility towards King Ghazi. Arab confederation became Nuri's weapon for return to power.

Although Hikmat Sulayman was ousted from the premiership in August 1937 Nuri was not included in Jamil al-Midfa'i's new government. Again Nuri appealed to the British and this time included in his programme both Syria and Lebanon and Saudi Arabia. The Levant countries had already initiated their treaties with France and were expecting to become independent when the French *Assemblée Nationale* ratified the treaties. As for Ibn Saud, Nuri pointed out that he was 'well respected, experienced and most efficient within his tribal areas, and well esteemed by all Arabs owing to his character as an Arab Noble and religious leader. His only weakness is lack of experience in administration of a modern state, with all its complication'. In contrast to Ibn Saud 'King Ghazi shows no capacity for kingship and little interest in statescraft. He is personally weak in character and not well esteemed by Arabs in general ... Were His Majesty King Faisal still living he would be the obvious and most conspicuously suited Arab leader to put the policy of an Arab Confederation of States into effect', but in the existing circumstances, the Arabs of Palestine, Trans-Jordan and Iraq should be asked in a referendum whether or not they agreed to the kingship of Ibn Saud. Nuri made it clear that although 'Abdallah was fairly popular in his country he had little support outside it. As for Iraq, Nuri alluded to the 'difficulties' of the last year, hinting that King Ghazi had been connected with the Bakr Sidqi–Hikmat Sulayman coup d'état and therefore had lost any claim to Nuri's loyalty.[200]

Even after the ousting of Hikmat Sulayman and the appointment of Jamil al-Midfa'i to the premiership, Nuri was still convinced that Iraq was standing on the brink of disintegration owing to the divisions within the army, the lack of stability and self-assurance by the Cabinet and the administration in general, and the increasing discontent in the tribal areas of the middle Euphrates and the desert. Therefore he decided to follow closely internal developments and to remain within easy reach of Iraq in his semi-exile in Cairo so that he might endeavour to reorganise the country when the disorders which he expected did, in fact, break out. In his endeavour to this end Nuri al-Sa'id decided to act in consultation and close cooperation with King 'Abd al-'Aziz Al Sa'ud.[201]

At the end of 1937 Nuri was prompted to act by the demonstrations against King Ghazi and the Hashemite dynasty which took place in Baghdad on the occasion of the opening of King Ghazi Street in Baghdad. He asked Mr Muwaffaq al-Alusi, formerly the Iraqi Consul in Beirut whose family had had close ties with the Saudi dynasty, to go and see 'Abd al-'Aziz Al Sa'ud, to put before him the true version of Nuri al-Sa'id's proposition regarding Palestine (since Nuri's rivals were spreading stories that Nuri had agreed to unlimited Jewish immigration into the whole area of his proposed confederation of Palestine, Trans-Jordan and Iraq) and to suggest to him that one of his (Ibn Saud's) sons should be nominated to the throne of Iraq.[202] To the British Nuri revealed only that he wanted to dispel Ibn Saud's apprehensions regarding the false story over Jewish immigration.[203]

But Ibn Saud was not impressed. He told Nuri's messenger 'not to reply to Nuri's suggestion and to disregard it absolutely', and he continued to be suspicious of Nuri al-Sa'id's intentions towards his inter-Arab activities. The Saudi monarch exerted pressure on the British Government to avoid any move that could be regarded as approval of Nuri's initiative and as always got favourable and reassuring British replies.[204]

Nuri's reaction to the Saudi negative attitude and pressure was an attempt to entice the British with a new idea. On 30 August 1938 he expressed his readiness to support the partition of Palestine if the Arab part of that country and Trans-Jordan were united with Iraq and if possible with Syria as well. Now, his preference for a Saudi leadership of that union was dropped and his new one was in the following order: Amir Zayd (the youngest brother of the late King Faysal, who was working in the Iraq diplomatic service), Amir 'Abd al-Illah (son of the late King 'Ali and nephew of King Faysal), King Ghazi and Amir 'Abdallah and Amir Sa'ud (son of 'Abd al-'Aziz Al Sa'ud) equal fourth. He added that if the British chose 'Abdallah the Arabs would accept it.[205]

Nuri got no reply from the British to his new suggestion. Not only did they not like his whole scheme, they were also at that period going back on their endorsement of the Palestine Peel Committee recommendation for the Partition of Palestine and searching for an alternative policy.[206] Consequently Nuri sought the support of Arab politicians. He went to Trans-Jordan, Egypt and Syria, met several politicians, including Amir 'Abdallah and al-Hajj Amin al-Husayni, the exiled Mufti of Jerusalem, and tried to convince them of the benefits that his proposition carried for the Arabs.[207] In October 1938 Nuri laid before the Syrian delegates to the Arab Inter-Parliamentary Conference on Palestine (see pp. 170–1) an enlarged version of his draft proposal for an Arab-Jewish agreement over the Palestine question. It envisaged an eventual unity of Syria and Iraq with an independent State of Palestine (including Trans-Jordan). And although the thorny question of the form of government – whether it should be a monarchy or a republic – was deferred for the future, the scheme failed to win the support of the Syrian delegates or that of Izzat Darwaza, the Palestinian leader. This was in spite of Nuri's boasts that he had secured the assent of Amin al-Husayni, the Mufti of Jerusalem and the President of the illegal Higher Arab Committee of Amir 'Abdallah, of the Saudi monarch, of the British authorities in Palestine and of many leading politicians in Britain, among those being Lord Lloyd, Colonel S. Newcombe, Lord Samuel, Sir Arthur Wauchope, Lord Winterton and others.[208]

During 1938 the Syrian public became disenchanted with the French since they were convinced that the French were not going to ratify the treaty with Syria. In Iraq itself Jamil al-Midfa'i could not stand up to the pressure of the factions which supported Nuri al-Sa'id. The Army lost much of its internal unity and self-confidence and could no longer prevent the return of Nuri al-Sa'id to power. Consequently in December 1938 he was once again appointed Prime Minister by King Ghazi. Thereupon the interest of the Iraqi Government and public in Franco-Syrian relations increased greatly. The government exerted pressure on Britain to persuade France to ratify the treaty. The press were publishing articles denouncing France, and expressing feelings of solidarity with Syria. Demonstrations to the same effect took place in various Iraqi towns and rumours circulated that Iraq was supplying Syria with weapons for eventual revolt against French rule.[209] Nuri al-Sa'id contacted 'Adil al-Azmah, one of the Syrian Nationalist leaders, and suggested to him that on 17 March 1939, when the Syrian Parliament was to be summoned, they should pass a resolution declaring union with Iraq and congratulating the King of Iraq on his birthday, 21 March.[210] It is true that the Syrian Parliament dared not take such a provocative line in their relations with France. But Nuri al-Sa'id was otherwise rewarded as Sa'dallah al-Jabiri, the Syrian Nationalist leader of Aleppo, and a group of prominent political and business leaders of that city expressed their support for Nuri's proposals and implored him and King Ghazi to bring about 'the Union of Syria and Iraq, under the shadow of the flag of the heir of Faysal for the realisation of the great Arab unity'.[211]

Concurrently with the initiative directed towards Syria Nuri did not forget Palestine. During the Palestine St James's Conference he personally, as well as other Iraqi officials, reminded the British once more of the 1936 Arab Federation scheme as a solution for the current troubles in Palestine. But once more the British were reluctant to make any such move which could jeopardise their relations with Ibn Saud.[212]

Suddenly an unexpected event took place which had strong bearings on Nuri al-Sa'id's activities. On 3 April 1939, King Ghazi was killed in a car accident. His son and heir, Amir Faysal, was still very young and consequently a Regent had to be appointed. With the full backing of the Army Nuri al-Sa'id backed the candidacy of the twenty-six-year-old Amir 'Abd al-Illah, nephew of King Faysal I, brother of King Ghazi's widow and uncle of the minor King, against the candidacy of the forty-one-year-old Amir Zayd, younger brother of King Faysal I, who was supported by several politicians. Nuri, with the support of the leading Army officers, carried the day and on 6 April the Iraqi Parliament proclaimed Amir Faysal as King Faysal II and Amir 'Abd al-Illah as Regent. Nuri and his military associates were assisted by Ghazi's widow, Queen Rajihah, who testified that Ghazi had before his death stated his wish that 'Abd al-Illah should become Regent.[213] This development cemented the cracking loyalty of Nuri al-Sa'id to the Hashemite dynasty and in the coming years Nuri once again devoted his energies to the enhancement of the position and prestige of Amir 'Abd al-Illah.[214]

Nuri al-Sa'id was well aware of the plans and attitude of Amir 'Abdallah regarding Arab unity and the future of Syria. 'Abdallah made no secret of it and on several occasions made it clear to the Iraqis and the British that he was the only legitimate successor to the claim of the House of Hashim to the Syrian throne and to the leadership of the movement for Arab unity. In the winter of 1939, when Nuri's inspired campaign over the future of Syria intensified, 'Abdallah again informed the British that he opposed Nuri's endeavours for the annexation of Palestine and Trans-Jordan to Iraq, in view of the instability of that country since the disastrous death of King Faysal, owing to the Assyrian incident, the Bakr Sidqi coup and the threat of the Iraqi Army to every government.[215]

Nuri realised that 'Abdallah's opposition weakened the Hashemite-Iraqi claim for a Confederation of the Arab countries of the Fertile Crescent and consequently in 1939, having healed the breach between himself and the Hashemites, he devoted a great deal of his energies, as far as this question was concerned, to coming to terms with 'Abdallah. Some time in the winter of that year Nuri tried to convince 'Abdallah that Hashemite plans regarding the future of Syria should be co-ordinated and the 'details of a scheme for establishing a Hashimite Kingdom in Syria and uniting Iraq, Syria, Trans-Jordan and ultimately Palestine also under the same royal house' should be elaborated. 'Abdallah's suspicion of Nuri al-Sa'id and of the Iraqi Regent was worked up by the British Resident so that he reacted to the Iraqi démarche in negative terms, although he agreed to receive Nuri for talks in 'Amman.[216] And when, some months later, Nuri did come to 'Amman and had talks with 'Abdallah, he tried to make it plain to him that 'if only the members of the Hashemite family could agree ... on a single representative their candidature would obviously be much strengthened against the rivalry of the Sa'udi family'. Nuri asked 'Abdallah to waive any pretensions of his own to the throne of Syria in favour of the infant King Faysal II. Nuri said nothing about his confederation scheme nor of the question of which of the Hashemites might become the sovereign of that confederation, thus enabling 'Abdallah in the future to claim this position for himself on the ground of being the senior member of the House of Hashim (in terms of age, of course, not of status). But for 'Abdallah this bait was not enticing enough and he rejected Nuri's proposition. 'He considered that he had the better claim to represent the Hashemite family and understood moreover that if the matter ever came to an issue, he had been promised British backing by Mr Winston Churchill.'[217] The only thing that Nuri could do was to prevent the Amir exercising any influence over his younger relatives of the Iraqi branch of his dynasty[218] and to hope for a better chance.

The circumstances prevailing in the Middle East after the outbreak of the Second World War were regarded by Nuri as opportune for pursuing his object although in somewhat modified way, and for a renewed attempt to coordinate his policy with that of 'Abdallah. The favourable reaction which Nuri encountered in 1939 among Syrian politicians and the continuous contacts which he had established since 1936 with the Palestinian Arab leader al-Hajj Amin al-Husayni no doubt had a strong influence on him.[219] The Arabs quickly realised that their bargaining power *vis-à-vis* Britain, relative to that of the Jews, dramatically improved once the war had broken out and they endeavoured to capitalise on this change (the first fruits of which they had already reaped in May 1939 in the form of the Palestine White Paper, when Britain dropped appeasement and began to prepare for war against Nazi Germany).

In March 1940 a meeting took place in Rutbah on the Iraqi–Trans-Jordanian border between 'Abdallah and 'Abd al-Illah, Nuri al-Sa'id and Mawlud Mukhlis. Nuri argued that it was a waste of time trying to effect a union with Syria or to secure the throne of that country for a Hashemite Amir as the French were unwilling to move in either direction, while the British Government were unwilling to agree to the early federation of Iraq, Palestine and Trans-Jordan but there was a possibility of their uniting Palestine and Trans-Jordan under the rule of 'Abdallah. Once this was done, it would be relatively easy to bring about closer connections between the Western and Eastern Hashemite kingdoms. Therefore 'Abdallah should pursue the aim of uniting Trans-Jordan and Palestine as energetically as possible, and Nuri al-Sa'id and his associates would support the scheme and, in addition, seek to obtain Egyptian sympathy. Nuri tried to get the Amir 'Abdallah to agree to a reconciliation with Amin al-Husayni, who was prepared to work for the ultimate federation of the three countries in question, but 'Abdallah refused to agree and said that he would act through his Arab friends in Palestine who were in opposition to the Mufti.[220]

The failure to obtain 'Abdallah's agreement to Nuri's scheme did not stop his endeavours. Iraq was passing at that time through troubled waters of nationalist tempests. A combined force of Army colonels, political supporters of Rashid 'Ali al-Kaylani, and young nationalists organised in *al-Muthanna* Club, over whom Amin al-Husayni had a strong influence, exerted heavy pressure on Nuri to exploit the favourable circumstances to the Arabs as far as their relations with Britain were concerned, and get Britain to concede to the Arabs on various points, including weapons for the Iraqi Army, the Palestine question and Arab unity.[221] Although Nuri failed to get 'Abdallah's endorsement for his new version of a smaller Arab Confederation, he began to exert pressure on the British to move towards meeting Arab demands on this point.

The fall of France gave Nuri and the Iraqi Regent a sense of urgency. They, like Amir 'Abdallah and King 'Abd al-'Aziz Al Saud were visualising apprehensively that a Turkish or Italian occupation of the Levant countries might follow the French armistice with Germany. Therefore they hoped that a British occupation would preempt such a negative eventuality and that such a British move would lead to the fulfilment of Arab aspirations for the independence of those countries with 'some kind of federal union with Iraq'.²²² But the consolidation of the Vichy-led French Government in Syria and Lebanon mitigated this apprehension and Nuri resumed for the time being his reserved attitude regarding the question of Syria being included in his proposed confederation.

Thereupon, Nuri approached C. J. Edmonds, the British Adviser in the Iraqi Ministry of the Interior, and repeated the proposition which he had recently put before 'Abdallah, adding that there would be no difficulty in including Palestine while still under mandate. However, he contradicted himself by including in his scheme the extension of the Anglo-Iraqi Alliance to cover all the members of the Confederation, thus implying the termination of the Palestine mandate as the Iraqi mandate had been terminated when the Alliance became effective in 1932. Nuri spelled out the substance of his Confederation proposal, and it turned out to be rather limited: removal of internal customs barriers for local produce and manufactures, currency union with notes issued in the name of the Confederation, unification of education for the Arabs, common military training and improvement of inter-state communications. Removal of customs barriers was regarded as particularly advantageous to Jewish industry in Palestine and as an economic means to obtain their agreement. Nuri was prepared to concede the choice of a king for the throne of Palestine to its population who would exercise this right in a free plebiscite. And as the only candidates would presumably be scions of the House of Hashim and Al Sa'ud, representatives of Iraq and Saudi Arabia would appropriately be included in the body supervising the plebiscite. However, he explained that while the Iraqi Government did not press the Hashemite claim he personally felt little doubt that Amir 'Abd al-Illah, the Iraqi Regent, would get a ninety per cent majority. Contrary to what he had told 'Abdallah several months earlier, Nuri expressed his view that 'Abdallah had little chance of getting the throne of Palestine but this would not prevent his continuing as at present ruler of Trans-Jordan within the proposed confederation. Here, for the first time a new element in Nuri's scheme was made crystal-clear. 'Abd al-Illah's Regency made him profoundly interested in the extension of Iraqi influence over the Fertile Crescent Arab countries, in the formation of the proposed confederation, and in finding a permanent throne for himself for the rainy day when he would have to transfer the reins of kingship to Faysal II. It should be added that when these propositions were made known to the British, the Iraqi press, no doubt instigated by official circles, were vehemently advocating the confederation as a panacea for all Arab ailments, including the Palestine question.²²³

This démarche was part of a more comprehensive pressure exerted on Britain by Arab governments and leaders which was interwoven with the growing Axis propaganda and prestige in the Middle East. This development and the coming to power of Rashid 'Ali al-Kaylani and his supporters, the pro-Nazi colonels, influenced the shaping of British policy in the Middle East in the spring of 1941 (see later, pp. 92–3 and 245–9). But before Britain made any move Nuri and the Regent were, in April 1941, swept away from their positions and had to flee from Iraq. Although their exile was short, the fact that they were brought back at the beginning of June 1941 to their former positions of power in Iraq by British arms weakened their position *vis-à-vis* the British, drastically curtailed their power of leverage on them and drove them to work mainly to consolidate their positions in Iraq. Only when this had been met, could Nuri resume his pursuit of the Arab confederation scheme.

During those hectic years of 1939 and 1940 Nuri's intensified activities were well known in the Middle East and aroused interest, but mainly apprehension, among neighbouring countries, rulers and politicians.[224] At the forefront of those enraged by Nuri's campaign was, naturally, the King of Saudi Arabia. Apart from his basic hostility to, and suspicion of, the Hashemite dynasty, he feared that Britain might support Nuri's designs and that Iraq, an ally of Britain, might use force to further her aims in Syria. When these had been obtained Iraq might then turn to her next goal, Hijaz, the cradle of the Hashemites, and even the Gulf principalities and then Najd, the Saudi heartland. Iraqi propaganda, originating from the Royal Palace when Ghazi was alive against Kuwait and Bahrayn, was cited by the Saudi king as indicative of Iraq's designs. As a counter-measure he let it be understood that one of his sons was regarded as a possible candidate to the throne of Syria. But when he was reassured that Britain did not contemplate any support for Nuri's design of Arab federation nor for the accession of any Hashemite prince to the throne of Syria, he relaxed and confessed that he had no designs regarding Syria and that his only interest there was negative: to thwart Nuri's project.[225]

The French, too, were not slow to express their discomfort over Nuri al-Sa'id's and other plans of Arab federation. After the Royal (Peel) Commission in Palestine had finished their work and submitted their reports, the French Government soon realised that the commission's recommendations had pan-Arab implications.[226] Consequently, the French Ambassador in London delivered a memorandum to the British Government in which he pointed out that encouragement of pan-Arab aspirations had a disturbing effect on the situation in Syria. He urged that it would be in the interest of both Great Britain and France to stabilise as soon as possible the existing situation in the Arab world. In October 1938, after the publication in the press, including *The Times*, of several articles containing allusions to the possibility of some form of Arab confederation receiving the blessing of the British Government, the French Ambassador again referred to that possibility and said that it had greatly disconcerted his government who hoped most earnestly that nothing of this nature would materialise.

ATTEMPTS AT FERTILE CRESCENT UNITY

The French Government's own position *vis-à-vis* Syria was always difficult, and any idea of a confederation could only add to their difficulties. Even if the inclusion of Syria in the proposed Confederation were not contemplated — and to this the French Government attached the utmost importance — nevertheless such a Confederation would act as a magnet and augment disquiet and agitation in Syria. Officials of the French Ministère des Affaires Etrangères added that their government wished Syria and the other Arab states to remain as individual entities within their existing frontiers and made it clear that they would oppose any idea of a large conglomerate Arab state under a sort of joint Franco-British mandatory regime, as had been mooted in the British press, or any other scheme of Arab federation.[227] This phenomenon happened more than once. Whenever a British newspaper, and especially a celebrated one such as *The Times*, published an article in support of Arab federation as a possible solution of the Palestine question or discussed the merit of this idea, French officials either in Paris or in the Levant countries would be incensed and ask their British counterparts uneasy questions. The British would answer that His Majesty's Government did not inspire these articles and did not share the views expressed.[228] The French would listen and would believe or not until the next disquieting press article was published.

Nuri al-Sa'id was once more nominated Prime Minister in October 1941 following a short transitional period of four months when Jamil al-Midfa'i held this position and presided over the rehabilitation of the Hashemite *ancien régime*. The first signs that under Nuri al-Sa'id's leadership Iraq had resumed its long pursuit of the Arab confederation scheme came in the summer of 1942. Arab nationalist circles in Beirut were then engaged in discussions with the Iraqi consul over a scheme of Arab federation of the Fertile Crescent.[229] It may have been that before going out full-speed Iraq tried to reach an agreement with probable opponents. We do not know the exact character of this scheme or the conclusions reached in these discussions, but it seems that they were not accidental and an atmosphere of soul-searching began to spread among Arab nationalists and those close to Nuri al-Sa'id.

Anyway, Nuri once more put his ideas before his associates and got an encouraging reaction from Taha al-Hashimi, who was then staying in Istanbul in quasi-exile. He wrote on 12 August 1942 to Nuri:

> ... the time has come to strongly demand a resolution of the Arab Question on the basis of a union which would include Iraq, Syria, Lebanon, Palestine and Trans-Jordan. Our aim before this War was to work to safeguard the independence of the Arab countries, provided that the issue of unity was left to them. The events of this War showed that the mere independence of the Arab countries

would not be useful if they did not unite with one another. Only union would safeguard their existence and independence in the best form. No glory and no pride can be derived from an existence which is miserable, humiliated and despicable. Taking into account what the Allied leaders had officially declared in respect of independence of the Arab countries and that they had been favourably disposed toward their unity [he was alluding, no doubt, to Anthony Eden's speech of 29 May 1941], it has become self-evident that we must work for the formation of this unity and to achieve it before this War has ended.[230]

Taha al-Hashimi's urgency turned out to be very timely indeed within several months of the overwhelming British victory at al-'Alamein during October–November, 1942. With the German threat gone and Britain once again sole master of the Middle East, Nuri al-Sa'id must have felt that his hour of grand action had at last come.

During 1942, and especially during the second half of that year, Zionist Jewish political activity in the United States intensified and became much more vocal. Various organisations united their efforts within the Emergency Council and the public pressure exerted on Britain to let the few Jewish refugees who had in one way or another succeeded in getting out from Nazi-occupied Europe enter Palestine became very bitter and hostile. Britain's retreat in 1941 from her previous promise to let the Jews establish fighting units of their own within the British Army triggered off a strong outcry for the establishment of a Jewish Brigade, a demand which Dr Chaim Weizmann made publicly known in his famous 'Foreign Affairs' article of January 1942. In May 1942 an emergency meeting of Zionist leaders in the Biltmore Hotel, New York, gave birth to the so-called Biltmore Resolution calling for Jewish free immigration to Palestine and for the establishment therein of a Jewish Commonwealth at the end of the war. With the adoption of this resolution by the Zionist Executive Committee in November of that year it henceforth became the cornerstone of Zionist policy.

This transformation was mainly brought about by the gradual and sporadic infiltration of horrible news from Eastern Europe that the Jews were systematically being murdered and that most of the Polish and Soviet Jews (in the Nazi-occupied part of the Soviet Union) had already been massacred. This incredible news could not after November 1942 be dismissed as exaggeration or mere propaganda fabrication since a group of Palestinian Jews caught in Poland at the outbreak of war were exchanged for a group of Germans living in Palestine. These people came and gave eye-witness testimonies about the operation of the German murder-machine which was in action in Poland. The Jews became bitter and enraged and their sense of helplessness and the indifference of most other peoples exacerbated their feelings.[231]

The Arabs were not deaf and blind. Like most other peoples they were not impressed by the dreadful news about the fate of European Jewry. What they did take notice of, and were impressed by, was the Jewish pressure in the United States which was directed towards Britain. It prompted Arab politicians who were pro-British, and thus had some degree of freedom of action, to exert counter-pressure. They felt that if the Arabs stood idly by doing nothing the Jews would obtain their objective,[232] and Nuri al-Sa'id even tried to arrange a joint Iraqi-Saudi approach to the British Government in protest against 'the formation of a Jewish Army'.[233]

The British military victory in al-'Alamein, Jewish-Zionist pressure and the Arab general feeling that something had to be done prompted Iraq, under the leadership of 'Abd al-Illah and Nuri al-Sa'id, to declare war in January 1943 against Nazi Germany and thus to gain a *locus standi* in a future Peace Conference which was widely believed to be the tribunal to decide the future of Palestine.[234] But that was not all. In anticipation of the final shaping of the political future of the Middle East Nuri reached the conclusion that he had better present his scheme for that future and gained widespread support for it among Arab and British politicians. Towards the end of 1942 he prepared a 'personal' Note in which he described and analysed the development of the Arabs and Palestine problems since the First World War and put forward his proposals for solutions. The Note was sent in mid-January 1943 to Richard Casey, the British Minister of State Resident in Cairo, but Nuri wanted to distribute it also among top British officials in the Middle East, the Dominions' representatives, some foreign governments and few Arab politicians, a move for which he had asked British consent. The British Government were not enthusiastic but did not judge it useful to object to the distribution of Nuri's Note, and thus about 300 copies were sent to its various intended recipients in February 1943.[235]

In his covering letter attached to the Note and addressed to Mr Casey, Nuri stressed Arab objection to the Zionist demands, viz., the establishment of a Jewish state in Palestine, free Jewish immigration thereto and the formation of Jewish fighting units within the British Army. He bitterly resented the growing Jewish-Zionist activities in the United States and Britain's promotion of these ends. But he stressed that within the framework of the solution which he had outlined in his Note there was a possibility 'to guarantee the future of the Jewish National Home as it exists at present in Palestine'. In the Note itself Nuri interpreted modern Arab history in such a way as to make his unity scheme look necessary, and politically and morally justified. He emphasised the various declarations made during the First World War and its aftermath by the Entente

Powers and the unjustified partition of the Arab countries which followed. Therefore he called upon the United Nations (the Allies fighting the Axis Powers) to declare there and then:

(1) That Syria, Lebanon, Palestine and Transjordan shall be reunited into one State.

(2) That the form of government of this State, whether monarchical or republican, whether unitary or federal, shall be decided by the peoples of this country themselves.

(3) That there shall be created an Arab League to which Iraq and Syria will adhere at once and which can be joined by the other Arab States at will.

(4) That this Arab League shall have a permanent council nominated by the member States, and presided over by one of the rulers of the States, who shall be chosen in a manner acceptable to the States concerned.

(5) The Arab League Council shall be responsible for the following: (a) Defence, (b) Foreign Affairs, (c) Currency, (d) Communication, (e) Customs, (f) Protection of minority rights.

(6) The Jews of Palestine shall be given semi-autonomy. They shall have the right to their own rural and urban district administration, including schools, health institutions and policy, subject to general supervision by the Syrian State.

(7) Jerusalem shall be a city to which members of all religions shall have free access for pilgrimage and worship and a special commission composed of representatives of the three theocratic [sic!] religions shall be set up to ensure this.

(8) That, if they demand it, the Maronites of the Lebanon shall be granted a privileged régime, such as they possessed during the last years of the Ottoman Empire. This special régime, like those to be set up in paragraphs 6 and 7 above, shall rest on an International Guarantee.[236]

At first sight it looks as though Nuri tried to combine his previous schemes of Fertile Crescent Confederation with Amir 'Abdallah's Greater Syria project by dropping the idea of a direct connection between Iraq and Syria and substituting a connection between Iraq and a *united* Syria after the latter had been established.

And indeed, on 18 February 1943, Nuri al-Sa'id sent a personal letter to 'Abdallah in which he stated that the 'Syrian and Palestinian problems will not be solved until Syria, Lebanon and Palestine are united' with special rights to Lebanon as in the Ottoman days and to the Jews in those areas of Palestine in which they formed the majority of the population.[237] Furthermore, Jamil al-Midfa'i, who was sent in the winter of 1943 by Nuri al-Sa'id to propagate Nuri's project, told the

British Resident in 'Amman that the Arab Federation idea really boiled down to the future of the four 'Syrian States'. But the fact that the kind of régime which would be set up in United Syria was left open dispels the impression of a co-ordinated endeavour with 'Abdallah. 'Abdallah was really crystal-clear in rejecting Nuri al-Sa'id's proposals. He dissociated himself from Nuri's initiative and told Jamil al-Midfa'i that 'it was not their [the Iraqis'] business to speak for the Syrian States while there were others with better qualifications and claims'.[238] Furthermore, a question necessarily raised is whether or not Nuri al-Sa'id was ready for the sake of Arab unity to give up the Iraqi-Hashemite claim to the throne of Syria and to accept the continuation of the republican form of government there.

When Nuri al-Sa'id tried to entice 'Abd al-'Aziz Al Sa'ud to support his scheme he repeatedly stressed that he did not intend to set up any particular king on the Syrian throne and that it would be left to the Syrians themselves to select the form of government they wished. In this question, he agreed, Iraq had no *locus standi*.[239] Jamil al-Midfa'i, who had just been appointed as Iraqi Minister to Saudi Arabia, personally assured the Saudi King 'that Iraq had no national or dynastic ambitions in Syria'.[240] And 'Abd al-Illah himself wrote to 'Abdallah and denied any rumours that he claimed the Syrian throne for himself 'as he had no intention of competing with his uncle in that matter''.[241] But in a personal conversation with Lieutenant-Colonel De Gaury Nuri al-Sa'id argued that 'Abd al-Illah was becoming the successor to King Faysal as a leader of the Arabs and that he should be King of Syria and Crown Prince of Iraq. To this end he intended to put a bill through the Iraqi Parliament to transfer the succession of the Iraqi Crown from the heirs and descendants of King Faysal I to Amir 'Abd al-Illah.[242]

'Abd al-Illah Hafiz, the Iraqi Minister for Foreign Affairs, was less cautious in speaking his mind. He admitted 'in strictest confidence' during a talk with the Saudi *chargé d'affaires* in Baghdad that the Iraqi Government aimed to place 'Abd al-Illah, the Regent of Iraq, on the Syrian throne.[243] And the Iraqi Minister in London, who was a Kurd and did not believe very much in pan-Arabism, told Mr M. Shertok [Sharett] in March 1944 that Nuri al-Sa'id 'thought of putting on the Syrian throne a member of the Iraqi dynasty'.[244] It seems safe to conclude that securing the Syrian throne for 'Abd al-Illah was a basic element of Nuri al-Sa'id's scheme. No less important is the fact that this was the impression of various foreign observers and it influenced their reactions to the scheme and had bearings on its eventual failure.[245]

Another interesting question is the real role allotted by the initiators of the Arab unity scheme to Saudi Arabia. We have already seen that Nuri tried to assure the Saudi monarch that neither he [Nuri] nor 'Abd al-Illah was interested in any personal gain in connection with the scheme.

Furthermore, in a conversation with the Saudi *chargé d'affaires* in Baghdad, Nuri improved the position of Saudi Arabia in his plan. Originally, Iraq and united Syria were envisaged to constitute the cornerstone of the intended Arab League, the proposed framework of the broader Arab unity which could be joined by any other Arab states at will. Now he suggested that Saudi Arabia would be placed on the same footing as Iraq and Syria and the three of them would be the constituent components of the loose Arab federal union.[246] But the Saudis were not impressed and as we shall see later on they did not change their critical and even hostile attitude to Nuri al-Sa'id's plan.

Anthony Eden's parliamentary reply of 14 February 1943, in which he repeated his statement of 29 May 1941, encouraged Nuri and gave a fillip to his endeavour.[247] First of all he decided to send Jamil al-Midfa'i to Damascus, Beirut, 'Amman and Jerusalem to have informal talks with Arab leaders there and to co-ordinate future plans with them. But at that stage Nuri made an extremely important decision to involve Egypt in his preparatory endeavours. After hesitating about whether or not to send Jamil al-Midfa'i to Egypt as well,[248] he decided to ask him to go to Egypt. Thereupon, on 17 March Nuri directly approached Mustafa al-Nahhas, the Egyptian Prime Minister, in a letter in which Nuri drew Nahhas' attention to Eden's last statement and suggested holding an official Arab conference in Cairo under the presidency of Nahhas, or a semi-official conference under the presidency of another distinguished Egyptian to be nominated by Nahhas. Apart from alluding to the advancement of the Arab cause the precise agenda and the date of the proposed conference were left open by Nuri for further consultation.[249]

We have no direct source which tells us why Nuri al-Sa'id took this fateful decision which proved very damaging to his policy. In the early days of March he learned from Sir Kinahan Cornwallis, the British Ambassador, that Britain took a very cool and reserved position in regard to his plan[250] (see also on p. 222). He may well have thought that according to Eden's statement Britain would support only an Arab unity scheme which would gain the support of all major Arab states. So he attempted to achieve a prominent role for Egypt in the preparatory stage in order to get Egypt's blessing for his plan. Then, possibly, Britain would have second thoughts.

Whatever the reasons, Jamil al-Midfa'i and another Iraqi politician Tahsin al-'Askari, the Minister of the Interior, reached Egypt in the second half of March and began to have talks with Egyptian leaders and public figures. On 27 March they met Mustafa al-Nahhas Pasha and discussed with him the question of Arab unity and the best means to achieve it. Despite what Nuri al-Sa'id had written to Nahhas on 17 March, the Iraqi delegates now agreed that unofficial representation in the proposed Conference was also necessary to meet the peculiar cases of Palestine and Syria, which were still under foreign control. Probably the Iraqis would also like to have unofficial Egyptian representation at the conference, in view of the fact that it was among opposition elements that the most ardent pan-Arabists were to be found, such as 'Abd al-Rahman 'Azzam Pasha, Muhammad 'Ali 'Allubah, Tawfiq Daws Pasha etc. Mustafa al-Nahhas, on the other hand, insisted that the proposed conference at Cairo be composed purely of representatives of the different Arab governments concerned. This position was certainly, in part at least, due to Nahhas' fear that if veteran Egyptian pan-Arabists of the opposition parties took part in the Conference, they and the Palace would overshadow the official Egyptian delegates in conducting discussions with the Arab representatives. The result was disagreement, and the disgruntlement of the Iraqis, and no agreement was reached.[251] Jamil al-Midfa'i decided to stay in Egypt no longer and left for Palestine and Iraq on 29 March. Before leaving, he declared himself in a statement to the press, to be in favour of Arab confederation and pleaded for the co-ordination of efforts in the cultural, social and economic spheres so that the various Arab countries could gain prosperity and defend their freedom and dignity. He did not indicate any controversy between him and the Egyptian Prime Minister, although he stressed that Egyptian leaders of all political opinions gave to the idea of confederation their 'attention, encouragement and appreciation'.[252] When Jamil al-Midfa'i returned to Baghdad he made it clear, though in a very cautious way, that agreement over the holding of a general Arab Conference was still to be reached, to Nuri al-Sa'id's disappointment.[253]

This Iraqi disappointment was exacerbated by Mustafa al-Nahhas' public reaction. On 30 March the Egyptian Minister of Justice, Muhammad Sabri Abu 'Alam, made a statement to the Senate, on behalf of Nahhas Pasha who was sick, in reply to questions tabled by two Senators of pan-Arab leanings. They wanted to know what was the reaction of the Egyptian Government to Anthony Eden's statement of 24 February. In his reply (to which we shall return on p. 260) Nahhas supported the idea of Arab unity, welcomed Eden's statement and emphasised that the intended Arab Conference should take place at Cairo under the presidency of the Egyptian Prime Minister and with only official representatives of the Arab governments.[254] Nuri desperately hoped that he could still salvage his initiative by a personal talk with Nahhas,[255] but when a meeting took place a few months later, it was within the framework of Mustafa al-Nahhas' initiative and based on his proposals.

Once again, in July 1943, Nuri tried to regain the lead by concentrating his endeavour in the direction of the Levant countries. He met various leaders and explained to them the necessity of building the foundation of Greater Syria as the preliminary to eventual Arab confederation.[256] He paid special attention to 'Abdallah, urging him once more to give up his separate claim to Syria,[257] but he failed. 'Abdallah subsequently never ceased to view with resentment and suspicion Nuri's activities in this sphere and strongly criticised his government.[258] Furthermore, a close inspection of the situation revealed to Nuri al-Sa'id the real magnitude of the obstacles represented by the French presence in the Levant, the attitude of the Maronites and the aspirations of the Jews in Palestine.[259]

In Syria itself the initial reactions to Nuri al-Sa'id's Note were far from enthusiastic. Syrian influential leaders questioned the right of Iraq or the Hashemites to rule there. What they were interested in was to gain complete independence and to govern themselves. In taking this position they counted on the support of the Saudi monarch and Egypt.[260] Nuri did not give way but continued his efforts to win over the Syrians. His main target was Jamil Mardam Bey, the Syrian Prime Minister, who had proved in his long career since the First World War that he was of an independent mind and capable of taking independent, less popular, positions. And indeed it seems that Jamil Mardam was inclined to accept Nuri's proposal, but other Syrian leaders of the National Bloc with Shukri al-Quwwatli at their helm were adamant. And if they needed any foreign encouragement for that stand they were abundantly receiving it from 'Abd al-'Aziz Al Sa'ud.[261] The Saudi king was all through the period under discussion as adamant in his hostile attitude to any Iraqi or Hashemite scheme to promote Arab Unity as ever. No Iraqi démarche of any kind could budge him from his intransigent position. Sometimes he was assured, as we have already noticed, that neither Nuri al-Sa'id nor 'Abd al-Illah was seeking personal advantage. However, even in acting in the United States for Palestine and other Arab courses, Nuri Pasha was motivated, if we accept Ibn Saud's view, by his personal ambition.[262] Ibn Saud also resented that Nuri had approached the Egyptian Prime Minister first with the proposal to convene a general Arab conference to discuss Arab unity; however, to judge by past developments a British Foreign Office official was confident that even if the Saudi king had been the first to be consulted, it would not have changed his position.[263]

The involvement of Egypt in this matter since Nahhas had launched his initiative on 30 March 1943 only aggravated Ibn Saud's anxiety and suspicion, because he neither trusted Nahhas Pasha nor accepted Egypt's leading role in the process of promoting Arab unity.[264] Although Ibn Saud used always to pay tribute to the idea of Arab Unity his policy was aimed at achieving the independence of each Arab state in such a manner that each would retain its own identity yet it would be impossible for them to commit acts of aggression against each other, and to ensure the

ATTEMPTS AT FERTILE CRESCENT UNITY

balance of power between them.[265] He was convinced that a Hashemite sitting on the Syrian throne would tilt the balance of power against Saudi Arabia and constitute a danger to his rule.[266] And this was the overriding factor for him.

The French too reacted negatively to Nuri's scheme, although mainly for a wrong reason. They suspected that the British were behind it.[267] Confronted with opposition from every corner including the British Government, Nuri began, in the summer of 1943, to despair. He realised that the Syrian leaders were interested in the consolidation of their independence and therefore he shelved for a while his initiative.[268] When he resumed his attempts half a year later on it was more in tune with political realities. It seems very clear that Nuri was now resigned to the fact that the Syrian leaders wanted a republican form of government and that they made it a *sine qua non* condition for their support for the formation of a united Greater Syria. Nuri was now ready to concede and 'Abdallah of course became furious, but it did not deter Nuri from proceeding.[269] When Nuri accepted this Syrian position his relations with the Syrian Government improved to the extent that, if we accept Nuri's word, he reached a verbal agreement with the Syrian President, the Prime Minister and the Minister for Foreign Affairs to the effect that if the proposed Arab Conference (expected then to be held in May 1944) produced no effective results, Iraq and Syria would enter into negotiations with each other.[270] 'Abdallah was really annoyed and urged his nephew 'Abd al-Illah, the Iraqi Regent, 'to counter the betrayal of the Hashimite House by Nuri Pasha in working for Arab unity on basis of republics'. 'Abdallah felt that Nuri, in attempting to outbid Nahhas accepted the view of the Syrian President and Prime Minister that Greater Syria should be a republic.[271] However, Nuri's concession could not change the course of events which were then proceeding in Nahhas' direction and when Nahhas' plans began to proceed smoothly, Nuri had no chance to stop them and to regain the lead.

2

The Ever-Present Panacea — Arab Federation as a Solution to the Palestine Question

The idea that the intractable Palestine problem could be solved by one form or another of Arab federation of which Palestine constituted a component accompanied the stormy development of the problem throughout the period of mandate. Protagonists of such a solution came from all the parties involved in the Palestine conflict — Jews, British and even a few Arabs — and they had in common two basic assumptions: that the inclusion of Palestine in a broader Arab framework would alleviate, in part at least, some of the fears that the Palestine Arabs felt as a result of the growth of the Jewish settlement in Palestine, and that a political fulfilment of the unity goal of Arab nationalism would counterbalance the partial loss of Arab national rights in Palestine. The scope of such a federation differed from one scheme to another, nor was its constitutional structure made clear, but these basic assumptions were usually there.

Jewish proposals

In the summer of 1933 at the eighteenth Zionist Congress a significant change took place in the balance of power within the Zionist movement. Labour became the biggest single party and, with three representatives in the Zionist Executive, including David Ben-Gurion and Moshe Shertok (later Sharett), the leading force. Ben-Gurion stressed the historical role of the labour movement to lay the foundation of Jewish independence and to implement Zionism by doubling within four to five years the Jewish *Yishuv* in Palestine.[1] On the other hand Ben-Gurion and other Jewish leaders were not blind to what was then developing among the Palestine Arabs. They noted the process of radicalisation, the dissolution of the Arab Executive and the first calls to resort to violent means in order to stop the advancement of the Jewish *Yishuv*.[2]

Ben-Gurion was especially impressed by the October 1933 demonstrations of the Palestine Arabs. He wrote to the members of the Zionist Executive in London:

The Arab activity has this time been carried out with diligence and discipline. It is skilfully led, undeterred by fatal casualties and might leave an enormous impression on world public opinion. [The Arabs] systematically do not attack Jews and fight only the Government. However, this attack, which uses new and fierce weapons, is of course directed against the Mandate and Zionism ... The Arab movement has in the last incident been revealed in a new light. It is no more an incited and instigated mob, aiming at looting, believing that 'the Government is behind him' and attacking the Jews in the belief that they are easy prey, but an organised and disciplined public, who present their national will through political maturity and capability of self-evaluation.[3]

The British authorities were then contemplating the establishment of a Legislative Council in Palestine as a means of resolving some of the Arabs' grievances.[4] Ben-Gurion's Labour Party supported its establishment if it were to be formed, as far as the question of national representation was concerned, on the parity principle. Ben-Gurion realised that this was not a realistic position. He was apprehensive that the government might establish a Legislative Council with an Arab majority and some moderate or non-Zionist forces within the Jewish community (the Farmers' Federation, Agudath Israel and part of the Sephardi community) would take part in it.[5] He therefore reached the conclusion that he should try to negotiate a comprehensive settlement directly with the Arabs.[6]

Ben-Gurion had four basic assumptions in mind:

1 It would be worthwhile to negotiate only with competent representatives of the Arab movement, thus ruling out any possibility of talks with 'sold-out' people.
2 The full truth of Jewish historical aims should be presented to the Arabs.
3 The Agreement should be based on full recognition of the aims of both peoples – 'great Zionism' on the one hand and the unity of the Arab people on the other. That is to say that once Palestine became a country with a Jewish majority, it would join an Arab Federation, without severing its connections with the British Empire.
4 A temporary and a permanent solution to the constitutional-political question of Palestine must be found.[7]

When Ben-Gurion tried to put this idea of negotiations into practice in the summer of 1934 the first question was whom to approach. The AE by that time had become almost completely moribund,[8] and a substitute had to be found. Ben-Gurion chose three Palestinian, one Lebanese and two Syrian leaders. They were: the highly respected Musa al-'Alami, who in 1933 had been nominated as Government Advocate and through family connections was close to Arab nationalist leadership in both Palestine and Syria (Musa al-'Alami was the son-in-law of Ihsan al-Jabiri, the Syrian leader and the brother-in-law of Jamal al-Husayni, the prominent Palestine leader); 'Awni 'Abd al-Hadi, the leader of the *Istiqlal* Party; George Antonius, who up to 1931 had served as a high-ranking official of the Department of Education and as Assistant Chief Secretary; Ri'ad al-Sulh, the prominent leader of the Sunni Muslim community of Lebanon; the Lebanese Druze Shakib Arslan and the Syrian Ihsan al-Jabiri, the last two being prominent anti-French leaders of the Syrian national movement and well known for their pan-Arab tendencies and activities. Sometimes accompanied by Moshe Shertok, Ben-Gurion met these people between summer 1934 and spring 1936. His proposals to his Arab interlocutors can be summarised as follows. There should be free Jewish immigration into Palestine, including Trans-Jordan, and once a Jewish majority had been achieved, this country would become an independent Jewish state. In return for Arab consent to this process, the Jews would support the formation of an Arab federation in the neighbouring countries and the independent Jewish state would be associated with the federation. Thus the Palestine Arabs, although becoming a minority in Palestine, would be connected with millions of Arabs outside it. Such a formation would not only safeguard the Palestine Arabs from any subjugation but would also fulfil their national aspiration for unity. For Ben-Gurion accepted the basic tenet of Arab nationalism that the Arabs of the Fertile Crescent and the Arabian Peninsula constituted one people and took Arab nationalist aspiration for unity seriously. Ben-Gurion added that until a Jewish majority had been achieved and the Arab federation been formed the mandate should continue to exist and the Palestine Jews and Arabs should participate on an equal basis in the government (and not in a Legislative Council, a proposition in the usefulness of which Ben-Gurion did not believe).[9]

According to Ben-Gurion, Musa al-'Alami's reaction was not an outright rejection of his ideas,[10] although he was sceptical over the association of the independent Jewish state with the Arab federation. He did not agree to British or League of Nations guarantees and without sufficient guarantee Jewish immigration to Palestine could not be countenanced. He suggested a reversal of order: first of all a federation had to be formed, then the Jews would enjoy the right of free immigration not only to Palestine but also to other parts of the federation.[11] Musa al-'Alami also expressed some misgivings over the question of Jewish immigration during the next ten years and proposed that it would be restricted so that at the end of this period the number of Jews in Palestine would not exceed one million. But on the whole his attitude was inclined to be positive and he expressed his belief that within a general

Arab framework a solution might be found. In order to reach it Amin al-Husayni, the Mufti of Jerusalem, and Arab national leaders outside Palestine should be approached and talked to. At one talk Musa al-'Alami was even able to tell Ben-Gurion that he had spoken with the Mufti and that even this arch-enemy of Zionism had not rejected Ben-Gurion's ideas out of hand but rather asked for a public declaration that could influence Arab public opinion and create a different atmosphere. Musa al-'Alami advised Ben-Gurion to meet with Ihsan al-Jabiri and Sahkib Arslam and promised to report to them the content of his [al-'Alami's] talk with the Mufti.[12]

Years later Sir Geoffrey Furlonge, Musa al-'Alami's biographer, admitted that 'they [B.G. and M. 'A] parted on superficially friendly terms, and Musa had been favourably impressed by Ben-Gurion's forthrightness. Nevertheless the conversation marked the final stage in his education on the nature and aims of Zionism ... He [M. 'A] had heard these leaders [B.G. and Shertok], who were not reckoned extremists, making crystal clear that they were aiming at nothing less than the complete control of the country'.[13] This rather reserved description should not be dismissed as wisdom from hindsight. Already in autumn 1934 Musa al-'Alami told a Jewish acquaintance: 'I don't think B.G. [in his talks with Musa al-'Alami] went any length at all or that he gave anything away'. Musa became so pessimistic about the possibility of reaching an Arab-Jewish understanding that he decided to wash his hands of politics and let things drift. The Jewish interlocutor of Musa al-'Alami, who knew Ben-Gurion's rather optimistic impressions of his talks with Musa al-'Alami, attributed the *volte-face* in Musa al-'Alami's attitude to the talks Musa al-'Alami had conducted with Arab leaders.[14]

'Awni 'Abd al-Hadi, who was first and foremost a pan-Arab nationalist, was enthusiastic about Ben-Gurion's proposal and agreed to unlimited Jewish immigration provided the Arabs had reached unity. However, on second thoughts he adopted a sceptical attitude and asked: 'Who would guarantee us? In the meantime you would be four millions in the country, whereas we would remain with the English and the French and with your promise. Do you think that we can rely upon your promises and declarations?'[15]

Riad al-Sulh, another pan-Arab activist, who in the past had shown rather a moderate attitude towards Zionism, accepted Ben-Gurion's proposals as a basis for negotiations.[16] But unlike him, Ihsan al-Jabiri and Shakib Arslan reacted unfavourably. Shakib Arslam dismissed the idea of Jewish support to the achievement of Arab unity because the very idea of unity was either only a dream or alternatively it was so solid that its implementation was assured anyway. In both cases the Arabs did not see why they should agree to Jewish immigration into Palestine. And in order to strengthen, so it seems, their negative attitude, in November

1934 Arslam and Jabiri published in their Geneva-based magazine *La Nation Arabe* their version of the talk with Ben-Gurion, although they had initially demanded that the meeting remain secret.[17]

Whatever was said in the talks no agreement was reached. It seems that in autumn 1934 Ben-Gurion was dissuaded from continuing these attempts by the public rebuff he got and this seems to be the reason for the interval of a year and a half before the resumption of the attempt with George Antonius in April 1936. Antonius agreed with Ben-Gurion's basic assumption that Arab-Jewish understanding could not be found within Palestine which was too small a country. But, unlike Ben-Gurion, surprisingly enough, Antonius expressed very sceptical views regarding a broad Arab unity and stressed that only Greater Syria from the Taurus Mountains to the Sinai Desert should be considered as the proper area. This land constituted one unit and should be reunited. Within Greater Syria Antonius agreed that a small part of Palestine could be established as a Jewish federated and autonomous province, but Jewish immigration must be limited even there. Ben-Gurion could not accept such limitations of the Zionist goals and therefore nothing ensued.[18]

However, Ben-Gurion was not deterred. On 19 May 1936, during a discussion of the Arab problem by the Zionist Executive he shared his views with his colleagues. For the first time he clearly stated before the highest authority of the Zionist movement what he regarded as a solution of the Palestine problem: a Jewish state associated with an Arab federation. And since this federation must be under tutelage of the British Empire, the Arab states which had already been placed within the British sphere were the first candidates for the association.[19] In addition Ben-Gurion twice brought the same message before the central committee of his Labour Party, stressing that only through Arab federation might the Arabs' fear of becoming a minority be relieved.[20] Although these views were not officially endorsed by the Zionist Executive or by his party, the ZE Political Department regarded them as guidelines and acted accordingly. But this time the addresses were different. It seems that the heads of the Jewish Agency in Jerusalem realised that the chances of reaching an agreement with leaders of the Palestine Arabs which would trade Palestinian Arab consent to free Jewish immigration to Palestine for a Jewish agreement to the inclusion of a future Jewish Palestine within an Arab federation were very slim indeed. Therefore they tried to circumvent them by an approach over their heads to the main Syrian political forces: the National Bloc on the one hand, and the opposition leader, Dr 'Abd al-Rahman Shahbandar on the other. During the spring and summer of 1936 Syrian representatives were engaged in talks with the French Government about the question of terminating the French mandate over Syria, and the heads of the Jewish Agency may have assumed that at such an hour the Syrians would behave in a statesmanlike way in order to prove their political maturity and win the support of the Jews for their country's independence.

From the end of May 1936 until September of that year Dr Bernard Joseph [Dov Yossef of later days] and Nahum Vilensky had been holding a series of talks in Cairo with Dr Shahbandar and some of his associates, including Amin Sa'id, a Syrian journalist on the *al-Muqataam* newspaper.[21] Joseph told Shahbandar that the Jews 'were even willing, on certain terms, to have Palestine form part of an Arab confederation', the terms being, as always, unrestricted Jewish immigration and land purchases in Palestine. Joseph clearly expressed the basic assumption of Ben-Gurion and other Jewish leaders, that the Jews of Palestine were part of a larger body — the Jews of the world — all of whom had the same right to come to Palestine and that the Arabs of Palestine, too, were only part of a larger Arab group together with which they would always be a majority over the Jews no matter how many Jews came into Palestine. Shahbandar, so Joseph noticed, regarded Joseph's attitude as reasonable but the stumbling blocks of immigration and the eventuality of the Jews becoming a majority in Palestine could not be surmounted.[22]

However, such contacts and talks with Shahbandar and his followers were resumed a year later at the end of 1937.[23] Shahbandar strongly opposed the National Bloc government in Syria on the question of the Franco-Syrian treaty and may have hoped to enhance his position by bringing about a rapprochement with the Jews. And indeed the talks between Shahbandar and his followers on the one hand and representatives of the Jewish Agency, on the other, were carried on intermittently up to Shahbandar's murder in 1940. By this stage Shahbandar and his followers were more forthcoming. They realised that the Jews could not be expected to agree to remain in a permanent minority position in a Palestine which had joined an Arab federation and were ready to defer this question to a future discussion after a transitional period of five years had elapsed.[24]

Concurrently another attempt, perhaps more serious, was carried out with the representatives with the Syrian ruling National Bloc. In June 1946 the Political Department of the Jewish Agency decided to use the opportune moment brought about by the change of government in France for such an attempt. Léon Blum's new Popular Front government decided to resume negotiations with the National Bloc over granting independence to Syria. The chief Syrian interlocutor Jamil Mardam realised the importance of having Zionist support for the Syrian national cause. He was aware of Léon Blum's pro-Zionist activities, including the latter's participation in 1929 in the formation of the enlarged Jewish Agency and, no less important, he (Mardam) shared the belief (or so at least JA officials thought) that the Palestine problem could be solved within a general Jewish-Arab agreement.[25] Taking part in the talks which began in July 1936 were the supreme leaders of the National Bloc including Shukri al-Quwatli, Lufti al-Haffar, etc. and Jewish Agency officials headed by Eliyahn (later Elath) Epstein. These were, in summary, the Jewish proposals:

1. Immigration according to economic capacity of absorption without injuring the Arabs;
2. Land purchases without depriving those who earn their livelihood from agriculture;
3. A non-overpowering regime, which might take the form of equality in parliament and administration;
4. Jewish positive attitude to Arab federation provided that Jewish interests were safeguarded;
5. Jewish positive attitude to Syrian independence provided that Lebanese independence and minorities rights were safeguarded;
6. British support of the negotiations and agreement.[26]

The Jewish negotiators made it clear that they regarded Syria as the oracle of the modern Arab National Movement and therefore the Syrian Nationalists were considered more competent to deal with the Palestine question than any other part of the Arab National Movement. They added: 'If the political and national aspirations of the Arabs lead ultimately to an Arab Federation we do not object to it in principle, provided it is based on harmony and understanding among the parties concerned'.

The Syrian negotiators heartily agreed with the description of their role in the Arab National Movement and stressed their historical mission in furthering Arab unity. They expressed their readiness to be instrumental in solving the Arab-Jewish conflict within a general Arab-Jewish agreement, but, as usual, when it came to discussing the details of the solutions to the thorny question of Jewish immigration into Palestine and land purchases nothing could bridge the gap.[27] According to Elath, Amin al-Husayni learned about the talks and exerted pressure on the Syrians to be adamant. And since Shukri al-Quwatli and his friends knew only too well that without the Mufti's consent no useful purpose could be served by continuing the talks with the Jews, even if some useful advantages to the general Arab cause and in particular to the Syrian one could be gained, they washed their hands of the talks.[28]

In spring 1937 Shertok tried again to convince Palestine Arab leaders of the usefulness of the Jewish basic approach. Both Jews and Arabs were expecting the report of the Royal (Peel) Commission and rumours that the Commission had recommended partition were widespread. The Arabs were very strongly opposed to it and the Jews not very enthusiastic either. Shertok told 'Abd al-Hadi in April 1937 that there was only one way to prevent partition and that was the agreement with the Jews based

THE EVER-PRESENT PANACEA – ARAB FEDERATION 65

on the often repeated Jewish proposals. But 'Awni was not won over. His reaction was very typical.

> You are not in a position to grant me Arab Federation and I am now not in a position to bring it about. It lies somewhere in the future and in the meanwhile I must take care of this country. And if some day such a Federation is formed, we shall be interested to attach to it Palestine as an Arab country. What interest shall we have in a Jewish Palestine attached to an Arab Federation?[29]

The last time that Ben-Gurion (explicitly) and Shertok (implicitly) made that proposition to Arab representatives was in the winter of 1939, towards the end of the Palestine St James's Conference held in London. On 7 March 1939 Malcolm MacDonald, the Colonial Secretary, arranged an unofficial meeting between the British, Jewish and Arab States (excluding the Palestinian Arab) delegates as a last-minute attempt to find an outlet from the apparent deadlock. During the talk Ben-Gurion reiterated his often repeated arguments, that if a Jewish Palestine became part of a larger body encompassing the neighbouring countries, the Palestine Arabs would not regard themselves a defenceless minority. Ben-Gurion got the impression 'that there was a "movement" between the three Arabs [the interlocutors], and Tawfiq al-Suwaydi [the Iraqi delegate] distinctly got excited'.[30] However, we have at our disposal al-Suwaydi's description of that meeting and proposal and he makes it crystal-clear that he was moved by the sophisticated presentation of the demand for a Jewish state in an enticing packing![31] Be that as it may, the main obstacle was the question of Jewish immigration over which no agreement could be reached between the Jews who insisted upon its full continuation and the Arabs who demanded its stoppage or, at least, its drastic limitation.[32]

Certainly one has already observed that all these talks and contacts by the Zionist leaders with the Arab nationalist leaders with a view to finding a solution to the Palestine question by means of an Arab federation which would include a Jewish Palestine, or with the Hashemites in connection with their Greater Syria or Fertile Crescent schemes of Arab unity, took place without serious discussions and official resolutions by the Central Zionist authorities. This situation could not continue for ever. In the late 1930s and early 1940s the question was regarded as too serious to be allowed to be dealt with in an improvised way. The Arab voices demanding the implementation of Arab unity became louder and louder.

The 1939 St James's Conference on Palestine in which delegates of the independent Arab states were invited by Britain to take part was regarded as a turning point in the British attitude to that question. The Philby plan (see pp. 80–105 of this chapter) had persisted for several years and absorbed a great deal of the energy of Dr Chaim Weizmann, the President of the World Zionist Organisation and of the Jewish Agency. Then in 1940 the Zionist Executive in London was faced with another initiative, this time of Professor H. A. R. Gibb (see below, pp. 79–80) who was then working in a semi-official capacity as the director of the Middle East section of the Royal Institute of International Affairs, whose staff were mobilised for the war effort as analysts and propagandists. Gibb's proposal that the British Government should declare that Syria, Iraq and Palestine should be federated including a Jewish unit was not rejected out of hand by the Jewish interlocutor, Professor S. Brodetsky of the London Zionist Executive, but he gave the non-committal reply 'that a great deal depended upon what was meant by a Jewish unit – its size, competence etc'. When this was reported to the London Zionist Executive it did not bring about a comprehensive discussion of the question, but only a trivial comment by B. Locker, the Labour representative, that it might be that someone else encouraged Gibb to call upon Brodetsky and the latter was satisfied with his reaction that the unknown might be the Foreign Office.[33] Such an evasive position could not be maintained for long.

In those days the point of gravity in the Zionist movement had already passed from London to Jerusalem, and in the Jerusalem Zionist Executive we have to look for an answer to the question of what the Zionist leadership really thought about Arab Federation as a solution to the Palestine problem. In the early and mid-1930s when the Zionist leaders enquired whether that approach was feasible it was clear that the animating spirit in that endeavour was David Ben-Gurion, the chairman of the Zionist Executive in Jerusalem since 1935. He began his attempt in 1933 upon his election as a member of the Executive and intensified it in 1935 when he was elected chairman. Moshe Shertok, the head of the Political Department, on the other hand, was more reserved and sceptical. Being very well acquainted with Arab affairs and the Arabic language he had strong doubts whether any kind of Arab unity was possible in the foreseeable future. In December 1940 when, in the face of the Arab bargaining strength *vis-à-vis* isolated Britain, the Arab federation was looked upon as certain to materialise after the war, Shertok expressed his agony: 'Whatever our attitude to the Federation idea may be, it is evident that the greater the Arab majority, the greater the instinct of oppression. The Arab Federation entails on us terrible danger which only a child can ignore'.[34]

Ben-Gurion reached other conclusions. He thought that the war years should be used to strengthen the Zionist movement, to mobilise American Jewry, to get maximum support from the USA which would become the crucial factor in the post-war settlement and redefine Zionist goals in the light of the gathering storm which was sweeping the Jewish people.

He envisaged a mass Jewish immigration into Palestine which would become a Jewish state. These goals and the political means to attain them were presented by him to his colleagues in the Jerusalem Zionist Executive in a document named 'Basic Lines of Zionist Policy', in March 1941. Even this radical document which marked the adoption of 'fighting Zionism' revealed that Ben-Gurion was still loyal to his belief in the possibility of using the Arab federation concept for solving the Palestine problem. Article 3 said: 'If a federation or an alliance of the Near East states is established, and the Arab peoples agree to the formation of a Hebrew Palestine as a member of that federation Jewish Palestine will join this federation as an independent state as far as all the internal matters (immigration, settlement on the land, labour laws, security, etc.) are concerned, similar to a Dominion within the British Commonwealth'.[35] Some months later Ben-Gurion left for Britain to work for Zionist goals there, then he went on to the USA.

His colleagues in Jerusalem were left with Ben-Gurion's message which influenced their course of deliberations and thought. They had to discuss its items in light of current political developments in which the possibility of the formation of Arab federation looked rather serious. On 27 July 1941 Shertok reported to his colleagues in the Zionist Executive on his talks in Cairo with Oliver Lyttelton, the British Minister of State, with regard to Anthony Eden's famous speech of 29 May 1941. Shertok made it clear to him that the last thing the Jews wanted was for Palestine to be included within the area where Britain would support any move agreed upon by the Arabs towards unity, including political unity.[36]

A few months later Shertok became less alarmed. Through a penetrating analysis of the Eden declaration and in light of British recognition of the French position in Syria (see p. 33), he reached the conclusion that Arab federation was not on the agenda and that Britain was not going to form it. For him it was a big relief. However, being a skilled politician he distinguished between his real position and what had to be told to other actors in the political struggle. Therefore Shertok stressed that in talks with the Arabs a positive attitude to the Federation should be expressed.[37]

With the same approach he talked to British politicians. When he learned from Lyttelton in December 1941 that the British were only thinking of a sort of economic union, he did not see any real impediment to telling him that if an Arab federation were established, the Jews would not oppose an independent Jewish division joining it.[38] Later on even this reserved approach evaporated. In September 1942 Shertok had a meeting with Wendell Wilkie, the special envoy of the US President. When asked about Arab Federation Shertok replied that he saw the relations among the Arab countries in a different way; 'possibly a certain association but not necessarily a federative relationship'. Anyway, in the formative stage of that federation the Jews would not be willing to hand over ruling powers to the federation because they would want to look after their main interest: immigration and settlement on the land. Only after Palestine became Jewish would the country be more free in its relations with the Arab neighbours, who themselves were not yet prepared for unity within one state.[39]

This pessimistic, or rather realistic, evaluation of the chances of Arab unity were based on Shertok's low view of one of the main protagonists of that idea — Amin 'Abdallah.[40] On the other hand, Ibn Saud and the Egyptians whom he esteemed much more highly, did not want, according to Shertok's penetrating analysis, to work for the idea.[41] No doubt the only occasion during the war years in which Shertok was ready to negotiate with Arabs the possibility of supporting the formation of an Arab federation was in July 1941 when he still thought that the Eden declaration meant a serious shift in British policy. No less significant was the identity of the Arab interlocutor. When the same month Shertok visited Cairo he met Nuri al-Sa'id who was then serving as the Iraqi Ambassador to Cairo. It seems that Shertok had a high regard for Nuri al-Sa'id's personality and steadfastness in pursuit of his pan-Arab goal. He told Nuri that the war could lay the foundations of Arab unity, much as the last war had laid the foundations of Arab independence. 'But the Arabs on their own are not capable of attaining it; you can achieve very important aid, you can attain the Jewish world as an ally.... If you agree that Palestine will become Jewish the whole of America will stand by you'. Nuri al-Sa'id dismissed this idea out of hand and added that even the most moderate Arab personality would not agree.[42]

Shertok was Ben-Gurion's political partner and head of the Political Department and even he did not hide for long his differing news on the question of Arab Federation. Dr Joseph was less cautious in expressing his disagreement. Other Zionist Executive members from other parties, the right wing and religious ones, expressed their dissenting views more easily. On 17 August 1941 when the question was thoroughly dealt with, Mr Ussishkin, the nationalist head of the Jewish National Fund, expressed the view that only 'a strong Jewish State should join the Arab Federation and not a weak body standing on one foot'. By a strong state he meant one which 'included within its boundaries *at least* [my italics] Trans-Jordan' with a clear Jewish majority. I. Gruenbaum, the radical leader of the General Zionists' Party, added economic reasons to the case against joining any Arab Federation. He even substituted for that concept a diametrically opposed one: federation not with the Arabs but with other minorities in the Middle East, like the Druze, the Kurds, the Circassians and the Alawites. Rabbi J.L. Fishman (later Maymon), leader of the Mizrahi (Zionist religious) Party, did not hesitate not only to reject the very idea but also to criticise Ben-Gurion openly for his attitude.[43]

Ben-Gurion remained isolated enjoying only the cautious support of Shertok and the embarrassingly wholehearted support of W. Senator, a very moderate Zionist who had been elected to represent non-Zionist components in the Executive of the Jewish Agency.

During 1942 even Ben-Gurion's position changed. He succeeded in that year in passing the famous Biltmore resolution defining the Zionist goal 'that Palestine be established as a Jewish commonwealth integrated in the structure of the new democratic world'. In November the Biltmore resolution was endorsed by the Smaller Executive Committee of the Zionist Organisation. Ben-Gurion's concepts, his 'Basic Lines of Zionist Policy', were made into the official Zionist programme.[44] What was missing was his readiness to see Jewish Palestine joining an Arab federation. This concept fell victim to the change of mood among the Jews when news of the wholesale murder of Jewish people in German-occupied Europe began to penetrate through the German wall of secrecy and deceit.

The belief in the capacity of the Arab Federation approach to bring about a solution of the Palestine problem was not confined to the heads of the Jewish Agency. Some other Jewish personalities engaged in the promotion of Jewish-Arab agreement shared this attitude and from time to time took it up in their political activities.

In December 1937 H. M. Kalvarisky, the indefatigable searcher for Arab-Jewish understanding, held talks with Khalusi al-Khayri and other young Arab intellectuals. Khalusi al-Khayri accepted large-scale Jewish immigration if Palestine became independent and united with Britain by means of a treaty instead of a mandate, was admitted to the League of Nations and joined an Arab Federation. He repeated his views also to Dr Bernard Joseph of the Political Department of the Jewish Agency, but made it clear that Jewish immigration, which might exceed three million, had to be directed to the whole area of the Arab confederation and not to be grouped in one place. He stressed that they were Arabs and not Palestinians and had a share in Iraq no less than any Arab who happened to live there.[45] Dr J. L. Magnes, another persistent activist for Arab-Jewish understanding, thought in terms of having bi-national Palestine included in the Arab Federation and took every opportunity, including Press articles and brochures, of putting forward his ideas.[46]

Arab initiatives

Arab initiatives in the same direction based on the same belief were naturally not too numerous, since they accepted the basic Zionist demand of large-scale Jewish immigration to Palestine. Palestinian Arab leaders usually maintained a reserved attitude towards this question and only in response to other people's proposals did they express some positive reaction. One such rare occasion took place in Geneva in May 1939 when the two important Palestinian leaders Jamal al-Husayni and Musa al-'Alami met R.A. Butler, the British Foreign Under-Secretary. In a reply to Mr Butler's query they said that only within an Arab Federation between Palestine and the neighbouring Arab countries 'some sort of real safeguards could be afforded to as many as half a million Jews in Palestine'. Since the number of Jews living then in Palestine did not actually exceed 450,000 their statement could be understood to admit the recognition of a continued, although very small, Jewish immigration to Palestine as a *quid pro quo* for the formation of an Arab Federation.[47]

However, such positions were very rarely expressed by Palestine Arab leaders. Much more frequently they were typical of non-Palestinian Arab leaders who were engaged in attempts to promote the ideas of Arab unity, dynastic or state interests or to solve the thorny question of Palestine. We have already noticed (see ch. 1) how importantly this attitude figured in King Faysal's, Nuri al-Sa'id's and Amir (later King) 'Abdallah's schemes. Also Hikmat Sulayman, Iraqi Prime Minister under Bakr Sidqi's putschist regime and a sworn rival of Nuri al-Sa'id's, took the same line and carried it even further. In a talk with C.J. Edmonds, the British principal adviser to the Iraqi Government, held on 8 February 1937, Hikmat Sulayman expressed his view that the way to allow Jewish immigration to continue into Palestine and yet not make the Arabs a minority was to form a rather loose federation of Iraq, Trans-Jordan and Palestine under the Iraqi Hashemite crown. 'This would conjure the minority bogey and the Arabs would no longer worry if a million Jews came in.' The Baghdad-Haifa railway would follow as a natural corollary, and Great Britain could be given all the guarantees her vital political interests required. The reaction of the British Foreign Office this time was emphatic: they rejected H. Sulayman's idea altogether, regarding it as impracticable and even imaginary. It should be stressed that Hikmat Sulayman's view was not a private or incidental one; it was part of the Iraqi Government's attempt to present an acceptable solution to the Palestine question before the British Government when the Peel Commission were preparing their report and recommendations, and Dr Naji al-Asil, the Iraqi Foreign Minister, repeated the same view several days after Sulayman had expressed it.[48]

Another Arab personality who in 1937–8 was actively engaged in the same direction was the Egyptian Prince Muhammad 'Ali, the uncle of King Faruq. Serving during the King's minority (summer 1936 to July 1937) as the President of the Regency Council, he became upon Faruq's coronation free to cherish his special approach to the Palestine problem. During the spring of 1937 the possibility that the Palestine Royal (Peel) Commission would recommend the partition of Palestine was frequently repeated in rumours. Against this background Prince Muhammad 'Ali put forward a proposal to break the Palestine deadlock by the formation of a Greater Syria federation, including Palestine and Trans-Jordan. This federation would consist of cantons or states on the model of Switzerland or the USA, each of which would be governed by its own people, Druzes by Druzes, Alawites by Alawites and so on. The Jewish zone would be confined to the coastal plain and be put under British protection. Britain was to remain in Jerusalem and Haifa as France in Beirut and Tripoli. Prince Muhammad 'Ali assumed that the establishment of a large Muslim Arab zone within his federated 'Empire' would satisfy the Arabs. Another wishful assumption of his was his belief that Britain and France could reach agreement over his scheme.[49] These ideas were leaked to the Egyptian newspaper *al-Muqattam*, which was favourably disposed to Arab nationalism and got a cordial reception there. This newspaper even reported that this scheme aroused the interest of many Syrians and Palestinians who sent the Prince letters of congratulation and offered him the Throne of the Federation, although, the newspaper argued, Muhammad 'Ali himself had suggested that Amir 'Abdallah of Trans-Jordan would sit on this throne.[50] British reaction was negative (see pp. 203–5).[51]

Muhammad 'Ali did not despair. He tried to get the support of the Jews for his plan. Through the good services of Maître Alexander, a well-known Egyptian Jewish leader and M. 'Ali's personal lawyer, he met Dr Chaim Weizmann, the President of the World Zionist Organisation. Weizmann's reaction was favourable in principle, although what he really had in mind was unlimited Jewish immigration to that part of Palestine which would be allotted to the Jews; then, having become a Jewish state, this part of Palestine would join an Arab confederation. Weizmann promised to carry the Prince's views to London and talk them over with the British Government.[52] In London Muhammad 'Ali's proposal crossed lines with a similar proposal by Lord Samuel (see below, p. 107).

A similar idea was put forward in June 1942 by Shafiq Haddad (an Iraqi subject of Egyptian stock, the son of Jibra'il Haddad who during the First World War had served the British authorities in Egypt as an intermediary between R. Storrs and the Hashemite family) on behalf of Amir Zayd, the youngest surviving son of the late King Husayn of Hijaz and brother of Amir 'Abdallah. He came to Jerusalem and suggested to Moshe Shertok the formation of a Federation or a Union between Syria and Palestine with Zayd on the throne. Trans-Jordan might come in after the passing of the Amir 'Abdallah. In return Amir Zayd 'would be most accommodating in regard to Jewish aspirations'. Shertok's reply was far from encouraging. He said he was not interested in the personal implication of the throne allocation, but in any solution which included a fair provision for the aspirations of the Jews. Anyway, it was useless to come to an agreement with an emissary unless he could commit or influence Arab opinion. Moreover, under Article 4 of the Palestine Mandate the Jewish Agency had a special relationship with Great Britain which could not be ignored. This rebuff was sufficient to stop any further approaches.[53]

Unofficial British démarches

Outside the Foreign Office some prominent British personalities had for years been cherishing the same attitude and the flare-up of the 1936 Arab rebellion in Palestine encouraged them to intensify their activities. Foremost among them was Sir Herbert (later Viscount) Samuel, the first British High Commissioner for Palestine, who for many years had been a staunch believer in the ability of an Arab federation to solve or at least to discharge the Jewish-Arab conflict over Palestine. Following a two-month visit in Palestine in February–March 1920 in which he was able to witness the intensification of the Arab anti-Zionist activities there,[54] Samuel concluded not only that there existed a strong desire to see a closer connection between Palestine and its Arab neighbours, mainly Syria, but also that such a development would help in solving the Jewish-Arab conflict. In a letter and a memorandum written at the beginning of April 1920 to Lord Curzon, the British Foreign Secretary, he suggested 'the formation of a Confederation of the Arab-speaking states, each of which should be under its own appropriate government, but all of which should be combined together for common and economic purposes. The seat of such a Confederation should be Damascus and Faisal [then ruling Syria] might be recognised, not only as sovereign in his own State, but also as the Honorary Head of the Confederation.' Palestine would be included in the proposed confederation but it would be administered by Great Britain under a mandate which would embody provisions relating to the Jewish national home. Besides Syria which would be placed under French mandate and Palestine, the confederation would include the independent Hijaz under the sovereignty of King Husayn and Iraq under British administration and, if desired, under an Arab sovereign. Curzon dismissed this scheme out of hand, since he realised how complicated its implementation would be from an international point of view (different mandatory powers in Syria and Palestine, the involvement of the League of Nations, etc).[55]

Samuel's proposition was not the casual expression of a momentary inspiration. On the contrary it was the beginning of a long-range conviction and action as it was based on the fundamental assumptions of pan-Arabism. Nearly three years later Samuel found, so he thought, another suitable moment to put forward a similar scheme. During the second half of 1922 the Palestine Arab nationalists were very actively engaged in an attempt to force the government to drop their Legislative

Council proposal by organising a boycott of the proposed elections to that body.[56] Samuel thought that his proposed confederation might induce a large part of the Palestine Arabs to give up their opposition to co-operation with the mandatory government and take part in the Legislative Council elections. In a letter of 12 December 1922 to the Duke of Devonshire, the Colonial Secretary, Samuel suggested the formation of an Arab confederation, the nucleus of which would be Hijaz, Palestine and Trans-Jordan. Talks should be held with the French *ab initio* in order to bring about the joining of Syria, their mandatory country, to the confederation, whereas Najd and other Arabian principalities would be able to join if they wished. The confederation would be headed by a President and a council. The President would be Husayn, King of Hijaz, acting, as a rule, through one of his sons as deputy. The council would be composed of representatives of the member governments and would meet alternately in Jedda, Baghdad, Jerusalem and Damascus in order to look after what he regarded as common interests of the confederation such as communications, customs, extradition, culture, education and religion. Other subjects might be added from time to time. 'More important, however, than any specific functions of the Council', Samuel stressed, 'would be the fact of its existence. This in itself would give satisfaction to Arab national aspirations. The confederation would be a visible embodiment of Arab unity, and a centre round which the movement for an Arab revival — which is a very real thing — could rally. It would give leadership and direction to that movement, especially on its cultural side'.

A fundamental part of Samuel's scheme was 'that policy in relation to the Jews in Palestine should stand' and the Palestine Arabs would co-operate with the local legislature and the confederated council. Samuel was satisfied that in these conditions the Zionist movement would welcome his scheme. As for the French, Samuel was much more sceptical, since they might regard the scheme as a British manoeuvre to form a strong Arab bloc under British control, with their part being secondary. Therefore he did not regard the participation of Syria in the confederation as an essential condition for its formation. Both Devonshire and Curzon dismissed the suggestion as unworkable and the latter went even further, dismissing the advantages and desirability of 'reliance on the Arabs'.[57]

However strong the dismissal may have been, it did not kill off the scheme within the orbit of the British Government. Another problem, this time stemming from difficulties in the relations between Britain and Hijaz, gave it another lease of life. During the winter of 1922–3 the negotiations over the conclusion of an Anglo-Hijazi treaty reached a deadlock because King Husayn of Hijaz dropped an article (no. 17) from a draft treaty which a year before had been agreed between T.E. Lawrence, representing the British Government, and Amir 'Abdallah on behalf of his father King Husayn. This article required King Husayn to recognise Britain's 'special status' in Palestine and Iraq and thus, implicitly at least, waive any claim that the British mandate in those countries contradicted any possible promises which had been made by Britain to Amir (as he was then) Husayn during the First World War.[58]

At this juncture H. Young of the Colonial Office prepared a detailed minute with a view to extricating the negotiations from the deadlock which they had reached. Young adopted Samuel's basic idea although in a milder way. Instead of a confederation he suggested recognising the Arabs' desire for an 'association' between Palestine and its Arab neighbours provided that this association did not hurt Zionism. Thus Husayn (and the Arabs in general) would get a *quid pro quo* for his recognition of Britain's 'special status' in Palestine and Iraq. Young's suggestion was endorsed by the Colonial Secretary and was afterwards included in the new drafts of the treaty, although Samuel stuck to his original idea.[59] In the spring of 1923 it looked as though an outlet was found and the draft treaty was initiated by Lord Curzon and Dr Naji al-Asil, Husayn's representative.

However, soon afterwards it became clear that not the question of Palestine and the possible association or confederation of the Arab countries were Husayn's main aims but two oases between Hijaz and Najd which had in 1919 been occupied by Saudi forces. Since Husayn demanded that Britain should recognise Hijaz's boundaries as they had existed before the First World War and since Britain did not want to jeopardise its relations with its ally 'Abd al-'Aziz Al Sa'ud of Najd, no treaty was reached between Britain and Husayn's Hijaz and the latter was left to its own resources to stand up to the growing Saudi threat. In 1926 Husayn finally abdicated and left Hijaz for exile and Samuel's initiative thus came to an abortive end.

Samuel tried once again at a different juncture in early September 1936, when the first stage of the Palestine Arab rebellion reached its peak. The British Cabinet discussed how to crush the rebellion and decided to send another division to Palestine and to proclaim martial law at an appropriate moment. This tough decision was made public on 7 September.[60] Samuel apparently thought that a showdown between the Army and the rebels had to be prevented to avoid further deterioration of the relations between the Arabs and the government. Therefore on 8 September he met Mr Ormsby-Gore, the Colonial Secretary, and presented a new version of his old scheme. The main points were to limit the growth of the Jewish population in Palestine up to a limit of 40 per cent of the whole, to exclude specified areas from Jewish land purchase or colonisation; to establish a Legislative Council, consisting of one third of Arab representatives and one third of Jewish representatives to be chosen, in the first instance, by communal bodies already existing or to be established for the purpose, and one third of official and unofficial members nominated by the government; and to promote a Customs Union between Iraq, Saudi Arabia, Yemen, Palestine, Trans-Jordan, Syria and Lebanon with freedom of trade within its area. A Supervising Council representing those states would be established with Arabic as its official language. This agreement would cover the period to the end of 1950.

Samuel shared his proposal with Earl Winterton, a friend of Nuri al-Sa'id and a pro-Arab protagonist in the House of Commons, who had thought of sounding his friend.[61] Dr Chaim Weizmann and P. Rutenberg, President of the Jewish National Council in Palestine, suggested that Samuel's proposal be discussed with Nuri al-Sa'id.[62] The Colonial Office took Samuel's proposal quite seriously and brought it before the Cabinet. But the Colonial Secretary and his aides did not see the usefulness of Samuel's meeting Nuri al-Sa'id which could 'give the Arab leaders an impression that they could sidetrack the Royal Commission or buy off effective military action during talk'.[63] Sir John Maffey, the Colonial Permanent Under-Secretary, repeated this and other arguments in a talk with Samuel and convinced him that, since the meeting with Nuri could not be avoided the conversations with him should be very tentative and the proposal should not be formally presented.[64] Samuel was strongly advised to make clear to Nuri that he was acting on his own initiative and that the British Government were by no means a party to it.[65]

Sir Herbert Samuel and Earl Winterton met Nuri al-Sa'id on 19 September in Paris. They communicated their proposal to him in outline but Nuri did not consider that it would be acceptable to the Palestine Arabs. Nuri pointed out to Samuel that most of his (Samuel's) proposals implied continued Jewish immigration, though on a limited scale, while the remainder facilitated immigration in the interests of the Jews. Not a single point was for the advantage of the Arabs. As to the proposed Customs Union of the Arab countries, that, said Nuri, was already under negotiation among them; but the inclusion of Palestine was not at present contemplated, because here again the chief beneficiaries would be the Jewish industrialists in Palestine, who would be given a large and valuable protected market for the products of their 'enormous factories'. Nuri's alternatives were either 'to suspend immigration in the existing circumstances and not to think of continuing even limited immigration' or 'to unite Palestine, Transjordan and Iraq in one State in a suitable political form to be agreed to by the British Government. The Arabs would then be able to agree to immigration, subject to limitation as to number and zone. Only in such union can the Arabs find assurance that Palestine will preserve its Arab character and be satisfied that there is no fear of a Jewish State being set up in it'.[66] This response stopped Herbert Samuel from proceeding with his scheme for a while. Although the response was quite similar to Samuel's own original thinking on the subject, he may now have thought that for such a far-reaching solution he could not muster a Jewish or a British favourable reaction.

Samuel renewed his activities in that direction towards the publication of the Royal (Peel) Commission Report and recommendations. On 15 June 1937, several weeks before publication he sent a long memorandum to the Colonial Secretary in which he argued at length against the idea of partition of Palestine, the core of the Royal Commission's recommendations.[67] Upon the publication of the Peel Report and during a debate in the House of Lords (to which he was a newcomer having recently been ennobled), he made his proposal publicly known for the first time. This time he realised that a mere Customs Union would not be regarded by the Arabs as a sufficient concession for the continuation of a limited Jewish immigration up to a ceiling of 40 per cent of the whole population for an interim period of ten years. Therefore he resorted to his original idea of forming a Great Arab Confederation which would include Saudi Arabia, Iraq, Trans-Jordan, Syria and Palestine to be established eventually with the assent of France and the full co-operation of the Zionist Organisation.[68]

This time Samuel's proposal got a fierce Zionist reaction and a much more moderate one from the Arab side. Although after Samuel's initiative in September 1936, Dr Chaim Weizmann and Dr Z. Brodtsky of the Jewish Agency Executive in London had reacted to his proposals 'in a very reasonable spirit' and even told Samuel that the Executive in Palestine 'had been favourably disposed towards an approach to the problem being made in this manner',[69] the reaction of David Ben-Gurion, chairman of the Executive in Palestine, was totally negative, and in a circular to Zionist organisations outside Palestine he instructed them 'to protest vigorously against Samuel's treacherous conduct'.[70] On the other hand, Amin al-Husayni, President of the Palestine Higher Arab Committee, reacted in a very unusual moderate way. In a press interview, although he refused to comment on the specific issues raised by Samuel, he praised him for his liberal thinking and foresight. 'Such a position on behalf of the Jews', he ended his comment, 'had it been taken, would have been regarded as an advance that could help in solving the Palestine question.'[71]

It seems that the partition recommendation of the Peel Commission and its adoption in principle by the British Government brought about such strong opposition from Amin al-Husayni and his followers that they were ready to consider alternatives. A sovereign Jewish state comprising 15 per cent of Palestine was considered by them much more harmful than the continuation of Jewish immigration, although greatly restricted. However, the Colonial Office was then convinced that the Peel recommendations opened the way towards a fundamental and lasting solution. They did not want to consider any other alternative which had already been denounced by the Jews anyway.

THE EVER-PRESENT PANACEA – ARAB FEDERATION 77

A year later Samuel resumed his effort. By then he might well understand that opposition to the Partition plan within the British Government was growing and he could not but be impressed by the favourable reaction of Amin al-Husayni to his attitude. Therefore, so it is safe to assume, he tried to enlist the support and cooperation of some prominent Arab leaders. In March 1938 Samuel met the Egyptian Prince Muhammad 'Ali, who had himself been engaged in the same activities, and with the Palestinian leader 'Awni 'Abd al-Hadi. His proposals had been co-ordinated with the Magnes group in Palestine and the unofficial British Hyamson-Newcombe plan. Besides the basic formula of limiting the growth of the Jewish community in Palestine within the next ten years to a maximum proportion of 40 per cent of the whole ('The Forty-Ten Formula') and reserving specified areas in Palestine to Arabs, with prohibition of land purchases or settlement by Jews, once again the idea of 'encouragement of a Confederation of Arab States, in which Palestine would be a member' was put forward. Since Muhammad 'Ali was very enthusiastic about the idea of a union between Palestine, Trans-Jordan, Syria and Lebanon, he wholeheartedly supported Samuel's plan. 'Awni 'Abd al-Hadi, on the other hand, said that the Arabs would agree to it only if the 40 per cent formula became a permanent solution and not temporary.

A little later Samuel repeated his scheme before Muhammad Mahmud Pasha, the Liberal Constitutional Prime Minister of Egypt, who had no objection. He rather 'thought that some proposal on those lines should be sought. Probably the Arabs would not agree to the Jewish population being as much as 40 per cent, but they might agree to a 35 per cent, or something a little less'.[72] The Colonial Office were still convinced that 'Awni 'Abd al-Hadi was ready to reach agreement on those lines, but the Foreign Secretary, Lord Halifax, thought that Samuel's views merited serious consideration and expressed his wish that Samuel continue, although unofficially, to work for a direct agreement on those lines between Jews and Arabs.[73] As we shall see later on (see pp. 106 ff.) the British Government were then reaching the stage of reshaping their Palestine policy and Samuel's views were an important input in that process.

A similar activity was in 1937–8 being carried out by Lord Lloyd, a Cambridge-educated orientalist and former High Commissioner for Egypt, the then President of the Royal Central Asian Society and chairman of the British Council, and a future Colonial Secretary in Churchill's government (1940). He too was aroused by the possibility of Palestine being partitioned and tried during 1937 to get the cooperation of those Jews and Arabs who, like himself, opposed partition and were ready to find an alternative solution. In March and November 1938 he visited several Middle Eastern capitals including Jerusalem and held talks with

British Arab and Jewish personalities.[74] On 23 October 1938 he published an article in the *Sunday Chronicle* outlining an alternative solution to the partition plan. David Ben-Gurion who was then in London asked him to meet him and the meeting took place two days after the publication of the article.

Lord Lloyd was in the advantageous position of being trusted by the Arabs as their friend and by the Jews as a staunch opponent to the official appeasement policy over Czechoslovakia. In that meeting Lord Lloyd made it clear that his opposition to the partition of Palestine had become much less strong and went so far as to say that 'what I am proposing is in effect a partition, although I won't call it that'. The only way to enable the Jews to have their main demands – large-scale immigration and an eventual Jewish State – implemented was 'possible only if we bring the neighbouring Arab countries into the plan. A Jewish State can only exist with an Arab Federation'. Such a federation should comprise Palestine, Trans-Jordan and Syria. Ben-Gurion, who agreed in principle, preferred because of French and Turkish opposition, a federation comprising Palestine, Trans-Jordan and Iraq. Lloyd had some reservations since he realised that such a federation would benefit the Hashemites to the annoyance of the Saudi ruler. But on the whole he wanted to pursue such a line by bringing it to Dr Weizmann.[75]

Meanwhile in the autumn of 1938 the whole situation changed when the British Government upon receiving the Woodhead Commission Report rescinded its endorsement in principle of the partition solution and decided to convene a conference of Jews, Arabs (including the Arab countries) and British to discuss other solutions much more accommodating to the Arab point of view. Against such a background Lord Lloyd did not, so one is obliged to conclude, proceed, but about two years later when he was serving in Churchill's wartime government as Colonial Secretary he had to confront his very own ideas which were then presented to him as another link in the long chain of private initiatives.

In the meantime other people did not let this apparently attractive idea lie idle. In January 1939 A.W. Lawrence, brother of the late T.E. Lawrence, was acting on behalf of a group of British personalities who supported the Hashemites. He met Nuri al-Sa'id and Colonel Newcombe, the prominent pro-Arab lobbyist, and Ben-Gurion[76] in order to win their support for his scheme, which at the same time he brought before the Foreign and Colonial Offices. He proposed to terminate the Palestine and Trans-Jordan Mandate and to form Arab and Jewish autonomous provinces (according to the Peel Partition recommendation, with the Negev being allotted to the Jews) each of which would control immigration in its area. Palestine and Trans-Jordan would be united in an independent Federation which should at the end of the process include Syria reunited with the Lebanon.[77] But as in the past the British Government were still not convinced that such an approach was practicable.[78]

Wartime troubles did not lessen the attractiveness of this approach. On the contrary, they lent it new vigour. This time the initiative came from the eminent orientalist, the Laudian Professor of Arabic, H.A.R. Gibb of Oxford University who was an ardent supporter of Arab unity in one way or another. In July 1940 he privately met prominent Zionist leaders of moderate views, Professor S. Brodetsky and Leonard Stein, and discussed with them whether, in view of the gravity of the situation in the Middle East, there was any possibility of reaching a working agreement which might serve as a basis for an ultimate settlement of the Arab-Jewish problem. They reached the conclusion that 'the general lines of an agreement could be found in (a) the linking up of Palestine with other Arab states in a union or a Federation; (b) guarantees for Jewish autonomy with an area of reasonable size; and (c) Arab-Jewish military cooperation'. In view of Stein's and Brodetsky's insistence that the initiative must come from the British Government, Professor Gibb brought these ideas to the Colonial Secretary, who gave them a considerate hearing.[79]

As we shall see (below, pp. 89 and 115–17) Lloyd's attitude was rather similar to that of Gibb, but he could not overcome the objections of the Foreign Office. Gibb waited for another attempt. He then directly approached the Foreign Office and presented a comprehensive and thorough scheme for an Arab Federation of the Fertile Crescent. Although it was not focused on Palestine, it referred to it since Palestine would become one of the components of his proposed federation. Basically he envisaged the inclusion of the Jewish national home in Palestine as it then existed within the federation while ensuring another area somewhere in the world for settlement by European Jewish refugees. This solution should be backed by the Allied countries (the 'United Nations') and, if necessary, enforced by them on the quarrelling sides. Unfortunately this document reached the Foreign Office after they had made up their minds against any initiative in that field and so it did not matter very much.[80]

The feeling that Arab federation might lead to a solution of the intractable Palestine problem was not unusual. Influential personalities liked the idea. Kingsley Martin, the well-known editor of the *New Statesman*, thought in late 1940 that 'an Arab Confederation .... would be a good solution [of the Palestine question]',[81] whereas Lord Hankey, who since the outbreak of the war had been serving as a Government Minister, told Dr Chaim Weizmann at the beginning of 1941 'that some sort of Federation will have to come into being with a Jewish territory in Palestine big enough to admit of a considerable Jewish immigration'.[82] Lord Hankey's view was not uncommon inside the higher echelons of the

British Government. It was shared by people of the highest standing, including Churchill, the Prime Minister, who was converted to it through a joint and complicated enterprise of Jewish and British personalities which might be called the Philby Affair.

The Philby scheme, or the proposed Saudi-led federation

As we have more than once noticed, the main Zionist leaders themselves played with the same idea and from time to time came up with basically the same solution to the Palestine conflict. During the second half of the 1930s a new element emerged within this approach: the recognition that feelers of such a nature should be directed not only to Arab nationalist leaders of the Fertile Crescent but also to 'Abd al-'Aziz Al Sa'ud, the King of Saudi Arabia, who in 1936 had begun to be more involved in inter-Arab relations with his two agreements with Iraq and Egypt. This attempt reflected the Saudi King's growing importance in the Middle East, although the Jewish leaders were well aware of his religious fanatical character and that 'impermeable wall of religious fanaticism, blind hatred and of religious interdictions and injunctions that separate him and us'. However a step towards him was taken in March 1937, when Dr Weizmann, who believed in the necessity of making Ibn Saud partner to the solution of the Palestine conflict,[83] had a meeting in London with Captain Harold Courtney Armstrong who, having written a well disposed biography of Ibn Saud (*Lord of Arabia*), enjoyed good standing at the Saudi Court. Since Armstrong hinted in the meeting that he could use his good services to establish contacts with the Saudis and actually tried to do so, the Zionist leaders went one step further.[84] This time they tried to establish direct contacts with Saudi officials.

In April 1937 Eliyahu (later Elath) Epstein of the Political Department of the Jewish Agency in Jerusalem was sent to Beirut to meet Fu'ad Hamzah, the Director (or Deputy Minister) of the Saudi Foreign Ministry. In the early 1930s Mr Epstein had studied at the American University of Beirut and afterwards carried out research on the way of life of the Arabian bedouin tribes. Thus he established contacts with Fu'ad Hamzah who was engaged in the same kind of research while preparing his famous book *Qalb Jazirat al-'Arab* (*The Heart of the Arabian Peninsula*). Fu'ad Hamzah was a Lebanese Druze who had entered the service of the Saudi King as a teacher of his sons and latterly was moved to the Foreign Service. Through a local acquaintance (a Lebanese Druze) Epstein was able to arrange to meet Mr Hamzah who was then spending his vacation in his native country. Epstein asked Hamzah to meet an authoritative representative of the Jewish Agency who could put before the Saudi King the Jewish case in the Palestine conflict. Hamzah agreed and Epstein told him that the Jewish representative would be none other than David

THE EVER-PRESENT PANACEA – ARAB FEDERATION

Ben-Gurion, chairman of the Zionist Executive in Jerusalem. Hamzah, so it seems, was flattered by the readiness of Ben-Gurion to come to Beirut to see him, but made it clear that the meeting would be of an unofficial character, otherwise he would have to ask for his King's consent and to inform the French mandatory authorities of Syria and Lebanon and the British authorities in Palestine. Epstein agreed and a meeting between Hamzah and Ben-Gurion was set for 13 April.

In that meeting Ben-Gurion analysed the Palestine question in the context of the broader Middle Eastern perspective and the fact that Palestine was surrounded by Arab countries. For his part Hamzah stressed the division of the Arab world into several states, the fact that no one really knew when an Arab confederation, which would erase the barriers between Syria, Iraq, Saudi Arabia and Palestine, might be established and that the question should be dealt with from the angle of the Palestine Arabs. Anyway Fu'ad Hamzah promised Ben-Gurion to bring his views before Ibn Saud when he returned to Saudi Arabia.

Immediately afterwards Epstein went to London as a companion to I. Ben-Zvi who had been invited to represent the Palestine Jewish community at the coronation of King George VI. Being encouraged by the friendly attitude of Hamzah, Epstein tried to establish in London direct contacts with Amir Sa'ud, the Saudi heir apparent, and with Mr Yusuf Yasin, the private secretary of the Saudi King, who were representing their country at the coronation. But Epstein's displeasure was great. Although Fu'ad Hamzah promised to meet Amir Sa'ud in Port Said on his way to London and to persuade him to meet the Jewish Agency representatives, neither Sa'ud nor Yusuf Yasin agreed to it. Furthermore, the Lebanese Druze intermediary between Epstein and Hamzah explained to the latter that this episode caused Hamzah a lot of problems. When Amir Sa'ud was told by Hamzah about his meeting with Ben-Gurion Sa'ud was infuriated and condemned him strongly although the meeting had been of an unofficial nature. Yusuf Yasin, a Syrian Muslim who was active in the early 1920s in the political struggle of the Palestine Arabs, used this affair in order to undermine Hamzah's standing at the Royal Court. And although the Saudi King's reaction was less severe, Hamzah's career was impaired. Some time later, he was demoted to the position of Ambassador to Vichy France and Turkey and lost some of his standing, though as protégé of Amir Faysal, the younger brother of Amir Sa'ud, his total fall was prevented.[85]

For the Zionist leaders it was only the beginning of the affair, not the end of it. Ben-Gurion too went to London in May 1937 to attend the coronation as representative of the Jewish Agency and still under the influence of Captain Armstrong's encouraging reaction he decided to find new routes in the direction of the Saudi King. He therefore arranged a meeting with St John Philby and Captain Armstrong. Apart from his well-known friendly relations with King 'Abd al-'Aziz Al Sa'ud Philby had already been involved in 1929 in an attempt at mediating between the three parties involved in the Palestine Question.[86] Furthermore, in 1931 Philby had expressed to Arab personalities visiting Najd and Hijaz 'his belief in Arab unity and his desire to see it implemented at the hands of Ibn Sa'ud'.[87] Certainly, Ben-Gurion still remembered Philby's 1929 mediation attempt and might also have known his pan-Arab, Saudi-oriented beliefs.

On 18 May 1937 Ben-Gurion met Philby and Armstrong separately. In the talks Ben-Gurion stated his Zionist beliefs, and outlined his basic principles for an agreement: (1) unlimited Jewish immigration to Palestine; (2) internal independence for Palestine; and (3) association of Palestine with an Arab Federation or Confederation. He made it clear that the possible partners for such a federation were Palestine, Trans-Jordan and Iraq and that Ibn Saud's rule should not extend to Palestine. Philby reacted by stressing that only Ibn Saud could head the proposed federation which should become fully independent. Without direct authority over Palestine Ibn Saud would not be in a position to deliver his part in the bargain. Philby thought that it might be useful if Ben-Gurion met with the Saudi delegates then present in London and suggested enquiring whether it was possible.[88]

Eight days later they met again and Philby admitted that the Saudi King forbade his delegates to have any such dealings. However, Philby now took the initiative and tried to get Ben-Gurion's agreement to the text of a pact which would be initiated by them and published.[89] Ben-Gurion refused and prepared an alternative draft.[90] Philby's draft, based upon rejection of the partition solution, would put an end to the British mandate over Palestine, and proposed the union of Palestine and Trans-Jordan under the protectorate of Ibn Saud, and the right of everyone irrespective of his religion and race to immigrate to Palestine limited only by the economic capacity of absorption to be finally decided by a League of Nations arbitrator. Ben-Gurion's draft, on the other hand, made immigration virtually free, put the League of Nations in charge of overseeing the implementation of the proposed agreement and expressed readiness to see the affiliation of Palestine with an Arab confederation provided that the confederation recognised and guaranteed the rights of the Jewish national home as laid down by the League of Nations. In his letter to Philby Ben-Gurion also expressed his doubts whether it was desirable to exclude Great Britain completely from the agreement. Philby did not reply, but Armstrong reported that there was no way to bring the Zionist and the Saudi delegates together.[91] Two months later, after the Palestine Royal (Peel) Commission had recommended the partition of Palestine and the British Government agreed in principle, Philby was carried over to that solution[92] and for a while it looked as if the ground for the erstwhile 'Federation-cum-immigration' approach was completely undermined.

This lull continued for a few months only. It seems that Philby was anxious to renew his mediation which, if successful, might enhance his standing. In October 1937 he found means to let Dr Weizmann know that a settlement could be found. To some extent he modified his original proposition, but stuck to its basic idea, that the Arab states should reorganise themselves as a Federation with Ibn Saud at the top. As for the Jewish immigration question, they would be admitted without limitation other than economic capacity of absorption, precisely as Ben-Gurion demanded, although not to Palestine but 'to the entire Arabic lands, Transjordania, Iraq and Arabia'. The British mandate would be annulled. Although Philby had initially supported the partition recommendation he could not fail to realise how strongly Ibn Saud rejected it. The most abhorrent element for the Saudis, so Philby hinted, was 'the suggestion of throwing the remainder of Palestine [according to the Peel Partition Plan] into Abdullah's kingdom'. Therefore Philby tried to find an alternative solution to the Peel Plan which might have the support of both the Jews and the Saudis. Weizmann was not attracted by this proposition and its anti-British tone when there were chances of having the Partition Plan implemented and commented that he did not trust Philby and did not contemplate a settlement based on the supposition of England's exclusion.[93]

On the other hand, Weizmann was convinced that the Saudi King was the only Arab personality who should be taken into account, having no regard for the other Arab states. Ben-Gurion shared this attitude. Therefore when in summer 1938 someone proposed to arrange a meeting between Ben-Gurion and Hafiz Wahbah, the Saudi Minister in London, he agreed. In that meeting Ben-Gurion told Wahbah that in his opinion Ibn Saud was the only person in the Arab world who was strong enough 'to do something' and asked Wahbah to arrange for him to meet the Saudi King. Wahbah promised to write to the King. However, after four months Wahbah had to admit that Ibn Saud rejected any such possibility, but left some room for continuing the manoeuvre by telling the Zionist side that Ibn Saud might agree to such a meeting being held during the coming St James's Conference.[94]

At approximately the same time Malcolm MacDonald, the Colonial Secretary, became fully convinced that only through a comprehensive Arab approach might there be found a solution to the Palestine question (see below, pp. 110–13) and that Ibn Saud, 'the greatest Arab leader' who possessed 'much moral and political power' and was of 'tremendous influence in the Moslem world' had to be persuaded to reach an agreement and to reconcile himself to the Jewish national home. MacDonald told Ben-Gurion and Weizmann that the British would try to persuade Ibn Saud and 'perhaps you can also reach an agreement with him'.[95] At the end of 1938 the star of the Partition Plan was setting since the British Government finally disavowed their previous acceptance of the principle of partition. From the Jewish point of view the price to pay for an agreement with any Arab leader in terms of a better, British-supported solution did not exist any more. Therefore, when in the winter of 1939 during the deliberations of the St James's Palestine Conference Philby resumed his activities[96] the Zionist leaders, including Weizmann, responded favourably, remembering Wahbah's words. Philby then learned about the activities of the pro-Hashemite British group headed by A. W. Lawrence and he opposed it. It prompted him to renew his work for his own pro-Saudi solution.[97]

Philby met several Zionist leaders and British personalities and on 28 February in a lunch party at his home with Ben-Gurion, Weizmann and Fu'ad Hamzah, who participated in the conference, he made a new proposal. The novelty was that as a *'quid pro quo* in the way of Jewish immigration to Palestine — say 50,000 in the next five years'[98] the Jews would agree to have Amir Faysal, the younger son of 'Abd al-'Aziz Al Sa'ud, as King of Palestine. Some of Philby's British contacts got the impression that the coronation of Faysal as King of Palestine was desired by the Saudi King himself.[99] It may well have been that the Zionist leaders had not yet been fully convinced that Philby truly represented the Saudi King's views. A few days later they asked Abdel Aziz, the former President of the All Indian Moslem League, to go to Mecca and enquire about Ibn Saud's views.[100] But the collapse on 17 March of the Conference and the publication of the anti-Zionist British Statement of Policy two months later ruled out for the time being any possibility that the Arabs would concede to the Jews something beyond the limits laid on the Zionist enterprise by the British. Philby's renewed attempt had miscarried again.

With the outbreak of the Second World War in September 1939 Ibn Saud found himself in financial difficulties which were increased by the stoppage of the pilgrimage to Mecca and Madinah during the war.[101] The payment by the British Government to Ibn Saud of a small annual subsidy amounting to £100,000 could not offset the effect of the stoppage of the pilgrimage and of royalty payments by Standard Oil of California. In any case Philby did not then know about this British decision, which was kept secret. It seems that Philby believed that if he brought to Ibn Saud a remedy to his financial difficulties he might win over the Saudi King to the kind of comprehensive settlement of the Middle Eastern problems which he had been looking for. He may have been prompted to think so by the fact that sometime in September following the outbreak of the war Ibn Saud wired to Philby, through the Saudi Minister in London, to come to him 'on the wings of speed'. Philby wanted, so one may conclude, to come to the king with something tangible in his hand. Therefore, on 23 September 1939 he met at the Athenaeum Club in London Professor L. B. Namier, the well-known Manchester historian, who in 1929–31 had been Political Secretary of the Zionist Executive in London, remained an active Zionist and close associate of Dr Chaim Weizmann, and in 1939 again joined the ZE. He made his old proposition to Namier with one important amendment: in order to bail him out of his financial difficulties, Ibn Saud would get the sum of £20 million and armaments.[102]

Namier was attracted and within a few days arranged for Philby to repeat his proposal to the highest Zionist figure, Dr Chaim Weizmann. It seems that this talk also passed smoothly and all of them met for the third time on 6 October. This time they were joined by Moshe Shertok, who happened to be in London, and went through Philby's proposal in detail. 'Philby's idea was that Western Palestine [excluding Trans-Jordan] should be handed over to the Jews, clear of Arab population, except for a "Vatican City" in the old city of Jerusalem. In return the Jews should try to secure for the Arabs national unity and independence. Such unity could be achieved under Ibn Saud alone. Philby envisaged in the first place the handing over to Saudi Arabia of Syria and various small states on the Red Sea'. He also 'suggested the sum of £20 million for Ibn Saud in case the scheme was carried out in full'. Dr Weizmann emphasised that the Jews were ready to promise 'economic advantages' but could not give any valid political promise which they had no power to fulfil and could do nothing which might conflict with their loyalty towards Great Britain and France. However, he added three encouraging remarks:

> (1) British public opinion would certainly back a reasonable claim for a Jewish-Arab settlement, and even be prepared to make certain sacrifices to achieve it; (2) Very influential American support for such a settlement could be expected; (3) The world would be faced at the end of the war with a very serious Jewish problem – of Jewish populations being evacuated from East European countries – and the man who could supply a possible solution for this problem would have a considerable claim on the world for benefits in return.

Shertok had some moral or political misgivings over the fate of the Palestine Arabs and suggested that part at least of the £20 million should be used for development in connection with the transfer of the Palestine Arabs to other Arab countries. On the whole Shertok had serious doubts about the possibility of attaining full independence and unity for the Arabs. Namier was less sure than Weizmann that the cash could be found. He therefore suggested that the money would be given in goods, and if Ibn Saud required arms, they could be supplied over a certain period of time from Jewish armament works in Palestine. 'Philby entirely agreed that such a subsidy would have to be distributed over a number of years, and paid, to a very large extent, in the form of goods.'

Although this talk did not end in a formal agreement, considerable understanding was arrived at over this far-reaching scheme. 'Weizmann said that when in America he expected to see President Roosevelt and to gain his support for some big scheme of such a character.' He insisted that an official Saudi endorsement of the scheme should be forthcoming, telling Philby that when the latter had gained Ibn Saud's assent and support for his idea, 'he should send word to me through the Saudi Arabian Legation in London'. After Weizmann and Shertok had left, Namier once more emphasised to Philby that 'while we were not in a position to make binding political promises about things not under our control, they and we alike had to put our faith in creating circumstances which would favour such a scheme'.[103] On the whole, the London Zionist Executive were positively impressed by these talks; so much so that Mrs Blanche ('Baffy') Dugdale, who had since 31 August 1939 served as a member of the Political Bureau of the London ZE, could note in her diaries: 'Ibn Sa'ud is the one that counts'.[104]

A few months later Philby began to carry out his part of the understanding. In January 1940 he came to Saudi Arabia and on the eighth day of that month met the Saudi King and put forward the scheme. The King reacted in an oblique way. He told Philby 'that some such arrangement might be possible in appropriate future circumstances, that he would keep the matter in mind, that he would give me a definite answer at the appropriate time, that meanwhile I should not breathe a word about the matter to anyone – least of all to any Arab – and, finally, that if the proposals became the subject of public discussion with any suggestion of his approving them he would have no hesitation whatsoever in denouncing me as having no authority to commit him in the matter'. But at the same time the King did not forbid Philby to communicate his position to Weizmann once he realised Philby's intention to do so.[105]

Now, Philby committed two mistakes. In a communication to his wife Dora, intended to be transferred to Weizmann, Philby interpreted 'Abd al-'Aziz Al Sa'ud's position as an acceptance. And, secondly, and more gravely, a little later Philby foolishly told Yusuf Yasin (who, it will be remembered, was a Syrian with a past Palestinian nationalist activity) and Bashir Sa'dawi of the Royal entourage about his plan. That was enough to enable the King's courtiers to raise opposition to the deal. Philby tried again in May 1940, but by then he had incurred Ibn Saud's wrath on other counts and thus Philby's role came to an end.[106]

It should be added that even if we accept Philby's interpretation of Ibn Saud's position and in 1940 there was a chance that the Saudi King would accept Philby's plan, the reasons for that acceptance gradually disappeared during the next three years. In 1940 Ibn Saud was desperate for money. The financial crisis of his kingdom was so severe that the very foundations of it were shaken. However, during 1941 the situation began to improve. Britain's yearly grant-in-aid was gradually but very significantly being increased from £100,000 in 1939 to about £3 million in 1942 (indirectly financed by the United States). But even this sum was not enough. Ibn Saud exerted pressure on Standard Oil of California to pay him advances on account of future royalties. The company responded favourably and these annual payments reached about $3 million in 1942 and about $5 million in 1945. Under pressure from American oil companies the US Government decided to be active in that field directly and from 1943 Saudi Arabia was included in the 'lend-lease' programme.[107] The financial reason which in 1940 may have led Ibn Saud not to reject Philby's plan outright, no longer existed two years later.

Not only Philby took his plan seriously. The Jewish side too behaved in the same way. On 26 November 1939 David Ben-Gurion reported to the Zionist Executive in Jerusalem on the Philby plan. He made one remark and one omission. He made it clear that he did not believe in the possibility of the Palestine Arabs being forcibly transferred out of Palestine, although he believed that some of them might agree to move out. Significantly enough Ben-Gurion failed to mention that the Jews were obliged by that understanding to offer their support for Arab unity; he only mentioned Arab independence. It may have been that the question of unity was regarded by him as too fanciful. The crux of the matter for him was the question of the transfer of the Palestine Arabs and making Palestine into a Jewish state. He told his colleagues that the office of the Zionist Organisation in London was preparing informative material pertaining to population transfer.[108]

This material was certainly intended to help in convincing the US and the British Governments of the advisability of the Philby plan. Dr Chaim Weizmann, who had been the main Jewish partner to the understanding with Philby, regarded this task of convincing them as his main duty in the first years of the Second World War. One may understand his enthusiasm in dealing with this matter in view of his past activities and achievements during the First World War when he employed his personal talent and charm in the diplomatic effort which succeeded in securing the Balfour Declaration and the agreement with Amir Faysal Ibn Husayan of Hijaz.

The first step which Weizmann took was to approach the old 'gentile Zionist', Winston Churchill, who, immediately on the British declaration of war against Germany on 3 September 1939, had been appointed First Lord of the Admiralty and a member of the War Cabinet. This approach was made through the good offices of Brendan Bracken (ennobled in

1952 as Viscount Brendan-Bracken), who had been one of the few Tory MPs who supported Churchill in his wilderness years during the 1930s and acted as his assistant and also as a liaison officer with the Zionist leaders.[109] On 31 October Bracken reported to Churchill about Weizmann's talk with 'one of the leading Arab representatives', stressing the possibility that Palestine 'could obviously flourish as a Jewish State' and 'that in return for a subsidy of 20 million pounds he [alluding to Ibn Saud who was mistakenly described as the Emir of Trans-Jordan] will offer Arabs a much better home than they have ever had in Palestine'.[110]

This memorandum exhibits once more what the Zionist leaders took to their hearts out of the Philby plan, but as we shall see later, the other elements of the plan were passed to Churchill. Not less significant is the fact that Weizmann this time took Philby seriously to the extent that Bracken considered that 'Weizmann was very much attracted by this idea' and he (Bracken) was led to understand that Weizmann's interlocutor was a 'leading Arab representative'. This stands in marked contrast to Shertok's impression of Philby!

It was not long before Weizmann met Churchill on 17 December. According to Weizmann's account of the meetings,[111] he did not discuss the Philby plan in full detail but only mentioned that 'after the war the Zionists would wish to have a State of some three or four million Jews in Palestine', a wish with which Churchill agreed. It may have been that after the information had been passed to Churchill by Bracken, Weizmann did not see any need to be more specific. However, we tend to think that Weizmann deliberately used vague language, since he tried a little further on in his book to present Churchill's solution to the Palestine problem, which was very similar to the Philby plan, as having emanated from him (Churchill) without any previous attempt being made to convince him. Furthermore, Weizmann claimed that only in the late days of 1941 did he hear for the first time from Philby about his plan, a claim which is clearly unfounded.[112]

Encouraged by Churchill's attitude Weizmann went to the USA to enlist the support of President Roosevelt with whom he had an interview in early February 1940. Here again Weizmann was not too forthcoming in reporting the content of the meeting, although he admitted in his book that he 'tried to sound him [Roosevelt] out on the likelihood of American interest in a new departure in Palestine, away from the White Paper when the war was over'. Roosevelt 'showed himself friendly but the discussion remained theoretical'.[113] However, there is little doubt that Roosevelt had been told the essentials of the Philby Plan, since about a year later and before any further meeting with Weizmann, Roosevelt told Colonel Oliver Stanley (the last War Secretary in Neville Chamberlain's government and a future Colonial Secretary) that the Arabs were purchasable and that the whole Palestine question was merely a matter of a little bribe, possibly hinting at the £20 million component of the proposed plan.[114]

When Weizmann returned to England he sent a message to Philby assuring him 'of his confidence in securing acceptance of the plan'.[115] Thereupon he began a sustained attempt to gain the support of crucial members of the British Cabinet. Since May 1940 a new War Cabinet under Churchill's premiership had been in office and the prospects of a favourable response looked promising to Weizmann. The first to be approached were Lord Lloyd, the first Colonial Secretary in Churchill's government, who had in 1937–38 been engaged in finding a solution to the Palestine question by means of its inclusion in an Arab federation (see above, pp. 77–8), and Lord Halifax, the Foreign Secretary.

Weizmann met Lord Lloyd in late August 1940 and outlined to him the Philby scheme, although Weizmann modified it to some extent by the concession that the Jewish state to be included in the Arab Federation headed by Ibn Saud should be small. Lloyd apparently expressed approval only of the basic assumptions of the Arab federation solution to the Palestine problem, but Weizmann interpreted it as a positive reaction to the Philby scheme. Encouraged, he carried on and met Viscount Halifax on 28 August. Again he presented the scheme and revealed to Halifax the positive reaction he thought he had heard from Lloyd. Foreign Office records do not tell us what Halifax said to Weizmann. What we do learn is that immediately Halifax met Lloyd and ascertained his position. He learned that Lloyd indeed had voiced a favourable attitude to the idea of Arab federation and that when the war ended and Britain emerged victorious it would be in a position to dictate a peace settlement for the Middle East. This settlement would comprise an Arab federation and 'a small autonomous area somewhere in Palestine (perhaps a very small area – nothing like what the Zionists would hope and expect)' for the Jews.

The Foreign Office officials did not support Lloyd's position. Lacy Baggallay of the Eastern Department explained the weaknesses of the very idea of an Arab federation from a British point of view (see below, pp. 243ff.) but he was really alarmed at the possibility that Dr Weizmann and 'people like him' might get the slightest idea that Britain might insist on the Jews getting an autonomous area. Sir Horace Seymour, the Assistant Under-Secretary, fully agreed and even added more arguments against an Arab federation. Sir Alexander Cadogan, the Permanent Under-Secretary, initialled their minutes without any comment. However, the political heads of the office confined their critical approach to the Jewish aspect of this matter. R. A. Butler, the Under-Secretary, commented: 'I have always thought that success [in reaching an agreement between the Jews and the Arabs] can only be achieved if Dr Weizmann or the Jewish leaders negotiate with the Arabs themselves. I am quite opposed to our giving ... any pledge of our support. Dr Weizmann has frequently talked of going to see Ibn Saud. I hope one day he will go'. Viscount Halifax summed up the discussion by this comment: 'Lord Lloyd might be interested to see [the previous minutes]. He must clearly avoid adding to our embarrassments by promising what he cannot certainly perform'.

Accordingly, the Foreign Office's official position, expressed in a letter of 19 September signed by W. I. Mallet (Halifax's Private Secretary) and addressed to Christopher Eastwood (Lloyd's Private Secretary) avoided a serious discussion of the idea of Arab Federation but rather went to great lengths to warn against any inkling being given to the Jews about possible British support. *Inter alia* it said:

> Lord Halifax feels that there may be a good deal in these ideas [the Philby scheme], and that if they play their cards properly the Jews may be able to secure their autonomous area in some future settlement. It may even be possible for us to press the Arabs when the time comes to give them such an area. But in the meanwhile he thinks it is most important that we should not give the Zionists the slightest inkling that we could or would use such pressure ... [Furthermore, the Philby scheme adds] a further, artificial obstacle to the already sufficiently numerous natural obstacles to [Arab] Federation by saying that no scheme of federation will be passed unless it includes a Jewish area: and that is the position which Lord Halifax fears we may find we have adopted almost without knowing it, if we give even the most guarded promise of support to the Zionists in seeking such an [autonomous] area.

The Colonial Office acquiesced in this position, although they dissociated themselves from the sharply critical attitude of Zionism which had been expressed in the Foreign Office's letter, and explicitly accepted one of the basic assumptions of the Philby plan, namely that 'Ibn Saud is the only big statesman in the Near and the Middle East'.[116]

As already mentioned above, we do not know for sure what Halifax really did tell Weizmann when they met. But the interpretation that Weizmann made of Halifax's reaction to the Philby scheme seems to us unwarranted. Weizmann again interpreted Halifax's support for the view that an Arab confederation would lessen the Arabs' fear of being swamped by the Jews as a favourable opinion of the specific Philby scheme. It may well have been that having been personally attracted by the scheme he went too far in reaching comforting conclusions about other people's opinions. It may also have been that Weizmann needed such a convenient presentation in order to carry his Zionist Executive colleagues with him. This last possibility is strengthened if we take into consideration that Weizmann added when he reported to his colleagues that 'he thought that the Prime Minister would probably favour such a scheme',[117] which gives more credence to our view that during the contacts in autumn 1939 with Churchill, either directly or through Brendan Bracken, the Philby plan had already been presented to Churchill and his favourable reaction was noted.

Weizmann expected to hear more from Lords Lloyd and Halifax whose positions he interpreted as favourable. When he did not get any further signal he again approached Lord Lloyd, this time in writing, in the expectation – is it too far-fetched a conclusion? – of getting some definite reply in a written letter. In his letter to Lord Lloyd of 2 December 1940 Weizmann expressed readiness to see a Jewish state in Palestine entering a Federation with the neighbouring Arab states, provided that this Federation remained in close connection with the British Commonwealth.[118] Weizmann well understood that Philby's insistence on 'full independence' would deter such a self-confessed imperialist as Lord Lloyd. Unfortunately, a few months later Lloyd died without having replied to Weizmann.

In the meantime, in September 1940, Weizmann met Churchill too for the second time during the war. Churchill had now become Prime Minister and Weizmann tried to convince him of the advisability and advantages of the establishment of a Jewish fighting force composed of about 50,000 men recruited in Palestine within the British Army. Weizmann succeeded in doing so, although owing to the stiff opposition of the British military authorities, the Foreign Office, etc., the establishment of such units materialised very slowly and an undisguised Jewish Brigade was formed only four years later. Reporting on that meeting in his autobiography, Weizmann said nothing about whether or not the Philby plan was then raised.[119] But Oliver Harvey, Anthony Eden's Private Secretary, recorded in his *Diaries* (entry of 1 November 1941) that Weizmann 'told me that before he went to America last time, he had seen Winston [Churchill] who had sketched out his idea of an Arab Federation including a Jewish Palestine under the Suzerainty of Ibn Saud'.[120] Here again we are told that according to Weizmann the whole idea emanated from Churchill. Secondly, Weizmann's last trip to America preceding Harvey's diary entry took place in the spring of 1941. Therefore, if we assume that no secret meeting took place between Churchill and Weizmann, the meeting between the two which is referred to in Harvey's *Diaries* is the one which had taken place in September 1940, about which Weizmann told us in his autobiography only half the story.[121]

May 1941 was a critical month in the war history of the Middle East. In that month the tolerant attitude which the British had pursued towards the Vichy-French Government in Syria ceased. Already the fall of France in June 1940 had freed Britain of the necessity to take into consideration

French susceptibilities as far as British Middle Eastern policy was concerned. Now the change was going to be more drastic. Also during that month the British forces were reoccupying Iraq which under Rashid 'Ali al-Kaylani had become hostile. As a collateral the British became very uneasy over French rule in Syria. The fact that the latter enabled German aeroplanes to land in Syria *en route* to Iraq to help the anti-British forces there caused the British to reverse their policy over Syria and to contemplate its occupation. It looked a very grave moment in the history of the Middle East in which destinies could be decided one way or another.

Churchill, with his deep historical awareness, must have thought so. He made up his mind to try a new start in his Palestine policy, basing it on the Philby scheme of which he had learned from Weizmann in the autumn of 1939 or by September 1940 at the latest. On 19 May he prepared a personal note on Syrian policy in which he outlined the course which Britain should take in Palestine. He wrote:

> 7. I have for some time past thought that we should try to raise Ibn Saud to a general overlordship of Iraq and Transjordania. I do not know whether this is possible, but the Islamic authorities should report. He is certainly the greatest living Arab, and has given long and solid proofs of fidelity. As the custodian of Mecca, his authority might well be acceptable. There would, therefore, be perhaps an Arab King in Syria and an Arab Caliph or other suitable title over Saudia Arabia, Iraq and Transjordania. 8. At the time of giving these very great advancements to the Arab world, we should, of course, negotiate with Ibn Saud a satisfactory settlement of the Jewish problem; and, if such a basis were reached, it is possible that the Jewish State of Western Palestine might form an independent Federal Unit in the Arab Caliphate. This Jewish State would have to have the fullest rights of self-government, including immigration, and provision for expansion in the desert regions to the southward [The Negev or even beyond that?], which they would gradually reclaim.

This Note was sent to the Foreign Office and then printed and circulated to some other Cabinet members.[122]

The reaction of the alarmed FO, which led to Anthony Eden's Mansion House speech on 29 May, will be dealt with in detail in its proper place (see pp. 247–9). Here it suffices to say that they rejected Churchill's attitude and assumptions *in toto*. C.W. Baxter, the head of the Eastern Department, prepared on 22 May a detailed Minute in which he efficiently destroyed Churchill's positions: (a) a strongly pro-Zionist policy in Palestine would alienate the Arabs in Syria whom Churchill wanted to win over to the British side, whatever the British concessions in Syria or other parts of the Arab world 'for everything depends upon our future

THE EVER-PRESENT PANACEA – ARAB FEDERATION 93

Palestine policy'; (b) it would be impractical 'to try to raise Ibn Saud to a general overlordship over Iraq and Transjordan. I do not think that Iraq would stand for this'; and (c) while agreeing that the most satisfactory settlement of the Jewish problem would probably be that 'a Jewish unit should form part of the proposed Middle Eastern federation', Baxter pointed out that 'it would, however, be too much to hope that the Arabs would agree to allow it [the Jewish unit] unrestricted Jewish immigration, and further expansion later in the desert regions to the south'. Sir Alexander Cadogan endorsed Baxter's doubts and added that he did not know why Britain should work for the promotion of an Arab Federation, that it would have to come as 'a spontaneous Arab movement'; that no one knew whether Ibn Saud would agree to give the right impetus; and once a new government was formed in Iraq, the involvement in this matter might not enhance their prestige. Sir Robert Vansittart, the former Permanent Under-Secretary, who was employed as a special adviser at the FO, supported these remarks.[123]

Eden's public speech of 29 May totally overlooked the Jewish and the Palestinian aspect of Churchill's proposal. His speech and the Paper he circulated on 27 May among the Cabinet members, which were endorsed by them on 3 June, sufficed to block Churchill's move (see below, pp. 249–50). Therefore, Churchill tried a different, less direct approach. In the summer of 1941 he told Sir Firoz Khan Noon, a prominent pro-British Indian Muslim politician who had been serving since 1936 as India's High Commissioner in London, 'to go and have a talk with Weizmann about the Moslem Zionist deadlock'.

When this talk took place Weizmann presented to Firoz Khan Noon the Philby plan. Firoz Khan Noon was convinced that the Philby plan was good and practicable. When he reported to Leopold Amery, the Secretary for India, he added two points agreed upon with Weizmann, which had not been included in the original plan: (a) that the Jewish 'autonomous state' prescribed in the plan should come into existence in accordance with a treaty with Ibn Saud ('The King of Mecca') and by him 'so that no Moslem can blame England for having created a Jewish autonomous state in Palestine or part of Palestine', and (b) that the envisaged Arab Federation would include the whole of Arabia, including the Yemen and the southern and eastern coast of Arabia, in addition to Syria, Lebanon, Iraq, Trans-Jordan and Palestine. And if the rulers of Iraq and Trans-Jordan did not accept the suzerainty of 'the King of Mecca' their kingship could be abolished. But Amery, a very close associate of Churchill of many years, who conveyed to Churchill Firoz Khan's description of the talk, doubted the 'Levantine effendis of Baghdad, Damascus and Jerusalem submitting to the overlordship of what they regard as a mere "bedouin"'.[124]

Churchill, who must have been impressed by the agreement reached by

Firoz Khan Noon and Weizmann, disregarded Amery's scepticism. He even pressed the matter further. On 23 September he asked in a personal minute three top Secretaries of State (Foreign, India and Colonial) to meet with Oliver Lyttelton, the Minister of State resident in Cairo who was then on a visit to London, and 'take a look at this solution which in my opinion is full of interest and indeed the best I can think of'.[125] In order to prevent any false impression that it was nothing but a casual whim, the day after sending that minute he repeated his demand in the War Cabinet meeting which discussed the situation in the Middle East against the background of the general report submitted by the Minister of State and in his presence. Furthermore, now Churchill not only asked his colleagues 'to take a look' at the scheme but also to 'see whether this suggestion could be carried further'.[126] Churchill's mind, no doubt, was set for a drastic change of the whole situation in the Middle East.

In preparation for that meeting Eden referred the Philby–Firoz Khan Noon–Weizmann proposal to the Eastern Department, whose dislike of Churchill's views of the Middle Eastern situation had more than once been expressed. They could quite easily show that this scheme would jeopardise the British position in the Arabian coast sheikdoms; that it was totally unrealistic to expect the Hashemite countries to accept Ibn Saud's suzerainty; that it was very doubtful whether the people of Damascus would submit willingly to the overlordship of Ibn Saud; that the Christians of the Lebanon would have even greater misgivings at the prospect of being ruled by a Muslim king; and, finally, that such a solution would undoubtedly also be very unwelcome to the French.[127]

At the Colonial Office the study of that scheme was much more thorough. It was not the first time it had been brought to the knowledge of Lord Moyne who had been appointed as Colonial Secretary in February 1941 following Lloyd's death. Weizmann spent the spring of 1941 in the USA and since his contact with Lord Lloyd had not resulted in any formal reply he began the whole story again with Moyne on his return from the USA in the summer. Weizmann met Moyne twice, on 29 July and a few days later. According to Weizmann Lord Moyne already believed in the Arab Federation approach to the Palestine problem. Weizmann therefore had only to add the role of Ibn Saud, in accordance with 'what the Prime Minister had said to him before his departure for the States'. Weizmann admits that about that point Moyne expressed some reservations since Ibn Saud 'has written some letters which were hostile to Zionist aspirations in Palestine', but Weizmann reassured him 'that such an attitude was meant for public consumption; he thought Ibn Saud was a man with whom discussion was possible'. He then told Lord Moyne of his talks with Philby.[128] Another important point which emerged from Moyne in the interview was the recognition 'that some Arabs would have to be transferred [from Palestine] and wondered whether this could be done without bloodshed'.

Fortunately we have at our disposal Moyne's report of these interviews and it reveals a different picture. In brief, Weizmann came to Moyne to present the Philby plan. Weizmann succeeded in convincing Moyne that the Palestine problem was one of the stumbling blocks between Britain and the Americans. Moyne did not express to Weizmann any support for any component of that plan, but rather stuck to the official Palestine policy as outlined in the May 1939 White Paper.[129]

Whatever the exact truth of Moyne's reaction to the Philby scheme, he was not indifferent to it. He met Firoz Khan Noon, about whose involvement in the Philby scheme he must have heard, and Brendan Bracken, Churchill's right-hand in Zionist affairs. As a result Moyne was reinforced in his belief that the right approach to the Palestine problem was the Arab federation approach, although his idea of an Arab federation had no room for Ibn Saud's suzerainty over it nor for his participation.[130] As we shall see later (pp. 118–21), this conviction shaped his position regarding the question of Arab federation.

His next step was to bring the essential elements of the Philby plan to the knowledge of Sir Harold MacMichael after his talks with Weizmann. MacMichael's reaction was totally negative. He questioned the readiness of the politicians of Damascus, Iraq and Palestine to let themselves be ruled by Ibn Saud. He further expressed doubts over the stability of Ibn Saud's own kingdom after his death. Moreover, since Ibn Saud 'is genuinely conscientious and religious-minded', MacMichael 'did not see him taking a "loan" of fifteen or twenty million pounds as an inducement to Jewish designs in Palestine nor (if he were otherwise) could he afford to do so'. Lastly, MacMichael was not sure that Weizmann himself seriously saw 'Ibn Saud at the head of an enlarged Arab Federation'.[131]

Deeply influenced by this view Sir Cosmo Parkinson, the Permanent Colonial Under-Secretary, prepared a Note, which was sent to the Foreign Office, stressing that the scheme was 'impracticable', that 'no force can be used to impose one Arab suzerain over the rest of the Arab world', and that 'any scheme embracing Syria and Lebanon involves consideration of the special position of the French in those territories'.[132] But that is not all. The most abhorrent aspect of the Philby scheme, as far as the top officials of the Colonial Office were concerned, was the possible dismissal of 'Abdallah, the Hashemite Amir of Trans-Jordan. On 6 August 1941 the Middle East (Official) Committee discussed British policy in Trans-Jordan and Syria. In the wake of the Free French Declaration of Syrian independence, which was endorsed by Britain, 'Abdallah demanded that his Emirate be elevated to an independent kingdom. The committee thought it would be a mistake to grant him his demand because 'if an Arab Federation was ultimately to be created, *possibly under the* aegis of Ibn Saud, *the most powerful of Arab rulers* of the Middle East [my italics]', 'Abdallah would play only a minor role.[133] And as if that was not enough, a month later came Amery's letter to Churchill reporting the content of Firoz Khan Noon's agreement with Weizmann which explicitly envisaged the abolition of 'Abdallah's 'kingdom' (see above, pp. 93–4). Parkinson realised that not only 'Abdallah's rule was at stake but the Hashemite Kingdom in Iraq as well. And although he knew well that such ideas were being formed in 'high quarters', no doubt meaning the Prime Minister, he did not hesitate to act.

A few days before the crucial Ministerial Conference with the Minister of State he reminded Lord Moyne that eight years ago an official committee (the Middle East sub-committee of the Committee of Imperial Defence) had decided to stick to the *status quo* in the Middle East, that is, to keep the Hashemites and Ibn Saud in their respective dominions and to avoid any encouragement being given to any move towards the establishment of an Arab Federation of the Fertile Crescent (see below, p. 200). Besides that, his Deputy, Sir John Shuckburgh, formed a solid wall in defence of the Hashemites based upon historical and moral arguments.[134]

These strong views of the two offices concerned left their mark on the three Secretaries of State who met on 26 September in an official conference with the Minister of State in which David Margesson, the War Secretary, also participated. The conference adopted the Colonial Office's views that 'A scheme of federation in the form set out by Sir Firozkhan Noon must be regarded as impracticable'. The Foreign Secretary was invited on their behalf to write to the Prime Minister, which he did on 29 September 1941.[135]

Weizmann did not of course know this decision and what had influenced it. What he did realise was that several months had elapsed since Firoz Khan Noon reported to Amery and nothing had happened. However, he continued to show 'much interest [in the "plan"] and sees possibilities in it',[136] and decided again to press it on the Prime Minister, but this time in a different way through Philby.

During the second half of 1940 and up to March 1941 contact with Philby could not be maintained since he had been interned by the British authorities for his anti-war views. On his release in April 1941, he 'was frequently in touch with Professor Namier [Weizmann spent the spring of 1941 in the USA], and inevitably discussed with him, the somewhat faded prospects of the 1939 "plan" which incidentally he and his friends had by no means given up as hopeless'.[137] Weizmann and Namier in early November arranged a meeting between Philby and Sir John Martin, Churchill's Private Secretary and a friend of Weizmann, so that Philby could tell Martin Ibn Saud's reaction to Philby's démarche.[138] Martin hoped to get new information on Ibn Saud's position. But Philby could

THE EVER-PRESENT PANACEA – ARAB FEDERATION 97

only reiterate Ibn Saud's apparent acceptance in January 1940 of his plan. Philby added that the number of Palestinian Arabs to be transferred from Palestine could be reduced if the Jews agreed to give up the Galilee, which was inhabited by 250,000 Arabs, and to be compensated with Sinai, provided that the Egyptians would agree to hand it over to them. Philby also expressed his belief that all Arab leaders except 'Abdallah would agree to Saudi-Wahabi suzerainty and only 'Abdallah would have to be forced to.[139]

Martin's account of that meeting again aroused Churchill's interest. Although only five weeks earlier the Ministerial Conference had passed a negative judgement on the Philby plan, the Prime Minister referred the account to the Colonial Secretary Lord Moyne (another close friend and confidant of his) for his comment. Moyne's remarks were not favourable. First of all, he declared that 'Mr Philby's unsuitability as a negotiator in such matters is evident'. Secondly, as for the substance of Philby's plan, he quoted the opinion of Mr Stonehewer-Bird, the British Minister in Jedda, who ruled out any possibility that Ibn Saud 'could support the idea of federation'. However, Moyne expressed his sympathy with the idea of a 'smaller area of Federal System', e.g. in Greater Syria excluding Saudi Arabia.[140]

Under the combined effect of the decision taken by the Ministerial Conference, and Amery's and Moyne's views, Churchill realised that he could not carry his colleagues with him in his support of Philby's plan. Therefore he reacted to the latest comment of Moyne by minuting in its margin: 'All this is premature. I remain wedded to the Balfour Declaration as implemented by me [referring to his June 1922 Statement of Policy] ... It is better now to get on with the war.'[141]

It may well have been that Weizmann got some inkling of what was going on between Moyne and Churchill and interpreted it in a favourable way. Is it a mere coincidence that a few days later he informed Philby 'that the Prime Minister was again actively interested in the scheme, and that Dr Weizmann was shortly to see Mr Eden on the subject'?[142] Anthony Eden had since December 1940 been serving as Foreign Secretary and had not yet been approached by Weizmann with regard to the Philby scheme. Unfortunately he had to be satisfied with a meeting with Mr Oliver Harvey, Eden's Private Secretary, and Mr Harold Caccia of the Foreign Office's Eastern Department. Already in August 1941 Harvey must have learned about the Philby plan for he expressed a favourable view in his *Diaries* about its basic elements. When, on 1 November 1941, Oliver Harvey saw Weizmann he encouraged him 'to come to terms with Ibn Saud', although what Weizmann needed was a British official backing of the plan, not an encouragement to pursue it. About three months later when Weizmann met Harold Caccia he could not secure even that.[143]

In the meantime another change took place in the Colonial Office and Viscount Cranborne (Marquess of Salisbury from 1949) was appointed in February 1942 as Colonial Secretary instead of Lord Moyne. Weizmann had to try again and he did so on 18 March 1942 on the eve of his departure for the USA. It seems that he presented the Philby plan in very strong terms since Cranborne wrote of Weizmann that 'he had immensely been attracted by a plan which had been proposed in certain quarters, including Philby, for the creation of a great Arab Federation under Ibn Saud within which there should be a Jewish state'. In the discussion Cranborne avoided any comment, but preferred to revert to the question of censorship in Palestine.[144]

Once again we find a discrepancy between what the British interlocutor reported of the talk and what the Zionist side understood him to say. However, this time it was not Weizmann who was the Zionist source for Cranborne's position, but Mrs Blanche Dugdale, the gentile member (since August 1939) of the Political Bureau of the London Zionist Executive. On 2 October she reported to her colleagues the content of a talk she had with Lord Cranborne. According to her, he referred to his last talk with Weizmann and said that 'he [Cranborne] felt this [the Philby plan] was one of the most interesting and important things for future policy.'[145] One cannot help the impression that Cranborne who well knew MacMichael's hostility to the Philby Plan was not too forthcoming when he reported to him the content of his talk with Weizmann.

To what extent did Weizmann succeed in converting the British Cabinet to the Philby plan? As we have already seen (pp. 92–3), the basic ideas of the Philby plan played an important role in the British Government's attempt, induced by the Prime Minister, to shape a policy for the Palestine question different from the one laid down in the 1939 White Paper and more favourable to the Jews. Secondly, even from a stricter point of view Weizmann had some success. Before Weizmann departed for the USA in March 1942, he met Churchill. If we accept Weizmann's word in his autobiography it was then that Churchill on his own initiative repeated to Weizmann that he had a plan to solve the Palestine question after the war: 'I would like to see Ibn Saud,' Churchill told Weizmann, 'made lord of the Middle East – the boss of the bosses – provided he settles with you. It will be up to you to get the best possible conditions. Of course we shall help you. Keep this confidential but you might talk it over with Roosevelt when you get to America. There is nothing he and I cannot do if we set our minds on it.'[146]

What did Churchill mean by those words? It seems to us that having realised that he could not persuade his government to carry out the Philby scheme, Churchill advised Weizmann that the game should thenceforward be played mainly on the American ground. If Weizmann were able to enlist the support of Roosevelt for the plan it might help Churchill to succeed where he had failed – in his own backyard. Furthermore, it

THE EVER-PRESENT PANACEA – ARAB FEDERATION   99

may well have been that from the outset Churchill's adoption of the Philby scheme was connected with the American factor. When, during the summer and autumn of 1941, Churchill was pushing this scheme forward the USA had not yet become directly involved in the war. In one of those dark days (14 September 1941), when another British figure, Oliver Harvey, expressed his support of the scheme it was precisely for that reason! He told Weizmann that the envisaged Arab Federation, in which there would be room for a 'purely Jewish Palestine', should be under international control, 'not purely British, because the British taxpayer would not stand for it alone. Here was the chance for Jewish Americans. At the Peace Conference they must press for some generalised solution with American participation – as moreover in Europe also. We must have America "mixed up" in Europe after the war – even if only by a token. Equally they should be "mixed up" with us in the Middle East through strong basis and sharing controls.'[147] Such was Harvey's discourse with Weizmann. Is it too far-fetched to think that Churchill's mind was heading in the same direction?

Churchill's words were good news for Weizmann; not exactly a profession of creed, but rather an admission by Churchill that Weizmann's three-year attempt to win him over to the Philby plan bore fruit. (Weizmann could not know of course that Churchill's conversion had taken place much earlier, see above, p. 92.) Now, Weizmann surely felt that his efforts in Britain had already been exhausted and he had to devote most of his energies to the USA. Therefore, he needed British backing in order to strengthen his hand *vis-à-vis* the Americans, and Churchill was forthcoming. There is no doubt that Churchill not only supplied Weizmann with ammunition to be used in the American diplomatic battleground but really believed in the usefulness of the Philby plan and in his ability to implement it after the war.

A year later echoes of Weizmann's activities in America with regard to the Philby plan reached London. Especially disturbing in the eyes of the Foreign Office and the Foreign Secretary was 'that Dr Weizmann was making play with the Prime Minister's name' as the sponsor of the Philby scheme. Churchill angrily replied 'that Weizmann had no authority to speak for him, but that it was sufficiently known that the views which Weizmann expressed were in fact substantially those of Churchill'.[148] As for other members of the Cabinet we have Moyne's testimony from January 1942 that 'there are indications that this idea has considerable support in the Cabinet'.[149]

Armed with Churchill's support and perhaps with some knowledge that Churchill was not fully isolated in this stand, Weizmann went to the USA in March 1942 to fulfil his part in the understanding with Philby by winning US backing for the plan.[150] On his arrival in the USA Weizmann had a brief interview with Roosevelt, 'in fact little more than a friendly welcome'. The USA had been in the war for only a few months and certainly the President faced very important questions with regard to the conduct of the war. At that time Roosevelt saw in Weizmann only the scientist. (Weizmann came to America in connection with his chemical research work which had some bearing on the war effort.) No wonder that in those circumstances Weizmann did not discuss 'Mr Churchill's plan' with Roosevelt.[151]

In the months to come Weizmann devoted his energies to his scientific work and to the inter-Zionist leadership struggle with David Ben-Gurion, who was also in the USA campaigning to mobilise American Zionists' support to his 'fighting Zionism' concepts expressed in the Biltmore programme. Soon afterwards, Ben-Gurion directly challenged Weizmann's authority by denying him the right to conduct political negotiations with foreign representatives without having been authorised beforehand by the Jerusalem Zionist Executive. With the support of most of the American Zionist leaders Weizmann withstood Ben-Gurion's onslaught and virtually forced him in September 1942 to return to Palestine.[152] Only then and after two months of convalescence from illness did Weizmann resume his activities on the external front. He felt that time was running out for the Jews. The possibility that the Jews were being murdered on a wholesale scale in Europe became a probability in the summer of 1942 and by the autumn of that year a proven fact. The sense of urgency which was then driving Ben-Gurion was not wanting as far as Weizmann as well was concerned.

Philby, who must have been disappointed with the lack of any positive, real step by Great Britain regarding his plan, changed his mind and urged Weizmann to approach Roosevelt.[153] This urging by Philby did not fall on deaf ears since the Zionist authorities themselves got the same message directly from Churchill. Lord Melchett, an active Zionist and an important figure in the British scientific war effort, told the London Zionist Executive in January 1943 that Colonel Morton, Churchill's personal Military Assistant, had repeated to him virtually the same message which the Prime Minister had delivered to Weizmann ten months ago. Melchett added that Churchill's policy had not changed and that 'He [the P.M.] had tried to get some action, but there had been opposition both on the Federation scheme and also on the schemes for saving Jews. Probably some pressure might be useful'.[154] And who else was better placed to exert such a pressure than the US?

In December 1942 Weizmann approached Sumner Welles, the Under-Secretary of State and the only friend the Zionists had in the State Department. He told him the details of the Philby plan and significantly enough did not mention the source of the plan, but rather attributed it solely to Churchill. Weizmann even added that Churchill had told him that the US President was in accord on this subject. Here Weizmann committed

THE EVER-PRESENT PANACEA – ARAB FEDERATION 101

two important mistakes. The concealment of Philby's authorship and role would later on blow up in Weizmann's face, and as for Roosevelt's being in accord with the plan Welles immediately reacted by noting that 'I should mention that the President has never mentioned this matter to me'.[154] Doubts about Weizmann's sincerity could not help him.

From Weizmann's point of view the reaction of the State Department was much more devastating than Welles's low tone of scepticism which did not affect his basic pro-Zionist position. Wallace Murray, the Adviser on Political Relations who had since 1930 been Chief of the Division of the Near Eastern Affairs of the State Department, to whom the matter had been referred, reacted in a totally negative way. He doubted whether it was possible to make Ibn Saud 'boss of the bosses' in the Arab world and whether Ibn Saud was ready to reach an agreement about Palestine acceptable to Weizmann. For him the only solution to the Palestine question was one which safeguarded the Arab majority therein.[156] A direct talk between Weizmann and Murray did not change the latter's negative attitude, but even Sumner Welles was less than a full supporter of the Philby-Weizmann-Churchill plan. He approved the idea that Weizmann would proceed to Saudi Arabia in order to discuss with Ibn Saud a solution of the problem of Palestine, but he refrained from making any comment on the substance of the plan.[157] But even this, more modest, part of the plan was attacked by J. Harold Shullaw, the US *chargé d'affaires* in Saudi Arabia, who wrote that 'There is little likelihood that Ibn Saud under any circumstances would receive a Jewish Delegation'.[158]

Faced with such stiff opposition to his plan, Weizmann set out to attack the main source of it – the Division of Near Eastern Affairs. On 3 March 1943 a delegation of the Zionist leaders – Weizmann, Dr N. Goldmann, Louis Lipsky and Shertok – met with W. Murray, Paul H. Alling, Chief of the Near East Division, Gordon P. Merriam, his assistant, and William L. Parker, also of that Division. Shertok was called from Palestine to help Weizmann in his efforts.[159] Here Weizmann committed another mistake: he must have been ignorant of Shertok's real view on the Philby plan, and when it became clear to him the damage had already been done. In the meeting with the State Department officials Shertok, even before Weizmann raised the matter, had negatively analysed one of the main foundation stones of the Philby plan: the notion that Ibn Saud would be the suzerain of an Arab federation which would include Palestine. Shertok questioned the practicability of Arab federation in general, its usefulness as a means to solve the Palestine question and the readiness of Ibn Saud to assume the role which was ascribed to him. (One should add that in these talks as in all previous and later talks with the Americans the name of Philby, his connection with the idea and his 1940 mission to Ibn Saud were not mentioned.) On these matters Shertok and Murray were in full accord.

Faced with this unexpected situation Weizmann retreated and expressed agreement with Shertok that it would be premature for him to go to see Ibn Saud.[160] Indeed, Shertok, who had come, in his own words, 'to save the Zionist cause from a trap which the State Department laid (sending us to negotiate with Ibn Saud) and into which Weizmann and Nahum Goldmann almost fell',[161] fully succeeded in his mission, although not exactly in saving Weizmann from a State Department's trap but rather in the destruction of Weizmann's policy!

Weizmann concluded that the only possibility of achieving anything was by a personal and direct appeal to the President. Sumner Welles approached the President on his behalf and fixed it. It is illuminating to learn that Welles presented Weizmann's aim to the US President as a 'hope that the way can be prepared for him to meet with King Ibn Saud and to try to work out the basis for an agreement which would obviate in the future the dangers and difficulties of the past twenty-five years'.[162] Not a word was written by Welles on the substance of the proposed agreement. And if we remember that Welles had also refrained from commenting on that substance when Weizmann put the plan before him but only approved the idea of Weizmann's meeting with Ibn Saud (see p. 101), we may conclude that even Welles had his reservations about the plan.[163]

The meeting of Roosevelt with Weizmann took place on 11 June. We have at our disposal three versions of the proceedings of that meeting, all of which were prepared by Weizmann. The first one was published in his *Trial and Error*, p. 535; a second, an 'off the record' document for Weizmann's disposal, is preserved in the WA; and a third was prepared for the British FO and a copy of it reached the State Department and is included in *FRUS, 1943*, Vol. IV, pp. 791–4. The contents of the talks can be sorted into five categories and it is extremely illuminating to see how they were presented in the three versions:

1 In his book Weizmann reports that Welles did not go into details about the Jewish demand for Palestine; however, Welles 'had read my article in Foreign Affairs [published in January 1942 in which Weizmann demanded the establishment of a Jewish State in Palestine], in which I had outlined my views, and he was in agreement with them'. In the personal record Weizmann reports that he 'emphasized the fact that Palestine will never be an Arab country again', but no comment on that was made by either the President or Welles. In the published version the nearest formula used by Weizmann was 'Jewish rights to Palestine' and that the Jews should 'know that there is a future for them in Palestine'.

2 About the Philby plan Weizmann wrote in his book that he repeated to Roosevelt 'the substance of Mr Churchill's last statement to me' and the President 'asked me to convey to the latter his positive reaction'. This crucial matter, the main subject of Weizmann's activity, does not figure

THE EVER-PRESENT PANACEA – ARAB FEDERATION

at all, either in the personal record or in the published one, although the personal record has a very vague reference to 'the crystallisation of the general settlement of the post-war problems'.[164]

3 In the book Roosevelt is reported to have considered Ibn Saud 'fanatical and difficult'. In the personal version the abusive remarks of the President were directed towards the Arabs in general, 'that they had done very badly in this war; that while they are just sitting we are pouring out our blood; that the Arabs have done nothing. Then he said, they are purchasable, and Dr Weizmann said, I have heard something to that effect (the word bakshish used)'.

4 Both the personal and the published records tell us that Roosevelt stated that he had persuaded Churchill to agree to the idea of calling together the Jews and the Arabs with both of them. In his book Weizmann is absolutely silent on this subject.

5 On the question pertaining to the losses on their investments that the Jews incurred in their colonisation enterprise the two records tell the same thing, whereas the book version is silent.

There is no doubt that the book version should not be taken at face value. It was written several years after the event. It tried to justify Weizmann's effort in pursuing the Philby plan and stressed the President's favourable reaction. It emphasised the negative role of Ibn Saud. The personal 'off the record' document is naturally the most reliable. We learn from it that Weizmann had concluded from Welles's cool reaction to the substance of the Philby plan that there was no point in pressing it on the President. Therefore he did not raise it at all and the President could not agree to it. The published version that had originally been prepared for the British Foreign Office is generally a watered-down version which was meant to soothe their susceptibilities. Therefore nothing is mentioned there of the anti-Arab remarks and the Jewish claim to Palestine is put in a milder way.

But that is not the end of the story. At the meeting of the Zionist leaders with the State Department officials Shertok had objected to Weizmann's idea that he (Weizmann) or another Jewish delegate should negotiate with Ibn Saud. Shertok as has already been noticed, suspected that this idea was a trap laid by the State Department (see above, p. 102) to get Jewish legitimacy for Ibn Saud's involvement in the Palestine entanglement and to force the Jews into confrontation with the harsh realities of Arab opposition. Therefore he tried to turn the tables on the supposed trappers and suggested that 'a British or American representative could discuss matters with Ibn Saud'.[165]

This remark certainly strengthened Welles's conclusion that a delegation to proceed to Saudi Arabia was the only practical aspect of the plan. Therefore during Weizmann's inteview with Roosevelt, Welles suggested that the Americans should send someone to see Ibn Saud to prepare the ground for the Conference which the President had mentioned. The President agreed and the name of Colonel Harold Hoskins was suggested.[166] Weizmann 'felt reluctant to express doubts', but soon afterwards he wrote to Sumner Welles 'deprecating the proposed choice because I know Colonel Hoskins to be in general out of sympathy with our cause'.[167] This Weizmann knew since 'he [Weizmann] had seen the report which Colonel Hoskins had sent about conditions in Palestine [after his 1942 visit to that country] and had also had a talk with him'.[168] But it was too late. The President had already decided to send Hoskins to Ibn Saud. Thus the Hoskins mission was born and contrary to Shertok's expectations the tables were not exactly turned on the heads of the Americans.

Colonel Hoskins was a kind of personal representative of the President to the Middle East. Beirut-born, he was fluent in Arabic and in the autumn of 1942 he was appointed as a liaison officer with the British military headquarters in Cairo. Under their guidance he wrote a hasty report on the probability of new disturbances breaking out between Jews and Arabs in the coming spring.[169] The steps to send Hoskins back to the Middle East were taken immediately after the Roosevelt–Weizmann interview. The British were notified on 12 June. They agreed,[170] and Colonel Hoskins was subsequently directed to ask Ibn Saud whether he would agree to enter into discussion with Weizmann or another Jewish representative to seek a solution to the Palestine problem.[171] Thereupon Hoskins went to Saudi Arabia and at the end of August he sent from Cairo a report which was supplemented on his return with a much longer one.

Since Sumner Welles declined to consider the Philby plan, its foundations were shaken by Shertok in the joint discussion of the State Department officials and the Zionist leaders and Weizmann did not raise it in his crucial talk with the President, it was not brought to the knowledge of Colonel Hoskins who was only equipped with the 'published' record of Weizmann's talk with Roosevelt which Weizmann had prepared for the British FO. As we shall see it turned out to be another grave obstacle in the twisted route of that plan. In his first report Hoskins described his several talks with King Ibn Saud. The King made it clear that he would meet neither Weizmann nor any other Jewish representative. Furthermore, the King went on to explain his personal hatred of Weizmann. The reason was Weizmann's attempt to bribe him with £20 million, the payment of which would be guaranteed by President Roosevelt. The inclusion of Roosevelt's name in such a shameful matter only aggravated the matter. The intermediary who had put all of it before Ibn Saud was Philby. In his supplementary memorandum Hoskins went further and claimed that Ibn Saud had driven him (Philby) out and would never again permit Mr Philby to cross the frontiers of his kingdom.[172]

THE EVER-PRESENT PANACEA – ARAB FEDERATION

When in September 1943 Roosevelt had these reports and heard additional explanations from Hoskins he was infuriated by this one-sided description. He felt personally insulted by his name having been involved in such a disgraceful deal, and hastened to draw the far-reaching political conclusion that giving Palestine to the Jews or a large-scale Jewish immigration to it were not feasible.[173] Roosevelt was interested that Ibn Saud's real attitude towards Zionism be known both to the British Government and to Weizmann. Therefore he instructed Hoskins to go to London.[174]

A few weeks later Colonel Hoskins came to London and saw, among others, Sir Maurice Peterson and Weizmann and told them the outcome of his mission in all its dark colours.[175] Weizmann realised how great was the damage to the Zionist cause and embarked on a counter-attack, the aim of which was to prove the unreliability of Hoskins' report. Both Namier and Weizmann spoke to Philby and urged him to disprove Hoskins' report as far as the January 1940 meeting between him (Philby) and Ibn Saud was concerned. Philby met Hoskins and the latter had to retreat. He admitted that it was he who had concluded from Ibn Saud's reaction that Philby had been driven out of Saudi Arabia and would never again be admitted into it. Secondly, Philby easily proved that for six months after his meeting with the King he had remained in Saudi Arabia, staying within the precincts of the Royal Palace,[176] that he had continued to maintain friendly relations with the King and that he had just been in touch with Prince Faysal while the latter was staying in London. With this information at their disposal Namier and Weizmann decided to bring it to the knowledge of Roosevelt through Sumner Welles.[177]

The letter to Welles was written and sent by Weizmann in December 1943 with an outspoken request that it 'be brought to the attention of the President'.[178] But by then Welles had already left the State Department owing to a personal scandal, and it is very doubtful whether he could do anything substantially to repair the great damage which had already been done. In these circumstances Philby began to despair of the chance to carry out his plan and admitted 'that he had thought that the Jews had much greater influence in America', whereas Professor Namier still believed 'that they [the Zionists] could still use the Philby scheme with advantage'.[179] Certainly, Namier was then unaware of the dimensions of the damage which the Hoskins mission had brought to the Zionist cause in the US government.

Another blow which overcame the Philby plan and all other hopes for agreement was the vehemence and publicity with which Ibn Saud expressed his anti-Zionist and anti-Jewish positions. In March 1943 Ibn Saud gave an interview to a *Life* correspondent in which he made public his deep hostility to Zionism and to any accommodation with it.[180] In April he told the American Minister that Palestine was an Arab country and should get real independence in due course. He also made no secret of his hostility to Jews in general.[181] And if only to make his views look serious he repeated them in a personal letter of 30 April 1943 to President Roosevelt.[182] The 'attempted bribe' made by Weizmann through Philby, which for more than three years had been kept secret by Ibn Saud and which was disclosed by him for the first time as a reaction to Hoskins' enquiries, was now revealed to other foreign diplomats.[183]

The British FO officials could not conceal their satisfaction in hearing Ibn Saud's hostility to the Philby plan.[184] For Harold Caccia Ibn Saud's declaration that 'Palestine is an Arab Country' was 'another nail in the coffin of the Philby plan'.[185] These people had not liked it from the first moment they had heard about it from Churchill in May 1941 and did whatever they could to question its foundations and practicability (see above pp. 92–3). Even Churchill had changed, so it seems, his attitude to the plan. It is true that at the beginning of March 1943 he still expressed support for the plan (see above, p. 99) but two months later when staying during 12–26 May in Washington for an Anglo-American Conference and a speech to American Congress he declined Weizmann's request for a meeting. Weizmann noted: 'Mr Churchill did not want to see me – I am a reproach to him'.[186] It looks as though Churchill learned that in the USA too the amount of support that Weizmann could enlist for the plan was not great and therefore he reached the conclusion that it had to be abandoned. He may also have been impressed by an anti-Zionist declaration of Ibn Saud which was made at the end of March.

The Foreign Office officials in the Eastern Department and Sir Maurice Peterson, the Deputy Under-Secretary in charge, realised in the second half of 1943, when the Palestine Cabinet Committee were working, that in contradistinction to the situation of March 1943, they were no longer handicapped by the Prime Minister's attitude. Therefore Sir Maurice notified the Embassy in Washington about the rejection of the Philby plan and authorised their Minister there, Sir Ronald Campbell, to notify the Americans when an opportunity rose.[187] It was the final blow to the plan, yet it could not obliterate the effect that the plan had had on official British thinking regarding the attempts to solve the Palestine question by means of an Arab federation.

Official British thinking

The various proposals, including of course the Philby scheme, to solve the Palestine question by means of an Arab Federation including a Jewish unit (whatever it may have meant in terms of size and jurisdiction) in Palestine were usually addressed to the British Government. Also those proposals which were exchanged between the protagonists themselves took it for granted that in order to be implemented Britain's active support

THE EVER-PRESENT PANACEA – ARAB FEDERATION 107

had to be enlisted. Therefore, we now turn to this intriguing question – the reaction of British official circles to the various propositions of that kind.

When Sir Herbert Samuel first proposed the formation of an Arab Federation, Lord Curzon rejected it (see above, p.72) because of the international complications that such a scheme entailed. Furthermore, his considered view revealed some of the basic British arguments which in the following years continued to influence British policy. He pointed to the many practical problems which would have to be overcome and drew attention to the fact that if the initiative came from Britain, the whole scheme would be met with suspicion by the Arabs regarding the British motives. Therefore, 'His Majesty's Government are convinced that the only sure basis on which such unity can be established is the natural trust and friendship of the various Arab rulers who alone can fuse into one people the diverse elements over which they exercise control'. The second Secretary of State who was directly concerned was the Colonial Secretary. The Duke of Devonshire commented that Samuel's scheme would irritate the French, would arouse Ibn Saud's suspicions and would not please the Palestinians who wanted nothing else than abandonment of Zionism. Therefore he concluded: 'As an attempt to promote cooperation between a number of people who have little in common with one another and are torn by mutual jealousies, it would be very unlikely to succeed'.[188]

Samuel's much later attempt, in 1936 (see above, pp.74–6) achieved a little better reception. But since it unfortunately coincided with the beginning of the Peel Commission's work, the Colonial Office did not wish to support any move that might be regarded as prejudicial to their conclusions. However, while the merits of Samuel's scheme were being discussed, the first opposing voices could already be heard. When he analysed the economic advantages and disadvantages of a pan-Arab scheme, Mr Eastwood of the Colonial Office's Economic Department expressed his belief that the formation of a free trade area, some unification of Custom tariffs between Palestine and its Arab neighbours and the formation of an Arabic speaking supervisory Council 'would be welcomed by the Arabs in Palestine. They would regard it as the first concrete recognition of Pan-Arab solidarity ... and it would go a long way towards a settlement [of the Palestine question]'.[189] In a minute it was argued that Mr Eastwood's view did not apply to the Arabs in general, but 'only to the politically minded Palestinian Arab' and that was exactly what Mr Eastwood claimed.[190]

It should be noted that this view was held by an important figure outside the Colonial Office: the 'man on the spot' – Sir Arthur Wauchope, the High Commissioner for Palestine. He reacted to the Samuel scheme by noting: 'A Customs union embracing all the Arab countries and

Palestine with freedom of trade within its area is an attractive idea which could commend itself to the Arabs of Palestine who, looking to historical precedents, would probably hope that a Customs union ultimately would lead to a political federation'. Wauchope added that such an arrangement would commend itself to Jewish manufacturing interests as well.[191] However, given that all these arguments were true, 'the effect of such developments on British interests and the position of Britain in Palestine is more doubtful'.[192] And, indeed, the last-mentioned consideration naturally constituted the central factor in shaping the British policy and positions. Another point which should not be overlooked is that Samuel's 1936 scheme envisaged the limitation of Jewish immigration during the next 10 years so that its ratio did not exceed 40 per cent. In that respect the Samuel scheme constituted a link to the even more restrictive British proposals, which were based on the Arab federation approach and which were put forward in the late 1930s.

The discussion of the Samuel scheme took place at a very crucial moment in the history of the Palestine problem. The British Government and the Colonial Office in particular worried very much over the intensity of the Palestine Arab Rebellion and the necessity to suppress it by drastic military measures.[193] Against this background one can understand why the Arab federation approach to the Palestine question began to win adherents inside the Colonial Office and the Palestine Government. The Foreign Office, although not directly involved in the day-to-day problems of the administration of Palestine, became no less sensitive to that matter. Through their contacts with the representatives of the independent (or quasi-independent) Arab states they realised that the Palestine flare-up aroused general interest, unease and feelings of solidarity with the Palestine Arabs in the neighbouring Arab countries and these feelings could endanger British positions, interests and standing there.[194] This evaluation which was circulated to the members of the Cabinet signalled the direction in which the government was heading. But it did not mean that the Arab federation approach was soon to be adopted.

However, in the winter of 1937 the British Ambassador in Baghdad reacted negatively to the proposition of Hikmat Sulayman's government that the only solution to the Palestine problem could be found 'on the lines of a federation, in some form, of Palestine, Transjordan and Iraq'. Dr Naji al-Asil, the Iraqi Foreign Minister in Hikmat Sulayman's Government, used the same arguments to justify this proposal, much as Nuri al-Sa'id had done in October 1936. Dr al-Asil admitted that he foresaw that such a scheme might not be acceptable to Ibn Saud because, if the federation were placed under the King of Iraq, it would greatly increase the resources and prestige of the Hashemite dynasty. He thought, however, that Ibn Saud might be satisfied if it were indicated to him that it would always be possible for him to seek a compensatory increase of power and territory by further expansion within the Arabian peninsula.

The British Ambassador warned him that his proposal would raise a large number of serious political and economic difficulties, for which he could then see no solution, resulting from the impossibility of releasing Palestine and Trans-Jordan from the mandate. Secondly, he emphasised the certain Saudi opposition, which would not be mitigated by further Saudi expansion in Arabia. The British Ambassador did not mention to the Iraqi Foreign Minister that such an expansion would most likely lead Ibn Saud to clashes with the Arabian rulers under British tutelage and therefore, from a British point of view, had to be avoided.[195] G. W. Rendel, who several days later met Dr Naji al-Asil, did not mince words in telling him 'that the solution he had advocated would have no chance whatever of acceptance by His Majesty's Government'.[196] The proposal made in May 1937 by Muhammad 'Ali, the Egyptian Prince (see above, pp. 70–1), fared no better. Although it was regarded as 'far from being mere nonsense', it represented 'a stage in the political development of the Arab countries which will not be reached till a lot of intermediate ditches have been jumped'. Sir Robert Vansittart, the British Foreign Permanent Under-Secretary, fully agreed.[197]

On Halifax's appointment, the Foreign Office again had to deal with Prince Muhammad 'Ali's proposition. It is very clear that to a large extent the Foreign Office retreated at least temporarily to their traditional sceptical attitude. Baggallay again repeated the traditional reasons which had induced them in the past to reject that approach: the jealousy of Ibn Saud; the difficulty of combining Arab states under French tutelage with those under British tutelage or with independent states; the suspicions and hostility of the French; and the reluctance of the Jews. Baggallay was sorry that the practical difficulties were too great, but he could not help, and C. Bentinck solidified his negative reaction by drawing attention to the fact that no good 'will result from bringing the Egyptian Royal Family into discussions about Palestine', since their attitude would be mainly dictated by the wish to enhance the position of the 'House of Mohammed 'Ali' and 'enable King Farouk later on to arrogate to himself the title of Caliph'.[198]

What the British authorities became almost fully convinced of was that involving the Arab states in some way in Palestine affairs, but which still fell short of a unity scheme, would best serve British interests since the 'moderate Arabs outside Palestine' in general and Ibn Saud in particular could exert moderating pressure on the Palestine Arabs.[199] Concurrently, and even as a precondition, the FO was fighting to secure the abandonment of the partition plan and to substitute for it a solution much more acceptable to the Arabs.[200]

The new direction was signalled in November 1937. In a memorandum on a Suggested Alternative Policy for Palestine, Rendel proposed that the new commission, which should examine whether or not partition could be implemented, 'might well be authorised to embark on consultations not only with the non-Palestinian Jews but also with the non-Palestinian Arabs, who should be given opportunities no less favourable than the non-Palestinian Jews of expressing their views'.[201] In another memorandum prepared by the FO for the use of the Foreign Secretary at a Cabinet discussion of the Palestine problem it was stated even more clearly: 'The question of our future policy in Palestine cannot be considered in isolation. The Arabic-speaking Middle Eastern countries form an organic whole and are closely interdependent. Our policy in Palestine cannot fail to react on our whole position in the Middle East, and seriously to affect the course of our future relations with the Middle Eastern Powers, particularly Iraq, Egypt and Saudi Arabia – countries commanding our sea and air routes to the East'. This view was presented by Eden to the Cabinet and was instrumental in turning them against the partition of Palestine.[202]

Anthony Eden resigned from the Cabinet in February 1938 and Lord Halifax was appointed in his stead. The new Foreign Secretary was more conservative in his attitude to Middle Eastern problems and less ready to propose a radically new foundation for British policy there. But he could not stop a process which had already been under way before his appointment. That process was taking place within the Colonial Office.

The perception of non-Arabism as a force to be reckoned with crystallised in the second half of 1938 when the British policy-makers realised how intransigent was the position of the Palestine Arabs, how extreme their opposition to *any* concession with regard to the question of Jewish immigration, how strong, on the other hand, was the Jewish pressure for the continuation, nay the increase, of that immigration owing to the terrible situation which the Jews were facing in the late 1930s in Germany, Poland, Rumania etc., and how strong were the repercussions of the Palestine Arab Rebellion in the neighbouring countries.

The time of stock-taking came after May 1938 when William Ormsby-Gore, the Colonial Secretary who had whole-heartedly supported the policy of partition as recommended by the Peel Commission, resigned. He was succeeded by Malcolm MacDonald who decided to examine the Palestine question in depth. He contacted various Jewish and Arab leaders, heard their views, including those of the Egyptian Prime Minister, and paid a two-day visit to Palestine. He realised that partition was not a practical solution, as the Foreign Office had beforehand argued, since the Jews would not accept a further limitation of the area allotted to them by the Peel Commission, whereas for the Arabs the very idea of a Jewish state, whatever its size, was abhorrent. On the other hand, he was impressed by the fact that, generally speaking, the Egyptian Prime Minister had expressed his view that the Arabs would be ready to discuss a solution on the lines that Lord Samuel had outlined before him (see above, p. 77).[203] At this stage MacDonald had already been convinced that alternative solutions should be examined by a conference in which both Jewish and Arab representatives would participate. This course was encouraged by Sir Harold MacMichael, the High Commissioner for Palestine.[204]

Now MacDonald turned to the crucial question of what should be the British position to be presented at this conference. To decide that he invited representatives of the Departments of State concerned (Foreign, War and Air) and the Palestine Government, including the High Commissioner, to take part in the consultations, which were held in October 1938 by the heads of the Colonial Office (the Secretary of State, the Under-Secretary of State, the Marquess of Dufferin and Ava, the Permanent Under-Secretary Sir Cosmo Parkinson, the Deputy Permanent Under-Secretary Sir John Shuckburgh, the Legal Adviser Sir Grattan Bushe and F. H. Downie and J. C. Sterndale-Bennett of the Middle East Department). During these consultations it became evident that a new attitude was now guiding Britain in Palestine. It became clear to them that the Arab states should be invited to the joint conference on Palestine in order to secure their moderating influence on the Palestine Arabs who would be required to agree to a substantially curtailed Jewish immigration to, and the land purchases in, Palestine. It was assumed that 'when Arab Federation comes up, they [the Arab States] will in any case be concerned'. Palestine, in which the Jews would remain a minority, would gain autonomy and one day join this federation. MacDonald was not sure when this federation would emerge but he wanted it to be quickly. He may have thought that only with Arab Federation as a collateral to his new Palestine policy could he win the consent of the Palestine Arabs. Therefore he suggested that the proposed Palestine Conference discuss 'the whole problem leading up to the federation of the Arab States and relations of the Jews to that'.[205]

The conclusions of these consultations were summarised by the Colonial Office (P. (38)2) and served as the basis for the discussions of the special Cabinet Committee which was appointed to define British positions to be presented at the proposed Conference. This committee included the Prime Minister, Neville Chamberlain, as chairman, the Chancellor of the Exchequer Sir John Simon, the Secretary of State for India the Marquess of Zetland, the Minister for Co-ordination of Defence Sir Thomas Inskip, the Home Secretary Sir Samuel Hoare, the Colonial Secretary Malcolm MacDonald and the Minister of Health Sir Walter Elliott. The Foreign Secretary was represented by Sir Alexander Cadogan, his Office's Permanent Under-Secretary.

This Ministerial Committee accepted the conclusions of the interdepartmental official consultations that the Arab countries neighbouring Palestine should be invited to the proposed conference so they could exercise their 'moderating influence'; that Jewish immigration should be limited and confined to the Jewish part; that both communities should develop self-government in their respective areas; and that, ultimately, one form or another of cantonised Palestine in which the Jews would remain a minority would join an Arab federation. A few weeks before these discussions began the Prime Minister had received a letter of assurance from the Egyptian Prime Minister. It strengthened Chamberlain's and his colleagues' belief in the moderating capability and will of the Arab Governments and it eased the acceptance of the notion that 'Palestine had now become a Pan-Arab question'. The British acceptance of a pan-Arab dimension of the Palestine problem and the curtailment of the Zionist policy were not regarded as a prelude to independence, but rather as a means of safeguarding British strategic needs and positions and transport installations in the Arab countries and Palestine which should by no means be abandoned in view of the general world political situation.[206]

The committee's conclusions were brought on 2 November 1938 before the Cabinet, who adopted them. But unlike the tone of the committee discussions the conclusions did not refer to the desirability of Palestine being included in the future in an Arab federation. It seems that the Cabinet were reluctant to pass final judgement on such a far-reaching issue. But since this committee continued to function during the next six months, up till the convening of the Palestine Conference and during the course of its discussions, the Colonial Secretary continued to preach to his colleagues his view that 'in the long run any satisfactory solution of this matter probably depended upon Palestine being joined in some kind of Federation with certain neighbouring countries. If this was done, it was likely that the Arabs would agree to allow the Jews to have control over a larger area of Palestine than they would be prepared to concede'.[207]

The less-than-total support of this attitude by the FO was manifest in late November 1938. The Department were then making preparations for the Foreign Secretary's scheduled visit to Paris for ministerial discussions there. They assumed that the French would express their fear that in the proposed Palestine Conference the British Government 'should be working for a "confederation" of Arab States, including Palestine, Transjordan and probably Syria, in the hope of settling British difficulties in Palestine by a combination of this nature'. In a brief prepared for the discussion and finally approved by Halifax himself, it was stated that the French could be informed, if they expressed the fear,

> that it is not the intention of His Majesty's Government themselves to put forward such a scheme, but of course there can be no

THE EVER-PRESENT PANACEA – ARAB FEDERATION   113

guarantee that the Arab delegates will not put forward such proposals. There can be no doubt that Arab feeling in Damascus, Jerusalem and elsewhere in the Middle East is drifting towards the idea of confederation. It would be unwise for His Majesty's Government and the French Government openly to oppose the movement; and it should rather be our policy to recognise the fact that this idea of confederation is in the air, and to guide the movement as far as possible along lines which do not run counter to our interests.[208]

In the context of these developments Earl Winterton, who in 1936 had been a partner in Samuel's initiative (see above, p. 75) and was now serving in the government as Chancellor of the Duchy of Lancaster and since March 1938 as a member of the Cabinet, referred to his and Samuel's initiative and to their talk with Nuri al-Sa'id, and the authority of the latter strengthened MacDonald's argument. He put it very clearly 'that we should only obtain a satisfactory settlement if Palestine were to be included in some wider Federation'. In spite of MacDonald's persistence and Winterton's support, their view had not become a fully-fledged policy. It rather reflected a way of thinking which in those days became paramount chiefly in the Colonial Office. Viscount Halifax, the Foreign Secretary, was less enthusiastic, although he did not question MacDonald's basic assumptions and conclusion. He tended to assume that the federal authority in the proposed Arab federation would remain in British hands. Furthermore, he pointed out that a hostile Arab would say that this federal plan meant that the Palestine Arabs were the only Arabs not permitted to form a separate state.[209]

It should be added that Lord Halifax made his position clear after an internal Foreign Office debate. When MacDonald's paper summarising the Colonial Office consultations and recommendations (P (38)2) reached the Foreign Office, it was analysed by L. Baggallay of the Eastern Department, who reached the conclusion that for a long-term policy based on agreement with the Arabs 'nothing but the cessation of Jewish immigration will suffice (immigration is the only point that really matters)', implying that no scheme of Arab federation would do the trick. Anyway he did not believe it was possible to include a Jewish state in one Arab federation, which 'has clearly got to come but at present the Arabs are not united among themselves as to what form it should take and we do not want to offend any of them if we can avoid it by taking sides too openly at this stage'. This reserved reaction was fully endorsed by C. W. Baxter, the head of the Eastern Department. Halifax, however, realised that total suspension of Jewish immigration was not 'practical politics' and he could not present this opinion as an alternative to MacDonald's recommendation. Thus, he did not oppose them in full but rather expressed an implied reservation.[210]

On the eve of the St James's Palestine Conference the FO had a last-minute chance to examine again their attitude to the Arab federation approach to the Palestine question, since another scheme, this time of A. W. Lawrence (see above, p. 78), was brought before them. After a thorough discussion they concluded 'that the idea of federation, whatever its own merits', was not 'going to be of much help as regards the question of the Jewish National Home'. Accordingly, Vansittart informed Lawrence that they could not accept his proposition. Vansittart stated that even if an Arab federation were to be offered to the Arabs, there would be not much chance 'of the Arabs accepting the formation of a Jewish autonomous province in Palestine, with powers to control its immigration'.[211]

Given this attitude by the Foreign Office, MacDonald could not enforce his view. He conceded that the question would be brought again before the Palestine Cabinet Committee when they would be framing the precise policy to be submitted to the Palestine Conference.[212] This concession really ended the Colonial Office's initiative. When the Palestine Cabinet Committee were discussing British Palestinian policy concurrently with the Palestine St James's Conference it became evident that the goodwill of the Arab states could not be attained and that they could not exercise a moderating influence on the Palestine Arabs owing to the intransigent position of the Palestine Arab delegation.[213] Hence one of the basic assumptions which had led MacDonald to adopt a pan-Arab attitude to the Palestine problem was proved false. He, so one is led to conclude, left his ideas in abeyance and never again during his ministerial service raised the matter.

MacDonald's office as Colonial Secretary came to an end on the formation of the war-time coalition government headed by Winston Churchill. His successor was Lord Lloyd. As we have already noted (see above, pp. 77–8) Lord Lloyd had been engaged in 1937–8 in an attempt to find a solution of the Palestine problem by means of an Arab federation. Now he had to deal with that matter when the burden of authority and responsibility was laid upon his shoulders. In July 1940 the initiative of Professor H. A. R. Gibb (see above, p. 79) was put before him and he and the Foreign Secretary had to react to it.

The Foreign and Colonial Offices took up similar positions to those they adopted towards the Philby scheme, which was drawn up two months later (see above, pp. 94–6). The Foreign Office officials did not like it at all, whereas the Colonial Office was more moderate. H. M. Eyres of the Foreign Office's Eastern Department did not think Gibb's approach 'hopeful'. Lacy Baggallay did not believe that it 'would really secure the Zionists an autonomous area either large or small in the long run, whatever promises the Arabs might give them at the outset', in view of the jealousies of the Arab rulers, particularly Ibn Saud, the objections of the French authorities in Syria and possible doubts on the part of Turkey. But even if Gibb were right, he emphasised, 'I feel that we ought certainly not to accept the position that the initiative must come from His Majesty's Government. The question of federation is primarily for the Arabs and, if the Zionists think that federation would be an advantage for them, it is for the Zionists to carry out their negotiations with the Arabs themselves, indicating what they can do to help the federation (finance etc.) and what they would have to receive in return'.

According to Weizmann Lord Halifax, the Foreign Secretary, adopted a much more optimistic view of an Arab Confederation as a solution of the Palestine problem. He had told Weizmann that 'Arab Confederation ... would have two advantages, first the Arabs would not feel that they were in danger of being swamped by the Jews, and, secondly, the Jews would become a part of a great organisation which might give them an open door to the Near East'. However, Halifax's about-turn, if it were true at all, was irrelevant to the decision-making process which was going on inside the Foreign Office in August 1940. The matter was discussed and decided upon by not too high officials and, according to the relevant file, the senior authority to be consulted was Sir Horace Seymour, the Assistant Under-Secretary.[214]

The Colonial Office shared the view that the federation's initiative should not come from the government, but they thought that if the Jews once got into negotiations with the Arabs about federation the British Government, 'while they would not be able to bring pressure to bear on the Arabs, ... would use their influence – or their good offices – with the Arabs', or something of that sort. The Foreign Office opposed this formula and Sir John Shuckburgh, the Colonial Deputy Under-Secretary, and F.H. Downie gave it up. Accordingly, Lloyd's reply to Gibb was favourable in principle but totally non-committal. On 24 July he wrote:

> I am by no means out of sympathy with the idea of Arab federation and I realise that such a development might well assist in the solution of the Arab-Jewish problem. I incline to the opinion held by my predecessor [MacDonald], and by many others who have had to deal with the difficult problems of the Middle East that some form of federation is the ultimate destiny of the Arab states which formerly belonged to the Ottoman Empire.... Where I cannot agree is with the view that in the matter of Arab Federation the initiative must come from the British Government. On the contrary it seems to me essential that the impetus should come from the Arab peoples themselves.... As regard the Arab-Jewish problem in Palestine ... it is for the Jews themselves ... to obtain ... the agreement of the Palestine Arabs or, in the event of an Arab federation, the agreement of the Arab States.[215]

Lloyd's words strengthen the impression that one gets from his dealing with the Philby scheme in the summer of 1940 (see above, pp. 89–90) that his positive attitude to the Arab federation approach to the Palestine problem was stronger than Halifax's and that he was involved personally in framing his office's policy in this respect. This impression is corroborated by the words he used when he wrote about the latest development to Sir Harold MacMichael:

> We have had indications from one or two sources lately that Jewish minds are thinking on the lines of a self-contained Jewish unit in a federation, covering Palestine, Syria and, I suppose, Trans-Jordan. The idea is not without its attraction. I have always felt that there can be no real solution of the Palestine problem within the present territorial limits of Palestine, and it may be that, with the position as fluid as it is at present in Syria, an opening will occur which will make big political alterations possible in your part of the world.[216]

Gibb's initiative left its mark on a Colonial Secretary who had even before assuming office been supporting this approach. The change of fortunes in Syria reinforced his belief in the usefulness of that approach because it removed a friendly France from the system of factors that had to be reckoned with and because it led many people to believe that when victory came the government of Syria could not remain in the treacherous hands of Vichy Frenchmen. MacMichael's reaction was similar in principle to Lloyd's view. The former used historical and geographical arguments to show why Palestine and Syria constituted one country which should be reunited. However, he had one important reservation; the Jewish unit should be of 'reasonable size (say Sharon plus)' otherwise the Arabs were not going to agree to.[217]

This view did not stop Lord Lloyd from searching for a solution although it really made it clear that what the Arabs might be ready to concede stood a long way from the minimum the Jews might be satisfied with. It seems to us that one way or another Lloyd made his views known to Sir John Martin, Churchill's private secretary, who incorporated them in a note on 21 November 1940 prepared for his master on the Jewish refugee problem in the wake of the decision to intern on the island of Mauritius 1700 illegal Jewish refugees who that month had reached the shores of Palestine. He concluded that the only way to avoid the embarrassment caused by the establishment of 'a British Dachau' was to change course in Palestine. He continued:

> We must find some way to give the Jews an area in which they can be masters of their own fate and partly of their own immigration regulations. Partition within the limits of Mandated Palestine on

> the lines of the Royal Commission is not practical politics, but *the changed situation in Syria* [my italics] does give the opportunity to consider with new hope the possibility of some form of federation (embracing at least Palestine, Syria and Trans Jordan) in which the Jews (not necessarily confined to the coastal bloc alone) could have an independent Eretz Israel. They would have to sacrifice some of their immediate territorial ambitions in exchange for independence in a small area and the prospect of indirect influence throughout the wide limits of the federation. On the other hand, the Arabs of the larger areas will more easily be persuaded to concede the Jews an area which would seem an impossibly large amputation from the small territory of Palestine.[218]

Churchill did not react to that démarche, but it may have contributed to his decision to try to carry out the similar (Philby) plan of which he had heard from Weizmann (see above, p. 92).

The dramatic developments in the Middle East in May–June 1941 which induced Churchill to try a new opening in the search for a solution to the Palestine problem also drove other interested figures to act with the same aim. One of them was Professor H. A. R. Gibb who with the staff of the Royal Institute of International Affairs prepared a detailed memorandum on Arab Federation and submitted it to the Foreign Office in mid-June. He pointed out, *inter alia*, that the question of Jewish immigration was the most contentious issue between the Jews and the Arabs and it would form an insuperable obstacle to an agreement directly negotiated between representatives of the two peoples.

> But if it became possible for the British Government, either alone or in association with other Governments, to initiate negotiations on the future of the National Home *as an integral part of discussions directed towards comprehensive settlement in greater Syria* [my italics], the chances of reconciling Arab and Jewish claims would be immensely improved.

Gibb's memorandum was referred for comment to the Political Intelligence Department, with whom the RIIA were associated during the war. Its head, Humphrey Bowman, put the stress on a different aspect — the need to implement the 1939 White Paper. He added that 'to secure the Arab's acceptance [of that statement] we can now offer in addition Arab federation'. But, 'unless we implement the White Paper we shall have the latent hostility of the Arabs everywhere — and federation may be a danger' to Britain, since it would be instrumental in co-ordinating Arab efforts against Britain. But, on the other hand, 'the putting into force of the assurances contained in the White Paper goes a long way towards the restoration of such confidence on the Arab side'. Then it would be worthwhile to pursue a policy aiming at the formation of a federation of Syria, Lebanon, Trans-Jordan and Palestine, which would include a Jewish semi-autonomous state whose frontiers resulted artificially from 'a political bargain between Great Britain and France' and from the Balfour Declaration.

R. A. Butler, the Under-Secretary, well understood that so long as Churchill headed the Government there would be no chance of implementing the constitutional provisions of the White Paper because the 'Cabinet won't agree'. He accentuated the hopeless situation in which Bowman's policy was placed with a gastronomic example: 'I feel that any treatise on Federation should be of a more "toad in the hole" variety, e.g. the Jewish Home should definitely be ensconced in the batter. The above is most carefully worked out, but the teeth keep shoving the sausage to the side'. And in any case any British offer of Arab federation should be 'pretty vague'.[219]

In July 1941 when the occupation of Syria faced the British Government with another acute question — the future of Syria — the Foreign Office realised that it had become impossible to treat the Palestine problem in isolation. They reached the conclusion that 'the real problem before us is how, if at all, we can solve the Zionist problem within a wider framework than that of Palestine, i.e. by bringing Syria, the Lebanon and TJ, together with Palestine, into some comprehensive arrangement'.[220] And the combination of these latest two views really shaped the Foreign Office's attitude: only a Palestine in which the policy of the 1939 White Paper had been implemented could join an Arab Federation, since if such a policy had not been carried out, the general hostility of the Arabs would prevent any cooperation with Britain, which was an essential condition for the successful formation of an Arab federation, whether smaller or larger.

The Colonial Office, too, became alert to the changes which took place in the Middle East in May–July 1941 and to their possible repercussions. The Colonial Secretary Lord Moyne succeeded Lord Lloyd in February 1941. Probably his officials worried lest he stuck to Lloyd's positive view regarding Arab federation as a solution to the Palestine problem. At all events, upon Moyne's assuming office F. H. Downie prepared a detailed memorandum entitled 'Arab Federation'. Although this dealt mainly with the general question of Arab federation (see below, p. 242), it also referred to the Palestine aspect and stated unequivocally that the Arabs were 'so bitterly opposed to the creation of a Jewish state in any part of Palestine however small' and to Jewish immigration thereto that nothing, federation included, would induce them to change their hostile attitude.[221]

However, Moyne was more impressed by Lloyd's views as expressed in the exchange of letters between Lloyd and MacMichael of the previous

THE EVER-PRESENT PANACEA – ARAB FEDERATION   119

September–October, and remained loyal to Lloyd's opinion (see above, p. 116). His attitude was indicated on 3 June when a Zionist delegation composed of Professors Brodetsky and Namier came to complain that the Jews had not been mentioned in Eden's Mansion House speech of 29 May. In his reply he stated that Weizmann 'had favoured the idea of an Arab Federation as likely to work out favourably for Jewish aspirations', clearly implying that he held the same view.[222]

And indeed he soon set out to ascertain whether or not that view was realistic. A month later, with the concurrence of the Foreign Office, Lord Moyne sent a most secret private and personal telegram to Sir Harold MacMichael as follows:

> View has been expressed in various quarters that recent developments in the Middle East, and in particular promise of independence to Syria, afford opportunity for comprehensive settlement which would be more acceptable than the White Paper policy both to Arabs and Jews. *One possible solution might be some form of Arab federation in which Jewish enclave, within some such geographical limits as those proposed by Peel Commission, would take its place as autonomous unit* [my italics]. I am fully alive to all the difficulties of this or any other solution of the intractable problem of Zionism, but we shall certainly be pressed to find some way out of the present morass and I am anxious to lose as little time as possible in setting our ideas into order. I should be grateful for your views. Do you see any prospect in the changed circumstance of the Jews being able to persuade the Arabs to accept a solution on any such lines?[223]

MacMichael's reply was not encouraging. He thought that the Arabs might agree 'if only the Jews would be content with a small token state based on Tel-Aviv'; there was no doubt that they would not. 'Any attempt to give the Jews an enclave roughly coterminous with that suggested by the Royal Commission would undoubtedly lead to a fresh Arab revolt, as well as being open to objections which rightly led to the rejection of partition by His Majesty's Government'. MacMichael suggested implementation of the *principles* of the White Paper (an Advisory and later a Legislative Council instead of the nomination of Palestinians as Heads of Departments) and continuation of British rule. He added that a 'settled Palestine' one day 'could join a larger federation if such materialised'.[224]

MacMichael's view provided a lively discussion in the Colonial Office. His alternative solutions were not accepted, whereas Moyne's attitude was hardly backed by his officials who required that any initiative for Arab federation should come from the Arabs themselves. They pointed out that the Syrian question had not yet been settled and the proposed federation was premature. Sir John Shuckburgh summed up their views by stating that 'we had better carry on as we are and wait for more propitious times before attempting high issues of principle or policy'. And Sir Cosmo Parkinson added: 'Of course, if Jews and Arabs will get together and reach some agreement based upon a federal scheme, so much the better; naturally H.M. Government would welcome any such agreed scheme. But is there any serious hope of this coming to pass?'

Moyne was, it seems, disappointed by the reply and the following discussion. He remarked: 'I doubt whether a discussion at this stage is likely to prove very fruitful'.[225] Disappointed as he was, he was not discouraged. On 6 August he wrote a letter to MacMichael, mainly devoted to describing his talks with Weizmann about the Philby plan (see above, p. 95), but he used it to restate his views although indirectly. He stressed that the Arab federation of Philby's scheme could come in two stages, Saudi Arabia being excluded in the first one. Thus what would emerge in the first stage corresponded to Moyne's and his predecessor's concept. In another talk with protagonists of the Philby plan (Brendan Bracken and Firoz Khan Noon) Moyne stated his view more clearly that the position in regard to Syria and Lebanon should be kept fluid so that there would be a possibility of making some federal scheme for Syria and the Lebanon, Palestine and Trans-Jordan more attractive to Arabs by altering the southern boundary of Syria/Lebanon and transferring to Syria/Lebanon part of the northern area of Palestine which contained a large Arab population. Moyne went further and suggested that his idea should be discussed with General de Gaulle in his capacity as the head of the Free French authorities when he came to London.[226] In holding those views Lord Moyne was rather isolated in his office. And in view of the frequent changes in the political head of that office and the permanency of the top officials, this phenomenon was very significant indeed.

And indeed, being isolated, Moyne could not force his view. Both the FO and CO concluded that 'unless we are prepared to go ahead with the White Paper, there are no other immediate steps that can be taken'.[227] This joint conclusion was presented to the Minister of State resident in the Middle East as a basis for his Ministerial Conference in London. There is no doubt that the whole issue would thus have subsided but for the intervention of the Prime Minister in connection with his attempt at forcing an adoption of the Philby scheme (see above, pp. 93–4). As we have already seen, the Ministerial Conference rejected the Philby scheme against the wishes of the Prime Minister. But under his pressure they decided to view more favourably the basic assumption of the Philby scheme, i.e. Arab federation as a solution of the Palestine problem, and accordingly concluded: 'A scheme of Arab federation had considerable attractions and, if feasible, seemed to offer great advantages from the point of view of a solution of the Palestine problem'. They did not overlook the attendant difficulties and therefore decided not to sound the parties concerned in the meantime. They also took a practical step and invited the Middle East Official Committee 'to examine forthwith the various forms which a scheme of Arab federation might take, and to report on their advantages and disadvantages and their practicability. In making this examination the Committee *would pay special regard to the help which such a scheme would afford to a solution of the Palestine problem* [my italics]'.[228] This decision disregarded the White Paper policy and stood in direct opposition to the considered views of the FO and CO officials. This done, Moyne could feel that his approach was vindicated. He stuck to his original position and wrote to teh Prime Minister: 'If applied to a smaller area [namely excluding Saudi Arabia and Iraq] a federal system might be the means of achieving a partition scheme for Palestine, which would be more acceptable than that of the Peel Commission'.[229]

Not for long could Moyne enjoy that feeling. In October 1941 the Middle East Official Committee under the chairmanship of Sir John Shuckburgh began to discuss the matter in accordance with the decision of the Ministerial Conference decision. They had before them a memorandum and a cable expressing the views of MacMichael, the views of the Colonial Office despatches from the British Ambassadors in Cairo and Baghdad (Sir Miles Lampson and Sir Kinahan Cornwallis), the Foreign Office's views and a few other documents.

MacMichael questioned the very foundations of the Ministerial Conference's conclusion. He wrote:

> The likelihood that the path of Zionism would be smoothed by 'unification' or 'federation' would lessen the chances of solution by that method being found acceptable ... I doubt, therefore, whether Federation will provide a solution for our troubles or those of the 'Arabs' or the Jews. On the contrary, it is arguable that the 'Arabs' will be more susceptible of control and less dangerous if they remain divided into comparatively small units, ... and that we, for our part, shall find the task of furthering the good of both parties, while safeguarding our own interests, considerably eased if we retain whatever control we may now have in each unit ...[230]

And in another cable MacMichael stressed that whatever the practicability of the various suggestions to solve the Palestine problem everything was dependent on 'whether H.M.G. is willing to proclaim its intentions to stand by the policy of the White Paper in its broader aspects'. 'Otherwise', he added, 'H.M.G. will certainly be suspected of thinking of federation in terms of Jewish rather than Arabic Consolidation.'[231]

The Foreign Office was not too pleased with MacMichael's note which was regarded as 'rather too negative for what we want'.[232] Therefore in inviting the views of the British Ambassadors to Cairo and Baghdad they were implicitly but clearly guided to bypass the Palestine problem.[233] Therefore their replies mainly contributed to the discussion of the broader question of Arab federation on its own merits and not as a means of solving the Palestine question (see below, p. 253). When Lampson briefly touched upon that issue he advised confining the British rôle 'to vague expressions', and to reaffirmation and expedited implementation of the decisions embodied in the White Paper.[234] Cornwallis accepted MacMichael's judgement that among the Palestine Arabs 'interest in federation is waning because they suspect the motives of the Jews who are pushing it'.[235]

No wonder that C. W. Baxter, the head of the Eastern Department of the Foreign Office, could summarise these views as 'neither Jerusalem, Baghdad nor Cairo seem to have any constructive suggestions about the help which a scheme of federation might afford to a solution of the Palestine problem', and this view was endorsed by the Egyptian Department and by Sir Horace Seymour.[236] S. E. V. Luke, for the Colonial Office, quite naturally reached the same conclusions and gladly pointed out 'that Sir Kinahan Cornwallis makes the point that the internal political questions of Syria and Palestine must be settled first, i.e. that federation, far from being the solution for those problems, will in fact be gravely prejudiced unless a prior solution has been found. This seems to me to be the core of the whole question'.[237]

The Middle East Official Committee began their work on 8 October. They included Sir John Shuckburgh, in the chair, E. B. Boyd, S. E. V. Luke, Sir William Battershill and Sir Bernard Reilly (all of the Colonial Office), C. G. L. Syers (Treasury), Major L. P. Kirwan and Captain R. F. Stileman (War Office), Group Captain A. H. Willetts (Air Ministry), C. W. Baxter and H. A. Caccia (Foreign Office), Colonel R. W. Spraggett (Admiralty) and R. T. Pell (India Office). The composition of the committee gave the Colonial and Foreign Offices a natural advantage and it was no wonder that in the end their views prevailed. The discussion and the preparation of the committee report were mainly carried out between their representatives and finally adopted by the committee. The only factor that prevented these officials rejecting altogether the idea of Arab federation as a means of solving the Palestine problem was the positive attitude in its favour of Churchill and of the Ministerial Conference who had invited their (the officials') views.

Therefore the committee presented their conclusions in a somewhat cautious way. After having stated that 'we do not rule out all possibility that a scheme of Arab federation might assist in a solution of the Palestine problem', they admitted with resignation that this could not be squared with a Jewish state of anything like the Peel Report size. Therefore their general conclusion was that 'there is no great likelihood that any scheme for political federation which would include Palestine could be successfully launched unless the Arabs and the Jews in Palestine had acquired a greater readiness for compromise and collaboration than exists at present'.[238]

The Report should have gone to the Cabinet for a final consideration. But the Foreign Office preferred to wait first for the reactions of the Minister of State. Then in February 1942 Captain Oliver Lyttelton changed his job in the Cabinet, and the Report waited for the new Minister of State, Richard Casey, to take office and prepare his view. However, in April a comprehensive discussion of British strategic needs in the Middle East became more urgent, and in accordance with the view of M.A. Rucker of the Minister of State Office the discussion of the Middle East Official Committee Report was postponed indefinitely or, at least, until the Joint Planning Staff had submitted a report on British strategic needs in the Middle East during and following the war. This postponement did not mean the rejection of the Report, because it was decided by the offices concerned that the operative recommendations about the study of measures to promote economic and cultural cooperation among the Arab countries would be carried out (see below, pp. 231–2).[239]

This considered judgement changed the character of the discussion of the Arab federation as a solution to the Palestine problem. A month after it was submitted, Lord Moyne, the main protagonist of that view, left the government (to be appointed in August 1942 as Deputy Minister of State Resident in the Middle East) and his successor Viscount Cranborne did not follow MacDonald's, Lloyd's and Moyne's views. In a farewell memorandum on Palestine which Lord Moyne wrote on leaving office and which was mainly devoted to the *Patria* tragedy and to the broader issue of Jewish immigration to Palestine, Moyne admitted that there was no chance of implementing his preferred way. 'A solution for the Zionist claims', he wrote, 'must therefore be found within the British Mandate possibly with the addition of Syria.'[240] But now he went a step further. Up to now all the proposals for the formation of an Arab federation had assumed that a Jewish state in Palestine, whatever its size, would be part of a broader federation. Now, on the contrary, Moyne realised that this assumption would not work. In February 1942 the Zionist demand for a much freer Jewish immigration to Palestine mainly from Rumania and the Balkan countries gathered momentum, accentuated by the *Struma* tragedy which cost the lives of 762 Jewish refugees when the ship sank in the Black Sea after being refused entry to Palestine. Lord Moyne, who was personally responsible for the tragedy, drew a farreaching conclusion. He now suggested 'a division of the British Mandate between the Jewish State on the West and a combined Arab, Palestinian and Trans-Jordan Territory on the East'.[241]

Thus Moyne began a new phase in the search for Arab federation;

it should be a smaller one (Syria, Trans-Jordan and Arab Palestine) and the Jewish state would not be part of it. These ideas played an important role in the discussions of the Palestine problem which took place in the second half of 1943 (see pp. 128 ff). In the meantime, throughout most of 1942, the search for a solution to the Palestine problem through some kind of Arab federation did not stand still. The initiative this time came from Sir Harold MacMichael, the High Commissioner for Palestine, who realised that the handling of the problem could no longer be muddled through and that the British Government had to decide upon a permanent solution which should be implemented in the near future. In London at the end of 1941 the Colonial Secretary felt that thorough thought should be devoted to the subject. He was sure that in spite of the Middle East Official Committee's negative conclusions on the question of Arab federation, the circulation of their report would 'revive the discussion of federation as a possible solvent of the Palestine question'. He mentioned that Weizmann had 'long been preaching that within the framework of federation room can be found for a Jewish state and there are indications that this idea has considerable support in the Cabinet', alluding, no doubt, to the Prime Minister's support of the Philby plan and reflecting Moyne's own attitude to the conceptual basis of the Arab federation approach. In order to be able to face the growing Zionist pressure Moyne wanted MacMichael to come to London and take part in consultations about a possible solution.[242]

Already at the end of 1941 MacMichael had tried to force upon the government a drastic change in their Palestine policy. He suggested abolishing the Palestine Mandate and substituting for it a new mandate in which there would be no place for a Jewish Agency, or ruling Palestine as a Crown Colony.[243] Since he got no reply to this far-reaching proposal, he brought new ideas when he came to London in April 1942 for the consultations. These ideas were put in a memorandum entitled 'Zionism and Arabism in the Middle East' and MacMichael repeated them on 2 April before the Heads of the Colonial Office and the following day in a joint meeting with representatives of the Foreign Office. He realised 'that nothing could be done at present in the matter of the termination of the Mandate and the abrogation of the privileged position of the Jewish Agency based on the Mandate'. Therefore he suggested two basic principles: (a) continuation of foreign control for an indefinite period because of the paramount European, and British in particular, strategic interests; and (b) gradual union of Syria, the Lebanon, Trans-Jordan and a binational Palestine. The foreign control could take the form of a supreme supervisory committee composed of the representatives of Great Britain, France and the USA who would be responsible for defence and financial guarantees. He stressed that 'closer union of Syria, Palestine, the Lebanon and Trans-Jordan was in accord not only with the historic unity of these territories but also with the present conceptions of the lines on which a general post-war settlement would have to be made'. He preferred a federal union, but did not think that this was the sole form of closer union and had in mind that the bi-national state of Palestine would probably be built on a parity basis.

By the time the consultations took place Lord Moyne, who shared MacMichael's basic ideas, had already left the Colonial Office, and so MacMichael could not find any support either in the CO or in the FO, who did not like these ideas at all. Harold Macmillan, the Colonial Under-Secretary, pointed to the need to ensure 'generous emigration opportunities to Palestine' for European Jews in order to solve the European-Jewish problem and as 'one of the essentials of the post-war settlement'; Sir Maurice Peterson quoted the findings of the Middle East Official Committee to the effect that 'any federation had to arise from the spontaneous desire and effort of the Arabs themselves' and not to be imposed by the great Powers; C.W. Baxter raised the question of how Amir 'Abdallah would fit into the scheme; and the new Colonial Secretary Viscount Cranborne (who had just succeeded Lord Moyne) wanted to know whether this scheme met British commitments to the Free French movement. At the end it was agreed not to take any action but to invite the departments concerned to examine MacMichael's proposals in detail.[244]

When the Colonial and Foreign Offices made the required detailed examination their initial negative attitude was not mitigated. On the contrary, new negative arguments were now raised. In the Foreign Office they did not believe in the workability of a bi-national regime in Palestine, but on the whole they abhorred the idea of inviting the USA and France to share the control of Palestine. The French Department of the FO stated that the French had always been 'very suspicious of our attitude towards Arab Federation' and they 'can be expected to oppose any scheme of the kind'. And the American Department expected an American suspicious reaction lest the British tried to entangle the Americans. Furthermore the Foreign Office officials realised that inside the proposed foreign-controlled federation the Syrians would enjoy less independence than had been promised to them and they could be expected to oppose the scheme; and, decisively, in the midst of the discussion H. Caccia discovered that Britain's vital interests of oil and communications in the Middle East, which were far larger than those of the Americans or the French, might be endangered, because 'French and American oil interests could vote us down if they got together'. Sir Maurice Peterson, who was in charge of Middle Eastern affairs in the FO, summarised the discussion by stressing that any form of Arab federation under the supervision of three foreign States would be quite useless; that nothing should be told to the Americans; and that no fresh discussion should be re-opened by the Middle East Official Committee.[245]

This deliberation is one of the very rare occasions during Anthony Eden's office as Foreign Secretary in which he took part in discussion of a Palestine or a Middle Eastern question. His participation exhibits the importance of that discussion and it shed light on his views. He minuted his agreement with the necessity to prevent any possible damage to British oil interests by the French and the Americans; he endorsed the view that the Americans should not be informed; and in general he accepted Peterson's final summary.[246]

The Foreign Office's views were put in a letter to the Colonial Office and generally accepted by them. Accordingly, they prepared a draft reply to MacMichael which virtually rejected his proposals. The fact that in the meantime, on 7 June, MacMichael repeated his views in a more coherent way in a special despatch did not change anyone's views in the Foreign and the Colonial Offices, but only caused another round of oral and written discussions and another negative reply to MacMichael,[247] the tone of which was made less 'crushing' at the insistence of Viscount Cranborne.[248] MacMichael was unconvinced and on 5 September he again wrote to Lord Cranborne, expressing his belief 'that no satisfactory settlement [of the Palestine problem] can be achieved without unification and control in some form or another' and that 'unification is desired by Arabs and Jews alike and is "historically" inevitable'.[249] However, the FO refused to reconsider their position,[250] and Cranborne had to reject MacMichael's latest plea.[251]

Apparently, MacMichael tried to enlist Arab and Jewish support for his scheme. One of his subordinates, Alec S. Kirkbride, the British Resident in 'Amman, made no secret of his favourable attitude towards a scheme which was identical to MacMichael's and tried to convince both Arab and Jewish leaders of its usefulness.[252] But it never reached any serious stage of having a strong local following. The fact that the Palestine Arabs suspected that the Jews were behind such a scheme was enough to nip in the bud any possible support that it might otherwise have won among them.[253] Also Sir Edward Spears, the British Minister to Syria and Lebanon, reported to the same effect that the Syrians were very much afraid of a powerful 'Zion'. Consequently, he added that even those 'who are keenest on some form of union with the rest of the Arab world would for the most part fight shy of such a combination [i.e. a Federation including a Jewish unit in Palestine]'.[254] Thus by such reports any support for MacMichael's scheme that could have grown in London was extinguished.

Therefore, at the beginning of 1943 the Palestine question stood where it had been since 1939: the White Paper was still considered as the basis of British policy, although the implementation of its constitutional provision was frozen. However all other political circumstances had changed: (a) the Jewish demand for the abolition of the White Paper

THE EVER-PRESENT PANACEA – ARAB FEDERATION

(the Biltmore Resolution) and for the gates of Palestine to be opened to immigration was becoming stronger and stronger especially after the worst possible news on the situation of Jews in German-occupied Europe proved to be true; (b) the opposite move of Nuri al-Sa'id only succeeded in triggering off an Egyptian counter-move (see chapter 1, pp. 55–6); (c) Allied victories in Egypt and North Africa heralded in the autumn of 1942 negated any danger of German occupation and convinced all people concerned that Britain could again decide the fortunes of the Middle East countries and peoples; (d) the British became anxious as a result of the amount of support that the Jews could muster in the USA; and (e) British officials dealing with Palestine became aware of the approaching date, 31 March 1944, when all Jewish immigration to Palestine, in accordance with the White Paper, had to stop, unless Arab consent had been granted.[255]

British policy-makers were aware of all these developments and tried to find solutions. Outstanding among them beginning in March 1943 was a British attempt to come to an agreement with the American Government on a joint declaration to the effect that there was no British or American commitment to the establishment of a Jewish state, or, at least, that there was no room for any serious discussion of the Palestine problem before the end of the war, a move which was thwarted in Washington only at the last moment.[256] The British Foreign and Colonial Offices continued to discuss the situation and to look for possible solutions; the CO thinking mainly of an answer to the imminent question of finding a policy for the period following 31 March 1944, whereas the FO was more interested in reaching a permanent anti-Zionist solution based on the implementation of the White Paper policy. In April 1943 both Offices were trying to compose a joint memorandum which would serve as a basis for a Cabinet discussion of future Palestine policy.

This trend was suddenly and abruptly reversed by Churchill's intervention, which resulted in a new direction in the search for a Palestine policy within which the idea of an Arab federation, although a limited one, again figured. Churchill was well aware of what was going on and did not hide his disapproval.[257] Then he got an alarming letter from Weizmann which induced him to act. Written on 2 April 1943, while he was still in the USA, Weizmann's letter complained about declarations by Viscount Cranborne and Colonel Oliver Stanley, Colonial Secretary since November 1942, that the White Paper remained the established policy of His Majesty's Government with regard to Palestine and against other British steps intended to buy off Arab goodwill. He appealed to Churchill to arrest this 'fatal process'.[258] Churchill promptly reacted by asking Cranborne and Stanley, a copy having been sent to Eden, to comment on Weizmann's criticism before he circulated Weizmann's letter to the Cabinet.[259] The replies of Cranborne and Stanley did not quieten Churchill, whereas Eden prompted Churchill to initiate a comprehensive Cabinet discussion of Britain's Palestine policy.[260]

Mr. Leo Amery, the Secretary of State for India, and perhaps the closest and most loyal political associate that Churchill had, intervened in this exchange of notes and praised Churchill for raising the issue. But he went further and put forward his view of how to solve the Palestine entanglement. In brief, he suggested the partition of Palestine and the establishment of 'a loose Syria-Palestine-Transjordan Federation'.[261] In a letter to Anthony Eden Amery repeated once more the worn cliché that 'Arab or probably in the first instance Levant federation of a very loose kind is probably the only solution of the Zionist tangle'.[262] In a further letter to Nuri al-Sa'id he put forward the main argument in favour of the Arab federation approach to the Palestine problem. He wrote: 'I have always inclined to the belief that by fitting the Jewish National Home into the wider framework of an Arab Federation or commonwealth the fears of the local Arab population of Palestine would be most reasonably assuaged'.[263]

As he had promised on 27 April Churchill circulated to the Cabinet his Note with which he enclosed his May 1939 speech against the White Paper and in which he stressed that although Britain had certainly treated the Arabs very well by having installed the Hashemites on the throne of Iraq, by having maintained 'Abdallah in Trans-Jordan and by having asserted the right of self-government for the Arabs of Syria, the Arabs had reacted by the rebellion in Iraq. He ended by claiming that 'they have created no new claims upon the Allies should we be victorious'.[264]

It is worth noting that this time Churchill did not revert to his favourite solution – an Arab federation under Ibn Saud including a Jewish state. A few weeks earlier Ibn Saud had expressed his anti-Zionist views in an interview to an American journalist and the British policy-makers took note. Secondly, Churchill was certainly aware of the changing financial situation of Ibn Saud since he had put forward the Philby scheme before his colleagues in 1941. And, thirdly, Churchill may have realised that the Americans were not going to support the scheme and certainly not take part in its enforcement. More than a year had already elapsed since he had encouraged Weizmann to go to the USA and try to convert Roosevelt, and nothing had happened. The only logical conclusion he could draw was that Weizmann had failed in his mission. Therefore when the discussion in the British Cabinet began Churchill did not put forward this plan again.

Churchill's Note opened a discussion of the Palestine problem among the Cabinet members in the form of an exchange of memoranda, which took place in May–June 1943. The possibility of solving the Palestine problem by means of an Arab federation was mentioned in three of these papers. In the first, Viscount Cranborne, former Colonial

THE EVER-PRESENT PANACEA – ARAB FEDERATION 129

Secretary and now Lord Privy Seal, mentioned among four possible solutions (without preferring one to another) of the Palestine problem, two which are of interest to our discussion, namely, 'the creation of a Palestinian Jewish State with the present boundaries within an Arab Confederation, or a confederation of a more limited type, including Palestine, Trans-Jordan, Syria and the Lebanon, which could absorb a larger number of Jewish immigrants, though it would not be a specifically Jewish state; or a portion of Palestine, or a reversion to Crown Colony Government.'[265] Oliver Lyttelton's memorandum, which he had prepared a year earlier on his return from Cairo where he had been serving as first Minister of State Resident in the Middle East and which he thought was suitable to be read during the recent debate, did not regard the Federation idea as something which might bring relief to Palestine, since he did not 'see that to add the Jewish problem is going to ease its [the Arab Federation] delivery; on the contrary, it would surely miscarry'.[266] In the third, Sir Stafford Cripps, the Minister of Aircraft Production, thought that Britain had to persist in her 'attempt to establish a bi-national State (as we succeeded in establishing in Canada). If we can do it within wider federal grouping – including, Syria, Lebanon and Transjordan – so much the better'.[267]

This discussion must have encouraged Churchill since it revealed that he could hope to reverse the policy of the White Paper. On the other hand, it showed that support for the Arab federation approach was far from being overwhelming. Anyway, it sufficed to convince Churchill that he could arrest the process which the Foreign and the Colonial Offices were leading. Therefore the War Cabinet meeting of 2 July at Churchill's instigation passed a resolution to establish a special Palestine Cabinet Committee whose composition and terms of reference were practically left to Churchill to decide. No wonder that for both these reasons the committee reflected a Zionist bias.[268]

As members of the Committee Churchill appointed on 4 July Herbert Morrison (Home Secretary and a prominent Labour leader) as Chairman, Viscount Cranborne (Lord Privy Seal, Conservative), Colonel Oliver Stanley (Colonial Secretary, Conservative), Leopold Amery (India Secretary, Conservative) and Sir Archibald Sinclair (Air Secretary and the Liberal Leader). Anthony Eden, the Foreign Secretary, protested against the inclusion of Amery, the most pro-Zionist Tory politician, and the exclusion of the Foreign Office. He could not persuade Churchill to exclude Amery, who was too much of a Zionist for Eden's taste, for that was exactly the reason why Churchill appointed him, as well as Morrison and Sinclair who were also well known for their strong pro-Zionist views. But under Eden's pressure Churchill had to add a representative of the Foreign Office. And since Eden declined to take part, owing apparently to the committee's composition and direction, which indicated

Churchill's desired outcome, and against which he had not the guts to fight, his Parliamentary Under-Secretary, Mr Richard Law, was appointed in his stead. In October also Lord Moyne (serving then as Deputy Minister of State Resident in the Middle East) was added to the committee.

This composition reflected Churchill's views since he saw to it that opponents of the White Paper policy had an overwhelming majority. The committee were required by the Cabinet 'to consider the long term policy for Palestine' and Churchill directed them to start by examining the Peel Report.[269]

During the discussions of this committee, the Arab federation panacea was a main topic and we must turn to consider mainly this aspect of them now. Before the committee began their work Churchill had on 20 July circulated to them a telegram he had received from General Smuts, the Prime Minister of South Africa, who like other Dominion Prime Ministers took part in the meetings of the War Cabinet when he happened to be in London. In his telegram Smuts expressed a pro-Zionist view as far as immigration and the White Paper were concerned and argued that 'a Palestine Jewish State would have to be constituted as part of a larger Arab Confederation'.[270] Thus, Churchill indicated, if any indication were needed, where he was heading and what his preferred solution was. Ibn Saud's hostility to Zionism may have forced Churchill to drop his support for the Philby scheme, but its fundamental principles remained close to his heart.

And indeed the joining of a Jewish state in Palestine to an Arab federation or its formation alongside a Jewish state in Palestine as a palliative to the pains caused by its creation figured prominently in the work of the committee. Its first meeting took place on 4 August. The tone of the discussion was set by Leopold Amery's memorandum which was presented to the meeting and by his talk during the discussion. He very strongly supported the creation of a Jewish state in Palestine along the coastal plain up to the Egyptian border including the whole Negev, Jezreel Valley, Lower Galilee, Tiberias and the Hulah Valley. Since this state would not be able to absorb all the millions of uprooted European Jewish refugees (the Germans saved this trouble in their way ...), Amery also proposed to create Jewish colonies in the former Italian territories of Cyranaica and Tripolitania. The Arabs would have most of the interior, Western and Central Upper Galilee (Acre sub-district) would be linked up with the Lebanon, and the Samaria and Jerusalem districts seceded to Trans-Jordan. Amery based his approach on many, usually pro-Jewish and Zionist arguments.

For our discussion the most interesting one is the connection he saw between his scheme and the question of Arab federation. He said in his memorandum:

THE EVER-PRESENT PANACEA – ARAB FEDERATION 131

There is a further argument in favour of partition which has developed since the date of the Royal [Peel] Commission's report. The whole question has to be envisaged to-day in the light not only of the Palestine situation but of the wider position both of Arabs and Jews. The Arab world is undoubtedly looking forward to some form of closer union, whether only of Syria, Palestine and Trans-Jordan, or on a wider basis, after this war. In the light of this aspiration which will be greatly helped by the removal of direct French control in Syria, the existence of a Jewish State in part of Palestine may, like the existence of the Lebanon, be more readily acquiesced in. It is at least significant that the Prime Minister of Iraq, in his recent confidential memorandum to the Minister of State [see pp. 51–2] went so far as to say:

> 'If the Palestinian Arabs could be reunited with the Arabs of Syria and Trans-Jordan they would not be so apprehensive of Jewish expansion, and the Jewish communities now in Palestine would feel safer and more settled. They could be allowed a considerable degree of local autonomy under some form of international guarantee if that is considered necessary'.

It is true that General Nuri [al-Sa'id] qualifies this later on by describing it as 'semi-autonomy' and implies that the creation of a strong Arab State would be a condition precedent. All the same it seems clear that the isolation of the Jews in their own specific area and the linking up of the Arabs of Palestine with those of Trans-Jordan or of Syria might be accepted if accompanied by definite assurances of our sympathy with the ideal of Arab Unity and on the basis of the Jewish State forming at any rate a co-operative element in any scheme, economic or political, for furthering that unity.

Amery made it clear that he thought that such a scheme should be enforced by Britain.[271]

In support of the need to create a federation of Syria, Trans-Jordan and Palestine, a memorandum of Lieutenant-Colonel Victor Cazalet MP who had lately visited the Middle East was circulated to the committee.[272]

In the meeting itself Amery repeated his arguments and Herbert Morrison agreed that in considering partition a larger area, including Trans-Jordan, should be taken into account.[273] Only Richard K. Law, the FO's representative on the committee, expressed a dissenting view. He told his colleagues, although in a tentative way, that 'although the Arabs were keen on federation in theory, jealousy between the various Arab kings made its realisation very unlikely, and that it was certainly not something that they were so keen on that they would be prepared to make sacrifices in Palestine to achieve'.[274] With his colleagues at the FO Law was now frank in his contempt for the way of thinking of the committee's members. He described the talk in the meeting as 'high, wide and handsome. The general atmosphere was that the Zionists should take over Palestine and Transjordan and most of the North African continent. When it gets down to hard talks probably it won't be so wild.'[275] Sir Maurice Peterson was much sharper in his criticism of the committee's deliberations and especially of the Amery Plan the circulation of which had done 'mischief'. This view was endorsed by Sir Alexander Cadogan[276] but as we shall see later on it was not shared by Richard Law, who apparently for political reasons preferred not to defy Churchill's will. One should remember that Law was on 24 September promoted by Churchill from Parliamentary Under-Secretary of the Foreign Office to Minister of State in the Foreign Office!

However strong the FO's reaction was, the committee agreed that the Colonial Secretary would prepare, after consultation with the Palestine Government, a plan for the partition of Palestine. They also instructed the Colonial and Foreign Offices to request the Post-Hostilities Planning Sub-Committee of the Chiefs of Staff Committee to prepare a joint appreciation of the strategic needs of Britain in Palestine after the war, and the FO to prepare an appreciation of the political effects on the Arab world of the establishment of an autonomous Jewish community in Palestine and of the bearing of pan-Arab aspirations upon it.[277]

The military planning authorities supplied the committee with appreciations of British military needs in the four Levant States. It was stated that owing to their importance to the British Empire and Commonwealth's world network of communication and to the flow of oil their security and tranquillity were of the utmost importance. Therefore air bases and control of means of communication had to be kept in British hands.[278] The final report of the Chiefs of Staff Committee warned that the partition of Palestine was bound to complicate the military control and that any leakage of a partition scheme before the end of the war would require deployment of troops to ensure the security of the Middle East at the expense of operations against the enemy.

The FO reminded the committee that the question of a military presence in Syria and Lebanon had to be squared with British commitments to France and with the certain opposition of the local governments to any placing of troops beyond the limits set in the 1936 treaties between France and Syria and the Lebanon.[279] Whatever the importance of that aspect, it was not very prominent in the committee's discussions and work. Furthermore the final report of the Chiefs of Staff Committee was circulated *after* the committee had already prepared their report and naturally could not influence it.

THE EVER-PRESENT PANACEA – ARAB FEDERATION 133

Oliver Stanley, the Colonial Secretary, prepared his partition plan to counteract the Amery Plan.[280] It took him all the summer and autumn and he submitted it only on 1 November. He reverted to the Partition Plan recommended by the Peel Commission and truncated even further the proposed Jewish state by dropping about 400 square miles from it. The Upper Galilee and the Hulah Valley would be linked with Syria, whereas Samaria and most of the Judean hills with Trans-Jordan, Jerusalem and Bethlehem would be included in a separate Jerusalem state under British rule. The Negev would be reserved by the British rulers for further examination of its potential development. The future of Amir 'Abdallah and whether to connect partition with any scheme of broader Arab unity were sidestepped.[281]

The Foreign Office needed the same period for the preparation of their position. But, if the Colonial Office took their time to be able to consult with the Palestine Government,[282] the Foreign Office was torn between Richard Law, Sir Maurice Peterson and C.W. Baxter. The last named stuck to the FO's position of the late 1930s when they defeated any partition scheme regardless of the size of the proposed Jewish state.[283] Peterson thought that Baxter exaggerated, and that a 'token' Jewish state which would suffice to give Jewish citizenship to Jews in other parts of the world who might be interested in it had to be established. Such a 'token' state (mainly the coastal area north and south of Tel-Aviv, excluding Jaffa with about 225,000 Jews and 50,000 Arabs) would not arouse stiff Arab opposition. Peterson stuck to the Foreign Office's rejection of any British encouragement of Arab federation, unless the Arabs themselves initiated it. He thought that 'any attempt directly to link a Palestinian solution with Arab federation would merely be to hang a new kind of millstone round the neck of the Palestinian controversy'. Instead, he suggested that the whole of the rest of Palestine should be Arab and linked up with Trans-Jordan as a new Arab State under the Amir 'Abdallah, capable of joining in any Arab federation which might materialise.[284]

Richard Law was more well-disposed towards partition than Peterson. He thought that the partition line should be 'reasonable in itself' and that less attention should be paid to statistics of population. Those who objected to being on one side or other of the line should be allowed to clear out. Since he was sure that the Arabs would resist any Jewish state, 'token' or otherwise, he came close to Stanley's view.[285] Therefore, he did not like the draft memorandum which Peterson had prepared and demanded that it be completed by a résumé of the American angle. Peterson became frustrated since in the meantime Weizmann had got word of what was going on and was lobbying for a Jewish state, and also since nothing was presented to balance Amery's views. At the beginning of September in Law's absence (he had gone to the USA) he argued to Eden that the Cabinet Committee were more than conscious of the American angle. Eden agreed, encouraged Peterson to oppose Amery's views 'who has never been right on any subject' and to prepare a paper, subject to his consent.[286] But it seems that he did not want to overrule the newly promoted Mr Law and perhaps was reluctant to defy Churchill. Therefore, at the beginning of October the Foreign Office had not yet shaped their view to be presented before the committee.[287] Only in mid-October were the Foreign Office on the point of producing their paper.[288] They were then forced to make a decision since a new factor had entered in the person of Lord Moyne, the Deputy Minister of State Resident in the Middle East, and the Prime Minister was showing signs of impatience.

On 22 September the British Government was notified that Lord Moyne would arrive in London on the 27th bringing with him proposals for the partition of Palestine within the framework of a greater Syria. Moyne expressed his wish to see the Foreign Secretary.[289] Churchill who had already in 1941 and 1942 known Moyne's views promptly appointed him as a member of the Palestine Cabinet Committee.[290] On 2 October Churchill impatiently asked Sir Edward Bridges, the Secretary of the War Cabinet, how many times the Palestine Committee had met since its formation and demanded that Lord Moyne be given the opportunity to present his view in which Churchill was interested.[291] It may also have been that Churchill wanted a quick resolution of the question in order to help Weizmann in his struggle to retain his leadership in the Zionist Organisation. Anyway in November 1943 Smuts told Weizmann that Churchill was thinking of partition and that the government wanted to help him.[292] Under this instigation the wagon began to run fast.

Moyne brought with him a detailed plan which had been prepared through consultations with Sir Harold MacMichael and Sir Edward Spears. It was deeply influenced by Nuri al-Sa'id's memorandum (see ch. 1, pp. 51–2) which was presented in a special appendix to his paper. Briefly, Moyne's proposals, endorsed by Richard Casey, the Minister of State Resident in the Middle East, provided for the creation of a small Jewish state along the coastal shore, Jezreel Valley and Tiberias area, for a Jerusalem state under an international body, with a British chairman and consisting of British, French and American representatives, and for the fusion of the remaining Arab Palestine, Trans-Jordan and Muslim southern Lebanon with Syria into one Greater Syria State. Western strategic interests would be safeguarded and there would be considerable economic unity among the four states (Syria, Lebanon, Jewish and Jerusalem).[293]

When this plan reached the Foreign Office, Sir Maurice Peterson realised that on partition there was an accord of views between the Colonial Office and the Minister of State. Therefore, he gave in on that point and regarded the Jewish state which would be created by Moyne's plan as small enough to be regarded as 'token'. But on the other point of linking up Arab Palestine and Greater Syria he advised his superiors to resist because if it was carried out Britain would risk antagonising both the French and the Saudis. On 5 October Eden and Moyne met and agreed that a Departmental Committee composed of officials of the Colonial and Foreign Offices and Moyne's aides would discuss Lord Moyne's paper.[294]

At the meeting Peterson reiterated his view that only a 'token' Jewish state could be fitted into the whole structure of Britain's Middle East policy. He thought that the Colonial Office plan should be modified by the exclusion of the Hulah Valley and Haifa from the Jewish state. Then he opposed the Greater Syria collateral of partition which the Colonial Office's plan sidestepped but was a basic component of Moyne's plan. By giving the Hulah Valley to the Arabs the territorial continuity between the Upper Galilee and Muslim Syria would be safeguarded without resorting to the radical remedy of transferring Southern Lebanon to Syria.

The last point he made was that until Arab federation emerged Arab Palestine should be united with Trans-Jordan. This Ibn Saud would accept. Sir G. Gater, the Colonial Permanent Under-Secretary, noted with satisfaction that the FO were not against partition in principle and wished that a common view be framed. Lord Moyne defended the Greater Syria factor of his plan and explained that 'Nuri was much keener on the Greater Syria project as a step towards Federation'. He noted that Nuri al-Sa'id had recently become much more sympathetic towards the Jews. He thought that the French would get what they wanted by treaties with the Lebanon and Greater Syria and therefore would not oppose the creation of this new State. Ibn Saud too would not oppose it because there was not 'any real danger of a Hashemite dynasty being created in Greater Syria: the tendency would be rather towards a Republican régime.' He added that Tawfiq Abu al-Huda had recently told Mr Kirkbride 'that the Trans-Jordan Government would not let Abdullah's interests stand in the way of the establishment of a Greater Syria'.

At the end of his remarks he went so far as to tell his colleagues that Britain had to 'take into account the interpretation placed by Arabs on ministerial statements. Even Mr Eden's statement last year about Arab Federation was now described by the Arabs as a pledge' and therefore they now relied on Britain to see that it was carried into effect. Sir Douglas Harris, who represented the Palestine Government, strengthened Moyne's position by stating 'that the feeling of the Palestine Arabs would be much more favourable to the partition projects if they were to be included in a large State such as a Greater Syria and not merely lumped in with Trans-Jordan'. But Lord Moyne did not present this matter as a *sine qua non* condition for partition. As an alternative, he said, the Upper Galilee could be linked up with the Lebanon. But even so agreement was not reached.[295]

The Foreign Office hastened the preparation of their paper, which was circulated to the Cabinet Committee alongside the Colonial Office's and Moyne's papers at the beginning of November. Written from the point of view of the general British policy in the Middle East, it repeated Peterson's views and made it clear that the bounds of the 'token' Jewish state had to be 'considerably less extensive than those recommended by the Peel Commission'. Moyne's clarification that his Greater Syria project was not identical with 'Abdallah's project brought Peterson to soften in his paper the argument against it based on the certain objection of Ibn Saud.[296] But it did not influence his overall objection which was mainly based on his conviction that any such move was detrimental to Anglo-French relations. For him good relations with France were much more important than any advantage Britain might gain by fostering any project of Arab unity. This, one can add, was the reason he so fiercely resented Sir Edward Spears's policies in Syria and tried his best to have him sacked.

It seems that Richard Law did not agree with Peterson's attitude which had been endorsed by Cadogan and Eden. During Eden's presence in Cairo and in the Foreign Ministers' Conference in Moscow (11 October – 10 November) Law had prepared a separate memorandum in which he agreed in principle with the Colonial Office's position that Palestine should be partitioned and that Stanley's plan should be accepted with two territorial modifications. He was much less determined in his position with regard to the Greater Syria scheme. Unlike partition, which should be decided, authoritatively announced and decisively enforced, the other issue should be negotiated with all concerned. Therefore partition should not be linked too closely with the question of Greater Syria.[297]

These discussions were much more important than the committee's meetings in which usually the views expressed in the memoranda and in the informal meetings were merely briefly reiterated.

The committee's second meeting took place on 4 November. After the long preliminary deliberations and faced with a divided FO they easily adopted Colonel Oliver Stanley's plan and decided that the Hulah Valley but not the northern part of it would be included in the Jewish State. Thus a territorial continuity between the Arab Galilee and Syria was assured.[298] The question of Greater Syria was left to the third meeting which took place on 16 November. Moyne repeated his arguments in favour of the scheme stressing the need to check the French attempt to insist on a position far beyond what Britain had retained in Iraq according to the 1930 treaty. 'Within the Greater Syria scheme he had outlined, we could satisfy the French that we were not trying to oust them from the Levant in order to step [in] ourselves'. The scheme was compatible with treaties between France and Syria and the Lebanon if they resembled the Iraqi treaty. Richard Law agreed and Oliver Stanley only added that partition should be pursued even without Greater Syria, but he did not doubt that within it the chances of partition being implemented were greater. Therefore the committee adopted Moyne's plan with the addition which Stanley had made,[299] and the Secretariat prepared the final Report, which was discussed at the fourth and last meeting on 10 December. Meanwhile the Foreign Office and Lord Moyne reiterated their original views: the FO for a much smaller ('token') Jewish state, and Moyne with the backing of Richard Casey, the Minister of State, for regarding partition and Greater Syria as one integral scheme.[300]

The Eastern Department continued to reject any scheme of partition claiming that it would ignite a new revolt of the Palestine Arabs and was likely 'to set the whole of the Middle East in uproar'. A new, or rather old, argument was now put forward: a Jewish state in Palestine would be detrimental to the interests of the Jews themselves outside Palestine. The effect of the Balfour Declaration was deplorable, 'for by increasing their political Jewish consciousness, it was the original cause of many of the difficulties and indeed persecutions which they have since experienced'. Peterson fully endorsed this argument and added his amazement that 'a committee presided over by the Home Secretary should not even mention the problem of [the Jews'] dual nationality'.[301]

Finally the committee agreed their report, which espoused Moyne's and Stanley's views, while Law added a note of dissent. They recommended (a) the partition of Palestine along the Peel partition line, with the exclusion from the Jewish state of the Western Galilee and the addition of the southern portion of Beisan sub-district and Jaffa; (b) the creation of a Jerusalem territory under a British High Commissioner; (c) Western Galilee and Southern Lebanon would be linked up with Syria and the central parts of Palestine with Trans-Jordan. The enlarged Trans-Jordan should in turn be fused with Syria to form Greater Syria; and (d) the Negev would be retained by British rule for further investigation of the development possibilities, a formula which was understood to imply a future joining to the Jewish state.

The committee adopted the view of the 'authorities in the Middle East' 'that no scheme for the partition of Palestine will succeed unless it is linked to a further plan for the proper arrangement of the Levant States as a whole'. This arrangement spoke of the linking of Greater Syria 'in a loosely knit association of Levant States with the Lebanon, the Jerusalem Territory and the Jewish State'.

Laws's Note of Dissent stated that any partition scheme would not easily be accepted by the Arabs, but at least they should get the Hulah salient, the Beisan-Nazareth-Tiberias area, Jaffa and the Negev. Law sidestepped the Greater Syria factor of the scheme and the possible objection of Ibn Saud. In the former he acquiesced and as for the latter he had been satisfied that Ibn Saud had no basis for complaint since nothing in the Committee's plan hinted at 'Abdallah's being installed as the King of Greater Syria.[302]

Also the Minister of State Resident in the Middle East, Richard Casey, and his Deputy, Lord Moyne, were not too happy with the direction the discussions of the Cabinet Committee were taking. Casey tried to use Eden's presence in Cairo in order to put before him his view that 'partition plus Greater Syria is, in my opinion, the best solution of the general Levant problem that I have yet heard'.[303] Lord Moyne too did not rest idle. At the last meeting of the committee he suggested reducing the area to be allotted to the Jewish state but he was 'more or less shouted down'.[304] Secondly, he circulated a telegram from Casey presenting his view of 'the consequences of attempting partition without simultaneously creating a Greater Syria'.[305]

In addition to stressing the importance of that principle Casey, who had come to London, and Lord Moyne succeeded in removing a more practical barrier. After the committee's report had been drafted and confirmed they realised that it would be very difficult to detach the south from the Lebanon, which had just won an important battle in its struggle against the French authorities. Without the secession of southern Lebanon to Syria there would be no territorial continuity between the Arab territory of Western and Central Galilee and Syria. Their remedy was to provide a link between that area and Syria on the west and north sides of the Hulah Valley. After a meeting with Eden, Morrison and Stanley[306] this amendment was endorsed by the committee.[307]

The Foreign Office's objection to the committee's report was, it became clear later on, much more fundamental and with Eden's return to London in December the Foreign Secretary himself again headed the Office. They, including Law, were afraid that there might be a 'snap decision' of the Cabinet on the whole question and especially as to either the areas allotted to the Jewish state or the timing of the scheme. C.W. Baxter, head of the Eastern Department, suggested agreeing with Lord Moyne and Colonel Oliver Stanley the line to be adopted when the report came before the Cabinet. But Eden was less worried. He did not see any danger of a 'snap decision' by the Cabinet.[308] His tactics were different. Baxter put the stress on the danger of a general uproar and the damage that would be done to the Jews all over the world. Sir Alexander Cadogan pointed to a new obstacle: nothing could be done with regard to the States of the whole Levant so long as the mandates had not been terminated. And now, in wartime, there was no legally competent international authority to do that! Therefore, nothing could be done and the whole scheme should be abandoned. Eden agreed and noted: 'I have an impression of the eager amateur [Moyne, Amery, Churchill himself?] about these Palestine proposals which frankly alarms me'. And in another minute: 'I am depressed, rather than impressed, by this document [the committee's report]. It will clearly be vehemently resisted by Arabs everywhere, if presented as it now stands'.[309]

And, indeed, delay rather than an outright frontal attack was Eden's strategy. Peterson was asked to prepare for Eden a Note summing up all these arguments. When he did so, with Cadogan's approval he brought forward two new points (and indirectly, but clearly, dismissed Law's position): the Christian interest in the Holy Land and 'what we now know (since Colonel Hoskins's visit) of the [US] President's wishes, which are that partition should be dropped, especially in view of Ibn Saud's attitude'.[310] It seems that his last point aroused Eden's hope to be able to persuade Churchill, who had always used American and Roosevelt's views as a most important consideration to be reckoned with in a favourable way to the Jews. He minuted: 'I do not suppose that war Cabinet can take it [the Report] before P[rime] M[inister]'s return.'[311] What an irony that Churchill's and Weizmann's persistent efforts to implement the Philby plan which brought Roosevelt to send Colonel Hoskins to Saudi Arabia now blew up in Churchill's face![312]

Contrary to Eden's expectations, Churchill, on his return from North Africa, expressed his support of the committee's proposals. On 16 January he wrote to Sir Edward Bridges, the secretary of the War Cabinet: 'This is a very fine piece of work and I am in general accord with the views expressed by all the members with one dissentient'. Churchill quoted Casey's opinion 'that the "Greater Syria" plan was essential to the success of the scheme' and noted: 'I am in general agreement with this.'[313] And as though he were in need of strengthening he received the following day a personal telegram from Casey in which he told Churchill 'that the best solution in sight is partition in Palestine together with the creation of Greater Syria. I do not think that partition is a workable solution by itself, there would be too much Arab resistance and too much bloodshed. But the simultaneous creation of Greater Syria would provide the necessary bait and the necessary political offset to partition from the Arab point of view. I do not believe there is any objection to Greater Syria that cannot be overcome in practice'.[314] Casey did not repeat his objection to the attribution to the Jewish state of the Hulah Salient and the Lower Galilee and it seems that he was ready to swallow it provided the Cabinet approved the Greater Syria component of the scheme. Fortunately for the Foreign Office, Churchill left one gap in the wall through which the FO later succeeded in thrusting, when he expressed the opinion that 'it would be much better if possible to defer action until the defeat of Hitler'.[315]

By direction of the Prime Minister the War Cabinet was to discuss the report on 25 January 1944. Eden was furnished with a detailed Note which argued for the deferring of *any* Cabinet decision till after the war. It quoted the Chiefs of Staff Report (see above, p. 132), the need to have the views of the British Ambassadors in the Middle East about the possible reaction of the Arabs to the committee's plan, and the Foreign Office's doubts about the feasibility of the Greater Syria scheme (mainly the French aspect) and their scepticism about whether it really could assuage Arab objection to the partition of Palestine. It strongly underlined the need to fit British policy in Palestine into their policy in the whole Middle East, in view of the increasing importance of essential British interests there, i.e. oil and communications.[316]

Even now the Foreign Office did not speak with one resolute voice. The Cabinet in their discussion completely disregarded the negative view expressed by the Chiefs of Staff in their memorandum, while Morrison and Churchill expressed their positive view of the scheme. Richard Law, the Minister of State at the FO, referred to his Note of Dissent,[317] and said that his 'difference with his colleagues was one of degree and not of principle, referring specifically to the allotment of the Hulah area to the Jewish State'. Eden took part in the discussion as well, but here it is impossible to know what he really said. According to the first draft of the minutes of the Cabinet's discussion, Eden spoke in similar terms to Law,[318] whereas in the final version Eden 'wished to reserve his final view *as regards the scheme as a whole* [my italics], pending the result of the private reference which he had made to H.M. Ambassadors in Cairo and Baghdad'. In particular he was doubtful about the recommendations with regard to the Hulah Valley and the Negev. At the end the War Cabinet approved the report 'in principle', on the understanding that 'any particular details of the scheme could, if necessary, be further examined, before a final decision was reached'. The Foreign Secretary's reservation was noticed. It was also concluded that 'the existence of the scheme should not be publicly disclosed or action taken upon it until after the defeat of Germany'.[319]

The Foreign Office officials realised that the approval only 'in principle', the decision to keep the whole matter in full secrecy and to defer any action until after the end of the war gave them the needed chance to reserve the whole direction of the decided policy as they had done after July 1937 when the Cabinet approved the Peel Report 'in principle' and afterwards, under Foreign Office pressure, recanted. Furthermore, this postponement gave them the chance to convert Eden to their view, which was completely antagonistic to the Palestine Cabinet Committee's Report. It seems to us that their first success was to remove Richard Law from dealing with the matter; anyway judging by the relevant FO files, Palestine policy and the proposed Greater Syria scheme were not, after January 1944, dealt with by the Minister of State at the Foreign Office.

In accordance with his reservation, the Foreign Secretary on 1 February 1944 invited the British Ambassadors to Baghdad and Cairo to present their comments on the committee's report which had been sent to them under directives of extraordinary secrecy. The Foreign Office's negative attitude was made known to them and their attention was especially drawn to what the FO regarded as the outstandingly weak points of the report.[320] As expected, their reactions were wholly compatible with the Department's attitude and expectations. Neither Lord Killearn nor Sir Kinahan Cornwallis accepted the committee's evaluation that the neighbouring Arab states would swallow the partition of Palestine. Instead Killearn proposed to scrap the mandate and to instal direct British rule, owing to Palestine's importance in the Empire's defence and communication systems, whereas Sir Kinahan suggested that further consideration should be given to President Roosevelt's new idea of permanent international trusteeship over Palestine. Neither of them believed that the creation of Greater Syria might sweeten the sour pill. Cornwallis wrote that it would not 'soften the blow [of Partition], for the gift offered is far less than what the Arabs expect' and Killearn noted: 'I do not believe' that 'the bait of "Greater Syria" (and I share the Foreign Office doubt as to its practicability) will diminish opposition to partition'.[321]

Now Eden had to make up his mind whether or not to attack the committee's conclusions endorsed in principle by the Cabinet and supported by the Prime Minister. But he hesitated, and may have been reluctant to add another issue to his long controversy with Churchill. Several weeks had elapsed since the receipt of the above-mentioned dispatches and he did not move. R.M.A. Hankey, who was in charge of Palestine affairs at the Eastern Department, C.W. Baxter, the Head of the Department, and Sir Maurice Peterson immediately recommended the circulation of the despatches to the Cabinet. But Sir Alexander Cadogan, the Permanent Under-Secretary, realised that it was too delicate a matter and advised Eden 'to get the P[rime] M[inister]'s concurrence before circulating these letters to the Cabinet.'[322] Eden himself was very pleased with Cornwallis's letter which he defined as 'an impressive despatch'[323] and he noted: 'We shall have so many troubles after the war that I question whether we have a right to add to them by championing the Partition scheme. Certainly we cannot commit ourselves to it until the war with Germany is over when the whole problem should be revised afresh'.[324] Killearn's recommendation, on the other hand, did not arouse Eden's enthusiasm and his letter was not found 'very clear' by Eden.[325] This difference may have increased Eden's hesitations and he preferred to take his time. Only after Colonel Oliver Stanley, the Colonial Secretary, wrote to Eden on 17 April asking whether he had received the Ambassadors' replies and, if so, when and to whom he proposed to circulate them, did Eden send the replies to Churchill on 26 April and ask his consent to have them circulated to the Cabinet. On 8 May Churchill's concurrence was conveyed to Eden and only then, on 15 May, were the despatches circulated to the Cabinet.[326]

Over the next move too the FO was hesitant and divided. In his above quoted letter Stanley also asked 'what the position is now with regard to the proposal for the partition of Palestine?' as though he wanted to indicate his low opinion of Eden's hesitations. Baxter suggested sending a non-committal answer but emphasised that in his Department's view, when the matter came up for discussion at the Cabinet the Foreign Secretary should make it quite clear that the FO did not accept the Palestine Committee's scheme. Eden was not too happy and minuted in a questioning way: 'What other policy does Mr Baxter advocate'?[327] Eden knew of course that Baxter's preferred policy was a resolute implementation of the May 1939 White Paper policy. But he knew no less confidently that this course was out of the question as long as Churchill headed the government. Furthermore, in a minute on Moyne's letter to him of 9 May he confessed that 'the alternatives to partition ... do not greatly impress, provided we admit – as we must – that there will have to be some considerable Jewish immigration to Palestine after the war'.[328] For a more satisfactory alternative he looked elsewhere. It was found in an idea which had been elaborated by Sir Maurice Peterson and which had first been suggested by President Roosevelt and Sir Kinahan Cornwallis.

Peterson proposed as an alternative both to the White Paper and Partition to create a Palestinian state the sovereignty over which would lie with the United Nations who would devolve it on a British Governor General. This Governor would take his day-to-day instructions from the British Government. Jewish immigration would be permitted on a much larger scale than contemplated in the White Paper (75,000 from 1939 to 1944 as a final concession) until the Jewish population of Palestine came within 100,000 short of the Arabs. This would allow for the gradual entry of about 400,000 Jewish immigrants. Peterson's ideas pleased Eden who gave him a go-ahead signal to prepare a detailed paper,[329] but it prompted a lively debate with the Colonial Office which remained loyal to the Palestine Cabinet Committee's Report. The arguments for or against partition were reminiscent of those raised in 1937 in the wake of the Peel Report. At the end Eden decided not to circulate his alternative proposals in order not to heat furthermore the atmosphere[330] which had already been heated enough by Peterson having shared his views with Wallace Murray, the political adviser of the US Secretary of State, an occurrence which prompted Stanley to call the attention of Herbert Morrison, the chairman of the Palestine Cabinet Committee, to it.[331]

In the summer of 1944 Eden remained without a definite alternative to the committee's scheme which, under the pressure of his office, he could not swallow. On the other hand, he had not the resolution to sustain a frontal attack on the scheme which was backed by the Prime Minister and defended by the Colonial Office. In the circumstances he had to admit to Churchill that 'Whatever else happens it is not practicable to continue the White Paper policy after the war'.[332] It looked as though the partition plan, 1944 vintage, would be finally approved and carried out. But, concurrently with this soul-searching another setback was awaiting the scheme, this time with regard to its Greater Syria component.

At the beginning of 1944 Sir Harold MacMichael, the High Commissioner for Palestine, reached the conclusion that the sweetening pill that the Palestine Arabs should be given to swallow partition should be a union under Amir 'Abdallah with Trans-Jordan. The British Resident in 'Amman held a talk with Tawfiq Abu al-Huda, the Prime Minister of Trans-Jordan, and understood that if partition was 'not so unjust' the Arabs would acquiesce in it and would accept the unity with Trans-Jordan. The Resident remarked that these views confirmed the view which he had consistently expressed. He also explained that a partition plan which would allot the Jews the Rehovoth area in the southern coastal area, the Sharon Plain in its centre, the Jezreel Valley and probably the Hulah and Beisan Valleys might be regarded as 'not so unjust'.[333]

This proposal coincided with 'Abdallah's pressure that the Trans-Jordan Mandate be terminated and his country be granted or at least promised independence like the development which had taken place in Syria and the Lebanon. Secondly, MacMichael realised that it was impossible to create a Greater Syria either according to 'Abdallah's concept or according to the Palestine Cabinet Committee's Report, because, on the one hand, the Syrians would not agree to be ruled by 'Abdallah as their King and, on the other, the Amir would certainly never consent to the incorporation of Trans-Jordan in Greater Syria unless he were accepted as the ruling head of the whole. Thirdly, Britain could not terminate the mandate, get rid of 'Abdallah and create the Greater Syria because since 1928 it had been bound by its agreement with Trans-Jordan 'to recognise the existence of an independent Government of Trans-Jordan under the rule of His Highness the Amir of Trans-Jordan'. Furthermore, MacMichael argued that it should not be done 'having regard to the moral obligations which have been incurred by His Majesty's Government towards the ruling family of Trans-Jordan'. MacMichael's conclusion was that the constitution of the Greater Syria State had to be regarded as an eventual rather than an immediate objective, and that it was necessary 'to contemplate a transition stage, involving the creation, under the Amir, of a new state (which might be designated "Southern Syria") consisting of Trans-Jordan and the Arab areas of Central Palestine, as a first step towards the constitution of the Greater Syria'.[334]

The length of the transition period was understood by the Colonial Office as identical with the Amir's life-time.[335]

The Foreign Office were very reserved about these proposals. Peterson noted that they would 'deprive Greater Syria scheme of the little value which it possesses by making it a two-stage affair'.[336] They suggested waiting until the special meeting of the Middle East Defence Council which Lord Moyne intended to convene could discuss the matter.[337]

In January 1944 Lord Moyne, who had served as Richard Casey's Deputy, succeeded to his post as the Minister of State Resident in the Middle East. Casey had had a clear-cut view of the necessity to carry out the partition of Palestine with the collateral of the creation of the Greater Syria State. He realised that the step was not compatible with keeping 'Abdallah in his present position and he suggested granting him financial compensation.[338] Moyne had less rigid views and was easily convinced by MacMichael and by Sir Edward L. Spears, who added a new argument, since Moyne himself when he left the Colonial Office in March 1942 had put forward the same proposition! (see p. 123) Spears admitted that a Greater Syria State was a necessary condition to partition of Palestine. But while the Levant States were still nominally under French mandate this was impossible. Therefore, he also recommended that in the meantime Trans-Jordan should be increased by adding the Arab parts of Palestine.[339] Moyne accepted these arguments and added more force to them by claiming that the partition of Palestine had become more urgent and it was doubtful whether it could be postponed until after Germany had been defeated. And since Greater Syria could not be created quickly and easily MacMichael's and Spears's suggestion should be adopted. Moyne asked the authority of the Foreign Office to invite to a meeting in Cairo of the Middle East Defence Committee the Ambassadors to Egypt and Iraq, the Ministers to Syria and Saudi Arabia and the HC for Palestine.[340]

Since Sir Maurice Peterson and the other officials dealing with Palestine and Arab affairs in general liked this new scheme even less than the original one ('The "two-stage" proposal robs it of even this value' ... 'as a *palliative* [sic!] (no more) to the imposition upon the Arabs of a Jewish State in Palestine'),[341] he expressed his wish 'to keep Lord Moyne and Cairo out of this altogether, especially since we have now got the views of Sir K. Cornwallis and Lord Killearn'.[342] But Cadogan thought otherwise. He assumed that the FO could not keep Lord Moyne 'out of this', so he preferred that Moyne confer with Sir Kinahan Cornwallis and Lord Killearn.[343] Eden accepted this view 'since Lord Moyne had no rigid views on this matter'[344] and one can add, so Eden may have thought, that since he had recently been convinced one way perhaps he could also be convinced the other. The more so since, if he were not convinced at all, his new proposal could serve to wreck the

THE EVER-PRESENT PANACEA – ARAB FEDERATION   145

whole scheme of partition. Therefore the FO gave Moyne the authority he asked for.[345]

On 6 April this conference took place in Cairo. Cornwallis and Killearn repeated their views against large-scale Jewish immigration, against partition and for the continuation of British control, either overtly (Killearn's view) or under the guise of the United Nations (Cornwallis's view). All the participants agreed that 'while the project for Greater Syria should continue to have our cordial support, its establishment could not form part of our immediate policy; if partition is decided upon, the Palestine Arabs should in the first instance be joined with those of Trans-Jordan, Galilee going to Syria'. The conference accepted the argument against a union between Trans-Jordan and Syria that would jeopardise 'Abdallah's position. Secondly, since British 'policy regarding France in the Levant would result in French influence being predominant in Syria' [a big disappointment, no doubt, to those convened in Cairo!], 'it is considered both by the political and Service authorities to be against our interests that a Syria in which strong French influence would be claimed should extend half-way to Suez Canal; consequently it would be preferable not to take active steps towards the establishment of Greater Syria until we have a clearer view of France's future position in the Levant'. This argument was chiefly Spears's.[346] He and MacMichael agreed, although grudgingly, that partition was unavoidable and had to come first. The transition period would come to its natural end when 'Abdallah died, 'which might well coincide with the liquidation of the French' rule in the Levant. Then Greater Syria might be implemented.[347]

So the situation in the summer of 1944 was confused: the Foreign Office were hesitant, Lord Moyne reverted to a more modest plan whereas the Colonial Office remained loyal to the original scheme of the Cabinet Committee and pressed for a final decision.[348] Even Churchill for a while lost his enthusiasm. In the past he used to argue to his colleagues in the Cabinet that if only from a purely British interest of securing American goodwill anti-Zionist policies should not be pursued. When in early 1944 it became known to the British Government that President Roosevelt was considering an international trusteeship regime as a possible solution to the Palestine problem, the American stick could no longer be waved by Churchill over the heads of most of his more reluctant colleagues. It may well have been this consideration that drove him not to seek a quick and final approval of the Palestine Committee's Report. He wrote to Amery: 'It is my hope that the subject [the Committee's Report] will not be dealt with until the armistice or the peace conference'.[349] Eden, who underlined this sentence with his usual red-inked pen, could not but feel relieved.

Suddenly Churchill changed his mind, and apparently at the instigation of the Colonial Office he agreed that the committee would resume their work, study the situation in the light of new facts or information and would prepare an additional report to be presented to the War Cabinet.[350] This about-turn of Churchill cannot be accounted for by sources known to us. The gravity of the Jewish tragedy in Europe had already been known three months earlier when Churchill wrote the above quoted minute to Amery, and so had the massive deportation of the Hungarian Jews, the last sizable Jewish community in German-occupied Europe, to the death factory in Auschwitz.[351] We are not inclined to think that Churchill wanted to preempt the annual Conference of the British Labour Party by having a Cabinet backing to a pro-Zionist policy, since the extreme pro-Zionist resolution of the Labour National Executive Committee had already been passed in April and endorsed by the party conference only in December. Churchill may have been influenced by the growing pressure of American Jewry or by the intensification of the Jewish campaign of terror directed against the British authorities in Palestine. It is also possible that Churchill realised that Eden was hesitant and did not have the guts to stick to his office's conviction that the 1939 White Paper should be implemented.

Whatever the reason, the resumption of the Committee's work renewed the controversy between the Colonial and Foreign Offices. The CO prepared a detailed memorandum designated 'Possible Modifications in the Partition Scheme ...', which took into consideration the views of MacMichael, Killearn, Cornwallis and the Cairo conference. They stuck to the partition scheme, but accepted the postponement of the creation of Greater Syria and the immediate creation of Southern Syria (Trans-Jordan and Arab Palestine) which would include the Western Galilee. Since there was no more need for territorial continuity between the Arab Western Galilee and Syria the whole Hulah Valley up to the northernmost edge of Palestine was to be included in the Jewish state. The reasons for the postponement of the creation of the Greater Syrian state were exactly those which had been explicated by MacMichael and endorsed by Moyne and the conference he convened in Cairo on 6 April.

The FO rejected this scheme with no less vehemence than the previous one.[352] They stressed that the Greater Syria state was an essential part of the scheme and that Casey had indicated that if it was not practicable, 'he was doubtful whether it would be worthwhile attempting partition at all'. Therefore nothing could assuage the bitter pill that the Arabs would have to swallow, which would make them hostile to Britain and dangerous to vital British interests in the Middle East. Furthermore, the enlargement of Amir 'Abdallah's domain, instead of retiring him on a pension as was originally proposed by Casey, would irritate and offend Ibn Saud and Britain would 'lose the chance of obtaining his support'. The Foreign Office prepared a counter-memorandum which put the case against partition, using mainly Cornwallis's arguments. It seems that now Eden dared to fight openly against partition, and Moyne's retreat from the

Greater Syria proposal only helped him. The memorandum stressed the damage that would be done to British interests in the Middle East (oil and communications) and warned that creation of a Jewish state in part of Palestine would not achieve finality, since it would be regarded by the Jews as 'merely a stepping-stone towards the realisation of their wider hopes for a larger Jewish State covering the whole of Palestine and Transjordan'. Eden added to this memorandum a previous paper which had been proposed by Peterson six months earlier but which Eden had hesitated to circulate (see p. 142) in which he outlined his alternative proposal: international trusteeship exercised by a British Governor General.[353]

When on 19 and 26 September the committee met they authorised the Colonial Secretary to proceed in redrafting the report in accordance with the necessary modifications which had been presented in his paper and took note of the Foreign Office undertaking to arrange for discussions with the Colonial Office during the redrafting process in order to reach agreement.[354] These discussions did not, however, bring about any agreement and the Foreign Office prepared a new memorandum stating their objection both to the principle of partition and to the details of the specific scheme.[355]

At the single committee meeting in which Eden personally took part, on 26 September, he declared his intention to put before the War Cabinet when they considered the report of the committee, his views against partition and for an international trusteeship regime which would allow increased Jewish immigration to Palestine. But this warning was not needed since after such long and painstaking work the report was never even discussed by the War Cabinet. On 16 October 1944 the chairman of the committee forwarded to the Cabinet the final, revised report, based on partition and the creation of a Southern Syria, under 'Abdallah, including Trans-Jordan, Central Arab Palestine and Western Upper Galilee.[356]

Churchill's intention was to get Cabinet approval of the scheme and to postpone the announcement of it, so he told Weizmann, until after the end of the war with Germany and the General Election held in Britain had been completed.[357] Weizmann's detailed note of this conversation[358] reveals another interesting point: Churchill complained to Weizmann that he did not enjoy enough support inside his own Conservative Party for his Palestine policy. Possibly, he wanted to defer the announcement of his new Palestine policy until after a new Parliament had been elected because he was sure that in the new House he would enjoy a greatly increased following. The incumbent Parliament was still packed with appeasers elected in 1935 when Churchill had been isolated in the political wilderness. Certainly he hoped that the post-victory elections would result in a Conservative landslide and the new Tory members who would owe Churchill their election would back him fully.

It is noteworthy that precisely at that time Nuri al-Sa'id of Iraq reached similar conclusions. He told the British Resident in 'Amman that 'provided that the partition [of Palestine] was effected on equitable basis, it might perhaps be best to lose part of Palestine in order to confine the Zionist danger within permanent boundaries'. His definition of the 'equitable basis' was the cession to the Jews of those areas where they constituted a majority, but Jerusalem had to remain in British hands if it were impossible to place this 'holy city of Islam' under Arab control.[359]

However, the murder of Lord Moyne on 6 November thwarted Churchill's intention. He was so outraged that he ordered the report not to be put before the Cabinet. He felt 'that it would be impossible to discuss future plans for Palestine while those outrages were going on and gave instructions that the discussion on the report should stand over'.[360] Moyne's successor, Sir Edward Grigg, did not share his predecessor's views and did not support partition.[361] It was a serious setback for the scheme which was finally scrapped after the Labour Party had won the general election of July 1945. Thus, partition as a British position met the same fate as its Greater Syria collateral.

3

The Rise of Political Pan-Arabism

Unlike the ideological sphere, in which pan-Arabism had developed into a rather coherent concept, based upon the assumption that the Arabs constituted one nation and were therefore entitled to establish one state, the concurrent political developments were much more complicated and even twisted. They took place in different countries; they reflected varied and even conflicting interests – dynastical, personal, partisan, etc.; and since they were in close touch with reality they had usually never been too far-reaching in their vision of the future. When 'Izzat Darwaza, one of the main Palestinian pan-Arab activists, described in private the goals of the 1931 General Arab Congress (see ch. 1, pp. 14–17) he admitted that when the Congress Preparatory Committee discussed the question of Arab unity, 'they reached a unanimous view that every [Arab] country should preserve its existence and thus a Federation would come into existence. None of the committee's members thought of unity'.[1] Whatever the exact meaning of that term, pan-Arabism as a political force gained important ground with its advances in Egypt.

Pan-Arabism in Egypt[2]

From its beginning the evolution of Egyptian national identity was marked by ambivalence: on the one hand, there was a deep feeling of belonging and devotion to the Nile Valley, and on the other, a supra-Egyptian concept of belonging to a broader community, either religious, such as the Muslim Ottoman Empire, or linguistic, such as the Arab Nation.[3] The first trend resulted from the influence of modern Western civilisation, while the second was a direct outcome of Islamic views and ways of thinking. This ambivalence truly reflected the confrontation between traditional and modern collective loyalties.

The supporters of the latter desired to transform the Nile Valley into a modern nation-state, whose inhabitants would owe allegiance solely to their country which had been distinguished by its geography and climate, by the comparatively high homogeneity of its population, by its deep-rooted historical continuity since the Pharaonic time and by its autonomous regime which had been established in the early nineteenth century by Muhammad 'Ali and since then had been maintained by his successors. While the foundations of that outlook had been laid by Ahmad Lutfi al-Sayyid in the first decade of the twentieth century, it reached its zenith in the 1920s when territorial nationalism dominated Egyptian national thought.

This doctrine maintained that the boundaries of the Nile Valley constituted the outer limits of the Egyptian's loyalty to his homeland (*wataniyyah*) and, similarly, to his national group (*qawmiyyah*). It sanctified Egyptian territory, idolised its landscape and venerated all its ancient features. It called for the derivation of the modern Egyptian community's identity, values and national and cultural symbols from the uniqueness of the land of the Nile. It was there that the character of the Egyptian nation was shaped, with psychological and biological traits common to each of its members – kinship of blood and origin, similarity of temperament, mentality, speech and modes of behaviour. The historical roots of the Egyptian nation were nourished by the ancient Pharaonic civilisation.

The supporters of Egyptian territorial nationalism called on Egypt to shake itself free of all obligations to the competing framework of identity: the Islamic, the Arab cultural-linguistic, and the Eastern (*Sharqiyyah*) frameworks. They demanded the dissociation of the Egyptian national identity from all contents and values of a traditional, Islamic, Eastern or Arabic nature, by proclaiming that it was incumbent on Egypt to create for itself a new culture, history, art and even a unique language based on the Egyptian colloquial Arabic or, as a very few suggested, even by the revival of the old and now extinct Pharaonic language. For these nationalists the Egyptian nation was a Western nation. Its ancient culture was an organic part of Mediterranean civilisation – the cradle of Western civilisation – and thus the future of Egypt resided with the West which was the abode of progress, science, philosophy, freedom and justice.

In contrast, and simultaneously, national and cultural trends which were consolidated within the Egyptian national movement encouraged non-territorial, supra-Egyptian concepts of identity. These trends denied the possibility that the modern Egyptian community could define its collective identity without reference to traditional patterns. They were guided by the urge to create neo-traditional forms of identity, to resist any exclusive, parochial concept that proposed to base the Egyptian national identity exclusively on the territory of Egypt. They desired to establish Egypt's collective identity on spiritual, religious and broader cultural foundations; they were terrified of an idea, such as Egyptian territorial nationalism, that rested on 'secular' and 'materialist' foundations.

Some of them stressed the universal character of Islam and their belonging to the all-embracing Islamic community (*ummah*). Others fostered a distinctively Eastern orientation and propounded the idea that

Egypt was of the nerve and sinew of the nations of the East. From within this trend emerged the writers who hallowed the Arabic language and saw in Arabic culture the basis for Egyptian culture. All of them were stimulated by an anti-Western feeling and approach that denied the view that Egypt was an integral part of Western civilisation.

The first concrete signs of supra-Egyptian concepts of identity can be traced even before the First World War in the nationalist teachings of Mustafa Kamil and his successors in the 'National Party' (*al-Hizb al-Watani*). These concepts were embodied for them in the existence of the Islamic Ottoman Empire of which Egypt was still a formal part. After the Ottoman collapse and with the abolition in 1924 of the Caliphate new pan-Eastern and pan-Islamic concepts began to crystallise among the supporters of the supra-Egyptian trend. These ideas were based on the assumption that the Egyptian nation was not a separate territorial entity, but rather an indivisible part of a vast, extra-territorial, pan-Eastern, pan-Islamic or pan-Arab framework of identity. These concepts began to influence many circles, but so long as the territorial concept was paramount, they could not get widespread currency.

The decline of the territorial, secular Western-oriented concept of identity was, it seems to me, a direct result of the growing involvement of the masses in public life. The uneducated masses were much less aware of Western concepts of political-territorial communities and of non-religious integration of peoples around an accepted authority than of their gut feelings as Egyptian Muslims, tightly connected with other Muslims. Their allegiance was mainly directed to Islam.

The Arab dimension of that concept mainly emerged through Islam: the Arab language has always been Islam's holy language and the Arab people have had a special position and a role to play within Islam. The West in general and Western institutions and ideas in particular were discredited in Egypt in the late 1920s and early 1930s. Thus, the way was wide open for the Muslim masses, who by then had flocked in their millions from the country to the cities, to look for ideological and political expression for their feelings.

The first organisation to preach supra-Egyptian ideas was the 'Eastern Bond Association' (*Jam'iyyat al Rabitah al-Sharqiyyah*), established in February 1922. The founders adopted several principles as the basis for their organisation: to work for a close co-operation between Egypt and all other Eastern peoples in their struggle for national liberation, to establish an Eastern League of Nations, to promote cultural, scientific, economic and social bonds among the peoples of the East, to disseminate the 'Eastern Idea' and to rejuvenate the Eastern civilisation. The Association was founded mainly by secular intellectuals and could not command massive support. Nevertheless it succeeded in mustering considerable support among the better-educated strata. However, in the late 1920s the Association got into conflict with the much stronger trend of *Salafiyyah* and in 1931 it disintegrated.[4]

The *Salafiyyah* (*al-Salaf* in Arabic means forefathers) movement – the followers of Rashid Rida – became in the 1930s through various organisations one of the most important ideological but also political forces in Egypt. These people regarded the theories of Jamal al-Din al-Afghani and Muhammad 'Abduh, as developed by 'Abd al-Rahman al-Kawakibi and Rashid Rida, as the ideological basis for shaping the identity of Egypt and for curing its social illnesses.

Though religious, the *Salafi* organisations were popular nationalist movements, born in the climate of the national struggle, which saw the battle for the soul and character of the national cultural image of Egypt as their primary responsibility. These movements challenged both Western-oriented expressions of Pharaonic Egyptianism and conservative Islamic orthodoxy which, in their view, had failed to provide a satisfactory solution to the challenges of the new era. As a comprehensive alternative to the existing social and political frameworks and ideology which shaped the Egyptian regime they attempted to present a return to the original (as defined and even reinterpreted by them, of course) institutions, principles and values of the Islam of *al-Salaf*.

This school believed that a purified Islam would be able to lay the foundations for renewal of the unity of the Muslims, whose last vestiges had disappeared with the abolition of the Caliphate, to furnish the moral strength capable of facing the Western political, economic and cultural onslaught, and to provide better replies to the vital social questions of the day. For them Arab unity was a necessary stage in the process of effecting Muslim unity and Egypt had to find its place within it. From its outset this trend got the covert and overt support of the Egyptian Royal Dynasty. The Egyptian monarch aimed at the re-establishment of the Caliphate and the *Salafi* movement was regarded by him as an accessory to achieve the title of Caliph for himself.[5]

This trend gave birth to many organisations, three of which are noteworthy: the first, and of less importance, was 'the Association of Islamic Guidance' (*Jam'iyyat al-Hadayah al-Islamiyyah*) which was established in 1928, and the much more important 'Young Men's Muslim Association' (*Jam'iyyat al-Shubban al-Muslimin*) which was established a year earlier. The most important *Salafi* movement which in the 1930s virtually superseded all other *Salafi* organisations was the well-known 'Association of the Muslim Brethren' (*Jam'iyyat al-Ikhwan al-Muslimin*). Equipped with the *Salafi* doctrine these organisations propagated the idea that Egypt belonged to a wider world – the world of Islam – in which the Arabs held a special position and were entitled to a leading role. Arabic language and culture had no alternative. They should be preserved, developed and cherished and they provided the necessary basis for the cultural and even the political unity of all Arabs, Egyptians included.

It is true that for those Islamic fundamentalists Arab unity was only a stage on the road to a further goal — the unity of all Muslims — but concurrently with them Egypt of the 1930s saw the emergence of people who presented the idea of Arab unity in secular terms and as a goal in itself, and were working for its implementation.

One of the most important exponents of Egypt's Arab identity, mainly in cultural terms, was Zaki Mubarak. He stressed in his lectures and articles that 'we are Arabs although we are also Egyptians', like the Iraqis, the Najdis etc. He argued even that he was 'Arab first and Egyptian in the second place' and that fact was mainly determined by linguistic-cultural, historical and religious factors. Zaki Mubarak did not leave any room to doubt that the linguistic factor was the most important. He stressed that 'Egypt was the land of any Arabic-speaking person of all religions, even of paganism' and there was no doubt about its Arab identity. 'Any visit to Cairo reveals her Arab vitality which is so clearly manifest in Al-Azhar, the Egyptian University, the Academy of Arabic Language and the National Theatre'.[6]

Arab political identification in Egypt emerged from the basic concepts of Arabic cultural identity, and the indebtedness of the former to the latter was explicit. It was based on the assumption that the nation was a cultural-linguistic entity and that the Arab identity of Egypt was derived from its Arabic cultural values.[7] In the various versions of this concept elements of Eastern and Islamic identification were intermingled and when it was expressed in political-operational terms it became deeply influenced by the extremist integral Egyptian nationalism.

The proponents of the political Arab identity of Egypt aimed first and foremost at defining the Arab supra-Egyptian framework in political terms. They were determined to pour political content into the Arab national identity of Egypt and to endow it with all-Arab political goals. This trend was at first upheld by intellectuals who had begun their soul-searching by propagating Arab cultural identity, but gradually various politicians and organisations joined their ranks and even took the lead.

The powerful emergence of the *Salafiyyah* movement was a proper background for the various expressions of religious and political solidarity with the Palestine Arabs in connection with the Jewish–Muslim conflict over the Wailing Wall, which flared up in the summer of 1929. The first explicit expressions of the Arab political identification trend were voiced after Muhammad 'Ali, 'Allubah and Ahmad Zaki defended the rights of the Palestine Muslims before the International Commission of Inquiry, established by the League of Nations to enquire into the respective rights of Muslims and Jews in the Wailing Wall. In his testimony 'Allubah, himself an important Egyptian politician, a former minister and a veteran of the Egyptian national struggle for independence, called upon his country to renounce its Egyptian territorial particularist orientation and adopt the goal of Arab unity.

This call triggered off a public debate which lasted several years. 'Allubah was joined by 'Abd al-Rahman 'Azzam and both, together with representatives of YMMA, took part in the General Islamic Congress which was held in Jerusalem in December 1931. 'Azzam also participated in the all-Arab national meeting which was held in the wake of the Islamic Congress, in which a Pan-Arab National Charter was formulated.[8] Since then 'Allubah, 'Azzam and others, mainly people with *Salafi* leanings, went on working ceaselessly for the pan-Arab goals. Makram 'Ubayd, the deputy-leader of the *Wafd* party, and a Copt, became close to them and in the summer of 1932 made a tour of Palestine, Syria and Lebanon as an expression of support for the struggle of the Arabs of those countries. 'Azzam in October 1933 even approached the British Residency (the Office of the British High Commissioner in Egypt) and presented a memorandum in which he described the growing movement for Arab unity in the Arab world in general and in Egypt in particular. He called upon Britain to 'further it and profit by it', and, should Britain refuse, he warned against any attempt to stamp it out or retard it.[9] The first Egyptian pan-Arab organisations were also formed in those years: the first at the end of 1930 was named the Association of Arab Unity (*Jam'iyyat al-Wahdah al-'Arabiyyah*) and the second, the General Arab Federation (*Al-Ittihad al-'Arabi al-'Amm*), three years later. Although these associations did not survive the mid-1930s they were helpful in directing the Arab identification towards the mundane spheres of practical politics.

In 1936 a significant upsurge in pan-Arab feelings and activities took place in Egypt. In the autumn of 1935 the Egyptians launched a popular struggle against the British to force them to reopen negotiations for a treaty in place of the unilateral 1922 British declaration of (greatly limited) Egyptian independence. This struggle which took various forms of popular demonstrations and strikes brought many Egyptians closer to other Eastern peoples who were then engaged in the anti-imperialist struggle. There were Egyptians who concluded from this resurgence of feeling of Eastern solidarity that such feelings should be sustained and encouraged and that their only real foundation was unity of language, religion and history, viz. Islamic-Arab unity. By doing so Egypt would return to it — to the natural course of its cultural history.[10]

Important political events which took place in 1936 both inside and outside Egypt contributed to the strengthening of the feelings of Arab solidarity and even identification. In April 1936 King Fu'ad died and the new future King, Faruq, had to wait 15 months to reach the minimum age. Several weeks earlier the 1923 Constitution had been restored and thus the political parties could resume unhindered their political struggle with one another and/or against the Palace. As a result the biggest and most popular of them all, the *Wafd*, was returned to power in May 1936. The new government headed by Mustafa al-Nahhas, the *Wafd* leader, in August concluded the Treaty of Friendship and Alliance with Britain. With its relations with Britain settled and independence secured, Egypt could turn its attention to other problems, among which its relations with its Arab neighbours were prominent.

And, indeed, throughout 1936 there were various indications that Egyptian interest in Arab affairs was growing. Arab students were welcomed and hailed; Egyptians went much more than in the past to visit Arab countries; Egyptian students in European universities took an active part in the all-Arab student organisations there;[11] and the Syrian disturbances of January 1936 and the General Strike that ensued were keenly followed.[12] Those developments and of course the Palestine Rebellion (which is discussed below, see p. 162) reinvigorated the pan-Arab movement everywhere.[13]

These feelings and views were strengthened in Egypt by economic considerations as well. The most important locally-owned Egyptian financial institution – Bank Misr – had established branches in the neighbouring Arab countries which facilitated financial relations between Egypt and its Arab neighbours. Supporters of Arabism in Egypt welcomed this development and saw it as instrumental in the consolidation of fraternal relations with the Arabs.[14] The same attitude was held with regard to the development of telephone communications and air transportation between Egypt and Saudi Arabia, or, some years later, with regard to the completion of the Damascus-Baghdad road.[15]

This attitude became much more conspicuous after the outbreak of the Second World War. Commercial relations with Europe and especially with the Axis powers became very hazardous and the Middle East countries had to find local sources for various goods previously imported from Europe as well as local outlets for their exports. Economic cooperation with neighbouring Arab countries became vital to Egypt. Egypt was urged to develop its industries so that the neighbouring industries became complementary and not competitive. It was stressed that such a policy was compatible with cultural realities and had to culminate in the formation of an economic union. Egypt, so it was argued, should lead the movement toward such a goal.[16]

A very important point which was conspicuous in the intellectual and political advance of Arab nationalism in Egypt was the fact that both outside and inside Egypt those who pleaded that it was an Arab country and should form one kind or another of an Arab bloc of states or even the framework of an Arab union also exhorted Egypt to take the lead in such a body. In the first place, it was stressed that in the past

Muhammad 'Ali and his son Ibrahim, the founders of modern Egypt and the forefathers of the existing ruling dynasty, had established strong contacts with Syria and Lebanon. Secondly, since the days of Isma'il Egypt's material development had advanced far beyond that of its Arab neighbours who therefore used to regard Egypt as their older brother.[17] And, indeed, the geographical position of Egypt, being placed at the centre of the Arabic-speaking world, its cultural position and relatively large population were among the most important arguments proving Egypt's right to the leadership of the Arab world.

The importance of Egypt in this context lay especially in the great and growing influence of its press all over the Middle East and in the influential position of Egyptian universities and particularly al-Azhar.[18] Owing to all this, *al-Ahram* noted, 'Egypt holds the right of leadership of the Arab countries and every Arab country has become used to regard Egypt as her direction of prayer (*qublah*) and as her model'.[19] The fact that in 1936 Egypt regained its independence was of help to its Arab confrères in their national struggle,[20] but it also obliged Egypt to use its newly acquired position to help the Arabs to gain the same status. The Arabs expected Egypt to do so and to lead them in their struggle and if it failed it would forfeit this right, concluded *al-Muqattam*, an important daily newspaper of pan-Arab leaning.[21]

No small amount of Egyptian pride and feeling of superiority accompanied the ideological demand to strengthen Egypt's Arab unity. *Al-Ahram* noted with satisfaction that when 'an Egyptian came to one of the Arab countries he felt as though he moved from one Egyptian province to another. For the same reasons anyone of the Arab countries when he reached Egypt felt that he visited a country like his'. The Arab countries followed Egypt as far as their struggle for independence and cultural and economic revival were concerned. Therefore 'they are proud of everything Egyptian, of the courage and patriotism of Egyptian leaders, of the people of Bank Misr and their efforts, of the Egyptian professors and their research, of the Egyptian authors and their writings and of the Egyptian youth and their awakening'.[22]

It should be noted that Arab nationalists in general gave a very favourable welcome to this development in Egyptian national orientation, a welcome which in its turn was noted with satisfaction by Egyptian protagonists of this trend.[23] A special place in this respectful attitude was held by Sati'al-Husri, perhaps the most important propagator of secular pan-Arab ideology, who through all his prolific writings accredited Egypt with the right, or even the obligation, of leadership of the Arab world in its march toward unity.[24] In April 1936 Sati'al-Husri explained in an article that 'nature had endowed Egypt with all the attributes and virtues which imposed upon her the obligation of leadership and command in the awakening of Arab nationalism'. Egypt's geographical position, its size and the fact that it was the most advanced Arab country in its civilisation, in its wealth and in its cultural activities made it the 'natural leader of Arab nationalism'.[25]

A very important political factor which gave much force and credibility to Egypt's new Arab identity was the fact that during 1936 the *Wafd* and its leaders were to a large extent taken over by Arabism. The settlement of the question of relations with Britain and the restoration of the 1923 more democratic constitution left the *Wafd* with no other live issue to use in rallying the masses and in sustaining their support for the party. On the other hand, the Islamic fundamentalist organisations were attracting an increasing number of disenchanted *Wafdi* youths, and were using the Palestine issue (see below, pp. 162ff.) to embarrass the Wafdist government elected in May 1936.[26] Nahhas, the Wafdist Prime Minister, was caught between his feelings of solidarity with the Palestine Arabs and the need not to lag behind the Islamic organisations in championing the Arab cause in Palestine on the one hand, and his eagerness not to antagonise the British before and soon after the conclusion of the treaty with them, on the other. Therefore up to the summer of 1937 he refrained from any public utterances on the subject and exerted pressure on the press and on the Islamic organisations, as a result of British demands, to tone down their anti-British campaign on the grounds that this would prejudice his own efforts to bring about a settlement of the problem.[27]

However, even when Nahhas was careful not to let the agitation in support of the Palestine Arabs get out of hand and while maintaining a friendly attitude towards the British, he 'took every opportunity of passionately advocating the Arab cause in private conversation, using on one occasion the phrase, "we, too, are Arabs"'.[28] Later on in the summer of 1937 Egypt expressed its concern over the Palestine question no less vociferously than other Arab countries. It voiced its opposition to the Peel Commission's recommendation of the partition of Palestine, and the maiden speech of the Egyptian Minister of Foreign Affairs after Egypt's admission to the League of Nations dealt almost entirely with the Palestine question.[29] No wonder that in October 1937 R.I. Campbell, head of the British Foreign Office's Egyptian department, noted that 'Egypt (and particularly the Wafd) aspires to a political leadership among the Moslems in the Middle East'.[30] Later, in December 1937, Faruq, the new young king, dismissed Nahhas and thus freed him from all constraints. Thenceforward Nahhas and his party used pan-Arab feelings and the Palestine question in their struggle against both their internal political rivals and the British.[31]

Thus the question of Egypt's Arab identity and orientation became deeply intermingled with its internal political strife, all the more so since the Palace and the politicians connected with it did whatever they could to outbid the *Wafd* on the matter. Consequently, most Egyptian politicians made the identification of Egypt as an Arab country a cornerstone of their policy of achieving for Egypt a prominent and even the leading position in the bloc of Arab states and the exalted title of Caliph (or *Amir al-Mu'minin*) for its young king.

Some of the numerous newspapers and magazines which stressed the Arab cultural and historical identity of Egypt and its political consequences went further by pointing to the links that Muhammad 'Ali and Ibrahim Pasha, the founders of the Egyptian ruling dynasty, had established with Syria and the Lebanon.[32] *Al-Hilal*, one of the most important Egyptian cultural magazines which for years had been propagating Egypt's Arab identity, published in April 1939 a special issue called 'The Arabs and Islam in the Modern Era', which paid special attention to the Egyptian dynasty's role in that respect. It was pointed out that the late King Fu'ad, Faruq's father, had inherited from his forefathers his love and encouragement for everything Arab. Muhammad 'Ali's goal of forming a 'glorious Islamic-Arab Empire, the foundation of which would be Egypt', instead of the crumbling Ottoman Empire, was a living example to the present king. Muhammad 'Ali's rebellion against the Ottomans was nothing else than a vital point in the awakening Arab national movement.[33]

The implementation of Faruq's goal of becoming the leader of all Arab states or even the Caliph of the Muslims was entrusted to 'Ali Mahir Pasha, Sheikh Muhammad Mustafa al-Maraghi, the rector of al-Azhar and the tutor of the young king, and, to lesser extent, Muhammad Mahmud Pasha, the leader of the Liberal Constitutional Party and a friend of Sheikh al-Maraghi. These three persons co-operated with the Palace and did their best to bolster its position in order to decrease the position of the *Wafd*.

When in December 1937 the King dismissed Nahhas Pasha from the premiership and appointed in his stead Muhammad Mahmud Pasha to head a government from which the *Wafd* was excluded and 'Ali Mahir himself was appointed two months earlier as the head of the Royal Cabinet, Sheikh al-Maraghi used this political change to revive his old ideas about the Caliphate.[34] He sent Egyptian *'ulama'* to Muslim countries to propagate the idea of an Egyptian Caliph with vice-Caliphs in each of these countries and the establishment of a permanent Supreme Islamic Council in Cairo, participated in by representatives from all the Muslim countries, to discuss and formulate a common policy on all questions of interest to these states.[35] Al-Maraghi tried to paint Faruq's kingship in religious colours, drawing attention to the religious character of his coronation and to his leading the public in the Friday prayers in Cairo's central mosque, and thus seeking to enhance his prestige at home.

These attempts were at first thwarted by Nahhas's Wafdist government claiming that the King derived his authority from the Constitution and not from any other source. And this strife contributed to the growing tension between the *Wafd* on the one hand and the King and his entourage on the other,[36] and to the dismissal of the former's government. Consequently the King was less handicapped. When Muslim leaders from other countries gathered in Cairo Faruq was presented to them as *Amir al-Mu'minin* and *Khalifat al-Muslimin* and allegedly received their pledges of allegiance.[37] If Faruq became Caliph, al-Maraghi himself would become, so he hoped, *Shaykh al-Islam* (head of the religious establishment) on the late Ottoman model.[38]

Another public manifestation of Faruq's attitude and policy was his support for Islamic institutes of learning inside and outside Egypt.[39] A more covert manifestation was the King's financial support for the *Salafi* fundamentalist movements or for the ultra-nationalist Young Egypt Party which in one way or another propagated the idea of forming a broader unity of Middle Eastern countries with Egypt at its head.[40] 'Abd al-Hamid Sa'id, the leader of the Young Men's Muslim Association, and one of the beneficiaries of the King's benevolence, rewarded him by joining the propaganda campaign stressing the suitability of Egypt and its king for assuming the role of the Caliphate.[41]

However, the Caliphate campaign did not get very far, because it aroused the hostile reaction of Turkey and Saudi Arabia and the opposition of Britain.[42] Furthermore, its religious traditional character put it in an ambivalent position vis-à-vis the notion of Arab unity which was then inspired by more secular factors of common language, culture and history.

These developments notwithstanding, Egypt in the late 1930s had not become fully convinced that Arab unity was imminent and that it might in the near future be absorbed within a broader Arab framework. More often than not the term 'Arab unity' (*al-Ittihad al-'Arabi* or *al-Wahdah al-'Arabiyyah*) meant Arab solidarity against Zionism and the West, partnership of feelings, economic and cultural co-operation, etc.[43] But even those feelings were strong enough to influence the course of Egyptian policies deeply.

Pan-Arabism in the Fertile Crescent

The situation in the Fertile Crescent (Syria and Iraq) was rather a different matter. Except for Antun Sa'adah's Syrian Nationalist Party there was no attempt to challenge the basic assumptions and beliefs of pan-Arabism. Certainly there was nothing like, or similar to, the triumph of the concepts of territorial nationalism which had swept Egypt during the 1920s. The Hashemites both in Iraq and Trans-Jordan regarded themselves as an Arab dynasty whose source of legitimacy sprang from their traditional position in the past history of Islam and the Arabs and from their role in the Arab Revolt during the First World War and not from the allegiance of the population in those countries.

There are clear signs that during the late 1930s pan-Arab attitudes, as distinct from the Hashemite dynastic interests or Iraqi state aims, were strengthened in Iraq too. The educated public in Iraq were keenly following developments in the neighbouring Arab countries, and Syria's successful general strike in the winter of 1936 left its mark on them.[44] The Iraqi public was deeply impressed that Egypt in 1936 decided to send as minister to Iraq one of its most outspoken pan-Arab activitists, 'Abd al-Rahman 'Azzam Pasha, who during his sojourn in Baghdad was indefatigable in preaching the virtues of Arab unity.[45] This appointment was regarded in Egypt too as a clear indication of the growth of the pan-Arab mood in Egypt, 'since 'Azzam was one of the foremost Egyptians who were working for strengthening the ties between Egypt and her neighbours and who believed that Egypt had to adopt Arab and Oriental policy and that the Egyptian interest in getting closer to the Arab countries was stronger than in approaching Europe'.[46]

'Azzam used his office in Baghdad to establish contacts and propagate his ideas beyond the circle of Iraqi Ministers and public servants. He used to invite many intellectuals, journalists and other leaders of public opinion to the Egyptian Legation, which he transformed by his own admission into a 'club of Arab propaganda'.[47] The Iraqis were deeply influenced by 'Azzam's activities and the Baghdad press helped him to spread his message to the public at large. Concurrently, an important Egyptian pan-Arab ideologist, 'Abd al-Mun'im Muhammad Khalaf, was then teaching in a Baghdad high school.[48] His message was the same, and the combined effect helped to assure the Iraqis that pan-Arabism was becoming a very serious factor indeed.

Members of the Iraqi intelligentsia who shared the belief in Arab unity formed in 1935 a cultural-political club, *al-Muthanna*, which propagated this belief by means of public lectures, in which 'Azzam and other non-Iraqi Arab guests, many of them Palestinians, took part, and by brochures. This club, and Arab national circles in general, keenly interested themselves in political developments in the neighbouring Arab countries, Palestine and Syria in particular. As far as the latter was concerned the most important development was the secession of the Alexandretta district by the French mandatory authorities to Turkey. This act was regarded in Iraq as the first step in the dismemberment of Syria and aroused old-time dislike and even fear of Turkey.[50] Political leaders demanded that their government express their support of Syria and use their diplomatic means in Syria's favour, but the government and the Foreign Minister were usually rather cautious.[51] The public at large were, on the other hand, much more enraged. Several stormy mass demonstrations were organised in support of Syria's right to the Alexandretta region, but to no avail.[52]

One of the outstanding manifestations of the growing pan-Arab feeling in Iraq was the 15-strong delegation of Iraqi senators, deputies and other notables who left in March 1936 for a visit to Syria, Palestine and Egypt. The members of the delegation made speeches in which they stressed the fundamental unity of the Arabs and pledged the help and sympathy of Iraq to all their brother Arabs in the struggle for independence. Everywhere they were fêted and most hospitably entertained. Sa'id Thabit's speech in Nablus, Palestine, was especially extreme and aroused the indignation of the British.[53]

In Syria itself the most important sign of the rising tide of pan-Arabism was the formation of *'Usbat al-'Amal al-Qawmi* ('The Nationalist Action League'). This organisation was formed in 1933[54] as the political instrument of the uncompromising pan-Arab youth who rejected any compromise or co-operation with the mandatory authorities. The strongest branch of the League was in Hums in Syria; being loyal to its pan-Arab ideology it tried to extend itself to other Arab countries as well, but it seems that it succeeded in doing so only in Lebanon.[55] And indeed even its Constitutional Conference was held in Qurnayil, Lebanon, where its fundamental programme was adopted.

This programme had a strong anti-imperialist tone and it exhorted the Arabs to fight imperialism in all its forms: economic, political and moral. The League had two principal goals, claiming that 'the achievement of each of them is a necessary condition for the achievement of the other': (a) total Arab sovereignty and independence; and (b) comprehensive Arab unity. Generally speaking the League tried to present pan-Arab ideology in concrete political terms which could be accomplished by human means.[56] The two main leaders of the League were Sabri al-'Asali (a future Prime Minister of Syria on behalf of the National Party) and 'Abd al-Razzaq al-Dandashi, while in 1938 'Ali al-Maha'iri served as the League's General Secretary.[57]

In view of their opposition to any compromise with the French mandatory authorities, they totally rejected the 1936 proposed treaty with France which the National Bloc leaders negotiated with her, and repeated their pledge to carry on the struggle until full independence had been achieved and the 'greater Arab state' had been formed.[58] This kind of opposition brought the League to reject the policy and the leading role of the National Bloc. This opposition further stiffened as it became clear that the National Bloc had failed to get French ratification of the proposed treaty.

It seems that the League achieved the peak of its fame in connection with the Alexandretta affair. In the person of Zaki al-Arsuzi the League found an effective local leader in the Alexandretta region.⁵⁹ This person had been instrumental in organising the local resistance in Alexandretta to the cession of the region to the Turks until 1938 when the Turks took full control and Arsuzi had to flee and take refuge in Damascus. There he joined forces with other nationalists and participated in forming the nucleus of the future *Ba'th* Party.⁶⁰ It is true that the League could not survive the blows it incurred in the late 1930: the death of 'Abd al-Razzaq al-Dandashi in summer 1935, the expulsion from the party of Sabri al-'Asali owing to his readiness to stand for election to the Syrian Parliament and the desertion of the League by Arsuzi. But during the second half of the 1930s the League was influential and spread the ideas of pan-Arabism among the Syrian public.⁶¹

The leaders of the National Bloc themselves were mainly interested in promoting the independence of Syria, but from time to time they also interested themselves in advancing pan-Arab ideas. And although nothing concrete came out of their feelers directed towards King 'Abd al-'Aziz Al Sa'ud and the British, they were enough to keep the matter of Arab unity alive and gradually helped to convince the British that the pan-Arab movement was real and active.⁶²

The effect of the Palestine Arab Rebellion

However important those dynastical, political, cultural and ideological factors may have been, the effect of the developments in Palestine during the 1936–9 years stands as perhaps the single most important factor which contributed to the growth of pan-Arab ideology, to the feeling of solidarity among the Arab peoples and to the attempt at shaping a unified general Arab position and policy.⁶³

Interest in Egypt in the Palestine conflict had been growing since the late 1920s, when its religious aspect became more apparent with the Wailing Wall disturbances of 1939.⁶⁴ But after the outbreak of the 1936 revolt, there was a much more widespread feeling of solidarity with the Palestine Arabs. On the popular level it took the form of hundreds of protests, appeals, speeches and gatherings mainly organised by the Young Men's Muslim Association and the Muslim Brethren, Palestinian and Syrian émigrés, student groups and smaller opposition parties. These circles also collected money for the Arab victims of the British reprisals⁶⁵ and even tried to recruit volunteers for the fighting.

These activities were organised and co-ordinated by the 'Higher Committee for the Relief of the Palestine Victims', which was active from May 1936 until 1939 and which included 'Abd al-Hamid Sa'id, Hasan al-Banna' and Muhammad Husayn Haykal, the leaders, respectively, of the YMMA, the Muslim Brethren and the Liberal Constitutional Party and Hamad al-Basil, Vice-President of the *Wafd* and an active pan-Arabist. This campaign embarrassed the Wafdist government, who had to restrain themselves in view of the delicate stage in Anglo-Egyptian relations i.e. the negotiations for concluding the Anglo-Egyptian Treaty of Alliance, and it brought about some losses in the popularity of the *Wafd*.[66] The culmination of this outbreak of popular feeling was reached in July 1936 when both houses of the Egyptian Parliament passed resolutions in support of the 'Palestinian nation which is sacrificing its sons for freedom and honour'.[67]

Even the Wafdist government, although deeply immersed in the negotiations with Britain and extremely cautious to avoid any more which might erect new blocks in their path, could not remain totally aloof from the growing mood of support of the Palestine Arabs' struggle. Concurrently with restraining public opinion and preventing violent manifestations of pro-Palestinian feelings Mustafa al-Nahhas, the Wafdist Prime Minister, did not conceal his pro-Palestinian views although he expressed them moderately.[68] He warned the British in June 1936 that on the Palestine question they 'were sitting on an "oven" in Egypt and only a "miracle" and his own continuous influence prevented violent agitation with possible anti-Jewish outbreak'. He recommended that the British government temporarily suspend Jewish immigration to Palestine, a move which would enable the Royal (Peel) Commission to function at once.[69] Nahhas adhered to this same means – discreet approaches to the British – after the conclusion of the treaty with Britain, and during the latter half of 1936 he offered his good services as mediator between the Palestine Arabs and the British Government.[70]

In Syria as well, the same kind of propaganda campaign was carried out, mostly by the Society of Islamic Guidance (*Jam'iyyat al-Hidayah al-Islamiyyah*). A large amount of ammunition was smuggled from there to Palestine by bedouins.[71] However, the general effect of the Palestine Revolt on the Syrian public was not very strong, since the Syrians realised that mandatory Palestine had prospered under British tutelage and with the development of the Jewish National Home much more than their own country. Furthermore, they did not want to antagonise the British whom they wanted to mobilise against the French authorities in their country.[72]

In Iraq, which had already achieved independence in 1930 and therefore was much freer to express its feelings and to act, the reactions to the Palestine Arab Revolt were much stronger and more significant. As in Egypt, many manifestations of the Iraqi public's disapproval of British policy in Palestine and support for the demands of the Palestine Arabs were voiced and funds were collected for the victims of the struggle.[73]

The co-ordinating body of this campaign was the Palestine Defence Committee formed by Taha al-Hashimi, Muhammad Mahdi Kubba, Naji al-Suwaydi, a senator and former minister, and Sa'id Thabit, the Speaker of the Parliament, together with two visiting Palestinian leaders. This body used a very strong anti-British tone in their leaflets, in which extremely distorted news about the revolt in Palestine was printed. A special role in this campaign was played by the pan-Arab *al-Muthanna* Club.[74]

Strong pressure was exerted in 1936 by these organisations, Members of Parliament and delegates of the Palestine Arabs on the Government of Iraq to join this campaign, to interfere with the British Government and to help the Palestine Revolt in every possible way. Ostensibly at least, the Iraqi Government both for reasons of internal policy and for the sake of their good relations with Britain did not desire to be drawn into taking any action, but they could not resist this strong pressure for long. The government forbade public meetings and demonstrations but had to permit the organisation of days of mourning and flag days. A deputation of senators and parliamentary deputies visited the British Ambassador and handed to him a memorandum in which they expressed the grave anxiety of Iraq concerning the situation in Palestine.[75]

The Iraqi Government also protested to the German Government against the purchase by Dr Chaim Weizmann, the President of the World Zionist Organisation and himself a prominent chemical scientist, of chemical equipment from a Frankfurt firm to be used in the 'big chemical industry which had been established in Rehovoth' for armament purposes. But Tawfiq al-Suwaydi did not want to pursue that matter too far in order not to bring about a crisis in the relations between the Arabs and Germany.[76]

More important was the attitude adopted by the Iraqi Government towards the 200-strong contingent of volunteers from Iraq, Syria and Trans-Jordan headed by Fawzi al-Qawuqji which reached Palestine on 22 August 1936.[77] This contingent was organised by the Iraqi Palestine Defence Committee who had persuaded al-Qawuqji to resign his commission in the Iraqi army and lead the contingent. The Iraqi Government had initially agreed to al-Qawuqji's mission and even supplied the volunteers with rifles and automobiles to carry them to Palestine, although at the last moment Yasin al-Hashimi, the Prime Minister, had second thoughts. He realised that the British had learned about the contingent and since he wanted to avoid any quarrel with them, he tried to stop the contingent from going to Palestine. But it was too late.[78]

In addition to various manifestations of support and solidarity for the Palestine Arabs during their general strike and the first stage of their revolt (April–October 1936) which took place in the various Arab countries, the contingent jointly attempted to mediate between the Palestine and the British Governments. This attempt failed but the intervention of the Arab rulers gave the Palestine HAC a pretext for calling off the strike. The story of this intervention and the strains which accompanied it has already been told in a previous book and we do not intend to repeat it here.[79]

THE RISE OF POLITICAL PAN-ARABISM

The joint Arab intervention in the affairs and on behalf of the Palestine Arabs did not end in October 1936 when the general strike and the first stage of the revolt were called off. Already in July 1936 in response to the Saudi proposal that some sort of joint *démarche* should be made by Iraq, Saudi Arabia and the Yemen, Yasin al-Hashimi, the Iraqi Prime Minister, had prepared a draft memorandum presenting the Arab case in the Palestine conflict which he thought might be communicated jointly by the Iraqi and Saudi Governments to the British Government.[80]

Upon the cessation of the general strike of the Palestine Arabs, the Iraqi Government went further. In October 1936 they invited King Ibn Saud to send a delegation to Baghdad to consult with them with a view to adopting a common policy towards Britain over the Palestine question. But the British Government were reluctant to let such an eventuality materialise and agreed to accept only separate approaches from each government.[81] Ibn Saud himself was far from enthusiastic about the Iraqi proposal for joint action, but since Amin al-Husayni exerted pressure on him to act on behalf of the Palestine Arabs he decided to comply.[82] And, indeed, both Iraq and Saudi Arabia submitted to the British Government separate memoranda of their own in which the Arab point of view over the Palestine question was presented. Ibn Saud did not even communicate the content of his memorandum to the Iraqis. The memoranda and other approaches were brought to the notice of the Palestine Royal Commission and this indicated the importance that the British Government attributed to the Arab Governments' view regarding the Palestine problem.[83]

Another arena in which some Arab countries could act in favour of the interests of the Palestine Arabs was the League of Nations. Upon the conclusion in 1936 of the Anglo-Egyptian Treaty Egypt was admitted to the international body and joined Iraq who had preceded her there by four years. The representatives of the two countries coordinated the views they expressed there and in May 1937 the Egyptian delegate used one of his earliest statements to the General Council to express the Arab grievances over Palestine.[84]

The Palestine Arabs in their turn carried on all through the crucial years of 1936–9 a massive propaganda campaign in which they stressed that the questions pertaining to Palestine were no longer the concern of the Arab people of Palestine alone, but of Arabs and Muslims at large.[85] The defence of the Arab character of Palestine became the first duty of Arab nationalists anywhere. And, indeed, this attitude was echoed in very many publications of various Arab nationalist organisations all over the Arab world.[86] The campaign even reached remote parts of the Muslim world. Resolutions in support of the Palestine Arabs were passed in places such as Zanzibar.[87] The British could not but be impressed by the fact that developments in Palestine were being reported in the Hijazi press, discussed in Egypt, commented on in India and becoming a lively topic almost everywhere in the Islamic world.[88]

A very strong boost to this feeling of solidarity with the Palestine Arabs was given in the summer of 1937 in the wake of the publication of the Palestine Royal (Peel) Commission's recommendation for the partition of Palestine, and its endorsement, in principle, by the British Government. In Egypt the harsh reaction to the Peel Report was really a turning point in its attitude to the Palestine problem.[89] The proposed Jewish state, although very small in size, was regarded as an alien factor in its culture, a potential economic competitor to Egypt's young industries and a source of danger to Egypt's hold on the Sinai peninsula. Strong pressure was exerted on the Egyptian Government by the press, members of Parliament and various Muslim and pan-Arab associations to use their influence as an ally of Britain to deter the latter from implementing that recommendation. Most significant was that politicians opposed to the incumbent Wafdist government began to use the Palestine question as a political weapon against it. Muhammad Mahmud Pasha and Muhammad Hasayn Haykal of the Liberal Constitutionalist Party and Ahmad Husayn, leader of the Young Egypt Party, publicly expressed their support of the Palestine Arabs and repeatedly criticised their government for its inaction.[90] Faced with this pressure, the Egyptian Government responded by promising to consult other Arab governments and by expressing their opposition to the partition of Palestine to the British Government.[91]

The Iraqi reaction to the Peel Commission recommendations was even more forceful. The Iraqi Government was headed at that time by Hikmat Sulayman who had taken over by a *coup d'état* at the expense of the former pan-Arab leaders of Iraq (Nuri al-Sa'id, Yasin al-Hashimi etc.). Being of non-Arab descent and accused of indifference to pan-Arabism, Hikmat Sulayman used this opportunity to demonstrate that his loyalty to general Arab causes was not weaker than his predecessors'. And indeed his harsh reaction had strong echoes in Iraq and outside it and aroused a widespread wave of support.[92] The Iraqi Government also submitted a memorandum to the League of Nations in which they presented the Arab arguments against the partition of Palestine and claimed that Iraq had vital interests in Palestine originating from racial, political, religious and economic causes.[93] Such a tough position also influenced the Egyptian Government in making up their minds. However, it should be pointed out that after Hikmat Sulayman lost his position as Prime Minister in August 1937, Iraq's attitude towards the Peel recommendation became milder. Already in September 1937, Tawfiq al-Suwaydi, who was then representing his country in the League of Nations, 'privately' told G. Rendel and Sir John Shuckburgh that the partition plan should be amended so that the proposed Jewish state included only areas in Jewish ownership. And several months later, Jamil al-Midfa'i, Hikmat

Sulayman's successor, suggested that a scheme of cantonisation, which would 'allot to the Jews a number of small areas at present inhabited by them' might be considered as a substitute to the partition plan.[94]

The Saudi reaction was initially not sharp and was not made public. But it soon changed. Saudi representatives told British officials that the Saudi King found himself under strong pressure exerted by the 'Wahabis of Nejd'. They represented that it was against the principles of Islam that a Jewish state should be set up. The King was also receiving a constant stream of telegrams and messages from Muslims outside his dominions begging him to oppose the principle of partition.[95]

The fact that Iraq, Ibn Saud's rival, was so vocal in its rejection of partition embarrassed Ibn Saud. He did not want, on the one hand, to lag behind Iraq, but, on the other, he did not want to jeopardise his good relations with Britain which he had been cultivating over a very long period stretching over almost 40 years. His way out of this entanglement was to stress again and again that he was being pressured to oppose partition by the *'ulama'* of his kingdom who were using an Islamic anti-Jewish *hadith* (a fragment of Muslim tradition) in order to prove to him that it was his religious duty to do so. According to this *hadith*, a day would come when the Muslims would kill the Jews. The fleeing Jews would hide behind stones and trees, but they would cry: 'a Jew is hiding behind me; come to kill him'.[96] The King told the British that if the *'ulama'* published a *fatwa* declaring a *jihad* against partition he would not be able to restrain the Saudi tribes.[97] This kind of indirect threat had an important effect on British policy-making.

In Syria too protests were made against partition,[98] but since this country had not yet become independent it had little effect on Britain, although it completed the circle of general Arab rejection and solidarity.

Against this background of joint public Arab disapproval of the recommendations of the Peel Commission, King Ibn Saud suggested to Iraq and Egypt that they should adopt a common policy against the partition of Palestine. British advice to the contrary sufficed to dissuade Iraq from joining hands with Ibn Saud, and Mustafa Nahhas of Egypt had his own considerations in declining Ibn Saud's invitation.[99] However, the 'united Arab opposition to the partition of Palestine' was regarded by Major W. J. Cawthorn, an Intelligence authority at the War Office, as 'the first real example, since the Golden Age, of a movement which has stirred the whole Arab world at once'.[100]

But even this general hostile reaction to the Peel Commission recommendations did not erase the deep inter-Arab jealousies and rivalries. The fact that 'Abdallah's Trans-Jordan Emirate was to gain from joining the Arab parts of Palestine to his domains only strengthened Ibn Saud's opposition and increased his suspicion of, and hostility to, 'Abdallah.[101] And, indeed, since 'Abdallah had only to gain from these recommendations, he did not join the general Arab chorus of denunciation. Ibn Saud threatened that if Britain persisted in its declared intention to carry out the Peel recommendation and unite Arab Palestine and Trans-Jordan into an independent kingdom, he would not be able to continue to leave his claim to 'Aqaba and Ma'an, the southernmost little towns of Trans-Jordan, in abeyance.[102]

This feeling of widespread solidarity with the Palestine Arabs and the almost universal rejection of the Peel recommendations was used by the leaders of the Palestine Arabs as a means of solidifying the general Arab support of their cause. Apart from their persistent attempt to mobilise the diplomatic, political and military assistance of the Arab countries,[103] these leaders tried to organise a general Arab congress which would demonstrate the amount of support they enjoyed in the Arab world.

Their basic assumption was that the Palestine Arabs alone could not bring about a drastic change of course in British policy in Palestine. Therefore they had to excite the feelings of the Arab and Islamic worlds for action in their support. At first they turned their eyes towards Cairo. But there the idea was supported by the traditionally pro-Arab politicians, like Mahmud Basyuni, the President of the Senate, whereas the ruling *Wafd* government were reluctant to extend their support and hence to harm the good relations with Britain which followed the conclusion, in summer 1936, of the Treaty of Alliance.[104] Therefore they tried elsewhere. They approached Ibn Saud and requested his permission to hold a general Muslim congress in Mecca during the pilgrimage season 'in order to enlist the support of the Muslim World for the Arabs of Palestine'. But there too they got the same negative reply and for the same reason.[105] Repeated approaches by representatives of the Palestine Arabs did not change Ibn Saud's objection,[106] and Amin al-Husayni, the Mufti of Jerusalem who took part in the *Hajj* of spring 1937, had to confine his public utterances to purely non-political matters.[107]

In the summer of 1937 attempts to organise a General Arab Congress were made, helped by the publication of the Peel Commission recommendations and by the almost universal Arab indignation which they aroused. Discussions between Amin al-Husayni and the Syrian nationalists, organised by the Palestine Defence Committee during the former's visit to Syria, led to the resolution to call such a congress. Attempts were first made to assemble official delegates of Arab governments. These efforts proved abortive. Finally, the Syrian committee sent invitations to 500 personalities in the Arab world to attend the congress in Syria.[108] Two *'ulama'* (Amin al-Tamimi and Hasan Abu al-Sa'ud) were sent to Egypt to enlist public and official support, but favourable response came mainly from the ultra-nationalist *al-Hizb al-Watani* and the YMMA.[109]

On 8 September 1937 411 people attended the congress which took place in Bludan, Syria. Of these 160 were Syrians, 128 Palestinians, sixty-five Lebanese, thirty Trans-Jordanians, twelve Iraqis, six Egyptians and one Saudi Arabian. Naji al-Suwaydi of Iraq was elected president with Muhammad 'Ali 'Alluba (Egypt), Amir Shakib Arslan (Lebanon) and Bishop Ignatius Huraykah (the Greek-Orthodox Bishop of Hamah, Syria) as his deputies. The other participants included prominent politicians and pan-Arab activists, such as 'Abd al-Hamid Sa'id (president of the Egyptian YMMA), Makram 'Ubayd (deputy leader of the *Wafd* and known for his pan-Arab leanings), 'Abdallah al-Yafi and Riyad al-Sulh (Lebanon) and Lutfi al-Haffar and Nabih al-'Azmah (president of the Syrian Palestine Defence Committee) from Syria. The congress resolved that Palestine was an integral part of the Arab world, that partition and the establishment of a Jewish state therein should be resisted and that the struggle should continue until it had been liberated and Arab sovereignty over the land had been attained. The congress also adopted resolutions regarding economic and propaganda warfare against the Jews.

The radical pan-Arab delegates used this conference to organise a special meeting of their own in order to strengthen their co-operation and co-ordinate their activities. They decided to establish a united organisation of the various nationalist societies such as the Nationalist Action League (of Syria), *al-Muthanna* Club (of Iraq) and nationalist Scout groups in order 'to unite the Arab nationalist young men and to adopt a nationalist programme of the Arab nationalist youth from the [Atlantic] Ocean to the [Persian] Gulf'.[110]

By its effect on Arab public opinion, and since it was during its deliberations that the Palestine Arab leaders decided to resume their rebellion, this congress 'may be considered a landmark in the increasing involvement of the Arab world in the Palestine problem.'[111]

And, indeed, when on the resumption of the revolt at the end of September 1937, the British authorities in Palestine outlawed the Higher Arab Committee, arrested and deported its leaders, dissolved the SMC and forced its president Amin al-Husayni to take asylum inside the precincts of the *al-Haram al-Sharif* in Jerusalem in order to avoid arrest,[112] a wave of protest and indignation swept the entire Arab world.

In Iraq public opinion vehemently reacted against these measures and the government had to submit an official protest 'against rigorous measures taken by His Majesty's Government in Palestine'. A similar Saudi move followed and the Saudi diplomatic representatives in London repeatedly warned the Foreign Office that the policy of retaliation and punishment pursued by the Palestine Government would do harm to the relations between Saudi Arabia and Britain.[113]

In Egypt, too, there was a widespread hostile reaction which was mainly expressed by the traditionally pro-Palestine circles: the Muslim fundamentalists, the pan-Arab politicians and the anti-*Wafd* opposition leaders, such as Muhammad Mahmud Pasha and Isma'il Sidqi.[114] This last factor could not but jeopardise the standing of the Wafdist government which was then in a state of decline although its leaders aspired to a position of leadership in the Arab world.[115] Gradually people of various shades of opinion joined this movement and declared that they wished Britain to change its policy in Palestine since they regarded the Egyptian nation as 'closely related to the Palestine Arab people by the ties of language, religion, blood, tradition and neighbourhood'.[116]

As the Palestine Arab rebellion intensified, so the feelings of solidarity in Egypt grew. And if in 1936–7 the protests against British policy in Palestine had been couched in moderate terms laying stress on the friendship for Great Britain which the Egyptian people were now feeling for it as an ally, in 1938 most of these restraints were set aside. A fierce anti-British campaign was carried out, spearheaded by the Muslim Brethren.[117] Now that the *Wafd* Party was out of power its leaders had no hesitation in joining this campaign as though they were trying to beat Muhammad Mahmud with his own stick.[118] Two Palestinian leaders, Emil al-Ghauri and Munif al-Husayni, were staying in Egypt at the time and their activities contributed to the creation of the atmosphere.[119]

The same sort of development took place in Iraq as well. Public meetings were organised, special prayers were held in the mosques and donations were collected for 'the victims of British aggression in Palestine'.[120] All these actions were organised by the Iraqi Palestine Defence Committee, under the presidency of Naji al-Suwaydi. And it is very probable that Iraq was one of the main suppliers of money and weapons to the Palestine Arab Rebellion.[121] Under this pressure even the pro-British Iraqi Government under the premiership of Jamil al-Midfa'i felt bound to voice their objection to British policy in Palestine.[122]

Even in Syria, which was going through grave ordeals of its own (the secession of the Alexandretta region to Turkey and the failure of the French to ratify their treaty with Syria), the manifestations of solidarity with the Palestine Arabs were intensified.[123]

Ibn Saud, who was afraid lest other leaders take the lead in this campaign, joined it in his usual cautious style full of expressions of friendship for Britain.[124] In one of his memoranda he stressed that unless he made his opposition to British policy clear he might find himself in a difficult position before the Muslim and the Arab world.[125]

These campaigns culminated in the Inter-Parliamentary Congress held on 7 October 1938 in Cairo. It was organised after an appeal for aid from Amin al-Husayni by the Egyptian Palestine Defence Parliamentary Committee, established in May 1938 under the presidency of Muhammad 'Ali 'Allubah.[126] 'Allubah and his Egyptian associates were approached by Amin al-Husayni after a previous approach to

King Ibn Saud and the Syrian Government had failed to bear any practical fruit.[127]

The congress was well attended – many people came from a dozen Arab and Muslim countries, including India and Yugoslavia, and 60 Members of Parliament from Egypt (including the Speaker of the Egyptian Parliament), Iraq and Syria. No delegates were permitted to come from Trans-Jordan or Saudi Arabia.[128] King Ibn Saud 'persuaded notables and Ulema that it was unnecessary for them to take part in the Congress because [the] King was in continued communication with His Majesty's Government with regard to Palestine with a view to a just and equitable settlement'.[129]

Other Arab governments too sent no official delegates, but at least the non-Wafdist Egyptian Government regarded the delegates with due respect. The Egyptian Prime Minister arranged a large banquet in their honour in which he delivered a strong speech in support of the demands of the Palestine Arabs. The Egyptian *Wafd* Party, on the other hand, boycotted the congress for internal political reasons, but made known their full support of the Palestine Arabs.[130]

The discussions of the congress caused no surprise: rejection of Zionism and of the partition of Palestine were repeated again and again. However, two issues were rather unusual. King Faruq of Egypt tried his best to make the congress as dignified as possible and exerted pressure on his Prime Minister, who was under counter pressure from the British, to render the highest possible acts of honour to the participants.[131] What the King had in mind was to use the congress as a stage to put forward his claim for the Caliphate. And, indeed, through the good services of his supporters, headed by Shaykh al-Azhar 'Ali al-Maraghi, Faruq was greeted at the opening session of the Congress as 'Faruq the First, the Commander of the Faithful'.[132]

The second interesting issue was the content of the speech delivered by Faris al-Khuri, Speaker of the Syrian Parliament. He explained that Palestine had been illegitimately divided from Syria in order to facilitate the implementation of Zionism and that Palestine would never be able to stand on its own. It should be reunited with Syria while the special positions of France in Syria proper and of Britain in Palestine should be safeguarded in separate treaties. Thus Palestine would be rescued from Zionism. This view was rejected by the Iraqi and the Palestinian delegations on the ground that negotiations with two 'imperialist' powers would make settlement of the Palestine problem more difficult.[133] Although the congress did not bear any tangible fruit it gave further impetus to the feelings of Arab solidarity.[134]

However, Faris al-Khuri was not deterred by the failure of the congress to adopt his proposals. He tried to convince the British Ambassador at Cairo of the usefulness of his proposals and claimed that he had succeeded in doing so and let his compatriots know his alleged success. He wanted to pursue his campaign in London. But only then, when he realised that the British authorities did not want to receive him, did he understand that the British Government were marching on a different road.[135]

For their part the British Government were well aware of the growing involvement of the Arab governments in the Palestine conflict. By inviting them to take part in the St James's Conference on Palestine, in the winter of 1939, the British Government hoped to get their assistance in solving this thorny question and to have an influential voice inside the pan-Arab movement.

The story of this conference has already been told and needs no repetition here.[136] What should interest us is the phenomenon of inter-Arab consultations in order to form a collective Arab position to be presented at the conference and, after its conclusion, as a common Arab reaction to the British position. Representatives of the Arab countries (except Trans-Jordan) which had been invited by Britain to take part in the St James's Conference and of the Palestine HAC assembled on 17 January in Cairo for three meetings. They agreed on a common programme which would guide them in the conference and, indeed, the Arab representatives at the St James's Conference did not deviate from the agreed programme. From Nuri al-Sa'id's pan-Arab point of view the very pattern of inter-Arab consultation and the formation of a joint Arab front mattered more than any other aspect of the issue. During these talks he expressed his hope 'that this historical meeting would serve as the foundation stone for the establishment of an Eastern and Arab League ...'.[137]

Muhammad Mahmud Pasha too did not fail to express his view that the Arab countries interested themselves in the Palestine question 'by virtue of their common foundations in history and language'. And Amir Faysal Al Sa'ud, head of the Saudi delegation, praised the fact that 'for the first time in our history we witness this clear manifestation of co-operation and solidarity of the Arab countries. For the first time we stand united. Let us hope that this conference may serve as a useful precedent for solving other problems and strengthening the foundations of our unity'.[138]

This pattern, although in a more restricted way, was repeated in April, when the delegates of the HAC were invited by Muhammad Mahmud to Cairo to take part in the discussion of the final proposals which had been presented to the Egyptians. The Palestinian delegates, according to the instructions of Amin al-Husayni, adopted an intransigent position and forced the reluctant Arab governments to join them in rejecting the British proposals so that apparently, at least, the joint Arab position was maintained or even strengthened.[139]

Thus a persistent example was created of repeated *démarches* by the Arab governments, individually or collectively, on behalf of the Palestine

Arabs. These *démarches* looked rather serious after the outbreak of the Second World War. In the autumn of 1939 the Egyptian and Iraqi Governments began to exert pressure on Britain to reach an agreement with the Palestine Arabs. Britain was required by the Egyptian, Saudi and Iraqi Governments to declare a general amnesty in Palestine which would include the deportees, the exiles and the convicted. The ground would thus be prepared for the establishment of a Palestinian Government and for a full agreement between the British Government and the HAC.[140] Britain realised that following the outbreak of the war the goodwill and co-operation of the Arab countries had to be secured. And although it refused to commit itself to the gesture demanded by the Arab governments,[141] in February 1940 Britain let the first Palestinian deported leaders return to their country.[142]

This was not regarded as sufficient by the three Arab governments and for many months to come they persistently demanded the proclamation of a general amnesty.[143] But what looked more important was the question of implementing the Palestine policy outlined in the May 1939 White Paper. Here the Arab governments rightly found themselves on more solid ground, since Britain had officially committed itself to that policy and the Arab demand did not go beyond the British commitment. In return for a British declaration of intention of implementing the White Paper the Arab governments 'should make an appeal to the people of Palestine to co-operate with the Allies in the present war'.[144]

In carrying out this step the Saudi ruler took the lead, which almost automatically aroused the jealousy of Nuri al-Sa'id,[145] Prime Minister of Iraq up to the end of March 1940 and Foreign Minister until almost the end of that year. In order to regain that lead and to withstand the sweeping tide of pan-Arab, pro-Nazi, anti-British feelings in his country he tried hard to bring about a tangible change in Britain's Palestine policy for which he would be credited and thus score important points in his competition against his rivals in the Arab world and at home. The pro-Palestinian feelings of the Iraqi public greatly increased as a result of the sustained campaign which Amin al-Husayni, the former Mufti of Jerusalem, had been carrying out since his arrival in Baghdad soon after the outbreak of war.[146]

On 25 May 1940 Nuri al-Sa'id officially submitted his demands to the British Government. In return for Iraq's participation in the fight against the pro-Nazi propaganda campaign, the British and the French Governments were required to make 'a clear and unambiguous pronouncement guaranteeing immediately or at least at the end of the War, the execution of the promises already given for the organisation of self government in Palestine and Syria'.[147] In other words the British Government were required to implement the constitutional provisions of the White Paper, whereas the French were asked to implement the 1936 treaty with Syria which they had not ratified. The collapse of France in the following month and Italy's declaration of war against Britain made Nuri al-Sa'id's demand over Syria irrelevant, but as far as Palestine was concerned, he must have felt that the time was very opportune to exert pressure on Britain which had passed through its most dangerous war-time situation.

Since Nuri did not get the reply he hoped for (see p. 240ff.) he resumed his pressure. During a talk on 31 July with the chief British adviser to the Iraqi Government, he demanded that in addition to strict implementation of the limitations laid on Jewish immigration and land purchases, Britain should go further than simply the strict implementation of the constitutional clauses of the White Paper. He now required Britain to begin the transition of power in Palestine not from the bottom, that is, by appointing more officials up to heads of departments, but from the top by the choice of head of state, the formation of the Council of Ministers and the drafting of a constitution, in a manner which had been since 1921 pursued in Iraq.[148] The British Government under Churchill rejected these demands, but this kind of pressure was repeatedly exerted during the whole war period.

Several months after Nuri al-Sa'id's initiative Mr George Antonius, who in winter 1939 had played a major role in the St James's Conference, presented a detailed memorandum of his own. In this memorandum Antonius analysed the general Arab situation, British policy and the Palestine question. He too demanded from Britain the speeding up of the liberation of the remaining political detainees in Palestine; the raising of the ban on the entry into Palestine of the remaining members of the HAC and of other political exiles, and 'the early enactment of measures to give effect to the constitutional and administrative changes on the lines of the White Paper'.[149]

Nuri al-Sa'id once again returned to his demand in January 1941 when he told the British Ambassador in Iraq that unless Britain implemented the constitutional provisions of the White Paper nothing could prevent pro-Nazi feelings among the Arabs.[150]

During the later years of the war when the United States' role and importance became clear, a great deal of Arab pressure was directed to that country. Many dispatches, memoranda and talks were devoted to the task of persuading the US Government of the justice of the Arab positions with regard to Palestine and of the harm that might be done to US interests and prestige in the Arab world. These acts of pressure were usually carried out on behalf of each Arab government on its own[151] but there was also an attempt at a joint Arab action.

This attempt was precipitated by the growth, in 1942, of the Jewish propaganda campaign, especially in the United States against British policy in general and for the formation of Jewish fighting units within the British army in particular.

THE RISE OF POLITICAL PAN-ARABISM

In December 1942 Nuri al-Sa'id proposed to Ibn Saud to join the Iraqi Government in an approach to the British Government protesting against the possible 'formation of a Jewish Army in Palestine', as the Jews had demanded. Ibn Saud had replied that he accepted the British denial of the story and considered it most undesirable in the general interest of the Arabs to make a public protest to the British Government. In January Nuri repeated his proposal of a joint approach to the British Government and got the same negative reply. There is little doubt that Ibn Saud's suspicion of Nuri al-Sa'id's real intentions were stronger than any other consideration. Ibn Saud of course made his attitude known to the British and scored several points in his competition against Nuri over British friendship.[152]

Consequently Nuri slightly changed his proposal and in February suggested that the Arabs should start a propaganda campaign in the United States and should exert pressure on its government. This change rather satisfied the British Government who thought that it would be worthwhile for the Arabs 'to make their views known in some way to the United States Government and to the American people'.[153] When Ibn Saud persisted in his refusal and rejected even a plea from the Syrian Government to join the Iraqis,[154] the British could not conceal their disappointment and H.M. Eyres of the Foreign Office minuted: 'It is pity that Ibn Saud automatically rejects even a good suggestion if it comes from Gen. Nuri'.[155] On the other hand in Egypt Nuri al-Sa'id succeeded in getting Egyptian consent to his suggestion that the Arab governments should address a note to President Roosevelt explaining the justice of the Arab cause in Palestine and seeking American support.[156]

The growth of cultural co-operation

The rise of political pan-Arabism was being accompanied and mutually strengthened by a strong trend of cultural co-operation among the Arab countries. As presented and analysed by I. Gershoni in his various publications,[157] the triumphant consolidation of the Arab identity of Egypt had been made possible by the growing awareness of Egypt's Arabo-Islamic culture and of its being a partner in a broader Arab cultural community.

Egypt's cultural relations with the Arab countries had already in the late 1920s become evident with travels of Egyptian politicians, writers, journalists, university dons and students to the Arab countries, such as Palestine, Syria, Lebanon, Iraq and Hijaz. They were usually warmly welcomed by their hosts and when they returned to Egypt they praised this 'warm welcome for the Egyptians and the love for everything Egyptian'. They saw to it that when their Arab counterparts visited Egypt, the Arab visitors would be welcomed in the same manner.[158]

However, in the early 1930s this exchange of visits was not tantamount to sharing the same national feelings and ideology. As Sati al-Husri tells us in his memoirs, in 1931 a group of Egyptian dons and students could not but express their astonishment when they heard their Iraqi hosts speaking of Arab nationalism. The Egyptians were then still thinking in terms of territorial identity and nationalism (i.e. Iraqi, Egyptian etc.) and restricted the use of the term 'Arab' to a definition of a bedouin wanderer. The Egyptians also had difficulty in not offending some of the Shi'ite *'ulema'* they met in Iraq.[159]

However, these exchanges of delegations of educated people and the study of students from one Arab country in another very much increased during the 1930s and had significant results. Iraq took the lead in this respect when it started at the end of 1935 to employ teachers, university dons, legal experts and physicians from Syria, Palestine, but mostly from Egypt, in its public services.[160] An agreement was reached between Iraq and Egypt to send various important cultural figures to work in Iraq and to let graduates of Iraqi secondary schools join the Egyptian university.[161]

The Iraqi Government under the premiership of Yasin al-Hashimi was very interested in the consolidation of cultural relations between Iraq and Egypt. Accordingly twelve Egyptian university professors were invited to teach in Baghdad University.[162] Among them were Zaki Mubarak, who was given a post in the Faculty of Humanities of Baghdad University, and 'Abd al-Razzaq al-Sanhuri, the prominent Egyptian professor of law and author of the Egyptian civil code, who was nominated as principal of Baghdad Law School. Other prominent Egyptian intellectuals, such as the writer Ibrahim 'Abd al-Qadir al-Mazini, visited Iraq and gave currency to their view of Arab partnership, solidarity and unity in public lectures and meetings with top Iraqi politicians.[163]

The Iraqi intellectuals and especially those of pan-Arab inclinations, such as the members of *al-Muthanna* Club, welcomed these guests most warmly and praised the national ties with Egypt.[164] When members of the Barada youth club of Damascus visited al-Muthanna Club in February 1938, the meeting was used by one of the Iraqi members to make such an inflammatory speech against the Iraqi Government 'for the government's failure to help Palestine' that the speech became a subject of concern and intervention by the Minister of the Interior.[165] The far-reaching effects of this occurrence did not escape the attention of such a keen British observer of the Iraqi scene as Sir Archibald Clark-Kerr.[166]

The Egyptian newspapers and circles which were already committed to the cause of Egypt's Arab identity did not fail to express their full satisfaction with this process. They praised the Egyptian Minister of Education, Muhammad 'Ali 'Allubah, himself a keen pan-Arabist, who worked for the same purpose.[167] These circles stressed that the consolidation of these cultural relations among the Arabs 'is an important force in determining the destiny of these peoples' and 'a factor in generating the idea of the Arab association'.[168]

The spokesmen of this trend had no doubt that Egypt had to integrate itself into the Arab East culturally and politically and praised the Egyptian people and newspapers who had preceded their government in promoting this trend.[165] Within the ranks of these people a special organisation for the advancement of Arabic culture emerged called 'the Society of Arabic Culture' (*Rabitat al-Adab al-Arabi*).[170]

This tendency soon bore fruit. Egyptian intellectuals who visited Iraq in 1936 felt at home and were happy to realise how friendly were the feelings that their hosts cherished.[171] These Egyptian intellectuals felt that special attention had to be paid to the unification of the various manifestations of Arabic culture. They tried to bring forward the idea of the need to unify the school programmes and textbooks in the Arab countries and to have periodical cultural conferences.[172]

In undertaking this Egypt had, so they thought, a special role to play: 'Cairo fulfils in the modern age the obligation which was carried out by Baghdad in the Abbaside era'; and 'Egypt is today the fountainhead from which the Arab culture and knowledge is flowering out'.[173] This had become so because 'Egypt is now much ahead of all Arab countries in knowledge and culture'[174] and the 'Egyptian intellectuals are today the defenders of the Arabic language and the pillars of the [Arabic] literature and rhetoric. The excellency of Egyptian intellectuals are not a source of benefits only for Egypt but also for all the Arab peoples'. Zaki Mubarak was sure that all the Arab peoples accepted 'Egypt's cultural leadership in view of her efforts for the care of the Arabic language' and because of its prominence in the fields of literature, journalism and publishing.[175]

The Egyptian statesmen well understood that the question of cultural unification had far-reaching consequences. As Muhammad Husayn Haykal, Minister of Education in 1939, put it: 'the unification of culture is the first foundation and the solid pillar to rely on in the process of bringing about the desired association between the Arab peoples'.[176]

Another important manifestation of the trend to solidify cultural co-operation between the Arab countries was the growing number during the late 1930s and early 1940s of all-Arab professional conferences. Usually in Cairo, but to a lesser extent also in other Arab capitals, conferences of professional groups from all parts of the Arab world were organised. These all-Arab meetings of physicians, lawyers, engineers, teachers, etc., mainly discussed matters of concern to the public at large and not merely questions of interest to the participants or members of these organisations. They emphasised the need for Arab co-ordination in professional matters, for the fixing of accepted standards, for mutual recognition of professional diplomas and more often than not the need to bring Arabs closer in their cultural and social lives and to promote Arab unity. Current affairs collectively concerning Arabs, mainly the Palestine problem, were discussed at length and resolutions calling on Great Britain to solve this problem in accordance with Arab demands were adopted.[177]

In the autumn of 1941 the Egyptian Government made public their intention to work out a programme aiming at strengthening the cultural ties between the Arab countries.[178] Dr Muhammad Husayn Haykal, the Minister of Education, proposed in a memorandum submitted to his government to arrange for an all-Arab cultural congress to be held in Cairo in the autumn of 1942. The reason he gave for his initiative was 'the desire on the part of the Arab countries for closer cultural ties between one another, a desire which has resulted from the Arab renaissance'. Haykal emphasised that Egypt had taken a leading part in that movement.

The initial reaction of Iraq was favourable and in Syria both the educated circles and the president of the Republic praised the idea.[179] Privately the Egyptian Government explained that cultural unity between the Arab countries had to precede any political union or federation. Therefore efforts should be restricted to achieving three aims: (1) strengthening cultural relations, first between Egypt and Iraq, and afterwards between the other Arab states; (2) immediate co-ordination of education and public instruction in all Arab countries, and (3) the immediate signature of a cultural pact with all Arab countries.[180] In January 1942 the Egyptian Government let the British know that they proposed to ask the Arab countries, including those still under mandatory government such as Syria, Lebanon and Palestine, to send representatives to Cairo in order to discuss with the Egyptian Ministry of Education the practical steps that should be taken towards these aims.[181]

However, several weeks later on 4 February, the famous crisis in Anglo-Egyptian relations took place, resulting in the dismissal of Husayn Sirri's government and the appointment of Mustafa Nahhas, the leader of the *Wafd*, as Prime Minister.[182] It seems that the new government adopted a more practical attitude. Although they adhered to the basic aims of the proposed Congress they preferred to achieve them through the formation of a permanent office of cultural co-operation rather than through a widely attended congress which might become a rostrum for political, or even anti-British, agitation. Therefore since April the Ministry of Education in the new Wafdist government in which Taha Husayn, the famous writer, served as a technical adviser, started to work for a more modest aim: the formation of an Office for Cultural Co-operation between Egypt and Iraq, which would meet alternately in Cairo and Baghdad.[183]

In July 1942 the Egyptian Government approved the proposal and the following month the Minister of Education made his decision to establish the office, the objects of which would include 'proposals for all that would lead to complete co-operation in cultural and educational matters of interest' to Egypt and Iraq.[184] After several months of negotiations with the Iraqi Legation in Cairo the office was formed and included on the Egyptian side the Minister of Education and his Permanent Under-Secretary and on the Iraqi side also the Minister of Education and a representative of his Ministry. The first task of the office was to prepare the draft of the cultural pact between the two countries.[185] All other Arab countries were invited to join the office. The Syrians responded favourably, but the Saudis decided not to take up the invitation since Ibn Saud suspected that the formation of the office was connected with Nuri al-Sa'id's unity scheme.[186]

In fact the idea of a cultural pact between the Arab countries was not new. Already in March 1940 Dr 'Abd al-Razzaq al-Sanhuri, while serving as the Permanent Under-Secretary at the Ministry of Education, had proposed that the Arab countries should sign cultural agreements between themselves. He argued that the strengthening of cultural and economic ties would be the basis for strengthening the political ties too and that was exactly what had happened in Italy and Germany.[187]

In August 1943 the office met, discussed questions of exchange of teachers and students, recommended the encouragement of the publication of scientific books in Arabic and the formation of a committee to consider the question of unification of Arabic scientific terms, and confirmed the draft cultural pact. The office was due to meet again in March 1944 in order to conclude the negotiations.[188] But in spring 1944 the more comprehensive inter-Arab talks (see pp. 267ff.) were under way and the question of cultural co-operation became only one aspect of the broader question then being dealt with. Therefore it was not until the passing of the Charter of the Arab League in March 1945 that the question of cultural co-operation was resolved, although in the meanwhile Egypt tried to demonstrate its cultural ascendancy by the suggestion of establishing Egyptian schools in various Arab towns in the Fertile Crescent and Saudi Arabia. These schools, the Egyptians claimed, would implement the old desire for the unification of Arabic culture around common ideas, aims and hopes.[189]

Improvement of inter-Arab relations

The independence of Iraq marked not only the beginning of its pan-Arab policy aimed at creating unity among the Arab lands of the Fertile Crescent but also the attempt to improve its relations with its Arab neighbours on the basis of inter-state bilateral contacts. The first practical step was taken in February 1930 when, due to the efforts of the British

Government, King Faysal the First of Iraq and King 'Abd al-'Aziz Al Sa'ud, King of Najd and Hijaz (as he had then been titled) met on board the British ship *Lupin* and reached reconciliation. This reconciliation was made possible by Faysal's recognition of Saudi rule over Hijaz, which up to 1925 had been ruled by Faysal's father King Husayn Ibn 'Ali, a step which aroused the indignation of Faysal's brother, Amir 'Abdallah of Trans-Jordan.[190]

Towards the end of the year Faysal and his Prime Minister Nuri al-Sa'id went further. They contemplated negotiating with the Kingdom of Najd and Hijaz the conclusion of *bon voisinage* and extradition treaties. But from the outset Faysal made it clear that he did not see these treaties as an end in themselves but rather as a component in his broader 'object of laying the foundation of Arab Alliance (*al-hilf al'Arabi*)', which would include, in addition to Iraq and Najd-Hijaz, Trans-Jordan, Yemen and also Syria when a national government was set up in it. This alliance would not be inferior compared with the 'little entente' of central Europe or the Balkan Treaty.[191] An Iraqi delegation headed by Nuri al-Sa'id negotiated this matter in Jedda in the winter of 1931 and the following April signed three agreements: (1) a Treaty of Friendship and *Bon Voisinage*; (2) a Treaty of Extradition; and (3) a Protocol of Arbitration. These agreements, the aim of the first of which was 'to bring together the Arab Nation and to unite her world', helped to solve various practical questions between the two countries and marked a dramatic improvement in the relations between the previously unfriendly states.

The second step towards rapprochement was taken in 1935. King Ghazi, Faysal's successor, had not been continuing his predecessor's pan-Arab policy, but, on the other hand, had to stomach a government with two of the stauncher pan-Arabists at its helm. From the Saudi point of view the death of King Faysal made a great difference, although the Saudis were well aware of the fact that the rapprochement between the two countries had taken place during Faysal's reign.[192] With Yasin al-Hashimi as Prime Minister and Nuri al-Sa'id as Foreign Minister the Iraqi Government tried their best to transform the better relations with the Saudi Arabian kingdom (as the country was now renamed on the amalgamation of Najd and the Hijaz into one kingdom) into the nucleus of a real all-Arab treaty.[193] The Saudi authorities reacted favourably to the Iraqi démarche and from the outset both sides attached more importance to the proposed negotiations between the two countries than might be inferred from the specific subjects to be discussed (trade, border affairs, passports, etc.).[194]

The negotiations between Nuri al-Sa'id on behalf of Iraq and Hafiz Wahbah and Fu'ad Hamzah on behalf of Saudi Arabia reached, in June 1935, the stage of exchange of draft treaties.[195] At that stage the Saudis were rather far-reaching in their vision of their future relations and proposed the conclusion of a treaty of alliance, whereas the Iraqis were satisfied with a treaty of friendship.[195] The contacts continued in a protracted manner and at the end of 1935 no real progress had been made.[197]

However, when in early 1936 Nuri al-Sa'id went personally to Saudi Arabia, ostensibly for the pilgrimage, the negotiations were taken up seriously and quickly resulted in the conclusion of an agreement. From the beginning of the negotiations general Arab issues were conspicuous. In a preliminary draft of July 1935 it was stated in the preamble that one of the aims of the treaty was the promotion and strengthening of the brotherhood between the two kings in order to bring about an understanding regarding Arab affairs. In article 1 this aim was put in another form and both parties agreed 'to endeavour to strengthen the bonds of brotherly friendship between the Arab countries'. It was also stipulated in article 8 'that the Arab countries should participate in the mutual understanding and co-operation on which the provisions of the preceding articles of this treaty are based'.[198]

During the second stage of the negotiations in the winter of 1936, this aim was made clearer and more concrete. In addition to the various bilateral issues discussed, both parties speeded up the negotiations in order to create a 'bloc of Arab Powers in anticipation of developments in Europe in which the opinion of many Arab nationalists would compel interested European Powers to gratify Arab aspirations'.[199] The proposed treaty now took the form of a mutual defensive treaty against a possible aggression by a third party against either of the contracting parties (article 4). And both of them undertook 'to coordinate their objects in regard to the peoples of the neighbouring Arab countries and to exert peaceful efforts to help these peoples towards the realisation of their aspirations for independence' (article 6).[200] No doubt the Italian invasion of Abyssinia was regarded as a potential threat against Saudi Arabia and the struggle against the mandatory régimes in both Syria and Palestine left its mark on Iraq and Saudi Arabia.

The British Government opposed this draft since it might draw into a war an ally of Britain (see below, p. 231) and thus implicate the British themselves. Therefore the negotiating parties tried to circumvent British opposition by a clear definition of the cases in which the military obligation to come to each other's assistance would be operative. They also introduced provisions for unifying their 'military systems and army policy', for 'ensuring uniform methods of culture' and for the co-ordination of their relations with any third party.[201] But British opposition again prevailed and these provisions had to be dropped.

The result was that when the treaty of alliance between Iraq and Saudi Arabia was signed in April 1936 it contained a pan-Arab dimension mainly in a declarative, and less in a substantial form. The preamble referred to 'the ties of the Islamic faith and of national unity (*wahdah Qawmiyyah*) which unite them' and the treaty was named 'Treaty of Arab Brotherhood and Alliance'. The obligation to co-ordinate foreign policy was introduced only in a negative way: '*not* to enter with any third party into an understanding or agreement over any matter whatever of a nature prejudicial to the interests of the other high contracting party or to his country or its interests' (article 1). The obligation to come to the help of each other in case of aggression was replaced by an obligation to 'consult together regarding the measures which shall be taken with the object of concerting their efforts in a useful manner to repel the said aggression' (article 47).

The practical aspect of the pan-Arab dimension of the treaty was retained in article 6 which stipulated: 'Having regard to the Islamic brotherhood and Arab unity which unite the Kingdom of the Yemen to the high contracting parties, they shall both endeavour to secure the accession of the Government of the Yemen to this treaty. Any other independent Arab State shall on request be permitted to accede to this treaty'. In article 7 the two parties committed themselves to 'co-operate with a view to unifying the Islamic and Arab culture and military systems of their two countries'.[202]

The British Ambassador at Baghdad knew only too well that at first the Iraqi and Saudi negotiators wanted to conclude a treaty providing for 'a defensive alliance between all Arab States, a common Arab foreign policy, a common Arab culture and economy and the facilitating of intercourse between all Arab countries', and that it was only owing to British objection that a much more muted treaty was concluded. Therefore, he suggested that these matters should 'be accepted as the objectives which the leaders of the pan-Arab movement are striving ultimately to reach'.[203]

After the ratification of the treaty in November 1936 Iraq appealed to the Imam Yahya of the Yemen to get his accession to it. In addition to an official letter by King Ghazi to the Imam the Iraqi Government sent a delegation to him to discuss the terms of accession.[204] During the negotiations the Imam expressed his readiness in principle to accede to the treaty but was reluctant to become bound by those provisions which were in accordance with the Covenant of the League of Nations and other international instruments to which Iraq was a party and to which by the insistence of the latter an allusion was made.[205]

Consequently the Iraqi delegation proposed various vague formulae which in May 1937 finally enabled the Imam to accede to the Treaty excluding the Yemen from the application of the Covenant of the League of Nations and any other international instrument referred to in the Treaty, like the Kellogg Pact or the Anglo-Iraq Treaty of Alliance.[206] Therefore, Sir Archibald Clark-Kerr noted that such an accession appeared 'in fact to be little more than a gesture, the practical significance of which is limited to a demonstration of racial fellowship, sympathy and common interest between the two countries'.[207] But against the background of the growing feeling of Arab solidarity, such a gesture was not devoid of historical significance.

Indeed, when the treaty was publicly discussed, what was emphasised and praised was its pan-Arab aspect. Ibn Saud declared to an *al-Ahram* correspondent that the treaty 'would form a foundation for the union of the Arab nation' and he hoped that other Arab countries would join the alliance.[208] Pan-Arab activists reacted in the same way. *Al-Muqattam* newspaper, one of the main exponents of pan-Arabism in Egypt, wrote that the treaty bore witness to 'the feelings prevalent among the Arab peoples and their inclination towards association' and that that feeling was not imaginary but a living reality.[209] Amin Sa'id, one of the editors of *al-Muqattam* and one of the historians with a pan-Arab perspective writing in Egypt, noted that Arabs everywhere welcomed the treaty with joy and 'hoped that it would serve as the first step in the way of implementing their unity.'[210] Following the ratification of Yemen's accession to the treaty the Syrian Parliament 'greeted the dawn of a new era and expressed Syria's will to accede to this alliance which constituted the first practical step toward Arab unity'.[211]

The British too took this treaty seriously. Sir Archibald Clark-Kerr, Foreign Assistant Under-Secretary in charge of the Middle East, held the view that pan-Arabism was 'living in the mind of all literate Iraqis and, of late, it has been stimulated by the Treaty with Saudi Arabia'.[212] Even such a shrewd, sceptical and even cynical observer as Gilbert MacKereth, the British Consul in Damascus, reckoned that King 'Abd al-'Aziz Al Sa'ud 'has at last, after years of jealous hesitation, in signing a treaty with Iraq, taken the first tangible step in "Halaf Arabi" (Arabian Alliance) that was dear to the former King of Iraq'.[213]

The reality was in fact much less rosy. This treaty did not quickly develop into a broader or even a real alliance and even the bilateral relations between Iraq and Saudi Arabia, pertaining mainly to questions arising from border crossing by bedouin tribes, did not improve. Therefore about three years later another British Foreign Office official noted that the treaty was 'not, in point of fact, an alliance in the true sense of the word, but a consultation pact. So far this treaty represents almost the only step taken by the Arabs towards the realisation of Pan-Arab ideas. So far as is known, no attempt has yet been made to give effect even to the limited obligation assumed under this treaty'.[214]

Almost simultaneously Egypt too tried to improve its bilateral relations with Saudi Arabia which had been strained since the conflict in 1926 respecting the Egyptian usage of sending the *mahmal* (a decorated litter) to Mecca with her pilgrims. Such a move was especially urged by the *Wafd* and *al-Ahram* since they regarded the Italian threat as real and immediate.

When 'Ali Mahir's government initiated in 1936 the settlement of the dispute with Saudi Arabia they blessed the government for it.[215]

The Saudi authorities reached the same conclusion and in February 1936 made public, although in an unofficial way, their wish to normalise their relations with Egypt.[216] The Egyptian Prime Minister 'Ali Mahir responded favourably and convinced King Fu'ad that the relations between Egypt and Saudi Arabia had to be regulated. Thus, the greatest obstacle to the establishment of normal relations between the two countries – the personal reluctance of King Fu'ad to recognise Ibn Saud – was removed.

In April Fu'ad Hazmah, the Saudi Under-Secretary for Foreign Affairs, arrived in Cairo to represent his country in the negotiations. Within a month an agreement was reached. The fact that the thorny question of the *mahmal* was not included in the negotiations and in the subsequent agreement and the death of King Fu'ad helped in bringing a swift result. In the Treaty of Friendship signed on 7 May 1936 Egypt recognised Saudi Arabia as a free and sovereign state and arrangements were made for settling various questions pending between the two countries. The question of the *mahmal,* which was not discussed, was settled by a compromise six months later.

It is interesting to note that unlike the Iraqi-Saudi Treaty this treaty did not include any expressions of pan-Arab tendency, although the article dealing with the *Hajj* and the repair of two mosques in Mecca and Madinah by the Egyptian Government (article 5) was based upon 'Islamic solidarity and co-operation.' Nevertheless, the pan-Arabists hailed this treaty as well and expressed the hope that 'this Treaty would constitute a first step in accession to the future Arab alliance'.[217]

This treaty, it is true, settled the ten-year dispute between the two countries, but it did not lead to cordial relations. When in the late 1930s King Faruq's intentions with respect to the Muslim Caliphate became known, Saudi Arabia did not conceal its resentment and opposition to Faruq's pretension.[218] But it seems that Nuri al-Sa'id appreciated the merits of these treaties above their immediate practical value. He wanted to complete the triangle of treaties by having another treaty signed between Iraq and Egypt.

Another development drove Nuri al-Sa'id to seek an alliance with Egypt. The treaty of alliance between Egypt and Britain placed Egypt on the same footing as Iraq: both became allies of Great Britain and therefore 'could be considered, for defence and other purposes, as allies of each other'. The potential aggressiveness of Italy following the invasion of Abyssinia should be encountered, according to Nuri, by a consolidated front of Middle Eastern countries. Therefore, in August 1936 he proposed to strengthen the relations between Iraq and Egypt in three fields: (a) improvement of communications; (b) adoption of a common military

THE RISE OF POLITICAL PAN-ARABISM

doctrine; and (c) closer cultural intercourse.[219] But in October 1936 a *coup d'état* toppled Yasin al-Hashimi's government in which Nuri al-Sa'id had been serving as Foreign Minister, and the question of alliance with Egypt was shelved for a while.

But not for too long. In the winter of 1937 Dr Naji al-Asil, Foreign Minister in the new Iraqi government, again raised the question of alliance with Egypt with the Egyptian Ambassador in Baghdad, and the reaction of Mustafa al Nahhas, the Egyptian Prime Minister, was favourable.[220] Both sides obviously had in mind 'the idea of a larger entente between the Arabic speaking nations of the Near East'.[221] However, the Egyptian Prime Minister soon lost interest in the proposed alliance with Iraq,[292] and nothing of this sort was concluded.

Nuri al-Sa'id once again returned to the question in 1939 after he had recaptured his leading position in Iraqi politics. He used the consultations held in Cairo in January 1939 by the Arab delegates to the St James's Palestine Conference (see above, p. 172) to propagate his pan-Arab ideas and more specifically his former proposal of alliance between Iraq and Egypt. He also took the trouble to ask British advice repeatedly concerning this idea.[223] This time, Nuri al-Sa'id as Prime Minister was perturbed by the worsened relations between his country and Iran, which had gradually come more and more under German influence, and wanted to enlist Egyptian support against possible aggression of Iran against Iraq. The negotiations began and were well advanced in winter 1939 with a view to concluding a defensive alliance with provisions for reciprocal military support in war.[224]

But Egypt, whose Royal Family had maintained cordial relations and marital connections with the Pahlevi ruling dynasty of Iran, refused to be dragged into this potential conflict and declined the Iraqi proposal. The Egyptian Prime Minister stoically remarked that 'if the spirit of co-operation was there, that was all that really mattered' and he did not think any such instrument as a treaty of alliance was necessary.[225]

Nuri persisted in his bid for this alliance. Even in August 1940, when Egypt's military inability to defend itself against the Italians became evident, he put his proposition to the Egyptian Prince Muhammad 'Ali. But by then the chances of such a treaty were very dim indeed and it seems that Nuri did not even get a reply from the Egyptian Government.[226]

The Effects of the Early Years of the Second World War

Following the outbreak of the Second World War Britain requested Egypt to declare a state of war against Germany. Since Egypt was not exactly obliged by the treaty between itself and Britain to do so, but only to furnish 'facilities and assistance', the British request provided Egypt with a bargaining position. Some time before the war broke out 'Ali Mahir Pasha, the Egyptian Prime Minister, had appointed 'Abd al-Rahman 'Azzam to his government as Minister of *Awqaf*, and in that capacity 'Azzam Pasha decided to use the newly acquired bargaining power to advance his pan-Arab views.

'Azzam persuaded his colleagues against automatic compliance with the British demand after threatening to resign. He argued that Egypt should make its declaration of war against Germany subject to British consent to four conditions: (a) Britain should commit itself to complete evacuation of its forces from Egypt upon the end of the war; (b) Britain should pay Egypt's war expenses; (c) Britain should declare its acceptance of Egypt's demands in Sudan; and (d) Britain should declare its 'support of the aspirations of the Egyptian people for Arab unity'. Since the British refused to bargain, no Egyptian declaration of war was made and no Egyptian demand was met by Britain.[227]

Egyptian pan-Arabists were not the only party trying to exploit the war conditions for squeezing out from Britain a declaration in support of Arab unity. They were soon joined by Arab nationalists from the Fertile Crescent countries too. The background against which this pressure was exerted was the military weakness of Britain in 1940 and the fall of France, on the one hand, and the big strides which German propaganda was making among the Arabs, on the other.[228]

On 31 July 1940 Nuri al-Sa'id told C. J. Edmonds, the chief British adviser to his government, 'that he and his principal colleagues felt that the moment had now come to push forward with the idea of an Arab Confederation of Iraq, Trans-Jordan, Palestine, and, if possible, Saudia'. Syria would join later. The closer union could be achieved in the following fields:

(a) Extension of the Anglo-Iraq alliance to include the other states as well;
(b) Removal of all customs barriers;
(c) Unified public instruction;
(d) Unified currency;
(e) Common system of military training;
(f) Development of inter-state communications by co-ordinated programme etc.

The important point was that Nuri al-Sa'id thought that the British Government should 'take the initiative to set the Closer-Union ball rolling'.[229] Since the Iraqi Government did not get any British reply, Taha al-Hashimi, the Iraqi Prime Minister in the winter of 1941, raised the matter again in February.[230] One should remember that in 1939–41 Nuri al-Sa'id and his circle were beset by the growing pressure of the anti-British nationalists. A favourable British response to his demands would substantially improve his position.

A similar proposition came from George Antonius, the famous historian of Arab nationalism and former high-ranking official of the Palestine Government in the autumn of 1940. He argued in a memorandum, which was brought to the knowledge of the Colonial and Foreign Offices in London by the High Commissioner for Palestine, that in order to strengthen those Arabs who believed in Anglo-Arab collaboration and understanding Britain should make a unilateral declaration of principles defining its attitude towards Arab national aims. The declaration 'should contain some positive assurance that the British Government realise the harm caused by artificial frontiers arbitrarily drawn across lines of natural and economic intercourse, and that they would use their influence to secure their abolition if such be the desire of the populations concerned'. It should avoid all appearance of forcing one form of unity or another on the Arabs but rather emphasise Britain's 'readiness to co-operate with the Arab states in the building up of a new order based upon the broad principles enumerated in the declaration'. Antonius made it clear that he did not aim at forming a unified state at once but rather a gradual advance through political alliance, and economic and cultural co-operation.[231]

As we shall see in the next chapter Britain was not ready to go so far to meet Arab demands, but one can by no means argue that these Arab demands fell on totally deaf British ears.

This pressure was accompanied by, or even originated from, an internal process in Egypt of strengthening its Arab identity. To a large extent Egyptian newspapers and cultural magazines had become outspoken mouthpieces of Egypt's Arab identity and of the corollary need to involve it as a leading factor in the formation of Arab unity. A landmark in this campaign was the April 1939 issue of the monthly *al-Hital* which was completely dedicated to matters of Islamic and Arab unity. The issue was sub-titled 'The Arabs and Islam in the Modern Era' and contained special congratulatory letters from Kings Faruq of Egypt, 'Abd al-'Aziz Al Sa'ud of Saudi Arabia and Ghazi of Iraq, Amir 'Abdallah of Trans-Jordan and President Hashim al-Atasi of Syria. The articles included one by Makram 'Ubayd, the Coptic deputy-leader of the *Wafd*, explaining that Arab unity was necessary in order to face imperialism and the 'sweeping European stream' and analysing the objective factors that constituted the Arab identity and character of Egypt. The kind of unity he had in mind was not intended to be implemented in a unitary state, but rather in a 'greater homeland, from which several smaller homelands would ramify; and while preserving their special personalities, these homelands would be united in their national characteristics, and strongly associated with the greater homeland'.[232] Such a form of decentralised regime was popular among other pan-Arabists and Fu'ad Abazah too was propagating this kind of regime as the most suitable for future Arab unity. Other pan-Arab activists held similar views.[233]

Muhammad Tal'at Harb, the manager of Bank Misr, emphasised in his article the economic factor which was driving Egypt to espouse Arab unity. Dr 'Abd al-Rahman Shahbandar, the Syrian pan-Arab leader, carried a similar banner when he clarified in his article that beyond the fact that no one doubted that cultural factors (history, language, religion etc.) produced Arab unity, material factors as well, such as geography and economic structure, were driving the Arabs in the same direction.[234]

Al-Muqattam published various articles during 1940 on the practical aspects of the process of the formation of Arab unity. These articles stressed that various steps should be encouraged, such as the improvement of transportation and communication networks between the Arab countries, the promotion of all forms of cultural ties, the co-ordination of schooling programmes, the lowering and gradual abolition of customs barriers and treaties of alliance.[235] This intensive discussion was carried out by the press of Syria and Iraq too.[236] It was only natural that the tantalising events of 1940 in the Western, North-African and Middle Eastern fronts convinced Arab thinkers that the political structure of the Middle East had become obsolete and everything was open to new approaches and solutions.

At the end of 1940 *al-Hilal* devoted another issue to the question of Arab unity. This issue too, like *al-Muqattam*'s 1940 articles, dealt with the practical means of implementing the idea. An article by Muhammad 'Ali 'Allubah queried the practicability of one unitary Arab state. He suggested instead a consolidated alliance, which would ensure 'a firm co-operation in culture, trade, industry and defence, in whatever matter which would not prejudice the independence of any participating nation politically or geographically'. An important point was the stress he laid on Egypt's role as the leader of his proposed alliance.[237]

This Egyptian role was welcomed by many writers in the Syrian press and *al-Muqattam* quoted this favourable reaction with undisguised satisfaction. He quoted a Syrian writer, Mustafa al-Shihabi, who wrote that following the British victories over the Italians Egypt was no longer threatened by invasion. And since Egypt had already become independent 'they [the Egyptians] had no more excuse for not hurrying and assuming the leadership of this most important movement for the Arab countries [meaning the movement for Arab unity]'.[238]

A similar approach was upheld by the famous Egyptian writer Mahmud Taymur who explained why it was impossible to re-establish the past Arab Empire and that the only feasible programme was to bring about cultural and economic co-operation. Nicola al-Haddas on the other hand stressed the political aspect of the matter. He advocated the conclusion of an all-Arab treaty of alliance as the best means of enabling the Arabs to be weightily represented in the international arena when the form of world peace was decided at the end of the war. This alliance would necessarily develop into a federated state like the USA. His conclusion was: 'If the Arab nations succeeded before the end of the war in forming the United Arab Kingdoms in the manner of the United States of America ... their success in determining their destiny would be much assured'.

The weekly *al-Thaqafah* devoted its issues of December 1941 to that matter and published articles by prominent pan-Arabists (among them 'Abd al-Wahhab 'Azzam) of the same direction. The same attitude was conspicuous in the Egyptian press in late 1942 and 1943 following the British victory in al-'Alamein. The activities of Egyptian diplomatic representatives in Iraq for closer ties between their country and Iraq were reported in detail, praised and encouraged to be carried further.[239]

This strong tendency had political and organisational manifestations as well. The *Wafd* party while in opposition (up to February 1942) used the growing support for pan-Arabism to exert pressure on the government in the manner of the Iraqi nationalist opposition in 1939–41.[240] Less important but still significant as an indicator to the changes through which Egypt was passing in the late 1930s and early 1940s was the change of the name and programme of the extreme quasi-fascist Young Egypt (*Misr al-Fatah*) Party. In March 1940 this party adopted the name of Islamic Nationalist Party and a new programme as a last step in the party's defensive effort to combat the appeal of the Muslim Brethren on their own ground, that of the defence of Islam and identification with the Arab character of Egypt, a process which the party had begun in 1938.[241]

The party's new programme combined the political, cultural and religious themes of the pan-Arab movement. Among the four aims set out in the programme the second spoke of the need 'to form a union of all Arab States' and the fourth 'to achieve a spiritual Islamic unity and to revive the glory and spread the message of Islam'. As an intermediary stage the programme called for the formation of an Arab Alliance based on seven points:

1. Opposition to any form of imperialism in any part of the Arab World.
2. Lowering tariff barriers and abolition of passport visas.
3. Agreement on preference to products of Arab countries, and the final removal of all customs barriers.
4. Unification of education.
5. Unification of laws, to be derived from the *Shari'ah* (Islamic law).
6. Linking of the Arab States in treaties of mutual defence, exchange of military information and unification of foreign policy.

    7. Protection of Muslims in all parts of the world; attention to be paid to instruction, particularly in the field of Arabic.[242]

Another organisation which was formed in 1940 combined pan-Islamic and pan-Arab approaches. This was the Egyptian Oriental Union (*al-Ittihad al-Sharqi al-Misri*), the principal aims of which were 'to bring together Egyptians and other Islamic peoples' and 'to establish relations with Muslims in Palestine, Syria, Iraq, Trans-Jordan, Saudi Arabia and the Yemen and persuade them to join the Union and propagate its principles'.[243] The fact that only Muslims from Arab countries were called upon gives this Islamic organisation a distinct Arab flavour as well. In November 1942 law students at the Cairo Fu'ad the First University formed an organisation which was pan-Arab in both its structure and aims and called 'The Association of Arabism' (*Rabitat al-'Urubah*). They organised student meetings in which the need of Arab unity was advocated. Fu'ad Abazah, the prominent pan-Arabist, used to lecture at their meetings.[244]

The most important perhaps of all pan-Arab organisations of late 1930s and early 1940s vintage was the Club of Arab Union (*Nadi al-Ittihad al-'Arabi*). It had originally been established in 1930 in Cairo by a few young people from Syria, Iraq, Palestine and, naturally, Egypt. During its early years of existence this club tried to strengthen the social, cultural and neighbourly relations between Islamic and Arab countries. It did not entertain any political aims and did not enjoy any public influence.[245] Gradually it disappeared.

However, in February 1942 the club was re-established by Fu'ad Abazah, claiming that its aim was only cultural, social and economic ties among the Arab nations. In order to achieve these ties the club from its outset declared its desire to form branches in all Arab countries.[246] The club's office-holders were: Fu'ad Abazah Pasha, president; Sayyid Ahmad Murad al-Bakri (head of the Sufi Orders in Egypt), vice-president; Khalil Thabit, vice-president; Ahmad Najib Barradah, secretary; Muhammad Tawfiq Khalil, treasurer; Sayyid Muhammad Idris al-Sanusi (the exiled head of the Sanusi Order), Haqqi Bey al-'Azm (a former Syrian Prime Minister), Maître Maurice Arkash, 'Abd al-Hamid Abazah Bey (cousin of Fu'ad and known to the British Embassy as an agent of Amir 'Abdallah), 'Abd al-Sattar al-Basil Bey and Dr Muhammad As'ad Salhab.[247]

But quite soon the club, in addition to the individual activities of its prominent members, turned to the political sphere too. In February 1943 the club was complaining to the British Embassy in Cairo over the situation in Syria and Lebanon, where the promises given to the population in July 1941 during the British and French reconquest had not been carried out.[248] And several months later the club declared that it 'aimed at the combination of the Arab countries under one political government, while each of them would be able to choose the kind of regime and way of life she pleases'.[249]

In early 1943 it looked as if the club's all-Arab character would lead to the formation of branches in other Arab countries too. And, indeed, in the winter of that year various steps were taken to form a branch in Baghdad. It got the backing of high-ranking politicians who took part in its formation such as 'Abd al-Razzaq al-Azri, Minister of Social Affairs, Tahsin al-'Askari, Minister of the Interior and a former Ambassador to Cairo; and Tahsin 'Ali, Minister of Education. The Iraqi Government and the Regent virtually gave it their blessing too.[250]

The inauguration of the Baghdad Club took place on 27 March 1943 in the presence of Fu'ad Abazah, who had been invited by the Iraqi founders.[251] But from the outset the Baghdad branch was much more outspoken in its political orientation than the mother Cairene organisation. They adopted a much more political constitution and did not conceal their aim of 'forming an association working openly for Arab unity'.[252] The timing of this development and the official backing it got lead one to wonder whether this club was not an instrument of Nuri al-Sa'id and his associates who were precisely then working at full speed for the realisation of their Fertile Crescent Arab Unity Scheme (see ch. 1, pp. 51–5).

The more political character of the Baghdad Club was not the only difference between it and its mother organisation. There were Iraqi pan-Arabists who resented the Egyptian leadership of that organisation. Taha al-Hashimi stated that Fu'ad Abazah 'knew nothing of the Arab question' when 'he rejoiced in his statement that Egypt was the first to consider it [Arab unity] and to discuss it in the Caliphate Conference [held in 1926], in the Oriental League and in the Palestine Conference [meaning the inter-Arab consultations held in January 1939 in Cairo].' Fu'ad Abazah was a newcomer to pan-Arabism according to Taha al-Hashimi, and only recently converted to it from the concept of Nile Valley Unity. Therefore he lacked the necessary requirements of leadership.[253]

One has to add that however strong the wave of pan-Arabism may have been in early 1940, not every party and organisation in Egypt was carried along with it. The Sa'dist Party (which broke away from the *Wafd*) was of the opinion that 'the time for political co-operation between several Arab countries has not yet arrived'. Only cultural co-operation should be encouraged.[254] In Syria the anti-Arabist Syria Nationalist Party was a strong political force with a serious following among Army officers and students. Among the Maronites of Lebanon the theory of a distinct Lebanese nationalism was prevalent.[255]

The early 1940s wave of pan-Arabism was not confined to internal developments in Egypt and Iraq but was also reflected in the relations between the Arab States. In June 1940 the Egyptian Government headed by the pan-Arabist 'Ali Mahir had to resign under strong British pressure. Britain had now demanded that Egypt should take a tougher line against the Axis Powers following Italy's declaration of war on Britain and France and its intention to invade Egypt in order to oust the British. Instead of 'Ali Mahir, Hasan Sabri was appointed Prime Minister.[256]

Britain's military situation soon became very grave indeed. After France's ignominious capitulation and at the beginning of the Battle of Britain many people thought that German victory was imminent. 'Ali Mahir, 'Abd al-Rahman 'Azzam and Muhammad 'Ali 'Allubah approached Tahsin al-'Askari, the Iraqi Minister in Cairo and himself a staunch pan-Arabist, advocating a pan-Arab Conference with a view to entering into relations with Germany and Italy. The same idea was suggested by Muzahim al-Bachachi, the Iraqi Minister to Vichy France.[257]

The Iraqi Government under Rashid 'Ali al-Kaylani as Prime Minister with Nuri al-Sa'id as Foreign Minister and Taha al-Hashimi as Defence Minister willingly accepted the proposal to hold a pan-Arab Congress in Baghdad and the official Press Bureau saw to it that the Iraqi newspapers published articles advocating the idea of holding a congress for launching a scheme for Arab federation.[258] But they were reluctant, it seems, to work in conjunction with the disgruntled Egyptian group of pan-Arabists who had just been ousted from power. Instead the Iraqi Government approached the new Egyptian Government with a proposal to hold the congress. Unfortunately for the Iraqi Government, the new Egyptian Government, unlike their predecessors, were reluctant to be dragged into any pan-Arab matter.[259]

Nuri al-Sa'id's visit to Cairo not only did not bring about a change of heart by the Egyptian Government, but aroused the suspicions of Ibn Saud who, as always, never trusted the motives of the Iraqis. He lost no time in making known his rejection of the whole idea and in attributing it to Nuri al-Sa'id's personal motives and desire of self-aggrandisement.[260]

Despite this Egyptian and Saudi reluctance, the Iraqis persisted in keeping the matter alive. It seems that the Iraqis continued to keep in touch with pan-Arab unofficial circles in Egypt and conducted unofficial talks with representatives of the Egyptian Government. And although it was emphasised that only through an Arab Alliance would the Arabs be 'able to face the present dangerous circumstances', the Egyptian Government were not moved.[261]

Another attempt to achieve something tangible in the field of Arab unity was made by Rashid 'Ali al-Kaylani during his short-lived rule as head of the anti-British *coup d'état* government in April–May 1941. He had already begun contacts with the Germans in the summer of 1940 when he was serving as Prime Minister of an Iraqi constitutional Government.

Amin al-Husayni, who was then staying in Baghdad, did the same. Both wanted to extract from the Germans recognition of the independence of all Arab countries, abolition of the mandates, recognition of the rights of the Arabs to unite and a total liquidation of the Jewish National Home in Palestine, in the same manner in which the Jewish question was being solved in Germany itself.[262] In return Iraq promised resumption of diplomatic relations with Germany, oil concessions and pro-German policy.[263] But in 1940 Germany was reluctant to give such far-reaching promises since it had to take into account the contradictory aims of its ally Italy. Therefore these talks did not bear fruit.[264] In the winter of 1941 the Germans were more prepared to meet some of the Iraqi demands, mainly to supply them with arms, but even then the Germans could not overrule the Italian objection to the far-reaching nationalist demands of the Iraqi Government and Amin al-Husayni. They had also to reckon with the Vichy-France position with regard to the French mandate in Syria and Lebanon, which was naturally totally opposed to these Arab demands.[265]

After the *coup d'état* the government of Rashid 'Ali al-Kaylani resumed negotiations with the Germans, strongly demanded military assistance and again proposed a treaty with the Germans. In early May 1941 the Germans decided to supply the Iraqis with military aid by air using the Vichy-controlled Syrian airfields. But once more no treaty was signed because even now the Germans could not accede to the far-reaching Iraqi demands.[266]

Rashid 'Ali had some trouble in getting all his colleagues to accept his proposed concessions to the Germans, since the ultra-nationalist Yunis al Sab'awi rejected the German demand for oil concessions. The Iraqi draft treaty included a detailed programme of Arab unity which was to receive the German blessing. The programme consisted of the following points:

1 Annexation of Kuwait by Iraq.
2 A federation of enlarged Iraq, Syria, Lebanon, Palestine and Trans-Jordan.
3 Delegates of these 'petty states' would meet in Baghdad for the establishment of the Council of the Federation, which would elect its President.
4 Each government would enjoy internal autonomy.
5 The Council of the Federation would control matters of foreign, military and economic affairs.[267]

Against this background, during 1940 and early 1941, of intensive activity for unity it is interesting to examine the Arab reaction to Anthony Eden's speech on 29 May 1941 in which he promised to support Arab initiative for political unity. In Iraq which at the end of May 1941 was passing through the final stage of Rashid 'Ali al-Kaylani's anti-British campaign, few people paid any attention to Eden's statement, although the new Iraqi Government of Jamil al-Midfa'i officially noted it with satisfaction.[268] Even in Egypt which was then enjoying less disturbed relations with Britain the reaction was to some extent reserved, although basically positive. The Egyptians criticised the statement for passing over the Palestine question and for coming too late.[269] Even *al-Muqattam*, which expressed a favourable view of Eden's statement, did not overlook the fact that it had been made outside Parliament and therefore could not be endorsed by them.[270] *Al-Ahram* was more outspoken in its scepticism. This newspaper demanded a repetition of the statement in Parliament and reminded his readers that during the First World War the American President Wilson had promised independence but when the war ended the people of the Orient had remained subjugated to foreign rule.[271] This sceptical, although restrained, reaction was emphasised in further expressions.[272]

Only the British Embassy in Cairo could deceive themselves that Eden's statement had had an immense effect. But even the Ambassador realised that unless it was repeatedly reiterated, its effect could easily evaporate.[273]

The first official reaction from Saudi Arabia was very favourable to the extent that it embarrassed the British. Hafiz Wahbah, the Saudi Minister in London, not only expressed his satisfaction, but also demanded that Britain take the lead in the field and offer the Arabs a scheme of federation.[274] But rather soon it became clear that this was Wahbah's personal reaction and not his King's[275] who thought that 'this was not the time to discuss such matters'. The King stated that 'speculation on the future form of Arab lands was only a distraction from the main aim', which was winning the war.[276]

The Arab reaction to Eden's statement has been usefully summarised and accounted for by Taha al-Hashimi in his diaries. He wrote: Eden's 'statement did not arouse any hopes in the Arab circles when it was made. In those days the Allied Powers needed the goodwill of the Arabs much more than now [diary entry of 24 April 1943] because Rommel was then threatening Egypt and the German troops were advancing further into the Caucasus'.[277] Promises made in a dire hour could not impress the disillusioned Arabs any more.

In 1942 Arab politicians initiated several other steps in order to promote co-operation between the Arab states so that they could act and be regarded as one bloc. The first of these attempts originated from the leaders of the Syrian National Bloc who enlisted the support of the Lebanese Arab nationalist leader. They proposed that an all-Arab committee should be established in order to frame the demands that the Arabs would submit to the Peace Conference when the war was over. Such a step would in itself promote the desired Arab union, declared the Syrian Prime Minister, and would establish it in the real world. But, as on so many other occasions, the reluctance of Saudi Arabia to join the scheme destroyed its chances of implementation.[278]

Another idea originated from Egypt. Mustafa al-Nahhas, the Wafdist Prime Minister, contemplated in May 1942 approaching the independent Arab states in order to bring them to publish a general declaration supporting the democratic nations in their war. Syria and Lebanon would be approached only if 'more nationalistically representative Governments' were established there.[279] If that were achieved Egypt's role as leader of the pro-democratic Arab peoples and in bringing the fulfilment of the nationalist demands in Syria and Lebanon would thus be recognised. Here too Ibn Saud refused to join in a move which might be regarded as dictated by Britain, since if he were to do so, he would lose, so his associates claimed, his influence over the Muslims and it would only help the Axis powers.[280]

A different and closer question which aroused the interest and activities of Arab statesmen in that year was the status of Syria and Lebanon. Throughout 1942 and 1943 Iraq refused to recognise the governments of those countries unless the Free French authorities declared that the present arrangements were provisional and that at the end of the war the peoples of Syria and Lebanon would be entitled to choose their governments in free elections. In the meantime Iraq only recognised the independence of Syria and Lebanon.[281] King Ibn Saud joined Iraq in exerting pressure on the Allies to bring the Free French to agree to the establishment of nationalist governments there.[282]

Nahhas for his part meddled deeply in the political troubles of Syria and Lebanon. He met the leaders of those countries and suggested various proposals aimed at getting the Free French to swallow new elections to the Parliaments or, at least, the convocation of the old, but democratically elected, ones.[283] At one stage of these contacts Nahhas volunteered to be the president of the commission to arbitrate on the question of the *interêts communs* (customs, transportation facilities etc., from which the authorities in Syria and Lebanon derived most of their income), control over which was demanded by the Syrian and Lebanon Governments and which the French refused to cede.[284]

Such meddling continued until the end of 1943,[285] and it encouraged the Syrian and Lebanese leaders to confront the French. In return Bisharah al-Khuri, the prominent Lebanese leader of the Maronite community, gave a commitment not to keep Lebanon outside the all-Arab political association which was then so close to the hearts of the Arab leaders.[286]

Those dealings with Syro-Lebanese affairs and the meetings with the Lebanese, Syrian, Trans-Jordanian and Iraqi leaders throughout 1942 gave Nahhas opportunities to discuss the broader question of inter-Arab relations after the war.[287] Nahhas intended to reach agreement on a project for Arab federation in which Egypt would play the dominant role. The Lebanese disenchantment with the French and their readiness, even, to take part in such discussions struck observers of Arab political developments in the service of the British Embassy in Cairo. For Nahhas and his government, this involvement was a clear source of prestige.[289] After having been installed in government in February 1942 by British tanks he badly needed spectacular achievements. Inter-Arab relations looked like the fertile ground from which such achievements could be reaped. Nahhas did not hide his position that Egypt was entitled to lead the Arab world. In November 1942 he pleaded to Britain that Egypt should participate in the Peace Conference after the war, although it was not a combatant, since the neighbouring Arab states 'would certainly be looking to Egypt to lead a solid Arab bloc in peace discussions'.[290] Such an approach was then current among many important Egyptian intellectuals.[291] Should one be surprised to find that Ibn Saud, that highly cautious and conservative ruler, would have nothing to do with this trend? He preferred that the Arabs of each country look to the improvement of their own country first, their agriculture, their industry, and make themselves prosperous, strong and happy. 'Then let them use their natural ties of blood and kinship to bind themselves more closely one with another. It can be done – though it will take a long time – by treaties, by friendly understanding, by recognition of mutual interests'.[292] Even when some Syrians approached Ibn Saud and asked him to agree that one of his sons be installed on the throne of Syria he flatly refused to have anything to do with the proposal. The only thing he was interested in was negative: to prevent a Hashemite Prince being installed on that throne.[293] This position proved to be very difficult for the pan-Arab enthusiasts to overcome.

The various pan-Arab initiatives did not stop at the beginning of 1943 but rather gathered momentum and speeded up. But they took place under different circumstances. Winter 1943 was a watershed in the modern history of the Middle East. With the Allied victories everything looked and was perceived differently; therefore the continuation of our discussion should take place in its proper setting.

4

British Policy Regarding Pan-Arabism

The various forms of pan-Arabism, whether motivated by dynastic, political or ideological considerations, always required Britain to take up a position in reaction to the attempts to put it into practice. Between the two world wars Britain was the main foreign power in the Middle East and any move to change the political structure of that region had a direct bearing on British positions and interests and might change the status of local rulers enjoying British protection. As we have already seen with regard to the attempts to solve the Palestine question through various schemes of Arab unity, British involvement in that question had stretched over many years and had to take regard to the various interests, both internal and international, which were involved.

British reaction to Faysal's initiative

The first time Britain had to come to grips with an attempt to place Faysal I on the throne of Syria in addition to that of Iraq was in 1925, when the French were the animating spirit.[1] When the British realised at the end of 1925 that the French Consul in Baghdad was seeking Faysal's help in dealing with the Syrian Revolt and the possibility that the constitutional arrangement in force in Iraq would be installed in Syria, they were dismayed. But at that stage they could stop Faysal, without any need to express a substantive view, by simply stating that Faysal and his government had no right to enter into diplomatic discussions or correspondence with foreign Consuls. By taking this step, they nipped the French initiative in the bud.[2]

When Faysal on the eve of his country's independence put before the British for the first time his plan for Arab unity of the Fertile Crescent, including a scheme of solution for the Palestine problem, Britain's immediate negative reaction was mainly due to the Palestinian aspect of the plan. The Foreign Office were of the opinion that Faysal's proposal with regard to Palestine went 'much further than the degree of readiness for self-government in Palestine actually seems to warrant'. They realised that Faysal's ideas could help in solving the Palestine problem but had no doubt that Faysal 'still cherishes hopes of extending his dominion over Palestine and Syria as well as Iraq,' whereas Britain had by then become fully convinced of the usefulness of its sovereignty over Palestine.³

This question looked much more serious upon Iraq's gaining independence and the recurrent French démarches towards King Faysal and King 'Ali, ex-King of Hijaz and Faysal's eldest brother, who was very eager to secure a kingship for himself and therefore cultivated his French contacts.

In early 1931 'Ali was the main protagonist for the Syrian throne. Faysal did not like his brother's competition and asked for British advice. The Colonial Office, who were adamant against Faysal's succeeding to the throne of Syria, were to some extent divided over 'Ali's candidature. N. Hathorn Hall thought that 'Ali's rule in Syria would prevent Faysal letting Britain use Iraq to attack Syria should a war break out between Great Britain and France. He worried also that if 'Ali became King of Syria Faysal's objection to a Syrian outlet for the oil of Iraq, which the French demanded and the British were then reluctant to concede, would be likely to disappear. Sir John Shuckburgh on the other hand pointed out that 'if we had Ali in Syria, Faisal in Baghdad and Abdullah in TJ we ought to be able to settle the Syrian boundary'. Therefore on the advice of A. Wilson, the Under-Secretary, Lord Passfield decided to adopt a non-committal position.⁴ A letter was addressed to the Foreign Office stating that the Colonial Office first of all wanted the French Government to reveal their real intentions and so long as this had not been done 'it would be inadvisable for King Ali to commit himself'. At any rate 'the choice of a King or form of Government in Syria is clearly a matter for the French Government and the people of Syria'. The Foreign Office endorsed this position and Sir Francis Humphrys, the British High Commissioner for Iraq, answered Faysal's queries accordingly. Repeated requests by Faysal for a clearer and tougher British reaction did not make the British Government budge from their somewhat evasive position.⁵

When the question of 'Ali's candidature for the Syrian throne was again raised in the autumn of 1931 the British position continued to be non-committal. Sir Lancelot Oliphant, the Assistant Foreign Under-Secretary, expressed the opinion that Britain should not deprecate such a possibility and Sir Robert Vansittart, the Permanent Under-Secretary, agreed with him.⁶

But suddenly Britain had to deal with that question more seriously and thoroughly since it became clear not only that 'Ali was looking at Syria but also that Faysal was resuming his initiative to unite the countries of the Fertile Crescent, or at least Syria and Iraq, under his crown and that Iraq too had been approached by the French. This possibility was not at all to the liking of the Foreign Office, whatever concrete form the unity scheme might take. G. W. Rendel concluded that if Faysal succeeded in securing the Syrian throne for himself or for a member of his family and if this led to a gradual emancipation of Syria connected to France by treaty relations on the Iraqi model, 'a situation might develop in which Syria and Iraq might gradually amalgamate but still be separately "attached" to France and Great Britain respectively. This might lead to a most anomalous international situation, possibly ending in a direct French-British conflict of interest'.

Sir Lancelot Oliphant added that since two separate governments and parliaments would exist in Syria and Iraq, Faysal would live half the year in one of his dominions and the rest in the other. This situation would afflict Iraq with dangers. Furthermore Faysal was a unique personality, but his successors might be less successful and 'for them to ride these two horses would be beyond their capacity'. If that happened 'I cannot see that in the interests of His Majesty's Government this amalgamation would be other than risky or even dangerous'. Sir Robert Vansittart endorsed these views. He minuted: 'I should see nothing but trouble for such an idea — and trouble for Feisal too. The abler and more virile Syrians would soon be first penetrating and then running Iraq; and with them we should have French influence ousting ours'.[7]

Although the Foreign Office reached a clear position over this matter they felt the matter was too serious to be settled within their own precincts alone. Therefore it was decided to refer the whole question of Hashemite designs over Syria and other Fertile Crescent countries to the Standing Official Sub-Committee on Middle East Affairs of the Committee of Imperial Defence when the views of the Colonial Office (whose main representative, A.C.C. Parkinson, Colonial Deputy Under-Secretary, chaired the sub-committee), the Admiralty, the Air Ministry, the War Office, the India Office and the Treasury could be consulted.

On 20 October 1931 the Official Middle East Sub-Committee met in London and had before them various despatches and memoranda concerning the various schemes to instal a Hashemite on the throne of Syria and the ambiguous French position. In addition to the doubts which had already been expressed by the Foreign and Colonial Offices Sir Francis Humphrys added that owing to Damascus's better climate Faysal would probably reside there and would leave a Regent in Baghdad. This situation would further weaken his position in Iraq which had already become rather weak. Such a situation or a permanent transfer of Faysal's crown from Iraq to Syria would result in the usurpation of power in Iraq by the extreme nationalists, in a manner detrimental to British influence on Iraqi rulers. On the other hand, Humphrys saw advantages to Britain if 'Ali were invited to become King of Syria. A.C.C. Parkinson on behalf of the Colonial Office and G.W. Rendel on behalf of the Foreign Office supported Humphrys' views although Rendel enquired whether the same danger of Syrian influence penetrating into Iraq might not exist if the choice of a King for Syria should fall on ex-King 'Ali. Furthermore, he asked whether King 'Ali and King Faysal might not leave a joint heir and thus bring about in the future the amalgamation of the kingships into one. He recognised, however, that it would be difficult for the British Government to interfere in that case.

Consequently the Sub-Committee reached the conclusion that Britain should aim at the *status quo*. They decided 'to recommend:

1. that the outcome most likely to be to our advantage would be the Constitution of Syria as a republic with a Syrian as President.
2. that for a single individual to hold the crowns both of Syria and Iraq would be most undesirable and would in any case be likely to prove unworkable;
3. that any attempt by King Feisal to transfer his crown from Iraq to Syria would be contrary to British interests;
4. that should the crown of Syria be offered to ex-King Ali no grounds exist for opposing his candidature.'[8]

These conclusions were presented to the Standing Ministerial Sub-Committee For Questions Concerning The Middle East of the Committee of Imperial Defence who on 17 November 1931 fully endorsed them.[9]

Consequently Sir Francis Humphrys was instructed to advise and influence King Faysal in accordance with the Sub-Committee's conclusions. It was made clear to him that in the British Government's view any kind of amalgamation of Syria and Iraq would result in weakening Faysal's position in Iraq and damaging the British position there and in the subjection of Iraq to Syrian, and thus to French, influence and control. It also emphasised that Syria was then in a higher state of development, that its towns would attract the Iraqis and that the capital might be transferred to Damascus — all of which would result in the increase of French influence to the detriment of the British position.[10]

This decision was not officially made public. Therefore ambiguity over the real intentions of the British Government and their position regarding the Hashemite designs continued to exist for many years to come, leaving enough room for activities by all potential pretenders without too strongly antagonising Britain.[11]

At the same period of 1930–31 when King Faysal and ex-King 'Ali were engaged in attempts to secure for either of them the Syrian throne, the Hashemite rulers of Iraq and Trans-Jordan were conducting negotiations between themselves in order to unite their countries in a treaty of co-operation and friendship, as a first step, possibly, towards a more comprehensive Arab unity. The main practical aim of the treaty was laying the legal foundation for solving ordinary problems resulting from border relations, and for making a framework for commercial, postal, customs, residential, travelling and extradition agreements.

The preamble was to have mentioned that the contracting parties were to foster 'Arab understanding' between themselves, and this was the cause of the trouble. The British FO opposed this expression and also the first article of the proposed treaty in which King Faysal and Amir 'Abdallah would recognise each other's position, on the grounds that it would irritate both the French in Syria and Ibn Saud. Furthermore, the FO explained, there is 'a certain implication in this clause [referring to "Arab understanding"] that Iraq and Transjordan are, in their own opinion, the nucleus of An Arab Confederation, to which other more outlying, and perhaps less important, Arab states can possibly later on be expected to adhere'.

The Colonial Office, who were then still responsible for relations with Iraq and of course for the government of Trans-Jordan, were not party to the Foreign Office's anxieties for various reasons. First of all, they argued, the demand to delete this expression from the preamble 'would arouse possible suspicion and resentment in the minds of King Faisal and Amir Abdullah'. Secondly, after having insisted upon Faysal's cultivating friendship with Ibn Saud, it would be strange to oppose a similar tendency with regard to Hashemite Trans-Jordan. And thirdly, and most interestingly: 'one of the ostensible purposes which were aired at the time of entry into the War in the Eastern Theatre was to establish Arab freedom and Arab Nationalism, and a number of promises were made about freeing the Arabs and securing Arab unity and so forth. It seems a little cynical now to question so innocuous a restatement of our own professions of 1914 as that included in the preamble to the present draft'.

However, the view of the Foreign Office prevailed and the Iraqi Government were asked by the British High Commissioner to delete this expression but not the provision for mutual recognition of Iraq and Trans-Jordan. Iraq and certainly Trans-Jordan at that time could not resist a clear British demand and the final text of the treaty was made in accordance with the British position.[12]

In 1932–3 Britain again had to take up a position regarding the pan-Arab scheme following the attempt of pan-Arab nationalists from Iraq, Syria and Palestine to hold a congress in Baghdad which would join hands with King Faysal's endeavours. Sir Francis Humphrys, the British Ambassador, did not oppose in principle the holding of such a congress but warned King Faysal 'that if it were held in Baghdad the Iraqi Government would necessarily become responsible if anything were said or done to give offence to their neighbours, whereas if it were held elsewhere, for example Mecca, the Iraqi Government would have no responsibility for what occurred'. Privately, and before referring the matter to the Foreign Office, the Ambassador had suggested to the King that if 'His Majesty wished to avoid embarassment from the deliberations of the Congress', certain conditions should be imposed on the organisers, namely, the agenda of the Congress should be restricted to cultural and economic questions only; the utmost care should be taken to avoid inciting the Arabs of Syria against the French and the Arabs of Palestine against the Jews; and consideration should be paid to the susceptibilities of King 'Abd al-'Aziz Al Sa'ud. Humphrys advised the Foreign Office that if his conditions were met the British Government should have no objections to the congress being held in Baghdad.[13]

King Faysal assured the British Ambassador 'that by gathering together a number of representative Arab leaders in Baghdad he will be able, by demonstration, to convince them of the reality of independence which Iraq has achieved and thereby to wean many of them, especially the Palestinians, from their present suspicion of British policy in regard to the Arabs'. As regards the thorny question of Palestine, Faysal had other sweet words to tell the British: 'A country so closely connected with the three principal religions of the world should enjoy conciliatory treatment of an exceptional kind under the aegis of Great Britain.' The FO, however, were from the outset worried lest such a congress became a rostrum for anti-British and anti-French agitation concerning Palestine and Syria.[14]

Furthermore, Professor S. Brodetsky, on behalf of the Zionist Executive in London, approached the Colonial Office and demanded that the congress should not be used for stirring up feelings against Zionism, just as an agitation against a foreign Power (Italy's suppression of the revolt in Libya) had been prevented in December 1931 during the holding of the General Islamic Congress by the expulsion of the culprits from Palestine. The Foreign Office hesitated whether to exert too strong pressure on Faysal. J. C. Sterndale-Bennett remarked that 'to try to obstruct the Congress, or to come out openly against it would be the surest way of consolidating and directing against ourselves a movement which, if left to itself, may not after all prove very dangerous to us'. The British High Commissioner for Egypt, Sir Percy Lorraine, had a more cautious attitude. He argued that 'obviously, however, a really successful issue of the Pan-Arab Congress movement would be dangerous to British positions in Palestine, Transjordan and Iraq and would react unfavourably on our position in Egypt'. Finally the Foreign Office practically allowed Humphrys to deal with the matter in accordance with his judgement. And indeed the British Ambassador continued to insist that Faysal prevent any agitation or even a serious political deliberation of the very questions which interested the organisers of the congress and for the solution of which they nourished the idea of the congress.[15]

However, the Colonial Office were worried lest under Humphrys' pressure the organisers of the congress might abandon the proposal to hold the congress in Baghdad and select Jerusalem as an alternative venue. Since the General Islamic Congress had been held in Jerusalem in 1931 it would be difficult to forbid the proposed congress this time, although it would no doubt stir the feelings of the Arab public in Palestine against

Zionism and British policy and could trigger off inter-communal disturbances. Therefore the Colonial Secretary felt strongly 'that, so far from doing anything which may result in the transfer of the venue of the proposed congress to Jerusalem, the policy of His Majesty's Government should be actively to avoiding a conference in Jerusalem, even if this involves the holding of the Congress in Baghdad'.

After several weeks, under the pressure of Sir Arthur Wauchope, the High Commissioner for Palestine, the Colonial Secretary went further and opposed the holding of the congress even in Baghdad. He wrote to the Foreign Secretary: 'a Pan-Arab Congress, with all its extremist atmosphere and talk, would play directly into the hands of the extremists and would almost certainly give them control of Arab organisations in Palestine'. At first the Foreign Office disclaimed any knowledge of the intention to choose Jerusalem as an alternative venue, but under pressure from the Colonial Office, the Foreign Office adopted a more negative attitude to holding the congress even in Baghdad.[16]

This tougher position stiffened Humphrys' attitude and he succeeded in persuading Faysal to postpone the congress, at any rate, until the autumn.[17] And since Faysal suddenly died in September 1933 the whole idea was dropped without any need for further British pressure. Had Faysal not died and had the promoters of the congress stuck to their intention to hold it in the autumn of 1933, they would have confronted strong British opposition which had already been decided upon in June by both the Foreign and Colonial Offices and had in that month been made known to Faysal during his talks in London.[18]

Britain and 'Abdallah's Greater Syria project

On the deaths of Faysal (in 1933) and 'Ali in 1935 'Abdallah remained not only the oldest Hashemite prince but also, in his own eyes at least, the natural leader of the whole dynasty and the upholder of their claims. It is true that King Ghazi of Iraq enjoyed a superior status as an independent sovereign, but the fact that Ghazi avoided the pursuance of Faysal's policy helped 'Abdallah, from the mid-1930s, to raise again the banner of Arab unity under Hashemite leadership (as we have already seen above, pp. 22–38).

In the winter of 1936 the British Resident in 'Amman learned that 'Abdallah was engaged in the attempt to win over the leaders of the Syrian National Bloc to his plan of unity between Trans-Jordan and Syria under his crown. At first, the Resident thought that those manoeuvres were harmless, but after some time he reached the conclusion that 'Abdallah should be informed by the High Commissioner for Palestine and Trans-Jordan 'that His Majesty's Government do not wish him to proceed any further along the lines he has proposed towards the amalgamation of

Syria and Trans-Jordan.' The reasons which the Resident quoted as warranting his moves were:

1. 'Abdallah's policy 'may cause annoyance to and elicit a protest from the French';
2. The present Trans-Jordan Government was the best the country had had and the Amir was now seriously weakening its authority and strengthening that of his opponents;
3. The Amir was wasting 'a lot of money' in pursuance of his policy;
4. 'to remain silent would support the Amir's statement ... that a union of Trans-Jordan and Syria, under the rule of His Highness, is not unacceptable to the British authorities, and could encourage the Amir and those working with him to persevere to that end.'

Accordingly, Sir Arthur Wauchope sent a polite but crystal-clear letter to 'Abdallah demanding that he stop his activities in Syria.[19] 'Abdallah got the message and for several years stopped his meddling in the affairs of Syria.

In 1939 after several years of unexceptional relations between the Saudis and 'Abdallah they became tense again. First of all, news and rumours were published about renewed attempts on behalf of 'Abdallah to secure for himself the throne of Syria. Secondly, the Saudis were convinced that 'Abdallah stood behind the propaganda campaign against their rule over Hijaz. And thirdly, the French approached Ibn Saud enquiring about his reaction to the possible candidature of one of his sons to the Syrian throne.

The Saudis demanded that the British clarify their position, that they oppose 'Abdallah's designs and that they stop his propaganda campaign.[20]

The initial reaction of the Foreign Office to the news about the Saudi position and to the French move was quite favourable. Lord Halifax wrote: 'The proposal seems to offer certain advantages from the point of view of stability in the Near East, and therefore for the French Government and His Majesty's Government alike'. He mentioned several reasons warranting his positive reaction. 'In the first place, the existence of a [non-Hashemite] dynasty in Syria would create an obstacle in the path of any precipitate or premature efforts at union between Syria and Iraq .... In the second place, a King would provide an element of stability quite lacking in the Damascus politicans.' He also thought that a Saudi prince (the most favourable candidate was Amir Faysal) would have the necessary personal qualities. He concluded that if the French Government could 'succeed in imposing their choice on the Syrian Government, there seems no reason at all why His Majesty's Government, for their part, should wish to offer any opposition to the object, even if they were in a position to do so'. Halifax well knew that such a policy would arouse the hostility of the Hashemites of both Iraq and Trans-Jordan, but he virtually suggested ignoring it.[21]

However, the Foreign Office could not discount the position of the Colonial Office who did not want to hurt 'Abdallah and jeopardise his position.[22] Sir Lancelot Oliphant of the FO admitted in a minute: 'In judging the candidature on form, I myself feel that there would be better prospects under the Amir Feisal than under the Amir Abdullah – and my own preference would be to come out into the open in that sense. But I realize that the CO may or will have contrary views, which we must consider – though I am convinced that their *protégé* is not the better candidate.'[23]

Accordingly, the final position of the British Government reflected the existence of clashing interest groups in the Middle East and the parallel existence of conflicting attitudes within the British Government. In the exchange of views between the Departments of State concerned it was resolved to act on the assumption that if Britain had supported either 'Abdallah or a Saudi Amir, it would have been placed in a very difficult position with regard to the other protagonist. Therefore the British Government concluded that 'in all the circumstances it will probably be best for His Majesty's Government if the future King of Syria (if there is one) should be neither an al-Saud nor a Hashemite. Meanwhile it is evidently best that His Majesty's Government should commit themselves as little as possible on such controversial questions, where whatever they say may give offence to one side or the other'.[24] But since the pressures of both sides were mounting, the British resolved that the best way to keep their neutrality and good relations with both the Hashemites and the Saudis was to instal an Egyptian Prince on the throne of Syria, 'provided one could be found who would take a course independent of King Farouk' and 'if Ibn Saud and the Hashemites saw no objections.'[25] British officially-expressed neutrality and a clarification of 'Abdallah's pretensions for a while sufficed to calm Ibn Saud.[26]

Concurrently with his greater plan, in the late 1930s and early 1940s 'Abdallah encouraged his supporters among the Syrian Druze to bring about the secession of their area, Jabal al-Duruz, from Syria and its annexation to Trans-Jordan. The Foreign Office were alarmed when they first heard about these measures. For them the crucial consideration was 'that the French should have no grounds to suspect that we are intriguing with ['Abdallah]'. Gilbert MacKereth, the British Consul in Damascus, accordingly adopted a cautious attitude: on the one hand he made it clear to the pro-'Abdallah Druze leaders that they should not expect any British encouragement of their moves, but, on the other, he refrained from informing the French High Commissioner of the affair, lest the Druze were offended and stopped their co-operation with the British in preventing recruitment by agents of the Higher Arab Committee of Druze volunteers for the Palestine Arab Revolt.[27] The British Resident in 'Amman too suggested 'that the best way to safeguard against giving offence to the French is to explain the position to them and inform them that the Amir ['Abdallah] does not enjoy our backing in his manoeuvres.' Consequently, MacKereth was authorised to explain the British position to the French without of course revealing to them the information he had received from 'Abd al-Ghaffar al-Atrash, the Druze leader who was supporting 'Abdallah.[28] The French, however, were not fully convinced about the British intentions, and from time to time they suspected some British Intelligence officers of encouraging 'Abdallah's moves in Jabal al-Duruz.[29]

The British authorities in 'Amman shared the basic attitude of discomfort about 'Abdallah's Greater Syria scheme. But, on the other hand, they thought that 'so long as His Highness ['Abdallah] does not do anything indiscreet which would give the French just cause for complaint ... it would be a mistake to offend him. To do so would only embitter His Highness and even if the scheme fell through from sheer impracticability, he would always feel that it had failed solely because of our interference'. The Foreign Office accepted the Colonial Office's view, based on Kirkbride's dispatch, but the former insisted that 'our people in Palestine and Transjordan should be very careful to do or say nothing to encourage the Amir Abdullah in any way. After all, if the Amir did secure the throne of Syria, we might well have to insist upon his leaving Transjordan, if only to avoid arousing the enmity of Ibn Saud'.[30] And indeed, the British mandatory authorities in Palestine and Trans-Jordan declared that they 'would not tolerate any improper activities directed against French interests'.[31]

On the outbreak of the Second World War Britain encountered a much stronger pressure on behalf of 'Abdallah who was now using a new argument, the alleged commitment of Churchill of March 1921 (see ch. 1, p. 31). Initially the Foreign Office's reaction was totally negative. They proposed that 'Abdallah be told that Churchill's promise of 1921 did not amount to a British commitment to support by all means 'Abdallah's return to Syria. Secondly, both 'Abdallah and Ibn Saud should be warned off by telling them that in the opinion of the British Government it would be a good thing if the Syrian throne were filled neither by a Hashemite nor by a Saudi. This should be arranged, if possible, by a mutual self-denying agreement whereby both the Saudis and the Hashemites would renounce all claims to the Syrian throne. This had to be so since the whole situation in the Middle East had changed since 1921 when the Hashemites 'were the sole embodiment, at least in their eyes, of the idea of Arab independence and unity'.[32]

But the Colonial Office did not like this far-reaching attitude. They thought that the question of monarchy in Syria was primarily a matter for the French Government. They agreed that it was inconceivable that Britain 'should allow Abdullah to take on the kingship of Syria in addition to his present functions'. They also agreed with the Foreign Office's appreciation of the Churchill 'undertaking' of 1921. On the other hand, they felt 'that it would be a pity to run the risk of causing serious offence to Abdullah by damping down his Syrian aspirations until such a step is inevitable'.[33]

The Colonial Office's attitude was shared by the British Ambassador to Iraq. Sir Basil Newton argued that from the point of view of Iraq he felt 'obliged strongly to deprecate the proposed initiative' for it seemed to him to 'be rash, to run the risk of drawing upon ourselves the fire of the Arabs in Iraq, Transjordan, Saudi Arabia and probably also Syria, in a matter which primarily concerns the French Government and the Arab States themselves'. Finally Sir Basil objected to Britain's hands being tied. 'How can we foretell what we may find politic after the war?' he asked. 'If Saudi Arabia were to disintegrate, and a policy of federation for Palestine and Syria to become practicable and desirable we might one day think that a member of the Hashemite family was after all the most likely person to promote this policy on lines agreeable to ourselves and the French.'[34]

The Foreign Office were not easily convinced. Lacy Baggallay minuted on Sir Basil's despatch: 'If there is one thing that is clear in the Middle East today it is that we could not possibly allow either a Hashemite nor an Al Saud to ascend the throne of Syria as things are at this moment'. Nor was he convinced that Ibn Saud would oppose the proposed British position.[35] But under the combined attack the Foreign Office had to retreat. Sir Lancelot Oliphant decided that the matter was not worth 'a first class tussle with the CO at this stage'.[36] Consequently the FO notified the CO that they were informing their representatives in the Middle East that a non-committal position should be taken, namely, that whether or not Syria should have a king was a matter for the French authorities and the people of Syria to decide.[37]

This position was maintained through the stormy years of 1939–41, although the fall of France in June 1940 caused the Foreign Office to take less emphatic notice of the French negative position towards 'Abdallah's scheme. About a month after the French capitulation P.M. Crosthwaite of the Foreign Office minuted: 'We have of course no intention of trying to bring about a union of various States west of the desert, under the Emir Abdullah or anyone else, *though if the French were eliminated such a development would be reasonable enough.*' Lacy Baggallay, his superior, initialled that minute without comment.[38]

In Syria itself Mr Gardner, the British Consul, was less inhibited. He met in January 1941 Dr 'Abd al-Rahman Shahbandar's son and brother-in-law, whose pro-'Abdallah views were well known. His report of the talk is not too revealing but the general tone is of sympathy with their struggle against the National Bloc leaders who were then holding pro-Nazi views. The Consul was afraid that Shahbandar's party might disintegrate under their opponents' pressure. 'In any case more money than formerly', Mr Gardner stated, 'will probably be necessary now to keep it alive in face of increased Italian activity'. It seems that the Foreign Office were somehow surprised to learn that the British Consul was subsidising this pro-'Abdallah party. Crosthwaite minuted: 'Mr Gardner has at least committed us' and C. W. Baxter, the Head of the Eastern Department, only added his initials.[39]

However, when in May–June 1941 the British made preparations to eliminate the Vichy-French from Syria they did not allocate any role to 'Abdallah in their plans. As we have already seen (see ch. 2, pp. 92 ff.), Churchill preferred Ibn Saud to 'Abdallah, so much so that he virtually contemplated the end of 'Abdallah's rule over Trans-Jordan. The alarmed Foreign Office succeeded in nipping Churchill's project in the bud and the Colonial Office was able to save 'Abdallah's position as far as his Trans-Jordanian Emirate was concerned (see ch. 2, p. 95). But in such circumstances it was unthinkable that 'Abdallah would enjoy official British backing for his Greater Syria scheme.

'Abdallah did not of course know Churchill's views. He realised, however, that he had no part to play during the British and Free French military campaign in June–July 1941 for the occupation of Syria and that he was overlooked in the declaration made both by Free France and Great Britain promising independence to Syria and the Lebanon. His reaction, as we have already seen (see ch. 1, pp. 32, 36), was swift and required Britain to adopt a clear-cut position. This requirement became urgent since 'Abdallah demanded that the British mandate over Trans-Jordan be terminated and his Emirate become an independent state as much as Syria and the Lebanon.

The British Resident in 'Amman cautioned 'Abdallah not to make any move without the prior agreement of the British Government. The Foreign Office, surprisingly enough, at first felt 'some sympathy for the Amir'. They admitted that there seemed 'no possible way of getting round Ibn Saud's objections to H[is] H[ighness] becoming King of Syria, but the objections are not really reasonable'.[40] Four days later the Foreign Office further considered 'Abdallah's pressing demands. P.M. Crosthwaite minuted:

> From the point of view of the inhabitants there is *nothing* [original emphasis] to be said for the maintenance of the purely artificial frontier between Syria and Trans-Jordan, and Trans-Jordan is far

too small to be anything but a pure joke as an independent state. The union of the two would in fact be a great feather in our cap — but how could such a step be reconciled with (a) French interests in Syria, (b) our strategic requirements, and (c) Ibn Saud's wishes? There may be solutions to these questions or ways round them, if thought long and hard enough.

Therefore he proposed an official enquiry into these questions. This proposal was endorsed by C.W. Baxter, Sir Horace Seymour, the Assistant Under-Secretary, and Sir Alexander Cadogan, the Permanent Under-Secretary. The fact that the Official Middle East Committee was required to deal with questions pertaining to British policy in the Middle East, made easy the endorsement of the recommendation to open up an official inquiry, a move which might bring about far-reaching results.[41]

Rather soon, however, the Foreign Office had to change their minds. Ibn Saud reacted strongly against 'Abdallah's activities in Syria when he learned that the former had sent messengers to propagate his scheme in Syria. The Commander of Free French troops in Syria, General Catroux, also complained against 'Abdallah's intrigues.[42] In addition the Foreign Office realised that 'Abdallah's following in Syria was negligible and almost totally confined to the area of Hawran adjacent to his territory where he had traditionally enjoyed the support of Druze notables and bedouin sheikhs.[43]

These factors alone could put an end to the initial understanding of the Foreign Office in June 1941 of 'Abdallah's claims. But with them came the recommendations of the High Commissioner for Trans-Jordan which, practically speaking, dealt a mortal blow to 'Abdallah's chances. Sir Harold MacMichael did not 'see any justification for encouraging him ['Abdallah] in respect of Syria'. However, he advised caution in dealing with him, since 'if he is rebuffed he may do something dangerous', but if he was not he would 'be spurred to further foolishness and subsequently blame His Majesty's Government for letting him down'. Therefore, MacMichael proposed to reply to the Amir in general terms about Britain's sympathy with the idea of Arab unity and independence, but pointing out that the matter 'is one for consideration by the Arabs themselves when the field is clearer than it is now and that any approach to the Syrian or other Government, such as the Trans-Jordanian Government has in mind, should in the view of His Majesty's Government emphatically be deferred until the position is more stable'.

The negative attitude of the Foreign Office towards 'Abdallah was immediately resuscitated. After endorsing MacMichael's proposition H.M. Eyres minuted: 'If it leads to trouble with the Amir, we may in the end have to get rid of him, which would remove one obstacle in the way of a satisfactory settlement in the Near East'. Baxter agreed but was not pleased to 'continue with a purely negative attitude indefinitely' and repeated his suggestion 'to clear our minds about Arab Federation and the future of Syria, Trans Jordan and Palestine'. Meanwhile Sir Horace Seymour informed the Colonial Office that the Foreign Office concurred with MacMichael's proposition.[44]

But meanwhile the Colonial Office had made up their minds that 'Abdallah should be rewarded for his loyalty, and his disappointment regarding the Greater Syria scheme be alleviated by the termination of the British mandate over Trans-Jordan and its replacement by quasi-independence in the form of a treaty settlement. They added that if 'Abdallah were to call himself King instead of Amir, his action would be supported by them.

The Colonial Secretary Lord Moyne did not wait to have the opinion of 'the-man-on-the-spot', Sir Harold MacMichael and in a rushed, unco-ordinated and unprepared move on 11 July raised the issue for discussion by the Ministerial Committee for Middle East Affairs. He said that 'the Amir Abdullah might perhaps be rewarded for his friendship by the title of King and, if the Syrians would accept him, he might be offered the crown of Syria as well'. Leo Amery, the India Secretary, 'was generally in favour of this policy' since he hoped to solve the Palestine problem in a way satisfactory to the Jews through a federation of one sort or another. But without having before them the opinion of MacMichael and prior to a serious examination by the Middle East Official Committee, the Ministerial Committee deferred their decision.[45]

The Foreign Office were much more cautious and reserved. They reminded the Colonial Office of the Saudi factor and of the Saudi possible resurrection of the demand for Ma'an and 'Aqaba should 'Abdallah declare himself king. Accordingly the temporary position taken and cabled to MacMichael required him to express his views to 'Abdallah with regard to the question of ending the mandate.[46]

MacMichael strengthened the Foreign Office position since he too cautioned not to rush with declarations that might lead to a lapse of time between the promises and their fulfilment.[47] And when MacMichael was required to prepare a draft treaty of independence between Great Britain and Trans-Jordan, his proposal was based on the existing treaty of 1928 and not on the 1930 Anglo-Iraqi Treaty, and amounted to nothing more than continuation of the mandate under different cover. Consequently the Foreign Office resolved to oppose any change in the status of Trans-Jordan.[48]

These conflicting attitudes were to be reconciled by the Middle East (Official) Committee who met on 6 August. The chairman, Sir John Shuckburgh, repeated the Colonial Office arguments in favour of enhancing the status of 'Abdallah as a reward for his loyalty and as an alleviation of 'any disappointment he might feel over the frustration of his ambitions in regard to the Crown of Syria', but avoided any allusion to his accession to the throne of that country. On behalf of the Foreign Office C. W. Baxter emphasised that the future of Trans-Jordan should be decided as part of a much wider problem. Secondly, he argued that the possible effect on the Palestine Arabs of the proposed termination of the mandate over Trans-Jordan should be taken into consideration. And, thirdly, he did not fail to remind his colleagues of the objection of Ibn Saud. The Foreign Office were supported in their negative approach by the representatives of the War Office and the Air Ministry who emphasised the necessity of keeping a military presence in Trans-Jordan until the war ended.

Another argument raised during this discussion resulted from Churchill's memorandum on the Syrian policy of the previous May (see ch. 2, p. 92). Although Churchill did not originally find too much support for his proposal, it was now argued that 'if an Arab Federation was ultimately to be created, possibly under the aegis of King Ibn Saud, the most powerful of the Arab rulers of the Middle East, the Amir Abdallah would necessarily play a quite secondary part, and with this possibility in view, it might be a mistaken policy to inaugurate measures at this stage for raising the status of Trans-Jordan or its ruler'.

Consequently the committee concluded that for the reasons mentioned, the time 'was not yet ripe for terminating the Trans-Jordan Mandate or for raising the status of the country to that of a Kingdom'. Therefore, 'little purpose would be served by attempting to discuss the terms of a new treaty with Trans-Jordan'. And 'in all the circumstances it would be better to take no action in the present'.[49] In accordance with these conclusions and with the concurrence of the Foreign Office and of Anthony Eden personally, the Colonial Office informed the High Commissioner for Palestine and Trans-Jordan that Britain was not going to accept 'Abdallah's demands.[50]

British recognition on 27 October 1941 of Syrian independence, however theoretical that independence may have been, was a slap in the face to 'Abdallah. But Britain had anticipated an acrimonious reaction on the part of 'Abdallah and decided to disregard it as result of the decisions taken a month earlier.[51] And acrimonious the reaction was, to the extent that Sir Harold MacMichael soon felt obliged to initiate a new discussion of the subject. His recommendations were that the Syrian aspects of 'Abdallah's demands should be ignored but, on the other hand, the British Government should state that 'the grant of independence to Trans-Jordan after the end of the war is agreed in principle, but that in the circumstances of the present the conclusion of a treaty to replace the Mandate must be delayed until then'. Such a move would put Trans-Jordan on the same footing as Syria and Lebanon, where the declaration of independence had not terminated the mandates, which would continue to be in force until the treaties were concluded.⁵² Oliver Lyttelton, the Minister of State in the Middle East, fully supported this suggestion, arguing that Britain had to look after her friends. He added that MacMichael's formula met 'the immediate needs of the situation without raising awkward issues outside Transjordan or committing us to something which it may be impossible to fulfil after the war. If Transjordan is to attain independence it can hardly stand alone, but must do so as part of a larger unit or federation, embracing Syria and the Lebanon and the inclusion of Palestine. This issue cannot be tackled now, but the proposed formula leaves the way open for some such development later.'⁵³

In the face of this pressure, the Foreign Office began at the beginning of February 1942 to dwell upon this subject again. H.A. Caccia who opened the discussion pointed out, in the same way that MacMichael had already done, that 'from historic, ethnographical, geographical and economic points of view it would be most natural to join it [TJ] in some way to Syria — before the war it was part of the vilayet of Syria [more precisely — the vilayet of Damascus] whereas Palestine was not'. But he realised that there were 'great difficulties in this natural solution — difficulties with the French, difficulties because the Palestine and Trans-Jordan mandates are a single instrument, difficulties with Ibn Saud if Syria and Trans-Jordan were to be united under a Hashimite etc. etc. etc.' Therefore he suggested first of all getting 'some idea of what our post-war strategic requirements are likely to be in this area as a whole and in TJ in particular' and having a discussion in the light of those requirements.

However, Sir Maurice Peterson, who had replaced Sir Horace Seymour as Assistant Under-Secretary in charge of the Middle Eastern Departments (Eastern and Egyptian) was not convinced. He did not 'see the least need to be in a hurry over this. To take Trans-Jordan out of the common mandate while leaving Palestine in would be to thrust the problem of the latter anew and rudely upon the Arab conscience'.⁵⁴ Therefore the Foreign Office took no action.

In April the Colonial Office felt that they had to respond to the mounting pressure emanating from the Middle East and, since MacMichael was due to come to London, to have a thorough discussion of the problems of Palestine and Trans-Jordan. Consequently they hastily arranged a meeting of the Middle East (Official) Committee to discuss the proposals of MacMichael and Lyttelton. In anticipation the Foreign Office again discussed the matter and their negative attitude, which had been reinforced since Peterson took charge, was manifest. Caccia summarised the pros and cons and reached the conclusion that the latter were stronger than the former. Baxter agreed and Peterson went much further in his hostility towards 'Abdallah. He minuted:

My own opinion is that Transjordan is too far from a country ever to stand alone. Nor would Abdullah, who loves to spend its revenues on his private luxuries, last for 3 months [: 6 it did – Baxter's insertion] (in Amman most of the inhabitants live in caves). Also that much of the disturbances of the last 20 years leading to the war itself have been due to the creation of many small states which could not stand alone. The best answer to Abdullah is that Transjordan can only be 'independent' as part of a larger whole. That answer so Sir H. MacMichael pointed out, will convert him into 'an ardent separationist'. I don't agree with Sir H. MacMichael that we may safely promise Transjordan independence after the war.[55]

Peterson's quotation from MacMichael's telegram of 21 January 1942 (see above, p. 211) clearly reveals what Peterson meant. In the telegram MacMichael explained that 'any proposal that Trans-Jordan should become part of *a republic of Greater Syria* [my italics] would convert him into an ardent separationist'. Therefore one cannot escape the conclusion that when Sir Maurice Peterson, who since the beginning of 1942 had become the most important single individual in framing the FO's Middle East policies, stated that 'Transjordan can only be "independent" as part of a larger whole' he had in mind the possibility that either 'Abdallah could be dispensed with and Trans-Jordan could become part of a republican Syria or Trans-Jordan could continue its separate existence under British tutelage.

The Middle East (Official) Committee met on 17 April 1942 and discussed the proposals of MacMichael who was due to come to London very soon and expected a reply. C. W. Baxter summed up the arguments against termination of the Trans-Jordan mandate, as they had been prepared by his department. And since Sir William Battershill, the representative of the CO and the committee's chairman, also stated that the 'Colonial Office was at present doubtful about the proposal', 'the committee were unanimous in the opinion that the disadvantages of a declaration of independence, as suggested by the High Commissioner for Trans-Jordan, outweighed the advantages'.[56]

On 24 April the Colonial Secretary, Lord Cranborne, held a discussion of the Palestine and Trans-Jordan problems with Harold Macmillan, his political under-secretary, Sir Harold MacMichael and various top officials. The findings of the Official Committee were discussed. MacMichael outlined his plan for a Federation of Greater Syria including a bi-national Palestine. He also admitted that he was uncertain about the position of 'Abdallah within his scheme. On the one hand he was aware of Britain's 'great obligations' to 'Abdallah for his 'whole-hearted and unreserved support'. But, on the other, 'it was difficult to see how it would be possible to devise any settlement which would not be a bitter disappointment to the Amir's hopes'. Naturally he retracted from his demand to declare the termination of the Trans-Jordan mandate at the end of the war. He now realised 'that the grant of an assurance on the lines proposed might inspire Ibn Saud to revive his claims for Aqaba and Ma'an'. However, while agreeing that the committee's view had to be accepted he 'expressed the hope that the reply to the Amir might be so worded as not to suggest that his claims were being ignored or would never receive recognition'.[57]

Accordingly the Colonial Office prepared a formal reply to the previous proposals of MacMichael and got the Foreign Office's concurrence. And since the question of the future of Trans-Jordan was closely connected with that of Palestine, and since in winter 1942 Churchill was still striving towards the implementation of his preferred solution of the Palestine and more general Arab problems, J. Martin, his war-time private Secretary, had in January told the Colonial Office that the Prime Minister wished to see the proposed reply to MacMichael's telegrams. When Churchill was satisfied that nothing in the reply committed Britain to declare the independence of Trans-Jordan the reply was cabled on 17 June to MacMichael.[58]

All these discussions reveal that not only had 'Abdallah no chance of getting British backing for his Greater Syria scheme, but also his rule over his own territory was not taken for granted by the British. Then in July 1942, when Allied fortunes in general and British fortunes in the Middle East in particular were at their lowest ebb, the British learned from Tawfiq Abu al-Huda, the Trans-Jordan Prime Minister, that 'Abdallah was convinced 'that we had no intention of doing anything to further his ambitions, and that we were going to lose the war'. It seems that the Foreign Office were only waiting for such a *faux pas* by 'Abdallah. H. M. Eyres minuted: 'The Amir is rather an embarrassment to us ... If therefore his loss of confidence in the allied cause leads him to take action which gives good reason to remove him, it will not be altogether a matter of repel.' Caccia and Peterson approved this remark without reservation,[59] and since other indications were that 'Abdallah was looking for reinsurance with the Germans, Peterson remarked that 'the Hashimite stock is pretty rotten'.[60]

As with all other Middle Eastern matters, 'Abdallah's mood changed as a result of the British victories in the autumn of 1942 and he resumed his pressure on Britain. On 30 November he again wrote a friendly letter to Churchill in which he presented far-reaching demands (see ch. 1, p. 34). But now the British took hardly any notice of it. Eyres remarked: 'It is very difficult to know what place we can find for him in the post-war Near East, and if he plays the fool and gives us an excuse to eliminate his dynasty, so much the better'. This attitude was fully endorsed by Caccia and Baxter and the reply drafted by the Colonial and Foreign Offices reflected, barely politely, this British reluctance to do anything which could help 'Abdallah.[61]

For the Foreign Office and even the Colonial Office 'Abdallah remained a nuisance, a 'dreadful problem', who prevented a comprehensive settlement of the Palestine problem by means of a Federation of Greater Syria, which could have been agreed upon with the Free French and Syrian nationalists but for 'Abdallah. Furthermore, he was regarded as another obstacle who further reduced the already meagre chances of Nuri's plan being implemented.[62] Consequently, a resolution of the Trans-Jordan Government calling for Syrian unity and demanding that Britain fulfil her 'promises' did not receive any formal reply from the British Government. The offices concerned in London were content with the usually evasive or even negative replies that the High Commissioner for Trans-Jordan and the British Resident in 'Amman used to make on such occasions.[63]

During 1944 and up to the formation of the Arab League this negative attitude to 'Abdallah did not improve. The advances that Syria and Lebanon had been making since the autumn of 1943 towards real independence no doubt spurred 'Abdallah to insist upon the British letting him march at the same pace in the same direction as a preliminary move towards Syrian unity. In February 1944 he made these demands to the British Resident and the Colonial Office had to reply. The CO were not yet ready to concede 'Abdallah's demand. First of all they wanted to see the recommendations of the Palestine Cabinet Committee finally framed and endorsed by the Cabinet, so that they would know the exact details of the amalgamation of Arab Palestine and Trans-Jordan. Therefore they disregarded MacMichael's advice to give 'Abdallah an assurance that the Trans-Jordan mandate would be terminated after the war. In the Foreign Office Eyres and Hankey were this time ready to meet MacMichael's recommendation, but Baxter and especially Peterson vehemently rejected this proposition and suggested that it should first be considered by the conference of British authorities in the Middle East which Lord Moyne proposed to hold in Cairo in April 1944. Cadogan, the Permanent Under-Secretary, concurred with this view which was duly transmitted to the Colonial Office.[64]

Lord Moyne, the Minister of State Resident in the Middle East, intervened in this discussion by a personal letter to Eden recommending that the British Government should be persuaded to give in the first instance 'provisional effect to the abandonment of our Mandatory position in Transjordan'. Moyne recommended this because he was suggesting a gradual approach to the implementation of the recommendations of the Palestine Cabinet Committee, and the unity of Trans-Jordan and Arab Palestine as an independent state should, in his view, be the first step (see also ch. 2, pp. 89–145). Eden, who had to react personally, was not moved and his reply to Moyne was framed in the same terms as the Foreign Office's reply to the Colonial Office.[65]

It seems that 'Abdallah had some knowledge that only as far as his demand for independence was concerned did he enjoy the support of the British authorities in the Middle East, namely the High Commissioner for Palestine and Trans-Jordan and the Minister of State Resident in the Middle East. Therefore throughout 1944 he repeatedly demanded that his country be granted independence and virtually shelved his main demand for Syrian unity under his crown.[66] But up to the end of the war and the change of government in Britain, the British authorities refused to change their minds in respect of Trans-Jordan independence. The more far-reaching demand of 'Abdallah – for British support for his claim to the throne of a united Syria – no longer figured in the bilateral relations between 'Abdallah and the British. On his own, and especially since his country's independence in 1946, 'Abdallah never ceased to look for any opportunity to proceed with his aim, which he never succeeded in implementing.

British reaction to Nuri al-Sa'id's initiative

Although Britain did not regard Nuri al-Sa'id's Fertile Crescent unity scheme as contemptuously as 'Abdallah's scheme, practically speaking its reaction was not very much more positive. As we have already seen (see ch. 1, pp. 39–57), Nuri al-Sa'id became the standard-bearer of the Iraqi-Hashemite claim for Fertile Crescent unity under their crown for several years after the death of King Faysal I and especially after 1939 when 'Abdallah became Regent.

In late 1935 the British learned that Nuri al-Sa'id 'likes to think that the pan-Arab mantle of King Feisal has fallen on his shoulders'. He then proposed that a union between Iraq and Trans-Jordan be implemented as a first step in the direction of the broader aim of a unity scheme in which Syria, Lebanon and Palestine as well would be included. J. G. Ward of the Foreign Office commented: 'From the narrow point of view of British imperial interests, a union of the two countries would be most undesirable, as it would bring across the Syrian desert, and almost up to the walls of Jerusalem, the present rather offensive Iraqi Nationalism, with its suite of pan-Arab intrigues'. G. W. Rendel, the head of the Eastern Department, approved his attitude and stated that 'the present suggestion is ill-considered and inappropriate'. These remarks guided Anthony Eden, the Foreign Secretary, when he despatched his instructions to Sir Archibald Clark-Kerr, the British Ambassador to Iraq, on how to react to Nuri al-Sa'id's activities.[67]

It may have been that when in the summer of 1936 Nuri resumed his activities and proposed as a solution to the Palestine problem an Arab

Federation of the Fertile Crescent countries, he thought first of all in terms of promoting his basic idea and not so much of the Palestine problem itself. But at that time the British dealt with Nuri's proposal and involvement in the affairs of Palestine within their concrete political context and not so much against the more general background of Middle Eastern politics and British interests there.

Nuri's point of departure was that a lasting peace in Palestine could be made only within a broader framework. This would be achieved in the first place by a loose confederation, like the British Empire, based on a *Zollverein*, of Iraq, Trans-Jordan and Palestine. It is true that in October 1936 Nuri al-Sa'id was kicked out of power by the Bakr Sidqi *coup d'état*, but since the successor government left the impression on the British Ambassador that they too favoured Nuri's proposal,[68] the Foreign Office felt obliged to deal with the matter.

Nuri al-Sa'id's proposal included a strict limit to be imposed on the continuation of Jewish immigration to Palestine and land purchases there. The Foreign Office's reaction was that if such things were done, there would be no need to look for any far-reaching solution such as the one proposed by Nuri. But about the crux of Nuri al-Sa'id's suggestion the reaction was not unanimous. T. V. Brenan thought that there was 'a germ of an idea in the recesses of Nuri Pasha's mind' and 'the development of the idea of an Arab confederation will proceed whether we like it or not, and it would pay us hand over fist to father the movement as cordially as we can'. J. C. Sterndale-Bennett shared the same approach and thought that 'the idea of some sort of Arab federation has come to stay, and there seems no reason why we should set ourselves against it'. But G. W. Rendel kept the position in line with his view of the previous year and regarded all this as 'pure speculative'.[69] Thus the negative attitude of the Foreign Office held.

In August 1937 the *coup d'état* government of Hikmat Sulayman was ousted from power, but Nuri was not included in al-Midfa'i's government and had to fight his way back from his virtual exile in Cairo to power at the end of 1938, during which time he was propagating his Arab unity scheme mainly as a means for regaining his position (see ch. 1, pp. 41–3).

Nuri's proposal of September 1937 (see ch. 1, pp. 41–2), which for the first time designated Ibn Saud as the future sovereign of the Arab Federation, was thoroughly considered by the Foreign Office. Baggallay pointed out that the Palestine Arabs would oppose the continuation of Jewish immigration even if Palestine were included in a broader Arab federation. Rendel stated that the proposal necessitated the elimination of the present rulers both of Iraq and Trans-Jordan and that it was a 'very wild' scheme outside the framework of practical politics. In addition, it would be intensely unwelcome to the French who regarded any pan-Arab scheme as detrimental to their position in Syria. Cadogan regarded the whole scheme as an endeavour at self-aggrandisement and Eden approved Rendel's suggestion to acknowledge the receipt of Nuri's letter in a polite but as non-committal a manner as possible.[70]

It is not surprising that in such circumstances the British Ambassador in Baghdad thought that Nuri's activities were inopportune and refused to consider his ideas when they were put before him. Secondly, Sir Archibald Clark-Kerr thought that 'having regard to the present diversity of the individual political situation of the Arab States, his plan for their federation into a commonwealth, linked under one sovereign on the lines of the British Empire seemed to be lacking in an appreciation of realities as thus unworthy of serious consideration'.[71]

Nuri did not take this negative attitude as final and came to London to carry on his message and try to convince the British Government that only by means of his proposal could the Palestine problem be solved in a lasting way. Rendel, as usual, doubted 'whether Nuri would in fact have the power to carry out any of the schemes at which he has hinted', and which Rendel regarded as 'of an extremely complicated and rather shifting character'. Sir Lancelot Oliphant, the Assistant Under-Secretary, shared this scepticism and minuted: 'I wish that I had greater confidence in Nuri Pasha'. However, he was ready to make a small gesture to Nuri and suggested that Viscount Cranborne, the [political] Under-Secretary for League of Nations Affairs, might be able to see him for a few minutes, but he doubted 'whether H[is] L[ordship] would derive either satisfaction or really helpful information'.

Cranborne was 'not hopeful of anything useful resulting', but agreed to see Nuri. 'He strikes me,' Cranborne remarked, 'as a devious intriguer, with a passion for having his fingers in every pie. However, we can at any rate hear what he has to say, however unintelligible it may be'.[72]

And if there were any need for another factor counselling caution to the Foreign Office, the British Minister to Saudi Arabia reminded them of Ibn Saud's suspicion of Nuri al-Sa'id and of the Iraqi Government who 'tried to usurp first place in the Palestine negotiations'. Consequently, when Nuri came to London and discussed his proposal with William Ormsby-Gore, the Colonial Secretary, and Viscount Cranborne, 'nothing was done to give Nuri Pasha ground for claiming special position in regard to such discussions'.[73] Furthermore, Nuri must have got an inkling of how negative the Foreign Office's attitude was to his Arab confederation (or commonwealth) proposal. Therefore, during his talks with Cranborne and Ormsby-Gore and separately with Rendel he totally refrained from raising his far-reaching proposal and restricted himself to presenting the usual Arab case about Palestine. Such unexpected 'good behaviour' this time earned him a good mark from Rendel who minuted: 'Nuri is still a person of sufficient importance in Middle Eastern politics for anything he says to carry some weight'. But even this went too far for the Heads of the Office. Oliphant reminded Rendel (if such a reminder were needed!) of Ibn Saud's hostility towards Nuri al-Sa'id and his remark was concurred with not only by Sir Alexander Cadogan, the Deputy Permanent Under-Secretary, but also by Eden himself.[74]

On his return to power in late 1938 Nuri quite naturally resumed his activities with regard to his cherished proposal. Now that he was again acting from the strong position of Iraqi Prime Minister and Foreign Minister, the British could not dismiss him and his ideas as easily as they had done a year earlier. As always the most important single consideration which the British took account of, while they were framing their attitude, was the relentless Saudi opposition to any scheme of Arab unity which might lead to a Hashemite becoming King of Syria or Palestine. The British realised that the Saudi opposition went even further. When in June 1939 the Foreign Office cabled their instruction to Sir Reader Bullard, the British Minister to Saudi Arabia, on how to deal with the Saudi reaction to the renewed activities of Nuri, they made this analysis:

> [We] presume that Ibn Saud's real fear is the formation of a comparatively strong and influential bloc of the northern Arab States which might rapidly overshadow Saudi Arabia in political importance, and dispose, once and for all, of Ibn Saud's claim to be regarded as the political leader of the Arab world. It would from Ibn Saud's point of view be worse still if Iraq, Transjordan and Syria were all ruled by members of the Sharifian [Hashemite] family, who might possibly even attempt to stir up a revolt in the Hejaz or other parts of present Saudi territories.

The British conclusion was that 'the question of the Syrian throne ... is primarily a question to be decided by the people of Syria and the [French] Mandatory Power'.[75]

In June 1939 the British learned that Ibn Saud's apprehension lest a Hashemite should become King of Syria drove him to utter vague threats to 'retaliate' against Iraq. This was a real nightmare for the British, who wished at all costs to avoid being caught between a formal ally (Iraq) and a very close and loyal friend (Saudi Arabia). Therefore, the British Embassy in Paris was advised to let the French understand that their selection of a Hashemite prince for the Syrian throne was not liked at all by the British. 'From the point of view of British (and French) interests in the Middle East, it may be hoped that such difficulties will not arise.'[76] During that year, when the controversy between Iraq and Saudi Arabia intensified with regard to the Syrian throne (in addition to tense border relations resulting from uncontrolled crossings by Iraqi bedouin tribes), there were some views within the British Government, such as that of I. N. Clayton of the Intelligence Service, that Britain had to decide between a Saudi and Hashemite candidate. This demand was flatly rejected by the Foreign Office. They again stated that 'the attitude of His Majesty's Government at present is that they do not back either of these families against the other, whether it is the matter of the Syrian throne or supremacy in the Arab world generally and that they wish to avoid any pronouncement on the subject for as long as possible'.[77]

In 1940 Nuri, as we have already seen, was under strong pressure by the extreme nationalists, which resulted in the *coup d'état* which brought Rashid 'Ali al-Kaylani and the Golden Square of Colonels to power and in the flight of Nuri and the Regent. After the restoration of the Regent thanks to the British military operation, the British cautioned Nuri al-Sa'id not to resume his activities in connection with his Fertile Crescent scheme of unity. And, indeed, he had no alternative but to promise the British to do nothing without British consent 'regarding Arab Confederation and Palestine and Syrian questions during the war'.[78]

During the next year Nuri indeed kept his promise. The British position in the Middle East, and hence the position of all pro-British Arab politicians, was very precarious, and the aim was survival. But after October–November 1942, with the dramatic change in the course of the war and the recrudescence of Jewish pressure concerning Palestine, Nuri took his famous step of addressing his Fertile Crescent unity proposal to Richard Casey, the British Minister of State Resident in the Middle East (see ch.1, pp.51–2).

The Foreign Office learned about Nuri al-Sa'id's move on 26 January when they received a cable from their Baghdad Embassy giving the gist of the proposal and stating the possibility that copies of Nuri's long letter would be circulated to about 300 people.

The initial reaction was dismay and even anxiety lest Nuri's letter opened a propaganda campaign in the Middle East. P.M. Crosthwaite minuted: 'The time has come to quell Nuri up short'. If Nuri meant his letter for consideration by the British Government no copies had to be circulated to a third party, Crosthwaite remarked. Peterson agreed and, as usual, expressed his concurrence in colourful language: 'Iraq's declaration of war [which had by a few days preceded Nuri's letter to Casey] has emboldened its little man to be more tiresome than ever'. Accordingly Cornwallis was instructed to tell Nuri that the British Government were 'not prepared to consider or comment upon his letter unless it is treated as strictly confidential as between our two Governments and no copies circulated to any third party'.[79]

Since Nuri was interested in official British consideration of his proposal, he agreed to distribute copies of his letters only to representatives of the Dominions, the British Viceroy in India, the US Government, the High Commissioner for Palestine, the British Minister in Syria and Lebanon and a few other British personalities working in the Middle

East. This was agreed by the Foreign Office who demanded that they should themselves distribute the copies to officials of the United Kingdom.[80] It looked as if the road to serious consideration by the British Government had become open. But, as always with Hashemite initiatives, the Saudi factor immediately raised its head.

Sometime in February 1943 the Iraqi Foreign Minister admitted to the Saudi chargé d'affaires in Baghdad – 'in strictest confidence of course: – that placing the Regent of Iraq on the Syrian throne ... was in fact the policy of the Iraqi Government who had reason to suppose that it would be welcome to the Syrians'. Ibn Saud was, naturally enough, infuriated and informed the British. The outraged Foreign Office had to discuss the question of the Syrian throne in a more substantive way than before. Eyres thought that a general settlement of the Middle East would have to await the end of the war and in the meantime no undertaking could be given. 'We shall certainly not agree to any final settlement without full consultation with Ibn Saud; but if meanwhile Ibn Saud wishes to make his views known to those concerned, we would see no objection.'

Caccia went even further and thought that if Nuri really proposed to make 'Abd al-Illah King of Syria Britain should oppose his candidature since the Regent of Iraq had 'so much important work' in his own country 'for the next dozen years'. But he rejected Eyres' proposal to encourage Ibn Saud to make his views known to those concerned – i.e., to carry out anti-Hashemite propaganda in Syria.

Accordingly, the British officially promised Ibn Saud to consult him on that matter 'when there is any occasion to do so'.[81] As for Nuri al-Sa'id, Cornwallis was instructed to tell him that the British Government 'have not yet had an opportunity of studying his memorandum, but that they would in any case be strongly averse to any propaganda being undertaken to support the candidature of the Regent for the throne of Syria'. Furthermore, if there might be anything in the admission of the Iraqi Foreign Minister that his government intended to place the Regent on the Syrian throne, Cornwallis was asked to tell Nuri al-Sa'id that the British Government were against it, since the Regent would 'need to devote all his energies to his own country for many years to come'. Moreover, his candidature 'would undoubtedly cause Iban Saud and the Amir 'Abdallah to react strongly' and the British Government 'would greatly regret it if this question were allowed to cause dissension between their Arab friends'.[82]

Now the Foreign Office took it upon themselves to discuss Nuri's proposal, which had not explicitly advocated the accession of 'Abd al-Illah (or anyone else) to the Syrian throne.

Cornwallis thought that 'the Arabs were going too fast'.[83] Eyres in London proposed that a tough warning be given to Nuri against pursuing his scheme. He should be warned 'that his manoeuvres will probably end in one more of his hurried departures to Amman by RAF plane. It is very well for him to say that everything will be informal and confidential and will not be exploited for propaganda purposes, but his past dabbling in Pan-Arabism and his desire to offer the Mufti asylum in Iraq should have taught him that he cannot control these sort of movements as he likes.' Therefore Britain 'should impress upon Gen. Nuri that he is setting his foot on a very slippery slope'.[84]

Baxter proposed a less hostile reply. First of all he suggested that the British reaction be made orally by Cornwallis. Secondly, Nuri should be told that Great Britain and the United States (the United Nations of those wartime days) rejected his demand to make a declaration regarding the future of the Arab states and against a Jewish state in Palestine. The reasons for the rejection should be stated to Nuri as the need to discover some solution to the Palestine problem that would be accepted by at least moderate Jewish opinion and the fact that his scheme 'completely overlooked the necessity for Franco-Syrian and Franco-Lebanese treaties to be concluded eventually'. Nuri, according to Baxter, 'seems also to have overlooked Mr Churchill's pledge that the influence of France in Syria and the Lebanon shall be predominant over that of other European countries'.

However, Peterson approached the issue differently. He did 'not see any necessity to attempt a reply to Nuri's memorandum in the immediate future'. It seemed to him 'much better to do nothing' until a common Anglo-American position on Palestine had been reached, a view which Cadogan fully approved.[85] And indeed the British did nothing for about six months! Only in September 1943 when it became clear that the proposed Anglo-American statement on Palestine was stillborn and Nuri al-Sa'id intensified his activities 'in canvassing the idea of Arab unity or Federation all round the Middle East', only then did the FO authorise their ambassador to tell Nuri that his demand had been rejected.[86]

Nuri was not of course deterred and continued to use any possibility of propagating the need for a federation between Iraq and Syria. In February 1944 after another attempt by Nuri to gain the support of the Syrian nationalist leaders, the Foreign Office again had to react. As in the past Baxter recommended exerting pressure on Nuri to postpone his activities at least till after the end of the war and the termination of the Syrian mandate. Peterson in his traditionally scornful manner minuted: 'There is no need to take Nuri quite so seriously'. But this time Baxter's view prevailed and Cornwallis was instructed to 'warn General Nuri to go slow with regard to his idea of arranging a federation between Syria and Iraq' and to add that 'it would appear that the scheme had better be postponed until after the war when the French position can be regularised'.[87]

To a third party Britain preferred not to reveal its basically negative attitude to Nuri al-Sa'id's scheme. When in October 1943 Mr Maisky, the Soviet Ambassador in London, visited the Middle East, he asked many questions about Arab federation. Cornwallis replied 'that while Nuri Pasha's ideas would encounter many obstacles he would certainly persevere with them and that Arab Nationalism, whether we like it or not would have to be seriously reckoned with'.[88] Thus, the Soviet Ambassador may have understood that the British attitude towards Nuri al-Sa'id's scheme was much more favourable than it really was, and Britain's hands were not tied.

British attitude to Pan-Arabism

Apart from the sceptical reaction to the attempts to solve the Palestine question by means of one sort or another of Arab federation, and in addition to the negative attitude towards the various Hashemite schemes of Fertile Crescent unity or of accession to the throne of Syria, Britain gradually became cognizant of pan-Arabism as a political force, and the consequent need to adopt an official position. The attempts to form a bloc of Arab countries, the effects of political developments in one Arab country on the others, the meddling of Arab personalities and governments in the Palestine conflict, the attempts to form a confederation or even a federation of Arab countries, some of whom were official allies of Britain and where vital British interests were located — all these could not pass unnoticed by Britain, and indeed for many years Britain had been following this development and taking positions according to its understanding of its own interests and of the objective grounds of that movement. The trouble was that very rarely could pan-Arabism as a political force be separated from the state or dynastic interests of one protagonist or another. Therefore the reaction of other Arabs was usually connected with, or even resulted from, their own particular interests and necessitated Britain's taking account of the reactions of the various rival factors among the Arabs.

Ibn Saud, for example, always regarded with suspicion every call for unity among the Arabs. Any change in the *status quo* in the Arab world was deprecated by him, lest it enhance the position of other states at the expense of his own. And especially so, when the call for unity came from one of the Hashemite-ruled countries. And since Britain from the early days of the twentieth century had cultivated close and friendly relations with the Saudi ruler, it could not fail to suppress any friendly attitude towards a call for unity that it might otherwise have adopted. Thus when in 1930 Nuri al-Sa'id preached the idea of an Arab alliance (*al-Hilf al-'Arabi*) Sir A. Ryan, the British Minister in Jedda, warned that 'any attempt to spring it on Ibn Saud might arouse his worst suspicions', in addition to his appreciation that the project in itself was 'unrealizable at present'. This reaction was accepted by the Foreign Office and became a basic British tenet.[89]

More seriously and profoundly, Britain had to consider in 1933 the question of the attempt to promote Arab unity. In that year King Faysal was rebuffed by Britain after being involved in the attempt to convene a pan-Arab congress in his capital Baghdad. Faysal heeded the British advice to adjourn the congress but asked them 'to acquaint him with the general attitude of His Majesty's Government towards the ideal of Arab unity which he had so much at heart'. Faysal had the impression that in 1921 when he had been installed as King of Iraq by the British, Britain's attitude towards that ideal was favourable and he wanted to know whether since then Britain had changed its view. Since Faysal was expected to visit London, the Foreign Office were obliged to think through this question and to prepare a considered view which would be presented to Faysal during the talks with him.

The immediate reaction of Sir Francis Humphrys, the British Ambassador to Iraq, was polite but negative. He thought that even a purely public discussion of political unity of the Arabs 'could hardly fail to excite the suspicions of his neighbours'. Humphrys felt that Faysal 'could best serve the Arab cause by concentrating his energies on the development of his own country's resources and institutions, so that the Government of an independent and enlightened Iraq might serve as a model and as encouragement to other Arab countries'.

The position of G.W. Rendel too was negative. He admitted that a change had taken place in the British position.

> In 1921 the Hashemites were the only serious candidates in the field for sovereignty over the majority of the purely Arab countries. Since then, largely owing to the folly of the late King Hussein, Ibn Saud has established a powerful dominion over the greater part of Arabia, and it has become clear that there can be no question of any combination between the Arab countries under Hashimite and those under Saudi rule. This fact alone is likely to make Arab unity entirely unattainable from the political point of view for many years.[90]

In anticipation of Faysal's visit Rendel prepared a detailed memorandum discussing this issue. In the memorandum Rendel analysed the obstacles in the way of forming a 'single [Arab] State or a confederation of autonomous states, of all former Ottoman territories south of present day Turkey, which have a predominantly Arab population'. The first obstacle was the Saudi factor and the rivalry between the Saudi and the Hashemite dynasties. Only the disappearance of either of them could erase this obstacle. The second obstacle was the existence of other rulers in Arabia who were 'extremely jealous of each other and of their own independence, and have never shown any sign of capacity for political co-operation'. One may add that the decisive position which Britain had maintained in all of those territories (except the Yemen) did not render this situation unwelcome to Britain.

The third obstacle was the mandatory system in the 'French Levant State' and in Palestine. Rendel pointed out that any project for Arab unity had to come into conflict with these systems which neither of the mandatory powers was going to relinquish.

> The French, even if they were prepared to agree, on certain conditions, to the emancipation of the State of Syria proper, have made it clear that they have no intention of relinquishing their hold on the predominantly Christian Lebanon, or, for the present at any rate, on the curious non-Arab enclave of the Jebel Druse. His Majesty's Government are equally precluded from allowing Palestine to be absorbed in any way in any kind of predominantly Arab Union, if only in view of a Jewish national home, quite apart from their obligation to the other non-Arab or non-Moslem Communities and interests in Palestine proper.

It should be added that in an earlier draft of this memorandum Rendel cited the existence of non-Arab minority groups in Iraq itself (Kurds and others in Northern Iraq) as another obstacle.

The fourth obstacle was the fact that Trans-Jordan was covered by the mandate for Palestine, of which it technically formed an integral part. In order to include Trans-Jordan in any unity scheme, first of all this country had to be released from the mandate. It was most doubtful in Rendel's view

> whether Transjordan at present fulfils any of the conditions which have been laid down by the League of Nations as justifying the release of a territory from the mandatory régime. Added to this, the Amir Abdullah has proved a disappointing ruler, and has shown himself to be so shortsighted and untrustworthy that it is difficult to see how His Majesty's Government could recommend Transjordan for emancipation under his rule. At the same time it is difficult to see how he could be deposed or replaced, without unfortunate reactions on the Jew-Arab situation in Palestine.

The fifth obstacle was the French desire to safeguard their position and interest in Syria and the Lebanon even after these countries had been emancipated. Syria under predominantly French political and cultural influence would be in rivalry with Iraq bound to Britain. Furthermore, 'Syria is at present at a higher state of development than Iraq'. Therefore any scheme of unity could lead to the spread of Syrian, and thus French, influence to Iraq rather than *vice versa* and even the capital might be moved to Damascus. 'It is clear that the immediate interests of His Majesty's Government, particularly in regard to the safety of inter-Imperial communications, which have been so careful protected by the Anglo-Iraqi Treaty of 1930, would suffer serious injury as the result of such a development.'

To all these human obstacles Rendel added a sixth, natural one, and it was geographical.

> Notwithstanding its apparent homogeneity and compactness, there is no geographical unity in Arabia. The northern countries, such as Iraq, Syria, Palestine and Transjordan, all differ widely from each other in configuration, soil, climate and general character. Southern Arabia, although it appears to possess a certain unity from a first glance at the map, can really more accurately be described as an archipelago of human settlements in a sea of desert inhabited by tribes who are driven by the exigencies of desert life into becoming, as it were, land pirates ceaselessly preying on each other. Any idea of unity or confederation based on the ordinary European conceptions which such words suggest seems hopelessly inapplicable to an area of this type.

The conclusions that Rendel drew were that 'from the point of view of general international co-operation and understanding, of cultural development, and of economic prosperity', Britain could 'naturally only view with sympathy any movement which tends to bring the peoples of the Arabian countries into closer and more friendly relations with each other', but nothing beyond that.

> Should the question of the attitude of His Majesty's Government towards the question of Arab unity be raised in the course of King Feisal's impending visit to this country, it is submitted that it should be explained that the general attitude of His Majesty's Government will be one of friendly sympathy towards any constructive proposals for peaceful co-operation and for the development of close and friendly relations among the Arab countries; but that it should be left to King Feisal to explain in greater detail exactly what he has in mind.[91]

Sir Cosmo Parkinson, the Colonial Deputy Under-Secretary, reacted by insisting that the memorandum should state unequivocally that it was 'the policy of His Majesty's Government to support Ibn Saud's regime in Saudi Arabia and the Hashimite regime in Iraq and Trans-Jordan. That policy, having regard to the relations between Ibn Saud and the Hashimites, is not compatible with any scheme of Arab political unity which would embrace Saudi Arabia, Iraq and Trans-Jordan'. Furthermore he liked 'if possible to be rather more definite in indicating that

His Majesty's Government are not in favour of Arab *political* [original emphasis] unity'.[92]

Frank Laithwaite commented on Rendel's paper on behalf of the India Office, who were interested in safeguarding British interests in the Persian Gulf and Eastern Arabia areas. He emphasised that no development should let the dependent rulers of Eastern and Southern Arabia seek closer relations with Western Arabia at the expense of the traditional British position there and that Faysal should at all costs be excluded from operating there.[93]

Accordingly, the final version of Rendel's memorandum paid heed to these remarks, made reference following Parkinson's suggestion to the 1931 conclusions of the Ministerial Middle East Sub-Committee of the Committee of Imperial Defence against Faysal's accession to the throne of Syria (see above, pp. 199–200) and became the guiding instrument of the British Government in this respect for the coming years.[94]

One at least of those entrusted with the implementation of that policy was less than enthusiastic about it. Walter Smart, the very influential Oriental Secretary at the British Residency in Cairo, rightly summed up the document: 'The net conclusion of Rendell's [*sic!*] memorandum is that, to suit European political interests, the Arabian countries must remain divided'. Smart claimed that the argument 'regarding lack of geographical homogeneity is weak. From the administrative and economic points of view alone, it would obviously be advantageous that the Arabian countries should be administratively and economically one. The absurdities of the present divisions have been often pointed out.'

Smart believed 'that formation of a large unified Arab state would settle the Zionist question satisfactorily because the Arabs then being in no danger of submission would be prepared to give the Jews the necessary guarantees for a real "national Home", though not for a Jewish state. In the last year we seem to have evolved very far towards the Jewish state.' Smart also questioned Rendel's arguments which were related to the mandatory systems.

> The Anglo-French experiment in Arabian countries can only endure on the basis of force. It has no roots in the natural native factors of the area concerned. The Railway [from the Mediterranean to Iraq], the [oil] pipe-line, the aerial route, Zionism all constitute the most gigantic land commitment ever accepted by England outside India. France is no doubt prepared indefinitely to provide the necessary military support for the Syrian commitment, but France is a great military power with a clear-cut colonial policy. Will England, with her diminished land forces and her erratic public opinion, be similarly prepared in the event of serious Arab opposition to her policy?

Finally he added: 'Rather jejune? But interesting as an indication of policy'. It is clear that Smart thought that the natural course of the Arab world (including even Egypt?) was towards unity and only the sheer force of Britain and France stopped this march.

His superior, Ronald Campbell, the Acting High Commissioner, partly shared Smart's attitude. He noted that Britain should not enable the Jews in Palestine to have a state of their own. On the other hand, he was confident that Britain 'can always use our Air Force and satisfy the public conscience with regard to economy and "diminished loss of life"'. His final comment was: 'Acceptance of *raison d'état* as you say'.[95]

Following Faysal's death the forces of pan-Arabism were for several years at a standstill. Only in 1936 was Britain again faced with a resurgent wave of pan-Arabism in the various countries of the Fertile Crescent and in Egypt and with the repercussions of the Palestine Arab revolt in the neighbouring Arab countries. These developments brought about a lively discussion of the various aspects of pan-Arabism in which for several years the various arms of the British Middle East Foreign Service and the Department at home took part.

The main source of information about the growing force of the Arab movement for independence and unity everywhere in the Middle East was a pair of brothers, Samuel and Edward 'Atiyyah, who were employed as Intelligence officers by the Sudan Agency (nickname for a British-controlled Sudanese Intelligence unit) in Cairo. In a series of reports from early 1936 up to autumn 1937 these two men separately described the growing resentment of the Arabs against French policy in Syria, against the Zionist policy of Britain in Palestine, the strong repercussions that these developments had upon Egyptian public opinion and the dangers that this situation presented for Britain. These reports noted the change in the objective conditions in the Arab countries in the fields of higher education, better communication and the spread of cultural means of expression which were strengthening the ties among Arabs from various countries. They emphasised the advances that pan-Arabism was making in Egypt through the activities of the Islamic fundamentalist organisations and noted that 'Islamic tendencies and sympathies will be the chief factors in shaping Egyptian future policy and action'. Unless something were to be done by Britain, the high esteem it had previously enjoyed among the Arabs would be lost, to the benefit of the competing Italians.[96]

The brothers' recommendations to cure the situation were that France should follow, in its relations with the Syrian nationalists, British policy in Iraq, that British espousal of Zionism should be arrested and that Britain and France, acting jointly, should 'sponsor the creation of some sort of an Arab State Federation under their aegis',[97] otherwise the Arabs would look to the Italians to help them 'to organise themselves into an Arab Confederation (to become in future an Arab Empire)'.[98]

The Ambassador in Cairo, Sir Miles Lampson, and his Deputy D. V. Kelly, did not necessarily concur with everything reported and recommended by the 'Atiyyahs but the very fact that these reports were passed on to London indicated a certain degree of accord and it was understood in this way by the Foreign Office.[99] Thus, one can detect a direct line of continuity between Smart's reaction of 1933 to Rendel's memorandum and the position held by the Embassy in 1936–7. Lampson specifically agreed that British and French policies in Syria and Palestine had left a very bad impression in Egypt and suggested that the British Government 'have in mind the importance of conciliating Egypt and detaching her as far as possible from the anti-European formation in neighbouring countries'.[100] D. V. Kelly, the Acting High Commissioner (as he had then been titled up to the conclusion of the Anglo-Egyptian Treaty in 1936), accepted that the trend towards an Arab identity had been growing in Egypt and that the *Wafd* and its leader Nahhas Pasha had been swept by this wave.[101]

Lampson fully agreed that British policy in Palestine presented 'dangers to our position generally in the Near East' and that 'the Arabs will not acquiesce peacefully in any solution of the question which does not assure a continuance of Arab predominance in Palestine'. The Palestine policy cannot 'be examined in isolation from our whole position in the Near East' and therefore should change.[102] As for schemes of Arab unity the counsels of the British representatives in Cairo were less clear-cut. Kelly thought that the formation of an Arab bloc under Egyptian hegemony is not 'intrinsically fantastic' and 'might now be turned to our advantage with the help of Anglo-Egyptian treaty.... But it is a double-edged weapon which, in the event of its not being turned to our advantage, may contain elements of serious trouble'.[103] Lampson dissociated himself from the recommendation of the 'Atiyyahs concerning British espousal of Arab federation and noted: 'This, I may record, is an old dream which seems no more practicable now then seventeen years ago'.[104] But he conceded that 'the efforts of the young intellectuals in the different Arab countries' to effect an Arab Federation were 'interesting as showing the trend of thought of many people in these parts'.[105]

Some of the 'Atiyyahs' reports were considered important enough by the Foreign Office to be sent to the British representatives in the Middle East for their comments. Sir Archibald Clark-Kerr, the British Ambassador to Iraq, thought it was mainly Iraq that was interested in pan-Arabism and it fell to that country 'to inspire and direct the revival of the pan-Arab movement'. Clark-Kerr believed that the attitude of the leaders of the pan-Arab movement towards Britain was not 'unfriendly', including those in Syria, owing to 'the straightforward honesty of British policy in Iraq, our friendship with Ibn Saud, our stand for Abyssinia and the present hopefulness of the situation in Egypt'. Only British policy in Palestine embarrassed British relations with pan-Arabs, but they 'have not yet lost confidence in the desire and in the ability of His Majesty's Government to devise an equitable solution to this problem. If this can be done, I see no immediate reason why the pan-Arab movement should be in any way hostile to Great Britain, or why its aims should be inimical to British interests'.[106]

A different reaction came from Gilbert MacKereth, the British Consul in Damascus. He admitted that a pan-Arab movement existed but doubted its potentialities. He believed that as a political force this movement flourished only against foreign rule and 'always died in liberty'. He noticed the growth of the local nationalisms of the existing states and regarded the broader Arab nationalism as first and foremost a cultural phenomenon devoid of any practical importance, 'an abstraction suitable only for the entertainment of philosophers'. And although he did not spell it out clearly, the message he advocated was to disregard the pan-Arab movement as irrelevant.[107]

The Foreign Office in London did not overlook these various reports. At the beginning the tone was set by J.G. Ward who considered Mac-Kereth's despatch 'as an excellent statement of the position', a view with which Rendel, the head of the Eastern Department, concurred.[108] Naturally, Ward very much disliked the 'Atiyyahs' reports and thought that they should not have been printed at all. But here Rendel admonished him and thought that they had some importance at least as indicative of the direction in which Lampson's mind was turning.[109] Ward reacted in the same way to Clark-Kerr's despatch. He tried hard to emphasise the points of weakness of the pan-Arab movement quoted in the despatch, having overlooked the more positive remarks made in this respect. For Ward the main thing was that the despatch bore out 'Mr MacKereth's contention that the inherent factionalism of the Arabs will prevent any greater realisation of the pan-Arab ideal'. This time Rendel expressed his entire agreement with Clark-Kerr's despatch, but this time did not comment on his subordinate's minute.[110]

As for the despatches from Cairo the Foreign Office were mainly interested in their crystal-clear recommendation that British pro-Zionist policy in Palestine be reversed. This position was fully endorsed by the heads of the Foreign Office including Anthony Eden and the relevant passages were circulated to the Cabinet, although Eden realised that not everything that Cairo recommended about Palestine could be done. But Lampson's position that the Palestine policy should be decided in relation to the Middle East as a whole was accepted by the Foreign Office, although his somehow benign treatment of the pan-Arab movement was overlooked.[111]

There was only one clearly dissenting view within the Foreign Office in 1936, that of Sir Archibald Clark-Kerr. Having stayed in London after his office as Ambassador to Iraq ended that summer, he was able to express his views about pan-Arabism much more clearly than in his above-quoted despatch. He too dismissed the views of 'the wilder pan-Arabs of Baghdad' who 'talk of an Arab state stretching from the Tigris to Cape Spartil [near Tangier] and refuse to listen to any suggestion that neither the Egyptian nor the Moor is an Arab. But such views as these may of course be dismissed. More practical politicians think in terms of something compacter – Iraq, Arabia, Syria and probably Palestine and Trans-Jordan'. Within these limits 'there is, I think an inevitability about the formation of some sort of Arab Confederation which will oblige us to keep a watchful eye on the present movement and indeed to go with it'. And he makes himself undoubtedly clear: such a movement

> is indeed a thing which we may have to reckon with at any time now. Far from trying to discourage it we should, I think, move with it and show some sympathy towards it. For it will be only by doing so that we may hope to be able to shape its course a little. I see no immediate reason why we should be afraid of it, even though, as Mr Rendel points out, Palestine is a snag. Movement or no movement Palestine will be a snag and a formidable one.[112]

It is very clear from this thorough discussion that in the prevailing view of the Foreign Office, pan-Arabism as a political movement was not considered on its merits a serious phenomenon which required Britain to espouse or object to it. The Palestine problem modified this attitude only to a certain extent. They believed that the repercussions of the developments in Palestine on the other Arab countries, where Britain had very important interests, were detrimental to the British positions and influence and therefore the Palestine policy could not be judged in isolation from the other parts of the Middle East. This conclusion is borne out by the manner in which Britain reacted to various manifestations of pan-Arabism.

During the negotiations in 1935–6 for the conclusion of the Iraqi-Saudi treaty of friendship Britain exerted strong pressure to prevent this treaty from becoming an instrument of military co-operation and foreign policy co-ordination. Even its symbolic reference to pan-Arabism failed to please the British, who were afraid that it would lay the foundations of a possible common policy against Kuwait, the weaker neighbour but under British protection.[113] The British argued that since they were an official ally of Iraq, any military or political obligation that Iraq might assume under the proposed treaty could one day directly have bearings on Britain's international position.[114] Furthermore, since the British feared that the proposed co-ordinated foreign policy would be directed to exert pressure on them concerning Palestine and on the French with regard to Syria, they made it clear that they did not agree to anything of this kind and succeeded in having these objectionable provisions dropped from the draft treaty.¹¹⁵ When in April 1940 the Iraqi and Saudi Governments once again proposed to conclude 'some sort of military alliance' between them, the British reaction was as negative as ever. The existing treaty was regarded as 'quite sufficient' and the idea was dropped.¹¹⁶

The attempt in 1936 to conclude a similar treaty between Iraq and Egypt did not fare much better in the eyes of the British Government. At first glance such an proposed alliance might be useful from a British point of view as 'a bulwark against Italy' and Germany should a 'dangerous Anglo-Italian conflict in the Eastern Mediterranean' break out.¹¹⁷ But immediately the British felt uneasy over this proposed alliance owing to the ever-present Palestine question. Lampson made it clear that 'the conclusion of ententes between Egypt and Iraq or other Arab speaking countries must be disadvantageous to us as long as we are committed to a form of Zionism which the Palestinian Arabs will not accept. Such ententes would tend to intensify external co-operation with the Palestinian Arabs against Zionism and ourselves'. To this view, with which it was in full agreement, the Foreign Office added, of the Arab 'little entente', that 'in the years to come when the eventual agitation begins to grow up against our retaining any sort of special military position in the Near and Middle East its diplomatic weight might prove distinctly embarrassing'.¹¹⁸

But since Lampson and Clark-Kerr deprecated any frontal British objection the British position was restricted 'to insisting on being kept informed of developments' according to the treaties with Iraq and Egypt and endeavouring to supervise any draft instruments which might materialise so as to ensure that no potentially objectionable provision was included.¹¹⁹ With the approval of Eden the British Ambassadors were instructed to take such a position,¹²⁰ but to the relief of Britain the negotiations between Iraq and Egypt did not result in any agreement being signed.¹²¹

This line of policy persisted for several years. When in 1939 Nuri al Sa'id resumed the endeavour to conclude an Iraqi-Egyptian treaty of alliance, C.W. Baxter, Rendel's successor, emphasised that Britain had to 'adopt an attitude of general goodwill'. Oliphant added 'and nothing more should, in my opinion, be our line'. This reaction was approved by Cadogan, Vansittart and Lord Halifax.¹²² And, indeed, the British Ambassador did not openly come out against the proposed alliance. However, his reserved reaction sufficed to calm down the pan-Arab politicians in Iraq and Egypt and nothing materialised.¹²³

Britain had to react to a more far-reaching scheme of Arab unity originating from Bashir al-Sa'dawi, a Syrian nationalist of Tripolitanian origin. Allegedly on behalf of a group of Arab nationalists, including

Ri'ad al-Sulh of Lebanon and Hashim al-Atasi, the Syrian President, he approached the British Embassy in Cairo in March 1937 and told W. Smart, the Oriental Secretary, that his group were asking for help and a positive British policy regarding Arab unity. Their aim was to form a league of all Arab states in Asia, which would develop and expand from a cultural organisation into a political unity. Only if this help was forthcoming could Italian penetration be resisted; if not the Arabs would 'find it difficult to avoid coming to some sort of terms with what may prove to be the rising power from a "realpolitik" point of view in the Near and Middle East'. Lampson recommended the rejection of this approach since 'as long as our policy in Palestine remains entirely unacceptable to the Palestine Arabs, any sort of Arab unification must, it would seem, result in stronger Arab support of the Palestinian Arabs against our Zionist policy'. T. V. Brenan, a traditional supporter of pan-Arabism in the FO, recommended that the government make some declaration of benevolent support for the cause of 'Arab unity'. He argued that such a declaration would help Britain to counter Italian propaganda, it would be a substitute for supplying arms to Arab states [which Britain refused to do]; it would cause no harm since '"Arab unity" is probably anyhow an impossibility'; and it would help to solve the Palestine problem by securing the Arab goodwill. Lacy Baggallay presented the customary counter-arguments and stated that 'our policy' is 'to avoid any *appearance* [my italics] of lack of sympathy towards pan-Arab schemes, whether we feel enthusiastic or not, and if we were ever placed in a position when we had to give some indication of our policy, I think we could only say that the *principle* [my italics] of Pan-Arab Unity had our blessing'. But Rendel went further. He stated that 'if British policy in Palestine continued to be such as to drive the Arabs into open hostility the declaration would at least be suspect. It would in any case be useless'.[124]

MacKereth from Damascus went further, dismissing Sa'dawi's *démarche* lock, stock and barrel. He warned that even 'if we turned every Jew out of Palestine, quit the country ourselves and planted an Arab ruler there', Britain would gain no more than momentary Arab goodwill. 'Arab loyalty, as history and contact with them teach, is fickle to a degree and Arab appetites are insatiable.... The Arab above all loves to bear a grudge.' Baggallay thought that this dispatch presented 'an interesting point of view', but Brenan and Rendel dismissed it altogether.[125] However, practically speaking, Rendel was rather close to MacKereth since his evasive reaction to Sa'dawi's *démarche* prevailed and Britain did nothing that had been demanded by the group of Arab nationalists.

In September–October 1936 when the Arab Kings of Iraq, Saudi Arabia and Yemen and Amir 'Abdallah of Trans-Jordan called on the Palestine Arabs at the request of their leaders to call off their strike, the only concession that Britain was ready to make was to acknowledge their right to approach the British Government and the Royal (Peel) Commission of Inquiry, through proper diplomatic channels, on behalf of the Palestine Arabs.[126] As far as these countries were concerned their presentations of memoranda and protests became a daily matter. The Foreign Office regarded this activity as redressing 'the balance to some extent in favour of the Arabs', since up to then the Jews had easier access to the British Government and to the League of Nations.[127]

However, even in this respect the British did not go all along the road of acquiescence in the right of the Arab countries to do so. First of all up to 1938 they tried to prevent Egypt from joining in this activity.[128] Secondly, the Foreign Office, with Eden's approval, in continuance of their policy pursued during the Iraqi-Saudi treaty negotiations in October 1936, objected to an attempt to shape a joint Iraqi-Saudi position on Palestine for presentation to the British Government, and their advice to the Iraqi and Saudi Governments sufficed to nip this Iraqi attempt in the bud.[129] It seems that the British Government acquiesced in the intervention of the Arab countries in the affairs of Palestine only on an individual basis or, after 1938, only when called upon by Britain to do so and not on their own initiative. And, indeed, when in the summer and autumn of 1938 the pan-Arab politicians of Egypt were calling for and subsequently organising the Inter-Parliamentary Arab Congress in support of the Palestine Arabs, the British Government were dissatisfied. They did not want to come out openly against its taking place but exerted pressure on Egypt to withhold an official blessing from the Congress.[130]

We have already noted (see ch. 1, pp. 50–4) that although the Foreign Office in 1937–8 realised that the Palestine question could no longer be considered separately from the broader question of British policy in the Middle East as a whole, they were not convinced that a proposal to form an Arab federation would help to solve the Palestine problem. It should be added that the Foreign Office maintained their rather sceptical attitude to the practicability of Arab unity on its own merits without regard to the Palestinian dimension of that question. And if any change to a more favourable attitude was introduced at all it was not too marked.

In reaction to the Arab rebellion in Palestine and its effects on the other Arab countries, in 1938–9 the British Government resumed their consideration of pan-Arabism. We have already noted (see above, pp. 110–14) that at the insistence of the Colonial Office the British Government adopted a much more favourable attitude to pan-Arabism in the second half of 1938, having hoped to guide this movement and use it for moderating the Palestine Arabs. The Foreign Office and other departments of state were naturally much more interested in the broader ramifications of this attempted new approach and in its possible repercussions on British positions all over the Middle East. One should not forget that in February 1938 Halifax succeeded Eden at the Foreign Office. And if Eden had already been convinced in 1937 of the necessity of involving the Arab states in the Palestine conflict in order to facilitate a solution, Halifax was much more conservative and cautious.

In February 1938 the War Office awoke to the possibility of the Arab countries allying themselves in a military operation against Britain resulting from their opposition to the partition of Palestine and the establishment of a Jewish state. They concluded that if Britain was at peace the Arab countries might only 'connive at incursions into Palestine or against British communications, property or personnel in the Middle East' and would not be agitated into a fully-fledged military operation. 'In general, "a small war" might result, temporarily affecting our air communications and one source of our oil supply.' But 'the dangers and extent of Arab hostility might be greatly increased should Great Britain be at war with any of the great powers. A serious reverse or signs that Great Britain might lose the war might lead to definite hostile action by some of the Arab Governments'. It is significant that while the Colonial Office thought that Major Cawthorn's memorandum was 'most valuable and convincing' and had no comments to make on it, the Foreign Office held the view that in all the circumstances 'there is little or no likelihood of a military combination of forces against H[is] M[ajesty's] G[overnment]'. But one point was stressed by Baggallay: 'Palestine may do more than the writer thinks to unite the otherwise disunited'.[131]

This basic dismissal of pan-Arabism, and especially its military potential, as a serious force to be reckoned with continued to prevail in the Foreign Office's Eastern Department even when the British Government under the guidance of the Colonial Office were adopting a more favourable approach towards it. As Mr Crosthwaite of the Eastern Department noted:

> It will be a long time before a pan-Arab Federation can produce 20 divisions, trained and equipped for modern warfare and ready to march at the first sign of encroachment.... However, we cannot in present circumstances afford to lose patience with them or put too sharply to them [the Iraqi pan-Arabists] the issue between pan-Arab fancies and the fact of their alliance with us. Indeed, if only some tolerable solution could be found in Palestine, there seems no particular reason why the two should clash, since normally we could no doubt rely on the jealousy of the other Arab states to keep Iraqi pretensions within limits. But whatever the solution in Palestine, we cannot of course encourage the Iraqis to intervene in questions such as the Franco-Syrian Treaty negotiations or

Alexandretta, as long as we attach importance to friendship with the French and the Turks.[132]

And, indeed, even in autumn 1938, after the October 1938 formal *volte face* towards pan-Arabism, the Foreign Office stuck to their position that French misgivings should always be taken into consideration.[133]

But the new direction of British policy towards pan-Arabism as a result of the Colonial Office's conviction that it might be used in helping to solve the Palestine problem (see ch. 2, pp. 111–12) could not fail to influence the attitude of the Foreign Office too. And one of the first signs was their readiness to take less account of French apprehension with regard to pan-Arabism or even, temporarily as we shall see later on, to disregard it altogether.

In a reaction to a despatch by Sir Miles Lampson in which he had analysed the effects of the Inter-Parliamentary Arab Congress and the Arab Women's Congress, the Foreign Office accepted his warning that 'it would be imprudent to under-estimate the danger of this movement which has been provoked by our Palestine policy'. Mr Etherington-Smith of the Eastern Department minuted:

> It seems clear that the Pan-Arab movement is a force to be reckoned with in the Near and Middle East and one which is likely to gather strength as time goes on. H.M.G. have already accelerated its development and helped to give it cohesion by their Palestine policy. But it seems clear that we stand to lose far more than we should gain by openly opposing Pan-Arab aspirations as Sir M. Lampson points out in his despatch; our course should rather be far from trying to discourage the movement, to move with it and show some sympathy towards it. For it will only be by so doing that we may be able to shape its course a little.

This reaction indicated the new course of thinking. Lacy Baggallay agreed and C.W. Baxter, the new Head of the Eastern Department, suggested that Lampson's despatch be given very serious treatment by distributing it to the King, Cabinet and Dominions. D.V. Kelly, who had returned from the Cairo Embassy to head the Egyptian Department, stressed the mental aspect of pan-Arabism rather than its political aspect. However he too quoted various despatches of Lampson to show 'the potential importance of pan-Arabism as a mental attitude and the danger of its developing as a movement hostile to British influence and policy'. In this context he drew attention especially to Egypt. 'It may be true that the majority of Egyptians are not predominantly Arab in race but as Moslems and speakers of Arabic as well as from political vanity they are rapidly coming to regard themselves as such and to aspire to moral leadership.' Sir Lancelot Oliphant agreed and decided to distribute

Lampson's despatch to King and Cabinet, which act Sir Alexander Cadogan, the Permanent Under-Secretary, endorsed, and Lord Halifax, the Foreign Secretary, approved. However, Halifax added, as a very rare sign of interest, a minute saying: 'Recent events in Europe have increased the importance of Palestine to the British Empire', which meant, so one may conclude, to dissociate himself from any other dimension of pan-Arabism but the one intended to help Britain to solve the Palestine problem.[134]

And if pan-Arabism could help Britain to loosen the burden of Palestine from its mental preoccupation, even French and Saudi susceptibilities should be disregarded. The Foreign Office admitted in January 1939 on the eve of the Palestine St James's Conference, to which the Arab countries had been invited, that in spite of French hesitancies, Britain had to be sympathetic towards pan-Arabism, but to 'take as little initiative as possible, because of these hesitancies'. By reflecting this sympathy Britain would be in a position 'to endeavour to guide the movement [of pan-Arabism] along the right lines'.[135]

This position, which had been made known officially to Ibn Saud,[136] alarmed the India Office who were afraid lest the status of the Gulf sheikhdoms bound to Britain by treaties of protection might be jeopardised if a serious movement towards Arab federation had been set on foot.[137] The Foreign Office replied that no reference had been made, when Britain expressed her new and more favourable attitude towards pan-Arabism, to the minor Arab sheikhdoms.[138]

The General Officer Commanding, British Troops in Egypt, General R. Gordon-Finlayson, too expressed his opposition to any British espousal of pan-Arabism, since if this movement were to unite the Arabs against Britain, the latter could find herself in a difficult position. But in April 1939 the Foreign Office felt relieved of the danger that Britain would continue to uphold the idea of partition of Palestine. Therefore, the whole question of pan-Arabism began to look much less imminent and consequently the warning of General Gordon-Finlayson a little bit superfluous.[139]

A similar, but rather ambiguous attitude was taken at the same time by the Foreign Office in a talk with Comte de Caix de St Aymour, the French representative in the League of Nations' Permanent Mandates Commission. Lacy Baggallay explained to his French interlocutor that Arab federation was not practicable 'at present, because of the different degrees of political and economic advancement as yet attained by the various Arab countries, and because of jealousies, dynastic and otherwise between them'. He stressed that the British Government 'were at present neither for nor against it, but thought that if it came at all it should come as the result of a natural and a spontaneous growth'. If this happened 'it would be impolitic to oppose it'. Baggallay declined to admit that even concerning Palestine the British Government had been adopting a favourable attitude towards pan-Arabism, but confined himself to the remark that 'many circles in this country were indeed favourable to the idea of federation as a means of securing increased Jewish immigration' to Palestine, but not the government.[140] One cannot help the conclusion that since the St James's Conference had ended in mid-March 1939 without any agreement with the Arabs, and since the Arab Governments had not succeeded in exerting a moderating influence on the Palestine Arabs, the Foreign Office felt less inhibited about expressing their basic scepticism of pan-Arabism and of its Palestinian dimension as well.

It is true that the official records of the St James's Conference do not tell us whether or not the British delegates seriously suggested to the Arabs trading their agreement to the continuation of Jewish immigration to Palestine, albeit in a very restricted form, for British support of Arab federation including Palestine.[141] But a talk between R. A. Butler, the [political] Foreign Under-Secretary, and the Palestine leaders Jamal al-Husayni and Musa al-'Alami, following the conference, is illuminating. When these two Arab spokesmen expressed their rejection of British policy, Butler questioned them on the subject of federation and he 'was rewarded by some positive statements which had hitherto been lacking. They said they had plans already worked out for an Arab federation with the neighbouring States'.[142] But this Arab *volte face* came too late. By May 1939 the White Paper had already been issued and the possibility that the British Government would shelve it immediately upon its publication was very slim indeed.

The retreat of the Foreign Office to their original position of rather scornful scepticism of the internal strength of pan-Arabism became clearer in summer 1939. By then, it became fully evident that bringing the Arab countries to take part in the discussion of the future of Palestine had not softened Arab intransigence, since the Arabs rejected the May 1939 White Paper.[143] Now the Foreign Office would once again consider pan-Arabism only on its merits, regardless of the allegedly possible contribution of that factor to finding a solution to the Palestine problem which might be accepted both by the Arabs and the Jews. The new perception was stated in a comprehensive memorandum on pan-Arabism which was prepared in September 1939 by Lacy Baggallay of the Foreign Office's Eastern Department.

After having analysed the historical background of the goal to establish an Arab federation, the political, cultural and economic developments which had strengthened this trend and the various federation schemes which had in the past been put forward, Baggallay went on to consider the strength of the existing reality and found that it was true to state that nothing was 'inherently permanent about most of the present boundaries of the Arab countries', apart from those of Egypt and to a lesser extent of Iraq. Therefore he expected a tendency to re-arrange 'their political divisions and groupings' to emerge in the future. But, rather like Rendel in his 1933 memorandum (see above, pp. 224–7), he found four categories of obstacle in the way of implementing that tendency: (a) the jealousies and rivalries of the various Arab rulers and states; (b) France's position and interest; (c) Turkey; and (d) Great Britain.

In category (a) Baggallay emphasised the strong rivalry between the Saudis and the Hashemites and its negative bearings on any movement towards even closer co-operation among the Arabs. In category (b) he pointed out that the French categorically rejected any such notion, which might endanger their position in Syria and the Lebanon which was very important to them. Category (c) was to a large extent a novelty in the British official consideration of that subject. Although the Turks had in the past declared time and time again that they harboured no territorial ambitions, many people, including Baggallay, so it seems, did not believe them. The annexation of the Sanjak of Alexandretta indicated, so those people argued, that sooner or later Turkey would take steps to obtain control of Aleppo in Syria and Mosul in Iraq. 'If these latent ambitions do exist, an Arab federation might indeed appear to Turkish eyes as a prospective obstacle to Turkish interests, although it would be difficult for the Turkish Government to say this openly.' This allusion to a *possible* Turkish objection and the indifferent attitude towards a theoretical Turkish threat to a territory (Mosul) which is part of a country (Iraq) bound to Britain by a Treaty of Friendship and Mutual Defence reflected the growing strategic importance of Turkey to Britain upon the outbreak of the Second World War and the high price which Britain was ready to pay in order to keep the former outside the Axis orbit.

Category (d) was the most important. Here Baggallay analysed the pros and cons of an Arab federation from the point of view of British strategic requirements. First of all, he stated, it was impossible to have a comprehensive policy for the area as a whole, which was too fragmented and torn by internal divisions. Britain must look after her basic needs which were all too well known: lines of communication and oil. In order to safeguard these interests Britain must retain a high degree of influence in the area. And it was reasonable to assume that a number of smaller and weaker states would be more amenable to British influence than one strong single State embracing all or most of the existing Arab countries. Therefore the British should not of their own accord 'wish actively to promote and encourage Pan-Arab ideas, even if the attitude of the French Government left them free to do so, and even if their relations with the various rulers were of such a kind that they could support a policy which seemed to favour one among them without causing offence to the others'. On the other hand, Britain should not actively oppose that idea, but take the line that any initiative to form a federation 'should and must come from the Arabs themselves'. If that point were to arise Britain should, instead of 'displaying active opposition or open lack of sympathy, endeavour to guide the movement along lines which should ensure that the ensuing federation or union was friendly to Great Britain'. Baggallay concluded that a British attempt to promote Arab federation 'would be a very risky experiment' owing to the above-mentioned factors and 'that a positive declaration on the subject should be avoided as long as possible'.

This memorandum was concurred with by Oliphant, Cadogan and Halifax himself. But the Heads of the Office believed that under the new strains of war the Memorandum should not be presented to the War Cabinet but rather distributed to King, Cabinet and Dominions, namely to other interested Departments of State, Dominions and, on Halifax's suggestion, to concerned posts abroad.[144]

From within the Foreign Office came two reactions, both of which strengthened the anti-federation tone. P. S. Havard, the British Consul in Beirut, stated that 'were an attempt made to include the Lebanon in any Arab federation and an Arab federation would necessarily mean one that was preponderantly Moslem, the Lebanese Christian communities would resist it by every means in their power';[145] whereas G. MacKereth, the Consul in Damascus, emphatically endorsed the conclusion against Britain's being drawn into the matter and went much further in defence of the French position and interests in Syria and Lebanon, since French military presence there enhanced the value of France and Britain in Turkish eyes.[146]

It seems that the other interested Departments of State were too deeply immersed in the conduct of the war and except for the War Office no reaction reached the Foreign Office. The War Office generally scoffed at the basic notions of pan-Arabism and regarded it as an ideology 'upheld by the intellectuals less as a conviction than as a convenient banner and a useful weapon against further European encroachment'. And since the Arab world was divided between rival dynasties Britain had to wash its hands of the contest for the leadership of the Arab world so as to avoid prejudicing its position and influence in either of the conflicting camps.[147]

Since all these comments generally corresponded with the tone and conclusions of the Foreign Office's memorandum, no change was introduced in it, and after it had been printed it served as a guiding instrument of the British Government until it was superseded two years later by another instrument.[148]

We have already noted that after the outbreak of World War II the Arabs began to exert pressure on Britain to meet Arab demands over Palestine and to make a positive declaration concerning Arab unity (see ch. 3, pp. 185–7). We must now turn our attention to the effects that this pressure had on British thinking and ascertain to what degree it changed the course of British policy. Not only Arab statesmen demanded that Britain declare its support for Arab unity or federation in one form or another; correspondents of Arabic newspapers in London posed the same questions and called upon the Foreign Office to prepare considered replies. It seems that until the summer of 1940 the British position, as stated in the September 1939 memorandum, held. In March 1940 such a reply was prepared by the Eastern Department to be given by R.A. ('Rab') Butler to John Leggitt, *al-Misri's* London correspondent.[149] About the same time Sir Harold MacMichael had a talk with M. Puaux, the French High Commissioner for Syria and Lebanon. Replying to a question about the British position on Arab federation as a possible solution to the Palestine conflict, MacMichael stated that 'an effective federation of the Arab States is a dream which will not be realised within any period of which account need be taken'. He went further: after pointing out the basic deficiencies of the existing Arab governments, he stated that nothing 'would notably be enhanced if [federation were] applied to a congeries of states, containing a heterogeneous medley of racial types...'. MacMichael's remarks, one should add, were fully endorsed by both the Colonial and the Foreign Offices.[150] Both offices, outwardly at least but not publicly, continued through 1940 to express the view that the time had not come for Britain to take any initiative in promoting Arab unity and that the British Government 'would naturally view with sympathy any projects for collaboration between Arab States which would be acceptable to all these states themselves'.[151]

That question of the French High Commissioner was typical of French opposition to any scheme of Arab federation and of the deep French suspicion of British intentions. Any article in one of the British newspapers favouring such a scheme was enough to arouse French apprehension and to cause them to pose questions to British representatives. Up to the French collapse in June 1940 Britain was careful to give no reason to the French to doubt their ally's sincerity,[152] but afterwards a different situation came about. It is true that even after the constitution of the Vichy regime in France Britain continued to take into account French sensitivities over its Empire in general and Syria and the Lebanon in particular, but it is evident that by now their weight was not the same as before.[153] Furthermore, in the Foreign Office a conviction was growing that if, on the French collapse in Europe, they 'were eliminated' from Syria, a new situation would then be created and 'a union of various States west of the desert, under the Emir Abdulla or anyone else ... would be reasonable enough'.[154] The Colonial Secretary, Lord Lloyd, an old-time believer in Arab federation, was now convinced that 'we should have much to gain by giving the Arabs definite encouragement over the question of federation, and giving it now, especially as France could be counted out so far as Syria was concerned'.[155]

This was only one of the changes which had been gradually taking place in the British consideration of Arab unity since summer 1940 in the face of growing Arab pressure, and in the light of the French collapse. Another change was caused by the combined effect on Arab public opinion of the French collapse, the German military successes, the achievements of German anti-British and anti-Jewish propaganda in the Middle East and the Italian declaration of war against Britain. Sir Miles Lampson reacted to this situation in July 1940, by sending an alarming despatch to the Foreign Office, which enraged the military authorities. This upholder of Arab positions over Palestine within the Foreign Office establishment, who in the past had expressed a clearly sceptical approach to Arab unity, now thought that the Arabs were strongly encouraged by these developments, that new hopes for independence were raised in Syria and that a 'strong movement is on foot for some sort of confederation of independent states in Northern Arabic world, e.g., between Iraq, Syria, Trans-Jordan and Palestine'. His main practical recommendation was a rapid implementation of all parts of the May 1939 White Paper on Palestine.[156]

Sir Basil Newton, the British Ambassador in Baghdad, also emphasised, although in a lower key, the ability of the Arabs to 'make trouble' all over the Middle East. He confirmed that the Arab leaders, with Iraqi pan-Arabists at their helm, were contemplating the formation of a confederation. He recommended that the British Government, 'as a counter-move against Axis Powers ... make it known that they would regard with benevolent sympathy any move towards federation which might be initiated by the Arab States themselves. In return we could ask for some public expression and tangible evidence of solidarity with His Majesty's Government'.[157]

Sir Harold MacMichael, High Commissioner for Palestine, also reacted to Lampson's warning. Dismissing Lampson's evaluation altogether, he wrote:

> There is a vast nucleus of variegated intrigue afoot throughout the Arab countries. To speak of it as 'a strong movement for some confederation of independent states' suggests a unity which is very far from existing. The idea of the confederation is by no means generally shared and the chief features exhibiting unity are first mutual distrust and second unanimity of desire of each part concerned not to miss the chance of getting ahead of others and to gain political kudos at home. They know perfectly well that Arab federation is at present a dream which would resolve itself into a nightmare though they keep getting some promises of encouragement which might prove useful.

He stressed that French collapse in Europe did not eradicate their military power in Syria; he explained Arab approaches as an attempt to examine British intentions and stated that Arab friendship would be secured through military victory in the war and not by appeasing them.[158] MacMichael stuck to his low opinion of pan-Arabism consistently. In October of that year he rejected a pan-Arab proposal put to him by George Antonius and questioned the basic assumption of Arab unity on which Antonius's proposal had been based.[159]

The Foreign Office in London discussed these views thoroughly, considering them far more dispassionately than Lampson or Newton. It is true that Baggallay agreed that 'a movement for some sort of confederation is undoubtedly on foot', but he doubted 'whether it is yet a "strong" movement'. He realised that 'the Arab rulers especially are far from united as to what form the confederation should take, and Ibn Saud for one is probably against one in any form'. He well understood the political change that had resulted from Churchill's accession to the premiership and concluded that a further anti-Zionist stand in Palestine 'from the point of view of practical politics is out of the question'. He suggested that the British representatives should be informed that Britain could not go beyond the White Paper and that its constitutional provisions would be implemented only after the war.[160]

Lord Lloyd, the Colonial Secretary, who in principle supported some form of Arab unity and thought that 'geographical, economic and strategical factors all point to the advantages of some kind of union', rejected the notion that the initiative had to come from the British Government.[161] Thus the first attempt to deviate from the policy outlined in 1939 by the Statement of Policy and by the memorandum on Arab federation was foiled, but new attempts were soon made.

Already in August 1940 Lampson repeated his demand for an immediate implementation of the Palestine White Paper *in toto*. This time he did not refer to the question of Arab unity. But this demand was also flatly rejected by the Foreign Office and by Halifax personally.[162]

About the same time Colonel Newcombe, who had been sent by Lord Lloyd 'ostensibly on a mission for the British Council' to Iraq 'for the purpose of rallying Arab support through the medium of his contacts in Iraq', responded favourably to the demands of the Iraqi pan-Arab leaders and of Amin al-Husayni, the deposed Mufti of Jerusalem, and urged his government, in addition to British concessions in Palestine, to declare their support of a closer union, federal or economic, of any Arab states which might eventually desire it. In such a union Iraq and Saudi Arabia, he argued, would be able to use their influence to silence anti-British propaganda regarding Palestine. And although Newcombe's recommendation coincided with the view of both Ambassadors Newton and Lampson the Cabinet under Churchill's guidance rejected it.[163]

A few months later Newcombe again put his proposal to the Colonial Office, suggesting that the federation should include Syria, Palestine, Iraq, Saudi Arabia, Yemen and Trans-Jordan. Representatives of these countries would sit in a Federal Council which would control certain matters, to the exclusion of defence and foreign affairs which would be controlled by Great Britain and possibly France. The Colonial Office discussed this proposal thoroughly. However, they concluded that 'in Arabia centrifugal tendencies are very strong and real union between Arab states will not be easy to attain'. Their negative reaction was summed up in a detailed note prepared by F.H. Downie, which the Colonial Secretary read 'with much interest'.[164]

But the steadfastness of the Foreign Office in the face of growing Arab pressure for a British declaration of support for Arab unity did not last long. In December 1940 Anthony Eden was again appointed Foreign Secretary. Halifax who in 1938–9 had not been enthusiastic about a policy of support for pan-Arabism was now replaced by Eden who in 1936–7 had advocated approaching the Palestine problem as part of the Middle East as a whole and not as a problem on its own. Furthermore, in the winter of 1941 anti-British forces in Iraq were daily stepping up their pressure on the Regent and on other pro-British politicians. It seems that these developments caused the Foreign Office to become more pliant to the counsels of their Middle Eastern Ambassadors. On 20 January 1941, C.W. Baxter informed the Colonial Office that 'the Foreign Office have *recently* [my italics] been giving some thought to the desirability of making some declaration on policy covering the Middle East [and not only Palestine]'. This declaration, he said, should be considered in the near future. Its main object would be 'not to win over the anti-British extremists, but to show our friends in the Middle East exactly what our views and intentions are towards the Arab world. For this purpose, any declaration would probably have to go further than the vague assurances suggested in paragraph 7 of Antonius's memorandum'. Since Antonius had demanded (see p. 243 of this chapter) a British declaration of sympathy with Arab goals of independence and unity in whatever form, Baxter's letter carried a far-reaching proposal to make a British public statement of policy of support for pan-Arabism.[165]

This shift did not result from a conviction that the Arabs should be compensated for British policy in Palestine. In February the High Commissioner for Palestine suggested proceeding with the implementation of the White Paper by nominating three Palestinians (two Arabs and one Jew) as Heads of Departments in the Palestine Government, and publicly declaring the intention to carry out the constitutional provisions of the White Paper. Those steps should be taken simultaneously with the announcement of the formation of a Jewish fighting contingent in the British Army as a counter-gesture to the Arabs. But since the British Government decided to postpone the formation of that contingent, MacMichael's advice was not taken,[166] although it had initially aroused a positive reaction, whereas the trend towards making a declaration over British policy in the Middle East was soon to gather momentum.

In the same month the Foreign Office found an occasion to discuss the question of the British position regarding Arab federation. Since a new British Ambassador had been appointed to the Baghdad Embassy the department wanted to furnish him with an authoritative statement of British positions regarding the Arab world to be signed by the Prime Minister and despatched to the Ambassador. As for Arab federation the despatch, which was prepared by the Eastern Department and approved by R. A. Butler, the Parliamentary Under-Secretary, after having been agreed by the Colonial Office, did not go much further than the position stated by the Foreign Office's memorandum of 28 September 1939: sympathy with the aspiration of the Arabs to promote unity among their countries, but reluctance to take the initiative in drawing up any scheme for it, which should come from the Arabs themselves. An earlier draft of the despatch went further, pointing out that this question was not necessarily dependent upon the solution of constitutional problems in Syria and Palestine, since Iraq and Saudi Arabia, for example, could 'establish as close a form of co-operation or federation as may be mutually acceptable to both countries'. And if such an arrangement were successful, these countries 'might consider whether their arrangements could be extended to other Arab countries, e.g. Egypt and the Yemen'. However, Baxter did not like this paragraph and suggested leaving it out and Seymour agreed.[167] The Foreign Office were not yet ready to change their traditional position and Eden had to wait.

The growing German pressure and the military reversal of the British in North Africa enabled Sir Miles Lampson to launch an attack. In late April 1941 he advocated his view in an official telegram and in a personal letter to Sir Horace Seymour, which had a strongly critical tone directed against Sir Lancelot Oliphant, the former Assistant Under-Secretary who had in the past 'squashed' Lampson's pro-Arab proposals. Now Lampson warned that Britain was in 'danger of reaping the whirlwind of our neglect' unless a change of policy was immediately introduced. He attributed the success of German propaganda to British espousal of Zionism and the danger felt by the Arabs of being dispossessed by the Jews, to Anglo-French domination and to the division of Arab lands into separate units which were economically and administratively not viable. This could be compared with expressions of German sympathy for the Arab nation and statements 'that Germany was the only country which was able to give the Arabs independence' from the British and French yoke, which were made by German diplomats to Arab leaders. Therefore he suggested that Britain issue a declaration which would 'contain definite guarantees for the stoppage of Jewish immigration, for Arab administrative predominance in Palestine, for real Syrian independence and assurances of our practical sympathy with Arab Federation'. Ibn Saud should get guarantees for his own territory, Turkish opposition to Arab unity should be disregarded, British commitment to Free France as far as Syria is concerned 'may very easily prove a mill-stone on our necks', and as far as the Zionist issue was concerned the major difficulty was pro-Zionism in London rather than the US position.[168]

Lampson was not the only source of reports about the devastating effects of German propaganda and activities. Both Sir Basil Newton and Mr Stonehewer-Bird, the British Minister in Saudi Arabia, had reported in January and March that the Germans were making approaches to Ibn Saud and promised to support the independence of Syria.[169] And in April immediately on taking office in Baghdad Cornwallis drew the Foreign Office's attention to a new German declaration of sympathy with the Arabs, which, according to his suggestion, should be met by a British counterstroke 'stressing British feelings of friendship for Arabs'.[170] In addition to these British-originated alarms, on 9 May Nevile Butler, the former head of the Foreign Office's American Department, now serving as a Counsellor in the Embassy in Washington, informed the Foreign Office about a talk with Wallace Murray, in which his American interlocutor expressed his fear of 'a general flare up in the Arab states'.[171]

The first serious consideration by the British Government of the possibility of making some conciliatory step towards the Arabs was made on 8 May. On that day the War Cabinet Defence Committee composed of the Prime Minister, the Lord Privy Seal (Clement Attlee), First Lord of the Admiralty (A. Alexander), Air Minister (Archibald Sinclair), War Secretary (D. Margesson), Foreign Secretary (Anthony Eden) and the three chiefs of Imperial, Naval and Air Staffs with the attendance of the Colonial Secretary (Lord Moyne) and the Air General Officer Commander-in-Chief, Middle East, met to discuss Churchill's demand to find means 'to prevent the Germans getting a footing in Syria ... without minding what happens at Vichy'.[172] In view of the fact stated during the discussion that the 'only British force available for use was the Brigade Group which was being prepared to go to Iraq' to crush the hostile regime of Rashid 'Ali al-Kaylani and of General Wavell's reluctance to use the Free French, 'Mr Attlee suggested that it might be possible to take advantage of the Arab feeling to change our policy towards Syria and to support openly the idea of an Arab Federation'. Thus the Arabs might support Britain in conquering Syria. Lord Moyne emphasised how impracticable the whole notion of Arab federation was. 'The most we could do would be to let it be known that we should not oppose a Federation.' He added that the Syrians might welcome the British 'if we could promise them a similar Treaty' to the one which the French had signed but never ratified. But even that was too far-reaching a concession for Churchill. Eager for action he stated that 'the time had passed for trying to liquidate matters by political settlements or promises to the Arabs'. He proposed to supply the Free French with the lorries they needed but badly lacked and to advise General Catroux to try to win over to the Free French cause the Vichy-French troops commanded by General Dentz in Syria. At the end it was agreed to let General Catroux lead the invasion of Syria when the Germans landed there so that he might win the support of the Vichy-French troops.[173]

Immersed in the nervous atmosphere caused by Lampson's letter and the alarming reports from other parts, including Washington, but certainly unaware of the rejection of Attlee's proposition by the Defence Committee, the heads of the Foreign Office began to discuss their reaction. On 20 May C.W. Baxter more or less rejected Lampson's suggestion regarding Palestine and Syria. With respect to the question of Arab federation he stuck to the conventional Foreign Office views: 'The difficulty is to evolve some scheme showing our practical sympathy with Arab federation, we have always taken the line that it is for the Arabs to work out for themselves their schemes for Arab federation. Certainly if we were to try to work out such a scheme we should encounter formidable difficulties, and it is doubtful whether we should in fact improve our position in the Arab world'. This negative reaction was on the following day supported by Sir Horace Seymour.

But within a day or two everything was reversed. Churchill's bombastic Note of 19 May was analysed on 20 May and shown to be virtually unrealistic by Baxter (see ch. 2, pp. 92–3) but for one thing — Arab federation. Now Baxter must have recollected his letter to the Colonial Office of 20 January, written on Eden's appointment as Foreign Secretary, and jumped at Churchill's support of a kind of Arab unity. He noted that 'what we should work for is an Arab federation which is what the Arabs always say they want'. But he opposed raising Ibn Saud to a general overlordship over the proposed Arab federation and rejected Churchill's notion, which was one of the main goals of the whole proposal, that in return the Arabs would agree to unrestricted Jewish immigration to a self-governing Jewish Palestine. Churchill's Note struck Cadogan too, and he followed Baxter. He accepted that 'our ultimate object would be to work for Arab Federation'. But in the meanwhile he was full of doubts how to do it and whether Ibn Saud or the new Iraqi Government would give the impetus. One thing he took for granted: the federation should come as 'a spontaneous Arab movement', implying a rejection of Churchill's idea to impose Ibn Saud's overlordship on the Arabs. A day later when he dealt with Baxter's and Seymour's negative reactions to Lampson's proposals of 26 April, he accepted their basic approach but drew Eden's attention to the fact that 'the Prime Minister's recent paper contemplated an Arab Federation', although, he added, 'there may be difficulty in bringing it about'. The fact that Churchill's proposed federation was to be headed by Ibn Saud in return for a most far-reaching pro-Zionist solution of the Palestine question was overlooked by Cadogan too. Eden read those minutes on 25 May and added his own: 'Discussed at meeting today'.[174]

It is not clear with whom Eden discussed the matter and what decisions were arrived at. What we do know is that the department began, in a very urgent and even hasty way, to work along two parallel paths: preparing a Note in reaction to Churchill's Note and formulating the text of a public speech for the Foreign Secretary. The Note was to have been used by Eden as the basis of his position in a discussion with the Prime Minister of the latter's Note. But Eden introduced several changes in it and instructed that it be distributed to the Cabinet without prior consultation with the other Departments of State concerned. Since such a procedure was very unusual and outraged the Colonial Office, Cadogan had to admit that it had been done 'as a matter of the greatest urgency and many of us were surprised to see it in print as a Cabinet Paper shortly afterwards'.

The Note itself combined Eden's own desire *to make public* his sympathy with the idea of Arab independence and those points in Churchill's Note which could be used to buttress Eden's view. It even accepted Churchill's proposal to let the Turks occupy Aleppo in order to safeguard their neutrality. But it totally disregarded Churchill's pro-Zionist proposals and the idea of Ibn Saud's overlordship. As for Arab federation Eden adhered to his office's view that it was not 'practical politics'. But since the 'Arabs generally agree that some form of "Arab federation" is desirable' Eden advised 'not only to refrain from opposing such vague aspirations, but even take every opportunity of expressing publicly our support for them', and to leave to the Arabs to work out the concrete terms of a federation.[175]

This last point may help us to understand Eden's sense of urgency and the hasty treatment. He certainly remembered that only about three weeks earlier the War Cabinet Defence Committee had rejected a milder proposal of Lord Moyne 'to let it be known that we should not oppose a Federation'. Therefore, he may have worried lest the Cabinet again reject the same position and he wanted to present them with a *fait accompli*. Consequently, the Eastern Department prepared a text of a speech which Eden delivered in the Mansion House, London, on 29 May without any discussion and authorisation of his Note by the Cabinet.[176] In that speech Eden did not mention any of Churchill's pro-Zionist ideas. On the other hand, he emphasised that the violent suppression of Rashid 'Ali al-Kaylani's regime in Iraq would not harm the long friendship between Britain and the Arabs. Then he passed to the crucial question of the British attitude to Arab unity aspirations and stated his view in a rather cautious way in which the term 'Arab Federation', unlike in his Cabinet Note, did not occur. After expressing his sympathy with Syria's aspirations for independence he went further:

> The Arab world has made great strides since the settlement reached at the end of the last war and many Arab thinkers desire for the Arab peoples a greater degree of unity than they now enjoy. In reaching out towards this unity they hope for our support. No such appeal from our friends should go unanswered. It seems to me both natural and right that the cultural and economic ties between the Arab countries and the political ties too, should be strengthened. His Majesty's Government for their part will give their full support to any scheme that commands general approval.[177]

It seems reasonable to assume that Eden's speech presented a serious dilemma for Churchill. Eden had publicly committed the British Government to a proposal that had been rejected both by the Defence Committee and by the Prime Minister personally. The only way to retreat from such a commitment would amount to a public admonishment of Eden which could probably lead to his resignation. Certainly, Churchill did not wish to see the departure from his government of one of the few close and intimate associates he had inside his own Conservative Party. Therefore, he chose a different approach. The day after the speech Churchill wrote a Personal Minute to Eden in which he disregarded the latter's speech altogether, and restated his basic pro-Zionist beliefs. On the other hand Churchill reminded him that he (Churchill) still 'should like to have some answer' to his Note of 19 May, implying that he did not regard Eden's speech as a satisfactory reaction. Eden replied on 2 June. He dealt with the Zionist question only and ignored Churchill's Note.[178] Instead, Eden's Note 'Our Arab Policy', was on 3 June discussed by the Cabinet who 'gave general approval to the Foreign Secretary's recommendations' including his fifth recommendation for 'Public support of the idea of Arab federation, the terms of which it must be left to the Arabs to work out'. Churchill's idea of making Palestine Jewish within an Arab Caliphate under Ibn Saud's overlordship was not discussed at all, and no change in favour of Zionism was approved as far as Palestine was concerned. That aspect, so it seems, was Eden's most important aim, much more than any appeasement of the Arabs, since another recommendation of his – 'in default of a Free French occupation' of Syria to 'promote, if possible, the occupation of Aleppo by the Turks' – could by no means be regarded as a conciliatory step towards the Arabs.[179]

Now that the speech had been made and its principles approved by the

Cabinet, first the Foreign Office and then other concerned Departments of State began to analyse its content, to realise what Eden meant and to examine the possibility of going further in the direction of giving encouragement to more concrete pan-Arab schemes. The first attempt was made by Professor H.A.R. Gibb and his war-time 'task force' ('Foreign Research and Press Service') at Balliol College, Oxford. In a memorandum presented on 9 June Gibb pointed out that Eden's speech should be made into a cornerstone of a comprehensive policy which must be initiated in the near future and progressively put into execution aiming at bringing about stabilisation of the whole Near East. This stabilisation could be achieved, he argued, by reunification of Greater Syria and gradual abolition of foreign control. Then this reunited Syria would join with other Arab countries in 'a triple system of cultural collaboration, economic and military agreements, and finally a constitutional linking-up of the whole'. As for the Jewish National Home Gibb too thought that it could be squared with his proposed federation and Weizmann's espousal of the same principle (in connection with the Philby scheme) was for him a source of encouragement.

The Political Intelligence Department reacted to Gibb's memorandum on 1 July. They were not great believers in Arab federation but thought it was politic for Britain not to discourage it. Furthermore, they regarded the implementation of the 1939 Palestine White Paper as the keystone to any British policy in the Middle East. And in order to secure its acceptance, they recommended adding to it the offer of Arab federation. Humphrey Bowman of the department submitted a different Note which pointed to the same conclusion, although in different language. He too claimed that unless Britain were ready to implement *in toto* the Palestine White Paper, there would be no point in promoting Arab federation which could become a danger for Britain. R.A. Butler, Eden's Parliamentary Under-Secretary, reacted to these papers in a very typical way. His remarks carried the message that any British offer of a federation should be 'pretty vague', but more importantly he stated that 'Cabinet won't agree' to fully implement the White Paper and therefore that all discussion remained academic.[180]

But the question could no longer be shelved. In August Hafiz Wahbah, the Saudi Minister, approached Eden (without his King's approval became clear a little later) and asked for British active participation in formulating a scheme of federation. From the Foreign Office reaction, including that of Eden himself, it emerges that they were all a bit embarrassed. They stated that when the Middle East was still very much a theatre of war very little, if anything at all, could be done.[181] Nevertheless, the need to give thorough thought to the question was fully grasped. As C.W. Baxter minuted on another occasion: 'we cannot continue a purely negative attitude indefinitely, and I would much like to clear our minds about "Arab Federation" and the future of Syria, Trans-Jordan and Palestine'.[182]

This need coincided with the need to react to 'Abdallah's plea that he be supported in his bid for the Syrian crown and his Emirate be declared independent (see above, pp. 205–12). The Colonial Secretary, who thought that Britain should accede to 'Abdallah's demand for independence, brought the question before the War Cabinet Middle East (Ministerial) Committee who resolved to refer it to the Middle East (Official) Committee for examination and report.[183] But the FO's Eastern Department were of the opinion that the demand should be discussed as part of 'the whole question of the future states of Syria, the Lebanon, Trans-Jordan and Palestine' and how Arab aspirations could 'best be fitted in with the interests and obligations of His Majesty's Government'. And although Sir Horace Seymour was not enthusiastic about this approach, Eden endorsed their view.[184] When the committee met, Baxter on behalf of the FO repeated his view that the future of Trans-Jordan was part of the broader Arab problem. But he went further. He pointed out to his colleagues that 'bearing in mind Mr Eden's Mansion House speech ... it was incumbent upon us to take the initiative in formulating a positive policy towards the Arab States in general'. The committee resolved that measures pertaining to separate Arab states, such as terminating the mandate over Trans-Jordan, would be desirable 'only if it can be reconciled with the general Arabian policy that His Majesty's Government may have adopted in the interval'.[185] Accordingly, MacMichael was notified that so long as no comprehensive Arab policy had been shaped nothing positive could be promised to 'Abdallah.[186]

The Foreign Office realised that this amounted to doing nothing since no such general policy was being discussed. Both Seymour and Eden expressed reluctance over 'doing nothing'[187] and it seems that Eden tried to hasten the process of shaping a comprehensive Arab policy. Anyway several days later when the War Cabinet discussed the situation in Syria and the tense relations with the Free French, the subject of the general Arab question was raised. It can be inferred from the short résumé of that meeting that the Prime Minister did not care for Eden's approach. Eden had no choice but to acquiesce in Churchill's view and the Cabinet concluded that 'the question of a settlement of the Arab question generally raised far more difficult issues, and it would probably be premature to attempt to deal with it at the present time'.[188] It seems that Churchill had learned a lesson from Eden's Mansion House speech which had been made without prior authorisation, and he saw to it that Eden's hands would thenceforward be bound by a clear Cabinet decision.

Since the subjects of British policy towards the general Arab question and whether or not Britain should be more active in shaping a scheme of Arab federation had repercussions on several other matters, they did not remain undiscussed for long. As a result of Churchill's pressure on his colleagues to discuss the Philby plan and the agreement reached over it between Weizmann and Firoz Khan Noon (see ch. 2, pp. 93–6) the Ministerial Conference with the Minister of State decided to invite the Middle East (Official) Committee to discuss the question of Arab federation as a means of solving the Palestine problem (see ch. 2, pp. 121–3). In order to be able to pass judgement the committee had to examine 'the various forms which a scheme of Arab federation might take'. Therefore the committee again resumed discussion of whether or not Britain should encourage the movement towards Arab federation not only within the context of the Palestine question.

From the start the Foreign Office stressed that the matter should be considered with regard to essential British strategic requirements in the whole of the Middle East and asked for a clear statement of these.[189] However, Sir Horace Seymour, the Foreign Assistant Under-Secretary in charge of the Middle East, thought 'that the Arabs when they talk of federation, do not really contemplate anything approaching so drastic as a federation'.[190] Consequently the committee had to take this important view into consideration.

The Colonial Office, too, had a reserved attitude to the question. Immediately following the Ministerial Conference's resolution they reminded the Foreign Office that 'no force can be used to impose one Arab suzerain over the rest of the Arab world, to bring about federation in any form'. Secondly, they drew attention to the French factor if the federation scheme were to embrace Syria and the Lebanon.[191] Since the committee was chaired by Sir John Shuckburgh, Parkinson's deputy, it is no wonder that those views very much influenced their work.

When in October 1941 the committee began their discussion they had before them the Foreign Office's September 1939 Note on Arab Federation, Gibb's memorandum of the previous June and the material prepared by the Colonial and Foreign Offices.[192] The Colonial Office put before them a memorandum prepared by Sir Harold MacMichael. He thought that federation or political unification in any shape was 'little more than a chimera' although there were 'directions in which differences in the field of culture and economics could be removed or minimised'. 'The improbability of success for any form of political unification' arose in MacMichael's view from big differences in race, religion, nationality and dynasty. In a further note MacMichael explained that if economic and cultural cooperation were ever to lead to political union the obvious field for the process would be Greater Syria, the division of which had been 'a defiance of history'.[193]

The Foreign Office invited British diplomatic representatives in Cairo, Baghdad and Jedda not only to analyse the difficulties in the way of any scheme of Arab federation, but to express their views as to what the future of the various Arab territories and the ultimate aim of British policy in those territories ought to be. Their view would help the British Government to decide whether 'they should attempt to take the initiative of drawing up some practicable scheme of bringing about some form of federation or closer cooperation between the Arab States'.[194] These questions clearly reveal the direction in which the Foreign Office wanted to lead British policy: an active British-led movement towards Arab unity regardless of the Palestine question.

In his reply Lampson stressed that a political federation was not at present a practical possibility, owing mainly to the internal Arab rivalries. But some cultural or economic federation might be more feasible and the first step should be some form of *Zollverein*. However, he added that the success of that course depended on giving a large measure of independence to Palestine, taking a different line with regard to Zionism and 'forcing the French to restrict their special rights in Syria and the Lebanon'. He added that political federation might in the future endanger British interests such as oil and communications and accepted MacMichael's view that the separation of Palestine from Syria was artificial.[195]

Cornwallis suggested that it was in British interests 'to move with the stream and to continue to show sympathy towards the movement [of Arab federation] as it develops strength'. But his practical proposition was not far-reaching. The first step should be the removal of the artificial cultural and economic barriers not only within Greater Syria but also with Iraq.[196]

Telegrams from Jedda made it clear that although Ibn Saud had sympathy with the idea of Arab unity and wanted to see close co-operation between the Arab countries, he nevertheless regarded the whole issue as premature and impracticable, a view which strongly impressed the Foreign Office.[197] The Minister of State Resident in the Middle East endorsed Cornwallis's view and suggested that one of his office's experts should examine the economic barriers between the Arab states that had to be removed.[198]

The committee was strongly influenced by these views. As the Foreign Office wished, they considered the question of federation not only as offering a possible solution of the Palestine problem, but also as being in itself a desirable object.[199] Their report[200] which had been prepared through consultations with the Foreign and Colonial Offices was presented to the government in January 1942 but, as we have already noted (see ch.2, p.123), it was never discussed and approved by the Cabinet. The committee found that the possibility of forming a political federation was remote. However, they did recommend instructing British representatives in the Middle East 'to draw up schemes for closer economic co-operation and removal of economic barriers between Syria, the Lebanon, Palestine and Trans-Jordan'. These representatives should be invited to consider also what non-political cultural contacts between the Arab states deserved encouragement. As for the political sphere the most extreme step which the committee recommended was to raise no objection to the extension of the 1936 Treaty of Arab Brotherhood between Saudi Arabia and Iraq by the addition of other Arab states, such as Syria and the Lebanon, and even to encourage them to do so.

The Foreign Office reacted by expressing readiness to carry out immediately the practical steps which the committee had recommended. Eden may have been disappointed, since when Sir Maurice Peterson expressed too strongly his belief that the Arabs 'never will' form a federation, he minuted: '"Never" is a dangerous word even in Arab politics. Muhammad did it once'.[201] And, indeed, as the Minister of State had previously suggested, he was now assigned the task of making the necessary enquiries.[202] Eden did not try again to preempt his colleagues. In April 1942 he wrote to Lord Cranborne, the new Colonial Secretary, explaining that the extension of the Treaty of Arab Brotherhood 'should be initiated by the Arab countries themselves' and he doubted whether Britain 'should do more than encourage such proposals if made by the Arabs themselves'. Lord Cranborne agreed[203] and the issue was practically closed since the enquiries in the Middle East had not yet resulted in anything tangible.

The examination of the possibility of bringing about closer economic co-operation did not lead to any practical moves beyond those taken out of necessity by the British authorities in the Middle East in order to assure minimum supplies of food and raw material, which culminated in the formation and successful operation of the Middle East Supply Centre with full American participation. The cultural aspect of the enquiries required by the Middle East (Official) Committee's Report proved far less practicable as far as British policy was concerned.[204]

If nothing happened in those fields where encouragement to pan-Arab tendencies should have been given, it is only natural that no change occurred in other spheres of Britain's Arab policy either. For example, when Nahhas Pasha tried in spring 1942 to initiate an all-Arab declaration in support of the democracies in their war against Nazi Germany and Fascist Italy, the British reaction was reserved, cool and even negative. Walter Smart noted that if the Arab countries were to co-operate among themselves in one sphere, however desirable, it would be very difficult to prevent them from doing the same in other less desirable spheres. And indeed, with the authority of the Minister of State in Cairo the British Embassy exerted pressure on the Egyptian Government to avoid such a step.[205] Another attempt by Egypt in the autumn of that year to form a solid Arab bloc of states under Egyptian leadership did not score a better British reaction.[206]

When at about the same time a suggestion came from Miss E. Monroe, the head of the Middle East Department of the war-time Ministry of Information, that the Prime Minister declare his support for Arab wishes and praise their past glories, the Foreign Office accepted with Eden's approval only a small part of the suggestion while Churchill rejected it altogether. More far-reaching suggestions from the same quarter were dismissed.[207] Another British enthusiastic supporter of pan-Arabism, Professor H.A.R. Gibb, once again presented in December 1942 a detailed memorandum in which he suggested that the Fertile Crescent be united within a thorough political, economic and cultural federation based not upon the existing states but upon a democratic federation of 12 provinces comprising Iraq, Syria, Lebanon, Palestine and Trans-Jordan. The lead should come from Britain who would be awarded 'for patronizing an Arab Union either a more extensive political control of the Middle East, or a large increase of Jewish immigration into Palestine and other Arab countries, or both'. Baxter in the Foreign Office thought that Gibb's paper, though interesting, was 'not likely to be practical politics'. But his superior Sir Maurice Peterson dismissed it altogether and regarded it as a 'disappointing paper'.[208] Needless to say no practical move was taken beyond sending copies to the British Embassies in the Middle East. Although the Embassies did not send any reaction, we know that in Cairo Walter Smart expressed a very similar view to his colleagues' views in London and added that such 'ideal proposals ... cannot become practicable until one native power can impose itself by force on the whole of the eastern Arab world'. And another Embassy man noted that from Baxter's covering letter one could have 'the feeling that at home they are not seriously bothering about what they will do when definite proposals [for unity] come from the Arabs'.[209] No doubt in the Cairo Embassy a more favourable approach to pan-Arabism than the official one in London was noticeable.

At this juncture and against an official British reluctance to give impetus to pan-Arab schemes came, surprisingly enough, Eden's statement in Parliament in February 1943 in which he repeated his May 1941 Mansion House speech. In that month Mr Price, a Labour Member of Parliament and a politician known to be pro-Arab, put a Parliamentary question to Eden in which he asked 'whether any steps are being taken to promote greater political and economic co-operation between the Arab States of the Middle East, with a view to the ultimate creation of an Arab Federation'. We don't know what prompted Mr Price to put his question; he may have learned something about Nuri al-Sa'id's letter and memorandum addressed a little earlier to Mr Casey. What one can know for sure, at least according to the relevant British archival material, is that this question had not been prearranged or initiated by the Foreign Office themselves.[210]

The Foreign Office prepared a reply which said nothing beyond what had been said by Eden in his earlier Mansion House speech. They could not add more substance if they wanted to keep within the lines taken by the British Government since 1941.[211] But at the same time they could not say less. Moreover, if in May–June 1941 Eden's speech did not arouse a general tremor in the Middle East, the situation in February 1943 was totally different. Britain by the latter date was again master of the Middle East and not an isolated country fighting against all odds for control of the Middle East and even for its life against the rising tide of Nazism. Consequently, the Parliamentary reply aroused a much wider interest in the Middle East, was taken much more seriously and triggered off a process which no one in the Foreign Office had expected in February 1943.

5

The Formation of the Arab League

The impact of Eden's February 1943 statement: the inter-Arab consultations

Unlike Eden's Mansion House speech of 29 May 1941, his February 1943 Parliamentary reply was well received in the Arab countries, owing to the change of military fortunes in the Middle East. Many press articles and comments were published, which usually stressed Eden's stipulation that the initiative should be taken by the Arabs themselves.[1] In some quarters the statement was understood as 'an open invitation to the Arab rulers to start working for Arab unity'.[2] It was stressed that in contrast to the British pledges to the Arabs during the First World War which had not been fulfilled, this time the case was different, 'because the mentality and elements who are going jointly to determine the destinies of peoples are unlike the mentality and elements of previous times'.[3]

This faith in British goodwill was to large extent made possible by Britain's support of Syria's and the Lebanon's demand for independence.[4] It seems that the positive Arab reaction was carried even further than might have been expected by the unanimous welcome everywhere in the Arab world.[5] Noteworthy was 'Abd al-Rahman 'Azzam Pasha's reaction. He deprecated Britain's declining to take any initiative and pointed out that not all Arab countries enjoyed self-government and had authoritative mouthpieces to speak on their behalf. However, the Arabs had to grasp that opportunity, and to gather a conference to discuss their future actions with representatives of public organisations to speak for the countries which had not yet reached independence. He exhorted his fellow Arabs to take the initiative so that Eden's statement did not pass once again unheeded.[6] This exhortation fell on fertile ground and many other Arab leaders of public opinion, including Muhammad 'Ali 'Allubah, favourably responded and published their own calls.[7]

Amidst this exchange of calls a group of Palestinian Arab leaders added a proposal of their own to convene in Cairo a representative Arab conference to discuss the question of Arab unity. And Amir 'Abdallah did not lag behind and added his own call for such a conference to be convened under his presidency in 'Amman, his capital.[8]

As we have already noted (see ch. 1, p. 54), the idea of calling an all-Arab Conference to discuss the matter of Arab unity in reaction to Eden's statement was put by Nuri al-Sa'id to Mustafa al-Nahhas in March 1943. The latter, who viewed Nuri al Sa'id's activities in that field 'with some suspicion and jealousy',[9] realised that he had been offered a golden opportunity to take the lead. And if Nahhas needed any more urging to take the initiative he may have realised that King Faruq was then interested himself in the matter of Arab unity and was trying to promote a conference on that subject in Cairo.[10] That the King took this line could not surprise anyone owing to his espousal of pan-Islamic tendencies since his coronation and his personal ambition for the Caliphate. Muhammad 'Ali 'Allubah, who for years had been very active in promoting the idea of Arab unity, enjoyed the full support of the King.[11]

The relations between King Faruq and Nahhas were tense since the latter had been forced on the King as Prime Minister by the British in February 1942.[12] Nahhas paid his debt to the British by unflinching loyalty to the Anglo-Egyptian alliance and by the use of emergency powers to curb pro-German activities. The British victory at al-'Alamein strengthened his position *vis-à-vis* the King, known for his pro-Axis inclinations, who did not give up his desire for revenge.[13]

Although the *Wafd* party under Nahhas's leadership had been enjoying overwhelming support in the country, it lost in the early 1940s part of its standing owing to corruption, nepotism and abuse of power which seeped into the *Wafd*'s leadership. This decline was reflected in several by-elections which the party lost in 1942. Furthermore, at the end of March 1943 Makram 'Ubayd, recently the *Wafd* Deputy Leader, published a pamphlet (nicknamed the 'Black Book') in which he marshalled against the government a series of charges of corruption, favouritism, illicit influence exercised by the family of Nahhas and administrative manipulation. There was little doubt that this attack, which looked formidable, had been prepared with the full co-operation of the Palace.[14]

In such circumstances and in view of Eden's statement and Nuri al-Sa'id's activities and the invitation extended to him, Nahhas could not let any other party take the lead in the movement towards Arab unity and he reacted swiftly. On 30 March 1943 a statement on his own behalf (see ch. 1, p. 35) was made to the Senate in which the Arab governments were called upon to send representatives to Cairo to discuss with Nahhas the matter of Arab unity. Following those consultations a general conference of official representatives would be convened to take the necessary decisions.[15] Thus Nahhas succeeded in fact in taking the reins out of the hands of Nuri al-Sa'id and in preempting any move that Faruq might have made.

He made it clear that the level of the proposed consultations and conference would be of official representatives and thus assured for him or for his delegates the leading role, at the expense of the Egyptian

Opposition and Palace. The latter apparently favoured the Iraqi proposition of holding a conference of representatives of unofficial organisations in order to allow the pan-Arab politicians of the Egyptian Opposition parties who were close to the Palace to play a prominent role.[16]

And indeed the various pro-Arab politicians in Egypt did not give up their activities. On the contrary, they intensified them in the wake of Nahhas's declaration, organised public meetings and even tried to co-ordinate their efforts with the Iraqi politicians whom Nuri al-Sa'id had sent to Egypt in March.[17] Also not everyone in the Fertile Crescent was satisfied with Nahhas's statement. It is true that openly the reaction was favourable and encouraging and the Egyptian press hastened to take notice of it,[18] but not everyone had been fully convinced of Egyptian goodwill. As Taha al-Hashimi put it in his diaries: 'It is rather strange that Egypt starts to uphold the Arab question, while she has only recently abstained from mentioning the Arab nations and preferred to rely on the Oriental nations and countries'.[19]

Amir 'Abdallah of Trans-Jordan was even more reserved in his reaction. He issued a statement addressed to the 'people of Syria from the Gulf of Aqaba to the Mediterranean Sea and Upper Euphrates' in which he called on the leaders in the 'Syrian Countries' to work for the formation of a comprehensive Syrian unity and to meet in a special conference in 'Amman to discuss the implementation of that project. Nahhas's call was totally disregarded. His Council of Ministers was induced by him to pass a resolution calling upon Britain to carry out its obligation to the Arabs by supporting Syrian unity and this resolution was officially presented to the British authorities.[20] 'Abdallah wanted his statement to be broadcast by the British-controlled Near East Broadcasting Station located at Jaffa, Palestine, but the High Commissioner for Palestine refused permission.[21]

'Abdallah's Prime Minister Tawfiq Abu al-Huda was more positive and accepted Nahhas's invitation to take part in the proposed consultations but he too emphasised that the Arabs were expecting the independent Arab states to help the various countries constituting Greater Syria by every available means to achieve their independence and unity.[22] 'Abdallah's deep resentment was fuelled by his conviction that he and the House of Hashim in general did not get their due from the British for their loyalty whereas others got more than was due to them.[23] It seems that he suspected that the British were standing behind Nahhas's initiative. King 'Abd al-'Aziz Al Sa'ud of Saudi Arabia too was very much resentful of Nahhas's initiative. He felt that he should have been consulted before and not after Nahhas's statement was made and he did not conceal his suspicions of Nuri al-Sa'id's intentions.[24]

Nahhas was not deterred and took steps to enhance his initiative.

In June he sent 'Abd al-Fattah al-Tawil Pasha, the Minister of Transport, to Syria and Palestine to propagate the idea of a general Arab Congress and soon afterwards went there himself. He was well received by the public, and the local press viewed his idea with favour.[25] In mid-June Nuri al-Sa'id made a statement which signalled his approval of Nahhas's initiative,[26] and indeed in July Nuri came to Cairo and thus the consultations began. They were carried out with the representatives of the various Arab countries through the autumn of 1943.[27] In addition to his talks with Nuri al-Sa'id, Nahhas had talks with Tawfiq Abu al-Huda, the Prime Minister of Trans-Jordan, with Sa'dallah al-Jabiri and Jamil Mardam, respectively the Syrian Prime Minister and Foreign Minister and Salim Taqla, the Lebanese Foreign Minister.

In order to include representatives of all Arab countries in the talks the Egyptians had to solve the question of the representation of Palestine and the non-independent North African states and to persuade the Saudi monarch to be less suspicious of the whole process and to send his delegate to Cairo. Initially Nahhas had said in his statement to the Senate on 31 March 1943 that only delegates of governments would participate in the consultations. But he found himself under public pressure to invite representatives of the Palestine Arabs and the North African countries as well.[28] Furthermore, he may have realised that by inviting them to the consultations he would enhance their international standing and thus his own in the eyes of the Arabs in general.

But he had to face a serious dilemma: whom should he invite to talk on behalf of the Palestine Arabs? If he repeated the precedent of the Palestine Arab delegation to the 1939 St James's Conference, the delegation would include Jamal al-Husayni and Amin al-Tamimi who were then interned by the British in Rhodesia. Therefore the Egyptians began to exert pressure on the British to release the interned Palestinian leaders and to let them and the North African delegates come to Cairo.[29]

However, the British were strongly against the release of the interned Palestinian leaders under Egyptian pressure and refused to budge over North African participation in order not to antagonise the French.[30] Since the Palestinian leadership insisted that Jamal al-Husayni should lead the Palestinian delegates,[31] no Palestinian Arabs took part in those consultations, and even in the Alexandria Conference in October 1944 Jamal al Husayni and Amin al-Tamimi could not participate. (The latter died in that month still interned in Rhodesia.) Nor, owing to the British position, did any delegates of the French-controlled North African countries – Tunisia, Algeria and Morocco – take part and Nahhas had to make the excuse that independent governments had not yet been formed in these countries.[32]

The British also refused to agree to the participation of the Libyan leader Muhammad Idris al-Sanusi, although before the war Libya had not been a French-controlled area but Italian and no French susceptibility had to be taken into account. Al-Sanusi's presence in exile in Egypt made the question of his participation even more acute. But the British held the view that Libya was an occupied enemy territory, the status of which had to be decided by the post-war Peace Conference and refused to recognise its leader as its temporal head or view favourably his persistent attempts to assert his country's right to independence.[33]

The question of Saudi Arabia's participation in the consultations was completely different. At the beginning Ibn Saud was adamant about participation. He argued that he should have been consulted before and not after Nahhas's statement to the Senate. Since such prior consultations had indeed taken place with Nuri al-Sa'id, he, Ibn Saud, was reduced to a secondary position. He also feared that if a decision to hold a general conference ensued, the question of Palestine was bound to be raised and his representatives would be placed in the most embarrassing situation of having either to listen in silence, which would be difficult, or to agree with what was said, which Ibn Saud refused to contemplate since it would damage his relations with Britain. Furthermore, Ibn Saud's policy, which he had outlined in his messages to Nahhas, was to achieve the independence of each Arab state in such a manner that while each state would retain its own identity, it would be impossible for them to commit acts of aggression against each other and so ensure a balance of power between them.[34] Therefore, he rejected the invitation and turned to the British for advice.[35]

Ibn Saud was very suspicious of Nuri al-Sa'id's motives and the fact that Nuri had indeed made his views and proposals known beforehand to Ibn Saud did not lessen his apprehensions.[36] However, the British let Ibn Saud understand that they would much prefer his participation in the consultations (see below, p. 295) and in the end Ibn Saud sent Yusuf Yasin to represent him in the talks. This decision was taken only when he realised that the Hashemites were not being backed by Britain or Egypt in their bid for the thrones of Syria and Palestine, that the general Arab consultations were regarded by Britain and the USA as a move which did not 'delay or obstruct the Allied war effort or the establishment of a just peace after the war',[37] and that Egypt was not going to support the formation of a real federation but rather a loose association of independent states.[38] The circle of participants was completed when the Imam of the Yemen followed the lead of Ibn Saud and also decided, out of deference to the latter's position, to send a delegate to the consultations.[39]

If we analyse the content of these consultations we will find various issues which generally engaged Arab minds in those days: Who were the Arabs? And which Arab countries should be consulted? These questions were put by Mustafa al-Nahhas to Nuri al Sa'id at the beginning of their talks. It was resolved — contrary to Nuri's view expressed in his January 1943 letter to Casey ('The Blue Book') — that Egypt, Saudi Arabia, Sudan and the North African countries should be included. Nuri admitted that Nahhas's statement of 30 March 1943 had completely changed the situation. It was stressed that the world at large and especially USA and Great Britain concluded from the stormy world situation which had led to the outbreak of the Second World War that small nations with affinities should group in federations with a view to economic and political co-operation and defence against aggression.[40]

The question of the type of federation the Arab countries would form necessarily arose. Was there to be a central government and, if so, what were to be its relations with and power over the regional governments? Or was there to be an executive council formed of delegates from different countries whose decisions would have to be executed? Was the regime of the federation to be monarchical or republican? In the first case, in what way would the King be selected and how could the different desires of the Saudis and the Hashemites be reconciled? Nuri and Nahhas reached the conclusion that union under a central government should be ruled out as unrealisable owing to external difficulties and internal differences and disagreements.[41] Thus, the demands which Ibn Saud had made to Mustafa al-Nahhas before and during the consultations were met.[42]

This approach was accepted also by Tawfiq Abu al-Huda, the Prime Minister of Trans-Jordan, whose interests were different (see later on).[43] Yusuf Yasin on behalf of his King Ibn Saud not only rejected any notion of political unity, however loose it might be, but even refused to commit his King to anything by refusing to sign the minutes of his talks.[44] It goes without saying that the Lebanese delegation emphasised the necessity of retaining the independence of each Arab state, although they expressed their readiness to co-operate as part of the Arab world with other Arab States, 'within the cadre of Lebanese independence'. Even this co-operation should take an economic and cultural rather than political form. To their satisfaction the Lebanese found the Egyptians to be in full accord with their own views.[45]

The only exception was the view of the Syrian delegation. Although they were eager to present a joint position with Ibn Saud they nevertheless regarded political unity as a practical goal and as a means to ensure general Arab backing in their struggle against the French. The Syrians excluded from the proposed Arab union Sudan and the North African countries leaving Egypt, Iraq, Greater Syria — including Lebanon, Palestine and Trans-Jordan in addition to Syria proper — Saudi Arabia and the Yemen. They expressed their readiness to give Nahhas *carte blanche* to suggest forms of unity which they would implement without hesitation.[46]

One cannot be a hundred per cent sure that the Syrian position was not also prompted by tactical considerations. In theory, the content of the Nuri–Nahhas talks was not made known to the public or to the other parties in the further consultations, except in official communiqués which did not reveal too much. But the Syrian Government, who were mostly interested in forestalling any move towards a possible implementation of 'Abdallah's Greater Syria project or Nuri al-Sa'id's Fertile Crescent unity scheme, sent Ahmad al-Shuqayri, the Palestinian leader, as a special representative to Cairo to follow on their behalf the course of the consultations between Egypt and the other Arab states. Shuqayri succeeded in obtaining the minutes of the Nuri–Nahhas talks and sent them to Damascus.[47] Thus, when the Syrians were making their far-reaching proposal in favour of full political unity they knew that this view had already been rejected both by Nuri and Nahhas. They could therefore score points in the contest for the leadership of Arab nationalism without having to bear any practical consequences of their proposal.

Nuri al-Sa'id's Fertile Crescent unity scheme was raised and discussed during his talks with Nahhas. But Nuri realised that once Egypt had joined the movement towards Arab unity his scheme became obsolete and he virtually gave up any attempt to force his idea upon the Egyptian Prime Minister. But this concession was not enough for Nahhas. Since the local press published a statement attributed to Nuri, expressing the desire of Iraq to have a port on the Mediterranean, Nahhas asked Nuri for an explanation. Nuri duly explained that he meant only the construction of a railway line connecting Iraq with the Mediterranean in agreement with the countries situated on the passage of the line.[48]

Disappointed as Nuri may have been, he turned to Ahmad al-Shuqayri. He told him to inform Shukri al-Quwatli, the Syrian President, that the Egyptians were not interested in Arab unity but only in their control of the Arabs. Therefore, no good would come from these consultations and Iraq and Syria should reach agreement between them. But Shuqayri gave him the Syrian negative reply on the spot, explaining that that course was impossible since Iraq was a monarchy and Syria a republic and the former was bound by a treaty to Britain, whereas the latter was free of any contractual obligation to any foreign power.[49] And indeed, the Syrians raised the question of Iraq's intentions regarding their country in their talks with Nahhas, although in an indirect way, and required the Egyptian interlocutors to take a position.[50]

The question of the Greater Syria project was prominent in the consultations. In the Nahhas–Nuri talks it was decided that, if Syria, Lebanon, Palestine and Trans-Jordan wished to unite in a single state, that would not prevent a more extensive co-operation among the various Arab states.[51] Nuri al-Sa'id publicly made it clear that he supported a Greater Syrian unity only if the people of those countries so desired.[52] Thus, although indirectly, he dissociated himself from 'Abdallah's position which was based on historical and dynastical factors and not on popular will.

Naturally enough, the demand to form a Greater Syria state and to regard its formation as the main manifestation of Arab unity was made by Tawfiq Abu al-Huda, the Trans-Jordan Prime Minister, who argued that Greater Syria had been unduly divided in the past into four states and asked Nahhas to help them to get their independence and to unite. The united 'Syrian Bloc' might then join a union formed by agreement among the other Arab states. Abu al-Huda made it clear that owing to the intransigent position of the Maronites in Lebanon he was just as ready to give up the inclusion of Mount Lebanon, namely, the Ottoman autonomous *sanjaq* of Lebanon, inside Greater Syria, as to ensure a special autonomous regime to the Jews in certain areas of Palestine. Alternatively, he did not rule out the formation of a federation similar to the United States of America or the Swiss Confederation as a possible framework of unity among the four 'Syrian countries'.

An extremely important question was the form of the regime of the proposed Greater Syria. Abu al-Huda made no secret of his preference for a monarchy and added that he knew that many Syrians favoured a monarchical regime. Asked by Nahhas whether Trans-Jordan would agree to a King chosen among the Syrians, if Syria opted for a monarch, Abu al-Huda replied that only descendants of kings could aspire to the throne.[53]

Yusuf Yasin on behalf of Ibn Saud flatly rejected that approach. He supported a republican regime for Syria. The question of uniting Syria and Palestine under a republican government was, according to him, for the people of these two countries to decide, but King Ibn Saud thought that the decision should be postponed until after the Jewish danger had been removed from Palestine. Even then they should only take such steps as they thought fit to achieve what measure of unity they wanted on condition that no other party's rights were infringed and that the resulting form of union was not to anyone's disadvantage. Yusuf Yasin explained that this condition was a safeguard against the establishment of a Syro-Palestinian monarchy with a Hashemite on the throne. On the other hand he declared that Ibn Saud approved of anything tending to draw Syria and the Lebanon into closer co-operation.[54]

Greater Syrian unity was thoroughly discussed between Nahhas and the Syrian delegation headed by Sa'dallah al-Jabiri, the Syrian Prime Minister and Jamil Mardam, the Foreign Minister. Here, for the first time Nahhas revealed his scepticism over the possibility of forming a Greater Syrian unity in any form, either as a unitary state or as a confederation. Sa'dallah al-Jabiri adopted a different approach. He stated that Syria, the Lebanon, Palestine and Trans-Jordan should naturally be united, but the republican regime of Syria had to be maintained and Damascus should become the capital.[55]

Going to any length to preserve Lebanon's independence and sovereignty, the Lebanese delegation, headed by Ri'ad al-Sulh the Lebanese Prime Minister, rejected any form of a Greater Syrian unity and stuck to the republican form of government.[56] For the Lebanese no less threatening was the possibility that the Syrians might revive their demand to incorporate Lebanon within a republican Syria. On that question Nahhas and Nuri decided to leave it until the former had sounded Lebanese opinion.[57] However, Sa'dallah al-Jabiri asserted in his talks with Nahhas that the great majority of the Lebanese, including the Christians and all the Muslims, desired incorporation with Syria. As a second best al-Jabiri argued that if a union between Syria and Lebanon was ruled out, Syria must recover the regions which had in 1920 been detached by the French, namely, the Sunni Muslim coastal towns of Tripoli and Sidon and the mainly Shi'ite Muslim area of eastern and southern Lebanon.

On the other hand, al-Jabiri admitted that Syria had recognised Lebanese independence and supported it on condition that, like Syria, the Lebanon claimed absolute sovereignty (*vis-à-vis* the French of course!), copied Syria in preserving its Arab character and came to an agreement with Syria regarding the administration of 'common interests'[58] (*les intérêts communs* — the various revenue-generating services, including the customs, of the mandatory government). All these conditions had already been met and virtually been included in the 1943 Lebanese National Charter, the foundation-stone of independent Lebanon. The question of the common interests had also been settled with the establishment of a common council for their administration.

It goes without saying that Ri'ad al-Sulh in his talks with Nahhas repeatedly insisted on Lebanon's right to independence and sovereignty within its present boundaries although he emphasised Lebanon's Arab character and its readiness to co-operate fully with its Arab neighbours. The Lebanese may have learned that the Syrians had adopted the contradictory attitude of at one and same time recognising Lebanon's independence and demanding its incorporation, *in toto* or at least its new Muslim areas, with Syria. Therefore during the talks Ri'ad al-Sulh reminded Lord Killearn, the British Ambassador to Cairo, that Britain and he personally had guaranteed the independence of Lebanon.[59]

The Palestine question was necessarily raised from the beginning of the consultations. First of all, there was the question of who could speak on behalf of the Palestinian Arabs in the next stages of the inter-Arab negotiations. Secondly, it was necessary to ascertain their views with regard to the future of their country. Nuri and Nahhas went no further than to authorise Nahhas to find answers to those two questions without laying down any specific procedure on how to do it. It is worth noting that Nuri repeated one of the tenets of his Fertile Crescent scheme, that the Palestine Arabs would accept the 1939 White Paper provided they were sure of their entry into 'Greater Syria' and that the Jews would only have a quasi-autonomous government in zones where they formed a majority, excluding Jerusalem. He emphasised that the Jews had to remain a minority in Palestine, which should retain its Arab character.[60]

All other participants in the consultations usually shared the same approach, namely, the need to safeguard for Palestine its independence some time in the future and its Arab majority. The imprecise and even evasive treatment of that subject is striking. To some extent Ri'ad al-Sulh on behalf of the Lebanon was more emphatic than other Arab interlocutors in his demand that the Arab states adopt measures to stop Jewish immigration to Palestine and land purchases there and to form a Palestinian national government.[61] In public the other delegations too usually took a much tougher line and stressed that the Palestine question was 'the corner-stone of the Arab problems, its solution as the basis for the preservation of Arab interests is the chief goal of all'.[62]

The only practical step which was discussed in the consultations was the idea of convening a Preparatory Conference to discuss in detail the form of future Arab unity. The possibility of convening such a conference was first mentioned at the negotiations between the Egyptian Government and Ibn Saud which had preceded the latter's readiness to join the inter-Arab consultations initiated by the former. But Ibn Saud favoured Mecca as the venue of the future conference, while Nahhas insisted on Cairo, claiming that Iraq and the Christian Arabs would oppose Ibn Saud's suggestion.[63] Ibn Saud also wanted to limit its deliberations to cultural and economic subjects only, whereas Nahhas insisted that political questions too should be included in the agenda.[64] But with the support of the Iraqis and the Syrians Cairo was fixed as the proper venue, although initially the Syrians sounded the possibility that the preparatory work would be done by a commission sitting periodically and in turn in each of the Arab countries.[65]

The most important conclusion that may be drawn from these consultations is rather contradictory. On the one hand, only Syria expressed its wish to see a real federation of the Arab States formed. And the Syrian Parliament went so far as to adopt by acclamation a formal resolution calling upon the Syrian Government to work for the attainment at present of a confederation of Arab states and their unity in the future.[66] But, on the other hand, various signs indicated that the Syrians were eager to be in full harmony with Ibn Saud,[67] to whom Shukri al-Quwatli was personally attached[68] and who most persistently opposed any notion of Arab political unity. Therefore it seems to us that the Syrians went so far in proposing a comprehensive Arab unity only with the knowledge that Nuri al-Sa'id and Mustafa al-Nahhas had already expressed their views against such an eventuality and thus they could embarrass them without jeopardising their relations with Ibn Saud.

More sincere, so it looks to us, were Syria's and Lebanon's declarations that they accepted Egypt's leading role within the Arab world.[69] No doubt, both countries regarded Egypt as a bulwark against any Hashemite design with regard to their independent states. These close relations established between Syria and Egypt prompted Taha al-Hashimi to note in his Diaries that 'Iraq lost her position to Egypt among the Arab countries'.[70] It should be added that in addition to the only too clear reasons which enhanced the position of Egypt, the procedure of the consultations enhanced it also. Since they took the form of bilateral talks held separately between Egypt and the representatives of all other Arab countries no one (except, that is, the Syrians owing to the success of Ahmad al-Shuqayri in laying his hand on the minutes of the Egyptian-Iraqi talks) knew[71] the content of the consultations with the others except the Egyptians. Thus the Egyptians enjoyed an enormous tactical advantage which they used to their benefit.

From the consultations to the Preparatory Committee

Iraq's leaders Nuri al-Sa'id and 'Abd al-Illah were not content with the emergence of Egypt as the leading Arab power especially as it became known that Nahhas opposed any union between Syria and Iraq, and owing to the Iraqi leaders' belief that Nahhas tended to arrogate the leadership of the Arab world to himself. Nahhas feared that an Iraqi-Syrian union might take the place of Egypt as the predominant local power in the Levant.[72] It seems that the Iraqi leaders decided to launch a counter-attack. At the end of 1943 the Iraqi Government entertained in Baghdad an official Syrian delegation, the composition of which may be of interest in discussing Arab unity. It included Jamil Mardam, the Syrian Foreign Minister, 'Abd al-Rahman al-Kayyali of Aleppo, the Minister of Justice and 'Adnan al-Atasi, a deputy from Hums.[73] All these three Syrian politicians were much closer to Iraq's policies than the Damascus-based ruling National Bloc and Shukri al-Quwatli, the President. And although the statement which was published at the end of the talks did not reveal anything substantial[74] it looks as though Nuri al-Sa'id was encouraged to carry on his counter-moves.

During the second half of January 1944 Nuri al-Sa'id visited Syria, the Lebanon, Palestine and Trans-Jordan. He was fêted at both Beirut and Damascus, and at Damascus allegedly reached an agreement, although a verbal one as he later admitted, with the Syrian President, Prime Minister and Foreign Minister that Iraq and Syria would federate and have a common policy regarding foreign affairs and defence, whatever the other Arab states did. They could gradually join the federation if they so wished.[75] But after careful scrutiny Sir Edward Spears, the British Minister in the Levant States, informed the Foreign Office that no such an agreement had been reached; that owing to the firm personal attachment of the Syrian President ('who is really the power in Damascus') to Ibn Saud such an agreement was totally out of the question; and that it was possible that Nuri derived a misleading impression of the Syrian attitude from Jamil Mardam, the Foreign Minister, whose loyalty to the Syrian President was not above suspicion.[76]

In 'Amman too Nuri al-Sa'id did not score more points. He proposed to 'Abdallah forming a common front with Iraq, Syria and Palestine Arab leaders and presenting a joint memorandum to the British Government asking for the early formation of Greater Syria. In reply to 'Abdallah's question Nuri admitted that since the proposed memorandum only dealt with the union of Syria, Egypt was not directly concerned at the moment, but could join a wider Arab union later.

'Abdallah went on to enquire about his own claim to the Syrian throne. Nuri replied that the position was difficult since the Syrians were emphatically demanding a Republic of Greater Syria. He tried to placate 'Abdallah, who was very angry, by saying that when the reunion of the 'Syrian Territories' was complete a plebiscite would be held to ascertain the desire of the majority as regards the final form of regime. 'Abdallah could not be satisfied, since his notion of his right to sit on the Syrian throne was not derived from a democratic concept of government. He accused Nuri before the British Resident in 'Amman of betraying both himself and Nahhas and hinted that he might in the future co-operate with the latter 'in order to check Nuri's trickery'. He asserted that Trans-Jordan must now 'look to her own interests' and dwarfed any hopes that Nuri might have about close co-operation with 'Abdallah.[77]

Furthermore, 'Abdallah tried to undermine Nuri al-Sa'id's position at home. 'Abdallah met his nephew 'Abd al-Illah, the Iraqi Regent, and told him that they had to form a united Hashemite front and that Nuri had betrayed the Hashemite house in working for Arab unity on behalf of republics. 'Abdallah felt that Nuri, having failed to gain ascendancy over Nahhas in the inter-Arab consultations, was endeavouring to bypass him by attempting himself to take the lead in a more limited scheme, almost identical to his original proposal, embracing Greater Syria and Iraq.[78]

Both Nuri and Nahhas had to cope with internal political repercussions in their own countries, but in that sphere Nahhas had a far rougher reception. The Baghdad press generally reacted favourably to Nuri's consultations with Nahhas in July–August 1943. The practical obstacles in the way of Arab unity were not overlooked and the need for patience and gradual approach was stressed.[79]

However, Nuri did not enjoy universal support and had to take into

THE FORMATION OF THE ARAB LEAGUE

account a certain amount of personal jealousy and opposition. The Regent did not want to let Nuri become the sole acknowledged leader of Iraq. When 'Abd al-Illah realised that the British were regarding with reservation (see below, pp. 290–303) the advances that the movement towards more unity among the Arabs was making he volunteered to the British his view 'that in Iraq there had from the outset been considerable feeling against Nuri Pasha for pressing Arab Union at this stage'. The Regent left the impression on the British that he was 'disposed to pour cold water' upon the idea of convening a general Arab Preparatory Conference. It seems logical to assume that Nuri al-Sa'id's resignation from the premiership in May 1944 resulted from the Regent's cool attitude to him,[80] although his successor Hamdi al-Bajahji declared upon assuming office that 'every Arab man is striving for the interests of his country and for Arab unity just as much as Nuri al-Said himself'.[81]

But the very concept of Arab unity was rejected, according to various people inside Iraqi Government machinery, by the non-Sunni-Muslim-Arab groups of Iraq such as the non-Arab Kurds and the Arab Shi'ites. Da'ud al-Haydari, the Iraqi Minister in London and a Kurd himself, advised the Regent against pursuing a pan-Arab policy and to 'be content with Iraq which was quite a big enough job for him'.[82] The Kurds were apprehensive of Arab federation, fearing that it would decrease their importance and lead to their interests being even more neglected, and the Shi'ites disliked the idea because they foresaw that if put into effect it would reduce them from numerical equality with the Sunnis to a minority position. But among the Sunni politicians of Iraq who constituted the ruling élite of that country, there was considerable enthusiasm for pan-Arab ideals.[83]

As for Egypt the situation was much more complicated and delicate. Nahhas's serious opponents – King Faruq, Makram 'Ubayd, his former Deputy as the *Wafd* leader, his former associates in the *Wafd* leadership who had left it, such as 'Abd al-Rahman 'Azzam, Muhammad 'Ali 'Allubah, etc. – had preceded him in their espousal of pan-Arabism. Nahhas and his *Wafd* party, tarnished by the way they had been brought to power by the British and passing through the storm which the publication of Makram 'Ubayd's 'Black Book' had stirred up, did whatever they could to capitalise on the inter-Arab consultations initiated by Nahhas to their own advantage. The Wafdist newspapers published news and articles showing that the neighbouring Arab countries regarded Nahhas as the leader of Arab unity and he was labelled 'the leader of the East and of pan-Arabism'.[84] The Wafdists emphasised the need for all progress towards Arab unity to be made through official delegates. A case in point was Nahhas's and his supporters' repeated demands that in the future Preparatory Conference only government representatives should take part. Thus the danger of the members of the Opposition, who were better acquainted with pan-Arabism, overshadowing the government in the conduct of the discussions would be prevented.[85]

The King and the Opposition did not stand idle in the face of Nahhas's inter-Arab activities and internal political manoeuvres. The King, in addition to being connected with Makram 'Ubayd's 'Black Book', tried to preempt Nahhas in the pan-Arab field. He encouraged the formation of an Arab Unity Committee composed of veteran pan-Arabists of his entourage, such as 'Abd al-Rahman 'Azzam, Muhammad 'Ali 'Allubah and Sheikh 'Ali al-Maraghi, the Rector of al-Azhar, who desired to be the main Egyptian representatives in handling contacts with the other Arab countries.[86] But when the King realised that the lead had been firmly taken and held by Nahhas he began to express his doubts about the drive for Arab unity. Faruq kept himself aloof from the inter-Arab consultations which he regarded as a 'show of Nahhas' or, at best, a mere competition between Nahhas and Nuri.[87] Faruq did not disguise his attitude from other Arab delegates to the consultations and his *Chef de Cabinet* went so far as to define Nahhas to the Lebanese delegation as 'the Egyptian Emile Eddé'.[88]

The alternative endeavour of Faruq's supporters in 1943–4 to revive the Egyptian King's claim to the Islamic Caliphate was not widely supported in Egypt and even less so outside it.[89] But Faruq's attempts were not confined only to that long term goal. He used all means at his disposal to undermine Nahhas's authority and popularity. Both were engaged in campaigns throughout Egypt's provinces and they competed with one another through various means of patronage. Each tried to appoint his own people to important positions in the Army, in the legal system and al-Azhar. But being backed by the British who in May 1944 directly intervened in his favour, Nahhas withstood the King, who could not easily get rid of him.[90] In the summer of 1944 the struggle between the King and Nahhas reached its climax when the Egyptian Government dismissed, against the King's explicit wish, Ghazali Bey, the Director of Public Security and one of the King's people. The King finally got his way and on 7 October dismissed Nahhas.[91]

The Opposition leaders joined the campaign against Nahhas with regard to his conduct of the inter-Arab consultations. As we have already seen they demanded a broadening of the framework so that non-official pan-Arabist leaders could participate and hinted that Nahhas was not qualified to lead in that field.[92] Others adopted a completely different position of hostility towards the inter-Arab consultations. They argued that the British, through their agent Nahhas, were behind his initiative, which was intended to disguise Britain's real interest in arranging, during the war, economic co-operation among the Middle Eastern countries. Furthermore, they accused Nahhas of referring to pan-Arab matters only as a trick in his quarrel with his political rival Makram 'Ubayd who was a Copt. Nahhas wanted to give the impression, so these opponents argued, that only when Makram 'Ubayd left the *Wafd* would the party be free to deal with Arab and Muslim matters without the hindrance which had hitherto prevented it from doing so.[93] These circles concluded that the question of Arab unity should be postponed until all the Arab countries had achieved their independence and the question of Palestine had been solved. Thus the British would not be able to attain their goal.[94]

This internal struggle seriously tainted the Egyptian intervention in the Lebanese crisis of November 1943. It is true that since Egypt was conducting the inter-Arab consultations and working to consolidate its position as the leader of the Arab bloc of states, it could not fail to intervene in the crisis and exert pressure on Britain to stand up against the harsh French measures. But the struggle between the King and the Prime Minister influenced the form and tone of Egyptian behaviour. The reaction of the Egyptian press following the arrest on 11 November of Bisharah al-Khuri, the Lebanese President, was very fierce and General Catroux, the chief Free French authority in the Middle East, attributed the sharpness of the reaction to Nahhas himself.[95]

In his declarations of 6 December 1943 Nahhas thanked Britain and the USA for their intervention in favour of Lebanese rights and the pressure they had exerted on Free French authorities to release the Lebanese President and restore the Parliament. He emphasised that the Arab bloc as a whole had played an important role in solving the crisis, and left the clear impression that Egypt and he himself were the leading factors of that bloc.[96]

Faruq did not allow the matter to be dealt with or utilised by Nahhas alone. He too immediately took action. He sent a telegram to the Lebanese President declaring that Egypt was behind Lebanon in its struggle. He also invited the British and American Ambassadors in Cairo to his palace and urged them to intervene. And after the resolution of the conflict in Lebanon's favour Faruq sent a Royal Delegation of Honour to Beirut carrying a special message of congratulation to the Lebanese President.[97] This competition was conspicuous from the very beginning of the Lebanese crisis. According to Prince Muhammad 'Ali, Nahhas's 'words and actions in regard to the Lebanese crisis had been excessive'.[98]

This internal problem did not distract Nahhas from his main goal which was to prepare the ground for the convention of the Preparatory Conference to lay the foundations of the very limited unity framework discussed and agreed upon during the inter-Arab consultations. A successful accomplishment of that goal could substantiate Egypt's already expressed pretension to speak on behalf of the whole Arab world and to approach the British Government about matters concerning other Arab countries.[99]

The first serious obstacle that Nahhas had to clear was again the question of how to bring about the release of Jamal al-Husayni and Amin al-Tamimi from their internment in Rhodesia and their participation in the Preparatory Conference. On the one hand the British refused to budge on that matter, and, on the other, the Palace and the anti-Wafdist Opposition were exerting pressure on the Egyptian Prime Minister not to yield. Nahhas dealt with the problem by utilising it to enhance his position as the standard bearer of Palestine Arab rights. He told the British that everything boiled down to the question of Palestinian representation in the process, failing which the conference would be indefinitely postponed and the responsibility for that would be laid on the British. If the British retreated Nahhas might gain an enormous personal achievement; and if they did not, he would be regarded as a tough fighter for Arab rights. Thus the memory of February 1942 might fade.[100]

A second problem was the demand from Iraq and Syria to convene the conference as early as possible. In dealing with that pressure Nahhas could more than rely on Ibn Saud who objected to any premature calling of a general conference. The latter argued that such a plenary conference had no chance of success and might only embarrass the Allies if Arab positions with regard to Syria and Palestine were voiced.[101]

Ibn Saud was ready to be a party to the proposed conference provided that three conditions were observed:

1. that his special position in the Arab world was recognised and priority given to no other ruler or person:
2. that the conference took no decision which might embarrass Britain or her Allies in the prosecution of the war; and
3. that there should be no question of Syria, Lebanon or Palestine becoming attached to either Egypt or Iraq and that their status as independent state should be preserved.[102]

In other words Ibn Saud was ready to take part only if he had been assured in advance that the Hashemite position would not be advanced, that no hedge would be inserted between him and the Allies and that the *status quo* in the Arab world would be preserved. For Ibn Saud Arab unity meant no more than some degree of solidarity and co-operation among independent Arab States.

As a result of his attitude both the Egyptian and the Lebanese Prime Ministers proposed to form a Preparatory Committee which would lay down the principles of Arab unity and only when their work had been completed would a general conference be called. Ibn Saud agreed but still demanded that the proposed committee avoid discussing any controversial political issues, as, for instance, Palestine and Syria. Finally he suggested that Nuri should write to Nahhas and put forward the proposal for a committee, leaving it to Nahhas to issue invitations to the countries

THE FORMATION OF THE ARAB LEAGUE

concerned. A British diplomatic representative in Jedda, Mr Jordan, thought that Ibn Saud hoped by the above suggestions to postpone indefinitely the preliminary meeting as he felt sure that the relations between Nuri and Nahhas were such as to prevent Nahhas accepting any proposals from Nuri.[103] But, as we shall see later on, Nahhas did not exactly wait for that proposal to come from Nuri.

In the meantime the Christian Lebanese, and especially the Maronite community, were being encouraged by the Saudi policy in their stand for complete independence from their Arab neighbours. In a direct talk with Ibn Saud an official Lebanese delegation headed by Ri'ad al-Sulh learned that both countries objected to virtually any change in the *status quo* in the Arab world. When in the wake of that meeting Ibn Saud recognised Lebanese independence within its present boundaries it was regarded as a 'very important development in Lebanon's political life'.[104] This Saudi position fortified the Lebanese Christians, including the President Bisharah al-Khuri, who feared a federation but could not afford to say so.[105] It was immediately reflected in their public statements. On 19 April 1944 Habib Abu Shahla, the Lebanese Minister of Justice and the Acting Prime Minister, declared that Lebanon objected to any plan of Arab unity which involved any modification of Lebanese independence and sovereignty which had lately been achieved. He agreed only to economic and cultural co-operation.[106] A little later Ri'ad al-Sulh went even further when he declared that 'the most important goal of the Arab unity Conference was to safeguard the complete independence of each Arab country'.[107]

The only serious counter-move was an attempt by the Syrian Foreign Minister Jamil Mardam to persuade Ibn Saud to change his mind. Jamil Mardam went to Saudi Arabia at the request of Nuri al-Sa'id who had also asked Ri'ad al-Sulh to do the same.[108] It seems that Ibn Saud's position was regarded by Nuri as a golden opportunity to enhance his own status as a champion of Arab unity. Nuri al-Sa'id realised that although the Syrian President was a close ally of Ibn Saud, Shukri al-Quwatli would not be able to refuse a demand to send his Foreign Minister to Jedda. And if the Syrian President opposed it, he would be under strong fire from his Foreign Minister who was known at one and the same time for his personal ambitions and for his good relations with Nuri al-Sa'id.

During his visit to Saudi Arabia Jamil Mardam tried to persuade Ibn Saud to use his influence to bring about a conference on Arab unity at an early date. He stated that now was the time to press Arab demands on the Allies, who were preoccupied with the prosecution of the war and the Arabs would therefore be able to get more out of them than later. But Ibn Saud rejected this argument altogether. He repeated his position that the Arabs should wait until the war was over, that the Syrians should put their 'own house in order first and desist from clamour for Arab unity'. Syria owed a lot to Britain and should not embarrass the country while it was at war. The fact that Jamil Mardam went on to ask Ibn Saud about his attitude towards Nuri al-Sa'id could not fail to arouse the former's suspicions of Jamil Mardam's motives and erased any hope of success, if such hopes there had been.[109]

The conflicting attitudes of the various Arab countries and the British attempt to slow the pace of calling the Arab Unity Preparatory Committee (see below, pp. 296–9) necessarily lessened Nahhas's resolution to act swiftly. Another rather old problem was whether the French-controlled North African countries and Libya should be invited to take part in the Preparatory Committee. In April 1944 Nahhas addressed a note to General de Gaulle suggesting such participation, asking for the release of imprisoned leaders and expressing the hope that France would recognise the independence of Algeria, Morocco and Tunisia. The French regarded this demand with apprehension and declined to accept it. They even tried to persuade the British to exert pressure on the Egyptian Government not to publish Nahhas's Note and the French rejection of it.[111] This Egyptian demand could only exacerbate the deeply suspicious French attitude towards the Arab unity movement, which was reflected in official French demands to the British Government that the North African countries be excluded from the intended pan-Arab Conference.[112]

The British themselves rejected a similar demand to be represented in the Preparatory Committee by Idris al-Sannusi, the exiled ruler of Libya, since they did not want to imply in advance of the post-war peace settlement what their position regarding the future status of the former Italian colonies might be.[113] These negative positions of Britain and Free France only added to Nahhas's difficulties because the Opposition at home and Nuri al-Sa'id[114] exerted pressure on him to stand fast and not budge from those demands.

This pressure which came from various sources bore fruit. In mid-June Nahhas made up his mind to proceed with the steps necessary for the calling of the Preparatory Committee. He prepared a draft letter that he intended to address to the governments of Iraq, Trans-Jordan, Saudi Arabia, Syria, Lebanon and Yemen. In the draft he stated that the consultations with Palestinian representatives had to be completed before any further step and that there were no alternative Palestinian personalities to speak on behalf of the Palestine Arabs other than Jamal al-Husayni and Amin al-Tamimi. However, since he had failed to secure their release, Nahhas suggested that the Preparatory Committee meet in Cairo at the end of July or the beginning of August. And although the British objected to the despatch of the letter Nahhas decided to disregard this objection and on 22 June he sent the letter to the Arab governments.[115]

The change in the Iraqi Government did not change Iraq's position.

THE FORMATION OF THE ARAB LEAGUE

Hamdi al-Bajahji, the new Prime Minister, reacted favourably to Nahhas's letter. He thought that Nahhas's proposal to call a Preparatory Committee and shortly afterwards a general Arab conference was 'the natural culmination of the negotiations which had been taking place over the last two years and that it was important that the Arab states should lose no time in coming to an agreement' over foreign policy, security and economic and cultural relations. It seems that in order to emphasise the continuity of policy the Iraqi Government appointed Nuri al-Sa'id as one of their delegates to the Preparatory Committee.[116] Naturally enough, the Syrians also accepted Nahhas's invitation and even 'Abdallah adopted a positive attitude.[117] But Ibn Saud reacted differently.

The Saudi ruler continued to doubt the sincerity of Nahhas and Nuri and his representatives left a clear impression that their master would not be a party to the future steps proposed by Nahhas.[118] However, he tried to avoid giving Nahhas a final answer until he had received a definite reply from the British Government as to whether he should accept or refuse. But the British did not want to be regarded as responsible for wrecking the process and they refused to advise Ibn Saud to reject Nahhas's invitation.[119]

Therefore Ibn Saud was facing a real dilemma. He suspected everyone else; he did not want to be forced to take a position with regard to Syria and Palestine; and he feared the formation of an Egyptian-Iraqi bloc in opposition to himself with Syria holding the balance.[120] On the other hand, he did not want to remain the only Arab independent ruler who decided to stay outside the new framework of Arab unity. A good reason for refusal which the British could supply him remained wanting. This lack of clear guidance from the British annoyed him since he believed that in his negative attitude to Nahhas's moves, he was acting in British interests. Meanwhile since the definite reply of Ibn Saud to the Egyptian invitation had not yet come, Nahhas postponed the date of the Preparatory Committee's meeting to 25 September,[121] although he was under persistent pressure from the Iraqis and the Syrians for an early convocation.[122]

But Ibn Saud did not easily budge from his refusal to send a delegate to the Preparatory Committee. On 20 July he even sent a negative reply to Nahhas.[123] However, two weeks later the first indication came that Ibn Saud might decide to participate. Various explanations were put forward by the British Foreign Office officials for the possibility that Ibn Saud might after all change his mind. Several days earlier the Arab public had become excited following the strong pro-Zionist resolution adopted by the ruling Democratic Party in the USA. It may have convinced Ibn Saud of the necessity to present an Arab common front against the pro-Zionist forces. Another, more plausible explanation was Ibn Saud's fear of being left out in the cold, a threat which became serious indeed when Ibn Saud realised that no Arab country, including Syria whose President was so close to him, followed his lead.[124] Ibn Saud tried to impose conditions to his possible consent such as that the discussions of the Preparatory Committee be kept secret and that the decision to hold the general Arab Conference should be taken only by unanimous vote of the delegates,[125] but to no avail. All other parties to the process were inclined to proceed even if Ibn Saud remained outside and they did not accept the Saudi conditions.

Ibn Saud's final positive decision was taken only at the last minute, when all other delegates had already come to Egypt. It seems that by then he realised how strong was the British interest in his participation. He may also have been flattered by another approach from Nahhas. And when he did decide, his decision was unconditional.[126] Nahhas was so interested in Saudi participation that he exerted pressure on the Iraqi Government not to send Nuri al-Sa'id as their delegate to the Preparatory Committee. And although the Iraqi Government rejected that demand[127] it may have left a good impression on Ibn Saud.

It seems to us that his way of taking the decision and making his consent known only when all other delegates had already come to Egypt was needed by Ibn Saud as a means of enhancing his prestige and position in the Arab world following the prominence which Nahhas had gained in the previous months. He may also have been influenced by Shukri al-Quwatli, the Syrian President who had joined in the attempt to persuade Ibn Saud.[128]

According to S. R. Jordan, the British *chargé d'affaires* in Jedda, the Arab leaders were so interested in the convocation of the Preparatory Committee even against the explicit wish of Ibn Saud only as a countervailing factor to the French desire to retain their position and influence in Syria and Lebanon.[129] Anyway, when the Saudis came to Cairo, the Yemenis, who always followed the Saudi lead, followed suit and sent a delegate.[130]

The joint position of Syria and Iraq in favour of an early convocation of the Preparatory Committee — Syria wishing to buttress its position in the face of French pressure and Iraq seeking to capitalise on Ibn Saud's reluctance to participate — helped to bring about, for a while at least, the emergence of a Syrian-Lebanese-Iraqi bloc. Thus they could present a counter-force to Nahhas's leading role which they resented.[131]

This development together with the appointment of Nuri as the Iraqi delegate could only irritate the Egyptian Government. Newspapers under Nahhas's influence reacted by publishing unfriendly comment and rude cartoons, alleging that Iraq was endeavouring to exploit Syria, Lebanon and Trans-Jordan so as to bring them under the Iraqi yoke and thereby secure for Iraq direct access to the Mediterranean.[132]

Against this background 'Abdallah, in a last-minute attempt to stop

Nahhas from becoming the leader of the Arab bloc, suggested to the Iraqi leaders — 'Abd al-Illah the Regent, Hamdi al-Bajahji, the Prime Minister, Arshad al-'Umari, the Foreign Minister, and Nuri al-Sa'id — the formation of a Hashemite bloc for the purpose of adopting a common policy at the imminent conference, to work for the liberation of Hijaz, the Hashemite ancestral patrimony, from Saudi occupation and for the creation of a Hashemite monarchy covering Greater Syria. The Iraqi Ministers objected to those proposals, pointing out that it was out of the question in the present circumstances to start conflicts between various Arab territories. They also pointed out that the formation of Greater Syria was beyond the power of the Arabs themselves without the approval of the USA, Britain and France. The Iraqis declined to agree to 'Abdallah's proposal to issue a joint communiqué announcing that a meeting had taken place at 'Amman. They excused their refusal by saying that Nahhas was already suspicious regarding the activities of Iraq.[133] One may add that the Iraqis were equally anxious to avoid any move that might arouse the suspicions of the Syrians, whose goodwill the Iraqis had lately succeeded in gaining.

With the objection of Ibn Saud overcome and the counter-measures of the two Hashemite countries not having gone far enough to disrupt the process, the Preparatory Committee was able to be convened on 25 September 1944, in Alexandria. As in the 1943 inter-Arab consultations the question of who would represent the Palestine Arabs was not easy to solve, owing to the lack of acknowledged and constituted leadership and the imprisonment of Jamal al-Husayni. After long deliberations the leaders of the Palestine Arab parties chose Musa al-'Alami as their delegate in the Preparatory Committee.[134] The Egyptians insisted on the British not opposing his participation owing to Musa al-'Alami's known moderation. If he were not allowed to take any part at all in the work of the committee, they argued, there was a danger that the position of the more extreme elements among the Palestine Arabs would be considerably strengthened.

At the beginning of the work of the Committee Musa al-'Alami was recognised as an observer only, although in public he was regarded as a 'delegate', like all other participants. Musa al-'Alami was not satisfied with this duplicity. He demanded to be recognised as a full member. He based his demand on the precedent of the 1939 St James's Conference when Palestine delegates had sat on an equal footing with the representatives of the Arab States. He threatened to return to Palestine rather than abandon that precedent. That threat alarmed the delegates[135] and through consultations with the British authorities in Egypt the Egyptian Government agreed to recognise him as a 'member representing the Arabs of Palestine'. In no way could he be considered as representing or committing Palestine as a whole or as a government. He would not take part in any decision or sign any resolution.[136] That arrangement was accepted by all parties concerned and Musa al-'Alami joined the Preparatory Committee in that capacity in its third session.[137] Husayn al-Kibsi, the representative of Imam Yahya of the Yemen, preferred to participate as an observer only.[138]

With all preliminary questions settled, the committee began their work from 25 September to 6 October. The subjects tackled and the views expressed very much resembled those of the previous consultations.[139] The most important subject discussed was how to adopt a scheme of inter-Arab co-operation rather than of political union. Again, as in the past, Syria was the only Arab country favouring the strongest form of co-operation, that is, a central government, and if that presented difficulties the Syrian delegation proposed some other form of federation or agreement or alliance. Failing that eventuality the Syrian Prime Minister Sa'dallah al-Jabiri suggested that at least in the sphere of foreign relations the Arab countries should adopt one united policy and that 'no member of the Arab States should depart from that policy'. And Jamil Mardam, his Foreign Minister, added: 'Military and Defence organisation should also be unified'.

All other countries, except Egypt, objected to these views and when the Egyptian delegates were called upon to reveal their views they had to admit that they too opposed the formation of a central government. On the other hand a near unanimity of views on co-operation in cultural and economic matters and communications emerged. The only reserved reaction came from Sheikh Yusuf Yasin, who refused to commit Ibn Saud before prior consultations with him, especially with regard to cultural problems. This was virtually a polite way of voicing Saudi Arabia's opposition to co-operation in cultural matters, since Saudi education was based on religion and not on a lay foundation. Yusuf Yasin was very reserved over economic co-operation too, since the economic conditions of his country were quite different from those of Egypt and the northern Arab states, but since he did not want his dissenting view to be recorded in the protocol he adopted his evasive attitude.[140]

Iraq and Trans-Jordan favoured forming a union, meaning an organisation with executive power and a council in which the members would be represented. An executive committee would assist the union in all phases of political, economic, cultural and social co-operation. Syria supported any idea which might promote Arab co-operation. But the representatives of Saudi Arabia, Yemen and Lebanon, with the backing of Egypt, rejected any suggestion that could diminish their countries' independence and sovereignty. Therefore it was resolved to form a union whose resolutions would be binding only on those who accepted them. Nuri al-Sa'id put forward a compromise formula that the non-obligatory nature of the council's resolutions would be

in force except for three matters where the decisions would be binding. These were:
1. Prohibition of the use of force to settle disputes between one Arab state and another.
2. Avoidance of a foreign policy detrimental to the policy of the Arab States as a whole.
3. Due regard to international engagements entered into by the majority of the Arab States and based on the general interest.

But even these suggestions, except for the second, failed to gain universal endorsement. There is no doubt that the insistence of Ri'ad al-Sulh, the Lebanese Prime Minister, on the complete independence of his country helped all other delegates who for one reason or another refused to go beyond the formation of a loose framework of cultural and economic co-operation.[141]

The question of Lebanon's independence had important bearings on the discussions since its chief delegate made it clear that his country would not agree to any diminution of its sovereign rights. The Lebanese Foreign Minister made that position crystal-clear in his declaration during the inaugural session of the Preparatory Committee, when the only concession he made was to repeat those elements in the Lebanese National Charter which required Lebanon 'not to be a focus for imperialism, nor a corridor for colonisation of its brothers, the other Arab countries'.[142]

During the discussions Ri'ad al-Sulh went further and emphasised that the desired co-operation among the Arab countries would only be possible so long as it was compatible with the independence and sovereignty of each one of them. The greatest service that Lebanon had rendered to the Arab cause was refusing, like Syria, to sign a treaty with France. Facing this staunch position the other representatives had to admit that the formation of any tight machinery for inter-Arab co-operation in the fields of foreign policy or security would leave Lebanon outside the proposed framework of Arab unity, and in such an eventuality Lebanon's Christians, especially the Maronites, might revert to their past attitude of reliance on France. For this reason they accepted the Lebanese position, and for those who had anyway opposed any serious advance towards real unity the Lebanese position was a very comfortable pretext.

In order to eradicate any suspicion that various elements among Lebanese Christian communities, notably the Maronites, still maintained towards Lebanon's participation in the Arab unity talks, the Preparatory Committee, at the Syrian delegate's suggestion[143] adopted a special resolution recognising Lebanon's independence within its present frontiers after it had adopted 'the policy of independence', namely the policy outlined in the Lebanese National Charter. But since that recognition was conditional upon Lebanon's following 'a similar policy in its foreign relations to that of the other [Arab] States', and since a resolution had been passed that the Arab countries should be forbidden to pursue a foreign policy which might prove detrimental to the Arab States as a whole sooner or later, it became clear that that recognition was not enough.[144]

The problem of the French in Syria and the Lebanon was not formally discussed during the discussions, though outside it the Syrian delegates expressed their complete opposition to any treaty with France. It may have been that after the French failure in the previous November to force their will on the Lebanese Parliament there was no need for any further demonstration of Syria's and the Lebanon's independence. Perhaps more important was the Syrian and Lebanese willingness to do nothing that could embarrass Britain who had so much helped them to gain their independence. And if we remember that the British wish that the Syrian question should not be raised in the discussions was strongly endorsed by Ibn Saud we can understand that silence.[145]

Even the Greater Syria project of 'Abdallah was much less prominent in the work of the Preparatory Committee in comparison with the previous inter-Arab consultations. It seems that 'Abdallah well understood that with no British backing and against the combined opposition of the whole Arab world he had no chance to further his cherished idea. The Syrians were encouraged by their triumph and even before the opening of the Preparatory Committee discussions they made their position clear to the Jordanians.

In September 1944 the new Trans-Jordan Consul at Damascus paid his first official visit to the Syrian Prime Minister, who took the opportunity to express his country's attitude towards 'Abdallah's idea without mincing his words. Sa'dallah al-Jabiri told him that the Syrian Government favoured the formation of Greater Syria but on a republican and not a monarchical basis. Syria regarded Trans-Jordan as integral part of itself and would welcome reunion in the form of a republic. If necessary the wishes of inhabitants of *both* territories [the ratio between the inhabitants of the two being about 9 to 1 in Syria's favour!] with regard to a republic could be tested by a plebiscite if Trans-Jordan and Syria were reunited. Furthermore, in direct refutation of 'Abdallah's basic beliefs, the Syrian Prime Minister went on: 'Some people seemed to think they had a monopoly on Arab nationalism and could claim credit for the Arab revolt against [the] Turks. Syrian people had played a major part in the Arab revolt.'[146] (This was obviously directed at Amir Abdullah.)

Therefore it is not surprising that unlike the inter-Arab consultations Tawfiq Abu al-Huda, the Trans-Jordan Prime Minister, did not bring the subject up in the Preparatory Committee. Nuri al-Sa'id was the first to raise it. He admitted that Lebanon and Palestine could not unite inside Greater Syria, but if the people of Syria proper and Trans-Jordan wanted unity that was their affair. It is very doubtful that Nuri al-Sa'id was suddenly converted to support 'Abdallah's scheme. We incline much more to think that Nuri wanted to give the Syrians the opportunity to repeat their hostility to 'Abdallah's ideas. Thus Nuri may have hoped to further consolidate Iraq's recently-established good relations with the Syrian leaders.

And indeed the Syrian Foreign Minister used the opportunity to repeat his country's basic belief that Lebanon, Trans-Jordan and Palestine constituted parts of Syria which had been cut off. However, he admitted that in the present political circumstances this act could not be rectified. Therefore any discussion of Greater Syria unity was premature and the only thing that should be done was to help Trans-Jordan to get its independence. Tawfiq Abu al-Huda reacted to that insinuation by pointing out that Trans-Jordan was at least partially independent and could develop its relations with Syria, but the Syrian delegates refused to contemplate any special relationship with Trans-Jordan until after Trans-Jordan had been fully liberated from the British mandatory regime. But when pressed Jamil Mardam had to repeat his country's adherence to its republican regime and its aim to include in Syria those parts which had been cut off.

This resolute Syrian position could have put an end to the discussion on this matter. But it seems that 'Abdallah, who must have had been informed about it, decided to retain for himself some degree of liberty for his future endeavours. Towards the end of the Preparatory Committee's work, he sent a telegram which Nahhas read to the delegates. He expressed his blessing to the committee and his belief that the Arab nation was interested in unity and that 'that aim would gradually ensue'. The delegates understood it as a demand to reopen the discussion of the forms of Arab unity and the Syrian and Lebanese delegates jumped to their feet to reiterate their views. But the Egyptians intervened and succeeded in putting an end to the discussion in accordance with the previous resolutions.

Towards the beginning of the Preparatory Committee's work various public statements were made in which it was emphasised that the Palestine problem would figure prominently on the agenda and strong protests were made against 'foreign aggression' in Palestine.[147] But when the talks began it became clear that the participants tried to keep away from that question as much as possible, apparently out of deference to British requests. But everything changed with the appearance of Musa al-'Alami and his admittance to the talks at the third session, although a more extreme representative could have exacerbated the situation even more. On 4 October Musa al-'Alami delivered a long and emotional speech. And although he made it in a quiet tone he moved all the delegates deeply and brought the Syrian Prime Minister to tears.

He gave a historical analysis of the Palestine problem from an Arab perspective and complained that even the 1939 White Paper had not been fully implemented. He tried to put the blame for the original rejection of that White Paper on the whole Arab world and pointed out that the Palestinians agreed to accept it with some modification during Jamal al-Husayni's talks in Baghdad with Colonel Newcombe in July 1940. He called upon the Arabs to stand by their Palestinian brethren and to supply them with money to safeguard their lands and send delegates to Western capitals to propagate the Palestine Arab case. It should be added that Musa al-'Alami did not simply reiterate the traditional Palestine Arabs' demand for clear-cut independence as an Arab country. He used vaguer language, saying that various solutions had been suggested in the United Nations for the partition of Palestine into two parts or into a number of cantons, or for placing the Arabs and Jews on a basis of equality in numbers for the moment, or leaving the Arabs with a small nominal majority of a few thousand, thus enabling a large-scale Jewish immigration. 'The last solution appears to be favoured by them [the Arabs] at present', claimed al-'Alami.[148] Nuri al-Sa'id was more forthcoming and in a talk with A.S. Kirkbride, the British Resident in 'Amman, he admitted that he accepted the partition of Palestine 'provided the partition was effected on an equitable basis'. Furthermore he revealed that partition had been discussed by the Preparatory Committee in an informal manner but that no positive decision had been reached, and it had been felt that if the British Government embarked upon partition, the Arab states should judge the merits of the policy by the basis adopted for the partition.[149]

The formal resolution adopted by the Preparatory Committee did not mention such an eventuality, of course. Instead it adopted a vague formula calling for safeguarding the rights of the Arabs, demanding that Britain honour its engagements involving the cessation of Jewish immigration and land purchases and the progress of Palestine towards independence (namely the foundation of the 1939 White Paper), rejecting the Zionist argument that the suffering of European Jewry justified the Zionist claim to Palestine, and referring the question of fund raising for rescuing Arab lands in Palestine for further examination. These decisions were unanimously approved, but Yusuf Yasin, the Saudi delegate, opposed their publication. Another decision which was unanimously approved was to accept Musa al-'Alami's suggestion to establish Arab propaganda bureaux in London and Washington.

The various resolutions passed by the Preparatory Committee were collected together in one document known as the Alexandria Protocol, referring to the venue of the Committee's sessions. It was prepared by a sub-committee and on 7 October was approved by the committee itself. It called for the formation of the League of Arab States, the aim of which was to consolidate inter-Arab ties and to direct the Arab countries towards the welfare of their peoples and the realisation of their aspirations. The League was expected to co-ordinate political plans and to protect the independence and sovereignty of the member states by suitable means against any aggression. It was forbidden for any member state to adopt a foreign policy which might be prejudicial to the policy of the League as a whole or to an individual member. Membership was confined to independent Arab states who wished to join. The decisions would bind only those members who had supported them when they were passed by the council of the League. The Protocol expressed the wish to promote co-operation in all non-political fields and a sub-committee of experts was established for that purpose. A political sub-committee was also formed to prepare the draft of the statutes of the League. On Lebanon and Palestine the Protocol embodied the resolutions which had earlier been discussed: (a) 'respect for the independence and sovereignty of the Lebanon within her present frontiers ... after the Government of the Lebanon had declared their adoption of a policy of independence in a ministerial statement which received the unanimous approval of the Lebanese Parliament on the 7th October 1943'; and (b) support for the rights of the Palestine Arabs, demand to see the principles of the 1939 White Paper carried out, and the formation of an 'Arab national fund' for the preservation of Arab lands.[150]

The conditional nature of the recognition accorded to Lebanese independence did not pass unnoticed by *al-'Amal* newspaper, the mouthpiece of *al-Kata'ib* (*les Phalanges*) organisation, the staunch defender of Lebanese independence.[151]

Although the Protocol did not go far towards Arab unity and that term was not even mentioned in it, the Saudi delegate objected to its publication until his and the Yemenite rulers had been informed of its content. The Saudis held the view that keeping secret the resolution of the Preparatory Committee was a clear commitment, and a condition of their agreement to participate in its work.[152] Yusuf Yasin feared that a Saudi refusal to endorse the Protocol after publication would leave a clear impression of disagreement. He stressed that Ibn Saud agreed to send a delegate only to a committee of a preparatory nature whose resolutions would be kept secret and would be submitted to the General Arab Congress.

Sheikh Yusuf Yasin could not do anything else, since his King had instructed him not to sign any protocol and to refuse any kind of co-operation even in economic and cultural spheres. Since the formation of an Arab League was regarded by Ibn Saud as premature he had instructed his delegate not to bind him 'even by one word' and to refer everything back to him.[153] The Yemenite delegate, who had become a full delegate instead of an observer only at the end of the Preparatory Committee's work, followed the Saudi lead and adopted the same position.

However, Nahhas, who wanted to crown himself with success, and the Syrians, decided to publish the Protocol and to present the Arab world with a *fait accompli*, although without the signatures of the Saudi and Yemenite delegates.[154] A British observer remarked that that development indicated the low prestige of Ibn Saud owing to his poor financial situation and his reliance on foreign aid and the general realisation that he had virtually nothing to contribute in the field of inter-Arab co-operation.[155]

The new Egyptian Government (see below) and King Faruq regarded Saudi Arabia's joining the Arab League with much more interest than Nahhas. They appointed the veteran pan-Arabist 'Abd al-Rahman 'Azzam as Minister Plenipotentiary in the Egyptian Foreign Ministry to deal with Arab unity. He was also appointed *Amir al-Hajj* (Commander of the Pilgrimage) and thus he was given a good pretext to go to Saudi Arabia. Ibn Saud immediately realised that this appointment was intended to produce means to persuade him to join.[156] In the meantime Ibn Saud indicated that he was ready to join a system of inter-Arab alliances which would guarantee political co-operation among the Arab countries while leaving out the suggestions for cultural and economic collaboration.

The combined pressure of Egypt and Britain succeeded in persuading Ibn Saud to sign the Protocol, although he still argued that he could not contemplate committing himself to anything that might affect his religious principles or to any action which was directed against Britain. In the end, on 7 January 1944, he authorised Yusuf Yasin to sign the Protocol and the Yemen followed suit.[157]

The formation of the Arab League

A day after the Preparatory Committee had successfully concluded their work King Faruq dismissed Mustafa al-Nahhas and appointed in his stead Ahmad Mahir as Prime Minister. For a moment it looked as if the movement towards the formation of the organisation for closer inter-Arab co-operation had been dealt a severe blow.[158] The fact that a week later changes of government occurred in Syria and Trans-Jordan too strengthened the impression that the whole edifice which Nahhas had so assiduously built was falling apart. German propaganda was quick to blame the British for that sequence of events.[159]

Nahhas's dismissal originated from the worsening relations between him and the King who realised that with the imminent victory of the Allies Britain would be less insistent on the retention in power of its trustworthy friend in Egypt. His successor included in his government and entourage some of the most prominent Egyptian pan-Arabists who had been excluded by Nahhas from the inter-Arab consultations and negotiations such as 'Allubah, 'Azzam and Makram 'Ubayd. No wonder that Mahir

THE FORMATION OF THE ARAB LEAGUE

pledged to continue the process which Nahhas had initiated.[160] The fact that Salah al-Din, the Egyptian Foreign Under-Secretary, was kept in office was a special case in point even in Nuri al-Sa'id's view, since the former had played a very useful part in the work of the Preparatory Committee and had shown a real interest in Arab unity.[161]

The sub-committee which had been entrusted by the Preparatory Committee with the preparation of the constitution of the Arab League began their work only in early 1945 after Ibn Saud consented to sign the Protocol. During their work it became clear that the Lebanese and Saudi delegates used whatever means and arguments they could to emasculate the corporate identity of the League, and to attenuate any executive function of it. The fact that the Lebanese Government had a new Prime Minister, 'Abd al-Hamid Karamah, enabled the Maronite Foreign Minister, Henri Fir'awn, to be very intransigent.

The Lebanese were very touchy about their independence and 'were inclined to regard the whole scheme, not as a racial Arab, but a religious Islamic, institution'. This they expressed in so many words to 'Abd al-Rahman 'Azzam.[162] The Lebanese and the Saudis remained within the organisation only when their views were accepted with Egypt's support. Those attitudes were manifest in the discussion of the specific issues.[163]

Nuri al-Sa'id was trying in the discussion, largely through the wording of the articles, to get closer to Iraq's original idea of Arab Federation. The Lebanese were strongly opposed to it and emphasised their demand to retain the complete independence of each member state. For that reason they opposed any formation of machinery of obligatory arbitration among the member States. The Lebanese were also anxious to emphasise that the League could not take action as a corporate body on behalf of individual states, who should retain their independence of action and the right to leave the League. 'We do not want the Arab League to become a State above the [member] States or a federation', declared the Lebanese Foreign Minister. The decision adopted (articles 12 and 13 of the Pact) laid down the procedure to be followed in case of disputes between member states and dealt with the thorny question of arbitration. The decision of the League's Council would be binding as regards disputes about which an appeal was made to the League except in matters relating to the independence of the state and its sovereignty or the security of its territory: these questions could not be subject to arbitration. The Saudi delegate supported the Lebanese position and Egypt, who played the role of an arbiter, in the end supported them. Consequently, the League became devoid of any corporate power.[164]

The Lebanese tried to go even further than the Alexandria Protocol and to prevent any possible agreement constituting a Greater Syrian unity. They proposed to forbid any member state of the League to conclude an agreement or a treaty with another member, a move which might be regarded as unfriendly to any other member state. But here they were not supported by anyone else and that demand was dropped.

The Lebanese opposed the participation of Musa al-'Alami and representatives of the North African countries in the discussions of the sub-committee. Since the British supported that demand it was accepted.[165] But over the future of those territories Lebanese reluctance and Saudi hesitation to include that question in the Pact of the Arab League could not stem the strong positive attitude of all the others. For its own part Britain exerted pressure to avoid that subject or to adopt a very mild formula, but its pressure was not fully effective. Egypt was strongly interested in having the backing of its Arab neighbours against any return of the Italians to Libya as it considered their presence there to be a danger, and at the insistence of 'Azzam Pasha it demanded that support be expressed for the Palestine Arabs.[166] Consequently special annexes were added to the Pact of the Arab League, which in a rather moderate way supported the 'international existence and independence' of Palestine and took 'into account the aspirations of the Arab countries which are not members', namely, were not yet independent. Any reference to the participation of Palestine in the League on an equal footing with other members was dropped in the final draft, largely as a result of British pressure. Instead the council of the League was asked to 'take charge of the selection of a representative from Palestine to take part in its work'.[167]

Between the convocation of the Preparatory Committee and the formation of the Arab League in March 1945 and during the work of the drafting sub-committee rather important political developments were taking place in the Arab countries which served as a background to the work of the sub-committee. The first was the strengthening of the French attitude against relinquishing their position in Syria and the Lebanon without treaties with these countries. After the liberation of France and the formation of a fully-fledged independent French authority in France, the power of that country was much increased and to the same extent the British necessity to take into account French views. The Arabs exerted counter-pressure but at the same time realised how important British support was for them.[168] The strengthening of Jewish pressure over Palestine, and the beginning in 1944 of an anti-British campaign of terror carried out by two extremist organisations, strengthened the Arab realisation that they could assure for themselves a favourable British attitude to that question and at least an early implementation of the 1939 White Paper *in toto*.[169]

Internal developments inside the Arab world also shed their light over the proceedings of the drafting sub-committee. In Lebanon there were voices from among the Maronites that the Protocol had gone too far in the direction of a federation. The fact that Parliament on 15 October 1944 approved by an overwhelming majority against only three votes[170] the positions taken by Ri'ad al-Sulh did not quieten those circles. On the contrary, opposition grew in strength and was one of the factors which contributed to the fall of Ri'ad al-Sulh's Government in mid-January 1945.

His mainly Maronite opponents claimed that by the terms of the Protocol Lebanon would become bound indirectly at least to the foreign policy of the other signatories; that no way was provided to leave the League if Lebanon once decided to do so; and that the Protocol clearly indicated that it was only a first step towards complete Arab unity. This campaign gained considerable strength when the Maronite Patriarch indicated that he supported it.[171]

The Saudis, on the other hand, although they too were resolute in their desire to preserve their full independence, after Ibn Saud's readiness to sign the Protocol modified their attitude to the process leading to the formation of the Arab League. It seems that Ibn Saud at last realised that Egypt was no more interested than himself in real Arab unity. The fact that since autumn 1944 the Egyptian Government was headed by Ahmad Mahir (and after his assassination in February 1945 by Fahmi Nuqrashi) and not by Nahhas, who had cherished far-reaching aspirations of leadership of the whole bloc of Arab states, certainly alleviated Ibn Saud's anxieties.[172] In adopting that attitude of co-operation with Egypt while retaining his full independence Ibn Saud rightly hoped to nip in the bud any possibility of Nuri al-Sa'id or any other Hashemite personality becoming a prominent leader of the new body. That development was possible since the personal relations between King 'Abd-al-'Aziz Al Sa'ud and King Faruq of Egypt had become very close.[173]

This change in the nature of the relationship between the two Kings was really far-reaching; in the past the relations between Ibn Saud and King Fu'ad, Faruq's father, had been marked by a scornful attitude of the Egyptian monarch towards what he regarded as a 'bedouin King'. Now King Faruq realised that Ibn Saud's attitude could help Egypt to consolidate its position in the Arab world. In January he arranged to go to Saudi Arabia to meet Ibn Saud ostensibly as an act of friendship and 'in order to make personal acquaintance'. That move could also enhance Faruq's position in Egypt itself and the Egyptian Prime Minister did not like it at all, but Faruq was resolute enough to carry the day.[174] And indeed when Faruq returned from Hijaz he was welcomed by public demonstrations on a considerable scale. It was stressed that the meeting of the two Kings contributed to the strengthening of relations between Egypt and Saudi Arabia.[175] And the relations were so improved that Ibn Saud subsequently proposed to sign a Treaty of Alliance of his country with Egypt and Syria. Such a treaty would have presented the new Arab League with an emerging bloc of states unfriendly to the Hashemites and it could have been a 'sizeable nail ... driven into the coffin of the Arab League'.[176]

Faruq's visit was followed by Shukri al-Quwatli visiting both Saudi Arabia and Egypt. The leaders of these three countries issued a joint declaration boasting that their discussions were expected to have a great impact on the history of Arab world. It seems that the Syrians adjusted their position to that of the Saudis. If a month earlier the Syrian Foreign Minister still declared that his country was 'ready for every concession necessary for the achievement of the greater unity' and added that he 'preferred to be a low-ranking official in the Greater Arab State to being a Minister or a President of the Republic in smaller Syria', the joint communiqué published following the meeting of Shukri al-Quwatli and Ibn Saud simply stated that both rulers 'fully agreed to promote whatever might be found useful for the Arabs and their national aspirations'. No wonder that the Hashemite rulers became perturbed. 'Abdallah invited 'Abd al-Illah, the Iraqi Regent, to visit him. The Regent, accompanied by Nuri al-Sa'id, visited Trans-Jordan on 5 February. This meeting produced an important change in Iraq's position with regard to the proposed League's obligatory arbitration power. If up to then Iraq had supported closer Arab co-operation and stronger power to the League, its enthusiasm suddenly became modified.[177]

When the drafting sub-committee had finished their work the scene was ready for it to be concluded with the formal approval of their proposals. The Egyptian Foreign Minister issued invitations to his colleagues in the other Arab countries to come to Cairo on 17 March for a plenary session of the Preparatory Committee. The draft prepared by the sub-committee was approved by the plenary committee with minor amendments introduced by Mr Badawi, a legal expert of the Egyptian Foreign Ministry. Consequently the Preparatory Committee transformed themselves into a General Arab Conference and on 23 March they signed the Pact of the League of Arab States. Since no Yemeni delegate was present the Pact was sent to San'a for signature.[178] Thus the League was formed.

Article 8 of the Pact which deals with the machinery of the League called for the appointment of a Secretary General to head a permanent Secretariat. Already in autumn 1944 Nuri al-Sa'id suggested that the Syrian Faris al-Khuri be appointed to that task.[179] Nuri may have thought that his candidate being a Syrian would enjoy the support of Saudi Arabia, when it joined the process, and being a Christian, the support of Lebanon. Thus Egypt's predominance would diminish and Iraq's influence would be increased with a Secretary General known for his friendly attitude. But the Egyptians had different views of course. Since the departure of Nahhas, 'Abd al-Rahman 'Azzam appeared to be the main Egyptian spokesman on Arab affairs and the closest adviser of King Faruq on that subject. His prestige had been enhanced when, as the Egyptian *Amir al-Hajj*, he had helped to persuade Ibn Saud to sign the Protocol and he was the only Egyptian politician who accompanied Faruq in his travel to Saudi Arabia and was present at the latter's meeting with Ibn Saud. He was Faruq's natural choice. 'Azzam boasted that not only had he got the full backing of Ibn Saud as well, but that the latter had agreed to sign the Protocol and to join the League on condition that 'Azzam was appointed as its Secretary.[180] 'Azzam was in full support of the Syrian concept of Greater Syrian unity. He did not see any justification for the independence of Lebanon, a small country of one million people who would not be able to stand alone, and suggested uniting it with Syria, Trans-Jordan and Palestine but *without* giving 'Abdallah any role to play.[181] No wonder that with the backing of Egypt and Saudi Arabia and the unanimity of views with Syria he got the job.

The Pact established a very loose framework for co-operation in various fields. It did not lay the foundations of Arab unity, a term which was not even mentioned in it. It was an act of compromise between keen pan-Arabists, like the Syrians, suspicious separatists like the Christian Lebanese, conservatives who resented any change in the *status quo* like the Saudis, protagonists of partial unity of the Fertile Crescent, like the Iraqis, or of Greater Syria, like 'Abdallah, and those who wanted no more than the formation of an Arab bloc of states under their leadership, like the Egyptians. The desire to include all states necessarily lessened the degree of unity achieved. If Lebanon had been dropped that degree could have been increased since the Lebanese were the most stubborn opponents to unity during the earlier stages of inter-Arab talks and even more so during the final stages. Their stubbornness was largely responsible for the Pact going in some respects even less far in the direction of unity than the Protocol of Alexandria. For example, the Protocol called upon the member states to 'co-ordinate policies'; it limited the right of the member states to conclude only international agreements which were not in conflict with the Protocol or its spirit; it forbade the member states to pursue a foreign policy prejudicial to the policy of the League or that of any member state. All those points were omitted from the final text of the Pact.[182]

That weakening of the binding character of the Pact was subject to criticism from the *Wafd* party in Egypt, largely, so it seems, for reasons of party politics, and from pan-Arab elements in Syria and Iraq. When the Pact was laid before the Syrian Parliament for ratification, some members criticised the changes which had been introduced into the Pact as compared to the Protocol. One of them was critical of the decision about Palestine and of the fact that it had not been included in the Pact itself but rather in a special annex. Another member declared that the ratification should not be considered as acceptance of the present Syrian borders, especially with Lebanon. But in the end the Syrian Parliament, like all the other Arab Parliaments, ratified the Pact unanimously.[183]

The Palestine Arabs were very disappointed. First of all, they got a very moderate decision, from their point of view, on the Palestine question. Secondly, they were denied representation on an equal footing in the League. And, thirdly, they needed a real instrument of pan-Arab solidarity as the main weapon in their struggle against the Jews over Palestine. Instead they got, in the words of Musa al-'Alami, a body which 'had now been reduced to a debating society'.[184]

The British attitude: the final stage

The dramatic turn in the war in the Middle East in the late autumn of 1942 and winter 1943, Eden's Parliamentary reply of February 1943 and the strong impact which those developments had on public opinion in the Middle East brought about a reconsideration of British interests and policies in that area. The door which had been closed in January 1942 with the acceptance of the Middle East (Official) Committee's Report was now open again. That process of official thinking, which had been initiated by Richard Casey, the Minister Resident in the Middle East, was the background against which the British Government was reacting through summer 1943 up to winter 1945 to the inter-Arab talks and conferences.

The first step had already been taken by Casey in December 1942 when he approached various Departments of State and asked for their views on 'long-term policy for the Middle East'. Both the Ministry of Transport and the Colonial Office stressed the need for economic co-ordination among the various Middle Eastern countries but were reluctant to recommend any move which might have direct political implications.[185]

The second move was made when the Middle East War Council (composed of the highest British political and military authorities in the Middle East) was called by Casey to meet in Cairo in May 1943 to discuss various aspects of Britain's Middle East policy, but mainly the Palestine and Syria problems. The basis for their deliberations was Casey's memorandum, which did not tackle the Arabs' desire for unity and what should be the British attitude to it. But other memoranda did consider that question. MacMichael's memorandum deprecated the division of Greater Syria into four units after the First World War, the French control of Syria and the Lebanon and the Zionist policy. He went further, emphasising that 'the problem of the Levant States cannot be treated piecemeal, for they are in all essentials of a single unit'. Therefore he suggested an economic unification of those countries 'whether it leads to any form of political confederation or not'. On the other hand, the memorandum of the General Officer Commanding, Palestine, which was circulated by direction of the Commander-in-Chief, Middle East Forces, pointed out that 'the present move towards creating some form of

Federation of Arab States' implied 'the development of organised opposition to Zionist policy which may be initiated and maintained by Arab influences and actions outside Palestine'. That Memorandum indirectly led to the conclusion that unless the Arabs' goodwill over Palestine had been won, Britain might not get any advantage from a closer unity of the Arabs.

In their deliberations the MEWC virtually adopted those approaches. They recommended against any deviation from the 1939 White Paper, as far as Palestine was concerned, and they called upon Britain to change its policy and evict the French from Syria and the Lebanon, since 'the continued presence of France in the Levant is incompatible with our political and military interests in the Middle East, as well as with the peaceful development and well being of the Arab countries'. Furthermore, 'any form of closer political association between the Arab States or even between the States of "Greater Syria" (i.e. Syria, Lebanon Palestine and Transjordan), a development to which His Majesty's Government have declared themselves sympathetic, is hardly possible as long as the French maintain any direct influence, political or military, in Syria and the Lebanon'. On the other hand, on the broader question of Arab unity the council adhered to a more cautious thinking. They concluded that 'the political confederation of Arab countries on a wide scale is impracticable at the present moment owing to the conflicting aspirations of the various countries and to the present peculiar status of Palestine and Syria. While the initiative must be left to the Arabs, the most practical course is to encourage efforts toward economic and cultural unity, out of which some form of political confederation, at least in "Greater Syria", may ultimately emerge'.

These recommendations which were referred to the Prime Minister and the Foreign Office at home were not liked at all by the latter. Except for the recommendation to stick to the anti-Zionist policy in Palestine, the FO rejected everything else. The Eastern Department refused to consider any policy which would antagonise the French authorities and the French people before the liberation of France had been achieved, and thus to forfeit their support, which was regarded as vital for the success of the future military operations of the Allies in France. As for Arab unity they stated that

> [while] we should avoid blame among the Arabs for not facilitating the process of Arab unity ... it is very difficult to see any hope of the practical realisation of any sort of Arab federation as yet and certainly not any hope at all of practical Arab contributions to the war effort. Moreover, unless we change our Palestine policy or at least stick to the White Paper, we are going to have the Arabs against us any way; and in that case it is perhaps better not to have any large measure of Arab unity.

The French Department of the Foreign Office – Sir Maurice Peterson, Sir Alexander Cadogan and Anthony Eden himself – went further in stressing the need to maintain the commitments which had been given to the French. They realised that any eviction of the French from the Levant States would sooner or later jeopardise Britain's position in Iraq. Casey was blamed by Peterson that he had 'sold himself to Sir E. Spears much in the manner of Dr Faustus', implying that Spears was the Devil himself. No wonder that in his official reaction Eden notified Churchill that he fully rejected the anti-French recommendations of the MEWC. And since the eviction of the French had been regarded by the MEWC as a precondition for any closer unity among the Arab countries, at least those of 'Greater Syria', Eden's position amounted to a rejection of the Arab aspects too of the policy recommended by the MEWC. Such a divergence of views required serious discussion and both Eden and Casey suggested that Casey should come to London to discuss the whole matter.[186]

It was decided that Casey would come to London at the end of June 1943 to discuss the various questions of British policy in the Middle East. In anticipation of that visit the FO prepared various papers summarising their views. Consequently Casey came to London and brought with him Sir E. Spears. Both of them met Cadogan and other Foreign Office officials. Both Casey and Spears tried to persuade the heads of the Foreign Office to adopt a new policy in the Middle East. Casey dressed up his suggestion that Britain should turn out the French from the Levant States by putting forward the idea of receiving 'some kind of a mandate from the United Nations for the safeguarding of the entire Middle East area including the Levant States'. Casey made it clear that in order to safeguard its vital interests in the Middle East, such as oil and communication lines, Britain should make its 'influence felt in the Middle East as a whole'. He went further and stated 'that the best means of promoting unity in the Middle East was on the economic side', namely by lifting customs barriers, including the Levant States in the sterling area and keeping the Middle East Supply Centre even for the post-war period. Such a policy would much further improve the utilisation of local resources for both the war effort and the well being of the local population. Spears fortified Casey's view by the time-worn notion 'that if we treat the Arab world as a whole, Palestine can be made to appear so small that we can do anything we like with it – even give it to the Jews'.

The Foreign Office rejected these concepts, except for the economic ones. Sir Maurice Peterson suggested an alternative policy 'to content the Arab countries by stopping short of making Palestine a Jewish State and by reducing the French position on the Levant to one corresponding with our own in Iraq. (An arrangement which would constitute no obstacle to Arab federation)'. He rejected the eviction of the French from the Levant since it would endanger British positions and interests elsewhere in the Middle East. He thought that a United Nations mandate was completely impracticable, and from his experience he had learned that the Arabs would not agree to trade off Palestine for a British encouragement of some form of Arab federation.

Eden fully agreed with him and approved Peterson's notion that the policy of treaties such as those reached with Iraq and Egypt should be the model. Since on that crucial question (unlike more technical questions of currency policy and grain supply) no agreement was reached, the Foreign Office were instructed to prepare a memorandum outlining future British policy in the Middle East. Such a paper could help Casey in his daily management of British policy in the Middle East 'as a whole' and in his dealings with the Americans.[187]

In the Memorandum the Foreign Office repeated their view that the French position in Syria and the Lebanon should after the war be regularised in a manner similar to that of Britain in Iraq. In the field of Arab unity the Foreign Office repeated Eden's position, which had twice been made in public (May 1941 and February 1943) and the only concession to Casey's view was a statement that the British Government were then examining whether any progress in the direction of economic unity of the Middle East was possible.[188]

Casey had no choice but to retreat, since his intervention in the preparation of the Foreign Office's Memorandum was to no avail. In a Memorandum of his own which he had prepared even before the Foreign Office's Memorandum was finally drafted, he limited himself to the economic aspect of the matter and endorsed a programme of development by stages of a Middle East Economic Council. Other remarks by him on relations with the Americans in the Middle East were scorned by Eden, who noted that those matters were 'not his business' but 'for our Ambassadors to do'. Casey's and Spears's earlier proposals to evict the French in order to pave the way towards an Arab federation under British tutelage were not even hinted at in the Memorandum.[189]

The Foreign Office's attitude was crowned with full victory when the War Cabinet approved the FO's and Casey's latest Memoranda and asked the Foreign Secretary to draw up a series of recommendations giving effect to the policy outlined in the memoranda. That Eden did in another Memorandum which dealt with the gradual development of the Middle East Supply Centre towards a Middle East Economic Council with US co-operation. This very limited scope, in which Britain was now prepared to encourage Arab co-operation, was further limited by the War Cabinet. When they discussed and approved the latest of Eden's memoranda, the War Cabinet added that 'this development ... should be carried out cautiously'.[190]

This policy continued for the whole war period and was reflected during the work of the Palestine Cabinet Committee and in further Cabinet memoranda which served as a basis for discussion of Middle Eastern problems with the Americans.[191] In a Foreign Office Memorandum, presented to the Palestine Cabinet Committee, it was clearly put that 'the assistance which we can render towards Arab Federation, represents a very limited credit indeed' for British interests. Furthermore, it seriously doubted whether the Arab rulers were interested at all in any kind of unity.[192] But of more importance to our discussion is the direct bearing which that negative attitude of the London government to any official British encouragement of Arab unity had on British reactions to the inter-Arab consultations which Nahhas initiated in the summer of 1943 and the practical moves which during 1944 gave birth to the Arab League.

As we have already seen, British reaction to Nuri al-Sa'id's was reserved (see ch. 4, pp. 217–22). When in March 1943 it became clear that Nuri proposed to convene a general Arab Congress of pan-Arab activists, both official and unofficial, to discuss ways and means to promote Arab unity, C. W. Baxter, the head of the FO's Eastern Department, reacted: 'I think that we might take the line that a Conference would be premature, but if the Arab leaders want to engage in confidential discussions, without publicity, regarding the preparation of some plan, they can surely do so by authorising their representatives at some Arab capital to take part in such confidential discussion'.

That attitude was endorsed by the Egyptian Department and approved by Peterson. The Colonial Office concurred. Consequently the British diplomatic representatives were instructed to do their best to discourage the holding of that Conference but not to 'openly oppose' it, in order not to give offence to Arab feelings.[193] It should be remembered that the highest British authority in the Middle East, Richard Casey, had some reservations. He thought that the Arab unity movement if 'properly guided' should 'not be to our disadvantage', and he certainly shared the Foreign Office's reluctance to come out openly against holding the conference. As an alternative on 25 March 1943 he suggested advising the Arab States 'to clear the ground first by direct contacts between themselves before convening any kind of conference'.

This basic attitude remained for two more years and was reinforced by the decision which the British Cabinet took in July 1943 as a result of the Minister of State's initiative. It was reflected on each actual occasion when some Arabs initiated a move which was intended to advance Arab unity. Thus, the formation in Baghdad of a local branch of the Cairo-based Arab Unity Club was regarded by the Foreign Office as 'a thorn in ... our flesh',[194] although the reaction to Nahhas's statement of 30 March 1943 and his subsequent actions fared better with the British, since, unlike Nuri, Nahhas preferred inter-government consultations and not a public gathering of more hot-headed unofficial politicians.

THE FORMATION OF THE ARAB LEAGUE

Even that kind of discussion was believed by the Foreign Office officials in London to be 'more likely to reveal Arab dissension' than to promote Arab unity, but not as dangerous as a public gathering which would necessarily have raised the questions of Syria and Palestine in a way embarrassing to Britain.[195] The Foreign Office officials clearly expressed their feelings of satisfaction when they realised that Faruq was trying to capture the first role for himself if a conference were to be convened in Cairo, that Nuri was not easily going to concede the leading part to Nahhas, and that 'Abdallah proposed that a more proper place for the future conference was not Cairo but 'Amman.[196] The fact that Nahhas's suggestion was very similar to Casey's and came several days after Casey had himself suggested his ideas to the Foreign Office left an impression of co-ordination between the two.[197]

Since Ibn Saud's reaction to the proposal to hold a general Arab Conference was negative, his position was initially not unwelcome to the Foreign Office. The British realised that Ibn Saud's attitude would help them to slow down the pace of the movement towards possible Arab unity in whatever form.[198] On the other hand, when in August 1943 it became known that Ibn Saud refused even to send a representative to the consultations with Nahhas, the British were facing a dilemma. A successful conclusion of the process which Nahhas had initiated without the participation of Saudi Arabia could have forced them to choose between two competing blocs of Arab states, both of them friendly to Britain. A traditional element in British Arab policy was to do anything possible to avoid such a choice. Therefore from the very first moment when the British Minister in Jedda realised that Ibn Saud was reluctant to react favourably to Nahhas's invitation to send a delegate to the consultations, he advised the former against sending a definite reply and asked him 'to leave the door open for the future'. His prompt reaction was approved by the Foreign Office and became the guiding principle in the future dealings of Britain on that question.[199]

Consequently, Ibn Saud changed his mind and in October 1943 sent Yusuf Yasin to the consultations with Nahhas in Cairo. The latter was instructed by his master to maintain close contacts with the British Embassy in Cairo and to report to them on his talks with Nahhas. At the end of those talks Yusuf Yasin refused to commit Ibn Saud to anything; nor did he agree to sign the minutes. The British representative in Cairo refused at the beginning to encourage Ibn Saud's envoy to sign. On the other hand, the possibility that Ibn Saud would be left out of the new framework of Arab unity if he persisted in his attitude of self-denial could not be ruled out and disturbed the British.[200]

At the same time the Foreign Office continued to feel rather strongly against a quick calling of a general Arab Conference, evolving out of the inter-Arab consultations. They were fearful lest such a conference were used to embarrass the British Government over the Palestine question and the future of the Levant States. The British representatives in the Middle East were advised about the undesirability of an early conference and were asked to do their 'best to discourage any idea of a general Conference', although in a very subtle and polite way.[201]

The Colonial Office asked that that position be officially communicated to the Arab rulers. But the Foreign Office were reluctant to go that far and convinced the Colonial Office that it was enough to let the British representatives know what the British position was and let them decide in what ways to discourage the Arab governments from 'going fast' on the road to a general Arab Conference.[202]

To some extent Eden was embarrassed by his office's position. He spent most of October 1943 in Moscow and Cairo and only in the latter place did he realise that the Foreign Office 'are now anxious that we should discourage the Conference'. He reacted by minuting: 'I should not have thought that we could discourage overtly at least'.[203] And indeed the British discouragement did not become an open action, but, on the other hand, the pressure of Mr Price, the pro-Arab Labour MP, to come out publicly in support of the steps already taken by the Arab leaders was rejected by the Foreign Office.[204]

It should be added that an important factor which contributed quite a lot to the adoption of a cautious position with regard to Arab nationalism and the movement for Arab unity was the personal attitude of Sir Maurice Peterson. Since he had succeeded Sir Lancelot Oliphant as the Foreign Office's Assistant Under-Secretary in charge of the Middle Eastern Departments, a conservative and cautious attitude was brought into Foreign Office thinking. That attitude was reflected in his minutes, in his counsels against any move which had the slightest facet of adventurism, in his long and persistent opposition to the anti-French policy pursued in Syria by Sir E. Spears and in a very far-sighted reaction to one of Casey's proposals. When in January 1944 Peterson advised against any British encouragement of a Greater Syrian unity he wrote: 'The danger [for Britain, of course] is not from Kings and P[rime] M[inister]'s but from the Tito's or Fauzi's of the Arab world.'[205]

The Saudis were of course only too pleased to learn that the British position over the question of holding a general conference was identical to their own.[206] It stiffened their opposition to any prompt calling of a conference and it consequently caused its postponement for about a year.

Britain had to make that position felt by the Arab rulers and especially by Nahhas when in June 1944 he decided to invite the Arab Governments to send delegates to a general Preparatory Conference which would lay the foundations of the organisation of Arab unity in the very restricted form which had been agreed upon in principle in the 1943 inter-Arab consultations. When in February 1944 the British heard that Nahhas and Nuri contemplated marching forward with the idea of the conference and calling it for April, Peterson thought that it should not be taken too seriously. He seemed to be content with the previous implicit warnings against holding the conference and did not deem it necessary to take any action, but to get more information. However the British Government had already made up their minds not to oppose directly and openly the holding of the conference and thus to draw upon themselves the blame for any failure to achieve Arab unity. The main British concern was 'that the Conference should not degenerate into a demonstration against our Policy in Palestine'.[207]

That approach was strengthened by Lord Killearn's objection to any step that might now be regarded by Nahhas as British opposition to holding the Conference. Eden approved Killearn's view and it was resolved to concentrate on means of preventing the conference from degenerating 'into a Pan-Arab condemnation of our Palestine policy' rather than trying to cause its postponement.[208]

The Eastern Department's officials were not happy. They continued to think that 'Lord K[illearn] should not have much difficulties in riding off the Conference till the summer, by which time there may be other things to occupy people's minds'. Peterson fully agreed with them and drew the attention of his superiors to the French worries about the proposed conference.[209]

In that approach the Eastern Department and Peterson were helped by a factor which was not usually highly regarded by the former. On 6 April 1944 Lord Moyne convened in Cairo a conference of the top British personalities working in the Middle East; Moyne's own assistants, the Ambassadors, the High Commissioner for Palestine and Trans-Jordan and the C.-in-C. Middle East Forces. This meeting, which was otherwise scorned by Peterson as 'a very "cock-eyed" meeting reminiscent of "Alice in Wonderland"', also reached a conclusion that 'the proposed Arab Conference should be postponed if possible'.[210]

Soon afterwards it looked as if Peterson's view would prevail rather than Eden's and Killearn's.[211] Even the latter tried 'to press Nahas Pasha to stall' and asked the British representatives in Beirut, Damascus and Baghdad to persuade the Syrian, Lebanese and Iraqi Governments 'to go slowly about the convocation of Arab Conference' and to avoid exerting pressure on the Egyptian Government. It is safe to assume that the British resolution not to release Jamal al-Husayni and Amin al-Tamimi from internment in Rhodesia was strengthened by that development – Nahhas did not want to convene the conference without Palestinian participation. And since the two interned Palestinian leaders had participated in the 1939 St James's Conference, he regarded them as authorised Palestinian representatives. Therefore their continued internment could help the British to achieve their goal of postponing the conference.

At the beginning of June Killearn realised that subtle means of persuasion and the attempt to thwart the Iraqi and Syrian pressure on Nahhas had failed. Therefore contrary to his former judgment he took measures 'to warn Nahas Pasha to go slow over proposed Arab Conference'. Killearn was persuaded to take that step since he could not 'see how the vexed question of Palestine could be avoided' if the conference were to be convened. Secondly, now that Nuri al-Sa'id had been ousted from office Killearn hoped that Nahhas was no longer afraid of Nuri's competition and could agree to let the idea of the conference quietly peter out.[212]

But Nahhas preferred to disregard the British view. During spring 1944 he was under the heaviest fire directed at him by the combined forces of the Palace and the Opposition. He remained in power only thanks to the British counter-pressure,[213] and it seems that he could not afford to be seen by the public as bowing to British pressure. He may have realised that for the British he was still the best Egyptian Prime Minister and therefore he enjoyed a good defence against them. In mid-June (see above, pp. 274–5) he issued the invitations to the Arab governments for the proposed Preparatory Committee. With that action taken the British were faced with a *fait accompli*. Their reaction was pragmatic: rather than obstruct the conference they decided to influence its process so that they should not be embarrassed by accusations and extreme decisions over the Palestine and Syrian problems. Pressure exerted by the Jewish Agency on the Foreign Office that they oppose the holding of the conference was totally disregarded.[214] The second practical step they took after realising that the committee was going to be convened was to ensure that Saudi delegates would participate and that no animosity would develop between Saudi Arabia and Egypt.

The British advice about Palestine and Syria was conveyed to the various Arab governments and was well received.[215] At that stage the Arabs were eager to secure continued British adherence to the 1939 White Paper Policy in Palestine and British backing against any French attempt to force upon Syria and the Lebanon a treaty as a pre-condition for complete evacuation of the Levant States. Therefore the proceedings and decisions of the Preparatory Committee when it met in October 1944 were much more moderate than the usual positions and resolutions that Arab gatherings used to pass those questions. Nahhas, no doubt, realised that there was a clear limit to his ability to defy the British whose pressure on King Faruq was the only factor that was keeping him in office. The Syrians were usually very vocal regarding Palestine, but Syria proper was closer to their hearts than Palestine. Sir E. Spears pointed out to the Syrian Prime Minister and the Foreign Minister that 'Syrians had been given such support from the British that this justified me in asking that no difficulties should be raised for us as regards Palestine'. These words were not merely a request for Syrian gratitude. They could be easily understood as a hinted threat to stop that support of which the Syrians were still in dire need. Therefore it worked very well and the Syrian Prime Minister promised Spears 'that not only would Syrians not raise this [Palestine] question themselves but that they would do their best to prevent it being raised otherwise'.

That promise was too far-reaching to be fulfilled. It soon became clear that the question of Palestine would be raised in the committee after all, although in a moderate way. Nahhas claimed, and the British accepted, that in view of strong pro-Zionist resolutions passed in summer 1944 by both major American parties he could no longer disregard the matter, and other Arab governments followed Nahhas' lead.[216]

Regarding the question of Saudi participation the British were facing a dilemma. Although they were in favour of it when they were convinced that Nahhas was going to convene the conference, they did not want to be seen as supporting the convocation of the committee. Consequently, the initial British advice to Ibn Saud in favour of participation was rather vague.[217] On the other hand Ibn Saud was reluctant to take part in a committee which would demonstrate his secondary position among the Arab states, unless he had been clearly advised to do so by the British.[218] The British were reluctant to explicitly tell Ibn Saud anything beyond the statement that they did not object to his taking part and carrying responsibility for his decisions.[219] Ibn Saud changed his mind and decided to send Yusuf Yasin to the Preparatory Committee only when he got 'a clear indication' from the British that they much preferred his participation and in order to present a united Arab front in face of the pro-Zionist resolutions passed by the American parties.[220]

The crucial moment for Ibn Saud was the British rejection of his demand that the British Government should exert pressure on Nahhas against calling the committee.[221] This made him realise that the British were serious in their desire to avoid any possibility of being blamed for blocking the committee, and thus the road for his participation was clear. At the same time he and the Arab public at large were able to learn from a report by the *al-Ahram* correspondent in London that, according to well-informed circles, the British were not expecting that the Preparatory Committee would bring about a political union of the Arabs, but that the committee could at best promote cultural and economic ties only.[222] Such an admission in public, although not from an official source, that the British did not take too seriously the attempt to promote Arab unity may also have helped Ibn Saud to decide in favour of participation in the committee, which he did only when the delegates convened in Alexandria had already begun their deliberations.

While the Preparatory Committee was sitting from 26 September to 6 October 1944, the British knew little of the content of its deliberations which were being held *in camera*. Therefore they could not influence it very much. The main thing that interested them was the Palestine question and they asked the Saudi delegate when he joined the discussion to see to it that the discussion and resolutions were not directed against them.[223]

On the whole the Foreign Office were surprised by the success of the Preparatory Committee in laying down the foundations of an inter-Arab organisation for political co-operation. It 'goes very much further than anything we have hitherto been led to expect as likely to emerge from the Arab Unity Conference', minuted R. M. H. Hankey. 'Arab Unity in one form or another is here to stay', was the reaction of Brigadier I. N. Clayton, the Adviser for Arab Affairs of the Minister Resident in Cairo. 'There are doubtless disintegrating elements in it', admitted that 'man on the spot', 'but anything which is construed as foreign aggression against any of its members will at once strengthen it enormously'.[224]

That impression of the Arab demonstration of unity was reinforced by the latter's practical nature. 'Divisions and jealousies as well as the instability of the Arab States concerned may militate against effective implementation of the resolutions', warned T. Shone, the British Minister at the Cairo Embassy, 'but, nevertheless, it is clear that discussions which have been taking place for over a year between the Arab States have cleared the ground of impracticable ideas such as those of immediate administrative unions or federations and led the Arab States in the more practical direction of Arab co-operation, political as well as economic, cultural and social'.[225] That attitude was fully endorsed by Lord Moyne who added another point. 'There is little doubt that the direction [of the newly formed organisation] envisaged at present is that of co-operation with Great Britain. The Middle East group as a whole is willing and indeed anxious to co-operate with Great Britain on a basis of independence and free association'.

Unlike that view, which was shared by Sir Kinahan Cornwallis as well,[226] the Foreign Office in London were less enthusiastic. They were still apprehensive lest the Arab world unite against Britain over Syria and Palestine. They knew only too well that as long as Churchill was heading the British Government there was very little chance that the strict implementation *in toto* of the 1939 White Paper on Palestine would become the official post-war policy. And the British authorities in the Middle East themselves warned that such a policy and a full support of Syria and Lebanon against France was a *sine qua non* condition for the preservation of the present Arab friendliness towards Britain. Secondly, the FO officials were still thinking that Shone and Moyne 'may rather overplay the measure or permanence of the unity achieved in Cairo'.[227]

That more cautious attitude was contrary to the information and advice coming from the Middle East. The Political Intelligence Centre, Middle East stated:

It is the general feeling among the delegates [of the Preparatory Committee] that the next step must be taken by H[is] M[ajesty's] G[overnment]. The ball was originally set rolling by the declaration of Mr Eden in 1941: the Arabs have now risen to the suggestion and produced their plans; and the plan itself is formed on the lines envisaged by him as desirable. Thus, while the delegates feel that the task of making the new 'Commonwealth' work devolves upon themselves they expect that HMG will take up an attitude towards it which will have beneficial effects upon its development.

Brigadier Clayton reached the conclusion that in view of British interests in the whole area of the Middle East (oil, communication lines, military bases and installations and naval facilities) 'the sympathy shown towards Arab Unity is encouraging. A measure of encouragement given to the States in their efforts to achieve it would be helpful. It might be done by a question and answer in Parliament'.[228]

Nuri al-Sa'id, too, brought a similar message to the British Embassy in Cairo. He told Smart that 'it must be obvious that all this [the Arab League when established] could not work without the help of Great Britain, which was essential'. And he went further and in a very frank gesture explained why the Arabs were then so eager to secure British goodwill: 'There could be no Arab League if the British insisted on France having a predominant situation in Syria', implying very clearly that by ousting the French from the Levant States Britain could secure for herself a leading position in the Middle East.[229]

Those prospects were forcefully presented and analysed in a despatch from Sir Kinahan Cornwallis in Baghdad. He explained that the solution of the Palestine conflict like the guarantee of the independence of Syria and the Lebanon were

> an integral part of their [Arabs'] scheme for Arab Unity, a movement which we have undertaken to support.... If we are ready to support the plan fully and openly, *and to respond to the invitation which has been given to us to act as guide and mentor of Arab World* [my italics], then I see every reason to hope that Imperial interests in the Middle East will be maintained and safeguarded more securely than ever before, and that a period of stability and prosperity lies before us.

That despatch strongly impressed the Foreign Office. It was shown to Eden, who decided to circulate it to the Cabinet.[230]

However, not all aspects of those recommendations became official policy and were carried out. What the British Government did was to ensure that Arab countries under British tutelage or friendly to Britain would not remain outside the new Arab organisation. They decided to enable Trans-Jordan, still under British mandate, to sign the Protocol reached at the end of the Preparatory Committee work at Alexandria. That decision was taken without too strong qualms since both the Colonial and Foreign Offices took note of the fact that the resolutions of the Arab League would only be binding on those countries which accepted them. It was made clear to the Trans-Jordan Government that they 'should not accept any specific obligations which might involve taking action contrary to the policy of His Majesty's Government whether in regard to Palestine or some other respect'.[231]

Secondly, the British advised Ibn Saud to instruct his delegate to sign the Protocol and to take part in the Constituent Conference of the Arab League so that he could 'guide the discussions on the right lines'.[232] In the traditional British way of thinking, Sir Walter Smart, the very influential Oriental Counsellor in the Cairo Embassy, pointed out that 'the danger of course, is that if Ibn Saud refuses to agree to the proposals, he may be isolated in the Egypto-Arab world and be accused of working against the Arab cause in the interests of Great Britain'.[233] That British advice was identical to the Egyptian one and between them they succeeded in convincing Ibn Saud. 'Abd al-Rahman 'Azzam, the special Egyptian envoy to Saudi Arabia, 'doubted whether his mission would have been successful had it not been for His Majesty's Government's advice to Ibn Saud of which he had learnt from the King himself'.[234]

On the other hand, the more specific advice to react to the process of forming the Arab League by an open declaration or a Parliamentary Reply in which Britain would bless the development or declare its support for it was not taken up by the Foreign Office. Instead Britain continued to have a behind-the-scenes favourable approach to the new organisation, using its influence to prevent extreme resolutions over Palestine and Syria. That attitude was fully manifest during the last stage of the formation process of the Arab League, when the British authorities in Cairo did nothing beyond the attempt to ensure that the resolutions passed in the form of the Pact of the Arab League be as moderate as possible, especially those dealing with the support that should be given to non-independent Arab countries in their struggle for independence.[235] Secondly, the British objected to the Pact being signed by Musa al-'Alami who had participated in the Preparatory Committee as a 'member representing the Palestine Arabs'. Their objection prevailed and only the representatives of the various Arab states signed the Pact.[236]

In the end the Pact did deal with the questions of Palestine and the non-independent Arab countries contrary to the expressed British wish.[237] But since the resolutions were rather moderate and the Pact even retracted a little bit as far as the authority of the League as a corporate body versus that of its member states was concerned, the Foreign Office could only express their satisfaction. Hankey minuted:

'A Conference of European States would hardly have been much more business-like. It's a surprising achievement for the Arabs'. Baxter added his initials without any reservation.[238] Several days later when the Pact was looked at thoroughly, Hankey and his colleagues stuck to their initial positive evaluation. They held the view that the formation of the Arab League and its Pact were a 'surprisingly practical outcome'. 'The pressure of Zionist agitation is largely responsible for the unusual degree of agreement and for the rather unfortunate reference to Palestine. It remains to be seen what the Arab States will make of it'.[239]

Meanwhile that development had the first practical effect on British policy. On 30 March 1945 Oliver Stanley, the Colonial Secretary, joined with Sir Edward Grigg in demanding to reconsider the recommendations of the Palestine Cabinet Committee, which had favoured the partition of Palestine. 'The marked success of the Pan-Arab Conference' was one of Stanley's arguments for his proposed reconsideration.[240]

British policy in the Middle East: image versus reality; London versus 'the men on the spot'

The fact that the Foreign Office in London regarded the formation of the Arab League as a surprise rather than as a culmination of their own efforts to promote Arab unity or, at least, a culmination of Arab leaders' efforts, which had been encouraged by Britain, is rather intriguing. For many years historical writings of the other non-British players in the Middle East 'games of nations' have been used to attribute to Britain a much larger measure of responsibility for the formation of the Arab League.

Among the Arabs both historians and politicians hold the same view. According to Ahmad al-Shuqayri, 'Britain devoted huge efforts to transform Arab unity into one of her weapons' during the Second World War, in a form of 'organisation which would include every Arab country and would be called Arab union'.[241] 'Abd al-Rahman 'Azzam Pasha was sure that the Foreign Office had arranged the Parliamentary Question of Mr Price in February 1943 in order to give Eden an opportunity to repeat his statement of 29 May 1941. To that he added the British encouragement of Saudi Arabia to take part in the formation of the Arab League and easily reached the conclusion of British responsibility.[242] In their defence one has to state that both those politicians were personally involved in the process only in its later stages, the first being a Syrian observer in Cairo in the summer of 1943 and the latter serving at the end of 1944 as a special Egyptian envoy to Saudi Arabia.

Two Muslim historians, writing before the British archives were open for historical inspection, held similar views. In 1951 the Egyptian 'Abd al-Rahman al-Rafi'i simply stated that 'the Arab League had been formed by British instruction'.[243] And several years later Mohamed Abdul Aziz of Dacca University in Bangladesh (East Pakistan of those days) claimed that Eden's 'repeated statements pledging support for the scheme of Arab unity had been mainly responsible for creating a wide-spread interest in the Arab world towards the formation of an Arab union'. He quoted and concurred with the Jewish pro-Zionist Jon Kimche's view that 'the Arab League was born with British help and encouragement, and to some extent as a result of British pressure'.[244]

It is a very rare occurrence for the views of Jews and Muslims, Arabs and Israelis to converge, as over the British responsibility for the formation of the Arab League. Aharon Cohen, an Israeli Marxist historian, wrote that in addition to the desire of the ruling circles in the Arab countries to strengthen their position by means of unity 'the idea of Arab Unity had got strong encouragement by the British Government who tried to offer the Arab peoples a substitute in form of a "unity" under the leadership of Britain, in order to strengthen her position in the region and to form a barrier in face of undesired political influences'. That was the background for Eden's speech of May 1941 and the Parliamentary Reply of February 1943.[245]

Ya'acov Shim'oni, a keen Israeli observer of Arab affairs, as late as 1977, wrote:

> In 1941 during the crisis days of the world war, Britain decided to initiate an alliance of Arab States, which would serve as a loyal ally of Britain during the war.... The British initiative resulted from the hope that the gradual realisation of the aspiration for Arab unity and the crystallisation of a conservative and homogeneous Arab nationalism would create among the Arabs an atmosphere of moderation, self-confidence and gratitude to Britain instead of the extreme and erratic nationalisms of the separate and small Arab States.

He thought that Nuri al-Sa'id's scheme had apparently got the British blessing, and only when it became clear that that scheme did not enjoy widespread Arab backing did the British decide to pin their hopes on Egypt's leadership of the Arab unity movement. The Egyptian Prime Ministers were not at all enthusiastic to play the role allotted to them by the British, who had strongly solicited them until they agreed.[246]

French writers, who bore a grudge against the British for their policy in the Levant States, usually held a very similar view. General Catroux wrote that the policy of pan-Arabism corresponded with the objects of British policy in the Middle East.[247] And another French writer, Michel Laissey, went so far as to claim that Eden's May 1941 statement was part of a more general British attempt 'to persuade the Arab States that they had a community of interests which should become durable and strong'.[248]

As we hope to have shown, British policy as shaped in London was generally different. The British Government were resolute against initiating changes in the political *status quo* in the Middle East and refused to give their blessing to Arab initiatives in that direction. Eden's May 1941 statement reflected to some extent a belief in the advantages of closer unity among the Arabs, but was mainly made in order to forestall a pro-Zionist proposal made by Churchill. Most importantly it did not signal a practical change in British Arab policy which was maintained in its former, traditional paths. What can account for that wide gap between reality and image? The fact that the Arab League disappointed many Arab nationalists no doubt contributed to the tendency to lay the burden of responsibility on British shoulders. Was it not natural that an organisation which had been formed at the instigation of the British should not develop into a real framework of Arab unity? Arab nationalists used to ask. Furthermore, the fact that the Egyptian Prime Minister who was involved in the formation of the Arab League, Mustafa al-Nahhas, had been installed in power by the British, created an impression of British backing or even responsibility for his moves.

Those explanations may have some force, but we think that they are not the sole and most important explanations. There are more than enough hints to suggest that the views and moves of the British authorities in the Middle East itself had a lot to do with the emergence of this imaginary view about British policy. On some occasions the view of British officials in the Middle East differed from the positions decided upon in London. Sometimes it looks as if it did not matter at all. For example, when in 1933 Walter Smart was rather reserved in his reaction to Rendel's negative Memorandum on the British attitude towards Arab unity,[249] we did not come across any indication that anyone outside the British Government had any inkling of it.

We know very clearly that highly important figures such as Moyne, Lyttelton, Casey, Kirkbride and MacMichael favoured the idea of establishing a greater Syrian unity. It is true that usually those who suggested such an arrangement did not deem it necessary, desirable or possible that 'Abdallah should assume the kingship of Greater Syria.[250] But at least once, in July 1941, when the conquest of Syria was approaching its final stage, Lord Moyne in his capacity as Colonial Secretary suggested rewarding 'Abdallah 'for his friendship by the title of King and, if the Syrians would accept him, he might be offered the crown of Syria as well'.[251] The effect that Kirkbride's personal views may have had on the Arabs in general and 'Abdallah in particular is clearer. In a talk with Tawfiq Abu al-Huda, Trans-Jordan Prime Minister, Kirkbride asked him 'how he thought, in the event of a just partition [of Palestine], the Arabs of Palestine would react to being placed under His Highness the Amir ['Abdallah]'.[252] It is very probable that Abu al-Huda interpreted

Kirkbride's question as an indication of the latter's support of 'Abdallah's Greater Syria plan.

Kirkbride's implied position was expressed even more clearly. He admitted in a talk with Mr Shertok: 'When Arabs came to see, he told them that Arab unity in the widest sense was a myth. The only practical policy was to unite Palestine, Syria, Lebanon and Trans-Jordan'.[253] It is true that 'Abdallah's kingship over that united Greater Syria was not mentioned by Kirkbride. But if we added to this that in 1940 the British Consul in Damascus gave a subvention to Shahbandar's party, which opposed the National Bloc and supported 'Abdallah (see ch. 4, p. 208) we should not be surprised to see that 'Abdallah and his assistants used to claim that the British were backing his Greater Syria scheme. Such a claim was made in June 1940 by 'Abdallah in an interview with Syrian leaders,[254] and he and Tawfiq Abu al-Huda repeated it in messages or in talks with Jewish or Arab leaders throughout the war. The only reservation that 'Abdallah claimed to find in the favourable British attitude was that the actual formation of Greater Syria should be deferred until after the end of the war.[255]

Nuri al-Sa'id's Fertile Crescent unity scheme was surrounded by similar conditions. Although officially not liked by the British Government, there was a group of British personalities who supported its basic concepts, like Lord Lloyd, Colonel Newcombe, Lord Samuel, Lord Winterton and others.[256] Lord Lloyd served as Colonial Secretary in 1940 and so Nuri and others could imagine that their scheme was now enjoying British favour.

With Lord Moyne there was no need to stretch the imagination too far. He supported the unity of Greater Syria and he regarded that unity as a first step in the implementation of Nuri's Fertile Crescent unity. More significantly he made no secret of his view and in November 1943, on his own admission, told no less a person than 'Abd al-Illah, the Iraqi Regent, that he 'agreed with Nuri's "blue book" [in which Nuri's plan had been published] that Greater Syria would have to come first'. It is true that Moyne refused to answer the Regent on whether he 'thought the Syrians would want a king' and preferred the non-committal view that on that matter he 'had no idea, that it did not concern us and would be for Syrians themselves to decide'.[257] But the very fact that the British Deputy Minister Resident in the Middle East, the highest British authority there, volunteered to a concerned party his favourable attitude to the gradual formation of a Fertile Crescent unity in which the formation of Greater Syria would constitute the first step could be reasonably understood by his interlocutor as an indication of which direction the wind was blowing in London.

It should be added that in the preparation of the 'blue book' Nuri was helped by British officials then holding positions as advisers with the Iraqi Government.²⁵⁸ Much more importantly, during the final stage of its preparation, Nuri told Lieutenant Colonel De Gaury (who was serving during the war as an intelligence officer in the Persian Gulf area) that 'Mr Casey [the then Minister Resident] had encouraged him' to prepare a paper about the need to form a Levant state.²⁵⁹ When the 'book' was published the British authorities objected to its public circulation. Therefore they agreed to distribute it themselves to British high ranking officials in the Middle East and outside it. In itself that move was intended to prevent public reaction to Nuri's plan, but it could also be interpreted as semi-official British backing.²⁶⁰ A comment by Cornwallis to Maisky, the Soviet Ambassador to London, 'that while Nuri Pasha's ideas would encounter many obstacles he certainly would persevere with them',²⁶¹ might easily be understood even by a less suspicious listener than a Soviet official as a favourable attitude to Nuri's scheme.

All these hints and pointers were heard, noticed, inflated out of all proportion and laid the foundations of the persistent myth that if the Hashemite schemes of unity had not been invented by the British Government they at least enjoyed their full support. It should be borne in mind that the British conclusions, reached repeatedly by officials and committees and approved by the political authorities, that no useful purpose would be served, as far as British interests or the need to solve the Palestine problem were concerned, by supporting the Hashemite schemes, were never brought in a clear and unequivocal manner to the knowledge of the promoters of those schemes. On the other hand, Nuri, 'Abdallah, etc. used to tell the British what their plans were. Usually the British advised against hasty actions or vigorous propaganda campaigns, avoiding substantive comments. No wonder that in such conditions even the British Ambassador in Baghdad reached the conclusion that 'it is not unnatural that he [Nuri al-Sa'id] should assume that no fundamental objection [of the British Government] exists to their adoption [referring to Nuri's ideas]'.²⁶² If that was Cornwallis's attitude one should not be surprised that he had been suspected by the Saudi *chargé d'affaires* in Baghdad of giving 'some measure of support' to those schemes. Cornwallis's denial certainly did not dispel the Saudi misgivings.²⁶³

That behaviour was apparently much more widespread and Moyne's and Casey's espousal of the Greater Syria and Fertile Crescent unity schemes was part of a wider phenomenon. On the outbreak of the Second World War a new Ministry of Information was formed by the British Government. Gilbert MacKereth, the British Consul in Damascus, easily understood the significance of the appointments made in that Ministry and reacted: 'In this connection I view with some misgiving the appointment of Britons notoriously zealous in the Arab political cause under the Ministry of Information in the Middle East and at home'.²⁶⁴ It is apparent that those 'zealous' propagandists went quite a long way in making promises to the Arabs. When in December 1942 Professor H.A.R. Gibb put forward his detailed proposal that Britain form an Arab federation, he argued that 'a special obligation rests upon the British Government to take the lead' in that direction, in view of, inter alia, 'the undertakings implicit ... in British propaganda to the Arab World in the course of this War'.[265]

On one occasion many important British officials in Iraq were quoted by the Saudi *chargé d'affaires* as openly expressing support of Greater Syria unity. It was taken as another evidence of the British position and it is doubtful whether the Arabs to whom the official denial was directed were assured that those officials had been misquoted and that Britain did not support the plan.[266]

That tendency of many important British officials in the Middle East was noticed not only by local observers. When the proceedings and decisions of the Middle East War Council reached London, R.M.A. Hankey on 5 June 1943 prepared a detailed analysis of them. He remarked, *inter alia*: 'The hope, avowed or unavowed, of all the British experts in the Middle East is, in my experience, that as the result of the war the French will be eliminated from Syria and that the Arab countries can then be united in some sort of loose federation under our leadership'.[267]

There were several occasions on which Hankey's impression could be formed. Hankey no doubt remembered that several days before 30 March 1943, when Nahhas made his statement in the Egyptian Senate about Arab unity, Casey had sent a telegram to London suggesting similar ideas (see above, pp. 294–5). He and all other concerned people in the FO knew that the Middle East War Council in May 1943 had passed a resolution in support of taking measures that would promote the unity of Greater Syria.[268] Hankey certainly knew that during the inter-departmental consultations over Britain's Palestine policy held in October 1943, Lord Moyne had emphasised that Britain had to take into account not only its own interpretation of British ministerial statements but also that placed on them by the Arabs. Moyne told the gathering that 'even Mr Eden's statement last year about Arab Federation was now described by the Arabs as a pledge. The Arabs knew very well that they could never effect Arab Federation as a result of their own efforts. They felt that Britain was committed to this statement and they relied on her to see that it was carried into effect'.[269]

Not all the pillars of the British edifice in the Middle East were thinking and acting like Casey and Moyne. Although the Embassy in Cairo kept up continuous pressure on the British Government to pursue as pro-Arab a policy in Palestine as possible, they by no means shared Casey's and Moyne's attitude to Arab unity. In June 1943 after Nahhas had set in motion the machinery of inter-Arab consultations, Walter Smart reacted:

> Ibn Saud's warnings about the proposed Conference and/or discussions about Arab Unity tally with remarks I have several times made in minutes, namely that our encouragement of Arab unity movements must bring up for discussion the questions of the French in Syria and the Jews in Palestine and that unless we are prepared to give the Arabs satisfaction on these two issues it is not clear why we want to promote discussion of them, unless we are playing the Macchiavellian game of having our hands forced.

Lord Killearn initialled that minute without any specific reaction of his own.[270]

The position of the British Government with regard to the dilemma presented in Smart's minute was to slow down the pace of the inter-Arab consultations and, on their conclusion, the calling of the Preparatory Committee and its work. Having failed to achieve that goal, the British representatives all over the Middle East tried their best to ensure that the questions of Palestine, Syria and the French presence in North Africa would not be raised at all, and if they were raised, that the discussions and resolutions would be as moderate as possible. On the other hand, the British were resolute in their determination to see Saudi Arabia taking part in that process — in the consultations, in the work of the Preparatory Committee and in the final formation of the Arab League — in order to avoid the need to choose between Saudi Arabia and the newly formed body. Britain also hoped that Ibn Saud would bring a permanent source of moderation into the inner counsels of the Arab League and that through him Britain would have a very co-operative channel of influence.

Over that last aspect of British policy the Cairo Embassy were 'zealous' too. After the rather successful conclusion of the inter-Arab consultations, Killearn expressed a manifest objection to any British move that could then be interpreted as directed against Arab endeavours. He wrote on 24 February 1944: 'In the circumstances I feel bound to record that I gravely doubt the wisdom of any attempt now to prevent the proposed conference for which Nuri Pasha is apparently actively pressing'. The turn-about in the 1943 attitude of the Cairo Embassy is crystal-clear. One should add that Killearn's latest position had got the receptive ear of Eden, who minuted: 'Why do we want to prevent it?'[271] However, as we have, we hope, clearly shown, the Foreign Office, and especially Sir Maurice Peterson, continued their attempts to slow down the Arab unity process and were caught by surprise when they realised that they had failed.

Sir E. Spears too noticed Killearn's change of heart. After a meeting of the top British personalities working in the Middle East, held in Cairo on 7 December 1943, with Eden, in which various aspects of British Middle Eastern policy were discussed, Spears noted: 'Lord Killearn laid stress on how Arab Federation Movement, *which he had been inclined to treat lightly* [my italics], was in fact very important'.[272] It is evident that Killearn realised that the British policy pursued in 1944 of 'encouraging the Arab Union' was 'diametrically opposing' the British policies of promoting Zionism in Palestine and safeguarding French predominance in Syria. In December 1944 he rejected the notion that Britain could at one and the same time 'run with the hare and hunt with the hounds'. He demanded that British policy regarding Syria and Palestine be brought into line with the encouragement given to the Arab unity movement.

This telegram raised a thorough discussion in the Foreign Office in which Eden himself took part. At the end the latter could state in his reply to Killearn that as far as Syria was concerned 'you have somewhat misunderstood our policy. Having underwritten the French promise of independence we have no intention of pressing those States to sign it away.' Eden stressed that Britain would support only an agreed settlement between France and the Levant States and would oppose any French attempt to impose resolution by force. On the other hand even Eden had to caution Killearn, although in a very subtle way, not to go too far in his espousal of Arab unity. On the latter aspect Eden wrote:

> I think you are in agreement with our present policy, which is one of general sympathy with the desire of the Arab States to reduce the barriers between them. To put the issue in its crudest form, I feel sure that if we were to adopt any other policy, we should very quickly be condemned by the whole Arab world as responsible for the breakdown of their discussions which might or might not have had useful results. We should arouse all the latent xenophobia of the Arabs. In general we cannot ignore the ideals and aims of the Arab Unity Movement and in view of our great strategic and other interests in the area we must try to guide it into spheres where we can co-operate [namely, as remote as possible from the Palestine embroglio].[273]

That authoritative exposition of British policy was much more similar to the traditional and actual British policy which had been pursued up to 1943 than to the actual steps taken by Casey and Moyne, and in 1944 by Killearn too.

In addition to those perplexities inside the British official machinery of government there was another factor which contributed to the misunderstanding of the real British policies and aims in the Middle East. The Arab nationalists and pan-Arabists could always find in London 'distinguished private persons who have shown an interest in furthering Arab ideas', from whom they got encouragement.[274] From time to time the British press, including the influential *Times*, published articles in support of some form or another of Arab unity. Such articles more often than not aroused the suspicions of the French, who regarded them as unofficial but true expressions of British aims in the Middle East.[275]

The combination of all those factors analysed above left the persistent impression that Britain initiated the political moves which culminated in the formation of the Arab League, an impression which can still be found in historical writings not based on the British primary sources, and which is only very slightly corroborated by them.

Conclusions

Britain did not create the Arab League, nor did it deliberately encourage its formation; at best it may have indirectly contributed to the process of its formation. The Arab League came into being as a result of various inter-Arab processes and rivalries and of the belief that the Palestine question could more easily be solved if a broader framework of Arab unity existed.

Members of the Hashemite dynasty and their supporters proposed various schemes of Arab unity. Faysal I of Iraq and Nuri al-Sa'id after him wanted to see unity established between the various countries of the Fertile Crescent. They were first of all motivated by the state interests of Iraq. They wanted to secure for their country safe access to the Mediterranean coast and to ensure that the pipe-line to Haifa and Tripoli passed through friendly territory. They were also driven to seek security within a greater Arab state because they felt threatened by the not-so-friendly neighbouring states of Turkey and Iran; the first had hardly given up its claim to the Iraqi oil-rich district of Mosul and the second had never ceased questioning its boundary with Iraq nor meddling in the affairs of the Iraqi oppressed Shi'ite community. Arab nationalism rather than Faysal's personal and dynastical right to the Syrian throne was evoked as justification for that policy.

Faysal and Nuri al-Sa'id repeatedly tried to entice the British Government to support their schemes but to no avail. They promised that within their unity scheme the Palestine problem could be solved and that awesome burden be taken off Britain's shoulders. But the autonomy promised to the Jews was much less than the Zionists were ready to accept and too much of a compromise for the Palestine Arabs to stomach.

The French usually opposed such schemes although from time to time they spread rumours about their support for a Hashemite Prince acceding to the Syrian throne in order to frighten the Syrian nationalists and force them to agree to French demands. And, indeed, here one can find the greatest obstacle that the Hashemites had to confront: the political elite of Damascus preferred independence as a separate state to any unity with one of the Hashemite countries, and even Faysal who in 1918–20 had ruled Syria could not overcome their resistance. Other Hashemite pretenders, like 'Ali, Faysal's eldest brother, had much less

CONCLUSIONS 313

chance of winning their hearts. His separate attempts could only spoil Faysal's.

'Abdallah, the Amir of Trans-Jordan, more strongly opposed Faysal's attempts. He confined his vision to Greater Syria only and regarded himself as the true successor to the Hashemite-led Arab Revolt of the First World War. He regarded Greater Syria as the mother-country of Arabism, the unity of which was a *sine qua non* for any further Arab unity. After Faysal's death in 1933 he devoted much of his energies to the fulfilment of that scheme. But he had even less support in Syria and he could rely on the co-operation only of some Druze leaders, bedouin sheikhs and the few followers of Shahbandar in Damascus. 'Abdallah believed that he had a solid claim on British support and his disappointment was much greater than Faysal's when that hoped-for support failed to materialise.

'Abdallah was ready, too, to reach a compromise with the Jews over Palestine and he went much further than any other Arab state in that direction. He hoped to get their active support for his plan. But that stand and his dependence upon the British forestalled the possibility of achieving a serious co-operation with the Palestine Arabs.

'Abdallah and Nuri al-Sa'id never co-operated with one another, nor did they co-ordinate their schemes which look rather complementary. Nuri also did not always put at the head of his endeavour the dynastical interests of the Iraqi Hashemites. But after 1939, Prince 'Abd al-Illah, the Iraqi Regent, entered the arena in order to secure a permanent throne for himself.

The revolt of Rashid 'Ali al-Kaylani stopped their efforts for a couple of years but Nuri resumed his activities in the winter of 1943 after the British victory at al-'Alamein. But then he could no longer overlook Egypt and he invited Mustafa al-Nahhas to take part in the attempt to promote a scheme of Arab unity. It may well have been that Nuri thought that if he gained Nahhas's approval of his scheme, the British would regard it as a fulfilment of their basic condition for giving their support: that the scheme of Arab unity should enjoy the support of all interested Arab quarters. But that move of Nuri al-Sa'id proved to be a terrible mistake, since it encouraged Nahhas to propose a scheme of his own and to initiate inter-Arab consultations which blocked Nuri al-Sa'id's way.

It was not only the Hashemites who believed that within the framework of Arab unity the Palestine problem could be more easily solved. Many Jewish leaders, British prominent personalities and even some Arabs shared the basic assumption of that approach, namely, that the Palestine Arabs would agree to make concessions to the Jews in return for the inclusion of Palestine in one scheme or another of Arab unity. In such a way, so those people believed, the Palestine Arabs would get some satisfaction of their national aspirations and would be assured of becoming a minority in Jewish Palestine. Furthermore, most of the Palestine Arab leaders did not believe in the eventuality of Arab unity and did not see why they should make the required concessions. Some of them and some Syrian leaders did not reject such propositions out of hand but the concessions they were ready to make fell short of the minimum Jewish demands.

The British Foreign Office too did not reject that approach altogether, but they realistically and accurately appreciated the Palestine Arab reaction and concluded that there was no chance of securing the consent of the nationalist circles among the Palestine Arabs. However, since that approach was raised and discussed many times within the corridors of the British Government it helped to make the question of Arab unity a serious matter.

Among the various attempts to implement that approach the Philby Plan stands out. Its significance is derived from the fact that Dr Weizmann, the most prominent Zionist leader in London, espoused it and succeeded in 1939–40 in convincing Churchill of its usefulness. When Churchill became the British Prime Minister he tried hard for about three years to implement it. Only when he became convinced in early 1943 that the plan was doomed to failure did he try another means and formed the Palestine Cabinet Committee. Weizmann renounced in his autobiography any responsibility for the Philby Plan, but the evidence we have gathered clearly points the other way.

Meanwhile during the ten years 1935–45 Arab nationalism became a strong popular belief and force. In Egypt that ideology gradually replaced all other alternative approaches to the question of Egypt's national identity. The Egyptian ruling dynasty encouraged that process, as did the organisations which worked for the spread of Arab nationalism and Islamic revivalism. It was easily pointed out that the Arab identity of Egypt and Arab unity corresponded with Egyptian national interests since Arab nationalists in the Fertile Crescent accepted Egypt not only as an important centre of Arabic culture but also as the political head of the Arab world.

In the Fertile Crescent Arab nationalism won the battle much more easily. The Arabic language and Arab history were almost universally regarded as the sole criteria of national identity. The first organisations to shape that ideology in concrete political terms emerged and became very instrumental in extending support to the Palestine Arabs during their 1936–9 Revolt.

That wave swept the Egyptian *Wafd* too. In order to retain his popularity *vis-à-vis* the Palace and Muslim fundamentalist organisations Nahhas became involved in the affairs of the Arab countries. The more he was attacked at home by his political adversaries, the more he turned to the Arab world for easy gains.

CONCLUSIONS

The combined front that the Arab world presented to Britain with regard to Palestine brought the British Government in 1939 to retreat from its pro-Zionist policy. That victory strengthened the inclination to meddle in the affairs of Palestine and thus a pattern was set up. The conclusion of several treaties among various Arab countries which used pan-Arab language and symbols further led the public to believe that the chariot of pan-Arabism was moving fast. The more so during the years of the Second World War when the requirements of the war drove Britain to occupy Syria and the Lebanon and to bring about the elimination of the French from that area.

But Britain was far from being committed to pan-Arabism or to any scheme of Arab unity. Faysal's and Nuri al-Sa'id's schemes of unity were rejected by Britain as impractical. Furthermore, they knew too well that the French would not welcome them in Syria and that the French might interpret this or other Hashemite schemes of unity as disguised British endeavours to oust them and to take their place. Therefore the British tried very hard not to give offence to French susceptibilities.

The British had even more sensitivity regarding the Saudi rock-solid opposition to any scheme of Arab unity which might enhance the position of the Hashemites. The guiding British principle was to avoid a situation in which they would have to choose between those two opposing Arab dynasties. Consequently the safeguarding of the *status quo* in the Arab world became a paramount British interest.

'Abdallah's scheme was totally rejected by Britain and his low popularity in Syria accounted for much of the British reaction. It is true that the unity of Greater Syria was regarded by many British officials as a natural development dictated by history, geographical conditions and economic necessities, but that view did not mean support for 'Abdallah's claim to the Syrian throne. On the contrary, there were moments when favourable British approaches to Greater Syria unity and to the elimination of the French from there raised doubts in London about the advisability of keeping 'Abdallah – 'a dreadful nuisance' – in power even in his smaller Emirate of Trans-Jordan. Only the conviction of the Colonial Office that 'Abdallah had faithfully served the British interests and that he had a just claim to British gratitude nipped in the bud any scheme ruling out the continuation of 'Abdallah's rule.

Attempts at Arab unity devoid of any Hashemite component could in theory at least fare better in British eyes. But Ibn Saud did not like such schemes either, since he suspected a Hashemite hand behind them and he resented any change. Therefore, the Saudi factor brought Britain to keep herself at arm's length from any scheme of Arab unity.

More importantly, even without the Saudi factor, all British official analysts who in the 1930s and early 1940s dwelt on the question of the British attitude towards Arab unity reached negative conclusions. They did not see its practicability for geographical, social and economic reasons. They did not believe that British strategic interests – oil and communications – would be better served if a framework of Arab unity were formed. Even more, they feared that a greater Arab state might endanger British interests. So long as the Palestine question was not solved in a satisfactory way to the Arabs and Arab resentment of British policy in Palestine continued unabated, any move towards greater Arab unity was regarded by the British Government as dangerous. Therefore the British saw to it that the bilateral treaties among various Arab countries did not include any provisions of a practical nature in respect of inter-Arab unity.

On the other hand, Britain made up its mind not to oppose Arab unity *publicly* and to let the Arabs know through proper diplomatic channels that any scheme of Arab unity which the Arabs themselves initiated and which enjoyed the support of all Arab countries would gain British support.

The developments in Palestine since 1936 drove Britain to modify that approach somewhat. First of all, the Foreign Office under Anthony Eden was inclined to believe that the Palestine question should be dealt with as part of the Middle East as a whole and Malcolm MacDonald in 1938 was convinced that pan-Arabism was a real force and that Britain should both encourage and guide it. Thus the panacea for the solution of the Palestine problem would be available. But the failure of the 1939 St James's Conference and of the White Paper to get Arab consent dealt a mortal blow to that belief and nothing remained of it inside the Colonial Office. Furthermore, with Halifax at the helm since early 1938, the Foreign Office too returned to the traditional British distrust of pan-Arabism.

However, during 1940 and early 1941 when the British position in the Middle East became very precarious, the British Ambassadors in Cairo and Baghdad exerted very strong pressure on the Foreign Office to meet Arab demands concerning Palestine and unity. At first that pressure was repelled, but in December 1940 Eden returned to the Foreign Office and a change could be detected. In January 1941 the Foreign Office informed the Colonial Office that 'the Foreign Office have recently been giving some thought to the desirability of making some declaration on policy covering the Middle East'.

Clement Attlee, the Labour Leader and a Cabinet member, reached a more far-reaching conclusion. In a discussion in the Cabinet Defence Committee in early May 1941 he suggested that in order to win over the Arabs of Syria to the British side Britain should declare its support for Arab federation. Lord Moyne, the Colonial Secretary, suggested a less far-reaching proposal: only to declare *publicly* that Britain did not object to the formation of Arab federation. But Churchill rejected both

CONCLUSIONS

proposals and carried the committee with him in support of a military invasion of Vichy-controlled Syria. But then came Churchill's Note of 19 May 1941 in which he put forward his revolutionary proposal to make Palestine a Jewish state and to include her in an 'Arab Caliphate of Islam' under the overlordship of Ibn Saud, thus adopting the Philby plan. Eden and his office objected to it vehemently. They prepared a Memorandum for circulation to the Cabinet, but without prior discussion and approval by the Cabinet Eden made public the content of that Memorandum in his famous Mansion House speech of 29 May. In that speech Eden repeated Moyne's proposal which had been made several weeks earlier in the Defence Committee and had been rejected by Churchill and by the Committee. It seems to us that Eden decided to present a *fait accompli* to his colleagues fearing that otherwise he would not achieve their endorsement. Only thus did Eden secure Cabinet approval of his Memorandum the first aim of which was to nip Churchill's pro-Zionist scheme in the bud and to give some satisfaction to Arab feelings. The speech did not herald any new British approach to Arab unity and in the months and years that followed British policy in that respect was formulated and carried out as in the past.

The Arabs were not much impressed by Eden's Mansion House speech. But when Eden had to repeat its content in Parliament in February 1943 as a reply to a Parliamentary question, the Arabs were much more impressed. The change of British military fortunes fully accounted for that change. Nahhas had been driven into a corner by his internal enemies, and he regarded Eden's declaration and Nuri al-Sa'id's invitation as a golden opportunity to regain his popularity at home and to thwart Nuri al-Sa'id's endeavour.

In doing that Nahhas had apparently been encouraged by Richard Casey who had a more favourable attitude towards Arab unity (and a much more hostile attitude to the continuation of the French rule in Syria) than the government in London. It seems that Casey was fully aware of the precarious position in which Nahhas found himself as a result of the combined attack of the King and the Opposition and wanted to secure his position, as the best Prime Minister that Britain could have in wartime Egypt.

Thus Nahhas initiated the inter-Arab consultations during much of 1943 which brought about the convocation of the Preparatory Committee in September 1944 and the formation of the Arab League in March 1945. During those consultations and discussions it became apparent that the Hashemites were interested only in their schemes of unity. And when they realised that those schemes did not stand any chance of success, they adopted a very reserved attitude to any proposal to give real authority to the future Arab League. Lebanon was ready to join the process only after its independence had been recognised. In order not to make Lebanon nervous about its independence the Charter of the Arab League was further diluted and the new body was a far cry from even a loose confederation.

Ibn Saud was reluctant to join the process and tried his best to prevent its taking place. Only under British pressure did he finally agree to send his delegate and to sign the Protocol of the Preparatory Committee and the Charter of the League.

The Egyptians were only too happy that their aim was advanced by others. They tried during the discussions to keep all options open but at the end all those who agreed to the formation of the Arab League joined only if it did not infringe any of their sovereign rights. Only the Syrians demanded the formation of a framework of real unity and even they made their proposals knowing that the others had completely different views.

Consequently the League did not herald a new era of unity. Rather, it exhibited a common Arab front concerning the Palestine question and the French insistence on retaining their positions in Syria and the Lebanon.

Casey and his subordinates in the Middle East supported the formation of the League as well as other schemes of Arab unity. Therefore they tried their best to eliminate the French from Syria in order to facilitate the gradual formation of one form or another of Arab federation. However, the British Government in London had different views. They resolved to impede the process of inter-Arab consultations and discussions and eventual Arab unity at least until after the war was over. One of their main reasons for adopting such a reserved and cautious position was their fear that any Arab gathering would be used to exert pressure on Britain to implement *in toto* the 1939 White Paper on Palestine, to adopt an anti-French position regarding Syria and to promise independence to the North African countries. Unlike Casey, Spears and Co., the London government realised that France would emerge after the war as a major European power and they believed that maintaining good relations with France very much outweighed any benefit that Britain might gain from adopting a pro-Arab and anti-French position in Syria. Furthermore, the Foreign Office in London well understood that the elimination of the French from Syria would become a precedent which would be detrimental to the British position in Iraq. As soon as France was being liberated that consideration prevailed and in December 1944 Spears was sacked from his position in Syria.

But meanwhile the inter-Arab consultations brought about the decision to convoke the Preparatory Committee. Only then did the Foreign Office instruct their representatives not to try any more to bring about the postponement of that convocation but rather to try to influence the participants to avoid any declaration or resolution which might be embarrassing to Britain. Since the Arabs at that time badly needed the

CONCLUSIONS

goodwill of the British on Syria, they to a large extent complied with the British requests and passed a rather moderate resolution concerning Palestine.

On the other hand, it is undeniable that, when Britain realised that the Arab League was going to be formed after all, it wanted its loyal friend Ibn Saud to participate in its formation; and that Casey and his subordinates encouraged Nahhas to begin his initiative, regarded the Greater Syria unity scheme (although without 'Abdallah!) favourably and expressed their consent to the scheme of Fertile Crescent unity (although, again, dissociating themselves from 'Abd al-Illah's possible accession to the Syrian throne!). These were the facts which, for years, left the impression that Britain had initiated those schemes and had been behind the process which culminated in the formation of the Arab League.

NOTES

TO CHAPTER 1

1 'Note on the present Orientation of Pan-Arab Policy in Iraq', Enclosure in Bagdad Despatch, no. 410, 29.8.38, E 5393/45/93, FO 371/21847.
2 'Ali Jawdat, *Dhikriyyat, 1900–1958* (Beirut, 1967), pp. 221–2.
3 Sati 'al-Husri, *Mudhakkirati fi al-'Iraq, Vol. I, 1921–1941* (Beirut, 1967), pp. 585–90.
4 Sir Francis Humphrys [British Ambassador to Iraq] to Sir John Simon [British Foreign Secretary], No. 1164, 21.12.32, E 6888/4478/65, FO 371/16011.
5 Tawfiq al-Suwaydi, *Mudhakkirati* (Beirut, 1969), pp. 152–5.
6 'Abd al-'Aziz al-Qassab, *Min Dhikriyyati* (Beirut, 1962), pp. 252–6.
7 Al-Suwaydi, pp. 179–80. See also al-Husri, I, pp. 504ff. On the various sects see al-Qassab, pp. 273–4. Humphrys to Simon, no. 1164, 21.12.32, E 6888/4478/65, FO 371/16011.
8 Taha al-Hashimi, *Mudhakkirat, II, 1942–1955* (Beirut, 1978), pp. 278 and 296.
9 Al-Suwaydi, p. 180.
10 Taha al-Hashimi, II, pp. 278 and 296–7. 'Record of Conversation between King Feisal and Sir John Simon at the Hyde Park Hotel on June 22nd, 1933', E 3728/347/65, FO 371/16855.
11 Extract from 'Record of Conversation between King Feisal and Sir John Simon at the Hyde Park Hotel on June 22nd, 1933', E 3728/347/65, FO 371/16855. Procès-Verbal de la cinquième Séance tenue le jeudi 5 août 1943, E 5376/506/65, FO 371/34961.
12 Nuri al-Sa'id's words to Moshé Shertok, Head of the Political Department of the JA, as quoted by the latter in his report to the JA Executive, 23.8.43, ZA, Executive Protocols.
13 'Note of Conversation between Sir F. Humphrys and King Faysal at the Hyde Park Hotel on the 13th July, 1933', E 6221/347/65, FO 371/16855.
14 Note on a conversation with General Haddad, 21.4.21, E/4708/482/89, FO 371/6458.
15 Z. N. Zeine, *The Struggle for Arab Independence* (Beirut, 1960), pp. 119–27. For a fuller treatment based for the first time on French official archival documents see Dan Eldar, *French Policy in the Levant and its Attitude Towards Arab Nationalism and Zionism, 1914–1920* (in Hebrew; unpublished PhD dissertation, Tel Aviv Univesity, 1978), pp. 392–409; and Jan Karl Tanenbaum, 'France and the Arab Middle East, 1914–1920', *Transactions of American Philosophical Society*, Vol. 68, Part 7 (1978), pp. 36–7.
16 HC for Iraq to Colonial Secretary (copy), 26.2.24, E 1843/218/89, FO 371/10160.
17 French archives are silent as far as this and many other similar talks are concerned. But bearing in mind that many French official files were destroyed during the transfer of French Government to Bordeaux in June 1940 such a paucity of evidence does not explain much.
18 Dobbs, HC for Iraq, to Colonial Secretary (copy), no. 609, 18.11.25, FO 371/10852; minutes, 7.1.26, E 8131/357/89, FO 371/10852; A. C. C. C. Parkinson [of the CO] to G. Rendel [of the FO], no. 89059/31, 3.11.31, E 5485/206/89, FO 371/15364.
19 HC to Colonial Secretary (copy), 29.2.26, FO 371/10160. See also Ali Mahafzak, 'La France et le mouvement nationaliste arabe de 1914 à 1950', *Relations Internationales*, no. 19, automne 1979, p. 307.
20 'The Throne of Syria', Annex no. 21 in Dhuqan Qarqut, *Tatawwur al-Harakah al-Wataniyyah fi Suriyah, 1920–1939* (Beirut, 1975), pp. 293–6.
21 M.E.(M)9, 9.11.31, CAB 51/1.
22 Qarqut, n. 108, quoting a French report.
23 Qarqut, p. 108 (and note 33) and 110.

NOTES

24 C.H.F. Cox, British Resident in Amman, to HC for TJ (copy), No. 2465, Secret, 22.1.31, E 925/206/89, FO 371/15364. See also I. Rabinovitch, 'The Syrian Monarchy', *Zemanim*, no. 3, p. 98.
25 Sir F. Humphrys's Memorandum, 10.9.31, ME(O) 26, CAB 51/5. For the historical background of the hostility of the Istiqlalist faction of Syrian nationalists towards the Hashemites, see Philip S. Khouri, 'Factionalism Among Syrian Nationalists During the French Mandate', *IJMES*, Vol. 13 (1981), pp. 441–69.
26 P.W. Ireland, *Iraq* (London, 1937), pp. 412–4.
27 As reported in E 4971, FO 371/14508.
28 See his report in E 3087, FO 371/14506.
29 Taha al-Hashimi, *Mudhakkirat, Vol. I, 1919–1943* (Beirt, 1967), p. 259.
30 See Y. Porath, *The Emergence of the Palestinian-Arab National Movement, 1918–1929* (Frank Cass, London, 1974), ch. 7, and M.E. Lundsten, 'Wall Politics: Zionist and Palestinian strategies in Jerusalem, 1928', *Journal of Palestine Studies*, Vol. VIII, no. 1 (Autumn 1978).
31 Faysal to H. Young, Acting HC, 8.12.29, enclosed with Humphrys to Lord Passfield, Colonial Secretary (copy), Conf. A 16.12.29, E 444/44/65, FO 371/14485. See also Enclosure with Bateman [of the British Embassy in Baghdad] to A. Eden, Foreign Secretary, no. 422, 31.8.36, E 5484/94/31, FO 371/20024.
32 Passfield to Humphrys (copy), Conf. A, 22.1.30, E 444/44/65 and FO officials' minutes, FO 371/14485.
33 G.W. Rendel [Head of the Eastern Department of the FO] to Sir H. Young [British Ambassador in Baghdad], No. 586, Secret, 3.11.32, E 5752/4478/65, FO 371/16011.
34 C.H.F. Cox, British Resident, to HC for Palesstine (copy), no. 151/sec., 3.12.30, E 342/342/65, FO 371/15281. Faysal believed in the fragility of the Ibn Saud's kingdom up to the end of his (the former's) life. See Rendel to Young, No. 586, Secret, 3.11.32, E 5752/4478/65, FO 371/16011.
35 On shaping British policy in respect of this question see pp. 197–202.
36 E 2380/250/65, FO 371/15281. The 250/65 group of sub-files in this volume is dedicated to the negotiations, British position, etc. See also E 42/2/25, FO 371/15285.
37 HC in Egypt to A. Henderson, Foreign Secretary, no. 211, Secret, 27.2.31, E 1205/1205/65, FO 371/15282. One wonders whether the name al-Hakimi is a misspelling of al-Hashimi.
38 *Al-'Iraq*, 16.2.31. A cutting is to be found in E 1117/2/25, FO 371/15285.
39 Longrigg, *Syria and Lebanon under French Mandate* (London, 1958), pp. 183–7.
40 Khaldun S. Husry, 'King Faysal I and Arab Unity, 1930–33', *Journal of Contemporary History*, Vol. 10 (1975), p. 325.
41 Humphrys to Passfield (printed for circulation for Cabinet Members), Secret E, 1.5.31, E 2627/294/89, FO 371/15364.
42 Khaldun Husry, 'King Faysal ...', p. 326.
43 M.E.(M)9, 9.11.31, CAB, 51/1.
44 Humphrys to Passfield (copy), Very Secret, 30.1.31, E 851/206/89, FO 371/15364. Cox to HC for Palestine (copy), 3.12.30, E 942/342/65, FO 371/15281.
45 Memorandum by Sir F. Humphrys, 10.9.31, ME(O) 26, CAB 51/5.
46 FO to Sir G. Clark (British Ambassador to Turkey), Teleg. no. 50, 4.11.31, E 5483/206/89, FO 371/15364. Humphrys to Sir P. Cunliffe-Lister [Colonial Secretary] (copy), Secret C, 3.12.31, E 406/226/89, FO 371/16086.
47 E.C. Hole [British Consul in Damascus] to Foreign Secretary, no. 66, Conf., 29.6.31, E 3916/206/89, FO 371/15364.
48 See Ihsan al-Jabiri's testimony as reported in Qarqut, p. 233, note 29.
49 ME(O), 11th meeting, 20.10.21, CAB 51/2. FO to Sir G. Clark, teleg. no. 50, 4.11.31, E 5483/206/89, FO 371/15364.
50 *Al-Muqattam*, 2 and 6 October, 1931, as quoted by Qarqut, pp. 110–111.
51 See Longrigg, pp. 190–2.
52 Humphrys to Simon, No. 17, Secret, 5.1.33, E 347/347/65, FO 371/16854.
53 *Al-Ikha' al-Watani*, 14.7.32, as quoted by Khaldun Husry, p. 327.
54 H. Satow [British Consul in Beirut] to FO, No. 54, 27.5.33, E 2965/2689/89, FO 371/16976; Frank H. Todd [British Consul in Damascus] to FO, No. 35, 7.6.33, E 3195/2689/89, *ibid*.

55 Jalal al-Urfahli, *Al Diblumasiyyah al-'Iraqiyyah wa-al-Ittihad al-'Arabi* (Baghdad, 1944), p. 215.
56 Humphrys to Simon, No. 17, Secret, 5.1.33, E 347/347/65, FO 371/16854.
57 Rendel to Humphrys, Secret and Personal, 16.11.32, E 5988/226/89, FO 371/16086.
58 Khaldun Husry, p. 338.
59 Rendel to Young, No. 586, Secret, 2.11.32, E 5752/4478/65, FO 371/16011.
60 King Feisal and Dr Weizmann: Memo by J. Hathorn Hall, 26.6.33, E 3452/3289/31, FO 371/16931; Suggested Meeting Between King Feisal and Dr Weizmann: Memo by G. W. Rendel, 19.6.33, E 3974/3289/31, *ibid.*
61 Extract from record of conversation between King Feisal and Sir John Simon at the Hyde Park Hotel on 22 June 1933, E 3728/347/65, FO 371/16855; Note of Conversation between Sir F. Humphrys and King Feisal at Hyde Park Hotel on 13 July 1933, enclosed with Humphrys to Sterndale-Bennett, 5.10.33, E 6221/347/65, *ibid.*
62 M. A. Young, Officer Administering the Government of Palestine, to CO, Secret B, 30.5.31, CO 733/204/87156/1.
63 For details see Y. Porath, *The Palestinian Arab National Movement, Vol. II, 1929–1939: From Riots to Rebellion* (Frank Cass, London, 1977), pp. 9–13.
64 Report by T[aysir] D[awjah], 4.2.32, ZA, A/113, 23/A. The Executive Committee's circular, 26.2.32, ISA, Division 66, 'Awni 'Abd al-Hadi's Papers, 165(28). Memorandum on the proposed Arab Congress, 30.12.32, enclosed with Sir Percy Loraine [British HC for Egypt] to Sir Lancelot Oliphant [of FO], Secret, 20.1.33, E 955/347/65, FO 371/16854, 'Izzat Darwaza, *Hawla al-Harakah al-'Arabiyya al-Hadithah*, III, (Sidon, 1950), pp. 83–4 and Annex no. 5, pp. 301–3.
65 'News by Gad [Taysir Dawjah]', 4.5.32, ZA, S/25, 4122.
66 Humphrys to Simon, no. 85, Conf., 2.2.33, E 863/347/65, FO 371/16854; Loraine to Oliphant, Secret, 20.1.33, E 955/347/65, *ibid.* For the reason of that split, see Marius Deeb, *Party Politics in Egypt: The Wafd & its Rivals, 1919–1939* (London, 1979), p. 247.
67 A. H. Cohen's report, 15.2.32, ZA, A/113, 23/A. A Talk with T[aysir] D[awjah], 28.2.32, ZA, S/25, 4122. *Al-Jami'ah al-'Arabiyyah*, 12.6.32.
68 News by Gad, 29.6.32, ZA, S/25, 4122.
69 Appreciation Summary no. 37/32 for week ending 17 September 1932, E 5584/226/89, FO 371/16086. Memorandum enclosed with Loraine to Oliphant, Secret, 20.1.33, E 955/347/65, FO 371/16854. See also Darwaza, *Hawla al-Harakah*, III, p. 83.
70 Darwaza, *Hawla al-Harakah*, III, p. 84. Qarqut, p. 110. Loraine to FO (copy), 24.12.32, enclosed with FO to CO, 12.1.33, CO 732/58/18136.
71 Appreciation Summary for week ending 17 September 1932, E 5584/226/89, FO 371/16086. Humphrys to Simon, No. 17, Secret, 5.1.33, E 347/347/65, FO 371/16854; Memorandum, 30.12.32, enclosed with Loraine to Oliphant, Secret, 20.1.33, *ibid.* See also the favourable, although rather vague, reaction of the Palestinian nationalist newspaper *al-Jami'ah al-'Arabiyyah*, 22.9.32.
72 Qarqut, p. 110.
73 Memorandum, 30.12.32, enclosed with Loraine to Oliphant, Secret, 20.1.33, E 935/347/65, FO 371/16854. Gad's News, 14.11.32, ZA, S/25, 4122. *Al-Karmil*, 14.1.33. *Al-Jami'ah al-'Arabiyyah*, 22.9.32.
74 C. G. Hope Gill [of the British Legation in Jedda] to FO (quoting an interview given by the King to *Sawt al-Hijaz*, 12.9.32), No. 399, 23.9.32, E 5267, 2814/25, FO 371/16027.
75 Memorandum, 30.12.32, enclosed with Loraine to Oliphant, Secret, 20.1.33, E 955/347/65, FO 371/16854. Periodical Appreciation Summary no. 7/33, 28.2.33, E 1485/111/31, FO 371/16926.
76 Periodical Appreciation Summary no. 6/33, 18.2.33, E 369/111/31, FO 371/16926.
77 Humphrys to Simon, no. 85, 2.2.33, E 863/347/65, FO 371/16854.
78 Darwaza, *Hawla al-Harakah*, III, pp. 84–85. Humphrys to FO, Teleg. no. 30, 25.2.33, E 1091/347/65, FO 371/16854.
79 Darwaza, *Hawla al-Harakah*, III, p. 85. Periodical Appreciation Summary no. 2/34, 15.1.34, E 897/271/31, FO 371/17878. Same of 10.1.35, no. 1/35, E 820/154/31, FO 371/18957. Same of 27.2.35, no. 6/35, E 1839/154/31, *ibid.*
80 Humphrys to Passfield (copy), Very Secret, 30.1.31, E 851/206/89, FO 371/15364.

NOTES

81 H. W. Young, Acting HC, to Colonial Secretary, 11.9.31, included in ME(O) 25, CAB 51/5. Humphrys to Simon, No. 17, Secret, 5.1.33, E 347/347/65, FO 371/16854.
82 Satow to HC for Iraq (copy), No. 1 (81/10/31), 13.1.31, E 657/206/89, FO 371/15364; HC for Iraq to Colonial Secretary (copy), teleg. no. 20, 10.1.31, E 206/206/89, *ibid.*; Humphrys to Passfield (copy), Very Secret, 30.1.31, E 851/206/89, *ibid.*
83 Al-Suwaydi, pp. 212–14.
84 HC for Iraq to Colonial Secretary (copy), Very Secret Teleg., 10.1.31, E 206/206/89, FO 371/15364; Satow to HC for Iraq (copy), no. 1, 13.1.31, E 6575/206/89, *ibid.* Rendel to Humphrys, 16.11.32, E 5988/226/89, FO 371/16086. Humphry's Memorandum, 10.9.31, ME(O)26, CAB 51/5. Taha al-Hashimi, II, pp. 89–90 (speaking of 'Adil Arslan).
85 P. Cunliffe-Lister [Colonial Secretary] to Sir A. G. Wauchope [HC for Palestine and TJ] (copy), Secret, 19.2.32, E 514/296/89, FO 371/16086. See also the minutes by P. J. Dixon (of the FO), 3.11.31, E 5443/206/89, FO 371/15364.
86 Humphrys to Simon, No. 17, Secret, 5.1.33, E 347/347/65, FO 371/16854.
87 Taha al-Hashimi, II, p. 90.
88 Wauchope to Cunliffe-Lister (copy), Secret, TC 75/32, 24.9.32, E 5762/375/31, FO 371/16056. On the *Istiqlal* see Porath, *From Riots ...*, pp. 123–7.
89 Humphrys to Wauchope (copy), Personal, 7.3.33, E 2009/347/65, FO 371/16854; same to same, 22.3.33, *ibid., ibid.* For the Ghawr al-Kabd land lease deal see Porath, *From Riots ...*, pp. 72–4.
90 Press extract, 23.3.32, E 2070/226/89, FO 371/16086. Qarqut, p. 109.
91 Taha al-Hashimi, I, p. 358.
92 Qarqut, p. 113. This faction included Shukri al-Quwatli, who was to become the most important Nationalist leader in Syria.
93 Shakib Arslan to Ibn Sa'ud, Ramadan 1349 (1931), as quoted by Khaldun Husry, p. 328.
94 G. W. Rendel, 'Attitude of His Majesty's Government Towards the Questionn of Arab Unity', 27.3.33, E 1732/347/65, FO 371/16854.
95 Intelligence report by Flight Lieutenant L. F. Pendred of the Air Staff in Palestine, 22.10.32, E 6355/76/25, FO 371/16017.
96 Telegram of 13.7.32, E 3531/76/25, FO 371/16015.
97 Sir G. Clark to FO, Conf. Teleg. No. 65, 3.11.31, E 5485/206/89, FO 371/15364.
98 Loraine to FO, Conf. Teleg. No. 8, 29.11.31, E 6079/206/89, FO 371/15364; same to same. Most Conf. Teleg. no. 23, E 6413/206/89, *ibid.* Same to same, Conf. Teleg. No. 11, 28.1.32, E 460/226/89, FO 371/16086. Sir M. Lampson [British Ambassador in Cairo] to FO, Teleg. No. 119, 1.3.38, E 1182/47/89, FO 371/21913.
99 James Morgan [of the British Embassy in Angora] to Simon, No. 433, 23.12.31, E 6376/206/89, FO 371/15364. Clark to Simon, No. 13, 6.1.32, E 226/226/89, FO 371/16086.
100 Clark to Simon, No. 42, 15.1.32, E 439/226/89, FO 371/16086; Loraine to Simon, Conf. No. 74, 20.1.32, E 514/226/89, *ibid.*; on the coordination of activities between 'Abbas Hilmi and the Turkish Government, see Loraine to Simon (and enclosure), Conf., No. 225, 5.3.32, E 1336/226/89, *ibid.*
101 Loraine to Simon, Conf. 16.3.34, E 1928/95/89, FO 371/17944.
102 Humphrys to Simon, No. 683, 26.10.33, E 6747/5250/93, FO 371/16924.
103 Humphrys to FO, Teleg. No. 384, 22.9.33, E 5635/2689/89, FO 371/16976.
104 British Consul in Damascus to FO, Teleg. No. 69, 28.12.33, E 339/95/89, FO 371/17944.
104a On this conflict see C. Ernest C. Dawn, *From Ottomanism to Arabism* (Urbana, 1973), pp. 4–5.
105 Humphrys to Rendel, 14.12.33, E 7939/2689/89, FO 371/16976; Tyrrell to Simon, No. 1782, 28.12.33, E 8021/2689/89, *ibid.* Humphrys to Satow (copy), 1.1.34, E 374/95/89, FO 371/17944; see also the files of group 95/89 in *ibid.*
106 Archibald Clark-Kerr [British Ambassador in Baghdad] to Samuel Hoare [British Foreign Secretary], No. 319, 11.6.35, E 3891/150/89, FO 371/19021. Houstoun-Boswall [of British Embassy in Baghdad] to C. W. Baxter, 31.5.39, E 4099/284/65, FO 371/23194.
107 Humphrys to FO, Teleg. No. 384, 22.9.33, E 5635/2689/89, FO 371/16976. Same to same, No. 683, 26.10.33, E 6747/5250/93, FO 371/16924.
108 Munib al-Madi & Sulayman Musa, *Ta'rikh al-Urdunn Fi al-Qarn al-'Ishrin* ('Amman, 1959), pp. 132–6.
109 A. S. Klieman, *Foundation of British Policy in the Arab World. The Cairo Conference*

of 1921 (Baltimore, 1970), pp. 74–5, 105–138. Sulayman Musa, *Al-Harakah al-'Arabiyyah; al-Marhalah al-Ula lil-Nahdah al-'Arabiyyah al-Hadithah, 1908–1924* (Beirut, 1977), pp. 596–599.

110 'Report on Middle East Conference Held in Cairo and Jerusalem (secret), March 12 to 30, 1921', p. 8, FO 371/6343.
111 'Abdallah Ibn Husayn, *Mudhakkirati* (Jerusalem, 1945), pp. 179–82. It should be remembered that 'Abdallah's Memoirs were published in 1945, many years after the recorded conversation had taken place. It is clear that Sulayman Musa himself does not believe 'Abdallah's claim. His first book, *Ta'rikh al-Urdunn*, which he co-authored with Munib al-Madi and which accepts 'Abdallah's claim (see p. 147) is a kind of an official history. But in his scholarly book, *al-Harakah al-'Arabiyyah*, he fully accepts the British version (see p. 598).
112 For a thorough treatment of this subject see I Gershuni, 'The Arab Nation, The House of Hashim and Greater Syria in the Writings of 'Abdallah' (in Hebrew), *Hamizrah Hehadash*, Vol. XXV (1975), pp. 1–26 and 161–83. Except when a specific source is quoted, this paragraph is based on this article.
113 'Abdallah to Kamil al-Qassab (copy), 7th Jumada al-Ula, 1358 (26.6.39), enclosed with A. S. Kirkbride [British Resident in Amman] to HC for TJ, 19.9.39, in Sir H. MacMichael to Malcolm MacDonald (copy), 29.9.39, E 7102/6697/89, FO 371/23281.
114 'Abdallah to the HC (copy), 18.5.43, enclosed with CO to FO, 77241/43, 16.8.43, E 4861/506/65, FO 371/34960.
115 Al-Husri, *Mudhakkirati*, pp. 24–5.
116 D. Ben-Gurion, *Meetings With Arab Leaders* (in Hebrew; Tel-Aviv, 1967), pp. 54–5.
117 A. S. Kirkbride to J. Hathorn Hall, Acting HC for TJ (copy) No. 210/7/Sec. 20.9.33, enclosed with A/HC for TJ to Colonial Secretary (copy), No. TC 103/33, Secret, 6.10.33, E 6608/347/65, FO 371/16855. Humphrys to Simon [with enclosure] No. 609, 21.9.33, E 5852/5250/93, FO 371/16924.
118 C. H. F. Cox, British Resident in Amman, 'Report on the Political Situation for the month of October 1933' (copy), Secret, 1.11.33, E 7188/169/31, FO 371/16927.
119 See Longrigg, pp. 215–18.
120 British Resident in 'Amman to Wauchope (copy), No. 43/Sec, 26.3.36, enclosed with Wauchope to CO (copy), Secret, TC/33/36, FO 371/20065 (p. 221).
121 A. C. Kerr to FO, Teleg. No. 37 (and minutes), 22.2.37, E 1140/1140/65, FO 371/20787; same to Rendel, 23.3.37, E 2154/140/65, *ibid*; same to Anthony Eden [Foreign Secretary], No. 149, 14.4.37, E 2307/1140/65, *ibid*; W. Ormsby-Gore [Colonial Secretary] to Wauchope (copy), 7.7.37, E 3009/1140/65, *ibid*.; see also E 4670 and E 4977 at that volume.
122 Longrigg, pp. 232–7. Al-Suwaydi, p. 286.
123 See Porath, *Palestinian-Arab National Movement 1929–1939*, pp. 220–32 and 278–9.
124 'Abdallah's Memorandum is enclosed with Sir H. MacMichael [HC for Palestine and Trans-Jordan] to MacDonald (copy), Secret A, 11.6.38, E 3866/38/31, FO 371/21885.
125 A. C. Trott [the British *chargé d'affaires* in Jedda] to Viscount Halifax [British Foreign Secretary], No. 133, 22.8.39, E 6447/549/25, FO 371/23271; Fu'ad Hamzah, Sa'udi Foreign Secretary, to Trott, 4.5.39, enclosed with Trott to Halifax, No. 138, 6.9.39, E 6627/549/25, *ibid*.; and other files in this volume. See also Kirkbride to HC for TJ, Secret no. 332, 19.9.39, enclosed with Harold MacMichael to Malcolm MacDonald (copy), No. TC/58/39, 20.9.39, E 7102/6697/89, FO 371/23281.
126 On this opposition and the Sa'udi pressure on Britain to avoid from any support to 'Abdallah in this respect see, for example, Trott to Halifax (and enclosures), No. 122, 18.7.39, E 5392/246/25, FO 371/23269.
127 Sir R. Bullard [British Minister in Jedda] to Halifax, No. 154, 29.10.39, E 7604/549/25, FO 371/23271.
128 Trott to Halifax (and enclosures), No. 122, 18.7.39, E 5392/246/25, FO 371/23269.
129 Bullard to FO, Teleg. No. 5, 15.4.39, E 2803/5/89, FO 371/23276.
130 FO to Bullard, Teleg. no. 99, 23.6.39, E 4246/1809/25, FO 371/23273; Sir Basil Newton [British Ambassador in Baghdad] to FO, Teleg. no. 225, 18.6.39, E 4423/1809/25, *ibid*.; Bullard to Baxter [of the FO] No. 1304/483/14, 27.6.39, E 4584/1809/25, *ibid*.
131 E. Sasson to M. Shertok [Head of the Political Department of the JA] (according to conversations by the former with Nasib al-Bakri), 15.5.39 and 30.6.39, ZA, S/25, 9900.

NOTES

132 *Al-Ahram*, 15.8.39. See also later on, pp. 44 ff.
133 G. Mackereth [British Consul in Damascus] to FO, Teleg. no. 47, 30.12.38, E 18/5/89, FO 371/23276; same to same, Teleg. no. 5, 9.1.39, E 260/5/89, *ibid.*; Cox to HC for TJ, No. 380/Sec. 7.1.39, enclosed with HC to Colonial Secretary (copy), Secret, 14.1.39, E 811/5/89, *ibid.*
134 See all the correspondence from 1939 in E 5653/2143/89, FO 371/23280.
135 Lampson to FO, Teleg. no. 1003, 29.8.40, E 2553/103/89, FO 371/24591.
136 Edward Spears, *Fulfilment of a Mission* (London, 1977), p. 140 and General Catroux, *Dans la Bataille de la Méditerranée* (Paris, 1949), p. 174. These two famous opponents are in complete accord over this point!
137 A. L. Kirkbride to MacMichael, 10.6.39, enclosed with MacMichael to Sir John Shuckburgh [Deputy Under-Secretary, Colonial Office] (copy), Secret, 14.6.39, E 4826/2143/89, FO 371/23280; and 'Ali Mahafzah, 'La France ...', p. 309.
138 Col. G. S. of the ME Intelligence Centre, 'A Record of a Conversation with Shahbandar', 30.1.40, F 599/599/65, FO 371/24548. E. Sasson, *On the Way to Peace* (in Hebrew; Tel-Aviv, 1978), pp. 187–8.
139 B. Newton [British Ambassador in Baghdad] to FO, Teleg. No. 375, 19.6.40, E 2027/953/65, FO 371/24548.
140 *Al-Ahram*, 16.8.39. On This Party and the Connections with 'Abdallah, see Porath, *From Riots to Rebellion*, pp. 62–75.
141 See MacMichael to Sir Cosmo Parkinson [Permanent Under-Secretary of the CO] (copy), Secret, 5.7.39, E 5308/2143/89, FO 371/23280.
142 E. Sasson, *On the Way to Peace*, pp. 187–8.
143 Protocols of JA Executive, 19.6.40, ZA.
144 MacMichael to Parkinson (copy), Secret, 5.7.39, E 5308/2143/89, FO 371/23280. Protocols of JA Executive, 21.6.40 (Shertok's words), ZA.
145 Moshé Sharett [Shertok], *Political Diaries, Vol. V, 1940–1942* (in Hebrew; Tel-Aviv, 1979), p. 55–6.
146 Sasson, pp. 227–8.
147 Protocols of JA Executive, 22.11.42, ZA.
148 Sir B. Newton to Halifax, No. 474, 23.8.39, E 6118/54/93, FO 371/23199. Same to same, No. 612, 20.11.39, E 7218/6697/89, FO 371/23281.
149 HC for TJ to CO (copy), Secret Teleg. No. 63, 11.10.39, E 7102/6697/89, FO 371/23281.
150 For the shaping of British policy see chapter 4.
151 HC TJ to CO (copy), Teleg. No. 51, 1.7.40, ME(O)(40) 24, 3.7.40, CAB 95/1; ME(O)(40) 6th Meeting, 14.7.40, *ibid.*
152 HC to CO, Teleg. No. 822, 9.6.41, E 3026/62/89, FO 371/27295. Kirkbride to HC (copy), Secret No. 390, 10.6.41, E 4225/53/65, FO 371/27044; same to same (copy), 11.6.41, *ibid.*
153 *Al-Ahram*, 17.7.41.
154 HC to CO (copy), Teleg. No. 61, 6.7.41, E 3715/53/65, FO 371/27044. See also *Al-Kitab al-Urdunni al-Abyad: Al-Watha'iq al-Qawmiyyah fi al-Wahdah al-Suriyyah al-Tabi'iyyah* ('Amman, n.d.), pp. 21–35.
155 HC to CO (copy), Secret teleg. No. 53, 17.6.41, E 3225/62/89, FO 371/27296.
156 HC to CO (copy), Secret teleg. No. 75, 23.7.41, E 4251/62/89, FO 371/27303.
157 Longrigg, pp. 322–3.
158 Kirkbride to MacMichael (copy), 19.9.41, E 6781/62/89, FO 371/27313.
159 See Spears, *Fulfilment, passim.*
160 HC for TJ to CO (copy), Most Secret teleg. no. 56, 14.7.42, E 4488/876/31, FO 371/31382; Kirkbride to MacMichael (copy), Secret, 20.7.42, E 4829/876/31, *ibid.*
161 Copies are enclosed with CO to FO, Secret, 23.12.42, E 7578/49/65, FO 371/31338. See also in E 1108/506/65, 4.12.42, FO 371/34955.
162 *Al-Ahram*, 17.1.43.
163 *Al-Aharam*, 3.3.43 and 18.3.43.
164 *Al-Aharam*, 8.4.43.
165 HC for TJ to CO, Secret Teleg. No. 47, 16.4.43, E 2290/506/65, FO 371/34957. A full translation is to be found in E 4861/506/65, FO 371/34960; MacMichael to CO (copy), Secret, 12.6.43, E 4861/506/65, *ibid.*

166 See the relevant documents of November 1943 in E 7083/506/65, FO 371/34963; E 7272/506/65, ibid. And E 1425/95/31, FO 371/40133.
167 Minute by H. M. Eyres [of the FO], 1.8.42, E 4488/876/31, FO 371/31382.
168 HC for TJ to CO (copy), Teleg. No. 40, 22.2.43, E 1749/506/65, FO 371/34956.
169 HC for TJ to CO (copy), Secret Teleg. No. 1138, 8.9.44, E 5580/41/65, FO 371/39990.
170 See in E 2352/3/65, FO 371/45238.
171 Sir Kinahan Cornwallis [British Ambassador to Iraq] to FO, Teleg. No. 303, 11.4.44, E 2244/41/65, FO 371/39987.
172 See the enclosures in CO to FO, 77241/41, 25.7.41, E 4225/53/65, FO 371/27044.
173 HC for TJ to CO (copy), Secret Teleg. No. 8, 21.1.42, E 541/541/31, FO 371/31381. Same to same (copy), Secret Teleg. No. 96, 15.11.43. E 7083/506/65, FO 371/34963 (full text in E 1425/95/31, FO 371/40133). See also in E 2307/95/31, FO 371/40135.
174 See report of 27.12.41. E 1316/49/65, FO 371/31337.
175 Cornwallis to FO, Teleg. No. 58, 19.4.43, E 2291/506/65, FO 371/34957.
176 *Al-Ahram*, 16.3.44.
177 See for 1942 the French exaggerated claims and British replies in FO 371/31465. See also E 2380/762/89 and E 3364/762/89 in FO 371/45611.
178 On this Party see Labib Zuwiyya Yamak, *The Syrian Social Nationalist Party: An Ideological Analysis* (Harvard, 1966).
179 HC for TJ to CO (with enclosures) (copy), Secret, 23.7.42, E 4837/876/31, FO 371/31382.
180 See Longrigg, pp. 328–33.
181 HC for TJ to CO (copy), Secret Teleg. No. 49, 12.9.44, 48(2), 44/117, FO 921/221. Sir E. Spears [British Minister in Beirut] to FO, No. 587, 22.9.44, E 5813/41/65, FO 371/39990.
182 Kirkbride to HC for TJ (copy), Secret Teleg. 19.12.44, 48(2) 44(198), and 44(176), FO 921/222.
183 I. Rabinovich, 'The Compact Minorities and the Syrian State, 1918–1945', *Journal of Contemporary History*, Vol. 14, No. 4 (October, 1979), p. 707.
184 HC for TJ to CO (copy), Secret Teleg, No. 53, 17.6.41, E 3225/62/89, FO 371/27296. Same to Same, Secret Teleg. No. 87, 1.9.41, E 5477/259/31, FO 371/27134.
185 See, for example, a disparaging Egyptian treatment dated August 1944, in E 5581/5581/65, FO 371/40026.
186 Stonehewer Bird [British Minister in Jedda] to FO, Teleg. No. 325, 4.11.41, E 7243/53/65, FO 371/27045. See also same to same, Conf. Teleg. No. 228, 5.7.41, E 3981/62/89, FO 371/27301.
187 Ibn Sa'ud in his third conversation with Col. G. De Gaury, in 14.11.41, E 8551/8551/25, FO 371/27278.
188 Wikeley [of the British Legation in Jedda] to FO, Teleg. No. 121, 21.3.43, E 1686/506/65, FO 371/34956.
189 Kerr to Sir Samuel Hoare [British Foreign Secretary], No. 597, 13.11.35, and minutes, E 6911/6911/31, FO 371/18965.
190 Doris May to Weizmann, 5.6.36, and Henry Rose to same, 6.6.36, WA, Rehovoth.
191 On this Commission see Porath, *Palestinian Arab National Movement 1929–1939*, pp. 220–5.
192 'Arab-Jewish Tension in Palestine: Nuri Pasha's Views' (FO's Note – copy), 11.6.36, CO 733/294/75113/Part II; Kerr to Rendel (copy), 16.6.36, ibid.; Weizmann to Ormsby-Gore, 28.6.36, ibid. D. Ben-Gurion, *Memoirs, III, 1936* (Tel-Aviv, 1973; in Hebrew), pp. 251–2, 293, 310 and 494.
193 HC to Colonial Secretary, Teleg. No. 638, 22.8.36, CO 733/314/75528/44/Part I. For the Arabic text see Darwaza, *Hawla al-Harakah*, III, pp. 135–6.
194 *Filastin*, 27.8.36.
195 Colonial Secretary to HC, Private and Personal Teleg. 2.9.36, CO 733/314/75528/44/Part II. For full details of this episode, see Porath, *Palestinian Arab National Movement 1929–1939*, pp. 207–11.
196 Moshé Sharett, *Political Diaries, 1936* (in Hebrew; Tel-Aviv, 1968), pp. 271–5.
197 Kerr to Rendel (with enclosure), 7.11.36, E 7219/94/31, FO 371/20029.
198 Taha al-Hashimi, II, p. 271.
199 See M. Khadduri, *Independent Iraq* (London, 1960), pp. 85–8.
200 Enclosure with D. V. Kelly [of British Embassy in Cairo] to Eden, No. 1067, 9.9.37,

NOTES

E 5538/22/31, FO 371/20813. Nuri made his memorandum known to Taha al-Hashimi, the Iraqi Chief of Staff from 1930 through Bakr Sidqi's coup d'état in October 1936, and he included the gist of it in his memoirs. (See Taha al-Hashimi, I, p. 225.)

201 H. Hindle James, Squadron Leader, R.A.F. (Retd.) [of the British Embassy in Cairo], 'Interview with General Nuri ...', 8.1.38, enclosed with Lampson to Eden, Secret, No. 37, 13.1.38, E 592/10/31, FO 371/21873.
202 Taha al-Hashimi, I, p. 472. As'ad Daghir, *Mudhakkirati 'ala Hamish al-Qadiyyah al-'Arabiyyah* (Cairo, 1959), p. 204. Bullard to FO, Teleg. No. 16, 11.1.38, E 227/10/31, FO 371/21872.
203 Lampson to FO, Teleg. No. 20, 11.138, E 257/10/31, FO 371/21872.
204 Muwaffaq al-Alusi to Khaldun Sati'al-Husri [the editor of Taha al-Hashimi's Diaries], Taha al-Hashimi, I, p. 472. Bullard to FO, Teleg. No. 28, 23.1.38, and FO to Bullard, Teleg. No. 19, 2.2.38, E 452/10/31, FO 371/21872. G.W. Rendel, 'Palestine: Saudi Enquiries about Nuri Pasha', 4.2.38, E 725/10/31, FO 371/21873.
205 Cox to MacMichael, Personal and Secret, 30.8.38, enclosed with MacMichael to CO (copy), Secret, 2.9.38, E 5677/10/31, FO 371/21881.
206 See Porath, *Palestinian Arab National Movement, 1929–1939*, pp. 277–81.
207 Kerr to Eden, No. 514, 28.12.37, E 175/10/31, FO 371/21872; same to same, No. 515, 28.12.37, E 176/10/31, *ibid.*; Lampson to FO, Teleg. No. 20, 11.1.38, E 257/10/31, *ibid.* H. H. James, 'Interview with General Nuri ...', 8.1.38, enclosed with Lampson to Eden, Secret, No. 37, E 592/10/31, FO 371/21873. 'A Talk with M[uhammad] U[nsi]', 6.9.38, ZA, S/25, 3051.
208 See report of the meeting dated 3 October 1939, ZA, S/25, 9900. One of these delegates was Nasib al-Bakri, President of the Syrian National Bloc in Damascus. He had for a long period maintained close relations with officials of the JA and supplied them with invaluable information about the activities of the Arab nationalists in Damascus. (See ZA, S/25, 3156; see also Porath, *Palestinian Arab National Movement, 1929–1939*, p. 365, note 75.)
209 Houstoun-Boswall to FO, Teleg. No. 99, 31.3.39, E 2402/5/89, FO 371/23276; same to same, Teleg. No. 102, 31.3.39, E 2410/5/89, *ibid.*
210 Bullard to FO, Teleg. No. 38, 20.3.39, E 2049/5/89, FO 371/23276. Taha al-Hashimi, II, p. 71.
211 A. W. Davis [British Consul in Aleppo] to Halifax, No. 20, 16.3.39, E 2225/5/89, FO 371/23276. Al-Suwaydi, *Mudhakkirati*, p. 286. Taha al-Hashimi, *Mudhakkirat* II, pp. 71 and 271.
212 See the alarming cables from Sir R. Bullard, the British Minister to Jedda, 18 and 21 February 1939, CO 733/406/75872/11. See also Houstoun-Boswall (Baghdad Embassy) to FO, 17.4.39, CO 733/410/75872/80 and last to first, 27.4.39, *ibid.*
213 Salah al-Din al-Sabbagh, *Fursan al-'Urubah fi al-'Iraq* (Damascus, 1956), pp. 83–84. Taha al-Hashimi, I, pp. 304–305. See also Khadduri, *Independent Iraq*, pp. 140–41.
214 In the late 1940s Nuri adopted a much more critical approach to 'Abd al-Illah but nevertheless retained his loyalty towards him. (See Taha al-Hashimi, II, pp. 104, 134 and 240.)
215 'Abdallah to the HC, enclosed wtih MacMichael to MacDonald, Secret A, 9.2.39, CO 733/406/75872/4.
216 MacMichael to Parkinson (copy), Secret, 6.4.39, E 3092/5/89, FO 371/23276.
217 Basil Newton [British Ambassador in Baghdad] to Halifax, No. 474, 23.8.39, E 6118/54/93, FO 371/23199.
218 Kirkbride to HC for TJ, Secret, 19.9.39, enclosed with MacMichael to MacDonald (copy), No. TC 58/39, 29.9.39, E 7102/6697/89, FO 371/23281.
219 On Nuri's meddling in Palestine affairs since 1936 and his contacts with Amin al-Husayni see Y. Nimrod, *The Role of J. L. Magness in Cancellation of the Peel Plan* (unpublished MA Thesis, Tel-Aviv University, 1977; in Hebrew), *passim*. See also Khadduri 'Nuri's Flirtations ...' *MEJ*, Vol. 16 (1962), p. 331.
220 Kirkbride to MacMichael, Secret and Personal, 9.4.40, enclosed with MacMichael to Shuckburgh (copy), 11.4.40, E 1626/1282/31, FO 371/24569.
221 Khadduri, *Independent Iraq*, pp. 144 ff.
222 Newton to FO, Teleg. No. 280, 20.6.40, E 2170/2170/89, FO 371/24592 and many other telegrams in that file. On Nuri's apprehensions see also Taha al-Hashimi, I, p. 341 ff.

223 J.C. Edmonds, 'Present Pan-Arab Activity in Iraq', 31.7.40, enclosed with Newton to FO, No. 362, 3.8.40, E 2283/2029/65, FO 371/24549.
224 See, for example, Shertok's reports to the JA Executive on 1.9.40 and 22.9.40, ZA, JA Executive Protocols.
225 This is based on the telegrams, despatches and minutes from the spring and the summer of 1939 in files E 2827/117/25 and 5392/246/25, FO 371/23269; E 4229/1809/25, E 4246/1809/25 and 4584/1809/25, FO 371/23273; and E 6783/6697/89 and E 6959/6697/89, FO 371/23281.
226 On this point see Porath, *Palestinian Arab National Movement, 1929–1939*, pp. 225–8.
227 FO to Sir E. Phipps (British Ambassador in Paris), 4.11.38, E 6341/10/31, FO 371/21883. Minute of 1.2.39 in E 712/712/93, FO 371/23213. 'Arab Federation', 28.9.39, E 6357/6/31, FO 371/23239.
228 H.F. Downie [of the CO] to FO (enclosing a secret despatch of MacMichael to MacDonald, 3.4.40), 75238/40, 14.5.40, E 2027/953/65, FO 371/24548.
229 E[liyahu] E[pstein – later Elath] to JA (enclosing the draft scheme), 24.7.42, ZA, Z/4, 14765.
230 Taha al-Hashimi, II, pp. 33–4.
231 On this process see Amitsur Ilan, *America, Britain and Palestine* (in Hebrew; Jerusalem, 1979), pp. 80–104.
232 See, for example, Wikeley to FO, No. 66, 18.2.43, E 1050/506/65, FO 371/34955.
233 Scott, 'Note of Proposals by General Nuri Pasha ...'. 4.2.43, CO 732/87/Part I, 79238/3 (Part I) (1943).
234 See, for example, Wikeley to FO, No. 8, 2.3.43, E 1524/506/65, FO 371/34956.
235 See telegrams of February 1943 in E 538 E 636 and E 794/506/65, FO 371/34955.
236 Enclosure of 14.1.43 in Minister of State to FO, 11.2.43, E 1196/506/65, FO 371/34955.
237 MacMichael to CO (copy), Teleg. No. 24, 24.2.43, E 1193/506/65, FO 371/34955.
238 HC TJ to CO (copy), Teleg. No. 40, 22.3.43, E 1749/506/65, FO 371/34956.
239 Wikeley to FO, Teleg. No. 66, 18.2.43, E 1050/506/65, FO 371/34955. G.H. Thompson [Acting Counsellor at the British Embassy in Baghdad] to FO, Teleg. No. 757, 12.8.43, E 4775/506/65, FO 371/34960.
240 Wikeley to FO, Teleg. No. 8, 2.3.43, E 1524/506/65, FO 371/34956.
241 HC TJ to CO (copy), Teleg. No. 38, 16.3.43, E 1596/506/65, FO 371/34956.
242 De Gaury, 'Note on Conversation with Nuri Pasha on 25th December, 1942', 29.12.42. CO 732/87 Part I, 79238/3 (Part I).
243 Wikeley to FO, Teleg. No. 78, 23.2.43, E 1132/506/65, FO 371/34955.
244 Shertok's report to ZE in London, 14.3.44, ZA, Z/4, 302/28.
245 See, for example, the sceptical reaction of Tawfiq Abu al-Huda, The Prime Minister of TJ, to Nuri al-Sa'id's statement that the Iraqi Regent 'had no desire to increase his responsibilities', in MacMichael to CO (copy), Teleg. No. 887, 24.7.43, E 4391/506/65, FO 371/34960.
246 Wikeley to FO, Teleg. No. 66, 18.2.43, E 1050/506/65, FO 371/34955.
247 The parliamentary question was tabled by a pro-Arab Labour M.P. Mr Price. It would be interesting to know whether or not Mr Price had learned about Nuri's scheme and wanted to ascertain the British reaction to it; and if so, whether or not he had been urged to do so by the Iraqis. To the British Deputy Minister of State in Cairo it was evident that Nuri based his activities on Eden's statement of 24 February 1943. (See Deputy Minister of State to FO. Teleg. No. 1750, 27.7.43, E 4394/506/65, FO 371/34960.)
248 Cornwallis to FO, Teleg. No. 201, 28.2.43, E 1227/506/65, FO 371/34955; same to same, Teleg. No. 227, 5.3.43, E 1309/506/65, *ibid*.
249 Nuri to Nahhas, 17.3.43, enclosed with Embassy to FO, No. 107, 24.3.43, E 2027/506/65, FO 371/34956.
250 Cornwallis to FO, Teleg. No. 227, 5.3.43, E 1309/506/65, FO 371/34955.
251 Lord Killearn [Sir Miles Lampson previously] to Eden, No. 574, 16.6.43, J 2855/2/16, FO 371/35536. See also Lampson's immediate telegram no. 665, 4.4.43, J 1519/2/16, FO 371/35531. We are able to render here small methodological service by pointing at the files of the British Embassy in Cairo which contain the original reports of a local informant (the Egyptian journalist, Habib Jamati) and the remarks of the Oriental Secretary Sir Walter Smart, who tells us that besides these reports he had a direct talk

with Tahsin al-'Askari. These files are 149/37/43 and 149/39/43, both of FO 141/866 (Part I).
252 Cutting from *Le Journal d'Egypte*, 28.3.43, enclosed with Terence Shone [for the Ambassador] to Eden, No. 319, 1.4.43, E 2096/506/65, FO 371/34957.
253 Embassy to FO (with enclosure), 22.4.43, E 2606/506/65, FO 371/34958; Thompson to FO, Teleg. No. 434, 12.5.43, E 2820/506/65, *ibid.*
254 Cutting from *Journal d'Egypte*, 31.3.43, enclosed with Shone to Eden, No. 319, 1.4.43, E 2096/506/65, FO 371/34957.
255 Cornwallis to FO, Teleg. No. 309, 31.3.43, E 1894/506/65, FO 371/34956.
256 Lord Moyne (Deputy Minister of State) to FO, Teleg. No. 1750, 22.7.43, E 4394/506/65, FO 371/34960.
257 MacMichael to CO (copy), Teleg. No. 887, 24.7.43, E 4391/506/65, FO 371/34960.
258 HCTJ to CO (copy), Teleg. No. 15, 9.2.44, E 1024/41/65, FO 371/39987. J. V. W. Shaw [Acting HCTJ] to CO (copy), 6.5.44, E 2814/41/65, FO 371/39988.
259 Wikeley to FO, Teleg. No. 509, 29.7.43, E 4631/506/65, FO 371/34960.
260 Wikeley to FO, Teleg. No. 4, 8.2.43, E 1231/506/65, FO 371/34955.
261 Al-Suwaydi, *Mudhakkirati*, pp. 244–6. See also Shertok's report to ZE, 22.8.43, based on a talk with Shafiq Haddad, the prospective Iraqi Military Attaché at Washington, ZA, protocols of ZE.
262 Wikely to FO, Teleg. No. 113, 15.3.43, E 1543/506/65, FO 371/34956. See many other examples in volumes 34957–34960.
263 See telegrams and minutes in E 1789/506/65, FO 371/34956.
264 See Ibn Sa'ud's Note of May 1943 in E 3595/506/65, FO 371/34959.
265 Wikeley to FO, Teleg. No. 316, 3.8.43, E 4361/506/65, FO 371/34960.
266 Wikeley to FO, Teleg. No. 78, 24.2.43, E 1132/506/65, FO 371/34955.
267 Minister of State to British Legation in Beirut, Teleg. No. 165, 31.7.43, E 4650/506/65, FO 371/34960. The French were not included in the list of persons to whom Nuri sent his Note, but they succeeded in getting a copy.
268 Shertok's report, 22.8.43, ZA, ZE protocols.
269 HCTJ to CO (copy), Teleg. No. 11, 31.1.44, E 785/41/65, FO 371/39987.
270 Cornwallis to FO, Teleg. No. 155, 25.2.44, E 1330/41/65, FO 371/39987.
271 HC for Palestine to CO (copy), Teleg. No. 447, 10.4.44, E 2283/41/65, FO 371/39987. It is almost certain that now again Jamil Mardam, the Syrian Foreign Minister, was a sort of intermediary between Nuri and Shukri al-Quwwatli. (See Sir E. Spears to Minister of State, Teleg. No. 28, 22.4.44, E 2500/41/65, FO 371/39988.)

TO CHAPTER 2

1 See in his *Memoirs, 1933*, pp. 656–8.
2 On this process see Porath, *Palestinian Arab National Movement*, Vol. II, pp. 109–39.
3 Ben-Gurion, *Memoirs, 1933*, p. 683.
4 On this proposition, see Porath, *Palestinian Arab National Movement*, Vol. II, pp. 143–58.
5 Ben-Gurion, *Memoirs, 1934–1935*, p. 149.
6 *Ibid.*, p. 163.
7 *Ibid.*, p. 149.
8 On the death of this body see Porath, *Palestinian Arab National Movement*, Vol. II, pp. 47–8.
9 Ben-Gurion, *Meetings*, pp. 20, 22, 31, 40, 48 and 49 (or in *Memoirs, 1934–1935*, pp. 164, 165 and 169).
10 Ben-Gurion, *Meetings*, p. 21.
11 *Ibid.*, p. 31.
12 Ben-Gurion, *Meetings*, pp. 21, 31 and 34–7.
13 Geoffrey Furlonge, *Palestine Is My Country: The Story of Musa Alami* (London, 1969), p. 103.
14 A. Pelmann to Ben-Gurion (copy), 28.10.34, enclosed with Pelmann to Dr. Brodetsky, 6.11.34, ZA, S/25,3051.

15 Ben-Gurion, *Meetings*, p. 24.
16 *Ibid.*, p. 22.
17 *Ibid.*, pp. 39–42.
18 *Ibid.*, pp. 54, 55, 59, 64 and 67.
19 ZA, ZE protocols, 19.5.36 (reproduced in Ben-Gurion, *Memoirs, 1936*, p. 206).
20 *Ibid.*, pp. 280 and 443.
21 See a resumé of these talks in ZA, S/25, 9166.
22 'Minute of Conversation with Dr Shahbandar and Amin Eff. Said at Cairo, 21.9.36', ZA, S/25, 3435. Sharett, *Political Diaries, III, 1938*, pp. 10–12.
23 *Ibid.*, Wilensky to Shertok, 17.12.37, ZA, S/25, 10095. Nimrod, *Magnes' Role* ... pp. 95–6. Sasson, *On the Way to Peace*, pp. 106–08.
24 Sharett, *Political Diaries, III, 1938*, pp. 25 and 35–7. Sasson, *On the Way to Peace*, pp. 138–40. 'Talks with N[asib] B[akri]', 31.3.40, ZA, S/25, 3500. This last report is reproduced in a falsified way in Sasson's book (pp. 187–9) and the printed version should not be trusted. This is rather exceptional. Usually Sasson's reports, which were reproduced in his book, were not changed although slightly abridged. See also C. H. Bateman, for British Ambassador in Cairo, to Viscount Halifax (copy), no. 381, 5.4.39, CO 733/398/75156/14.
25 E. Elath, *Return to Zion and the Arabs* (in Hebrew; Tel-Aviv, 1974), p. 288.
26 'Articles of Reply to the Secretariat of the National Bloc in Syria', ZA, S/25, 3267.
27 The minutes of the talks and Epstein's reports are to be found in ZA, S/25, 3267. Some of them were reproduced as enclosures to Elath's [Epstein's] book, *Return to Zion*.
28 *Ibid.*, pp. 291–2. See also M. Sharett, *Political Diaries, II, 1937* (in Hebrew: Tel-Aviv, 1971), p. 189.
29 Sharett, *Political Diaries, II, 1937*, pp. 112–13.
30 Ben-Gurion, *Meetings*, p. 262 and Sharett, *Political Diaries, IV, 1939*, p. 121.
31 Al-Shwaydi, *Mudhakkirati*, p. 321.
32 Ben-Gurion, *Meetings*, pp. 263–5.
33 Meeting of ZE in London, 12.7.40, ZA, Z/4, 302/23.
34 From his speech to the Central Committee of the Labour Party, 15.12.40, in his *Political Diaries, 1940–1942*, p. 149.
35 Attached to the protocol of ZE meeting, 23.3.41, ZA, ZE protocols.
36 Meeting of ZE, 27.7.41, ZA, protocols of ZE.
37 ZE meeting, 26.10.41, ZA, protocols of ZE.
38 Shertok's report in the meeting of ZE, 21.12.41, *ibid.*
39 Shertok's report to the ZE, 15.9.42, ZA, protocols of ZE.
40 ZE meeting, 22.11.42, ZA, protocols of ZE.
41 This can easily been detected in his published *Diaries*.
42 Shertok's report, 27.7.41, ZA, protocols of ZE.
43 ZE meeting, 17.8.44, ZA, protocols of ZE.
44 M. Bar-Zohar, *Ben-Gurion* (in Hebrew; Tel-Aviv, 1975), Vol. I, pp. 440–67.
45 H. M. Kalvarisky to Shertok, 3.12.37, ZA, S/25, 10095; B. Joseph's memorandum, 22.12.37, *ibid.*, 3052.
46 See Nimrod, *Magnes's Role*, p. 22. N. Katzburg, *The Palestine Problem in British Policy, 1940–1945* (in Hebrew; Jerusalem, 1977), pp. 38–9.
47 E. Phipps to FO (copy), 26.5.39, CO 733/408/75873/30 (Part I).
48 See letters and minutes of February–March 1937 in E/1146/22/31, FO 371/20804 (copy in CO 341/75528/44).
49 Muhammad 'Ali to Sir Robert Vansittart (Permanent Under Secretary of the FO), 11.5.37, E 2920/22/31, FO 371/20806.
50 *Al-Muqattam*, 28.6.37 and 7.7.37.
51 See Baggallay's minute and Vansittart's letter of 26 and 27 May in E 2920/22/31, FO 371/2/806.
52 Miles Lampson to A. Cadogan (with enclosure), 24.2.38, E 1438/10/31, FO 371/21874. Sharett, *Political Diaries, 1938*, p. 36.
53 CS of the Palestine Government to Boyd (including two reports), 27.6.42, no. 44, CO 732/87 (Part I), 79238 (1942).
54 For which see Porath, *Emergence*, pp. 53–100.

55 Samuel to Curzon *DBFP, 1919–1939*, First Series, Vol. XIII, no. 235, pp. 241–6. See also E. Kedourie, 'Sir Herbert Samuel and the Government of Palestine', in his *Chatham House Version* (Frank Cass, London, 1974), pp. 77–9 and Viscount Samuel, *Memoirs* (London, 1945), pp. 145–50.
56 On the whole affair, see Porath, *Emergence*, pp. 147
57 Samuel to Duke of Devonshire, 12.12.22; last to Curzon (copy), 10.1.23; and first to last (copy), ISA, CS, 128.
58 On these negotiations see Y. Porath, 'The Palestinians and the Negotiations for the British-Hijazi Treaty, 1920–1925', *Asian and African Studies*, Vol. 8, no. 1 (1972), pp. 20–48. When no other source is quoted the following paragraph is based on this article.
59 Young's minute and further developments are to be found in CO 733/42.
60 Porath, *Palestinian Arab Nationalist Movement*, Vol. II, pp. 198–9.
61 Ormsby-Gore to Wauchope, 8.9.36, CO 733/315/75528/58.
62 Weizmann to Samuel, 14.9.36, ISA, Samuel Papers, 100/18.
63 Ormsby-Gore to Samuel, 15.9.36, CO 733/315/75528/58. For the shaping of the Office's position see the minutes there.
64 Maffey's note of the talk, 16.9.36, CO 733/315/75528/58.
65 Maffey's note, 18.5.36, CO 733/315/75528/58.
66 Copies of both Samuel's Note on this talk, dated September 20th, and Nuri's report to the Iraqi Prime Minister, dated September 26th, are to be found in CO 733/315/75528/58. Nuri's account is much more detailed but the substance is identical in both accounts.
67 Samuel to Ormsby-Gore, 15.6.37, ISA, Samuel Papers, 100/18.
68 *Parliamentary Debates: House of Lords*, 5th Series, Vo. CVI, cols. 641–3.
69 Maffey's Note, 18.9.36, CO 733/315/75528/58. It must be stated that this claim is contradictory to what is known from all other available sources about views held by the JA Executive in Palestine over the question of limiting Jewish immigration and placing the Jewish community in a fixed minority position.
70 Ben-Gurion, *Memoirs IV, 1937*, p. 310. Idem., *Letters to Paula* (Vallentine, Mitchell & Co., London, 1971), p. 135.
71 *Davar*, 30.7.37 (reproducing the text of the interview published in the *Daily Telegraph* on 29.7.37).
72 MacDonald's Memorandum, 21 August 1938, CP 190(38), CAB 24/278.
73 See the correspondence of spring 1938 in E 2668/10/31, FO 371/21876.
74 Nimrod, *Magnes*, pp. 8–9.
75 Ben-Gurion, *Letters to Paula* (London, 1971), pp. 198–205.
76 Nigel Wingate to Weizmann, 14.2.39, WA. Ben-Gurion's report to the ZE in Jerusalem, see meeting of ZE, 26.11.1939, ZA, protocols of ZE.
77 See the memorandum of January 1939 in E 1274/29/31, FO 371/23245.
78 Vansittart to Lawrence, 15.2.39, *ibid.*
79 Gibb to Lloyd (copy), 12.7.40, E 2289/2289/31, FO 371/24565. Although Gibb did not make it clear that he initiated the meeting, FO officials concluded it from the tone of his second letter of 7 August (see *ibid.*). Brodetsky's report to the ZE in London is emphatically positive on this point. (See meeting of 12.7.40, ZA, Z/4, 302/23.)
80 Gibb's memorandum. 'A Plan of Arab Federation', 16.12.42, E 7433/49/65, FO 371/31338.
81 Weizmann's report to the ZE in London, 6.11.40, ZA, Z/4, 302/24.
82 Ditto, 7.1.41, *ibid.*
83 A note of a talk between Weizmann and W. Ormsby-Gore, 25.2.38, WA.
84 Sharett, *Political Diaries, II, 1937*, p. 79 and *Political Diaries, III, 1938*, p. 310.
85 Ben-Gurion, *Meetings*, pp. 130–6; idem., *Memoirs, IV, 1937*, p. 122. Elath, *Return to Zion*, pp. 322–7.
86 Porath, *Palestinian Arab National Movement*, Vol. II, pp. 20–1.
87 Taha al-Hashimi, *Mudhakkirat* Vol. I, p. 109.
88 Ben-Gurion, *Memoirs, IV, 1937*, pp. 179–83; idem., *Meetings*, pp. 137–43.
89 Ben-Gurion, *Meetings*, pp. 145–7. See also ZA, S/25, 10095.
90 This draft as is clear from the context cannot but be Ben-Gurion's. Its attribution to Philby in Hattis, *The Bi-National Idea*, p. 175 and Ben-Gurion, *Memoirs, IV, 1937*, pp. 193–4, is mistaken. (See in ZA, S/25, 10095.) Gomaa's treatment of this episode is confused and

based on indirect sources (see pp. 11–12 of his book) such as Yusuf Yasin's report to G. W. Rendel of what Philby had told Yasin about Ben-Gurion's suggestion. A copy of Yasin's report to Rendel of 31.5.37 is to be found in CO 733/341/75528/44.

91 Ben-Gurion to Philby, 31.5.37, ZA, S/25, 10095. See also Ben-Gurion, *Meetings*, pp. 147–50.
92 H. St John B. Philby, *Arabian Jubilee* (London, 1952), p. 207.
93 Salaman to Weizmann (and latter's remarks), 26.10.32, WA.
94 D. Ben-Gurion, *Memoirs, V, 1938* (in Hebrew; Tel-Aviv, 1982), pp. 115, 235, 238 and 422.
95 Ben-Gurion, *Letters to Paula*, entry of 20.9.38, p. 170. See also Sharett, *Political Diaries, III, 1938*, p. 310.
96 Nigel Wingate to Weizmann, 14.2.39, WA.
97 Ben-Gurion's report to the meeting of ZE in Jerusalem, 26.11.39, ZA Protocols of ZE.
98 Philby to Dora, his wife, as quoted by Monroe, *Philby*, p. 219. See also Philby, *Arabian Jubilee*, p. 208 and Sharett, *Political Diaries, IV, 1939*, p. 97.
99 Wingate to Weizmann, 14.2.39, WA.
100 Prof. Brodetsky to the ZE in London, session of ZE, 9.5.39, ZA, Z/4, 302/23.
101 Prof. L. B. Namier's memorandum on the talk with Philby, 6.10.39, WA. See also Monroe, *Philby*, p. 221.
102 Namier's note of the meeting, 24.9.39, ZA, Z/4, 14615.
103 Namier's memorandum, 8.10.39, WA. Sharett, *Political Diaries, IV, 1939*, pp. 374–6. Philby published a different version of that talk (see *Jubilee*, p. 213). But we preferred Namier's and Sharett's accounts which were written on the same day of the talk and which were corroborated by further developments.
104 N. A. Rose (ed.), *Baffy: The Diaries of Blanche Dugdale, 1936–1947* (Vallentine, Mitchell & Co., London, 1973), p. 161.
105 Philby's memorandum, 17.11.1943, WA.
106 Monroe, *Philby*, pp. 222–3; Philby, *Jubilee*, p. 214.
107 These developments are presented and analysed in Aaron David Miller, *Search for Security: Saudi Arabian Oil and American Foreign Policy, 1939–1949* (Chapel Hill, 1980), pp. 32–91.
108 ZE meeting, 26.11.39, ZA, protocols of the ZE. Shertok's Diaries reveal the same thing. The sole important political point which Shertok had found in the Philby plan was the transfer of the Arabs and giving the whole of western Palestine to the Jews. (See Sharett, *Political Diaries, IV, 1939*, p. 376.)
109 Sharett, *Political Diaries, 1939*, p. 373. See also a Note on Weizmann's meeting with Churchill, 17.12.39, WA.
110 Bracken's 'Memorandum to the First Lord', 31.10.39, PREM, 4/51/9. E. Monroe's quotation (*Philby*, p. 223) from that memorandum includes a part which does not appear in the original document.
111 Chaim Weizmann, *Trial and Error* (London, 1949), p. 514.
112 Weizmann, *Trial and Error*, p. 526. Weizmann's interest in claiming that the Philby plan, although being identical with later ideas of Churchill, was not connected with them stemmed from his later embarrassment. When in late 1943 he realised that the plan had collapsed he tried to explain why he had attached considerable importance to it. His explanation was that the very same 'plan' had been mentioned to him 'quite independently, and without any knowledge of Mr Philby's view, by the Prime Minister [Churchill]'. (See Weizmann to Judge Samuel Rosenman, Roosevelt's Jewish Adviser, 4.1.44, WA.)
113 Weizmann, *Trial and Error*, p. 516.
114 Stannley's report, July 1941, E 6097, FO 371/31379.
115 Philby, *Jubilee*, p. 214.
116 All the minutes and exchange of letters of September–October 1940 are included in E 2635/2635/31, FO 371/24569. See also Lloyd to MacMichael, 24.9.40, CO 733/444 I/75872/115.
117 Weizmann's report to the London ZE, 29.8.40, ZA, Z/4, 302/24.
118 Weizmann to Lloyd, 2.12.40, WA, and E. B. Boyd's minute, 25.7.41, CO 733/444I/75872/115. See also M. Cohen, *Palestine: Retreat from the Mandate* (London, 1978), p. 210, n. 52 where the date of the letter is wrongly given as 22.11.40.
119 Weizmann, *Trial and Error*, pp. 521–2.
120 John Harvey (ed.), *The War Diaries of Oliver Harvey* (London, 1978), p. 59.

121 See also Note of Interview of Weizmann with Lord Moyne, 29.7.41, WA, where Weizmann admitted that Churchill had revealed his plan to him before Weizmann's Spring 1941 travel to the US.
122 See in E 2685/53/65, FO 371/27043, = PREM 4/32/5. One cannot avoid the conclusion that there is a great similarity between the October 1939 understanding between Weizmann and Namier and Philby (see pp. 84–6 of this chapter) and Churchill's Note. Even the term 'Western Palestine' as a description of Palestine excluding TJ, which was usually used mainly by Zionist writers and which occurred in the October 1939 understanding is here repeated by Churchill.
123 See these minutes in E 2685/53/65, FO 371/27043.
124 Amery to Churchill, 10.9.41, E 6189/53/65, FO 371/27045, (= PREM, 4/52/5).
125 Prime Minister's Personal Minute, No. 923/1, 23.9.41, E 6189/53/65, FO 371/27045.
126 WM (41) 96th Conclusions, Minute 1, Confidential Annex, 24.9.41, CAB 65/23.
127 See minutes of 25.9.41, E 6189/53/65, FO 371/27045.
128 A Note of Interview with Lord Moyne, July 29th, 1941, WA.
129 Moyne to MacMichael, 6.8.41, CO 733/444I/75872/115. We shall return to this letter later on (see ch. 2, p. 120) to see how Moyne used this episode to put forward his idea of a smaller Arab Federation as a solution to the Palestine Problem.
130 Parkinson's minute, 20.8.41, CO 733/444I/75872/115.
131 Moyne to MacMichael, 6.8.41, and last to first, Secret and Personal, 1.9.41, CO 733/444I/75872/115.
132 Shuckburgh (transmitting the Note) to Sir Horace Seymour, Foreign Assistance Under-Secretary, 25.9.41, E 6189/53/65, FO 371/27045.
133 ME(0) (41) 14th mtg, 6.8.41, E 4464/374/31, FO 371/27137 (= CAB 95/1).
134 See the exchange of minutes between Parkinson (22.9.41), Boyd (24.9.41) and Shuckburgh (24.9.41) in CO 732/87I/79238 (194).
135 MSC 41(14), 26.9.41, E 6189/53/65, FO 371/27045, and Eden to Prime Minister, 29.9.41, ibid.; see also Shuckburgh to Seymour, 25.9.41, ibid.
136 Harvey, *Diaries*, p. 59.
137 Philby, *Jubilee*, p. 215.
138 Harvey, *Diaries*, n. 59.
139 Martin to Prime Minister, 3.11.41, PREM 4/52/5. See also G. Cohen, *Churchill and the Question of Palestine* (in Hebrew; Jerusalem, 1976), p. 50. Cohen is mistaken about the date of the Weizmann-Churchill meeting. It took place in March 1942 and not 1941.
140 Moyne's Note to the Prime Minister, 6.11.41, CO 732/87I/79238 (1941) (= PREM 4/52/5).
141 Churchill's minute of 9.11.41 as reported on 11 November by F. Bowman to C. H. Thornby of the CO, CO 732/87I/79238 (1941).
142 Philby, *Jubilee*, p. 215.
143 Harvey, *Diaries*, pp. 28, 38, 59 and 89.
144 Cranborne to MacMichael, 23.3.42, CO 733/444I/75872/115.
145 B. Dugdale's report to London ZE, 2.10.42, ZA, Z/4, 302/25.
146 Weizmann, *Trial and Error*, pp. 525–6. Weizmann dated this meeting as the date of his departure to America which took place on 11 March. But clearly this could not be so, since on 18 March he was still in London and had an interview with Viscount Cranborne!
147 Harvey, *Diaries*, pp. 41–2.
148 Halifax to Eden, 2.2.43, E 826, FO 371/35031; Eden to Prime Minister, 3.9.43, E 2342, FO 371/35033; Prime Minister to Eden, 2.3.43, *ibid.*; Peterson to Cadogan, 25.3.43, E 1196, FO 371/34955. See also G. Cohen, *The British Cabinet and Palestine* (in Hebrew; Tel-Aviv, 1976), pp. 35–6.
149 Moyne to MacMichael, 24.1.42, CO 732/87I/79238 (1942).
150 May we add that in pursuing that policy Weizmann did not enjoy the full support of all of his colleagues. Shertok at least opposed it from its outset (see his *Political Diaries, 1939*, p. 395) to the end (see M. Sharett, *Personal Diaries* (Tel-Aviv, 1978), p. 182). Inside the London ZE, on the other hand, he enjoyed stronger support and Philby kept in touch with members of the ZE. (See London ZE meeting, 29.4.42, ZA, Z/4, 402/25.) In January 1943 Shertok took part in their meeting. Prof. Namier asked: 'Now that the Arabs were losing their nuisance value, should they [ZE] not press for a statement by the Prime Minister and President Roosevelt on the lines of the Philby Scheme?' To that Shertok replied 'that

the Philby Scheme was only one of the possibilities'. He also added that 'he was not prepared to place his trust in Ibn Saud and put his head into a noose'. Prof. Brodetsky too expressed scepticism (see meeting, 16.1.43, *ibid.*) and it shows that the support for Weizmann's policy even on his home ground was weakening.

151 Weizmann, *Trial and Error*, p. 527.
152 A detailed description and analysis of that rift is to be found in Bar-Zohar, *Ben-Gurion*, pp. 440–61 and M. Cohen, *Palestine: Retreat from the Mandate* (London, 1978), pp. 131–9.
153 Namier's words in the London ZE meeting, 18.1.43, ZA, Z/4, 302/26.
154 London ZE meeting, 18.1.43, ZA, Z/4, 302/26.
155 *FRUS, 1942*, pp. 550–1.
156 *FRUS, 1942*, pp. 553–6.
157 Memorandum of Conversation between Weizmann and S. Welles (copy), 26.1.43, WA.
158 *FRUS, 1943, IV*, pp. 780–1.
159 Sharett, *Personal Diaries*, p. 184. This travel of Shertok to the USA was fateful as far as his relations with Ben-Gurion were concerned. The latter interpreted it as though Shertok sided with Weizmann in his struggle to win over American Zionist leadership and never forgot or forgave. (See Bar-Zohar, *Ben-Gurion*, pp. 459–61.)
160 *FRUS, 1943, IV*, pp. 757–63.
161 Sharett, *Personal Diaries*, p. 182.
162 Welles to the President (copy), 10.5.43, WA.
163 Certainly, Weizmann referred to this issue when he wrote of Welles that he 'had been somewhat cautious and reticent in our private conversations'. (See *Trial and Error*, p. 534.)
164 Only half a year later Weizmann did claim in a personal letter to S. Welles that he had mentioned to the President the scheme 'originally put to me by Mr. St. John Philby'. (See Weizmann to Welles, 13.12.43, ZA, Z/4, 14615.)
165 *FRUS, 1943, IV*, p. 761.
166 This is according to the personal record. The published version has the same description, but in his book Weizmann tried to make a completely different impression. He tells us about a meeting between himself and Hoskins and then about Hoskins' travel to the Middle East without any connection between this journey and the interview with the President. (See *Trial and Error*, p. 531.) Weizmann's apologetic description is persistent!
167 Weizmann to Welles, 13.12.43, ZA, Z/4, 14615.
168 Weizmann's report to the London ZE meeting, 11.11.43, ZA, Z/4, 302/28.
169 *FRUS, 1943, IV*, pp. 782–5. For general background see Ilan, *America, Britain and Palestine*, pp. 115–18.
170 *FRUS, 1943, IV*, pp. 795–6.
171 *Ibid.*, pp. 796 and 800–01.
172 *FRUS, 1943, IV*, pp. 807–10 and Hoskins's Memorandum, 3.11.43, E 6823/506/65, FO 371/34963.
173 *FRUS, 1943, IV*, pp. 811–14. See also Ilan, *America, Britain and Palestine*, pp. 132–5.
174 Hoskins' memorandum, 3.11.43, E 6823/506/65, FO 371/43963.
175 Weizmann's report to the London ZE, 11.11.43, ZA, Z/4, 302/28.
176 Philby, 'Note to Interviews with Colonel Hoskins', 15.11.43, ZA, Z/4, 14615; London ZE meeting, 16.11.43, Z/4, 302/28.
177 Namier's report, 2.12.43, *ibid.* A photo-copy of King 'Abd al-'Aziz Al Sa'ud's letter to Philby of 4 Muharram, 1363 H (31.12.43) can be found in WA.
178 Weizmann to Sumner Welles, 13.12.43, ZA, Z/4, 14615. Another copy can be found in FO 371/40139, E 206/206/31.
179 Namier's words, London ZE meetings, 7.1.44 and 25.1.44, ZA, Z/4, 302/28.
180 See text E 2079/506/65, FO 371/34956.
181 Wikeley to FO, teleg. no. 171, 24.4.43, E 2395/506/65, FO 371/34957 and *FRUS, 1943, IV*, pp. 768–71.
182 *Ibid.*, pp. 785 and 795.
183 Record of Conversation with the British Minister, 20.9.43, E 6264/506/65, FO 371/34962.
184 See for example their minutes on Wikeley's telegram of 31.3.43, E 2079/506/65, FO 371/34956.
185 Caccia's minute, 26.4.43, E 2395/506/65, FO 371/34957.
186 'Off the Record' Note, 11.6.43, WA. In the published memorandum Weizmann was

less outspoken. He explained Churchill's refusal by his having had 'very little to tell me'. (See *FRUS, 1943, IV*, p. 793.)
187 Peterson to Campbell, 25.1.44, E 206/206/31, FO 371/40139. See also the minutes in that file.
188 Curzon to Duke of Devonshire, the Colonial Secretary (copy), 18.1.23, ISA, CS, 128; last to first, 10.1.23, *ibid.* See also Kedourie, *Chatham House Version*, pp. 78–9.
189 Eastwood's paper, 21.9.36, CO 733/315/75528/58.
190 G. I. Ranson's minute, 22.9.36, *ibid.*
191 Wauchope to Ormsby-Gore, 22.9.36, *ibid.*
192 J. Martin's minute, 30.9.36, *ibid.*
193 See Porath, *Palestinian Arab National Movement*, Vol. II, pp. 195–9.
194 FO's Memorandum, 20.6.36, CP 178 (36), CAB 24/263.
195 Kerr to Eden, 17.2.37, E 1427/22/31, FO 371/20805.
196 Same to same (with enclosures), 19.2.37, E 1428/22/31, *ibid.*
197 See the minutes of May 1937 in E 2920/22/31, FO 371/20806.
198 Lampson to Cadogan (with enclosure), 24.2.38, and minutes, E 1438/10/31, FO 371/21874.
199 Wauchope to Ormsby-Gore, 8.4.37, CO 733/311/75528/Part VII.
200 An analysis of Rendel's role, although attributing to him perhaps an inflated importance, is E. Kedourie's article, 'Great Britain and Palestine: The Turning Point', in his *Islam in the Modern World* (London, 1980), pp. 93–170.
201 See Rendel's memorandum, 3.11.37, E 6470/22/31, FO 371/20819.
202 Note for Use, 16.11.37, E 6751/22/31, FO 371/2082); see also the papers included in E 6773/22/31, *ibid.*
203 MacDonald's Memorandum, 21.8.38, CP 190(38) CAB 24/278. See also Michael J. Cohen, 'Appeasement in the Middle East: The British White Paper on Palestine, May 1939', *The Historical Journal*, Vol. XVI, no. 3 (1973), pp. 576–7 and N. Katzburg, *From Partition to White Paper* (in Hebrew; Jerusalem, 1974), pp. 48–55.
204 MacMichael to MacDonald, 24.9.38, CO 733/386/75872/1.
205 The minutes of these consultations are kept in E 6217/1/31, FO 371/21864.
206 See the Committee's minutes in E 6379/1/31, FO 371/21865.
207 Cabinet Conclusions 52(38), 2.11.38, E 6471/1/31, FO 371/21865.
208 See the Brief of 19.11.38, E 7128/6389/65, FO 371/21839.
209 Cabinet discussions 52(38), 2.11.38, E 6471/1/31 and 54(38), 9.11.38, E 6672/1/31, FO 371/21865; and the third meeting of the Committee P(38) 3rd mtg., 14.11.38, E 6824/1/31, *ibid.*
210 See their minute of 20 and 21 October, E 6572/1/31, FO 371/21865.
211 See all the material in E 1274/29/31, FO 331/23245.
212 See note no. 198.
213 See M. Cohen, *Palestine: Retreat from the Mandate*, pp. 72–82.
214 Weizmann's report to ZE, 29.8.40, ZA, Z/4, 302/24. For shaping the FO's view see in E 2289/2289/31, FO 371/24569.
215 The exchange of letters of July–August 1940 between Prof. H. A. R. Gibb and Lord Lloyd, the minutes, and the interdepartmental consultations are to be found in E 2289/2289/3, FO 371/24569.
216 Lloyd to MacMichael, 24.9.40, CO 733/4441/75872/115.
217 MacMichael to Lloyd, 4.10.40, CO 733/4441/75872/115.
218 See the memorandum of 21.11.40, PREM 4/5/51. I am indebted to Dr Ron Zweig for drawing my attention to this document.
219 Gibb's memorandum of 9.6.41, Bowman's Notes of 5 and 7 July and Butler's comments are to be found in E 3824/53/65, FO 371/27044.
220 Baxter's minute, 23.7.41, E 3937/53/65, FO 371/27044 and Caccia to Boyd, 19.9.41, E 6277/53/65, FO 371/27045.
221 F. H. Downie, 'Arab Federation', 12.2.41, CO 732/871/79238 (1941).
222 Moyne to Anthony [Eden], 5.6.41 (transmitting a Note of that talk held on 3.6.41), E 3101/53/65, FO 371/27044.
223 Moyne to MacMichael, 11.7.41, CO 733/4441/75872/115. It is no coincidence that in this file a copy of the Lloyd–MacMichael correspondence of September–October 1940 was placed as a background to Moyne's move.

224 MacMichael to Moyne, 13.7.41, *ibid.*
225 See minutes by S. E. V. Luke (of 21.7.41), E.B. B[oyd], (of 25.7.41), J. E. S[huckburgh] (of 25.7.41), A. C. C. P[arkinson] (of 30.7.41) and by M[oyne] (of 4.8.41) in *ibid.*
226 Parkinson's minute addressed to the Colonial Secretary, 20.8.41, CO 733/444I/75872/115.
227 MSC (41) 1, 22.9.41, CAB 95/8. On the preparation of that document see E 5477/259/31, FO 371/27134.
228 MSC 41(14), 26.10.41, E 6185/53/65, FO 371/27045 (= CAB 95/8).
229 Moyne to Prime Minister (copy), 6.11.41, CO 732/871/79238 (1941).
230 H. MacMichael, 'Note on the Prospects of "Federation" As a Solution of the Palestine Problem', 13.9.41, E 6210/53/65, FO 271/27045.
231 MacMichael to Moyne (copy), 7.10.41, E 6488/53/65, FO 371/27045.
232 Baxter's minute of 3.10.41 endorsed on the same date by Seymour, in E 6210/53/65, *ibid.*
233 FO to Cairo and Baghdad, 4.10.41, *ibid.*
234 Lampson to FO, 14.10.41, E 6636/53/65, FO 371/27045.
235 Cornwallis to Eden, 4.10.41, E 6881/53/65, *ibid.*
236 Baxter's minute, 20.10.41, the Egyptian Dept., 3.12.41 and Seymour's, 3.11.41, E 6695/53/65, *ibid.*
237 Luke's minute, 24.10.41, CO 732/871/79238 (1941).
238 The Minutes of the Committee (MEO (41) 5–10) and their Report (MEO (42)4) are to be found in CAB 95/1. On the preparation of the Report see in CO 732/871/79238 (1941) and E 436/49/65, FO 371/31337.
239 See in E 838, E 976 and E 2583, FO 371/31337.
240 Moyne's memorandum, 'Palestine', 2.3.42, CO 733/444I/75872/115 (1942).
241 *Ibid.*
242 Moyne to MacMichael, Personal and Secret, 24.1.42, CO 732/871/79238 (1942).
243 See the minutes of Luke (2.4.42), Boyd (6.4.42), Battershill (7.4.42), Parkinson (8.4.42), Harold Macmillan (Under-Secretary, February–December 1942; 9.4.42) and Viscount Cranborne (14.4.42), CO 733/444I/75872/115.
244 Documents nos. 7 and 8 of 23–24/4/42, CO 733/444I/75872/115.
245 See the minutes of May 1942, E 2723/49/65, FO 371/31337.
246 See minutes of late May, E 3121/49/65, FO 371/31338.
247 Caccia to Boyd, 9.6.42, *ibid.*
248 MacMichael to Cranborne, 7.6.42, *ibid.* See also for the CO's similar views in CO 732/871/79238 (1942).
249 MacMichael to Cranborne, 5.9.42, CO 732/871/79238 (1942).
250 Peterson to Battershill, 17.10.42, E 5802/49/65, FO 371/31338.
251 Cranborne to MacMichael, 23.10.42, CO 732/871/79238 (1942).
252 Shertok's reports to London ZE, 16.12.42, ZA, Z/4, 302/26 and his report to Jerusalem ZE, 22.12.42, ZA, ZE Protocols.
253 This view was held by MacMichael (see his memorandum, 13.9.41, E 6210/53/65, FO 371/27045) and by Luke (his minute, 13.11.41, CO 732/871/79238 (1941)).
254 Spears to FO, 25.2.43, E 1176/506/65, FO 371/34955.
255 For a thorough analysis of this situation see G. Cohen, *British Cabinet*, pp. 26ff. When no source is quoted we used this book.
256 See also Ilan, *America, Britain and Palestine*, pp. 107–25.
257 Caccia's minute, 13.4.43, E 2341, FO 371/35033.
258 Weizmann to Churchill, 2.4.43, Cohen, *Cabinet*, doc. no. 1, p. 85.
259 Churchill's personal minute to Cranborne and Stanley, 18.4.43, *ibid.*, no. 2, p. 88.
260 Docs. 3–5 in *ibid.*
261 Amery to Churchill, 29.4.43, PREM 4/52/1. See also Katzburg, *The Palestine Problem in British Policy* (in Hebrew; Jerusalem, 1977), doc. no. 2, pp. 20–1.
262 Amery to Eden, 10.5.43, E 2810/506/65, FO 371/34958.
263 Amery to Nuri al-Sa'id, 10.5.43, *ibid.*
264 Churchill's Note on Palestine, WP (43) 178, 28.4.43, E 2742, FO 371/35034 (= doc. no. 6 in Cohen, *British Cabinet*).
265 WP (43) 187, 4.5.43, CAB 66/36 (= G. Cohen, *British Cabinet*, doc. no. 8, p. 104).
266 WP (43) 265, 23.6.43, CAB 66/38 (= *Ibid.*, doc. no. 12, p. 137). Lyttelton was serving then in the War Cabinet as Minister of Production.

NOTES

267 WP (43) 288, 1.7.43, CAB 66/38 (= *Ibid.*, doc. no. 14, p. 144).
268 *Ibid.*, doc. no. 16, p. 152.
269 W.M (43) 92nd Conclusions, 2.7.43, CAB 65/39 and P(M)(4)1, 20.7.43, CAB 95/14. See also G. Cohen, *British Cabinet*, pp. 78–82 and M. Cohen, *Palestine*, pp. 164–5.
270 WP(4) 337, 20.7.43, CAB 66/39.
271 P(M)(43)3, 31.7.43, CAB 95/14 (= E 4336, FO 371/35036).
272 P(M)(43)5, 2.8.43, CAB 95/14.
273 P(M)(43) 1st Meeting, 4.8.43, CAB 95/14.
274 Law's minute to the Eastern Department, 7.8.43, E 4336/87/31, FO 371/35036. Law's words are not mentioned at all in the official minutes of the Committee and it seems that this omission was a deliberate political act of his!
275 *Ibid.*
276 Peterson's minute to the Secretary of State, 5.10.43, E 6027/87/31, FO 371/35039.
277 P(M)43 1st Meeting, 4.8.43, CAB 95/14.
278 All these papers are to be found in CO 732/87II/79238 (1943).
279 P(M)(44)6, 22.1.44, E 666/95/31, FO 371/40133.
280 See Peterson's minute, 5.10.43, E 6027/87/83, FO 371/35039.
281 P(M)(43)14, 1.11.43, CAB 95/14 (= E 6616/87/31, FO 371/35040).
282 Peterson's minute, 5.9.43, E 5697/87/31, FO 371/35038.
283 Baxter's minute, 25.7.43, E 4336/87/31, FO 271/35036.
284 Peterson's minutes and draft memorandum, 23.7.63 and 8.8.43, E 4336/87/31, FO 371/35036. See also Peterson's words in consultations with the CO, 15.10.43, E 6027/87/31, FO 371/35039.
285 See his minutes in E 4336/87/31, FO 371/35036.
286 Peterson's minute of 5.9.43 and Eden's minute of 6.9.43, E 5697/87/31, FO 371/35038.
287 Peterson's minute, endorsed by Cadogan, 5.10.43, E 6027/87/31, FO 371/35039.
288 Peterson's words in the meeting with Moyne and CO officials, 15.10.43, *ibid.*
289 Minister of State to FO, 22.9.43, E 5697/87/31, FO 371/35038.
290 Katzburg (*Palestine Problem*, p. 77) attributes this appointment to Churchill's wish to be fair with those who opposed his views. We think exactly the other way round! From the outset Churchill tried to pack his Committee with supporters of a creation of a Jewish State in Palestine. Secondly, as we shall see it is illogical to expect an appointment of an opponent when one is trying to hasten the work of a Committee.
291 Prime Minister's minute, 2.10.43, PREM 4/52/1.
292 Weizmann's interviews with Smuts, 23.11.43, WA. See also Rose, *Baffey*, pp. 207–08 and M. Cohen, *Palestine*, p. 136.
293 P(M)(43)15 of 1st November 1943 is the final form which was presented to the Cabinet Committee. E 6027/87/31 of FO 371/35039 has also the original text which was brought from Cairo.
294 Peterson's minute, 5.10.43, E 6027/87/31, FO 371/35039.
295 Record of a meeting ... 15.10.43, E 6027/87/31, FO 371/35039.
296 P(M)(43)16, 1.11.43, E 6028/87/31, FO 371/35040 (= CAB 95/14). A detailed criticism from the FO's point of view of Moyne's and CO's plans can be found in E 6616/87/31, FO 371/35040.
297 P(M)(43)18, 2.11.43, E 6616/87/31, FO 371/35040 (= CAB 95/14). It should be added that on 23 November Eden with Sir Alexander Cadogan left Britain again for conferences in Cairo and Tehran and returned on 11 December. During these periods of absence Richard Law was in charge of the Office.
298 P(M)43, 2nd meeting, 4.11.43, CAB 95/14 (= E 6877/87/31, FO 371/35041).
299 P(M)43, 3rd meeting, 16.11.43, E 7344/87/31, FO 371/35041 (= CAB 95/14).
300 See FO's minute in E 7722/87/31, FO 371/35042 and Moyne's Note, including a telegram from Casey, P(M) 43(27) 9.12.43, *ibid.*
301 Minutes of 7–8 December 1943, E 7847/87/31, FO 371/35042.
302 P(M)(43) 29, 20.12.43, E 8139/87/31, FO 371/35042 (= CAB 66/44).
303 Casey to Eden, 6.11.43, E 6866/2551/65, FO 371/34976.
304 R. M. A. Hankey's minute of a talk with Moyne, 14.12.43, E 7344/87/31, FO 371/35041.
305 Casey's telegram of 28.12.43 is reproduced in P(M)(44)1, 4.1.44, 6(2) 44/12, FO 921/148 (= CAB 95/14).

306 Baxter's minute, 6.1.44, E 8139/87/31, FO 371/35042.
307 WP(44)50, 24.1.44, E 667/95/31, FO 371/40133.
308 Minutes of 14–16 December, 1943, E 7344/87/31, FO 371/35041.
309 Minutes of 16, 18 and 19 December 1943, E 7847/87/31, FO 371/35042.
310 Peterson's Note to the Secretary of State, 13.12.43, *ibid.*
311 Eden's minute of 18 December where he referred Cadogan and Peterson to an earlier minute of his of 18 December, *ibid.*
312 See the previous sections of this chapter.
313 Prime Minister's minute 16.1.44, P(M)(44)4, 21.1.44, E 665/95/31, FO 371/40133.
314 Casey to Churchill, 17.1.44, *ibid.*
315 Prime Minister's minute, 16.1.44, *ibid.*
316 Baxter's Note, 24.1.44, E 665/95/31, FO 371/40133.
317 This reference proves that the 'Minister of State' referred to in the Minutes is Law and not Casey, because only Law added to the Report a Note of Dissent.
318 WM(44), 11th Conclusions, Minute 4, 25.1.44, PREM 4/52/1 (= CAB 65/45).
319 *Ibid.* It appears that at the meeting Eden spoke in terms which were included in the draft minutes and the more negative approaches were inserted only afterwards on a second thought which was certainly influenced by his Office.
320 Foreign Secretary to the Ambassadors, 1.2.44, E 8139/87/31, FO 371/35042.
321 Cornwallis to Eden, 24.2.44, E 1494/95/31, FO 371/40134; Killearn to Eden, 16.2.44, E 1532/95/31, *ibid.*
322 Hankey's minute, 9.3.44; Baxter's minute, 11.3.44; Peterson's minute, 12.3.44; Cadogan's minute, 12.3.44; E 1532/95/31, *ibid.*
323 Eden's minute, 19.3.44, E 1494/95/31, *ibid.*
324 Eden's minute, 18.3.44, E 1532/95/31, *ibid.*
325 See Eden's minute of March 8th at the head of Moyne's letter to Eden of March 1st, E 1837/95/31, FO 371/40134.
326 See all these exchanges of letters of E 2829/35/31, FO 371/40135 and W(44)253, 15.5.44, *ibid.*
327 Baxter's minute, 12.5.44, *ibid.*
328 Eden's minute, 14.5.44, E 2987/95/31, *ibid.*
329 Peterson's minute, 12.3.44, E 1532/95/31, FO 371/40134. Peterson's Note of 18.4.44 and its discussion are to be found in E 3339 and 3340, FO 371/40136.
330 On this debate in June and July 1944 see in E 3968 and 4924/95/31, FO 371/40136.
331 Stanley to Eden, 17.4.44, E 2829/95/31, FO 371/40135.
332 Eden to Prime Minister, 1.6.44, E 3340/95/31, FO 371/40136.
333 HC for Palestine to CO, 16.1.44, in P(M)(44)3, 21.1.44, E 596/95/31, FO 371/40133 (= CAB 95/14).
334 MacMichael's memorandum, 4.2.44, E 1425/95/31, FO 371/40133.
335 Boyd to Baxter, 4.3.44, *ibid.*
336 Peterson's minute, initiated by Cadogan on 12.4.44, *ibid.*
337 Baxter to Boyd, 20.3.44, *ibid.*
338 Casey's telegram of 28.12.43, P(M)(44)1, 4.1.44, 6(2) 44(12), FO 921/148.
339 Spears' interview with Churchill, 9.12.43, St Antony's College, Private Paper Collection, Spears Papers, Box II, File 7.
340 Moyne to Eden, 1.3.44, E 1837/95/31, FO 37/40134.
341 Peterson's minute of 12.3.44 on which Eden noted: 'I agree', E 1493/95/31, FO 371/40134.
342 *Ibid.*
343 Cadogan's minute, 12.3.44, *ibid.*
344 Eden's minute, 14.3.44, *ibid.*
345 FO to Minister Resident, 16.3.44, *ibid.*
346 See in the enclosure with Moyne to Eden, 9.5.44, E 2987/95/31, FO 371/40135; see also the minutes of the Conference in *ibid.*
347 MacMichael's words in *ibid.*
348 Stanley to Eden, 25.5.44, E 3340/95/31, FO 371/40136; same to same, 18.7.44, E 4924/95/31, *ibid.*
349 Churchill to Amery (copy), M 579/4, 21.5.44, E 3145/95/31, FO 371/40136.
350 P(M)(44)8 and 9, 29.8.44 and 6.9.44, CAB 95/14.

NOTES

351 See Churchill to Eden, 11.7.44, *ibid.*
352 See in E 5658/95/31, FO 371/40137 for the CO's new proposal (P(M)(44)10, 11.9.44) and FO's criticism.
353 The minutes and FO's Memorandum P(M)(11) of 15.9.44, are in E 5660 and E 6188/95/31, FO 371/40137.
354 P(M)(44) 1st meeting, 19.9.44, E 5890/95/31, FO 371/40137 (= CAB 95/14); P(M)44 2nd meeting, E 6104/95/31, *ibid.*
355 See in E 5960, 6039 and 6188/95/31, FO 371/40137.
356 P(M)(44)14, 16.10.44, E 6372/95/31, FO 371/40137 (= CAB 95/14).
357 Martin to Gater, reporting the content of Churchill's talk with Weizmann, 4.11.44, PREM 4/52/3. See also next footnote.
358 Weizmann's Note, 4.11.44, WA.
359 A. S. Kirkbride to HC, 25.11.44, enclosed with Boyd to Baxter, 14.12.44, E 7855/41/65, FO 371/39991.
360 Morrison to Churchill, 26.2.45, PREM 4/52/1.
361 P(M)(45)1, 30.3.45, CAB 95/14.

TO CHAPTER 3

1 Taha al-Hashimi, *Mudhakkirat*, II, p. 40.
2 This section owes a lot to I. Gershoni, *The Emergence of Pan-Arabism in Egypt* (Tel-Aviv, 1981). Where no source is quoted, it is usually based on Gershoni's book.
3 See J. Jankowsky. 'Ottomanism and Arabism in Egypt, 1860–1914', *Muslim World*, Vol. LXX, no. 3–4 (July–Oct. 1980) pp. 226–59.
4 I. Gershoni, *Egypt Between Distinctiveness and Unity: The Search for National Identity, 1919–1948* (in Hebrew; Tel-Aviv, 1980), pp. 141–3.
5 Gershoni, *Egypt*, pp. 97–138 and his 'Arabization of Islam: The Egyptian Salafiyya and the Rise of Arabism in Pre-Revolutionary Egypt', *Asian and African Studies*, Vol. 13 no. 1 (1979), pp. 22–57.
6 Zaki Mubarak, *Wahy Baghdad* (Cairo, 1938), pp. 58, 61–2, 63, 64.
7 This subject is discussed here mainly in the footsteps of Gershoni, *Egypt*, pp. 232–4.
8 On those two meetings see Porath, *Palestinian Arab National Movement*, Vol. II, pp. 9–12 and 123–4.
9 'Azzam to Hamilton, 15.10.33, 834/1/33, FO 141/744.
10 *Al-Ahram*, 24, 25, 28.2.36.
11 See *al-Ahram* and *al-Muqattam* of those days.
12 See *al-Muqattam* from 18.1.36 onward.
13 See G. MacKereth's Memorandum, 15.5.36, E 3039/381/65, FO 371/19980. See also A. C. Kerr's minute, 23.9.36, E 5672/5672/93, FO 371/20017.
14 *Al-Muqattam*, 7, 9.1.36.
15 *Ibid.*, 11.1.36 and several March 1936 issues.
16 *Al-Muqattam*, 29.11.39.
17 *Al-Muqattam*, 10.2.40.
18 See the view of D. V. Kelly, of the Egyptian Department of the British FO, 11.11.36, E 6508/10/31, FO 371/21883.
19 *Al-Ahram*, 2.5.37. See also *ibid.*, 19.2.40.
20 *Ibid.*, 13.8.37.
21 *Al-Muqattam*, 28.2.36.
22 *Al-Ahram*, 28.2.36.
23 See, for example, *al-Muqattam*, 16.9.36.
24 Analysis of his writings can be found in W. Z. Cleveland, *The Making of an Arab Nationalist* (Princeton, 1972) and Bassam Tibi, *Arab Nationalism* (London, 1981).
25 Al-Husri, II, p. 476. See also his article, 'Misr wa-al-'Urubah' in his *Ara' wa-Ahadith fi al-Qawmiyyah al-'Arabiyyah* (2nd ed., Beirut, 1956), pp. 95–110.
26 Lampson to Eden, 16.8.36, FO 371/20023. See also Gomaa, pp. 37–8.
27 *Ibid.*

28 Kelly to Eden, 4.9.36, E 5831/381/65, FO 371/19980.
29 Gomaa, p. 38.
30 Campbell's minute, 15.10.37, E 5964/22/31, FO 371/20816.
31 Gomaa, p. 38.
32 *Al-Muqattam*, 10.2.40.
33 *Al-Hilal*, April 1939.
34 Kedourie, *Chatham House Version*, pp. 279–81, and Anwar al-Jundi, *Al-Imam al-Maraghi* (Cairo, 1952), p. 109.
35 Lampson to FO (and enclosures), 25.3.38, FO 371/21878. See also Gomaa, pp. 38–45 and Kedourie, *Chatham House Version*, pp. 198–207.
36 *Al-Balagh*, 24.7.37.
37 See for example, *al-Ahram*, 8.10.38 and 23.1.39.
38 On his political activities see al-Jundi, *Al-Imam al-Maraghi*, pp. 107–17.
39 *Al-Muqattam*, 10.2.40.
40 Gershoni, *Emergence*, p. 36.
41 *Al-Hilal*, April 1939.
42 Gomaa, pp. 40–1.
43 See Gomaa, pp. 49–52.
44 Kerr to Eden, 24.2.36, E 1173/381/65, FO 371/19980. Kerr's minute, 23.9.76, E 5672/5672/93, FO 371/20017. *Al-Ahram*, 6.11.36.
45 D. V. Kelly to Eden, 4.9.36, E 5831/381/65, FO 371/19980 and first to George [Rendel], 12.10.36, E 6696/381/65, *ibid*. Bateman to Eden, 21.8.36, E 5672/5673/93, FO 371/20017.
46 *Al-Ahram*, 5.4.36.
47 'Azzam's Memoirs, part III, *al-Usbu'al-'Arabi*, 31.1.72.
48 Jalal al-Urfahli, *Al-Diblumasiyyah al-'Iraqiyyah wa-al-Ittihad al-'Arabi* (Baghdad, 1944), p. 13. 'Abd al-Mun'im Muhammad Khalaf, *Ma'a al-Qawmiyyah al-'Arabiyyah fi Rub'Qorn* (Cairo, 1958), pp. 61–80. See also Gershoni, *Emergence*, p. 45.
49 See Majid Khadduri, *Independent Iraq* (London, 1965), *passim* and Muhammad Mahdi Kubbah, *Mudhakkirati fi Samim al-Ahdath, 1918–1958* (Beirut, 1965), pp. 54–7. The full name of this Club was al-Muthanna Ibn Harithah al-Shaybani, after the name of the Arab hero who had taken part in the conquest of al-Hirah in southern Iraq, the first acquisition of Islam outside the Arabian Peninsula.
50 C. J. Edmonds, 'Note on the present Orientation of the pan-Arab policy in Iraq', 23.8.38, enclosed with Houstoun-Boswall to Halifax, 29.8.38, E 5393/45/93, FO 371/21847.
51 *Al-Ahram*, 17.1.37, 25.4.37.
52 *Al-Ahram*, 1.4.39 and al-Suwaydi, pp. 280–2.
53 C. H. Bateman to Eden, 3.4.36, E 2306/381/65, FO 371/19980. On the visit of the delegation to Nablus and other Palestinian towns see Akram Zu'aytir, *al-Harakah al-Wataniyyah al-Filastiniyyah 1935–1939; Yawmiyyat Akram Zu'aytir* (Beirut, 1980), p. 51.
54 Longrigg dates its foundation to 1935, but the League's publications (some of which can be found in ZA, S/25, 9332) bear the date of 1933 as the formation year. See also Shibli al-'Aysami, *Hizb al-Ba'th al-'Arabi al-Ishtiraki, I, Marhalat al-Arba'inat al-Ta'sisiyyah, 1940–1949* (Beirut, 1975), p. 19.
55 We found traces of its activities (leaflets, brochures, demonstrations) only from Syria and Lebanon.
56 Qarqut, pp. 178–9.
57 According to the League's publications in ZA, S/25, 9332.
58 'Statement to the Fighting Arab Nation', in *ibid*..
59 An inflated description of Arsuzi's role in the League can be found in Olivier Carré, 'Le Mouvement Idéologique Ba'thiste', in André Raymond (ed.), *La Syrie d'Aujourd'hui* (Paris, 1980), pp. 186–7.
60 Sami al-Jundi, *Al-Ba'th* (Beirut, 1969), p. 20ff. 'Isam Nur al-Din, 'Nazarat fi Ara'Zaki al-Arsuzi fi al-Siyasah', *Al-Fikr al-'Arabi*, no. 22, October 1981.
61 Longrigg, p. 228; John F. Devlin, *The Ba'th Party* (Stanford, 1976), p. 7. On Dandashi's death see Akram Zu'aytir, *Yawmiyyat*, p. 4.
62 See E 2158/22/31, FO 371/20806 and E 3054/22/31, FO 371/20807, both of spring 1937.
63 See, for example, the intelligence Note by E. S. Attiyah, the Sudan Government Intelligence Officer, 31.10.36, enclosed with Lampson to Eden, 17.12.36, E 8028/381/65, FO 371/19980.

64 James Jankowski, 'Egyptian Responses to the Palestine Problem in the Interwar Period'. *IJMES*, Vol. 12 (1980). This article is heavily used in the following sections. See also Bayumi 'Abdallah, p. 72.
65 Lampson to FO, 3.7.36, E 4415/3127/31, FO 371/20035.
66 *Al-Muqattam*, 1.8.36. Gomaa, p. 37.
67 See the text in Lampson to FO, 22.7.36, E 4677/3217/31, FO 371/20035.
68 James Jankowski, 'The Government of Egypt and the Palestine Question: 1936–1939', *MES*, Vol. 17 (1981), p. 429.
69 Kelly to FO, 22.6.36, E 3598/3217/31, FO 371/20035.
70 Jankowski, 'The Government of Egypt', pp. 430–1.
71 For leaflets of that organisation see ZA, S/25, 9350; Arab Bureau News, 16.6.36; *ibid.*, 3139.
72 F. C. Ogden, British Vice-Consul in Damascus, to Eden, 22.8.36, E 5495/94/31, FO 371/20024.
73 Kerr to Eden, 27.5.36, E 3314/2585/93, Bateman to Eden, 14.7.36, E 4774/2585/93, FO 371/20016. Bateman to Eden, 17.8.36, E 5484/94/31, FO 371/20024. Kubbah, p. 59. Some of these leaflets are to be found in ZA, S/25, 9350.
74 For examples see Kerr to Eden, 19.5.36, E 3022/2585/93, FO 371/20016; Bateman to Eden, 25.6.36, E 3986/2585/93, *ibid*.
75 Kerr to Eden, 3.6.36, E 3399/2585/93, FO 371/20016. Bateman to Eden, 17.8.36, E 5484/94/31, FO 371/20024.
76 Al-Suwaydi, *Mudhakkirati*, pp. 283–4. It seems that al-Suwaydi alludes to the Sieff Institute which was then established in Rehovoth and which was afterwards renamed the Weizmann Institute for Scientific Research.
77 On this contingent see Porath, *Palestinian Arab National Movement*, Vol. II, p. 188ff.
78 In addition to the sources quoted in *ibid.*, see Khayriyyah Qasimiyyah (ed.), *Filastin fi Mudhakkirat al-Qawuqji*, Vol. II (Beirut, 1975), p. 14 and Taha al-Hashimi, *Mudhakkirat*, II, p. 128.
79 See Porath, *Palestinian Arab National Movement*, Vol. II, pp. 199–216.
80 Bateman to Eden, 17.8.36, E 5484/95/31, FO 371/20024.
81 G. W. Rendel, 'Palestine ...', 19.10.36, E 6600/94/31, FO 371/20027. See also in E 6745/94/31, FO 371/20028.
82 Bullard to FO, 25.2.37, E 1206/22/31, FO 371/20805.
83 Rendel, 'Palestine ...', 8.2.37, E 884/22/31, FO 371/20804 and E 1019/22/31, *ibid*. See also E 1428, E 1685, E 1707 and E 2012 of 22/31, FO 371/20806. The Iraqi memorandum is included in E 2174/22/31, FO 371/20806.
84 Al-Suwaydi, *Mudhakkirati*, pp. 277 and 298.
85 See, for example, the enclosures with MacMichael to MacDonald, no. 471, 30.6.38, CO 733/368/75156/23 I.
86 For many examples see the leaflets and brochures in ZA, S/25, 9332. See also 'Political News', 6.7.38, ZA, S/25, 10098.
87 See Hafiz Ibn Muhammad to the CS of Zanzibar (copy), 8.6.38, CO 733/367/75156/3 (Part II).
88 Examples are numerous. See for instance in CO 733/367/75156/6 and CO 733/408/75872/28.
89 Bayumi 'Abdallah, p. 73.
90 *Al-Ahram*, 14, 17, 21.7.37. Bayumi 'Abdallah, pp. 74–5. Rendel, 'Palestine: Egyptian Attitude', 13.7.37, E 4162/22/31, FO 371/20809; Lampson to FO, 21.7.37, E 4194/22/31, *ibid*.
91 *Al-Ahram*, 19, 21.9.37.
92 *Al-Ahram*, 12, 21.7.37. Kerr to Oliphant, 24.7.37, E 4455/14/93, FO 371/20795.
93 *Al-Ahram*, 1.8.37.
94 Rendel, 'Palestine: Iraqi Attitude', 13.9.37, E 5392/22/31, FO 371/20813. 'Palestine', December 1938, E 7141/22/31, FO 371/20821.
95 Rendel, 'Palestine: Ibn Saud's Reaction', 20.7.37, E 4167/22/31, FO 371/20809.
96 Baggallay, 'King Ibn Saud and Palestine', 20.8.37, E 4898/22/31 FO 371/20812. This *hadith* can be found in al-Bukhari, *Sahih* (Cairo, 1348h), IV, pp. 114–15.
97 Kelly to FO, 13.9.37, E 5390/22/31, FO 371/20813. See also the notes of 16.9.37 in

98 *Al-Ahram*, 14, 21.7.37.
99 Kerr to FO, teleg. no. 163, 19.7.37, E 4160/22/31, FO 371/20809. Lampson to FO, teleg. no. 427, 25.7.37, E 4320/22/31, FO 371/20810. Kelly to FO, teleg. no. 375, 20.8.37, E 4668/22/31, FO 371/20811.
100 His memorandum is enclosed with his letter of 9 February 1938, to R. G. A. Etherington-Smith of the Eastern Dept., E 788/10/31, FO 371/21873.
101 Bullard to FO, teleg. no. 1, 10.7.37, E 3885/22/31, FO 371/20808; same to same, teleg. no. 2, 14.7.37, E 4034/22/31 *ibid*.
102 Rendel, 'Palestine; Saudi Attitude', 14.7.37, E 4063/22/31, FO 371/20809. See also E 4458/22/31, FO 371/20810.
103 See Porath, *Palestinian Arab National Movement*, Vol. II, pp. 199ff.
104 See the interesting report by S. Atiyyah, of the Sudan Agency in Cairo, 30.12.36, enclosed with Lampson to Eden, no. 56, 13.1.37, E 577/351/65, FO 371/20786.
105 Mahmud Zada of the Saudi Legation in London, to Rendel, 2.1.37, E 38/22/31, FO 371/20804.
106 Trott to FO, teleg. no. 71, 27.8.37, E 5028/22/31, FO 371/20812.
107 Bullard to Eden, no. 33, 4.3.37, E 1639/201/25, FO 371/20839.
108 Porath, *Palestinian Arab National Movement*, Vol. II, pp. 231–2, and the sources quoted there. See also E. Kedourie, 'The Bludan Congress on Palestine, September 1937', *MES*, Vol. 17, no. 1 (1981). When no source is quoted we relied on those publications.
109 *Al-Ahram*, 9.9.37.
110 Akram Zu'aytir, *Yawmiyyat*, pp. 325–6.
111 Kedourie, 'The Bludan Congress', p. 107.
112 See Porath, *Palestinian Arab National Movement*, Vol. II, pp. 233–7.
113 Scott to FO, teleg. no. 232, 8.10.37, E 5872/22/31, FO 371/20816; see also E 5885/22/31, *ibid.*; Rendel, 'Palestine: Saudi Attitude', 12.10.37, E 5938/22/31, *ibid*. See also the files in FO 371/20818.
114 Kelly to Eden, 27.10.37, E 6586/22/31, FO 371/20819.
115 See the minute by R. I. Campbell, head of Egyptian Department, 12.11.37, E 6706/22/31, FO 371/20820. Bayumi 'Abdallah, pp. 73–5.
116 See the petition of 21.11.37, which is enclosed with Lampson to Eden, 9.1.38, E 443/10/31, FO 371/21872.
117 See, for example, Lampson to Halifax, 26.9.38, E 5898/10/31, FO 371/21881. Bayumi 'Abdallah, p. 76. *Al-Ahram*, 1.5.38.
118 See *al-Ahram*, 5.8.38 and 18.11.38.
119 See Porath, *Palestinian Arab National Movement*, Vol. II, p. 275.
120 *Al-Ahram*, 5 and 7.8.38, 10.11.38.
121 Porath, *Palestinian Arab National Movement*, Vol. II, pp. 275–6, and the sources quoted there.
122 Peterson to Halifax, 20.4.38, E 2324/10/31, FO 371/21875. Same to same, 19.11.38, E 7067/1/31, FO 371/2/21867. See also Baxter's minute, 2.8.38, E 4445/38/31, FO 371/21885.
123 *Al-Ahram*, 29.4.38, 30.4.38. A. W. Davis, British Consul in Aleppo, to Halifax, 3.10.38, E 5899/10/31, FO 371/21881.
124 Bullard to FO (copy), 14.3.38, CO 733/370/75156/67; same to same (copy), 19.3.38 *ibid.*; same to same, 20.4.38, *ibid*.
125 His memorandum of 21.4.38 is enclosed with Bullard to Halifax, 21.4.38. E 2780/10/31, FO 371/21876.
126 N. V[ilensky] to M. Sh[ertok], Cairo, 30.5.38, ZA, S/25, 3156. On the composition of the Committee see 'Allubah to Lampson, (copy), 24.6.38, CO 733/368/75156/16. *Al-Ahram*, 26.6.38 and 1.8.38.
127 MacKereth to Eden, 29.11.37, E 7179/22/31, FO 371/20821, Lampson to FO, telegram no. 409, 26.7.38, E 4441/10/31, FO 371/21879.
128 *Khutab Haflat al-Iftitah al-Kubra*.
129 Trott to FO, teleg. no. 139, 4.10.38, E 5791/10/31, FO 371/21881.
130 *Al-Ahram*, 9.10.38. Muhammad Husayn Haykal, *Mudhakkirat fi al-Siyasah al-Misriyyah*

(new ed., Cairo, 1977), Vol. II, p. 132.
131 Lampson to FO, teleg. no. 527, 10.10.38, E 5907/10/31, FO 371/21881.
132 *Al-Ahram*, 8.10.38.
133 See *Taqrir al-Wafd al-Niyabi al-Suri 'an al-Mu'tamar al-Barlamani al-'Alami lil-Difa' 'an Filastin*, p. 40 and Lampson to FO, teleg. no. 534, 11.10.38, E 5942/10/31, FO 371/21881.
134 See Lampson to Halifax, 24.10.34, E 6508/10/31, FO 371/21883.
135 MacKereth to FO, teleg. no. 38, 5.11.38, E 6491/10/31, FO 371/21883. Same to Halifax (copy), 19.11.38, CO 733/398/75156/14. Shuckburgh to Baxter, 31.10.38, E 6405/10/31, FO 371/21883.
136 See Porath, *Palestinian Arab Nationalist Movement*, Vol. II, pp. 281–94. M. Cohen, 'Appeasement in the Middle East: The British White Paper on Palestine, May 1939', *Historical Journal*, Vol. XVI, no. 3 (1973), pp. 571–96.
137 See Porath, *Palestinian Arab National Movement*, Vol. II, pp. 283–4, and the sources quoted there. See also Kamil Muhammad Khillah, *Filastin wa-al-Intidab al-Britani, 1922–1939* (Beirut, 1974), pp. 471–2; and Lampson to FO, teleg. no. 23, 24.1.39, E 712/712/93, FO 371/23213.
138 Zu'aytir, *Yawmiyyat*, pp. 555–6.
139 Porath, *Palestinian Arab National Movement*, Vol. II, p. 288. 'Awni 'Abd al-Hadi claims that he and the delegates of the Arab countries personally advocated during the London Conference and at the April 1939 Cairo Consultation the acceptance of the British proposals. He especially praised Muhammad Mahmud Pasha for 'his energetic endeavour at convincing the Arab countries to accept the White Paper'. [See Khayriyyah Qasimiyyah, *'Awni 'Abd al-Hadi – Awraq Khassah* (Beirut, 1974), p. 118.] Tawfiq al-Suwaydi, on the other hand, claimed the opposite. He wrote in his memoirs that Muhammad Mahmud enthusiastically supported the rejection of the White Paper for personal reasons. He was led to think that the acceptance of the White Paper would be regarded as a personal achievement of 'Ali Mahir Pasha, Head of the Royal Cabinet, who was the most prominent Egyptian representative to the St James's Conference from which Muhammad Mahmud had personally been excluded by King Faruq. Muhammad Mahmud was afraid that this personal achievement might have led 'Ali Mahir to the premiership at his expense! (Al-Suwaydi, *Mudhakkirati*, pp. 327–9.) On Muhammad Mahmud's exclusion from the Conference see Haykal, *Mudhakkirat*, II, p. 132.
140 *Al-Ahram*, 2, 3, 4, 12, 17, 11.39, 23, 24, 25.4.40, 2, 16,5.40.
141 Baggallay, 'Interest of Saudi Arabian Government in the Palestine Question', 3.1.40, E 50/50/31, FO 371/24565.
142 J.C. Hurewitz, *The Struggle for Palestine* (New York, 1976), pp. 115–16.
143 See many examples in the files, especially E 1952/50/31, of 1940 in FO 371/24566.
144 See Baggallay's Note, 3.1.40, E 50/50/31, FO 371/24565. See also the other files in that volume.
145 Newton to FO, teleg. no. 134, 29.4.40, E 1901/50/31, FO 371/24566.
146 Khadduri, *Independent Iraq*, pp. 162–211.
147 See in Halifax's memorandum, 'The Arab States and Palestine', WP(G) (40) 149, 12.6.40, CAB 67/6.
148 Edmond's Note, 'Present Pan-Arab Activity in Iraq', 31.7.40, enclosed with Newton to Halifax, 3.8.40, E 2283/2029/65, FO 371/24549.
149 G. Antonius, 'Memorandum On Arab Affairs' (copy), 3.10.40, enclosed with Downie to FO, 4.1.41, E 53/53/65, FO 371/27043.
150 Newton to FO, teleg. no. 16, 6.1.41, E 110/110/65, FO 371/27046.
151 See many examples in *FRUS*, 1943, Vol. IV, pp. 765, 769, 785 and 805; *FRUS*, 1944, Vol. V, pp. 564–5, 570–3, 577–8, 582–5, 590, 604–10, 621, 638–40, 648–9, and 652–4; *FRUS*, 1945, Vol. VIII, p. 2, 670 and 689. See also *al-Ahram*, 24.3.44.
152 See the Note by T. Scott, 4.2.43, CO 743/87 (Part 1) 79238/3 (Part i).
153 See the telegrams of February and March 1943, in E/1050/506/65, FO 371/34955.
154 Wikeley to FO, teleg. no. 8, 2.3.43, E 1524/506/65, FO 371/34956.
155 Eyres's minute, 17.3.43, E 1542/506/65, FO 371/34956.
156 Wikeley to FO, teleg. no. 7, 14.2.43, E 1234/506/65, FO 371/34955.
157 See his *Egypt* (in Hebrew); *The Emergence; Arabization*; and 'Major Trends in The

Evolution of the Egyptian National Self Image, 1900–1950', Occasional Papers on the Middle East, no. 16, Haifa University, August 1977.
158 Bayumi 'Abdallah, p. 86.
159 Al-Husri, II, pp. 66–9.
160 *Al-Muqattam*, 5, 14, 18.1.36, 9.4.36.
161 Bayumi 'Abdallah, p. 86.
162 *Al-Muqattam*, 23.2.36.
163 Kerr to Eden, 24.2.36, E 1173/381/65, FO 371/19980, same to same, 26.2.36, E 1175/381/65, *ibid*.; see also Lampson to Eden, 24.2.36, E 1326/381/65, *ibid*.; *Al-Muqattam*, 11.1.36.
164 *Al-Muqattam*, 16.2.36 and 15.3.36.
165 Taha al-Hashimi, *Mudhakkirat*, I, p. 243.
166 See his minute of 23.9.36 in E 5672/5672/93, FO 371/200017.
167 *Al-Ahram*, 28.2.36, *Al-Muqattam*, 1.3.36.
168 *Al-Ahram*, 2, 5, 7.3.36.
169 *Ibid.*, 24.2.36.
170 *Ibid.*, 29.2.36.
171 See Zaki Mubarak's impressions in his book *Wahy Baghdad* (Cairo, 1938), pp. 400, 410, 417.
172 Bayumi 'Abdallah, pp. 87–8. See also Lampson to Eden, 2.1.37, E 351/351/65, FO 371/20786.
173 Zaki Mubarak, pp. 56, 213 and 412.
174 *Ibid.*, p. 217.
175 *Ibid.*, pp. 61 and 269–70. See also Karim Thabit's similar view in *al-Muqattam*, 8.5.40.
176 Muhammad Husayn Haykal's article in *al-Hilal*, April 1939, p. 12.
177 See many descriptions in *al-Ahram*, 8.1.37, 29, 30.1.39, 20, 24.1.40, 24.12.41, 31.7.42, 18.12.42, 8.12.43, 9.7.44, 13, 22.8.44, 19.3.45; *Al-Muqattam*, 4.7.42. See also report of 24.1.43 ZA, S/25, 3544 and of 24.12.43 and 26.7.44, ZA, S/25, 3160. An article stressing the importance of these conferences by Muhammad 'Ali 'Allubah was published in *al-Hilal*, April 1939, pp. 50–2.
178 See the reaction of *al-Muqattam* of 11.11.41. This newspaper called upon the Egyptian Government to begin the long march towards Arab unity by acting in the cultural and economic spheres. Since this was exactly the view that was then being adopted by the British Government (see later, pp. 253–4), this identity of views gives credence to the claim of Jewish observers of Arab affairs in those days that *al-Muqattam* used to express the views of the British Embassy in Cairo. (See Sasson, *On the Way to Peace*, p. 249.)
179 Lampson to Eden, 1.12.41, E 8275/53/65, FO 371/27043. *Al-Ahram*, 20.11.41, 7.12.41.
180 See the report of 27.12.41 enclosed with Boyd to Baxter, 23.2.42, E 1316/49/65, FO 371/31337. See also the report of 20.6.42, enclosed with CO to FO, July 1942, E 4624/49/65, FO 371/31338.
181 Lampson to MacMichael (copy), 23.1.42, E 1786/49/65, FO 371/31337.
182 See Charles D. Smith, '4 February 1942: Its Causes and Its Influence on Egyptian Politics and on the Future of Anglo-Egyptian Relations, 1937–1945', *IJMES*, Vol. 10 (1979), pp. 453–79.
183 Bayumi 'Abdallah, p. 88. Lampson to Eden, 16.12.42, J 125/2/16, FO 371/35528. *Al-Muqattam*, 2.4.42.
184 Lampson to Eden, 2.1.43, J 490/2/16, FO 371/35528.
185 Lampson to Eden, 16.12.42, J 125/2/16, FO 371/35528. Lampson to FO, teleg. no. 2576, 13.11.42, J 4665/38/16, FO 371/31575. *Al-Ahram*, 15.11.42.
186 Wikeley to FO, teleg. no. 76, 22.2.43, E 1110/506/65, FO 371/34955. *Al-Ahram*, 26.1.43.
187 *Al-Muqattam*, 6.3.40.
188 Weekly Political and Economic Report, 12–18 August, no. 37, J 3731/2/16, FO 371/35537. Urfahli, p. 336. *Al-Ahram*, 8, 13.8.43. *Al-Muqattam*.
189 *Al-Balagh*, 13.5.43.
190 See Rendel's memorandum, 27.3.33, E 1732/347/65, FO 371/16854; See also Humphrys to Wauchope (copy), 22.3.33, E 2009/347/65, *ibid*.
191 See E 42/2/25 and E 1117/2/25, FO 371/15285 and Taha al-Hashimi, *Mudhakkirat*, I, p. 102.

NOTES

192 See the details in Urfahli, pp. 337–52. See also Ryan's Note on his talk with Fu'ad Hamzah, 31.3.36, enclosed with Ryan to Eden, 1.4.36, E 2110/52/25, FO 371/20056.
193 As an indicator to the greater degree of friendship and trust see Ryan to Simon, 4.2.35, E 1309/1309/25, FO 371/19017; and Bagdad Despatch, no. 105, 21.2.35, E 1456/1309/25, *ibid.*
194 Ryan to Simon, 11.4.35, E 2703/1309/25, *ibid.*
195 Kerr to Hoare, 24.6.35, E 3887/1309/25, FO 371/19017.
196 Rendel, 'Proposed Saudi-Iraqi Treaty', 3.7.35, E 4069/1309/25, *ibid.*
197 Kerr to Hoare, 11.12.35, E 7468/1309/25, *ibid.*
198 See the draft in E 4472/1309/25, FO 371/19017.
199 Ryan to FO, teleg. no. 1, 3.1.36, E 52/52/25, FO 371/20056.
200 See the draft in E 225/52/25, *ibid.*
201 See the draft in E 764/52/25, *ibid.*
202 See for the English text in E 1974/52/25 *ibid.* The Arabic text is to be found in E 2110/52/25, *ibid.* The term *wahdah qawmiyyah* was translated by FO officials as 'racial unity'. Today no doubt it would have been translated as 'national unity', although the objective 'national' does not differentiate between one's allegiance to one's state (like Iraq, etc.) and pan-Arab loyalty and identification.
203 Kerr to Eden, 28.5.36, E 3284/381/65, FO 331/19980.
204 Kerr to Eden, 16.12.36. E 8066/52/25, FO 371/20056; same to FO, teleg. no. 45, 29.12.36, E 56/56/25, FO 371/20838. On the ratifying legislation by the Iraqi Parliament and the ratification see in E 2846 and E 7751/52/25, FO 371/20056.
205 Kerr to Eden, 23.2.37, E 1431/56/25, FO 371/20838.
206 See E 1649, E 1921, E 2308, E 2592, E 3030 and E 3195/56/25, *ibid.*
207 Kerr to Eden, 27.5.37, E 3030/56/25, *ibid.*
208 Ryan to Eden, 28.4.36, E 2835/52/25, FO 371/20056.
209 *Al-Muqattam*, 23.3.36.
210 *Al-Muqattam*, 2.4.36.
211 *Al-Ahram*, 24.12.37.
212 Kerr's minute, 23.9.36, E 5672/5672/93, FO 371/20017.
213 MacKereth to Eden (enclosing a Memorandum respecting Pan-Arabism), 15.5.36, E 3039/381/65, FO 371/19980.
214 Baggallay, 'Arab Federation, 28.9.39, E 6357/6/31, FO 371/23739.
215 Hassan Ahmed Ibrahim, *The 1936 Anglo-Egyptian Treaty* (Khartoum, 1976), p. 54. *Al-Ahram*, 25.4.36. *Al-Muqattam*, 9.4.36.
216 When no other source is quoted this section is based on E 1132, 1898, 1909, 1914, 2199, 2487, 2491, 2628, 2980, 3198, 7300, E 7752/202/25, FO 371/20061.
217 *Al-Ahram*, 20.4.36. *Al-Muqattam*, 19, 20.11.36.
218 See, for example, in E 1109/1108/25, FO 371/23272.
219 Bateman to Eden, 21.8.36, E 5672/5672/93, FO 371/20017.
220 Kerr to Eden, 18.1.37, E 698/698/93, FO 371/20801.
221 Lampson to Eden, 1.2.37, E 987/698/93, FO 371/20801.
222 See in Kelly to Eden, 26.3.37, E 1870/698/93, *ibid.*
223 Lampson to FO, teleg. no. 23, 24.1.39, E 712/712/93, FO 371/23213; Baxter to Peterson, 24.2.39, E 1503/712/93, *ibid.*
224 Peterson to FO, teleg. no. 27, 4.3.39, E 1828/712/93, *ibid.*
225 Bateman to FO, teleg. no. 482, 30.8.39, E 6167/474/93, FO 371/23211.
226 Lampson to FO, teleg. no. 970, 24.8.40, E 2514/2514/93, FO 371/24562.
227 Jamil 'Arif (ed.), *Safahat min al-Mudhakkirat al-Sirriyyah li-Awwal Amin 'Amm lil-Jami'ah al-'Arabiyyah 'Abd al-Rahman 'Azzam*, 1st Vol. (Cairo, 1977), pp. 251–7. See also Haykal, *Mudhakkirat*, II, pp. 145–6.
228 See Lampson to FO, teleg. no. 718, 13.7.40, E 2283/2029/65, FO 371/24549.
229 See Edmonds' memorandum, 31.7.40, enclosed with Newton to Halifax, 3.8.40, E 2283/2029/65, FO 371/24549.
230 Newton to FO, teleg. no. 121, 9.2.41, E 426/53/65, FO 371/27043.
231 Antonius, 'Memorandum on Arab Affairs', 3.10.40, enclosed with Downie to Baxter, 4.1.41, E 53/53/65, FO 371/27043.
232 *Al-Hilal*, April 1939.

233 *La Bourse Egyptienne*, 20.9.41, 10.12.42, 21.12.43. *Al-Ahram*, 28.1.43.
234 *Al-Hilal*, April 1939.
235 See *al-Muqattam*, 10.2.40, 4.3.40, 6.3.40, 8.5.40, 16.7.40 and 18.8.40.
236 Sasson, *On the Way to Peace*, p. 190.
237 He repeated the same ideas in *al-Musawwar* in November 1942. (See Sasson, *On the Way to Peace*, pp. 257–8.)
238 *Al-Muqattam*, 20.2.41.
239 *Al-Muqattam*, 24.12.42. See also *al-Ahram* issues of winter 1943.
240 Lampson to FO, teleg. no. 268, 26.4.40, J 1335/92/16, FO 371/24625.
241 James P. Jankowski, *Egypt's Young Rebels, 'Young Egypt': 1932–1952* (Stanford, 1975), pp. 80–1.
242 See in E 9471/3/65, FO 371/45241.
243 See in *ibid*.
244 Sasson, *On the Way to Peace*, p. 258. *Al-Ahram*, 28.1.43.
245 *Al-Muqattam*, 15.6.31. Lampson to Eden (with enclosure), 13.1.37, E 577/351/65, FO 371/20786.
246 See the memorandum on 'The Club of Arab Union', 7.7.43, ZA S/25, 416. See also Lampson to Eden, 8.4.43, E 2274/506/65, FO 371/34957.
247 See the memorandum 'Comités arabes au Caire', 9.4.43, 149/46/43, FO 141/866 (Part I). See also Weekly Report, 8–14 April 1943, no. 19 J 1950/2/16, FO 371/35533 and Stone to Cornwallis (copy), 20.3.43, E 1875/506/65, FO 371/34956.
248 Embassy to FO (with enclosure), 10.2.43, E 1161/27/89, FO 371/35175.
249 Taha al-Hashimi, *Mudhakkirat*, II, p. 43.
250 Urfahli, pp. 291–3. Shone to Eden, 10.3.43, E 1749/506/65, FO 394/34956.
251 Lampson to Eden, teleg. no. 6, 31.3.43, E 2029/506/65, FO 371/34956.
252 See in doc. 149/39/43 of 30.3.43, FO 141/866 (Part I). See also Cornwallis to FO, teleg. no. 258, 13.3.43, E 1494/506/65, FO 371/34955 and same to same, teleg. no. 313, 1.4.43, E 1920/506/65, FO 371/34956.
253 Taha al-Hashimi, *Mudhakkirat*, II, p. 44.
254 See the report of 27.12.41 in E 1316/49/65, FO 371/31337.
255 See Khalil Zuwiyya Yamak, *The Syrian Social Nationalist Party: An Ideological Analysis* (Cambridge, Mass., 1966); John P. Entelis, *Pluralism and Party Transformation in Lebanon; Al-Kata'ib 1936–1970* (Leiden, 1974); and Hisham Sharabi, *al-Jamr wa-al-Ramad* (Beirut, 1978).
256 See in Haykal, *Mudhakkirat*, II, pp. 158–9.
257 Edmond's Memorandum, 31.7.40, enclosed with Newton to Halifax, 3.8.40, E 2283/2029/65, FO 371/24549. See also HC for TJ to CO (copy), 14.8.40, E 2418/953/65, FO 371/24548.
258 Newton to FO, teleg. no. 397, 1.8.40, E 2027/953/65, *ibid*.
259 Lampson to FO, teleg. no. 975, 25.8.40, E 2511/953/65, *ibid*.
260 Baggallay, 'Memorandum: Ibn Saud and Arab Politics', 6.8.40, E 2027/953/65, *ibid*.; Seymour's Memorandum, 13.8.40, E 2397/953/65, *ibid*.; Stonehewer-Bird to FO, teleg. no. 189, 16.8.40, E 2432/953/65, *ibid*.; same to same, teleg. no. 203, 3.9.40, E 2594/953/65, *ibid*.; same to same, teleg. no. 209, 7.9.40, E 2620/953/65, *ibid*.
261 *Al-Ahram*, 8, 11, 17.11.40.
262 *Documents on German Foreign Policy*, Series D, Vol. X, (London, 1960), pp. 556–60. See also L. Hirszowicz, *The Third Reich and the Arab World* (London, 1966), pp. 82–108.
263 Mahmud al-Durrah, *Al-Harb al-'Iraqiyyah al-Britaniyyah, 1941* (Beirut, 1969), pp. 136–47.
264 G. Warner, *Iraq and Syria, 1941* (London, 1974), pp. 36–66.
265 Hirszowicz, pp. 108–29. Al-Durrah, pp. 355–8.
266 Hirszowicz, pp. 144–6. 'Abd al-Razzaq al-Hasani, *al-Asrar al-Khafiyyah fi Harakat al-Sanah 1941 al-Taharruriyyah* (2nd ed., Sidon, 1964), pp. 151–2, 157–9.
267 Taha al-Hashimi, *Mudhakkirat*, I, p. 471.
268 Cornwallis to FO, teleg. no. 856, 31.7.41, E 4348/62/89, FO 371/27304. Al-Suwaydi, *Mudhakkirati*, pp. 422–3.
269 Gomaa, pp. 103–4.
270 *Al-Muqattam*, 30.5.41.
271 *Al-Ahram*, 31.5.41.

272 *Ibid.*, 6.6.41. See also Ahmad al-Shuqayri, *Hiwar wa-Asrar ma'a al-Muluk wa-al-Ru'asa'* (Beirut, n.d.), p. 63.
273 Lampson to FO, teleg. 1648, 3.6.41, E 2797/53/65, FO 371/27043.
274 See the Note of the talk between Wahbah and Eden in E 4761/53/65, FO 371/27044. See also Eden to Stonehewer-Bird, 15.8.41, *ibid., ibid.*
275 See in E 6636, E 6881 and 6995/53/65, *ibid.*
276 Stonehewer-Bird to FO, teleg. no. 333, E 7395/53/65, *ibid.*
277 Taha al-Hashimi, *Mudhakkirat*, II, p. 43.
278 See the docs. in 356/2/42, FO 141/840. See also *al-Ahram*, 28.3.42 and *al-Muqattam*, 27.3.42.
279 Lampson to FO, teleg. no. 1277, 10.5.42, E 2986/49/65, FO 371/31337.
280 Stonehewer-Bird through Lampson to FO, teleg. no. 1359, 21.5.42, E 3208/49/65, FO 371/31338. See also in 356/6/42, FO 141/840.
281 According to the material in FO 371/31469–31470.
282 See *FRUS, 1943*, Vol. IV, pp. 768–70.
283 Edward Spears to Minister of State (copy), teleg. no. 130, 4.6.42, E 3465/207/89, FO 371/31473; same to same, teleg. no. 167, 24.6.42, E 3812/207/89, *ibid.*
284 See in E 3998/207/89, *ibid.*
285 See the files in FO 371/35530.
286 Catroux, pp. 259–60. Catroux erroneously thought that Britain was supporting this pan-Arab effort and was encouraging Egypt in its meddling in Syro-Lebanese affairs.
287 See in Gomaa, pp. 153–4. See also Lampson to Acting HC for Palestine (copy), 19.4.42, J 2107/38/16, FO 371/31571.
288 See Habib Jamati's report, 10.6.42, 356/13/42, FO 141/840.
289 See Walter Smart's memorandum 'Egypt and the Arab World'. 3.5.43, 149/2/43, FO 141/866 (Part I).
290 Lampson to FO, teleg. no. 2591, 16.11.42, J 4692/38/16, FO 371/31575.
291 See Report no. 12, 19–24 February 1943, J 1321/2/16, FO 371/35530.
292 Stonehewer-Bird to FO, teleg. no. 52, 13.12.42, E 140/69/25, FO 371/35147.
293 Wikeley to FO, teleg. no. 59, 9.2.43, E 831/27/89, FO 371/35174.

TO CHAPTER 4

1 On Faysal's initiatives see ch. 1, pp. 4–22.
2 HC for Iraq to CO (copy), teleg. no. 609, 18.11.25, FO 371/10852 and the minutes of the interdepartmental meeting, 6.1.26, E 8131/357/89, FO 371/10853. I wish to express my gratitude to Prof. I. Rabinovich who supplied me with these two documents. See also J. E. W. Flood [of the CO] to Rendel, 3.11.31, E 5485/206/85, FO 371/15364.
3 See the minutes of January 1930 in E 444/44/65, FO 371/14485.
4 See the minutes of January 1931 pertaining to file 89059 (Part I) of 1931, CO 732/47.
5 See the exchange of letters and despatches of January–March 1931 in E 417, E 851, and E 1445/206/89, FO 371/15364.
6 Oliphant's and Vansittart's minutes, 30.9.31, E 4784/206/89, FO 371/15364.
7 See their minutes of 29 and 30 September, 1931, *ibid.*
8 ME(O) 11th meeting, 20.10.31, CAB 51/2. See also E 5485/206/89, FO 371/15364.
9 ME(M) 9, 3.11.31 and ME(M) 1st meeting, 17.11.31, CAB 51/5.
10 Cunliffe-Lister to Humphrys (copy), 27.11.31, E 5872/206/89, FO 371/15364. See also Husry, 'King Faysal ...' pp. 328–31.
11 See, for example, Cunliffe-Lister to Wauchope (copy), 19.2.32, E 514/226/89, FO 371/16086.
12 The exchange of letters between the two Offices, the despatches to Iraq, the dealings with the Iraqi Government and the draft and final text of the Treaty, of January–March 1931, are included in E 250/250/65 and the following files of FO 371/15281.
13 Humphrys to Simon, 21.12.32, E 6888/4478/65, FO 371/16011.
14 Humphrys to Simon, 5.1.33 and minutes, E 347/347/65, FO 371/16854.
15 See minutes and despatches of January–March 1933, E 578/347/65, E 905/347/65 and

E 955/347/65, *ibid*. See also Humphrys to Oliphant (enclosing a minute of a talk with Faysal), 23.1.33, E 773/347/65, *ibid*.; same to Simon, 2.2.33, E 863/347/65, *ibid*.
16 See the exchange of letters of Feburary–April 1933, E 1084/347/65, and 1544/347/65, *ibid*.
17 Humphrys to Simon, 5.3.33, E 1469/347/65, *ibid*.
18 See the documents of June 1933 in E 3119, E 3120, E 3728 and 6221/347/65, FO 371/16855.
19 Wauchope to CO, with enclosures (copy), 22.4.36, FO 371/20065.
20 Trott to Halifax, 22.8.39, E 6447/549/25, FO 371/23271.
21 Draft letter of Halifax to CO, April 1939, E 2803/5/89, FO 371/23276.
22 C.W. Baxter's minute, 31.8.39, E 5392/246/25, FO 371/23269.
23 Oliphant's minute, 1.9.39, *ibid*.
24 See the exchange of views between the FO and the CO and the despatch sent to Jedda of September 1939, *ibid*.
25 FO to Bullard, 25.9.39, E 6447/549/25, FO 371/23271.
26 Bullard to Halifax (with enclosure), 29.10.39, E 7604/549/25, *ibid*.
27 See telegrams and minutes of early January 1939, E 18/5/89, FO 371/23276; see also MacKereth to FO, teleg. no. 5, 9.1.39, and last to first, teleg. no. 2, 11.1.39, E 260/5/89, *ibid*.
28 Cox to HC for TJ (copy), 7.1.39 and minutes, E 811/5/89, *ibid*.
29 Catroux, p. 174, and the letters and minutes of November 1939, E 7365/2143/89, FO 371/23280.
30 A.L. Kirkbride to MacMichael (copy), 14.6.39 and Baxter to Shuckburgh, 17.7.39, E 4826/2143/89, *ibid*.
31 S. Moody, CS to the Palestine Government, to General Barker (copy), 24.8.39, E 7365/2143/89, *ibid*.
32 Baggallay to Downie and telegs. to Jedda nos. 138–40, 28.9.39, 6.10.39, E 6697/6697/89, FO 371/23281. See also Eyres's interpretation of these telegrams as 'statement of policy', 27.2.43, E 1132/506/65, FO 371/34955.
33 Downie to Baggallay, 3.10.39, E 6783/6697/89, FO 371/23281; see also CO to MacMichael (copy), 7.10.39, E 6880/6697/89, *ibid*.
34 Newton to Halifax, 14.10.39, E 7087/6697/89, *ibid*.; and his teleg. no. 382, 13.10.39, E 6917/6697/85, *ibid*.
35 See his minute of 28.10.39, E 7087/6697/89, *ibid*.
36 See his minute of 6.10.39, E 6783/6697/89, *ibid*.
37 Baggallay to Luke, 4.11.39, E 7102/6697/89, *ibid*.
38 See the minutes of 24.7.40, E 2027/935/65, FO 371/24548.
39 Gardner to FO, teleg. no. 3, 11.1.41, and the minutes, E 172/169/89, FO 371/27330.
40 HC for TJ to CO (copy), teleg. no. 822, 9.6.41 and minutes of 13.6.41, E 3026/62/89, FO 371/27295.
41 See the minutes on MacMichael's teleg., 24–25.6.41, E 3225/62/89, FO 371/27296.
42 Stonehewer-Bird to FO, teleg. no. 228, 5.7.41, and minutes of 21–24.7.41, E 3981/62/89, FO 371/27301.
43 HC for TJ to CO (copy), 23.7.41, E 4251/62/89, FO 371/27303.
44 HC for TJ to CO (copy), 6.7.41, and minutes, 10–12.7.41, E 3715/53/65, FO 371/27044.
45 ME(M)(41), 3rd mtg., 11.7.41, CAB 95/2.
46 Shuckburgh to Baxter, 28.6.41 and Seymour to former, 5.7.41, E 3407/374/31, FO 371/27137. See also CO to HC for Palestine, 10.7.41, 77241/41, CO 733/444 (Part I)/75872/115.
47 HC for Palestine to CO (copy), teleg. no. 1018, 12.7.41, E 3795/374/31, FO 371/23137.
48 HC for Palestine to CO (copy), 23.7.41 and minutes of July–August, E 4239/374/31, *ibid*.
49 ME(O) 4th mtg., 6.8.41, CAB 95/1.
50 E.B. Boyd to Baxter (and enclosure), 16.8.41, and the minutes of 22–24.8.41, E 4741/374/31, FO 371/27137.
51 See the minutes and Notes of 18–21.9.41, E 5477/259/31, FO 371/27134.
52 HC for TJ to CO (copy), 21.1.42, E 541/541/31, FO 371/31381.
53 Minister of State to FO, teleg. no. 6, 6.2.42, E 901/541/31, *ibid*.
54 See the minutes in E 541/541/31, *ibid*.
55 See the minutes of 15–16.4.42, E 2310/541/31, *ibid*.
56 ME(O)(42) 2nd mtg., 17.4.42, CAB 95/1.
57 The Note of the meeting is included in E 2723/49/65, FO 371/31337.

NOTES

58 See the telegram and exchange of letters between the concerned Offices in E 3063/541/31, FO 371/31381.
59 HC for TJ to CO (copy), teleg. no. 56, 14.7.42, and minutes, E 4488/876/31, FO 371/31382.
60 See his minute of 24.8.42, E 4829/876/31, *ibid.*
61 See 'Abdallah's letter and the minutes in E 7578/49/65, FO 371/31338.
62 See Baxter's minute, 23.3.43 and the draft despatch to the Minister of State, E 1196/506/65, FO 371/34955.
63 See Boyd to FO (and enclosure), 3.11.43, E 7029/506/65, FO 371/34963A. This volume (FO 371/34963A) contains only the part of the material originally included which was released for inspection. The remainder (FO 371/34963B) has not yet been released.
64 See the exchange of letters and minutes of March 1944, E 1425/95/31, FO 371/40133.
65 Moyne to Eden, 1.3.44, last to first, 29.3.44 and minutes, E 1837/95/31, FO 371/40134.
66 See many files of FO 371/40135 and 371/40136.
67 The minutes of 3–4.12.35 and the despatch of 3.3.36 are in E 6911/6911/31, FO 371/18965.
68 Kerr to Eden (and enclosure), 7.11.36, E 7217/94/31, FO 371/20029.
69 See the minutes in E 7217/94/31, FO 371/20029.
70 See the minutes of September 1937 in E 5338/22/31, FO 371/20813.
71 Kerr to Eden, 25.12.37, E 175/10/31, FO 371/21872.
72 See the minutes of January 1938, E 257/10/31, *ibid.*
73 Bullard to FO, teleg. no. 28, 231.1.38 and last to first, teleg. no. 19, 2.2.38, E 452/10 31, *ibid.*
74 See the Notes of the talks of January–February 1938 and the minutes, in E 473 and 502/10 31, *ibid.*
75 FO to Bullard, teleg. no. 99, 23.6.39, E 4246/1809/25, FO 371/232737; see also latter to former, 27.6.39, E 4933/1809/25, *ibid.*
76 Baxter to W. H. B. Mark [of the British Embassy in Paris], 11.7.39, E 4584/1809/25, *ibid.*
77 Baggallay to J. C. Sterndale-Bennett, 7.12.39, and Bullard to Baggallay, 7.11.39, E 7675/1809/25, *ibid.*
78 Cornwallis to FO, teleg. no. 1140, 8.10.41, E 6477/1/93, FO 371/27081.
79 See the exchange of telegrams and minutes, 22–27.1.43, E 538/506/65, FO 371/34955.
80 Cornwallis to FO, teleg. no. 111, 29.1.43 and last to first, teleg. no. 103, 5.2.43, E 636/506/65, *ibid.*
81 See the telegrams and minutes, 24.2–12.3.43, E 1132/506/65, *ibid.*
82 See telegrams and minutes, 28.2.–3.3.43, E 1331/506/65, *ibid.*
83 Cornwallis to FO, teleg. no. 252, 12.3.43, E 1405/506/65 FO 371/34955.
84 Eyres's minute, 21.3.43, E 1621/506/65, FO 371/34956.
85 See their minutes of 23.3.43 and 25.3.43, E 1196/506/65, FO 371/34955. The minutes of Minister of State Resident in the Middle East, with the concurrence of the British Embassy in Cairo, expressed the same attitude as the Ambassador in Iraq and recommended that Nuri be advised to proceed more slowly with his scheme, but his telegram reached the FO after Peterson and Cadogan had already decided. (See Minister of State to FO, teleg. no. 749, 27.3.43, 149/36/43, FO 141/866 Part I.)
86 See Hankey's minute, 7.9.43, E 1196/506/65, *ibid.*
87 FO to Cornwallis, teleg. no. 84, 18.4.44 and minutes of 16.4.44 and 18.4.44, E 915/41/65, FO 371/39987.
88 Cornwallis to FO, teleg. no. 947, of 7.10.43, E 6010/2551/65, FO 371/34976.
89 See Ryan to FO, teleg. no. 1, 2.1.31 and Baxter to CO, 15.1.31, E 42/2/25, FO 371/15285.
90 Humphrys to FO, 9.1.33 and Rendel's minute, 23.3.33, E 1469/347/65, FO 371/16854.
91 'Attitude of His Majesty's Government Towards the Question of Arab Unity', 27.3.33, E 1732/347/65, *ibid.*
92 Parkinson to Rendel, 11.5.33, E 2500/347/65, *ibid.*
93 Laithwaite to Rendel, 8.6.33, E 3014/347/65, *ibid.*
94 See in E 3119 and E 3120/347/65, FO 371/16855.
95 See their minutes of July 1933, file 834 (1933), FO 141/744.
96 These reports were included in Cairo despatches, 24.2.36, E 1326/381/65, FO 371/19980; 2.4.36, E 1886/381/65, *ibid.*; 17.12.36, E 8020/381/65, *ibid.*, 13.1.37, E 577/351/65, FO 371/20786; 5.11.37, E 6730/351/65, *ibid.*
97 See in E 8028/381/65, FO 371/19980.
98 See in E 6730/351/65, FO 371/20786.

99 See Rendel's minute and Oliphant's concurrence, 24.11.37, E 6730/371/65, FO 371/20786.
100 Lampson to Eden, 24.2.36, E 1326/381/65, FO 371/19980; see also same to same, 2.4.36, E 1886/381/65, *ibid.*
101 Kelly to Eden, 4.9.36, E 5831/381/65, *ibid.*
102 Lampson to Eden, 17.12.36, E 8028/381/65, *ibid.*
103 Kelly to Eden, 4.9.36, E 5831/381/65, *ibid.*
104 Lampson to Eden, 17.12.36, E 8028/381/65, *ibid.*
105 Lampson to Eden, 13.1.37, E 577/351/65, FO 371/20786.
106 Kerr to Eden, 28.5.36, E 3284/381/65, FO 371/19980.
107 MacKereth to Eden, 15.5.36, E 3039/381/65, *ibid.* Mr Ogdan, his Vice-Consul, repeated the same view in even stronger terms a few months later. See M. Cohen, *Palestine*, p. 140. M. Cohen was erroneous in his claim that the view of Ogdan (a Vice-Consul!) provided 'a fair summary of the British view'.
108 See his minutes of 11.6.36 and 14.6.36, E 3039/381/65, FO 371/19980.
109 See the minutes in E 5360/351/65 and 6730/351/65, FO 371/20786.
110 See the minutes of 11.6.36 and 17.6.36, E 3284/381/65, FO 371/19980.
111 See the minutes in E 5831 and E 8028/381/65, *ibid.*
112 See his minutes, 23.9.36, E 5672/5672/93, FO 371/20017.
113 See K. R. Johnstone's minute, 2.3.35, E 1309/1309/25, FO 371/19017.
114 See the minutes of July 1935, E 3887/1309/25, *ibid.*; Rendel, 'Proposed Saudi-Iraqi Treaty', 1.7.35, E 4063/1309/25, *ibid.*
115 See the minutes of January 1936 in E 225/52/25, FO 371/20056. See further in other files of this volume.
116 Newton to FO, teleg. no. 109, 3.4.40 and minutes, E 1488/166/25, FO 371/24586.
117 See Rendel's minute, 22.9.36, E 5672/5672/93, FO 371/20017 and Ward's minute, 19.2.37, E 987/698/93, FO 371/20801.
118 Lampson to FO, 1.2.37 and Ward's minute, 19.2.37, E 987/698/93, *ibid.*
119 See in *ibid.*
120 Eden to Lampson and Clark-Kerr, 11.3.37, E 1361/698/93, *ibid.*
121 Lampson to Eden, 26.3.37, E 1870/698/93, *ibid.*
122 See the minutes of January–February 1939, E 712/712/93, FO 371/23213; see also Baxter to Peterson, 24.2.39, E 1503/712/93, *ibid.*
123 See the exchange of cables and minutes of September 1939, FE 6320/47/93, FO 371/23211.
124 Lampson to Eden, 8.4.37 and minutes, E 2158/22/31, FO 371/20806.
125 MacKereth to Eden, 26.5.37 and minutes, E 3054/22/31, FO 371/20807.
126 See Porath, *Palestinian Arab National Movement*, Vol. II, pp. 199ff.
127 See Baggallay to Colonial Under-Secretary, 10.8.37, CO 733/352/75718/12.
128 Porath, *Palestinian Arab National Movement*, Vol. II, pp. 205 and 214. Gomaa, pp. 53–4.
129 See the material in E 6600/94/31, FO 371/20027 and Kerr to Rendel, 25.11.36, E 7647/94/31, FO 371/20029.
130 See the material of September 1938 in E 5651/10/31, FO 371/21881.
131 E. J. Cawthorn to R. G. A. Etherington-Smith (and enclosure), 9.2.38 and FO's minutes, E 788/10/31, FO 371/21873.
132 See his minute of 21.9.38, E 5393/45/93, FO 371/21847.
133 See the material in E 6341/10/31, FO 371/21883 and E 6962/1/31, FO 371/21866.
134 Lampson to Halifax, 24.10.38, and the minutes of 10–11 November, E 6508/10/31, FO 371/21883.
135 See the material of January 1939, E 1274/29/31, FO 371/23245.
136 Halifax to King 'Abd al-'Aziz Al Sa'ud, March 1939, E 2313/177/25, FO 371/23269.
137 IO to FO, 1.4.39, E 2428/177/25, *ibid.*
138 See in E 2537/177/25, *ibid.*
139 Lampson to Oliphant (with enclosure), 24.4.39 and minutes E 3416/3416/25, FO 371/23194.
140 'Record of a conversation with the Comte de Caix de St. Aymour'. 15.4.39, E 2655/284/65, FO 371/23194.
141 See the records in FO 371/23223–23225.
142 E. Phipps to FO (transmitting Butler's talk), 26.5.39, CO 733/408/75872 (Part I).
143 See Porath, *Palestinian Arab National Movement*, Vol. II, pp. 284–94.

NOTES

144 See in E 6357/6/31 of September 1939, FO 371/23239. See also Y. Porath, 'Britain and Arab Unity (Document)', *Jerusalem Quarterly*, no. 15, Spring 1980, pp. 36–50.
145 Havard to Baggallay, 14.11.39, E 7748/7314/65, FO 371/23195.
146 MacKereth to Baggallay, 15.11.39, E 7749/7314/65, *ibid.*
147 WO to FO, 1.11.39, E 7314/7314/65, FO 371/23195.
148 See further references to the memorandum as a guiding instrument in Baggallay to Downie, 28.5.40, E 2027/953/65, FO 371/24548; Churchill to Cornwallis, 11.3.41, E 694/1/93. FO 371/27061.
149 See the material in E 1117/953/65, FO 371/24548.
150 Downie to Baggallay (and enclosure), 14.5.40 and minutes, E 2027/953/65, FO 371/24548.
151 FO to Newton, teleg. No. 366, 3.8.40 (and minutes), *ibid.*
152 See, for example, in E 1117/953/65 of February–March 1940, FO 371/24548.
153 See the allusion to the French position in the FO's Memorandum, 'Syria and Lebanon', 1.7.40, M.E.(O) (40) 21, CAB 95/1.
154 See Crosthwaite's minute and Baggallay's consent, 24.7.40, E 2027/953/65, FO 371/24548.
155 See Baggallay's note, 5.9.40, E 2635/2635/31, FO 371/24569.
156 Lampson to FO, teleg. no. 718, 13.7.40, E 2283/2029/65, FO 371/24549.
157 Newton to FO, teleg. no. 408, 3.8.40, *ibid.*
158 HC for Palestine to CO (copy), teleg. no. 692, 22.7.40, *ibid.*
159 See MacMichael to Lloyd (copy), 7.10.40, E 59/53/65, FO 371/27043. In light of MacMichael's position one is not surprised to read that he did not hide from Antonius his dissatisfaction with the former's memorandum, even though Antonius had prepared it at MacMichael's request. (See Taha al-Hashimi, I, pp. 363–4 and on p. 4 of the Report on Arab Federation, E 436/49/65, FO 371531337.)
160 See the minutes and FO's telegrams of August 1940, *ibid.*, and FO to Newton, teleg. no. 416, 20.8.40, E 2289/2289/31, FO 371/24569.
161 Lloyd to Gibb (copy), 29.7.40, *ibid.*
162 See the material in E 2474/2029/65, FO 371/24549.
163 Downie, 'Arab Federation', 1.2.41, CO 732/87 (Part I)/79238 (1941). Gomaa, pp. 22–3. G. Cohen, 'Churchill and the Establishment of the War Cabinet Committee on Palestine (April–July 1943)', *Ha-Tzionut*, Vol. IV (1975), p. 264, note 16.
164 See the Note and minutes of February 1941 in CO 732/87 (Part I)/79238 (1941). One should add that Downie's Note repeated the basic assumptions and conclusions of Baggallay's memorandum of September 1939 (see this ch., pp. 238–40) from which it is quoted.
165 Baxter to Downie, 20.1.41, E 53/53/65, FO 371/27043. It is true that to judge by the minutes in the file Anthony Eden was not shown Antonius's memorandum (which is in that file) and was not consulted about the reaction to it. But the fact that Baxter suggested such a far-reaching step, contrary to the views of his subordinates (E. M. Eyres and A. V. Coverley-Price), to an outside agency strengthens our belief that in doing so he got backing from 'above'. Furthermore, in reaction to a report from Sir Basil Newton on 6 January 1941 about German activities in Saudi Arabia (see p. 246 of this chapter) Baxter minuted that the non-implementation of the White Paper prejudiced the position of Britain's friends in the Middle East and he proposed 'to submit shortly the question of making some declaration of the policy in the near future'. Seymour stated that 'as regards Palestine, so far as I know, His Majesty's Government would not be willing to make any further statement at present'. Seymour's view was endorsed on 11 and 12 January by both Cadogan and Eden. Baxter may have understood his superiors' opposition to making a statement on Palestine as agreement to making such a statement on the broader issue of British Middle Eastern policy and may have got oral clarifications from them. Anyway, it is unreasonable to think that he would have committed the FO – in writing! – to a view contrary to his Secretary of State's view. (See the minutes in E 110/110/65, FO 371/27046.)
166 See MacMichael to CO (copy), teleg. no. 245, 24.2.41, minutes, and latter to former (copy), teleg. no. 343, E 691/374/31, FO 371/27137.
167 The draft, the minutes and the despatch of 11.3.41 are to be found in E 694/1/93, FO 371/27061.
168 Lampson to Seymour, 26.4.41, E 2191/53/65, FO 371/27043. Lampson to FO, teleg. no. 962, 15.4.41, E 1550/194/65, FO 371/27048.

169 Newton to FO, teleg. no. 16, 6.1.41, E 110/110/65, FO 371/27046 and Stonehewer-Bird to FO, teleg. no. 91, 26.3.41, E 1162/194/65, FO 371/27048.
170 Cornwallis to FO, teleg. no. 60, 23.4.41, E 1795/1795/98, FO 371/27105.
171 Butler to Baxter, 9.5.41, E 2702/53/65, FO 371/27043.
172 W. Churchill, *The Second World War*, Vol. III (London, 1948), p. 289. See also Warner, p. 128.
173 War Cabinet Defence Committee (Operations), Minutes of Meeting, 8.5.41, CAB 69/2.
174 All these discussions and minutes are to be found in E 2191/53/65, FO 371/27043.
175 'Our Arab Policy', W.P. (41) 116, 27.5.41 and the minutes and letters there, E 2716/53/65, FO 371/27043.
176 Michael J. Cohen who interprets Eden's speech chiefly as an attempt to assuage any blow that the Arabs may have suffered as a result of the crushing by British hands of Rashid 'Ali al-Kaylani's regime, cannot explain why Eden acted so urgently in making his statement public prior to the approval of his Memorandum by the Cabinet. (See M. Cohen, 'A Note on the Mansion House Speech', p. 384.)
177 On the preparation of the speech see in E 2703/53/65, *ibid*. D. Carlton overlooked the Middle Eastern policy of Eden, but concluded that the relations between Eden and Churchill were often marked by competition and jealousy. (See D. Carlton, *Anthony Eden – A Political Biography* (London, 1981).)
178 Prime Minister's Personal Minute to Foreign Secretary, no. 598/1, 30.5.41 and Eden's reply, 2.6.41, E 2668/149/31, FO 371/27131.
179 War Cabinet Conclusions, 56(41), 3.6.41 and Eden's Memorandum, E 2716/53/65, FO 371/27043.
180 See the Memoranda and the minutes in E 3824/53/65, FO 371/27044.
181 See the material of August 1941, in E 4761/53/65, *ibid*.
182 Baxter's minute, 10.7.41, E 3715/53/65, *ibid*.
183 ME(M)41, 3rd mtg., 11.7.41, CAB 95/2.
184 Minutes of 24–25 June, E 3225/62/89, FO 371/27296 and minutes of 17 and 18 July, E 3795/374/31, FO 371/27137.
185 ME(O)(41), 4th mtg., 6.8.41, CAB 95/1.
186 On the preparation of the instructions to MacMichael in August 1941 see in F 4741/374/31, FO 371/27137.
187 See their minutes of 23 and 24 August, *ibid*.
188 Cabinet Conclusions, WM(41) 87th, 28.8.41, CAB 65/19.
189 FO's memorandum, 21.9.41, MSC(41) 10, 22.9.41, CAB 95/8.
190 Seymour's minute, 25.9.41, E 6189/53/65, FO 371/27045.
191 Parkinson's Note in Shuckburgh to Seymour, 25.9.41, E 6189/53/65, FO 371/27045.
192 ME(O)41(5), 2.10.41, E 62277/53/65, *ibid*.
193 MacMichael's Note (copy), September 1941, E 6210/53/65, and same to CO (copy), teleg. no. 1371, 7.10.41, E 6488/53/65, *ibid*.
194 FO to Embassies in the ME, 4.10.41, E 6277/53/65, *ibid*.
195 Lampson to FO, teleg. no. 3221, 14.10.41, E 6636/53/65, *ibid.*, see also his despatch of 2.10.41, E6864/53/65, *ibid*.
196 Cornwallis to FO, 4.10.41, E 6881/53/65, *ibid*.
197 See the telegrams and minutes of October–November 1941 in E 6995, E 7395 and E 7894/53/65, *ibid*.
198 Minister of State to FO, teleg. no. 98, 5.11.41, E 7282/53/65, *ibid*.
199 ME(O) 6–10, October 1941, CAB 95/1 and ME(O)(41) 5th and 6th mtgs., 8.10.41 and 18.12.41, CO 732/87(Part I)/79238 (1941).
200 ME(O)(42)5, 14.1.42, E 436/49/65, FO 371/31337.
201 See the minutes in *ibid*.
202 See the telegrams and minutes of February 1942, in E 838/49/65, *ibid*.; see also the material in E 976/49/65, *ibid*.
203 Eden to Cranborne, 1.4.42, E 976/49/65, CO 732/87 (Part I)/79238 (1942); C.H. Thornley, Cranborne's Private Secretary to O. Harvey, Eden's Private Secretary, 4.4.42, *ibid*.
204 See Gomaa, pp. 116–32.
205 See the material of April 1942 in file 356/6/42, FO 141/840.

NOTES

206 Lampson to FO, teleg. no. 2576, 13.11.42 and minutes, J 4665/38/16, FO 371/31575; same to same, no. 2591, 16.11.42, *ibid.*, *ibid.*
207 E. Monroe to Harold Caccia, 28.8.42 and minutes, E 5124/43/65 and the material in E 5631/49/65, FO 371/31338.
208 Gibb's memorandum, 'A Plan of Arab Federation', 16.12.42 and minutes, E 7433/49/65, *ibid.*
209 See the material of March 1943 in File 149/22/43, FO 141/866 (Part I).
210 This is clearly stated in an exchange of telegrams between Casey and Cadogan in March 1943, E 1587/506/65, FO 371/34956.
211 On the preparation of the reply see E 1143/506/65, FO 371/34955.

TO CHAPTER 5

1 Taha al-Hashimi, *Mudhakkirat*, II, p. 43. See also Weekly Report, 25.2.43 – 3.3.43, J 1322/2/16, FO 371/35530.
2 Al-Shuqayri, *Hiwar*, p. 63.
3 See *al-Ahali*'s leading article, 26.2.43, in E 1363/506/65, FO 371/34955.
4 Haykal, *Mudhakkirat*, III, p. 20.
5 *Al-Balagh*, 1.3.43.
6 *Al-Ahram*, 28.2.43. See also for further reactions in J 1322/2/16, FO 371/35530.
7 *Al-Ahram*, 1, 2.3.43. See also Taha al-Hashimi, *Mudhakkirat*, II, p. 37.
8 Cornwallis to FO, teleg. no. 235, 8.3.43, E 1382/506/65, FO 371/34955; see also E 1465, E 1513/506/65, *ibid.*
9 Lampson to FO, teleg. no. 629, 28.3.43, J 1431/2/16, FO 371/35530.
10 Lampson to FO, teleg. no. 533, 13.3.43, J 1203/2/16, FO 371/35530.
11 See the reports of February and March 1943 in J 1217 and J 1366/2/16, *ibid.*
12 See for details Haykal, *Mudhakkirat*, II, pp. 193–209.
13 See Gomaa, pp. 61–3.
14 Killearn to Eden, 16.3.43, J 2855/2/16, FO 371/35536. According to a detailed and convincing British intelligence report the Black Book damaged Nahhas's reputation mainly within the educated classes. (See in J 2928/2/16, FO 371/35536.)
15 *Al-Ahram*, 31.3.43. See also Lampson to FO, teleg. no. 639, 31.3.43, E 1888/506/65, FO 371/34956.
16 See the telegram and minutes of early April 1943 in E 1950/506/65, *ibid.* See also Shone to Eden, 1.4.43, E 2096/506/65, FO 371/34957.
17 *Al-Ahram*, 4.4.43. See also the material in file 149/46/43, FO 141/866 (Part I).
18 *Al-Ahram*, 4, 7.4.43.
19 Taha al-Hashimi, *Mudhakkirat*, II, p. 43.
20 MacMichael to CO (copy), 22.4.43, E 5821/506/65, FO 371/34962.
21 MacMichael to CO (copy), 16.4.43, E 2290/506/65, FO 371/34957. See also Taha al-Hashimi, *Mudhakkirat*, II, p. 47.
22 *Al-Ahram*, 8.4.43.
23 MacMichael to CO (copy), 24.4.43, E 2455/506/65, FO 371/34957.
24 Wikeley to FO, 10.6.43, E 3388/605/65, FO 371/34958.
25 Killearn to Eden, 20.6.43, J 2893/2/16, FO 371/35576; same to same, 4.7.43, J 3115/2/16, *ibid.* *Al-Ahram*, 11.6.43.
26 *Ibid.*, 17.6.43.
27 For a detailed analysis of the separate talks of Nahhas and the various Arab leaders see Gomaa, pp. 165–90.
28 Gomaa, pp. 188–9.
29 Nahhas to Killearn, 27.12.43, E 589/589/31, FO 371/40143; and all the 589/31 files in *ibid.*
30 Shone to Eden, 9.11.43 and minutes, E 7350/506/65, FO 371/34963A.
31 Killearn to FO, teleg. no. 5, 15.1.44, E 356/41/65, FO 371/39987; see also the material in E 1349/41/63, *ibid.*
32 Same to same, teleg. no. 62, 13.3.44, E 1817/41/65, *ibid.*
33 See in E 7489/506/65 of November 1943, FO 371/34963A.

34 Wikeley to FO, teleg. no. 316, 3.8.43, E 4631/526/65, FO 371/34960.
35 Wikeley to FO, teleg. no. 245, 10.6.43, E 3388/605/65, FO 371/34959 and his despatch of 12.6.43, E 3595/506/65, *ibid.*
36 Gomaa, p. 163.
37 Wikeley to FO, teleg. no. 349, 30.8.43, E 5194/506/65, FO 371/34961; Jordan to FO, teleg. no. 378, 12.9.43, E 5488/506/65, *ibid.* And mainly the material in E 6264/506/65, FO 371/34962. See further Gomaa, pp. 172–9.
38 Jordan to Eden (and enclosures), 2.10.43, E 6264/506/65, FO 371/34962.
39 Gomaa, pp. 187–8.
40 See minutes of Nuri's and Nahhas's talks, 31.7.43–6.8.43, E 5376/506/65, FO 371/34961.
41 *Ibid.*
42 On the talks between Yusuf Yasin and Nahhas see in E 8115/506/65, FO 371/34963A.
43 On his talks with Nahhas see in E 6291/506/65, FO 371/34962.
44 See in E 6707/506/65, FO 371/34963A.
45 Killearn to Eden, 23.1.44 and 21.2.44, E 737 and E 1349/41/65, FO 371/39987; G. Furlonge, British Consul General in Beirut, to Spears, 21.1.44, F 871/41/65, *ibid.*
46 Shone to FO, 9.11.43, E 7349/506/65, FO 371/34963A and the minutes of the talks in E 7981/506/65, *ibid.*
47 Shuqayri, *Hiwar*, pp. 64–6.
48 See *Minutes* of the second talk, 1.8.43, E 5376/506/65, FO 371/34961.
49 Shuqayri, *Hiwar*, p. 68.
50 See in E 7981/506/65, FO 371/34963A.
51 See in E 5376/506/65, FO 371/34961.
52 *Al-Ahram*, 16.3.44.
53 See in Shone to Eden (and enclosure), 6.10.43, E 6291/506/65, FO 371/34962.
54 Shone to Eden (and enclosure) 9.11.43, E 7349/506/65, FO 371/34963A.
55 Killearn to Eden (with enclosure), 8.12.43, E 7981/506/65, FO 371/34963A.
56 Same to same (with enclosure), 21.4.44, E 1349/41/65, FO 371/39987.
57 See in E 5376/506/65, FO 371/34961.
58 See in E 7981/506/65, FO 371/34963A.
59 Killearn to Eden, 23.1.44 and 21.2.44, E 737 and E 1347/41/65, FO 371/39987. See also *al-Ahram*, 4.1.44.
60 See in E 5376/506/65, FO 371/34961.
61 See in E 1349/41/65, FO 371/39987.
62 Weekly Political and Economic Report, 28.10.43–3.11.43, J 30/2/16, FO 371/35539.
63 See in E 6264/506/65, FO 371/34962 and in Shone to Eden, teleg. no. 1997, 23.10.43, J 4441/2/16, FO 371/35539.
64 Shone to Eden, 26.10.43, E 6706/506/65, FO 371/34963A, see also Baxter to Wahbah, 8.12.43, E 7797/506/65, *ibid.* Yusuf Yasin held to that proposition in the consultations (see E 8115/506/65, *ibid.*).
65 Killearn to Eden, 8.12.43, E 7981/506/65, *ibid.*
66 See the telegrams in E 5156/27/89 and E 5353/27/89, FO 371/35181.
67 C.-in.-C. Middle East to WO (copy), 14.10.43, E 6264/506/65, FO 371/34962. Shone to Eden, 26.10.43, E 5890/506/65, FO 371/34963A; and same to same, 9.11.43, E 7349/506/65, *ibid.*
68 Spears to FO, teleg. no. 95, 22.2.44, E 1209/41/65, FO 371/39987.
69 See in Killearn to Eden, 8.12.43, E 7981/506/65, FO 371/34963A and in E 1349/41/65, FO 371/39987.
70 Taha al-Hashimi, *Mudhakkirat*, II, p. 55.
71 On this tactical point in E 1349, E 1876 and E 1891/41/65, FO 371/39987.
72 Shone to FO, teleg. no. 303, 5.9.43, E 5353/506/65, FO 371/34961 and HC for TJ to CO (copy), 3.11.43, E 6721/506/65, FO 371/34963A.
73 Cornwallis to FO, teleg. no. 2, 1.1.44, E 41/41/65, FO 371/39987.
74 See in E 701/41/65, *ibid.*
75 Cornwallis to FO, telegs. no. 99 and 155, 8, 25.2.44, E 915 and 1330/41/65, FO 371/39987.
76 Spears to FO, teleg. no. 95, 21.2.44, E 1209/41/65, *ibid.*

77 HC for TJ to CO (copy), telegs. no. 11 and 15, 31.1.44 and 9.2.44, E 785 and E 1024/41/65, *ibid.*
78 HC for TJ to CO (copy), 10.4.44, E 2283/41/65, *ibid.*; and Cornwallis to FO, teleg. no. 303, 11.4.44, E 2244/41/65, *ibid.*
79 Cornwallis to Eden, 31.8.43, E 5375/506/65, FO 371/34961. See also al-Suwaydi, *Mudhakkirati*, pp. 403–05.
80 Killearn to FO, teleg. no. 1274, 26.6.44, E 3777/41/65, FO 371/39988. For the letter of resignation see 'Abd al-Razzaq al-Hasani, *Al-Usul al-Rasmiyyah li-Ta'rikh al-Wizarat al-'Iraqiyyah* (Sidon, 1964), pp. 193–7.
81 Thompson [of the Baghdad Embassy] to FO (with enclosure), 17.7.44, E 4448/41/65, FO 371/39989.
82 Baxter's Note, December 1943, E 7798/506/65, FO 371/34963A; and Moyne's Note, 15.12.43, E 7952/506/65, *ibid.*
83 Cornwallis to Maurice [Peterson], 11.1.44, E 521/41/65, FO 371/39987.
84 See a summary in the Weekly Report, no. 20, 15.4.43 – 21.4.43, J 1951/2/16, FO 371/35533 and the same, no. 28, 10.6.43 – 16.6.43, J 2786/2/16, *ibid.*
85 Killearn to Eden, 16.6.43, J 2855/2/16, FO 371/35536.
86 See Habib Jamati, 'Comités Arabes au Caire', 9.4.43, 149/46/43, FO 141/866 (Part I).
87 Killearn to FO, teleg. no. 294, 31.8.43, E 5352/506/65, FO 371/34961 and Weekly Report, no. 36, 5.8.43 – 11.8.43, J 3628/2/16, FO 371/35537. See also the Memorandum on Arab Unity, p. 38, E 9471/3/65, FO 371/45241.
88 Furlonge to Spears, 21.1.44, E 871/41/65, FO 371/39987. Emile Eddé had been a lifelong supporter of the French position in Lebanon and during the autumn 1943 crisis in Lebanon accepted a French nomination as *Chef d'Etat*, which ruined his position.
89 See the Memorandum, p. 38, in E 941/3/65, FO 371/45241.
90 On the British backing see Hankey's minute, 1.6.44, E 2793/41/65, FO 371/39988.
91 For this internal struggle see all the reports in FO 371/41316–41319.
92 See the Weekly Report, no. 19, 8.4.43 – 14.4.43, J 1950/2/16, FO 371/35533.
93 Killearn to Eden, 29.8.43, E 5376/506/65, FO 371/31961. See also Mahmud 'Azmi's claims as reported by D. Ben-Gurion to the JA Executive, ZA, ZE Protocols, 22.8.43, and 'Memorandum on Arab Unity', 1.10.43, para. 22, CO 732/88 (Part II) /79238 (1943–4).
94 In addition to the sources quoted above see in Weekly Report, no. 50, 11.11.43 – 17.11.43, J 4842/2/16, FO 371/35540.
95 See all the Egyptian newspapers following the arrest. See also Catroux, p. 412.
96 Weekly Report, no. 53, 2.12.43 – 8.12.43, J 5141/2/16, FO 371/35541.
97 Taha al-Hashimi, *Mudhakkirat*, II, p. 57. Al-Ahram, 15.12.43.
98 Shone to FO, teleg. no. 2161, 12.11.43, J 4690/2/16, FO 371/35539. Shone to Scrivener [of the Egyptian Dept.], 16.11.43, J 4799/2/16, FO 371/35540.
99 See, for example, Nahhas to the FO, 16.4.44, enclosed with Eden to Killearn, 5.5.44, E 2793/41/65, FO 371/39988.
100 Killearn to Eden, 10. and 16.3.44, E 1627 and 1734/41/65, FO 371/39987.
101 Moyne to FO, teleg. no. 682, 23.3.44, E 1924/41/65, *ibid.*; Killearn to FO, teleg. no. 603, 25.3.44, E 1947/41/65, *ibid.*
102 Jordan to Eden, 15.3.44, E 1881/41/65, *ibid.*
103 Moyne to FO, teleg. no. 682, 23.3.44, E 1924/41/65, *ibid.* Jordan to FO, teleg. no. 154, 19.4.44, E 2411/41/65, FO 371/39988.
104 In addition to the sources cited in the former note, see the talk with the Lebanese Consul in Jerusalem, in Sasson, *On the Way to Peace*, p. 322–3.
105 Spears to Moyne, teleg. no. 28, 22.4.44, E 2500/41/65, FO 371/39988.
106 Spears to Eden, teleg. no. 37, 28.4.44, E 2814/41/65, *ibid.*
107 *Al-Ahram*, 21.7.44.
108 Jordan to FO, teleg. no. 134, 19.4.44, E 2411/41/65, FO 371/39988.
109 Jordan to Eden (with enclosure), 1.4.44, E 2323/41/65, FO 371/39987.
110 Killearn to FO, teleg. no. 817, 22.4.44, E 2572/41/65, FO 371/39988.
111 Killearn to Eden, 21.4.44, Z 2996/87/69, FO 371/42170.
112 See the Note on the talk between Peterson and M. Viénot, 13.3.44, E 1704/41/65, FO 371/39987.

113 See the Note on the meeting between Lord Moyne and the Sannusi leader, E 6598/41/65, FO 371/39991.
114 Killearn to FO, teleg. no. 481, 10.3.44, E 1627/41/65, FO 371/39987.
115 Killearn to FO, teleg. no. 1202, 14.6.44, E 3516/41/65, FO 371/39988; same to same, 22.6.44, E 3675/41/65, *ibid.*; same to same, teleg. no. 1253, 23.6.44, E 3686/41/65, *ibid.*
116 Cornwallis to FO, teleg. no. 542, 5.7.44, E 3990/41/65, *ibid.* Thompson to FO, teleg. no. 590, 15.7.44, E 4313/41/65, FO 371/39989.
117 Spears to FO, teleg. no. 419, 11.7.44, E 415/41/65, FO 371/39988. HC for TJ to CO (copy), teleg. no. 56, 7.7.44, E 4100/41/65, *ibid.*
118 Ellison (from Jedda) to FO, teleg. no. 227, 6.7.44, E 4008/41/65, *ibid.*
119 Same to same, teleg. no. 229, 8.7.44, E 4015/41/65, *ibid.*, latter to former, teleg. no. 107, 13.7.44, *ibid.*, *ibid.*
120 Ellison to FO, teleg. no. 242, 14.4.44, E 4191/41/65, *ibid.*
121 Same to same, teleg. no. 245, 16.4.44, E 4203/41/65, *ibid.* Jordan to FO, teleg. no. 262, E 4439/41/65, FO 371/39989.
122 Killearn to FO teleg. no. 1466, 26.7.44, E 4478/41/65, *ibid.*
123 Jordan to FO (with enclosure), 20.7.44, E 4525, *ibid.*
124 Jordan to Moyne, and minutes, teleg. no. 143, 3.8.44, E 4680/41/65, *ibid.*
125 See in Jordan to Eden (and enclosures), 3.8.44, E 4840/41/65, *ibid.*
126 Jordan to FO, teleg. no. 301, 12.8.44, E 4854/41/65, *ibid.* For the gradual process of making that decision see the various files included in FO 371/39990.
127 Thompson to FO, teleg. no. 783, 13.9.44, E 5617/41/65, *ibid.*
128 See I. N. Clayton's memorandum on his talk with al-Quwatli, 20.8.44, 48(2), Vol. II, FO 921/220. See also al-Suwaydi, *Mudhakkirati*, pp. 426–7.
129 Jordan to Butler, 1.11.44, E 6910/41/65, FO 371/39991.
130 See in E 455/3/65, FO 371/45235.
131 Killearn to FO, teleg. no. 1466, 26.7.44, E 4478/41/65, FO 371/39989; Thompson to FO, teleg. no. 624, 28.7.44, E 4568/41/65, *ibid.* See also al-Suwaydi, *Mudhakkirati*, pp. 425–6.
132 Thompson to FO, teleg. no. 673, 10.8.44, E 4816/41/65, FO 371/39989. See also same to same, teleg. no. 783, 13.9.44, E 5617/41/65, FO 371/39990.
133 HC for TJ to CO (copy), teleg. no. 42, 48(2) 44/149, Vol. III, FO 921/221.
134 Officer Administering the Government of Palestine to CO (copy), teleg. no. 1219, 29.9.44, E 5923/41/65, FO 371/39990.
135 See Quillian's Report in E 6800/41/65, FO 371/39991.
136 Shone to Eden (with enclosure), 6.10.44, E 6328/41/65, FO 371/39990.
137 See the protocol of that session, E 455/3/65, FO 371/45235.
138 See the Minutes of the second session, *ibid.*, *ibid.*
139 The complete minutes of the Preparatory Committee are included in E 455/3/65, FO 371/45235. Unless other sources are quoted, reference is made to that file.
140 See his words to W. Smart in the latter's Memorandum, 10.10.44, 151/234/44, FO 141/949.
141 See the analysis in al-Shuqayri, *Hiwar*, pp. 68–89.
142 Shone to FO, teleg. no. 1922, 30.9.44, E 5892/41/65, FO 391/39990.
143 It was not coincidental that no other than the Syrian delegate made that proposition! (See Shuqayri, *Hiwar*, p. 93.)
144 See the talk between the Syrian delegate and Brig. I. N. Clayton, 6.10.44, 48(2)44/154, FO 921/221. See also Bisharah al-Khuri, *Haqa'iq Lubnaniyyah* Vol. II (Beirut, 1960), pp. 109–10.
145 See the report of Brig. C. D. Quillian, Head of Political Intelligence Centre, Middle East, enclosed with Shone to Eden, 24.10.44, E 6800/41/65, FO 371/39991.
146 Jerusalem to CO, reported to Minister Resident, Cairo, 12.9.44, 48(2)44/117, FO 921/221.
147 Cornwallis to FO, 25.9.44, E 5886/41/65, FO 371/39990.
148 See the Note on the 7th and 8th meetings, in Burrows to FO, 20.11.44, E 7358/41/65, FO 371/39991 and the full protocol mentioned above.
149 Kirkbride to HC for TJ, enclosed with Boyd to Baxter, 14.12.44, E 7855/41/65, FO 371/39991.
150 For the full text see E 6477/41/65, FO 371/39991. It was published in Gomaa, pp. 272–4.
151 See Fayez A. Sayegh, *Arab Unity: Hope and Fulfillment* (New York, 1958), p. 128.

NOTES

152 See Yasin's words to a British official in doc. 48(2) 44/153, FO 921/221.
153 For the exchange of telegrams between Ibn Saud and Yusuf Yasin see E 6478/41/65, FO 371/39991.
154 See Smart's Memorandum, 7.10.44, 151/234/44, FO 141/949. See also Nahhas's version on his unilateral step of publication in Muhammad 'Ali al-Tahir, *Zalam al-Sajin* (Cairo, 1951), p. 573.
155 See Quillian's Report, E 6800/41/65, FO 371/39991.
156 Jordan to FO, teleg. no. 456, 14.11.44, E 7003/41/65, FO 371/39991. See also Clayton's Note, 21.11.44, 48(2) 44/174, FO 921/222.
157 Minister Resident to FO, teleg. no. 169, 28.11.44, E 7340/41/65, FO 371/39991; see also in E 7621 and E 7636/41/65, *ibid*. See also the telegrams of December 1943 – January 1944 in E 88, E 144, E 156, E 402, E 486 and E 896/3/65, FO 371/45235. See also the colourful but twisted description in Jamil 'Arif, *Mudhakkirat 'Azzam*, pp. 263–7.
158 See the minutes of 10.10.44, E 6102/41/65, FO 371/39990. See also Quillian's Report, 16.10.44, E 6800/41/65, FO 371/39991.
159 Minister Resident to Eden, 1.11.44, E 6697/41/65, FO 371/39991.
160 See *al-Ahram* and *al-Muqattam* of October 1944. It is worthwhile to note that 'Azzam attributed to himself the continuation of the pan-Arab policy by the new Government. He claimed that he had convinced Ahmad Mahir of the usefulness of that course. (See the third part of his memoirs published by *al-Usbu' al-'Arabi*, 31.1.72.)
161 Shone to FO, teleg. no. 220, 8.11.44, E 7004/41/65, FO 371/39991.
162 Khalid al-'Azm, *Mudhakkirat*, Vol. I (Beirut, 1973), p. 256 and Husayn Haykal, *Mudhakkirat*, III, p. 20. See also 'Azzam's memoirs in *al-Usbu' al-'Arabi*, 7.2.72.
163 Killearn to FO, 28.2.45, E 1582/1582/31, FO 371/45415. Same to same, 23.3.45, E 2091/3/65, FO 371/45237. For a very detailed discussion see Gomaa, pp. 239–61.
164 Killearn to FO, telegs. nos. 413, 442 and 476, E 1275, E 1337 and E 1417/3/65, FO 371/45236. Same to same, 9.3.45, E 1930/3/65, FO 371/45237. *Al-Ahram*, 26.1.45.
165 *Ibid*.
166 Killearn to FO, teleg. no. 500, 2.3.45, E 1479/3/65, FO 371/45236; same to same, teleg. no. 506, 3.3.45, E 1484, *ibid*. See also in E 1495 and 1583 of the same volume and Killearn to FO, teleg. no. 587, 9.3.45, E 1668/3/65, FO 371/45237; Graftey-Smith [British Minister at Jedda] to FO, teleg. no. 145, 17.3.45, E 1870/3/65, *ibid*. Killearn to FO, teleg. no. 76, 22.3.45, J 1153/3/16, FO 371/45919.
167 Killearn to FO, 30.3.45, E 2335/3/65, FO 371/45238. A Note on that pressure of 2.3.45 is to be found in file 48(1)45(41), FO 921/323.
168 Gomaa, p. 238.
169 See Musa al-'Alami's hopes as reported by Smart in his Memorandum, 20.3.44, E 2184/3/65, FO 371/45238.
170 *Al-Ahram*, 16.10.44.
171 Shone (now British Minister at Damascus) to Eden, 19.1.45, E 830/3/65, FO 371/45236.
172 Haykal, *Mudhakkirat*, III, p. 20.
173 See 'Azzam's words as reported in Jordan to FO, teleg. no. 16, 5.1.45, E 144/3/65, FO 371/45235. See also Killearn to Eden, 23.3.45, E2091/3/65, FO 371/45237 and Smart's Memorandum, 20.3.45, E 2184/3/65, FO 371/45238.
174 Killearn to Eden, 22.1.45, E 738/209/25, FO 371/45542; same to same, teleg. no. 24, 31.1.45, E 739, *ibid*.
175 Killearn to FO, teleg. no. 243, 2.2.45, J 503/10/16, FO 371/45930. See also *al-Ahram*, 25.–30.1.45.
176 See Smart's minute, 15.3.45, 48(1)45/49, FO 921/323.
177 Gomaa, p. 236–7. *Al-Ahram*, 5.1.45, 6.–19.2.45. Cornwallis to FO, teleg. no. 6, E 749/209/25, FO 371/45542.
178 Killearn to FO, teleg. no. 593, 9.3.45, E 1664/3/65, FO 371/45237; same to same, teleg. no. 667, 19.3.45, E 1881/3/65, *ibid*.; same to same, teleg. no. 705, 23.3.45, E 2010/3/63, *ibid*.
179 Smart's Memorandum, enclosed with Shone to Eden, 1.11.44, E 6875/41/65, FO 371/39991.
180 Jamil 'Arif, *Mudhakkirat 'Azzam*, p. 266. Killearn to Eden, 9.3.45, E 1930/3/65, FO 371/45237. See also same to same, teleg. no. 57, 10.3.45, J 1021/3/16, FO 371/45519; same to same, teleg. no. 76, 22.3.45, J 1153/3/16, *ibid*.

181 Jordan to Eden, 14.12.44, E 157/3/65, FO 371/45235. 'Azzam confirmed it in his memoirs in *al-Usbu' al-'Arabi*, 7.2.72.
182 See for more details in Sayegh, pp. 125–9.
183 Gomaa, p. 263. Young to FO, teleg. no. 219, 2.4.45, E 2162/3/65, FO 371/45238.
184 Smart's Memorandum, enclosed with Killearn to Eden, 23.3.45, E 2184/3/65, FO 371/45238. See also the talk between Musa al-'Alami and the Palestinian journalist Nasir al-Din Nashahibi as reported by the latter in his *al-Hibr Aswad ... Aswad* (Beirut, n.d.), p. 42.
185 See in 79238/4 (1942–3), CO 732/87 Part I.
186 MEWC(43)2, 21.4.43 (= WP(43)246, 17.6.43), E 3577/2551/65, FO 371/34975; MEWC (43) 20, 9.5.43, *ibid.*, *ibid.*; MEWC(43)10, 2.5.43, *ibid.*, *ibid.*; WP(43)247, 17.6.43, E 3234/2551/65, *ibid.*; Eden to Churchill, 10.6.43, and minutes *ibid.* *ibid.*
187 Peterson, 'The Middle East and the Post-War Settlement', 25.6.43, E 3931/506/65, FO 371/34959. MSC(43)1 and 2, 29.6.43 and 2.7.43, E 3896/2551/65 and E 4081, FO 371/34975.
188 'British Policy in the Middle East', WP(43)301, 12.7.43, E 4079/2551/65, *ibid.*
189 'British Policy in the Middle East', WP(43)302, 8.7.43, E 4264/2551/65, *ibid.* Eden's remarks appear on the margins of Casey's Memorandum.
190 War Cabinet Conclusions, 99(43), 14.7.43, *ibid.*, *ibid.*; 'British Policy in the Middle East', WP(43)312, 15.7.43, and War Cabinet Conclusions, 101(43), 19.7.43, E 4265/2551/65, *ibid.*
191 See for example the material in E 6481 and 6486/2551/65, FO 371/34976; E 4336/87/31, FO 371/35036 and, especially, 'British Policy in the Middle East', enclosed with Eden to Moyne, 18.4.44, E 1580/16/65, FO 371/39984 and E 2099/16/65, FO 371/39985.
192 'Note on Palestine Question', 1.11.43, P(M)(43)16, E 6028/87/31, FO 371/35040.
193 See minutes of 23.–24.3.43, E 1640/506/65, FO 371/34956; FO to British representatives in the ME, teleg. no. 252, 26.3.43, *ibid.*, *ibid.*; see also the material in E 1685 and E 1701/506/65, *ibid.*
194 Casey to FO, teleg. no. 749, 25.3.43, E 1838/506/65, *ibid.*; see minutes of 7.–8.4.43, E 1920/506/65, *ibid.*
195 See the minutes of E. A. Chapman-Andrews of the Egyptian Department, and of P. Scrivener, the Head of that Department, 14.4.43, J 1644/2/16, FO 371/35531. See also Hankey's minute, 10.8.43, E 4686/506/65, FO 371/34960.
196 See Eyres's minute, 3.4.43, E 1919/506/65, FO 371/34956, and Peterson's minute, 2.5.43, E 2455/506/65, FO 371/34957.
197 See a slightly different approach in Gomaa, p. 162. Our interpretation is strengthened by 'Azzam who tells us that Nahhas made his declaration after he had been encouraged by the British to do so, but 'Azzam erroneously attributed that move to Lord Killearn and not to Casey. (See Jamil 'Arif, *Mudhakkirat 'Azzam*, p. 263.)
198 Caccia's and Peterson's minutes, 29.4.43, E 2434/506/65, FO 371/34957.
199 Wikeley to FO, teleg. no. 326, 9.8.43, and minutes of 10.8.43, F 4690/506/65, FO 371/34960. 'Record of Conversations between Ibn Saud, Sheikh Yusuf Yasin and His Majesty's Minister, 20.–21.9.43', E 6264/506/65, FO 371/34962.
200 Jordan to Cairo Embassy, teleg. no. 25, 5.10.43, E 5994/506/65, FO 371/34962. Shone to FO, 26.10.43, E 6706/506/65, FO 371/34963.
201 FO to ME Embassies, 8.10.43, E 5994/506/65, FO 371/34962.
202 Peterson's note, 6.10.43, E 6027/87/31, FO 371/35039.
203 Smart's Memorandum, 12.10.43, and Eden's Minutes, 13.10.43, 149/140/43, FO 141/866 Part 2.
204 See Price's Question, the Department's reply and the letter of Law to Price, 29.11.43, E 6897/506/65, FO 371/34963.
205 Peterson's minute, 28.1.44, E 596/95/31, FO 371/40133.
206 Shone to FO, 26.10.43, E 6706/506/65, FO 371/34963.
207 Peterson's minute and FO to Killearn, teleg. no. 243, 18.2.44, E 915/41/65, FO 371/39987; Dominion Office to Dominion Governments (copy), teleg. no. 339, 6.3.44, *ibid.*
208 Killearn to FO, teleg. no. 347, and Eden's minute, 24.2.44, E 1264/41/65, *ibid.*; FO to Killearn, teleg. no. 304, 2.3.44, E 1330/41/65, *ibid.*
209 See Eyres's minute of 13.3.44 which was concurred with by Hankey and Baxter, and Peterson's minute of 14.3.44, E 1627/41/65, *ibid.*

210 The proceedings of the conference are enclosed with Moyne to Eden, 9.5.44, E 2987/95/31, FO 371/40135.
211 See their minutes of 24.–25.3.44, E 1891/41/65, FO 371/39987.
212 Killearn to Beirut Legation (copy), teleg. no. 28, 20.4.44, E 2456/41/65, FO 371/39988; Killearn to FO, teleg. no. 1142, 5.6.44, E 3374/41/65, *ibid.*
213 See the minutes of 1.–2.6.44, E 2793/41/65, *ibid.*
214 See the material in E 3516, E 3627 and 3686/41/65, *ibid.*; Peterson, 'The Arab Conference in Cairo', 14.7.44 and Baxter's minute, 21.7.44, E 4216/41/65, *ibid.*
215 Cornwallis to FO, teleg. no. 542, 5.7.44, E 3990/41/65, *ibid.*; Ellison to FO, teleg. no. 229, 8.7.44, E 4015/41/65, *ibid.*; Killearn to FO, teleg. no. 1366, 10.7.44, E 4075/41/65, *ibid.*
216 Spears to FO, teleg. no. 419, 11.7.44, E 4155/41/65, *ibid.*; Killearn to FO, teleg. no. 1505, 31.7.44, E 4167/41/65, FO 371/39989; same to Eden, 16.8.44, E 5197/41/65, *ibid.*
217 FO to Wikeley, teleg. no. 107, 13.7.44, E 4015 and E 4076/41/65, FO 391/39988.
218 See the telegrams and minutes of July 1944, E 4203/41/65, FO 371/39989. See also the illuminating interview between Brig. I. N. Clayton and Shukri al-Quwatli on that subject, 20.8.44, 48(2), Vol. II, FO 921/220.
219 See the minutes of Young, Baxter and Peterson, 6.–8.8.44, E 4714/41/65, FO 391/33989.
220 Jordan to FO (and enclosure), 3.8.44, E 4840/41/65, *ibid.*; same to same, teleg. no. 301, 12.8.44, E 4854/41/65, *ibid.* See also Clayton's memorandum on his talks with Arab leaders, 24.8.44, and minutes, 48(2)44/108, FO 921/220; and his note of 5.9.44, 48(2)44/117, Ref. – /2, FO 921/221.
221 See the material of September 1944, E 6387/41/65, FO 371/39990; see also Moyne to FO, teleg. no. 2105, 7.9.44, E 5488/41/65, *ibid.*; and further files in that volume.
222 *Al-Ahram*, 28.9.44.
223 Yusuf Yasin to Ibn Saud, 6.10.44, enclosure with Wikeley to FO, 12.10.44, E 6478/41/65, FO 371/39991.
224 See his minute, 10.10.44, E 6137/41/65, FO 371/39990. Clayton's minute, 25.12.44, 48(2)44/197, 48(2) Vol. IV, FO 921/222.
225 Shone to Eden, 23.10.44, E 6477/41/65, FO 371/39991.
226 Moyne to Eden, 19.10.44, E 6697/41/65, *ibid.*; Cornwallis to same, 5.11.44, E 7213/41/65, *ibid.*
227 See the minutes of early November 1944, E 66971/41/65, *ibid.*
228 PICME Report, signed by Brig. C. D. Quillian, enclosed with Shone to Eden, 24.10.44, E 6800/41/65, *ibid.* Clayton's Note 8.1.45, 48(1)45/6, 48(1) Vol. I, FO 921/323.
229 Smart's Memorandum, enclosed with Cairo Embassy's despatch, 1.11.44, E 6875/41/65, FO 371/39991.
230 Cornwallis to Eden, 5.11.44, and minutes, E 7213/41/65, *ibid.*
231 See the material of November 1944, E 7010/41/65, *ibid.* See also Sir E. Grigg [the new Minister Resident] to FO, teleg. no. 6, 29.1.45, E 802/3/65, FO 371/45236; CO to HCTJ (copy), teleg. no. 398, 3.3.45, *ibid.*, *ibid.*
232 FO to Jedda, telegs. 288, 28.11.44, E 7003/41/65, FO 371/39991; Jordan to Eden, 30.11.44, E 7636/41/65, *ibid.*
233 Smart's Memorandum, 10.10.44, 151/234/44, FO 141/949.
234 Jordan to FO, teleg. no. 16, 15.1.45, E 144/3/65, FO 371/42535.
235 See, for example, Killearn to FO, teleg. no. 500, 2.3.45, E 1479/3/65, FO 371/45236; same to same, teleg. no. 510, 3.3.45, E 1495/3/65, *ibid.*; same to same, teleg. no. 524, 5.3.45, E 1583/3/65, *ibid.* Same to same, teleg. no. 575, 8.3.45, E 1636/3/65, FO 371/45237; see also in E 1668, E 1793, E 1839/3/65, *ibid.*
236 Killearn to FO, teleg. no. 508, 3.3.45, E 1483/3/65, *ibid.* FO to Killearn, teleg. no. 421, 10.3.45, E 1639/3/65, FO 371/45237.
237 Killearn to FO, teleg. no. 76, 22.3.45, J 1153/3/16, FO 371/45919.
238 See the minute of 20.3.45 and Baxter's initials of 22.3.45, E 1881/3/65, FO 371/45237.
239 See the minutes of 27.–28.3.45, E 2010/3/65, *ibid.*
240 Colonial Secretary's Memorandum, 30.3.45, P(M)(45)1, CAB 95/14.
241 Shuqayri, *Hiwar*, pp. 62 and 66.
242 Jamil 'Arif, *Mudhakkirat 'Azzam*, pp. 260–3.
243 'Abd al-Rahman al-Rafi'i Fi A'qab al-Thawrah al-Misriyyah Vol. III (Cairo, 1951), p. 141.

244 Mohamad Abdul Aziz, 'The Origin and Birth of the Arab League', *Revue Egyptienne de Droit International*, Vol. 11 (1955), pp. 56–7. He quoted Jon Kimche, *Seven Fallen Pillars* (London, 1953), p. 47.
245 Aharon Cohen, *Political Developments in the Arab World* (in Hebrew; Merhavia, 1959), p. 102.
246 Ya'acov Shim'oni, *The Arab States* (in Hebrew; Tel-Aviv, 1977), pp. 230–2.
247 Catroux, p. 220.
248 Michel Laissy, *Du Panarabisme à la Ligue Arabe* (Paris, 1948), pp. 100–03.
249 See in doc. no. 834 (1933), FO 141/744.
250 Lyttelton to FO, teleg. no. 6, 4.2.42, E 901/541/31, FO 371/31381.
251 ME(M)(41) 3rd mtg., 11.7.41, CAB 95/2.
252 HC for Palestine to CO, 16.1.44, P(M)44(3), 21.1.44, E 596/95/31, FO 371/40133.
253 Shertok's report to ZE in London, 16.12.42, ZA, Z/4 302/26.
254 Newton to FO, teleg. no. 375, 19.6.40, E 2027/953/65, FO 371/24548.
255 Sharett, *Political Diaries, 1940–1942*, p. 55. Shuqayri, *Hiwar*, p. 71.
256 See the report on the discussion of the Syrian delegation to the 1938 Inter-Parliamentary Arab Conference in Cairo, 3.10.38, ZA, S/25, 9900.
257 Moyne to Law (enclosing the report of his talk), 29.11.43, E 7575/506/65, FO 371/34963.
258 Gomaa, p. 70, n. 1.
259 De Gaury, 'Note On Conversation With Nuri Pasha on 25th December 1942', 29.12.42, 79238/3 Part I (1943), CO 732/87 (Part 1).
260 See the material in E 2315/506/65, FO 371/34957.
261 Cornwallis to FO, teleg. no. 947, 7.10.43, E 6010/2551/65, FO 371/34976.
262 Same to Eden, 24.2.44, E 1494/95/31, FO 371/40134.
263 Wikeley to FO, teleg. no. 78, 24.2.43, E 1132/506/65, FO 371/34955; Cornwallis to FO, teleg. no. 206, 1.3.43, E 1259/506/65, *ibid*.
264 MacKereth to Baggallay (and enclosure), 15.11.39, E 7749/7314/65, FO 371/23195.
265 Gibb, 'A Plan of Arab Federation', 16.12.42, E 7433/49/65, FO 371/31338. On the dismal effects of the British propaganda war against the propaganda of the Axis Powers see the memoirs of 'Abd al-Rahman 'Azzam, published in *al-Usbu' al-'Arabi* 31.1.72, p. 34. The files of the Ministry of Information in the Public Record Office generally contain material pertaining to the administration of the newly-formed Ministry and hardly anything of substance about the content of the propaganda itself carried by the Ministry in the Middle East!
266 Wikeley to FO, teleg. no. 66, 18.2.43, E 1050/506/65, FO 371/34955; Spears to FO, teleg. no. 133, 25.2.43, E 1176/506/65, *ibid*.
267 Hankey's minute, 5.6.43, E 3234/2551/65, FO 371/34975.
268 See in E 3234/2551/65, FO 371/34975.
269 'Record of a meeting held on 15 October 1943', E 6027/87/31, FO 371/35039.
270 See minutes of 16–17.6.43, 149/64/43, FO 141/866 Part I.
271 Killearn to FO, teleg. no. 347, 24.2.44, and Eden's minute, E 1264/41/65, FO 371/39987.
272 'A Meeting in Cairo ...', Box III, File 4, Spears Papers, St. Antony's College Documentation Centre.
273 Killearn to FO, teleg. no. 2713, 25.12.44, minutes of December–January, and FO to Killearn, teleg. no. 24, 4.1.45, E 7876/23/89, FO 371/40307.
274 An example of their effect see in MacKereth to Halifax (copy), 19.11.38, CO 733/398/75156/14.
275 Examples of their political repercussions can be found in E 6357, FO 371/23239 and E 2027, FO 371/24548.

BIBLIOGRAPHY

IN HEBREW

M. Bar-Zohar, *Ben-Gurion; A Political Biography* (three vols, Tel-Aviv, 1977).
D. Ben-Gurion, *Memoirs* (Tel-Aviv, 1971).
D. Ben-Gurion, *Memoirs Volume Two, 1934–1935* (Tel-Aviv, 1972).
D. Ben-Gurion, *Memoirs Volume Three, 1936* (Tel-Aviv, 1973).
D. Ben-Gurion, *Memoirs Volume Four, 1937* (Tel-Aviv, 1974).
D. Ben-Gurion, *Memoirs Volume Five, 1938* (Tel-Aviv, 1982).
D. Ben-Gurion, *Meeting with Arab Leaders* (Tel-Aviv, 1967).
Aharon Cohen, *Political Developments In the Arab World* (Merhavia, 1959).
Gavriel Cohen, *The British Cabinet and Palestine, April–July 1943* (Tel-Aviv, 1976).
Gavriel Cohen, *Churchill and Palestine, 1939–1942* (Jerusalem, 1976).
Gavriel Cohen, 'Churchill and the Establishment of the War Cabinet Committee on Palestine (April–July 1943)', *Ha-Tzionut*, Vol. 4 (1975).
D. Eldar, *French Policy in the Levant and Its Attitude Towards Arab Nationalism and Zionism, 1914–1920* (unpublished Ph.D. dissertation, Tel-Aviv University, 1978).
E. Elath, *Return to Zion and the Arabs* (Tel-Aviv, 1974).
I. Gershoni, 'The Arab Nation, The Hashemite Dynasty and Greater Syria in the Writings of 'Abdallah (Parts I, II)'; *Ha-Mizrah He-Hadash*, Vol. XXV (1975).
I. Gershoni, *Egypt Between Distinctiveness and Unity: The Search For National Identity, 1919–1948* (Tel-Aviv, 1980).
A. Ilan, *America, Britain and Palestine; The Origin and Development of America's Intervention in Britain's Palestine Policy, 1938–1947* (Jerusalem, 1979).
N. Katzburg, *From Partition to White Paper; British Policy in Palestine, 1936–1940* (Jerusalem, 1974).
N. Katzburg, *The Palestine Problem In British Policy, 1940–1945* (Jerusalem, 1977).
Y. Nimrod, *The Role of J. L. Magnes in the Cancellation of the Peel Plan* (unpublished M.A. Thesis, Tel-Aviv University, 1977).
I. Rabinovich, 'The Question of the Syrian Monarchy', *Zmanim*, Vol. 1, no. 3 (April 1980).
E. Sasson, *On The Way to Peace* (Tel-Aviv, 1978).
M. Sharett, *Personal Diaries* (Tel-Aviv, 1978).
M. Sharett, *Political Diaries, 1936* (Tel-Aviv, 1968).
M. Sharett, *Political Diaries, Vol. II, 1937* (Tel-Aviv, 1971).
M. Sharett, *Political Diaries, Vol. III, 1938* (Tel-Aviv, 1972).
M. Sharett, *Political Diaries, Vol. IV, 1939* (Tel-Aviv, 1974).
M. Sharett, *Political Diaries, Vol. V, 1940–1942* (Tel-Aviv, 1979).
Y. Shim'oni, *The Arab States; Their Contemporary History and Politics* (Tel-Aviv, 1977).

IN ARABIC

[King]'Abdallah Ibn Husayn, *Mudhakkirati* (Jerusalem, 1945).
Nabih Bayumi 'Abdallah, *Tatawwur Fikrat al-Qawmiyyah al-'Arabiyyah fi Misr* (Cairo, 1975).
Jamil 'Arif (ed.), *Safahat min al-Mudhakkirat al-Sirriyyah li-Awwal Amin 'Amm lil-Jami'ah al-'Arabiyyah 'Abd Rahman 'Azzam*, Vol. I (Cairo, 1977).
Shibli al-'Aysami, *Hizb al-Ba'th al-'Arabi al-Ishtiraki,* Vol. I, *Marhalat al-Arab'inat al-Ta'sisiyyah, 1940–1949* (Beirut, 1975).
Khalid al-'Azm, *Mudhakkirat* (Beirut, 1973).
Mahmud 'Azmi, *Al-Ayyam al-Mi'ah* (Cairo, n.d.).
'Abd al-Rahman 'Azzam, 'Dhikrayat 'Azzam Basha', *al-Usbu' al-'Arabi*, 17.1.72, 24.1.72, 31.1.72, 7.2.72.
As'ad Daghir, *Mudhakkirati 'ala Hamish al-Qadiyyah al-'Arabiyya* (Cairo, 1939).
'Izzat Darwazah, *Hawla al-Qadiyyah al-'Arabiyyah al-Hadithah* (Sidon, 1950).
Mahmud al-Durrah, *Al-Harb al-'Iraqiyyah al-Britaniyyah, 1941* (Beirut, 1969).
'Abd al-Razzaq al-Hasani, *Al-Asrar al-Khafiyyah fi Harakat al-Sanah 1941 al-Taharruriyyah* (Sidon, 1964).
Taha al-Hashimi, *Mudhakkirat, Vol. I, 1919–1943* (Beirut, 1967).
Taha al-Hashimi, *Mudhakkirat, Vol. II, 1942–1955; al-'Iraq, Suriya, al-Qadiyyah al-Filastiniyyah* (Beirut, 1978).
Muhammad Husayn Haykal, *Mudhakkirat fi al-Siyasah al-Misriyyah* (Cairo, 1977).
Al-Hilal, April 1939: *Al-'Arab wa-al-Islam fi al-'Asr al-Hadith*.
Al-Hilal, Vol. 49, 1st Part (December 1940).
Sati' al-Husri, *Ara' wa-Ahadith fi al-Qawmiyyah al-'Arabiyyah* (Beirut, 1956).
Sati' al-Husri, *Mudhakkirati fi al-'Iraq, Vol. I, 1921–1927* (Beirut, 1967).
Sati' al-Husri, *Mudhakkirati fi al-'Iraq, Vol. II, 1927–1941* (Beirut, 1968).
Anwar al-Jundi, *Al-Imam al-Maraghi* (Cairo, 1952).
Sami al-Jundi, *Al-Ba'th* (Beirut, 1969).
'Ali Jawdat, *Dhikrayat, 1900–1958* (Beirut, 1967).
'Abd al-Mun'im Muhammad Khalaf, *Ma'a al-Qawmiyyah al-'Arabiyyah fi Rub' Qarn* (Cairo, 1958).
Kamil Muhammad Khillah, *Filastin wa-al-Intidab al-Britani 1922–1939* (Beirut, 1974).
Bisharah al-Khuri, *Haqa'iq Lubnaniyyah* (Beirut, 1960).
Al-Kitab al-Urdunni al-Abyad: al-Watha'iq al-Qawmiyyah fi al-Wahdah al-Suriyyah ('Amman, n.d.).
Muhammad Mahdi Kubbah, *Mudhakkirati fi Samim al-Ahdath, 1918–1958* (Beirut, 1965).
Zaki Mubarak, *Wahy Baghdad* (Cairo, 1938).
Munib al-Madi and Sulayman Musa, *Ta'rikh al-Urdunn fi al-Qarn al-'Ishrin* ('Amman, 1959).
Sulayman Musa, *Al-Harakah al-'Arabiyyah; al-Marhalah al-Ula lil-Nahda al-'Arabiyyah al-Hadithah, 1908–1924* (Beirut, 1977).
Nasir al-Din al-Nashashibi, *Al-Hibr Aswad .. Aswad* (Beirut, n.d.).
'Abd al-Rahman al-Rafi'i, *Fi A'qab al-Thawrah al-Misriyyah*, Vol. III (Cairo, 1951).
Dhuqan Qarqut, *Tatawwur al-Harakah al-Wataniyyah fi Suriyah, 1920–1939* (Beirut, 1975).
Khayriyyah Qasimiyyah (ed.), *'Awni 'Abd al-Hadi – Awraq Khassah* (Beirut, 1974).
Khayriyyah Qasimiyyah (ed.), *Mudhakkirat Fawzi al-Qawuqji, Vol. I, 1914–1932* (Beirut, 1975).
Khayriyyah Qasimiyyah (ed.), *Filastin fi Mudhakkirat al-Qawuqji, Vol. II, 1936–1948* (Beirut, 1975).

'Abd al-'Aziz al-Qassab, *Min Dhikrayati* (Beirut, 1962).
Salah al-Din Sabbagh, *Fursan al-'Urbuah fi al-'Iraq* (Damascus, 1956).
Hisham Sharabi, *Al-Jamr wa-al-Ramad* (Beirut, 1978).
Ahmad al-Shuqayri, *Hiwar wa Asrar ma'a al-Muluk wa-al-Ru'asa'* (Beirut, n.d.).
Muhammad 'Ali al-Tahir, *Zalam al-Sajin; Mudhakkirat wa Mufakkirat Sajin Harib* (Cairo, 1951).
Tawfiq al-Suwaydi, *Mudhakkirati* (Beirut, 1969).
Taqrir al-Wafd al-Niyabi al-Suri 'an al-Mu'tamar al-Barlamani al-'Alami lil-Difa' 'an Filastin
Jalal al-Urfahli, *Al-Diblumasiyyah al-'Iraqiyyah wa-al-Ittihad al-'Arabi* (Baghdad, 1944).
Akram Zu'aytir, *Al-Harakah al-Wataniyyah al-Filastiniyyah 1935–1939, Yawmiyyat Akram Zu'aytir* (Beirut, 1980).

IN EUROPEAN LANGUAGES

Mohammed Abdul Aziz, 'The Origin and Birth of the Arab League', *Revue Egyptienne de Droit International*, Vol. II (1955).
D. Ben-Gurion, *Letters to Paula* (Vallentine, Mitchell & Co., London, 1971).
D. Carlton, *Anthony Eden, a Biography* (London, 1981).
General Catroux, *Dans la Bataille de la Méditerranée* (Paris, 1949).
Winston S. Churchill, *The Second World War*, Vol. III (London, 1948).
William L. Cleveland, *The Making of An Arab Nationalist; Ottomanism and Arabism in the Life and Thought of Sati' al-Husri* (Princeton, 1971).
Michael J. Cohen, 'Appeasement in the Middle East: The British White Paper On Palestine, May 1939', *Historical Journal*, Vol. XVI, no. 3 (1973).
Michael J. Cohen, 'A Note On The Mansion House Speech, May 1941', *Asian and African Studies*, Vol. II (1977).
Michael J. Cohen, *Palestine: Retreat from the Mandate, The Making of British Policy, 1936–1945* (London, 1978).
C. Ernest Dawn, *From Ottomanism to Arabism, Essays on the Origins of Arab Nationalism* (Urbana, 1973).
Marius Deeb, *Party Politics in Egypt: the Wafd and its Rivals, 1919–1939* (London, 1979).
John F. Devlin, *The Ba'th Party: A History from the Origins to 1966* (Stanford, 1976).
Documents On German Foreign Policy, Series D, Vol. X (London, 1960).
John P. Entelis, *Pluralism And Party Transformation In Lebanon: al-Kata'ib 1936–1970* (Leiden, 1974).
G. Furlonge, *Palestine Is My Country; The Story of Musa Alami* (London, 1969).
I. Gershoni, 'Arabization of Islam: The Egyptian Salafiyya And The Rise of Arabism In Pre-Revolutionary Egypt', *Asian and African Studies* Vol. 13 (1979).
I. Gershoni, *The Emergence Of Pan-Arabism In Egypt* (Tel-Aviv, 1981).
I. Gershoni, *Major Trends In The Evolution Of The Egyptian National Self-Image, 1900–1950*; Occasional Papers On The Middle East, no. 14, University of Haifa, August 1977.
Ahmed Gomaa, *The Foundation Of The League of Arab States* (London, 1977).
Great Britain, *Documents On British Foreign Policy*, First Series, Vol. XIII (London, 1963).
John Harvey (ed.), *The War Diaries of Oliver Harvey* (London, 1978).
Susan Lee Hattis, *The Bi-National Idea In Palestine During Mandatory Times* (Haifa, 1970).

L. Hirszowicz, *The Third Reich and the Arab World* (London, 1966).
J.C. Hurewitz, *The Struggle for Palestine* (New York, 1976).
Hasan Ahmed Ibrahim, *The 1936 Anglo-Egyptian Treaty* (Khartoum, 1976).
James Jankowski, 'Egyptian Responses to the Palestine Problem in the Interwar Period', *International Journal of Middle East Studies*, Vol. 12 (1980).
J. Jankowski, 'The Government of Egypt and the Palestine Question: 1936–1939', *Middle Eastern Studies*, Vol. 17 (1981).
J. Jankowski, 'Ottomanism and Arabism in Egypt, 1860–1914', *Muslim World*, Vol. LXX, no. 3–4 (July–October 1980).
E. Kedourie, *The Chatham House Version And Other Middle Eastern Essays* (Frank Cass, London, 1974).
E. Kedourie, *Islam In the Modern World* (London, 1980).
M. Khadduri, *Independent Iraq from 1932 to 1958* (London, 1960).
Philip S. Khouri, 'Factionalism Among Syrian Nationalists During The French Mandate', *IJMES*, Vol. 13 (1981).
Aaron S. Klieman, *Foundations of British Policy In the Arab World: The Cairo Conference of 1921* (Baltimore, 1970).
Michel Laissy, *Du Panarabisme à la Ligue Arabe* (Paris, 1948).
S.H. Longrigg, *Syria and Lebanon Under French Mandate* (London, 1958).
Mary Ellen Lundsten, 'Wall Politics: Zionist and Palestinian Strategies in Jerusalem, 1928', *Journal of Palestine Studies*, Vol. VIII, no. 1, (Autumn, 1978).
Ali Mahafzah, 'La France et le mouvement nationaliste arabe de 1914 à 1950', *Relations Internationales*, no. 19, automne 1979.
Aaron David Miller, *Search for Security: Saudi Arabian Oil and American Foreign Policy, 1939–1949* (Chapel Hill, 1980).
E. Monroe, *Philby of Arabia* (London, 1973).
H. St. J.B. Philby, *Arabian Jubilee* (London, 1952).
Y. Porath, 'Britain and Arab Unity (Document)', *Jerusalem Quarterly*, no. 15, Spring 1980.
Y. Porath, *The Emergence of the Palestine-Arab National Movement, 1918–1929* (Frank Cass, London, 1974).
Y. Porath, *The Palestine-Arab National Movement*, Vol. II, *1929–1939: From Riots to Rebellion* (Frank Cass, London, 1977).
Y. Porath, 'The Palestinians and the Negotiations for the British-Hijazi Treaty, 1920–1925', *AAS*, Vol. 8 (1972).
I. Rabinovich, 'The Compact Minorities and the Syrian State, 1918–1945', *Journal of Contemporary History* Vol. 14, no. 4 (October 1979).
A. Raymond (ed.), *La Syrie D'Aujourd'hui* (Paris, 1980).
N.A. Rose (ed.), *Baffy: The Diaries of Blanche Dugdale 1936–1947* (Vallentine, Mitchell & Co., London, 1973).
Viscount Samuel, *Memoirs* (London, 1945).
Charles D. Smith, '4 February 1942: Its Causes and its Influence on Egyptian Politics and on the Future of Anglo-Egyptian Relations, 1937–1945', *IJMES*, Vol. 10 (1979).
E. Spears, *Fulfilment of a Mission* (London, 1977).
J.K. Tanenbaum, 'France and the Arab Middle East, 1914–1920', *Transactions of the American Philosophical Society*, Vol. 68, part 7 (1978).
Bassam Tibi, *Arab Nationalism: A Critical Enquiry* (London, 1981).
United States of America, *Foreign Relations of United States, 1942*.
United States of America, *Foreign Relations of United States, 1943, Vol. IV*.
United States of America, *Foreign Relations of United States, 1944, Vol. V*.
United States of America, *Foreign Relations of United States, 1945, Vol. VIII*.

Chaim Weizmann, *Trial and Error* (London, 1949).
G. Warner, *Iraq and Syria, 1941* (London, 1974).
L. Z. Yamak, *The Syrian Social Nationalist Party; An Ideological Analysis* (Cambridge, Mass., 1966).
Z. N. Zeine, *The Struggle for Arab Independence* (Beirut, 1960).

INDEX

Abazah Bey, 'Abd al-Hamid, 190
Abazah Pasha, Fu'ad, 187–8, 190, 191
'Abd al-Hadi, 'Awni, 14, 16, 24, 60, 61, 64–5
'Abd al-Illah, Amir, Iraqi Regent, 38, 43, 44, 45, 46, 47, 51, 53, 56, 57, 221, 267, 268, 269, 277, 288, 306, 313, 319
'Abd al-Majid, 21, 22
'Abd al-Mun'im, 20
'Abdallah, Amin, 68
'Abdallah, Amir of Transjordan (later King), 4, 16, 18–19, 20, 70, 71, 73–4, 125, 128, 133, 135, 138, 143, 144, 146, 147, 167–8, 180, 187, 190, 198, 201, 216, 225, 233–4, 251, 257, 259, 268; and Arab Unity Preparatory Committee and Arab League, 275, 276–7, 280, 281, 288, 289, 295; Greater Syria project of, 22–39, 44–5, 52, 136, 203–16, 263–4, 268, 277, 280, 281, 305–6, 307, 313, 315; and Nuri al-Sa'id's Fertile Crescent scheme, 43, 44–5, 46, 47, 52–3, 56, 57; and Philby Plan, 95–6, 97
Abdel Aziz, 84
'Abduh, Muhammad, 152
Abdul Aziz, Mohamed, 303–4
Abu 'Alam, Muhammad Sabri, 55
Abu al-Huda, Tawfiq, 33, 35, 135, 143, 214, 259, 260, 262, 264, 280, 281, 305–6
Abu al-Sa'ud, Hasan, 168
Abyssinia, 229; Italian invasion of, 181, 184
al-Afghani, Jamal al-Din, 152
Agudath Israel, 59
al-Ahram, 156, 183–4, 194, 299
al-Alamein, battle of, 34, 50, 51, 189, 258, 313
al-'Alami, Musa, 59–61, 70, 238, 277–8, 281–2, 286, 290, 302
Alawites, 68, 71
Aleppo, 3, 239, 248, 249
Alexander, A., 246
Alexander, Maître, 71

Alexandretta, ceded to Turkey, 3, 28, 160–1, 162, 170, 236, 239
Alexandria, Arab Unity Preparatory Committee convened in (1944), 277–84, 298–302, 317, 318
Alexandria Protocol (1944), 282–4, 285, 286–7, 288–9, 302, 318
'Ali, ex-King of Hijaz, 5, 9, 17–18, 21, 22, 198, 199–200, 203, 312–13
Ali, Amir, 4
'Ali, Tahsin, 191
Alif Ba', 21
Alling, Paul, 101
'Allubah, Muhammad 'Ali, 55, 153–4, 169, 170–1, 176, 188, 192, 257, 258, 269, 270, 284
al-Alusi, Muwaffaq, 42
al-'Amal, 283
Amery, Leopold, 93–4, 96, 97, 128, 129, 138, 145, 146, 210; Plan of (1943), 130–1, 132, 133, 134
Amman, 12, 15–16, 29, 45
Anglo-Iraqi Treaty of Alliance, 13, 47, 182
Antonius, George, 24, 60, 62, 174, 187, 243, 244
'Aqaba, 168, 214
Arab Executive, dissolution of, 58, 59
Arab Federation, and Palestine, 58–148: Arab initiatives, 69–72; Jewish proposals, 58–69; official British thinking, 67, 106–47; Philby scheme, 80–106; unofficial British démarches, 72–80
Arab Inter-Parliamentary Conference on Palestine (1938), 43, 170–1, 234, 236
Arab League, 33, 36, 52, 54, 215, 257–311, 305, 312, 318–19; Alexandria Protocol (1944), 282–4, 285, 286–7, 288–9, 302, 318; British attitudes/policy, 290–304, 305, 308–9, 311, 312, 318–19; Charter, 179, 318; formation of, 284–90, 317, 319; from consultations to Preparatory Committee, 267–84; inter-Arab consultations, 257–67, 284, 308–9, 317, 318; Preparatory Committee, 266, 269, 271–84, 285, 286, 298–302, 317, 318

Arab Legion, Trans-Jordanian, 32
Arab nationalism, 24, 28, 176, 186, 187, 314; *see also* Pan-Arabism
Arab Revolt (1916–18), 23, 24, 28, 38, 160
Arab Unity Club, Cairo, 190–1; Baghdad branch of, 191, 294
Arab Unity Preparatory Committee *see* Arab League
Arab Women's Congress, 236
Arab Unity Committee, Egypt, 270
Arabic culture, 151, 152–3, 156, 176–9, 314
Arabic language, 150, 151, 152, 153, 314
Arkash, Maître Maurice, 190
Armstrong, Captain Harold Courtney, 80, 81, 82
Arslan, 'Adil, 12
Arslan, Amir Shakib, 12, 14, 16, 29, 60, 61, 62, 169
Arslan, Sharif, 19
al-Arsuzi, Zaki, 161–2
al-'Asali, Sabri, 161, 162
al-Asil, Dr Naji, 70, 74, 108–9, 185
al-'Askari, Tahsin, 54, 191, 192
Association of Arab Unity, Egypt, 154
Association of Arabism, Egypt, 190
Association of Islamic Guidance, Egypt, 152
Association of the Muslim Brethren, Egypt, 152
Assyrian incident, 45
al-Atasi, Adnan, 267
al-Atasi, Hashim, 187, 233
'Atiyyah, Samuel and Edward, 228–9, 230
al-Atrash, 'Abd al-Ghaffar Pasha, 27–8, 206
al-Atrash family, 32, 38
Attlee, Clement, 246, 247, 316
Auschwitz death camp, 146
al-Azhar university, 156, 158
al-'Azm, Haqqi Bey, 190
al-'Azmah, 'Adil, 15, 24, 44
al-'Azmah, Nabih, 15, 169
al-Azri, 'Abd al-Razzaq, 191
'Azzam Pasha, 'Abd al-Rahman, *Amir al-Hajj*, 15, 55, 154, 160, 186, 192, 257, 269, 270, 284, 285, 286, 302, 303; appointed Secretary-General of Arab League, 288–9
'Azzam, 'Abd al-Wahhab, 189

al-Bachachi, Muzahim, 192
Badawi, Mr, legal expert, 288
Baggallay, Lacy, 89, 109, 113, 114–15, 207, 217, 233, 235, 236, 237–40, 243
Baghdad, 15, 16, 17, 19, 21, 178; anti-Hashemite demonstration (1937), 42; Arab Unity Club, 191, 294; coup d'état (1936), 41, 42; University, 176

Baghdad Congress proposed (1933), 201–3, 224
al-Bajahji, Hamdi, 275, 277
al-Bakri, Fawzi, 28, 29
al-Bakri, Nasib, 5, 28, 30
al-Bakri, Sayyid Ahmad Murad, 190
Balfour Declaration, 7, 97, 137
Bank Misr, Egypt, 155, 156, 188
al-Banna', Hasan, 162
Barada Youth Club, Damascus, 176
Barradah, Ahmad Najib, 190
al-Basil Bey, 'Abd al-Sattar, 190
al-Basil, Hamad, 15, 162–3
Basyuni, Mahmud, 168
Ba'th Party, 162
Battershill, Sir William, 122, 213
Battle of Britain, 192
Baxter, C. W., 92–3, 113, 122, 125, 133, 138, 141, 142, 208, 209–10, 211, 212, 213, 214, 215, 222, 232, 236, 244, 245, 247, 250–1, 255, 294, 303
Bedouin sheikhs, 32
Beirut, 3, 71
Beisan Valley, 137, 143
Ben-Gurion, David, 58–62, 63, 65, 66–7, 68–9, 76, 78, 81–2, 83, 84, 87, 100
Bentinck, C., 109
Ben-Zvi, 81
Berthelot, M., 4, 5, 10
Bethlehem, 133
Bilad al-Sham, 24, 35
Biltmore Resolution (1942), 50, 69, 100, 127
Blum, Léon, 63
Bowman, Humphrey, 117, 118, 250
Boyd, E. B., 122
Bracken, Brendan, 87–8, 91, 95, 120
Brenan, T. V., 217, 233
Bridges, Sir Edward, 134, 139
Brodetsky, Professor S., 66, 79, 119, 202
Brodtsky, Dr Z., 76
Bullard, Sir Reader, 219
Bushe, Sir Grattan, 111
Butler, Nevile, 246
Butler, R. A., 70, 89–90, 118, 238, 241, 245, 250

Caccia, Harold, 97, 106, 122, 125, 212, 214, 221
Cadogan, Sir Alexander, 89, 111, 132, 136, 138, 139, 141, 209, 215, 218, 219, 222, 232, 237, 240, 247–8, 292
Cairo, 274; all-Arab professional conferences, 177–8; British talks with 'Abdallah (1921), 22–3; Club of Arab Union, 190–1, 294; Inter-Arab consultations (1943), 54–5, 257–67; Inter-Parliamentary Arab Congress

Cairo (contd)
(1938), 170–1, 234, 236; Middle East Defence Council Conference (1944), 144–5, 146, 297
Caliphate Conference (1926), 191
Campbell, R.I., 157
Campbell, Ronald, 228
Casey, Richard, 34, 51, 123, 134, 137, 138, 139, 144, 146, 220, 255, 262, 290, 292, 293, 294, 305, 307, 308, 310, 317, 318, 319
Catroux, General, 33, 209, 247, 271, 304
Cawthorn, Major W.J., 167, 235
Cazalet, Lieut-Colonel Victor, 131
Chamberlain, Neville, 111
Churchill, Winston, 34, 36, 77, 78, 80, 89, 114, 117, 118, 122, 127–30, 145, 174, 208, 211, 214, 222, 243, 246, 247, 248, 255, 292, 300, 317; and Eden's Mansion House speech, 248–9, 251, 305, 317; Note of 19 May 1941: 92, 211, 247, 248, 249, 317; Note of 27 April 1943: 127–8; and Palestine Cabinet Committee, 129–30, 134, 138–48 *passim*, 314; and Philby scheme, 87–8, 91, 92, 93–4, 96, 97, 98–9, 100, 102, 103, 120, 121, 124, 128, 314, 317; 'promise' to 'Abdallah, 22–3, 31, 32, 45, 206, 207
Circassians, 68
Clark-Kerr, Sir Archibald (later Lord Inverchapel), 176, 182–3, 216, 218, 229–31, 232
Clayton, I.N., 219, 300, 301
Clemenceau, Georges, 4
Cohen, Aharon, 304
Colonial Office, 74, 75, 76, 77, 83–4, 110–27 *passim*, 316; and 'Abdallah's Greater Syria project, 205–14 *passim*, 315; and Faysal's initiative, 198, 199, 201, 202–3; and formation of Arab League, 294, 296, 302; and Palestine Cabinet Committee, 133, 134–8, 142, 143, 144, 146–7; and Pan-Arabism, 226–7, 234, 235, 236, 241, 243, 244, 245, 247, 252, 253; and Philby scheme, 90, 94, 95, 96, 97–8, 290
Copts, 154, 187, 271
Cornwallis, Sir Kinahan, 54, 121, 122, 141, 144, 145, 146, 220, 221, 222, 223, 246, 253, 300, 301, 307
Cranborne, Viscount (later Marquess of Salisbury), 98, 123, 125, 126, 127, 128–9, 213–14, 218, 254
Cripps, Sir Stafford, 129
Crosthwaite, P.M., 208–9, 220, 235–6
cultural co-operation, Arab, 175–9
Curzon, Lord, 72, 73, 74, 107

Customs Union, Arab, 75, 76, 107–8

Daghir, As'ad, 14
Damascus, 3, 10, 12, 20, 200
al-Dandashi, 'Abd al-Razzaq, 161, 162
Darwaza, 'Izzat, 14, 24, 43, 149
Daws Pasha, Tawfiq, 55
De Gaulle, General Charles, 120, 274
De Gaury, Lieutenant-Colonel, 53, 307
Dentz, General, 247
Devonshire, Duke of, 73, 107
Downie, F.H., 111, 115, 118, 244
Druzes, 5, 12, 14, 28–9, 32, 38, 60, 68, 71, 80, 81, 205–6, 209, 225, 313
Dufferin and Ava, Marquess of, 111
Dugdale, Mrs Blanche, 86, 98

Eastern Bond Association, Egypt, 151–2
Eastwood, Christopher, 90, 107
Eden, Anthony, 34–5, 50, 54, 55, 94, 97, 110, 126, 127, 128, 211, 215–16, 218, 219, 230, 232, 234, 235, 244, 245, 246, 248, 250, 251, 254, 255–6, 292, 293, 296, 297, 301, 308, 309, 310, 316; Cabinet Note (May 1941), Mansion House speech (May 1941), 54, 67, 68, 92, 93, 119, 193–4, 248–50, 251, 255, 256, 257, 303, 304, 305, 317; and Palestine Cabinet Committee, 129–30, 134, 135, 136, 138–42, 144, 146–7; Parliamentary Reply (February 1943), 54, 255, 257–8, 290, 304, 317
Edmonds, C.J., 47, 70, 186
Egypt, 8, 14, 20, 35, 38, 68, 80; and Arab cultural co-operation, 175–9; Arab League, 286, 287–9, 304, 318; and Arab Unity Preparatory Committee, 271–84, 285; British Treaty of Friendship with (1936), 155, 163, 165, 168, 184; Inter-Arab consultations (1943), 54–5, 257–67, 268, 269–71; Inter-Parliamentary Congress (1938), 170–1; Iraqi relations with, 184–5, 192, 232; League of Nations' membership, 157, 165; and Lebanese crisis (1943), 271; Muhammad 'Ali's federation plan, 70–1, 109; and Nuri al-Sa'id's Arab unity scheme, 43, 54–5, 56, 127; and Palestine issue, 153–4, 155, 157, 162–3, 166, 168, 169–71, 173; Pan-Arabism, 149–59, 160, 169, 172, 173, 175–9, 183–6, 187–92, 194, 195–6, 228–9, 234, 236, 254–5, 269–70, 314; Saudi Treaty of Friendship with (1936), 183–4; and Second World War, 185–6, 188–9, 192
Eisenhower, General Dwight D., 34
Elliott, Sir Walter, 111

INDEX 369

Epstein, Eliyahu (later Elath), 64, 80–1
Etherington-Smith, Mr, 236
Euphrates tribes, 25, 39, 42
Eyres, H.M., 114, 175, 209, 214, 215, 221–2

Farmers' Federation, 59
Faruq, King of Egypt, 70, 109, 154, 157, 158, 159, 171, 184, 187, 205, 258, 269, 270, 271, 284–5, 287–9, 295
al-Fatah, 14
Faysal I, King of Iraq, 2, 3, 25, 39, 42, 44, 53, 70, 72, 224; Baghdad Congress proposal (1933), 201–3, 224; death of (1933), 12, 13, 17, 20–1, 22, 24, 180, 203, 216, 228; friction between 'Abdallah and, 18–19; London talks (1933), 13–14; and Pan-Arabism, 15–17, 180, 224, 226, 227; Syrian initiatives of, 4–22, 24, 28, 197–203, 227, 312–13, 315
Faysal II, King of Iraq, 44, 45, 47
Faysal Al Sa'ud, Amir, 19, 27, 38, 43, 81, 84, 105, 172, 204
Fertile Crescent see Iraq; Syria
Fir'awn, Henri, 285
Fishman (later Maymon), Rabbi J.L., 68
Foreign Office, 13, 79, 108–27 passim, 268, 275, 314; and 'Abdallah's Greater Syria project, 204–16 passim; and Faysal's initiatives, 197–203 passim; and formation of Arab League, 294–304; and Nuri al-Sa'id's Fertile Crescent scheme, 216–22 passim; and Palestine Cabinet Committee, 129–44, 145, 146–7; and Pan-Arabism, 224–56 passim; and Philby scheme, 89–90, 92–3, 94, 95, 96, 97, 106
Foreign Research and Press Service, Oxford, 250
France, French, 62, 71, 73, 92, 94, 109, 112–13, 125, 136, 137, 138, 144, 145, 161, 196; and 'Abdallah's Greater Syria project, 22–32 passim, 38, 204, 207, 209, 212; Alexandretta ceded to Turkey by, 160–1, 162, 170, 236, 239; and Arab Unity Preparatory Committee, 274, 276, 279–80; and British Middle East policy, 91–2, 290, 291–3, 300, 301, 304, 310, 311, 315, 318; Fall of France (1940), 32, 46, 91, 174, 186, 192, 207, 241, 242, 243; and Faysal's Syrian initiatives, 4–6, 7, 9–10, 11, 12, 13, 17–18, 19, 21–2, 197, 198, 199, 200, 201; and independence of Syria and Lebanon, 36, 62–3, 95, 195, 211, 215, 286; and Jabal al-Duruz, 205–6, 225; and Nuri al-Sa'id's Fertile Crescent scheme, 43–4, 48–9, 57, 217–18, 222; and Pan-Arabism, 225–6, 228, 229, 231, 235–6, 237, 239, 240, 241–2, 243, 252, 253; Syrian Treaty with (1936), 173–4, 235–6; Vichy Government, 31, 47, 91, 116, 192, 193, 208, 241; see also Arab League; Lebanon; Syria
Free French, 32, 33, 95, 120, 125, 195, 208, 209, 215, 246, 247, 251, 271, 274
Fu'ad, King of Egypt, 154, 158, 184, 287
Furlonge, Sir Geoffrey, 61

Galilee, 97, 136, 145; Central, 138; Lower, 130, 139; Upper, 130, 133, 135–6; Western, 137, 146
Gardner, British Consul in Syria, 207–8
Gater, Sir G., 135
General Arab Congress (Cairo 1943) see Arab League
General Arab Congress (Jerusalem 1931), 14–17, 149, 154, 202; Preparatory (Executive) Committee of, 14–15, 16, 149
General Arab Congress (Syria 1937), 168–9
General Arab Federation, Egypt, 154
General Zionists' Party, 68
George VI, King, 81
Germany see Second World War
Gershoni, I., 175
al-Ghauri, Emil, 170
Ghazi, King of Iraq, 21, 22, 24–5, 26, 29, 41, 42, 43, 44, 48, 180, 182, 203
Ghazali Bey, 270
Gibb, Professor H.A.R., 66, 79, 114, 115, 116, 117, 250, 255, 307–8
Goldmann, Dr Nahum, 101, 102
Gordon-Finlayson, General R., 237
Greater Syria projects, 62, 263–5, 266, 280–1, 285, 289, 290, 296, 305, 307, 308, 319; 'Abdallah's, 22–39, 44–5, 52, 136, 143, 203–16, 263–4, 268, 277, 280, 305–6, 313, 315; Palestine Cabinet Committee's, 134–8, 139, 140, 141, 143–4, 146–7; Prince Muhammad 'Ali's, 70–1; Republican, 264, 265, 268, 280
Grigg, Sir Edward, 148, 303
Gruenbaum, I., 68

Haddad, General, 4
Haddad, Jibra'il, 71
Haddad, Shafiq, 71–2
al-Haddas, Nicola, 188
al-Haffar, Lutfi, 64, 169
Hafiz, 'Abd al-Illah, 53
Haifa, 3, 71, 135
al-Hakimi, Taha, 8

Halifax, Viscount, 77, 89, 90, 91, 109, 110, 112–13, 115, 116, 204–5, 232, 235, 237, 240, 243, 244, 316
Hall, N. Hathorn, 198
Hamzah, Fu'ad, 80–1, 84, 180
Hankey, Lord, 79, 141, 215, 300, 302–3, 308
Harb, Muhammad Tal'at, 188
Harris, Sir Douglas, 135
Harvey, Oliver, 91, 97, 99
al-Hasani, Shaykh Taj al-Din, 6, 33
Hashemite dynasty, 2, 70, 78, 96, 108, 128, 224, 239, 307, 312; and 'Abdallah's Greater Syria project, 22–39, 203–16; and Faysal's Syrian initiatives, 4–22, 199–203, 312; legitimacy of, 159–60; and Nuri al-Sa'id's initiative, 39–57, 312
al-Hashimi, Taha, 49–50, 163, 186, 191, 192, 194, 259; *Diaries*, 7
al-Hashimi, Yasin, 10, 12, 15, 16, 17, 39, 164, 165, 166, 176, 180, 185
Havard, P.S., 240
Haydar, 'Ali, 21
Haydar, Rustum, 6, 11
al-Haydari, Da'ud, 269
Haykal, Muhammad Husayn, 162, 166, 177
Hazmah, Fu'ad, 184
Higher Arab Committee (HAC), 40, 43, 76, 164, 169, 172, 174, 208
Higher Committee for the Relief of the Palestine Victims, 162
Hijaz, 4, 5, 8, 13, 18–19, 27, 34, 48, 72, 82, 175, 287; British draft treaty deadlock, 73–4; Ibn Rifadah revolt (1932), 16, 20; Saudi occupation of, 2, 180, 204, 277
al-Hilal, 158, 187–8
Hilmi, 'Abbas, 20
al-Hizb al-Watani, Egypt, 168
Hoare, Sir Samuel, 111
Hoskins, Colonel Harold, 104–5, 139
Hulah Valley, 130, 133, 135, 136, 138, 139, 140, 143, 146
Humphrys, Sir Francis, 7, 9, 10, 13, 17, 25, 198, 199, 200, 201–2, 224
Huraykah, Bishop Ignatius, 169
Husayn Ibn 'Ali, Amir, Sharif of Mecca and King of the Hijaz, 21, 22, 32, 71, 72, 73–4, 180
Husayn, Ahmad, 166
Husayn, Taha, 178
al-Husayni, al-Hajj Amin, 43, 45, 46, 61, 64, 76, 77, 165, 168, 169, 170–1, 172, 173, 193, 243
al-Husayni, Jamal, 60, 70, 238, 260, 272, 274, 277, 282, 297
al-Husayni, Munif, 170
al-Husri, Sati, 156–7, 176

Hyamson–Newcombe plan, 77

Ibn Rifadah, 16
Ibn Saud, 'Abd al-Aziz, King of Saudi Arabia, 8, 9, 13, 16, 18–20, 22, 27, 38, 39, 44, 46, 56, 68, 74, 107, 108–9, 114, 128, 130, 135, 136, 138, 139, 146, 162, 170, 171, 175, 179, 201, 202, 214, 259, 315; and 'Abdallah's Greater Syria project, 204, 206, 207, 208, 209, 211, 212; Alexandria Protocol signed by, 283–4, 285, 287, 288, 302, 318; and Arab League, 283, 284, 287, 309, 318; and Arab Unity Preparatory Committee, 272–4, 275–6, 277, 278, 283, 295, 299; Faruq's relations with, 287–8, 289; and inter-Arab consultations (1943), 261, 262, 266, 268, 295, 309; and Nuri al-Sa'id's Fertile Crescent scheme, 41–3, 47, 48, 53, 56–7, 217, 218, 219, 221; and Pan-Arabism, 165, 167–8, 170, 171, 175, 179, 183, 184, 187, 192, 194, 195, 196, 223–4, 226, 229, 237, 246, 247, 248, 249, 253; and Philby scheme, 80–106, 128
Ibrahim Pasha of Egypt, 156, 158
Inönü, Ismet, Turkish President, 28
Inskip, Sir Thomas, 111
Iran (Persia), 1–2, 3, 185
Iraq, 1–3, 23, 66, 80, 92, 128, 226; and 'Abdallah's Greater Syria plan, 24–5, 36–7; Arab cultural co-operation, 176, 177, 178–9; and Arab federation proposals, 70, 76, 82, 83, 93, 96, 108–9; Arab League, 288, 289; and Arab Unity Preparatory Committee, 269, 272, 274, 275, 276, 277, 278–9; British Treaty of Alliance with (1932), 13, 47, 182; *coup d'état* (1936), 41, 42, 45; declares war against Germany (1943), 51; Faysal's Syrian initiatives, 4–22, 197–203, 312–13; inter-Arab consultations, 262–9; League of Nations' membership, 7, 12, 13; neighbouring countries' relations with, 1–3; Nuri al-Sa'id's Fertile Crescent scheme, 36–7, 39–57, 216–23, 263, 265–6, 306–7, 312, 313; and Palestine issue, 163–4, 165, 166–7, 169, 170, 173–4, 175–6, 233–4; and Pan-Arabism, 159–62, 169, 179–85, 186, 233–4, 239, 242, 243, 244, 245, 255; and Peel Report, 166–7; Rashid Ali's *coup d'état* (1941), 192–4, 220, 248, 313; Saudi relations with, 2–3, 8, 179–83; and Saudi Treaty of Alliance (1936), 180–3, 231–2, 234, 254; Transjordan Treaty of Friendship with (1931), 8, 200–1

INDEX

Iraqi Preparatory Committee, 15, 16, 17
Islam, 23, 149, 150, 151, 152
Islamic Nationalist Party, 189–90
al-Istiqlal (Independence) Party, 18, 24, 29, 60
Italy, Italians, 174, 181, 184, 185, 192, 202, 232, 242, 286

Jabal al-Duruz, 28–9, 205–6, 225
al-Jabiri, Ihsan, 60, 61, 62
al-Jabiri, Sa'dallah, 37–8, 44, 260, 264, 265, 278, 280
Jaffa, 133, 137
Jerusalem, 52, 71, 85, 130, 133, 134, 169, 203; 'Abdallah's talks with British (1921), 22, 23; General Islamic Congress (1931), 14–17, 149, 154, 202; Wailing Wall riots, 7, 153–4, 162; Zionist Executive, 66–7, 68, 76, 81, 87, 100
Jewish Agency (Jerusalem), 18, 30, 31, 40, 62–4, 66, 69, 76, 80, 81, 124, 298
Jewish Brigade, 50, 91
Jewish fighting units, 51, 174, 175, 244–5
Jewish immigration, 26, 30, 31, 39–41, 42, 50, 51, 60, 61, 62, 63, 64, 65, 67, 69, 70, 71, 74, 75, 76, 78, 82, 83, 84, 93, 105, 108, 110, 113, 114, 116–17, 123, 127, 129, 142, 145, 163, 174, 217, 238, 246, 247, 255, 266, 282; 'The Forty-Ten' Formula, 77
Jewish National Council, Palestine, 75
Jewish National Fund, 68
Jewish National Home, 8, 31, 51, 72, 79, 82, 83, 88, 93, 114, 117, 118, 119, 123, 128, 163, 193, 227, 228, 250
Jews, Jewish refugees, 7–8, 13, 26, 30–1, 50–1, 56, 67, 79, 100, 116, 123, 127, 130, 146, 282
Jezreel Valley, 130, 134, 143
Jordan, S. R., 273, 276
Joseph, Dr Bernard (later Dov Yossef), 30, 63, 68, 69
Jwadat, 'Ali, 15

Kalvarisky, H. M., 69
Karamah, 'Abd al-Hamid, 285
al-Kata'ib (les Phalanges), 283
al-Kawakibi, 'Abd al-Rahman, 152
Kawkab al-Sharq, 15
al-Kayyali (of Aleppo), 'Abd al-Rahman, 267
al-Kaylani, Rashid 'Ali, 22, 46, 47, 92, 192–3, 194, 220, 246, 248, 313
al-Kazimayn, 1
Kellogg Pact, 182
Kelly, D. V., 229, 236
Kemal, Mustafa (Atatürk), 151
al-Khadra, Subhi, 14
Khalaf, 'Abd al-Mun'im Muhammad, 160

Khalil, Muhammad Tawfiq, 190
al-Khayri, Khalusi, 69
al-Khuri, Bisharah, 195, 271, 273
al-Khuri, Faris, 10–11, 33, 171–2, 288
Killearn, Lord, 32, 121, 122, 141, 144, 145, 146, 229, 230, 232, 233, 236–7, 242, 243, 245–6, 247, 253, 265, 297, 298, 309–10
Kimche, Jon, 304
Kirkbride, Alec S., 126, 135, 206, 282, 305–6
Kirwan, Major L. P., 122
Kubba, Muhammad Mahdi, 163
Kurds, 2, 3, 68, 269
Kuwait, 48, 193

Labour Party, British, 7, 146, 148
Labour Party, Jewish, 58, 59, 62
Laissey, Michel, 304
Laithwaite, Frank, 227
Lampson, Sir Miles, *see* Lord Killearn
land purchases in Palestine, Jewish, 63, 64, 74, 77, 111, 174, 217, 266, 282
Law, Richard K., 130, 131–2, 133, 134, 136, 137–8, 139, 140
Lawrence, A. W., 78, 84, 114
Lawrence, T. E., 22, 73, 78
League of Arab States *see* Arab League
League of Nations, 1, 2, 10, 60, 69, 72, 82, 182; Egypt's membership of, 157, 165; Iraq's membership of, 7, 12, 13; Permanent Mandates Commission, 237; and Palestine Arabs, 165, 166; and Wailing Wall riots, 153
Lebanon, 10, 11, 12, 15, 21, 24, 26, 38, 77, 93, 94, 118, 120, 124, 132, 175, 190, 195; Alexandria Protocol, 283, 286–7; and Arab League, 285, 286–7, 289, 317–18; and Arab Unity Preparatory Committee, 272, 273, 274, 276, 278, 279–80, 281, 283; and Faysal's Syrian initiatives, 11, 12, 15, 21; and Greater Syria project, 263–5; independence of, 12, 36, 195, 211, 215, 257, 273, 279, 280, 283, 285, 286, 301; and inter-Arab consultations, 262, 263, 264–5, 266–7; Maronites, 14, 52, 56, 191, 195, 264, 273, 279, 285, 286–7; National Charter (1943), 265, 279; November 1943 crisis, 271; and Nuri al-Sa'id's Fertile Crescent scheme, 41, 49, 52, 216; and Pan-Arabism, 191, 195–6, 239, 240, 241, 251, 254, 255; and Partition of Palestine, 130, 134, 137; Vichy Government in, 47, 193
Leggitt, John, 241
Legislative Council in Palestine, British plans for, 59, 72–3, 74–5

Lépissier, Paul, 9, 10, 17–18, 22
Liberal Constitutional Party, Egypt, 158, 162, 166
Libya, 202, 260–1, 286
Life, Ibn Saud's interview in, 105
Lipsky, Louis, 101
Lloyd, Lord, 43, 77–8, 79, 89, 90, 91, 94, 114, 115–16, 118–19, 241–2, 243, 306
Locker, B., 66
Lorraine, Sir Percy, 202
Luke, S. E. V., 122
Lyttleton, Oliver, 67, 94, 123, 129, 212, 305

Ma'an, 22, 168, 214
MacDonald, Malcolm, 65, 83–4, 110–11, 113, 114, 316
MacKereth, Gilbert, 28, 183, 205, 230, 233, 240, 307
MacMichael, Sir Harold, 95, 98, 111, 116, 118, 119, 120, 121, 122, 124–5, 126, 134, 143, 145, 146, 209, 210, 211, 212, 213, 214, 215, 241, 242–3, 245, 251, 252, 253, 290, 305
Macmillan, Harold, 125, 213
Madinah, 84, 184
Maffey, Sir John, 75
Magnes, Dr J. L., 69
Magnes group in Palestine, 77
al-Maha'iri, 'Ali, 161
Mahir, Ahmad, 284–5, 287
Mahir Pasha, 'Ali, 158, 184, 185–6, 192
mahmal (decorated litter), 183–4
Mahmud Pasha, Muhammad, 77, 110–11, 158, 166, 170, 172
Maisky, Mr, Soviet Ambassador in London, 223, 307
Mallet, W. I., 90
al-Maraghi, Shaykh al-Azhar 'Ali, 171, 270
al-Maraghi, Sheikh Muhammad Mustafa, 158, 159
Mardam Bey, Jamil, 12, 19, 56, 63, 260, 264, 267, 268, 273, 274, 278, 281
Margesson, David, 96, 246
Maronite Christians of Lebanon, 14, 52, 56, 191, 195, 264, 273, 279, 285, 286–7
Martel, Comte de, 25
Martin, Sir John, 96–7, 116–17, 214
Martin, Kingsley, 79
Maurepas, M., 17
Mauritius, internment of Jewish refugees on, 116
al-Mazini, 'Abd al-Qadir, 176
Mecca, 16, 84, 168, 183, 184, 266
Melchett, Lord, 100
Merriam, Gordon P., 101
Middle East Supply Centre, 254, 292, 293
Middle East Economic Council, 293

Middle East (Official) Committee, 121, 122–3, 124, 125, 199–200, 209, 210, 212, 213, 227, 251, 252, 254, 290
Middle East War Council, 290–1, 292, 308
al-Midfa'i, Jamil, 15, 41, 42, 43, 49, 52–3, 54, 166–7, 170, 194, 217
Ministerial Conference, British (1941), 96, 97, 120–1, 122
al-Mirsad (Damascene newspaper), 6
Mizrahi Party, 68
Monroe, Miss E., 255
Montgomery, General Sir Bernard L., 34
Morrison, Herbert, 129, 131, 138, 140, 142
Morton, Colonel, 100
Moscow, Foreign Ministers' Conference in (1943), 136
Mosul, 2, 3, 239
Moyne, Lord, 94–5, 96, 97, 98, 99, 118–20, 123–4, 125, 130, 210, 215–16, 246–7, 248, 300, 305, 306, 308, 310, 316, 317; Cairo Conference convened by (1944), 144–5, 146, 297; and Greater Syria plan (1943), 134–7, 138, 144, 146–7; murder of, 148
Mubarak, Zaki, 153, 176, 177
Muhammad, Prophet, 23
Muhammad 'Ali, 20
Muhammad 'Ali, Egyptian Prince, 70–1, 77, 109, 149, 153, 156, 158, 185, 271
Mukhlis, Mawlud, 15, 46
al-Muqattam (journal), 63, 71, 156, 183, 188, 194
Murray, Wallace, 101, 142, 246
Muslim Brethren, Egypt, 162, 170, 189
al-Muthanna Club, Iraq, 46, 160, 164, 169, 176

al-Nahhas Pasha, Mustafa, 15, 35, 56, 57, 155, 157, 159, 163, 167, 178, 185, 195–6, 229, 254, 287, 308, 319; and Arab Unity Preparatory Committee and Arab League, 271–84, 295, 296–8, 299, 308–9, 313, 317; dismissed as PM by Faruq, 284; and inter-Arab consultations, 54–5, 258–71, 294, 295, 308–9, 313, 317
Na'if ('Abdallah's son), 28
Najaf, 1
Najd, 8, 23, 27, 48, 73, 74, 82, 180
Namier, Prof. L. B., 85–6, 96, 105, 119
al-Nashashibi, Fakhri (Nashashibi party), 29–30, 32, 38
al-Nashashibi, Raghib, 38
La Nation Arabe, 62
Nationalist Action League, Syria, 161–2, 169
Nazareth, 137
Near East Broadcasting Station, Jaffa, 35

INDEX

Negev, 78, 92, 130, 133, 137, 140
Newcombe, Colonel S., 43, 78, 243, 282, 306
Newton, Sir Basil, 207, 242, 243–4, 246
Noon, Sir Firoz Khan, 93–4, 95, 96, 120, 252
Nuqrashi, Fahmi, 287
Nuwayhid, 'Ajaj, 14

Office for Cultural Co-operation, Egyptian–Iraqi (1942), 178–9
oil industry, 3, 10, 84, 87, 126, 132, 193, 198
Oliphant, Sir Lancelot, 198, 199, 205, 207, 218, 219, 232, 236–7, 240, 245, 296
Oriental Union (*al-Ittihad al-Sharqi al-Misri*), Egyptian, 190, 191
Ormsby-Gore, William, 39, 74, 110, 218
Ottoman Empire, 1, 2, 149, 151, 158; *see also* Turkey

Pahlevi dynasty, Iran, 1, 2
Palestine, 7, 13, 18, 19, 24, 50; 'Abdallah's Greater Syria plan, 26–7, 29–31, 32, 34, 38, 213, 214, 215; Arab Federation as solution to problem of, 58–146; Arab Rebellion (1936–9), 39, 40, 72, 74, 108, 110, 155, 162–75, 228, 233–4, 314; Biltmore Resolution (1942), 50, 69, 100, 127; Faysal's Syrian initiatives, 7–8, 11, 12, 13, 197–8; 'Forty-Ten Formula', 77; Jewish land purchases, 63, 64, 74, 77, 103, 111, 174, 217, 266, 282; Legislative Council proposed for, 59, 72–3, 74–5; Nuri al-Sa'id's Fertile Crescent scheme, 39–41, 42–3, 44, 45–6, 47, 49, 52, 55, 216, 217, 218, 222; Wailing Wall disturbances, 7, 153, 162; *see also* Jewish immigration; Jewish National Home; Pan-Arabism; Partition; Peel Commission; St James's Conference; White Paper; Zionism
Palestine Cabinet Committee (1938), 111–12, 114
Palestine Cabinet Committee (1943), 129–48, 215, 294, 303, 314
Palestine Defence Committee, Iraq, 163–4, 170
Palestine Defence Committee, Syria, 168, 169
Palestine Defence Parliamentary Committee, Egypt, 170
Palestine Higher Arab Committee *see* Higher Arab Committee
Palestinian Arabs, 29–30, 40, 58–9, 313–14; formation of Arab League, 260, 265–6, 272, 274, 277–8, 281–2, 283, 286, 289, 290, 297, 298–9, 302; General Arab Congress (1937), 168–9; General Strike and Rebellion (1936–9), 39, 40, 72, 74, 108, 110, 155, 162–75, 206, 228, 233–4, 314; Inter-Parliamentary Congress (1938), 170–1; October 1933 demonstrations, 58–9; and Pan-Arabism, 162–75, 232, 233–4, 238, 257; and Philby scheme, 85, 87, 97; Wailing Wall conflict, 7, 153–4, 162; *see also* Palestine
Palestinian National Defence Party, 29–30, 32, 38
Pan-Arabism, 14–17, 25, 29, 48, 55, 72, 149–96, 314–15, 316; Baghdad Congress proposed (1933), 201–3, 224; British policy regarding, 197–256, 315; cultural co-operation, 175–9; in Egypt, 149–59; in the Fertile Crescent, 159–62; General Islamic Congress, Jerusalem (1931), 14–17, 149, 154, 202; improvement of inter-Arab relations, 179–85; National Covenant (Charter: 1931), 14–15, 154; Palestine Arab Rebellion, 162–75; and Second World War, 185–96; *see also* Arab League
Parker, William L., 101
Parkinson, Sir Cosmo, 95–6, 111, 120, 199, 226, 227
Parti Populaire Syrien, 37
Partition of Palestine, 26, 43, 64, 70, 76, 77–8, 82, 83, 84, 109, 110, 116–17, 128, 157, 166–8, 171, 235, 237, 282; Palestine Cabinet Committee's proposals, 130–44, 145–8, 303
'Party of the Free Hijazis', 27
Passfield, Lord, 198
Patria tragedy, 123
Peel (Royal) Commission Report (1937), 26, 39, 43, 48, 64, 70, 76, 78, 82, 83, 107, 110, 119, 121, 130, 131, 133, 136, 137, 140, 157, 163, 165, 166–8, 234
Pell, R.T., 122
Peterson, Sir Maurice, 105, 125, 132, 133–5, 136, 137, 139, 141, 144, 147, 212–13, 214, 215, 220, 222, 254, 255, 292–3, 294, 296, 297, 309
Philby, Mrs Dora, 86
Philby scheme (St John Philby), 65–6, 81–106, 114, 116, 117, 120–1, 124, 128, 130, 139, 250, 252, 314, 317
Ponsot, Henri, 9
Post-Hostilities Planning Sub-Committee Report, 132, 140
Preparatory Committee *see* Arab Unity Preparatory Committee; General Arab Congress
Price, Mr (Labour MP), 255, 296, 303
Puaux, M., 241

Qadri, Tahsin, 6
al-Qassab, Kamil, 19
al-Qawuqji, Fawzi, 164
al-Qawatli, Shukri, 15, 41, 56, 64, 263, 266, 267, 273, 276, 288

al-Rafi'i, 'Abd al-Rahman, 303
Rajihah, Queen of Iraq, 44
Rashid 'Ali *see* al-Kaylani
Raslan, Muzhir, 12
Rehovoth, 143, 164
Reilly, Sir Bernard, 122
Rendel, G.W., 109, 110, 166, 198, 199–200, 216, 217, 218–19, 224–6, 227, 229, 230, 231, 233, 305
Reynaud, Paul, 10
Rida, Rashid, 152
Roosevelt, President Franklin D., 86, 88–9, 98, 99–100, 101, 102–5, 139, 141, 145, 175
Royal Institute of International Affairs, 66, 117
Rucker, M.A., 123
Rutbah, 46
Rutenberg, P., 75
Ryan, Sir A., 223–4

al-Sab'awi, Yunis, 193
Sabri, Hasan, 192
Sa'adah, Antun, 159
Sa'dawi, Bashir, 86, 232–3
Sa'dist Party, Egypt, 191
Sa'id, Amin, 63, 183
Sa'id, 'Abd al-Hamid, 159, 162, 169
al-Sa'id, Nuri, 4, 8, 12, 13, 15, 28, 68, 70, 75, 78, 108, 113, 127, 128, 131, 135, 166, 172, 179, 258, 259, 285, 313; and Arab League, 285, 287, 288, 295, 301, 304; and Arab Unity Preparatory Committee, 266, 269, 272–3, 274, 275, 276, 277, 278–9, 280–1, 297; 'The Blue Book' (letter to Casey), 262, 306–7; *coup d'état* (1936) and exile in Cairo, 41–2, 217; Fertile Crescent scheme of, 36–7, 39–57, 68, 191, 216–23, 236, 265–6, 294, 304, 306–7, 312, 313; and inter-Arab consultations (1943), 54–5, 257–8, 261–9, 270; Note (1943), 51, 56, 134; and Palestine issue, 148, 173–4, 175, 282; and Pan-Arabism, 180–1, 184–5, 186, 191, 192, 232, 255; and re-appointed Prime Minister (1938), 43
St Aymour, Comte de Caix de, 237
St James's Conference on Palestine (1939), 44, 65, 83, 84, 112, 114, 120, 121, 172, 174, 185, 237, 238, 260, 277, 297, 316
Saint Quentin, Comte de, 21

Salafiyyah (Salafi) movement, 152, 153, 154, 159
Salah al-Din, 285
Salhab, Dr Muhammad As'ad, 190
Samaria, 130, 133
Samuel, Sir Herbert (later Viscount), 43, 71, 72, 306; Arab Federation proposals of, 72–3, 74–7, 107–8, 111, 113
al-Sanhuri, 'Abd al-Razzaq, 176, 179
al-Sanusi, Sayyid Muhammad Idris, 190, 260–1, 274
al-Sa'ud, 'Abd al-Aziz *see* Ibn Saud
Al Sa'ud, Amir *see* Faysal
Saudi Arabia, 20, 29, 76, 108–9, 155, 159; and 'Abdallah's Greater Syria plan, 27, 38–9, 204, 210; and Alexandria Protocol, 283–4, 285, 287; and Arab cultural co-operation, 179; and Arab League, 284, 285, 286, 287–9, 296, 302, 303; and Arab Unity Preparatory Committee, 272–4, 275–6, 278, 299; British wartime grant-in-aid to, 84, 87; Egyptian Treaty of Friendship with (1936), 183–4; Hijaz ruled by, 2, 180, 204, 277; Ibn Rifadah revolt against, 16, 20; and inter-Arab consultations (1943), 261, 262; Iraqi relations with, 2–3, 8, 179–83; and Iraqi Treaty of Alliance with (1936), 180–3, 231–2, 234, 254; and Nuri al-Sa'id's Fertile Crescent plan, 41–3, 53–4, 56–7, 219–20, 221; and Palestine issue, 165, 167–8, 169, 173, 175, 233–4; and Pan-Arabism, 165, 167, 169, 171, 172–3, 180–4, 194, 195, 231–2, 233–4, 239, 243, 244, 245, 250; and Philby scheme, 80–106, 120; and U.S. lend-lease, 87
al-Sayyid, Ahmad Lutfi, 150
Second World War, 31–6, 45–7, 50–1, 67–8, 79, 84, 91–2, 99, 100, 114, 117, 118, 123, 127, 155, 173–5, 185, 206, 208, 220, 258, 290–4, 303, 307; and Pan-Arabism, 185–96, 239, 240–56, 315
Senator, W., 69
Sephardic Jews, 59
Seymour, Sir Horace, 89, 115, 122, 209, 210, 212, 245, 247, 251, 252
Shahla, Habib Abu, 273
Shahbandar, Dr 'Abd al-Rahman, 5, 27–8, 29, 62, 63, 188, 208, 306, 313
Shertok (Sharett), Moshe, 30, 31, 40, 53, 58, 60, 64–5, 66, 67–8, 79, 71–2, 85–6, 101–2, 104, 306
al-Shihabi, Mustafa, 188
Shi'ites, 1–2, 3, 25, 176, 265, 269
Shim'oni, Ya'acov, 304
Shone, T., 300

INDEX

Shuckburgh, Sir John, 96, 111, 115, 119-20, 121, 122, 166, 198, 210-11
Shullaw, J. Harold, 101
al-Shuqayri, Ahmad, 263, 303
Sidqi, General Bakr, 41, 42, 45, 70, 217
Sidqi, Isma'il, 170
Simon, Sir John, 13, 111
Sinai, 97
Sinclair, Sir Archibald, 129, 246
Sirri, Husayn, 178
Smart, Walter, 227-8, 229, 233, 254, 255, 302, 305, 309
Smuts, General, 130, 134
Society of Arabic Culture (*Rabitat al-Adab al-Arabi*), 177
Society of Islamic Guidance, Syria, 163
Spears, Sir Edward, 126, 134, 144, 145, 268, 292, 293, 296, 298, 299, 309-10, 318
Spraggett, Colonel R.W., 122
Standard Oil of California, 84, 87
Stanley, Oliver, 127-8, 129, 137, 138, 141, 142; and Partition plan of, 133, 136, 303
Stein, Leonard, 79
Sterndale-Bennett, J.C., 111, 202, 217
Stileman, Captain R.F., 122
Stonehewer-Bird, Mr, 97, 246
Storrs, R., 71
Struma, sinking of, 123
Sudan Agency, Cairo, 228
Sufism, 190
Sulayman, Hikmat, 22, 26, 41, 42, 70, 108, 166-7, 217
al-Sulh, Riyad, 15, 16, 60, 61, 169, 233, 265, 266, 273, 279, 287
Sunni Muslims, 1, 3, 60, 265, 269
al-Suwaydi, Naji, 163, 169, 170
al-Suwaydi, Tawfiq, 65, 164, 166
Syers, C.G.L., 122
Syria, 1, 3, 66, 180, 190; 'Abdallah's Greater Syria project, 22-39, 203-16, 263-4, 280, 305-6; Alexandretta ceded to Turkey from, 160-1, 162, 170, 236, 239; Allied occupation of (1941), 31, 32, 33, 36, 92, 208, 246-7, 249, 315, 317; anti-French revolt (1925), 4-5; Arab federation proposals, 62-4, 71-2, 73, 76, 78, 116, 117, 118, 124, 125, 126, 131; and Arab League, 287, 288, 289; and Arab Unity Preparatory Committee, 272-81 *passim*, 284; British Greater Syria plan (1943), 134-8, 139, 140, 141, 143-4, 146-7; Constituent Assembly and Constitution, 5, 6, 9, 11; and cultural co-operation, 175, 178, 179; Faysal's initiatives, 4-22, 197-203; French Treaty with (1936), 173-4, 235-6; General Arab Congress (1937), 168-9; general strike and demonstrations (1936), 25, 155, 160; independence of, 12, 36, 62-3, 95, 195, 211, 215, 257, 280, 286, 301, 310; and inter-Arab consultations, 262-7; and Inter-Parliamentary Congress (1938), 171; and Nuri al-Sa'id's Arab unity scheme, 41, 43-4, 45, 46, 48-9, 52-3, 54, 55, 56-7, 216-23; and Palestine issue, 131, 132, 133, 134, 135, 136-7, 163, 167, 168-9, 170, 171-2; and Pan Arabism, 159-62, 167, 168-9, 183, 188, 191, 194-5, 229, 232-3, 239, 241-2, 243, 244, 245, 250, 251, 254; parliamentary elections (1931), 11, 12; and Philby plan, 92-3, 95, 120; Vichy government in, 31, 47, 116, 193, 208, 317
Syrian Congress (1919), 11, 24
Syrian Council of Representatives, 33
Syrian National Bloc (Nationalists), 9, 11, 12, 14, 17, 21, 22, 25-6, 27, 29, 33, 37, 38, 44, 56, 62, 63-4, 159, 161, 162, 191, 194, 203, 208, 264, 267, 306

al-Tamimi, Amin, 168, 260, 272, 274, 297
Taqla, Salim, 260
al-Tawil Pasha, 'Abd al-Fattah, 260
Taymur, Mahmud, 188
Terrier, Captain, 17
Thabit, Sa'id, 15, 161, 163, 190
al-Thaqafah, 189
Tiberias, 130, 134, 137
Transjordan, 3, 7, 8, 11, 13, 16, 18, 68, 159-60, 171; 'Abdallah's Greater Syria plan, 22-39, 203-16, 264-5, 313; and Arab federation proposals, 70, 71, 73, 76, 77, 78, 108, 109, 116, 118, 123, 124, 135, 137; and formation of Arab League, 262, 267, 268, 274, 276-7, 278, 280-1, 288, 289, 302; independence of, 211-12; Iraqi Treaty of Friendship with (1931), 8, 200-1; Jewish immigration into, 60, 83; and Nuri al-Sa'id's Fertile Crescent plan, 39, 41, 42, 43, 45, 46, 49, 52, 216, 217; and Pan-Arabism, 186, 225, 242, 244, 251, 254, 255; and Partition of Palestine, 130, 131, 133, 134, 135, 137, 143, 167-8; and Philby scheme, 82, 93, 95-6, 97, 120; proposed union of Palestine and, 26-7, 30, 46, 136, 167-8; Saudi relations with, 167-8, 180
Turkey (formerly Ottoman Empire), 1, 2, 3, 20, 28, 115, 159, 239, 246, 248, 249; Alexandretta ceded to, 3, 160-1, 162, 170, 236, 239
Turkomans, 2

Tyrrell, Lord, 21

'Ubayd, Makram, 154, 169, 187, 258, 269, 270–1, 284; 'Black Book' pamphlet by, 258, 269, 270
al-'Umari, Arshad, 277
United Nations, 142, 145, 282, 292, 293
United States, 125, 174, 175, 293, 294; Biltmore Resolution (1942), 50, 69, 100, 127; lend-lease to Saudi Arabia, 87; and Philby scheme, 87, 88–9, 98–105, 128; Zionist activity in, 50, 51, 66, 69, 127, 146, 174, 275
Ussishkin, M., 30, 68
'Utaybah tribe of the Hijaz, 22

Vansittart, Sir Robert, 93, 109, 114, 198, 199, 232
Vichy France, 31, 47, 91, 116, 192, 193, 208, 241, 247, 317
Vilensky, Nahum, 63

Wafd Party/Government, Egypt, 15, 154, 155, 157–8, 159, 162–3, 166, 168, 169, 170, 171, 178, 183–4, 187, 189, 191, 195, 229, 258, 269, 271, 289, 314
Wahbah, Hafiz, 83, 84, 180, 194, 250
Wailing Wall disturbances, 7, 153, 162
Ward, J. G., 216, 230
Wauchope, Sir Arthur, 18, 39–40, 43, 107–8, 203, 204
Wavell, General, 246
Weizmann, Dr Chaim, 13, 39–40, 66, 71, 75, 76, 78, 79, 80, 115, 119, 124, 127, 133, 134, 147, 164; 'Foreign Affairs' article (1942), 50; and Philby scheme, 83, 84, 85–6, 87, 88–91, 92, 93–106, 117, 120, 128, 250, 252, 314; *Trial and Error*, 102–3
Welles, Sumner, 100–1, 102, 103–4, 105
Weygand, General, 4, 5
Wilkie, Wendell, 67
Willetts, Captain A. H., 122

White Paper on Palestine (1939), 46, 98, 117–18, 119, 120, 121, 122, 126–7, 128, 129, 130, 142, 143, 146, 173, 174, 238, 242, 243, 244, 250, 266, 282, 283, 286, 291, 298, 300, 316, 318
Wilson, A., 198
Wilson, President Woodrow, 194
Winterton, Earl, 43, 75, 113, 306
Woodhead Commission (1938), 26, 78
World Zionist Organisation, 66, 71, 64; see also Zionism

al-Yafi, 'Abdallah, 169
Yahya, Imam of Yemen, 9, 182
Yasin, Sheikh Yusuf, 81, 86, 261, 262, 264, 278, 282, 283, 284, 295, 299
Yemen, 8–9, 23, 93, 180, 233–4, 244, 262; accession to Saudi–Iraqi Treaty, 182–3; and Arab Unity Preparatory Committee, 274, 276, 278, 283–4
Yossef, Dov see Joseph, Dr Bernard
Young, H., 74
Young Egypt Party, 159, 166, 189; see also Islamic Nationalist Party
Young Men's Muslim Association, Egypt, 152, 159, 162, 168, 169
Young Turks, 23

Zaki, Ahmad, 153
Zanzibar, 165
Zayd, Amir, 43, 44, 71
Zetland, Marquess of, 111
Zionism, Zionists, 50, 51, 74, 76, 79, 107, 119, 121, 123, 126, 171, 227, 228, 230, 232, 245, 249, 275; and Arab initiatives, 71–2; 18th Congress (1933), 58; Jewish proposals for Arab Federation, 58–69; and Philby plan, 80–106; see also Palestine
Zionist Executive, 58, 62, 66–7, 68, 76, 81, 86, 87, 98, 100, 202
Zionist Executive Committee, 50, 58, 69
al-Zirikli, Khayr al-Din, 14